Public Policy Issues for Management

Second Edition

ROGENE A. BUCHHOLZ
Loyola University of New Orleans

Prentice Hall, Englewood Cliffs, New Jersey 07632

Buchholz, Rogene A.
   Public policy issues for management / by Rogene A. Buchholz.—
2nd ed.
      p.   cm.
   Includes bibliographical references and index.
   ISBN 0-13-678087-3
   1. Business and politics—United States.   2. Social responsibility
of business—United States.   3. Industry and state—United States.
I. Title.
JK467.B83   1992
322'.3'0973—dc20   90-26563
                                                              CIP

Acquisitions editor: Alison Reeves
Editorial/production supervision and
    interior design: Brian Hatch
Cover design: 20/20 Services, Inc.
Copy editor: Linda L. Thompson
Prepress buyer: Trudy Pisciotti
Manufacturing buyer: Robert Anderson
Supplements editor: David Scholder

© 1992 by Prentice-Hall, Inc.
A Simon & Schuster Company
Englewood Cliffs, New Jersey 07632

Printed in the United States of America

10 9 8 7 6 5 4 3 2

ISBN 0-13-678087-3

PRENTICE-HALL INTERNATIONAL (UK) LIMITED, *London*
PRENTICE-HALL OF AUSTRALIA PTY. LIMITED, *Sydney*
PRENTICE-HALL CANADA INC., *Toronto*
PRENTICE-HALL HISPANOAMERICANA, S.A., *Mexico*
PRENTICE-HALL OF INDIA PRIVATE LIMITED, *New Delhi*
PRENTICE-HALL OF JAPAN, INC., *Tokyo*
SIMON & SCHUSTER ASIA PTE. LTD., *Singapore*
EDITORA PRENTICE-HALL DO BRASIL, LTDA., *Rio de Janeiro*

Contents

Preface

The importance of public policy to business executives and management students can hardly be overestimated. Indeed, in many situations, it seems fair to say that the environment in which business operates is more a function of public policy than it is of traditional free market forces. The aggregate economic conditions that a company faces as far as employment and income levels are concerned is largely determined by the fiscal and monetary policies of government. Specific industries are affected by trade policies, environmental regulation, safety and health concerns, and tax measures. Beyond the industry level, the fate of individual companies is oftentimes in the hands of government due to the necessity of obtaining a government contract or the need for some other kind of help from government.

Since public policy is so important, it is necessary for business executives and business students to have some knowledge of what public policy is all about and how it is formulated with regard to specific issues. Knowledge of how public policy shapes the business environment is important in order to analyze the impact specific measures might make on a particular company, industry, or the entire business sector. Public policy issues must be understood so business executives can know how and when to appropriately and effectively participate in public policy formulation with regard to these issues. To abdicate this role is to leave the fate of business up to government officials, public interest group leaders, and other participants in the public policy process. This hardly seems to be a responsible position for corporate management to take vis-à-vis stockholders, employees, consumers, or the public at large.

> Learning to understand the external environment, and to consider its impact in making management decisions, has become a most necessary skill for every successful manager...No business decision today can be based solely on traditional business rationale and be successful.[1]

[1] Rogene A. Buchholz, *Business Environment/Public Policy: Corporate Executive Viewpoints and Educational Implications* (St. Louis, Mo.: Washington University Center for the Study of American Business, 1980), p. 29.

There are various ways to approach environmental concepts and issues and integrate them into a managerial framework. My textbook, *Business Environment and Public Policy: Implications for Management and Strategy,* which is now in its fourth edition, is one of the few in the field to use the concept of public policy as an integrative concept. Specific issues are discussed as public policy issues rather than solely social or political issues. Management's response to these issues is analyzed in the context of a strategic planning process that integrates public policy concerns into strategy formulation, implementation, and evaluation.

The chapters in that textbook that deal with specific public policy issues have received many positive comments over the past several years. Many instructors expressed the desire that these issue chapters be published separately, since they teach the types of courses that deal mostly with public policy issues and do not deal very extensively with conceptual material related to the public policy process or strategic planning. These comments gave me the idea for a book that would take the issue chapters in the textbook, put them together with an introductory and a concluding chapter, and publish them as a separate volume. This idea was supported by Prentice Hall, who gave their blessing to the project. The book did well enough on the market to go into a second edition.

This book is intended for use in a comprehensive management course dealing with broad environmental matters of concern to business and management that focuses primarily on social and political issues affecting business organizations. The book might also be useful in traditional business policy and strategy courses that deal extensively with social and political issues. It could be used very nicely with a casebook that would illustrate concretely some of the issues discussed in the text material. The book can also be used in more specialized courses dealing with government regulation or business-government relations. Because of its managerial focus, it should also be of value to managers of business corporations and executive development programs, serving as a handbook of public policy issues and regulations. Finally, the book can also be used in schools of public administration that have courses focusing on public policy issues and impacts on business organizations.

The opening chapter of the book deals with the nature of public policy issues and their importance to management, the public issues life cycle, and says something about the nature of the public policy process. Then follow a series of eight chapters that focus on specific public policy issues including government regulation, antitrust, corporate governance, wealth and poverty, equal opportunity, occupational safety and health, consumer protection, and environmental protection. These chapters follow roughly the same format. They begin with a brief discussion of the issue, then describe the specific public policies and administrative processes that have been created to deal with the issue, and conclude with an extensive discussion of problem areas where certain dimensions of the issue are unresolved. All these chapters have been updated with current information and developments, and in some cases have been restructured for this second edition.

These eight chapters are followed by a chapter that treats international public policy issues, since business functions more and more in an international context. This international chapter includes a discussion of the international regulatory framework to give a student an idea of the ways in which public policy is formulated in an international context. This discussion is followed by a consideration of ethical issues in an international context and the difficulty of functioning in different cultures with different ethical standards. Several global environmental issues are also discussed to provide students with an awareness of the nature of global environmental problems. The chapter concludes with a discussion of the nature of public affairs in an international context.

Besides being updated with current information and restructured in some cases, this second edition also contains a case at the end of each chapter to illustrate the major themes and issues of the chapter. This case is long enough so that it can become the basis of an extended discussion if the instructor chooses to adopt this approach. Such cases provide a good vehicle for introducing issues to the class and allow the instructor to deal with concrete situations. These cases could also be assigned as class projects for instructors who want students to do further research into the issues presented in the cases.

It must be noted that macroeconomic issues such as employment and inflation are also public policy issues that affect business and could legitimately be included in this book. Equally important are labor issues related to collective bargaining, productivity, and quality of working life. These issues, however, form the basis for entire fields of study in their own right, as the study of macroeconomic policy and industrial relations has developed an extensive body of literature over the years. These issues are thus dealt with in other parts of the curriculum and cannot be adequately covered in a book of this nature.

Thanks are due to many people who were influential in the writing of this book. The intellectual debt of any author is enormous, and only a few who have made special contributions to the writing of this book can be singled out. William C. Frederick of the University of Pittsburgh is owed a great debt of personal gratitude for introducing me to the field of Business Environment and Public Policy and serving as my mentor during my years of study at that institution. Lee E. Preston and James E. Post deserve credit for introducing me to the concept of public policy in their book, *Private Management and Public Policy,* which was very influential in shaping my thinking.

Equally influential was Murray L. Weidenbaum, whom I worked with for 3 years at the Center for the Study of American Business (CSAB) at Washington University in St. Louis, Missouri. This association made me aware of the impact public policy has on business and the process of government regulation. My work with the American Assembly of Collegiate Schools of Business, who along with the CSAB sponsored the study of the Business Environment/Public Policy field that I conducted, acquainted me with many aspects of the public policy dimension of management.

The reviewers of the first draft of the book deserve thanks for making many helpful suggestions for improving the content and readability of the book. The people at Prentice Hall with whom I worked, especially Alison Reeves, the editor, provided a great deal of assistance and encouragement at every step of the process. Their interest in this project is greatly appreciated. Mohammed Allam, of the University of Texas at Dallas, provided invaluable assistance in tracking down references and providing other research assistance for the first edition. The support of my colleagues and the Dean at Loyola University of New Orleans, where I am presently located and where the second edition was prepared, is greatly appreciated.

Acronyms

CEQ	Council on Environmental Quality
CERCLA	Comprehensive Environmental Response, Compensation, and Liability Act
CETA	Comprehensive Employment and Training Act
CFA	Consumer Federation of America
CFCs	Chlorofluorocarbons
CME	Centre on Multinational Enterprises
CMEA	Council for Mutual Economic Assistance
COLA	Cost of Living Adjustment
CPA	Consumer Protection Agency
CPS	Current Population Surveys
CPSA	Consumer Product Safety Act
CPSC	Consumer Product Safety Commission
CRI	Consumer Research Institute
CSAB	Center for the Study of American Business
CSPI	Center for Science in the Public Interest
CTG	Control Technique Guidelines
CU	Consumer's Union

D

DISC	Domestic International Sales Corporation
DOE	Department of Energy
DSR	Division of Safety Research

E

EEC	European Economic Community
EFTA	European Free Trade Association
EIS	Environmental Impact Statement
EO	Executive Order
EEOA	Equal Employment Opportunity Act
EEOC	Equal Employment Opportunity Commission
EPA	Environmental Protection Agency
ERA	Equal Rights Amendment
ERISA	Employee Retirement and Income Security Act
ESOP	Employee Stock Ownership Plan
ETS	Emergency Temporary Standard

F

FAA	Federal Aviation Administration
FASB	Financial Accounting Standards Board
FCC	Federal Communications Commission
FCPA	Foreign Corrupt Practices Act
FDA	Food and Drug Administration

FEPA	Fair Employment Practice Act
FERC	Federal Energy Regulatory Commission
FIFRA	Federal Insecticide, Fungicide, and Rodenticide Act
FPC	Federal Power Commission
FTC	Federal Trade Commission

G

GAO	General Accounting Office
GATT	General Agreement on Tariffs and Trade
GCC	Government Coordinating Committee
GM	General Motors
GMP	Good Management Practices
GNP	Gross National Product

H

HEW	Department of Health Education and Welfare
HHI	Herfindahl-Hirschman Index
HHS	Department of Health and Human Services
HUD	Department of Housing and Urban Development

I

ICC	Interstate Commerce Commission
ICCR	Interfaith Center on Corporate Responsibility
ICIFI	International Council of Infant Food Industries
INFACT	Infant Formula Action Coalition
IRRC	Investor's Responsibility Research Center
IRS	Internal Revenue Service

J

| JOBS | Job Opportunities in the Business Sector |
| JTPA | Job Training Partnership Act |

L

LAER	Lowest Achievable Emission Rates
LAFTA	Latin American Free Trade Association
LIFO	Last-In, First-Out
LMSA	Labor-Management Services Administration

M

MBDA	Minority Business Development Agency
MESBIC	Minority Enterprise Small Business Investment Corporation
MCL	Maximum Contaminant Levels
MNC	Multinational Corporation

N

NAB	National Alliance of Businessmen
NACOSH	National Advisory Committee on Occupational Safety and Health
NAM	National Association of Manufacturers
NAS	National Academy of Sciences
NCL	National Consumers League
NEISS	National Electronic Injury Surveillance System
NEPA	National Environmental Policy Act
NESHAP	National Emissions Standards for Hazardous Air Pollutants
NFIB	National Federation of Independent Business
NHTSA	National Highway Traffic Safety Administration
NIH	National Institute of Health
NIMBY	Not In My Back Yard
NIOSH	National Institute for Occupational Safety and Health
NLRB	National Labor Relations Board
NMPC	National Minority Purchasing Council
NPDES	National Pollutant Discharge Elimination System
NPL	National Priorities List
NRDC	Natural Resources Defense Council
NSPS	New Source Performance Standard

O

OASDI	Old Age Survivors and Dependents Insurance
OECD	Organization for Economic Cooperation and Development
OFCCP	Office of Federal Contract Compliance Programs
OIRA	Office of Information and Regulatory Affairs
OMB	Office of Management and Budget
OMBE	Office of Minority Business Enterprise
OPEC	Organization of Petroleum Exporting Countries
ORD	Office of Research and Development
OSHA	Occupational Safety and Health Act
OSHA	Occupational Safety and Health Administration
OSHRC	Occupational Safety and Health Review Commission
OTA	Office of Technology Assessment

P

PAC	Political Action Committee
PCB	Polychlorinated Byphenyl
P&G	Procter & Gamble
PIC	Private Industry Council
PSD	Prevention of Significant Deterioration
PSIP	Private Sector Initiative Program

R

RCRA	Resource Conservation and Recovery Act

S

SARA	Superfund Amendments and Reauthorization Act
SBA	Small Business Administration
SEC	Securities and Exchange Commission
SIP	State Implementation Plan
SOCAP	Society of Consumer Affairs Professionals

T

TLV	Threshold Limit Values
TNC	Transnational Corporation
TSCA	Toxic Substances Control Act
TSD	Treatment, Storage, and Disposal Facility
TSS	Toxic Shock Syndrome
TWA	Trans-World Airlines

U

UNCTAD	United Nations Conference on Trade and Development
UNCTC	United Nations Centre on Transnational Corporations

W

WHO	World Health Organization

CHAPTER *1*

Public Policy Issues

Introduction

Numerous books and articles have been written over the past several years stressing the importance of public policy issues to the management of modern corporations. This importance does not have to be emphasized again. Corporations know all too well how public policy issues affect their companies; many, in fact, have become quite sophisticated in responding to public issues of concern to them and participating in the public policy process where such issues take shape. The past 20 years have seen the emergence of new organizational forms and functions that facilitate corporate involvement in the public policy process so that corporations can have some impact on the outcome of the debate about public policy issues.

The business institution has been reshaped and the managerial role redefined by many public policy measures designed to accomplish both economic and noneconomic goals and objectives of the larger society. Particularly over the last two decades, public policy has become an ever more important determinant of corporate behavior, as market outcomes have been increasingly altered through the public policy process in the form of new legislation and regulation designed to respond to public issues of concern to society.

These changes are making it increasingly clear that business functions in two major social processes through which decisions are made about the allocation of corporate resources. These are the market system and the public policy process. Both processes are necessary to encompass the broad range of decisions that a society needs to make about a corporation. The market mechanism and public policy process are both sources of operational guidelines and performance criteria for managerial behavior.

Throughout most of its history, business has not had to concern itself with the public policy process because it could assume with some confidence that the basic value system of American society was economic; thus whatever public policies resulted were generally supportive of business interests. There are exceptions to this, of course, but throughout most of American history public policy has by and large been designed to promote business rather than interfere with its functioning.

This has changed over the past several decades. With the social changes American society has experienced, business can no longer assume that public policy will be supportive of its interests. In fact, most—if not all—of the social responsibilities of business that are now public policy measures interfere with normal business operations and result, from a strictly economic point of view, in nonproductive investments. Public policy measures directed toward pollution control, safety and health, and other public issues interfere with the ability of business to fulfill its basic economic mission. Thus it is important for management to have a conceptual understanding of public issues and how the public policy process functions. Management also needs to understand the role that public policy plays in a market-oriented society.

Management's participation in the public policy process is generally the responsibility of a corporation's public affairs department, and there is some evidence to suggest that these departments have become more important over the past several years in managing a corporation's response to a public issue.[1] What is not so well known, however, is the extent to which the corporate community as a whole is using certain strategies to participate in the public policy process and how effectively its responses to public policy issues are being managed. It is not clear that corporations are engaged in strategic thinking when participating in the public policy process, as much of their activity seems to be, at least on the surface, short-term and reactionary in nature.

Part of the reason for this may be that corporate executives and students of business and management do not have as comprehensive a knowledge of public issues and the public policy process as they have of more traditional business subjects. This book is meant to correct some of this problem by presenting a comprehensive discussion and analysis of the major public issues that are affecting corporations in today's environment. These issues need to be taken into account by a concerned and informed management that recognizes the importance of developing a strategic response to public issues as well as more traditional business concerns.

The Nature of Public Issues

The idea of strategically managing the company's involvement in the public policy process implies the existence of a public issue affecting the corporation. This type of issue is distinct from one arising out of a more traditional business function (which does not require collective action and can be acted on by individual corporations in pursuit of economic objectives). Public issues result from the impact of a problem on society. Public issues affect many people, not just a few, and they require collective rather than individual action for a successful outcome. Thus from society's point of view, public issues are those that work their way into the public policy process because of their extensive impacts and collective nature, which requires society to develop a common course of action to deal with the problems involved. Public issues arise when the public has a problem that demands some kind of collective action and there is public disagreement over the best solution to the problem.[2]

From a business point of view, public issues can be defined as public policy questions that affect business corporations in such a way that business has both a legitimate right and a responsibility to help in developing a common course of action. Those issues that become the subject of collective action are placed on the public policy agenda. The specific course of action followed with respect to an issue is decided through the public policy process. Most public issues eventually result in some kind of public policy that seeks to address the problems involved and resolve them to the satisfaction of enough people or groups in society so that the policy will be accepted.

Public issues emerge in our society because of value changes that generate pressures on our institutions by causing a gap between public expectations and institutional performance. That which people desire and think is good for them and their society changes over time because of various influences. Values change in response to technological advances that make it possible to do things that never could have been done before or to do them easier or cheaper than before. New information changes the way we think and feel about products and our activities in society. Shifts in population have an effect on society's dominant value systems. Another factor influencing values is education. As people attain more formal education, they may question their desires and the values and ideas they were raised to believe were important. They may come to reject the traditional values appropriated from their families and adopt a new set of desires and goals to pursue.

Changes in basic institutions, such as the family and the church, affect values. Institutions often play a crucial role in the socialization of children and the transmitting of values from generation to generation. Finally, affluence causes values to change. As more and more people become affluent and fulfill their basic economic needs, other things may become important to them that were not within the range of possibility before. They may desire other goods and services besides economic ones and pursue other goals related to self-fulfillment or improvement of the quality of life for themselves and their children.

When a relatively homogeneous value system exists in a society over a period of time, that society is stable and experiences relatively little social change. When a homogeneous value system begins to break up and large segments of society begin to express nontraditional values, social change of some kind seems inevitable. New issues are raised that find their way onto the public policy agenda so that they deserve the attention of government and corporations. Social change of this sort usually brings about changes in the major institutions of society to incorporate these new values and reduce the gap between public expectations and institutional performance.

The structure of the social-political process also has a great deal to do with the kinds of problems that get attention and the issues that find their way onto the public policy agenda. Ours is a pluralistic society open to all sorts of influences and pressures from individuals and groups who wield influence in the public policy process. Many individuals join groups that can quite properly be called interest groups because they form around shared interests. People organize such groups and join or support them because they share common attitudes and values on a particular problem or issue and believe they can advance their interests better by organizing themselves into a group rather than pursuing their interests individually. These groups become political when they make claims on other groups or institutions in society.

These interest groups may become part of broader and more comprehensive social movements that spread throughout the entire society. A social movement can be defined as a large-scale, widespread, and continuing elementary collective action in pursuit of an objective that affects and shapes the social order in some fundamental aspect.[3] Such movements become the focal point for many groups and individuals interested in the same issue. The stages in the development of a social movement are as follows:

1. Dissatisfaction of a group
2. Dramatic events
3. Strategies for obtaining social change
4. Emergence of strong leadership[4]

In a pluralistic system, people who are concerned about a problem organize or join an existing movement to pursue an issue that has been raised. If the problem is of widespread concern and the group or groups dealing with it can attract enough financial and political support, the problem may eventually become public as more people become aware of it and show support for some kind of collective action. Eventually government or other institutions may translate the issues being raised into formal legislation or other policy actions.

In a pluralistic society, problems are identified and issues raised in a sort of bottom-up fashion—concern about a problem can begin at the grass-roots level and grow into a major public issue that demands attention. Public policy reflects the interests of various groups in the policy-making process and results from a struggle of these groups to win public and institutional support. Management must be aware of how issues are raised in our society and understand the stages through which issues pass on their way to affecting corporate behavior. Such knowledge is essential to anticipate the issues that will impact corporations in order to design corporate strategies that will be effective for both the corporation and society.

Public Policy and Public Issues

The collective action taken with respect to a public issue is appropriately called public policy. One way to define the term is simply to say that public policy is policy made by a public body, such as government, that is representative of the interests of the larger society. Government is the institution designed to make public policy, and thus whatever policy it formulates in the form of legislation, regulation, executive orders, court decisions, and so on, is public policy. Such a definition, however, does not do justice to the complexity of government or society and is unnecessarily restrictive.

Anderson, Brady, and Bullock state that a useful definition of public policy will describe it as a pattern of governmental activity on some topic or matter that has a purpose or goal. Public policy is purposeful, goal-oriented behavior rather than random or chance behavior. Public policy consists of courses of action, according to these authors, rather than separate, discrete decisions or actions performed by government officials. Furthermore, public policy refers to what governments actually do, not what they say they will do or intend to do with respect to some public problem.[5] With these criteria in mind, the authors offer the following as their definition of public policy.

> A goal directed or purposeful course of action followed by an actor or set of actors in an attempt to deal with a public problem. This definition focuses on what is done, as distinct from what is intended, and it distinguishes policy from decisions. Public policies are developed by governmental institutions and officials through the political process (or politics). They are distinct from other kinds of policies because they result from the actions of legitimate authorities in a political system.[6]

Theodore J. Lowi defines public policy as a government's expressed intention, which is sometimes called purpose or mission. Lowi further points out that a public policy is usually backed by a sanction, which is a reward or punishment to encourage obedience to the policy. Governments have many different sanctions, or techniques of control, to assure that their policies are followed.[7] Thomas R. Dye defines public policy as whatever governments choose to do or not to do. Dye argues that public policy must include all actions of government and not just stated intentions of either government or government officials. He also points out that public policy must include what government chooses not to do, as government inaction with respect to particular issues can have as great an impact on society as government action.[8]

Preston and Post offer a much different definition of public policy. They refer to policy, first of all, as principles guiding action, and emphasize that this definition stresses the idea of generality by referring to principles rather than specific rules, programs, practices or the actions themselves, and also emphasizes activity or behavior as opposed to passive adherence.[9] Public policy, then, refers to the principles that guide action relating to society as a whole. These principles may be made explicit in law and other formal acts of governmental bodies, but Preston and Post are quick to point out that a narrow and legalistic interpretation of the term public policy should be avoided. Policies can be implemented without formal articulation of individual actions and decisions. These are called implicit policies by Preston and Post.[10]

The first few definitions are unnecessarily restrictive. Government need not engage in a formal action for public policies to be put into effect. A good example is the debate that took place with respect to South Africa. Before the U.S. government took any specific actions regarding economic sanctions, various religious and secular groups in society brought pressure to bear by divesting themselves of stock they may have held in companies that were doing business in South Africa and did their best to persuade companies with facilities in the country to leave. Many companies responded to these pressures and changed their policies with respect to doing business with or in South Africa without needing the sanctions of formal public policy to motivate them.

The Preston and Post definition, however, confuses principles and action. Principles can guide action, but the principles themselves are not necessarily the policy. Policy more appropriately refers to a specific course of action with respect to a problem, not to the principles that guide the action. Current monetary policy follows a specific course of action taken by the Federal Reserve Board either to tighten or to loosen the money supply. The principles that guide this action are derived from monetary or economic theories, but these principles do not constitute the policy itself. Public policy involves choices related to the allocation of scarce resources to achieve goals and objectives. But policymakers cannot ride off in all directions at once and must make choices among contending allocations of scarce resources. These choices represent courses of action taken with respect to particular problems. _gov't_

Thus public policy is a specific course of action taken collectively by society or by a legitimate representative of society, addressing a specific problem of public concern, that reflects the interests of society or particular segments of society. This definition emphasizes a course of action rather than principles. It does not restrict such action to government, it refers to the collective nature of such action, and it does not claim that each and every public policy represents the interests of society as a whole. Enough interests have to be represented, however, so that the policy is supported and can be implemented effectively.

The specific course of action eventually taken with respect to a problem is decided through the public policy process, through which public policy is formed. Bear in mind there is no one single process in the United States.[11] Public policy is made by means of a complex, subtle, and not always formal process. Many agents who do not appear on any formal government organization chart nevertheless influence the outcome of the public policy process.[12]

The policy of the United States with respect to South Africa was formed through a process involving public opinion, interest groups, institutions, demonstrations, the media, and a host of other actors. When public policy is formalized by government, there still is no single process. Public policy can be made through legislation passed by Congress, regulations issued in the Federal Register, executive orders issued by the president, or decisions handed down by the Supreme Court. The process of making public policy begins in the society as problems and issues are defined. These issues may find their way into formal institutions for some policy decisions and then be returned to the society again for implementation.[13]

The public policy agenda is that collection of topics and issues with respect to which public policy may be formulated.[14] There are many problems and concerns that various people in society would like to have acted on, but only those that are important enough to receive serious attention from policymakers comprise the public policy agenda. Such an agenda does not exist in concrete form, but is found in the collective judgement of society, actions and concerns of interest groups, legislation introduced into Congress, cases being considered by the Supreme Court, and similar activities. The manner in which problems in our society get on the public policy agenda will be a subject of later discussion.

With these working definitions of some essential concepts in mind, we can turn to other considerations. Preston and Post state that the scope of managerial responsibility and the goals that management is to serve are determined through both the public policy process and the market mechanism.[15] Both public policy and the market mechanism are processes through which members of society make decisions about the allocation of resources for the provision of goods and services. But these processes are quite different in concept and operation, and it is necessary to have a thorough understanding of public policy and the nature of public issues in order to understand the strategic implications of these issues for corporations.

Public Issues Life Cycle

The notion of a public policy agenda suggests that public issues have a life cycle—they go through a series of stages as they evolve. Many models of the public policy life cycle identify four such stages (Figure 1.1). The life cycle begins with changing public expectations that create a gap between corporate performance and what the public expects from its institutions. These changes are most likely the result of structural shifts in society that cause strains between societal expectations and what is actually happening. The seeds of a new public issue are sown when the gap becomes wide enough to affect significant numbers of people and cause extensive dissatisfaction with corporate performance. The issue begins to be discussed at grass roots levels, when people begin to form opinions.

These new expectations may then become successfully politicized. As the issue becomes widely discussed in the media and becomes a concern for interest group discussion, it may be picked up by politicians and introduced into the formal public policy process. Perhaps a precipitating event, such as a major oil spill or chemical disaster, will occur to galvanize the issue and harden public opinion. Thus the issue is brought before the public, so to speak, and is placed on the public policy agenda, where it may become the subject of subsequent action.

The legislative phase refers to the time period surrounding the enactment of legisla-

Figure 1.1 The Life Cycle Concept

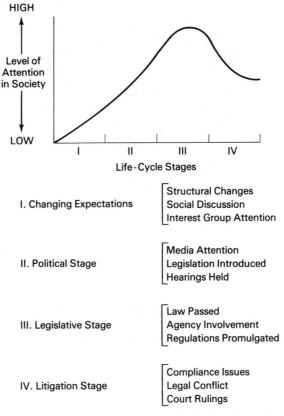

I. Changing Expectations

⎡ Structural Changes
⎢ Social Discussion
⎣ Interest Group Attention

II. Political Stage

⎡ Media Attention
⎢ Legislation Introduced
⎣ Hearings Held

III. Legislative Stage

⎡ Law Passed
⎢ Agency Involvement
⎣ Regulations Promulgated

IV. Litigation Stage

⎡ Compliance Issues
⎢ Legal Conflict
⎣ Court Rulings

Source: Rogene A. Buchholz, *Business Environment and Public Policy,* 4th ed. (Englewood Cliffs, N.J.: Prentice Hall, 1992), p. 511.

tion and regulatory requirements dealing with the issue and its implementation. This phase changes the rules of the game for business. New legislation may require considerable debate and bargaining and even be the subject of court rulings. At this stage, the issue has become institutionalized; society has altered the contract between business and society and expressed its expectations legislatively.

The last stage, the litigation phase, is one of implementing the new rules of the game. During this period, there may be many negotiations between government and business regarding enforcement standards and timetables for meeting the new requirements. If government agencies do not believe business is successfully meeting the new rules and negotiation breaks down, they may file suit in court to force compliance. In this stage, the adversarial relationship between business and government is most pronounced, and the opportunities for cooperation to meet public expectations severely limited. Figure 1.2 shows these four stages and illustrates how the ability to influence an issue narrows as the issue moves through its life cycle.

The author believes that a three-stage model of the public policy life cycle makes the most sense as far as corporate strategy is concerned. The three stages are public opinion formation, public policy formulation, and public policy implementation. This model combines the political and legislative phases of the models previously described

Figure 1.2 Public Issues Life Cycle

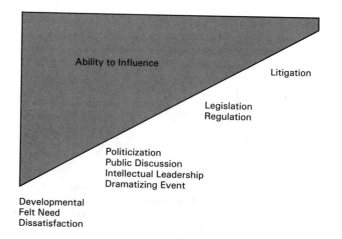

Ability to Influence

Litigation

Legislation
Regulation

Politicization
Public Discussion
Intellectual Leadership
Dramatizing Event

Developmental
Felt Need
Dissatisfaction

Source: National Association of Manufacturers, "The Public Policy Process—Part One: Shaping Future Agendas," *Perspective on National Issues,* June 1984, p. 2. Reprinted with permission.

because the process of introducing and passing legislation (statutory law) and the process of issuing regulations (administrative law) can both be considered part of public policy formulation. The remainder of this section is organized around the three-stage model and deals with specific corporate political strategies that may be useful at each stage.

PUBLIC OPINION FORMATION

The first stage of the three-stage public policy life cycle can be called public opinion formation. At this stage, the concern of the corporate strategist is with the emergence and development of public opinion. The primary focus is on emerging issues of concern to business. In this stage, the major strategic approach available to a corporation for influencing the public policy process is communicating its view on public issues to the public at large. Participation in the public policy debate gives the company the opportunity to present alternatives that could obviate the need for specific regulation altogether. From a corporation's point of view, the effect of a good communication strategy is that it reduces the need for other more expensive and potentially troublesome strategic options further along in the public issues life cycle.

Communication has long been an operational concern of corporations as evidenced by the vast amounts of time, money, and effort spent on advertising and public relations. It is a more recent phenomenon for corporate communication efforts to be considered a major component in a public policy strategy. In part, this transition reflects the extensive changes in the external environment of corporations that includes greater public concern over corporate activities and a concomitant increase in government scrutiny and regulatory control. Thus, we have seen corporations speak to societal groups through meetings or participation on radio/TV talk shows, issue press releases or hold press conferences, become involved in advocacy or image advertising, develop and support extensive economic education programs, and/or utilize formal corporate communications (the annual report, quarterly letter, or proxy statements) as communication vehicles, all in an effort to voice their opinions on public issues.

PUBLIC POLICY FORMULATION

The second stage of the public issues life cycle is public policy formulation. At this stage the concern is with specific legislative proposals introduced in Congress that will directly or indirectly impact on the business firm. The issues at this stage have become politicized and have taken on form and substance as proposed legislative enactments, and the primary strategic objective of the corporation at this point is to oppose or support bills depending on their impact or change them in some way so that they are more acceptable.

Principal approaches utilized by corporations at this stage are memberships in general business or trade associations designed to enhance the "voice" of business by the weight of group numbers, lobbying to obtain access to legislators and ensure that the firm's point of view is understood, and campaign contributions to help elect candidates who will be favorable to business interests. Lobbying as a strategic option assumes that personal contact and direct representation are more likely to get the firm's points across to those who could make a difference on the proposed legislation under consideration.

Of growing significance at this stage is the use of political action committee (PAC) monies as a means of influencing the electoral process. Although individuals may contribute to the candidate of their choice, the inherent limits of single contributions, particularly since they represent the viewpoint of a single person, do not always provide the needed leverage to offset the voices of other single contributors. As a consequence, the pooling of individual contributions and the distribution of those funds through a PAC has come to be viewed as a principal strategic option for corporations interested in influencing the formulation of public issues into acceptable legislative mandates.

PUBLIC POLICY IMPLEMENTATION

The last stage of the public issues life cycle is public policy implementation. At this point the statutory legislation has been enacted and regulations are being promulgated that will impose costs on the corporate community. Since the issues have become bureaucratized, with the emphasis being on administrative decision making, the primary objective of business at this point is to obtain regulations with which it can live and transfer the regulatory costs, to the extent possible, onto the consumer or other parties.

At this stage of the public issues life cycle, many options for business firms are closed or, at best, limited, and the firm's strategic response is no longer entirely in the hands of the firm's managers but increasingly involves its legal counsel. One primary strategy available to firms at this stage is judicial advocacy in court hearings before regulatory agencies by attorneys representing the firm's interest in a narrowly focused, adversarial, litigation proceeding. Firms can also choose a strategy of noncompliance at this stage and accept whatever penalties this strategy might involve.

Another option at this stage is to generate a new public policy issue, thereby forcing the problem back to the first stage of the public policy life cycle in the hopes of changing public opinion with resultant changes in the enabling legislation and implementing regulations. Something similar to this happened during the late 1970s and early

1980s as business became subjected to more and more regulations. Although business lost many battles over specific regulations, eventually the issue of government regulation as a whole was thrown back into the discussion stage and became a major factor in the presidential election of 1980, at which time a candidate was elected who promised to cut back on regulations that were hampering business.

Public Issues and Strategic Management

Figure 1.3 illustrates a strategic management model of the three-stage public issues life cycle and summarizes the strategic options that a firm might employ at each stage. The concept of a life cycle for public issues is important because different corporate strategies are called for at different stages. The options open to business for some kind of a response to the issues are different at each stage, which makes it necessary for corporations to concern themselves with "goodness of fit" between the life cycle of a public issue and the response of a corporation. The development of an appropriate strategy that takes this life cycle into account is important for the development of corporate strategy. For the corporate strategist, the question is not whether to participate in the public policy process, but how to participate effectively and efficiently—for instance, how to formulate, select, and implement corporate public policy strategies.

Figure 1.4 depicts the focus and the key actors at each stage of the public issues

Figure 1.3 A Strategic Management Model for Public Policy Issues

The Strategic Process	Strategic Options
Stage I: Public Opinion Formation	Communication Strategies Direct Meetings TV and Radio Talk Shows Press Releases Economic Education Programs Advocacy Advertising Image Advertising The Annual Report
Stage II: Public Policy Formulation	Participation Strategies General Business Associations Trade Associations Lobbying Honorariums Constituency Building PAC Contributions
Stage III: Public Policy Implementation	Compliance Strategies Cooperation with Agencies Legal Resistance Judicial Proceedings Creating a New Issue Noncompliance

Source: Mike H. Ryan, Carl L. Swanson, and Rogene A. Buchholz, *Corporate Strategy, Public Policy, and the Fortune 500: How America's Major Corporations Influence Government* (Oxford: Basil Blackwell Ltd., 1987), p. 45.

Figure 1.4 The Public Issue Life Cycle

Stages	I	II	III
Issue	Idea	Legislation	Law
Society	Public Interest Groups	Officeholders	Regulators

Source: Mike H. Ryan, Carl L. Swanson, and Rogene A. Buchholz, *Corporate Strategy, Public Policy, and the Fortune 500: How America's Major Corporations Influence Government* (Oxford: Basil Blackwell Ltd., 1987), p. 46.

life cycle. In the first stage, the issue is an idea that is being discussed. The issue is of concern to some people and may involve a change in corporate performance. The key actors in society championing this issue are public interest groups who seek to enlist broader support for their interests. They can use various strategies, including protests, boycotts, demonstrations, media coverage, and the like to gain attention and have their concerns placed on the public policy agenda. If corporations want to participate at this stage, they must become involved in the discussion.

In the second stage, the issue has been translated into particular kinds of legislation that are being considered to deal with the concerns raised in stage I by requiring some kind of change in corporate behavior. The key players at this stage are elected officeholders who introduce and debate the legislation and who eventually vote to support or defeat the legislation. For corporations to be involved at this stage means they must relate to these officeholders and their staffs in some fashion.

The third stage focuses on law, or the implementation of legislation that has been previously enacted. The original issue has now become institutionalized and the idea translated into specific legislation that has become the law of the land. The principal actors at this point are the regulators in government agencies, who are writing and enforcing rules to bring corporations into compliance with legislation. Corporations can choose to work with these regulators to write and interpret rules in order to take corporate interests into account, they can challenge particular rules in the courts, or they can adopt a strategy of noncompliance.

The actors at each stage of the public policy life cycle form the infamous iron triangle. The iron triangle consists of the public interest groups who have a significant stake in a particular issue or issues, the regulatory agency responsible for implementing legislation that has been passed with respect to the issue or issues of concern, and the particular subcommittee or committee of Congress that had primary responsibility for shaping the legislation and continues to exercise an oversight function regarding the regulatory agency. This iron triangle is seen as virtually impregnable by some commentators, particularly if each of the three parties has the same interest in the issue. Thus it is important for business to recognize the significance of these triangles and their implications for the formulation and implementation of public policy.

The importance of accepting some responsibility for public issues is not always apparent to corporations, but what is clear is that the strategic options—what a corporation can do to influence the course of public policy decisions—become more limited the longer the company declines to act on issues that will affect it in some significant fashion. Reacting to public policy issues only when they pose an immediate problem ensures the loss of many frequently more desirable alternatives. For this reason corporations must consider the options available for managing public policy participation at successive stages of the public issues life cycle as a strategic process, as the following indicates:

> Once an issue is the subject of prospective legislation, a company has relatively few options.

Usually the choices are to support, oppose or seek to amend the bill. As for laws and regulations, all a company can do is try to influence their administration so as to minimize their adverse impacts and capitalize on their favorable consequences. Dealing with issues in their later stages, public affairs officers complain of putting out fires, of crisis management. Like corporate planners, many of them want to develop early warning systems, procedures for detecting issues in an emerging stage when they are manifested in discussion and debate among opinion leaders, writers, journalists, social and natural scientists. In this stage . . . the company has many more options in reacting to or, preferably, influencing them to its benefit. It can be proactive, to use a common but deplorable term of jargon, rather than reactive. It can . . . choose whether to fight, where and when.[16]

Basic to each stage of the public issues life cycle is an understanding of the issue and the public policies that have been or are being formulated to deal with the issue. The following chapters discuss the major public policy issues about which corporations have to be concerned in today's environment. (This text does not discuss macroeconomic policy, which deals with inflation, levels of employment, and traditional labor issues related to collective bargaining. As stated in the preface these issues form the basis for entire fields in their own right; thus they are more appropriately the subject matter of other parts of the curriculum and cannot be adequately covered in a book of this nature.) The public issues discussed in the following chapters must be understood by management in order for corporations to effectively participate in the discussion about these issues and strategically manage the corporation's response to reduce the gap between public expectations and institutional performance.

Questions for Discussion

1. What changes have taken place in American society over the past several decades? How have these changes impacted the corporation and management? What new concerns have been introduced into the business school curriculum because of these changes?
2. What is a public issue? What is the relationship between a public issue and public policy? How do public issues arise in our society? What role do interest groups play in getting issues on the public policy agenda?
3. What is public policy? How does public policy differ from business policy? Is there is a relationship between public policy and business policy? Does public policy refer to principles derived from theory or to action taken with respect to a specific issue?
4. What is the public issues life cycle? Why is this an important concept as far as business is concerned? What strategies are useful at each stage of the public issue life cycle? What events herald the movement from one stage of the life cycle to the next stage?

Case: The Smoking Controversy

The tobacco industry has been a major employer in the United States since the founding of the country. It has almost always been a prosperous industry, but in recent years uncertainty has hit the markets of this once-thriving industry. Changing market trends have led to a decline in the sales of tobacco products. Total cigarette sales decreased by about 6 percent in 1983—nearly 40 billion cigarettes—and another 10.2 percent the following year. This trend continued through 1989, as cigarette sales kept declining.[1] The tobacco industry adopted several strategies to counter this trend, including increasing efforts to market its product in Third World countries, targeting specific groups, such as women and African Americans, in this country, and diversifying by merging with other companies.[2]

The factors behind this declining market have to do with changing consumer tastes, health concerns, and demographics. People are learning about the health hazards of smoking and becoming more aware of the health problems related to smoking. The American public today is more health conscious than in previous years and people are going to greater lengths to improve the general quality of their lives. Increased restrictions on where smokers can practice their habit also contribute to the decline in tobacco sales. The demand for cigarettes might decline still further as the male population ages and employment continues to shift toward the service sector.

The health issue regarding cigarette smoking began to be raised as early as 1953, when findings suggesting a connection between repeated cigarette use and lung cancer were presented at the annual meeting of the Dental Society. In 1954, *Reader's Digest* published an influential article based on medical research linking smoking with lung disease. In response to these medical reports, which were critical of cigarette smoking and its relationship to diseases such as lung cancer, expenditures for cigarette advertising steadily increased, making cigarettes one of the most heavily advertised products in the late 1950s and early 1960s. Public attitudes towards smoking, however, were changing, resulting in a requirement passed by Congress in 1966 that a health warning be placed on all cigarette packages. Since then not only has government become more active, but so have private citizen groups in support of increased legislation and restriction on smoking and the tobacco industry.

Much of the public's attention in recent years has focused on the effects of passive smoking on human beings. Involuntary, or passive, smoking can be defined as the exposure of nonsmokers to tobacco-combustion products in the indoor environment. James L. Repace, a physicist at the Environmental Protection Agency, and Alfred A. Lowrey, a chemist at the Naval Research Laboratory in Washington, D.C., reviewed 14 epidemiologic studies and reported that all but one study showed evidence of an elevated risk of lung cancer among nonsmokers exposed to cigarette smoke. Repace estimated that depending on the level of smoke one is exposed to "there may be between 500 and 5,000 deaths each year from this disease (lung cancer) among nonsmokers 35 or more years of age, simply because they were exposed to side stream tobacco smoke."[3]

Because of the concern with passive smoking, 40 states passed laws restricting smoking in public places. Thirty-three prohibit smoking in subways and 17 forbid it in offices and other workplaces. There are also about 800 local ordinances against the use of tobacco. These vary widely across the country. For example, in Cambridge, Massachusetts, smoking has been banned in nearly all public buildings. In Austin, Texas, every company is required to have a written policy on smoking, and if there is a dispute, the rights of the nonsmoker prevail.[4] Every week seems to bring new rules and regulations on where one can smoke.

Smoking in the workplace is also an issue of recent concern because of the passive smoking issue. Proponents of a smoke-free workplace argue that restrictions on smoking will save lives and money by reducing absenteeism, health insurance costs, property maintenance, and legal liability. The problem for employers is one of balancing the rights of smokers with nonsmokers and the responsibility of the employer to provide a healthy work environment. This is not an easy problem to solve, as many employers are discovering, but more and more companies are dealing with it in some fashion. A poll taken by the Administrative Management Society in 1986 found that 42 percent of the firms surveyed had some kind of smoking policy, up from only 16 percent at the beginning of the decade.[5]

Smoking is also becoming more hazardous to careers in business. Instead of being a socially acceptable practice, smoking is increasingly seen as a character defect indicating weakness and lack of self-discipline. Thus in some companies smoking is becoming an impediment to the climb up the corporate ladder.[6] In other cases, job seekers are finding that smoking can prevent them from getting work. Classified newspaper advertisements sometimes specify that employers are looking for nonsmokers only, and in other situations, one of the first questions asked of job applicants is whether they smoke.[7]

Employers justify these actions because they believe tobacco users take too many sick days and raise insurance premiums. Employees who smoke cost too much in health-care benefits, lost productivity, and office maintenance. Companies are revising their definition of work performed to include not only how well workers perform their jobs but whether they are good corporate citizens. The opponents of this practice believe that it results in discrimination against smokers and will, no doubt, lead to lawsuits. Thus far, however, employers have had wide latitude in regard to regulating company policy with regard to smoking. The federal courts have focused their efforts on employment discrimination based on race and sex and have not had occasion to establish a firm legal framework with regard to the smoking issue.[8]

Since 1971, there has been a ban on the advertising of cigarettes on radio and television. Antismoking groups want a ban on all forms of cigarette and tobacco advertising. A recently passed bill makes health warning labels mandatory on all tobacco products, not just cigarettes. Plaintiffs involved in lawsuits against tobacco companies have claimed that the cigarette warnings did not adequately warn them concerning the dangers or risks of contracting particular diseases by smoking. They also claim that industry advertisements directly challenge or criticize health warnings, encouraging smokers to disregard any warnings of health risks. These arguments are central to the product liability cases still pending.

In October 1985 a new law went into effect requiring four rotating health warnings. Representative Albert Gore, Jr. (D. Tenn.), called this legislation a true compromise between "keeping the essential elements of a comprehensive smoking education program while recognizing the legitimate concerns of the tobacco industry."[9] The new warnings specifically express a relationship between cigarette smoking and lung cancer, heart disease, and emphysema and warn pregnant women that smoking might result in fetal injury and premature birth.[10]

The federal government began regulating smoking on airplanes in 1973 when the now-defunct Civil Aeronautics Board required airlines to provide separate sections for nonsmokers. Ten years later, in 1983, all smoking was banned from small aircraft and cigar and pipe smoking was banned on large commercial flights. On April 23, 1988, smoking was banned on all domestic flights of two hours or less, and a year or so later, on all domestic flights, a policy that had been advocated for several years.[11]

There have also been smoking ordinances established in many other public places, such as hospitals and restaurants, where smoking is only allowed in designated areas. Thirty-eight states now have ordinances against smoking on public transportation and in public places including schools, hospitals, auditoriums, theaters, and government buildings. Five states and about a dozen cities or counties regulate smoking in the workplace, whether a public or private facility.[12] Smokers do not seem to have any kind of united front to retain these rights.

The primary factors initiating this confrontation between smokers and nonsmokers were the medical discoveries that smoking did indeed entail certain health risks. This caused a division between those who smoked and those who wanted smoking eliminated for health reasons. Despite this issue, the tobacco industry continues to be a profitable business, promoting the use of cigarettes and other tobacco products as if no serious problem existed. Meanwhile, the antismoking campaign persists and continues to cause problems for the tobacco industry.

In anticipation of a decline in tobacco sales, major tobacco companies have diversified. Philip Morris, marketer of Marlboro, the country's best-selling cigarette, acquired Miller Brewing Company in 1969. More recently, R. J. Reynolds acquired Nabisco, and Philip Morris merged with General Foods. These mergers represent diversifications into product areas or lines that fit closely with the strong consumer marketing required of cigarettes and utilize the same primary distribution channels. These responses by the tobacco industry, however, will not alleviate the pressures of the antismokers. These are more in the nature of defensive strategies designed to help the industry survive in case the tobacco market does collapse at some point.[13]

The future of the tobacco industry depends mainly on what the courts decide in the many product liability suits filed against major tobacco companies. Many analysts believe that no strong precedent has been set in the cases that have been decided thus far and believe that pending cases in Texas, New Jersey, and Boston will be the crucial tests. The industry's future also depends on how the general public responds to new research findings about the hazards of smoking and, more importantly, the hazards of inhaling secondary smoke.

The former surgeon general of the United States, Dr. C. Everett Koop, predicted that for all its enormous economic power, the cigarette industry will virtually disappear over the next 20 years. The tobacco industry is currently a formidable adversary and the biggest obstacle to the antismoking campaign in this country. But as per capita cigarette consumption continues to decline, the Surgeon General claims that the industry will become less and less formidable with every tomorrow.[14] Thus the threat of a smoke-free society is one that the industry cannot ignore, because its very existence is at stake.

Case Notes

1. Stuart Elliott, "Tobacco Firms Match Challenges," *USA Today,* May 24, 1988, p. B-1. See also Walecia Konrad, "If It's Legal, Cigarette Makers Are Trying It," *Business Week,* February 19, 1990, pp. 52–54.

2. Ibid. See also "Where There's Smoke There's Cash," *Insight,* January 15, 1990, pp. 34–35.

3. "Effects of 'Passive Smoking' Lead Nonsmokers to Step Up Campaign," *Journal of the American Medical Association,* Vol. 253, No. 20 (May 1985), pp. 29–37.

4. "Where There's Smoke," *Time,* February 23, 1987, p. 22.

5. Ibid., p. 23.

6. Alix M. Freedman, "Harmful Habit: Cigarette Smoking Is Growing Hazardous To Careers in Business," *Wall Street Journal,* April 23, 1987, p. 1.

7. "Thou Shalt Not Smoke," *Time,* May 18, 1987, p. 59.

8. Jube Shiver, Jr., "Smoking: A Burning Work Issue, *Los Angeles Times,* November 21, 1985, p. 1.

9. "4 Cig Warning Backed," *New York Times,* May 18, 1984, p. A-10.

10. Irvin Molotsky, "Congress Votes Stiffer Warnings Of Tobacco Risk," *New York Times,* September 27, 1984, p. A-1.

11. Laurie McGinley, "Ban on Smoking Sought for Flights by Airlines in the U.S.," *Wall Street Journal,* August 13, 1986, p. 6. See also "AMA Will Urge Ban On Smoking in Planes, Fines for Violations," *Wall Street Journal,* June 26, 1987, p. 9.

12. "Effects," *JAMA,* p. 2938.

13. "Tobacco Takes A New Road," *Time,* November 18, 1985, pp. 70–71.

14. Sharon Eglebor, "Koop: Smoking Costs Too High," *Dallas Times Herald,* March 28, 1987, p. A-1.

Chapter Notes

1. See Public Affairs Research Group, School of Management, Boston University, "Public Affairs Offices and Their Functions: Highlights of a National Survey," *Public Affairs Review,* Vol. II (1981), pp. 88–99.

2. Robert Eyestone, *From Social Issues to Public Policy* (New York: John Wiley, 1978), p. 3.

3. Kurt Lang and Gladys Lang, *Collective Dynamics* (New York: Thomas Y. Crowell, 1961), p. 490.

4. Frederick D. Sturdivant, *Business and Society: A Managerial Approach* (Homewood, Ill.: Richard D. Irwin, 1977), p. 101.

5. James E. Anderson, David W. Brady, Charles Bullock III, *Public Policy and Politics in America* (North Scituate, Mass.: Duxbury Press, 1978), pp. 4–5.

6. Ibid., p. 5.

7. Theodore J. Lowi, *Incomplete Conquest: Governing America,* 2d ed. (New York: Holt, Rinehart and Winston, 1981), p. 423.

8. Thomas R. Dye, *Understanding Public Policy,* 3d ed. (Englewood Cliffs, N.J.: Prentice Hall, 1978), p. 3.

9. Lee E. Preston and James E. Post, *Private Management and Public Policy* (Englewood Cliffs, N.J.: Prentice Hall, 1975), p. 11.

10. Ibid.

11. Anderson, Brady, Bullock, *Public Policy,* p. 6.

12. B. Guy Peters, *American Public Policy: Promise and Performance,* 2d ed. (Chatham, N.J.: Chatham House, 1986), p. vii.

13. Ibid.

14. Preston and Post, *Private Management,* p. 11.

15. Ibid., p. 13.

16. James K. Brown, *This Business of Issues: Coping with the Company's Environments* (New York: The Conference Board, 1979), p. 6.

Suggested Reading

AGULIAR, FRANCIS JOSEPH. *Scanning the Business Environment.* New York: Macmillan, 1967.

ANDERSON, JAMES E., DAVID W. BRADY, AND CHARLES BULLOCK III. *Public Policy and Politics in America.* North Scituate, Mass.: Duxbury Press, 1978.

ANSOFF, H. I. *Corporate Strategy.* New York: McGraw-Hill, 1965.

BAUER, RAY, AND KENNETH GERGEN. *The Study of Policy Formation.* Riverside, N.J.: The Free Press, 1971.

DUNN, WILLIAM N. *Public Policy Analysis: An Introduction.* Englewood Cliffs, N.J.: Prentice Hall, 1981.

DYE, THOMAS R. *Understanding Public Policy,* 6th ed. Englewood Cliffs, N.J.: Prentice Hall, 1987.

EYESTONE, ROBERT. *From Social Issues to Public Policy.* New York: John Wiley, 1978.

HEATH, ROBERT L., AND RICHARD ALAN NELSON. *Issues Management: Corporate Public Policy-making in an Information Society.* Beverly Hills: Sage Publications, 1983.

LINEBERRY, ROBERT L. *American Public Policy.* New York: Harper & Row, 1978.

OLSON, MANCUR. *The Logic of Collective Action.* Cambridge, Mass.: Harvard University Press, 1977.

PETERS, B. GUY. *American Public Policy: Promise and Performance,* 2d ed. Chatham, N.J.: Chatham House, 1986.

PRESTON, LEE E., AND JAMES E. POST. *Private Management and Public Policy.* Englewood Cliffs, N.J.: Prentice Hall, 1975.

POST, JAMES E. *Corporate Behavior and Social Change.* Reston, Va.: Reston, 1976.

SCHIPPER, F., AND M. M. JENNINGS. *Business Strategy for the Political Arena.* Westport, Conn.: Greenwood Press, 1984.

STARLING, GROVER. *The Politics and Economics of Public Policy.* Homewood, Ill.: Dorsey Press, 1979.

CHAPTER 2

Government Regulation

The regulation of business by the federal government became so pervasive and comprehensive in American society during the 1970s that it was the subject of a national debate. In fact, it expanded so much that it was difficult to find an area of business untouched by it. In the early 1980s, one of the main components of the Reagan economic program was a reduction in the regulatory burden to cut inflation and increase productivity in the American economy. Thus regulation became a public policy issue in and of itself.

Murray Weidenbaum, a former chairman of the Council of Economic Advisors, referred to this growth of regulation as a second managerial revolution, involving another shift of decision making regarding power and control over the corporation.[1] The first revolution, based on the separation of ownership and control, was first advocated by Adolph A. Berle and Gardiner C. Means, who argued that decision-making power in the modern corporation had shifted from the formal owners to a class of professional managers.[2] The second managerial revolution involved a shift of decision-making power from the managers of corporations to a vast cadre of government regulators who were influencing—and in many cases controlling—managerial decisions of the typical business corporation, including decisions about where products could be made and under what conditions they could be produced. These types of decisions, which became increasingly subject to government influence and control, were basic to the operation of a business organization.[3]

> No business, large or small, can operate without obeying a myriad of government rules and restrictions. Costs and profits can be affected as much by a directive written by a government official as by a management decision in the front office or a customer's decision at the checkout counter. Fundamental entrepreneurial decisions—such as what lines of business to go into, what products and services to produce, which investments to finance, how and where to make goods, and how to market them, and what prices to charge—are increasingly subject to government control.[4]

Government regulations affect every department or functional area within the corporation and every level of management. Top management in particular can spend a great deal of time on public policy matters that are regulatory in nature. Corporations also face varying and rising penalties under federal statutes. Some of the impacts that regulation makes on the functional areas of a corporation are described in the paragraphs that follow. Figure 2.1 shows in more detail the impact of regulation on the functional areas of a hypothetical corporation and the government agencies involved.

Research and development has been affected by a host of safety and health regulations. Thus a good deal of R&D effort now goes into what is called "defensive" research, directed toward meeting the requirements of government regulatory agencies rather than toward the development of new and/or improved products.

The *manufacturing* function has been affected by a host of regulations dealing with safety and health in the workplace and pollution control. Depending on the industry, some companies have to allocate a significant portion of their capital expenditures toward meeting these regulatory requirements.

Marketing is affected by regulations that deal with deception in advertising, disclosure of product characteristics believed to be of interest to the consumer, requirements for warning labels on certain products, and regulations pertaining to packaging. The marketing department is also responsible for a reverse distribution mechanism—product recalls that can be ordered by a government agency.

The *personnel* function is affected by regulations pertaining to equal opportunity for women and minorities, regulations related to age discrimination, and efforts of government agencies to promote the hiring of handicapped people. These regulations affect all aspects of the personnel function: hiring, firing, transfers, promotions, and the like.

The *finance* department is affected by demands for increased disclosure of information to shareholders and the Securities and Exchange Commission, as well as having to respond to increased demands for information from other government agencies.[5]

The volume of regulations that affect business is so large that no corporation in the country can comply with all the laws and regulations to which it is subject. Small companies in particular are probably not even aware of all the regulations affecting them. The National Council on Wage and Price Stability, for example, made a study in 1976 that listed 5,600 regulations from 27 different agencies with which steelmakers must comply.[6] The Federal Register, in which all proposed and final regulations are published, grew from 9,562 pages in 1960 to 74,120 pages in 1980. One survey determined that federal departments and agencies sent out more than 9,800 different types of forms and received 556,000,000 responses for several years during the 1970s.[7]

Types of Regulation

It is necessary at the outset of a discussion of regulation to look at the various types of government regulation in existence, since the regulatory activities of government are not all the same. Different types of regulation have different objectives, use different methods to accomplish these objectives, affect different segments of business, and involve different costs to society. The major types of government regulation are regulation of competitive behavior, industry regulation, social regulation, and regulation of labor-management relations. The list of agencies in Exhibit 2.1 is by no means exhaustive, but is representative of these different types of regulation.

Competitive Behavior. Since the Sherman Antitrust Act of 1890, the government has been regulating competitive behavior by investigating such illegal practices as price

Figure 2.1 Hypothetical Industrial Corporation and Federal Government Relations

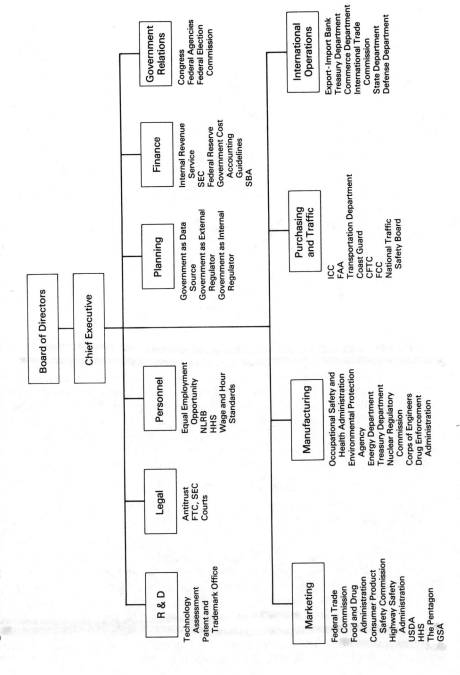

Source: Murray L. Weidenbaum, *Business, Government, and the Public,* 4th ed. (Englewood Cliffs, N.J.: Prentice Hall, 1990), p. 9.

EXHIBIT 2.1

Types of Government Regulation

I. Competitive behavior
   A. Justice Department (JD)
   B. Federal Trade Commission (FTC)

II. Industry regulation
   A. Utilities (FERC)
   B. Communications (FCC)
   C. Surface transportation (ICC)
   D. Finance and securities (SEC)

III. Social regulation
   A. Occupational Safety and Health (OSHA)
   B. Equal Employment Opportunity (EEOC)
   C. Advertising and deceptive practices (FTC)
   D. Product safety (CPSC)
   E. Physical environment (EPA)
   F. Food and drugs (FDA)
   G. Auto safety and economy (NHTSA)

IV. Labor-management relations
   A. National Labor Relations Board (NLRB)
   B. Labor-Management Services Administration (LMSA)

fixing and price discrimination and the structure of industries when they become highly concentrated. The agencies of the federal government involved in regulating competitive behavior are the Antitrust Division of the Justice Department and the Bureau of Competition in the Federal Trade Commission. This type of regulation is discussed in the next chapter, which deals specifically with this area of public policy.

Industry Regulation. This type of regulation is the oldest, beginning with the Interstate Commerce Commission (ICC), which was established in 1887 to provide continuous surveillance of private railroad activity across the country. While some states had practiced such regulation before the federal government, the inability of the states to regulate railroads effectively led to the passage of a regulatory act, which set the pattern for additional regulatory commissions of this type. Thus followed the Federal Power Commission (FPC), the Civil Aeronautics Board (CAB), and the Federal Communications Commission (FCC), all examples of industry regulation.

One reason for this type of regulation is the belief that certain natural monopolies exist where economies of scale in an industry are so great that the largest firm would have the lowest costs and thus drive its competitors out of the market. In other situations, one firm may be able to supply the entire market more cheaply and efficiently than several smaller firms. Since competition cannot act as a regulator in these situations, the government must perform this function to regulate these industries in the public interest.

Another reason for industry regulation is that an agency may be needed to allocate limited space, as was true of airlines and is still the case with broadcasters. The threat of predatory practices or destructive competition is another rationale for regulation, one often used to justify regulation of the transportation industry. Regulation may be needed, it is often argued, to provide service to areas that would be ignored by the market. An example was the provision of railroad and airline service to small towns and cities before the advent of deregulation. Finally, some argue that regulation is needed to prevent fraud and deception in the sale of securities.

This type of regulation focuses on a specific industry and is concerned about its economic well-being. Although the original impetus for regulation may have come from consumers who believed they needed protection, the so-called capture theory suggests that these agencies eventually become a captive of the industry they are supposed to regulate. This happens because of the unique expertise possessed by members of the industry or because of job enticements for regulators who leave government employment. The public or consumer interest is often viewed as subordinate as the agency comes to focus on the needs and concerns of the industry it is regulating.

Social Regulation. A new wave of social regulation appeared in the 1960s and 1970s in response to the change in the social values and concerns of society. This type of regulation is a radical departure from the industry type of regulation just discussed. Health and safety regulation, for example, affects virtually all of business, not just a particular industry, and thus is far broader in scope. The effects of ICC regulations are limited to surface transportation companies, whereas safety and health regulations apply to every employer engaged in a business affecting commerce. Thus social regulation is issue-oriented rather than industry-oriented.

Furthermore, this new style of regulation, rather than focusing on markets, rates, and the obligation to serve, affects the conditions under which goods and services are produced and the physical characteristics of products that are manufactured. The Environmental Protection Agency (EPA), for example, sets constraints on the amount of pollution a manufacturer may emit in the course of operations. The Consumer Product Safety Commission (CPSC) sets minimum safety standards for products. The Occupational Safety and Health Administration (OSHA) regulates safety and health hazards in the workplace.

These agencies are concerned with noneconomic matters and sometimes pay little or no attention to an industry's basic mission of providing goods and services to the public. Their impetus comes from social considerations related to improving the quality of life, and they sometimes ignore the effects of their regulations on such economic matters as productivity, growth, employment, and inflation.

Social regulation often means that the government becomes involved with very detailed facets of the production process, interfering with the traditional perogatives of business management. For example, OSHA sometimes specifies precise engineering controls that must be adopted. The CPSC mandates specific product characteristics that it believes will protect consumers from injury. The Federal Trade Commission (FTC) deals with specific advertising content in some cases. These activities involve the government in many more details of business management than industry regulation.

The pressures for this new type of regulation come primarily from a variety of interest groups concerned with the social aspects of our national life—environmentalists, consumer groups, labor unions, and civil rights organizations. The traditional capture theory—the idea that the industry captures its regulators—does not apply to this type of regulation. Industry, by and large, has shown no enthusiasm for social regulation because it interferes with the basic economic mission of business. If anyone comes to dominate these new functionally oriented agencies, it will be the special-interest groups concerned with the agency's specific task of regulation.[8]

One reason for this type of regulation is related to the nature of today's workplace and marketplace. It is often argued that when goods and technology are complex and their effects largely unknown, consumers are incapable of making intelligent judgments of their own, and workers may not know the risks they face on various jobs or may not be able to acquire the necessary information. Expert judgment is needed in these areas to protect consumers and workers from unnecessary risks that they cannot assess for themselves.[9]

Another reason for this type of regulation is the existence of externalities when the actions of a firm have a harmful effect on third parties. The cost of external diseconomies such as air and water pollution cannot be voluntarily assumed by firms unless a government agency exists to enforce standards equally across all firms in an industry. Voluntary assumption by some firms would place them at a competitive disadvantage; regulation is needed to make all companies meet the same standard, leaving them in the same competitive position.

Labor-Management Relations.   This area of regulation grew out of the depression years, when the Wagner Act established the right of employees to form unions and bargain collectively with management over wages and working conditions and other aspects of labor-management relations. A full discussion of this aspect of regulation is more properly the subject of an industrial relations course. The two principal agencies involved in this aspect of regulation are the National Labor Relations Board (NLRB), which was created by the Wagner Act to administer the laws related to collective bargaining between companies and labor unions, and the Labor-Management Service Administration, which regulates certain aspects of union activity and shares, with the Internal Revenue Service, the administration of legislation pertaining to benefit plans of corporations.

The Growth of Regulation

Many of the more traditional industry regulatory agencies were created during the New Deal era, but there is little doubt that regulation was a growth industry during the 1970s, with the leading product being the newer areas of social regulation. Figure 2.2 shows the growth in the number of agencies from before 1900 to 1979, the end of the last period of rapid agency growth.

This growth is also shown in Tables 2.1 and 2.2 (on pages 25 and 26), which list the expenditures on federal regulatory activities from 1970 to 1980 (administrative costs contained in the federal budget) and the increases in the staff of these agencies over the same time period. Overall regulatory expenditures in 1980 were more than four times the 1970 level, and staff increased by 62 percent over the 1970 level. These tables also show that the major growth took place in social regulation (consumer safety and health, job safety and other working conditions, and environment and energy).

During the 1960s and 1970s, Congress enacted more than a hundred laws regulating business activity. In addition, existing or new federal agencies issued thousands of rules and procedural requirements. The Reagan administration came into office promising to cut back or at least slow the growth of this regulatory onslaught. Immediately upon taking office, it froze dozens of regulations that were promulgated during the final

Figure 2.2 A Historical Perspective to Agency Growth

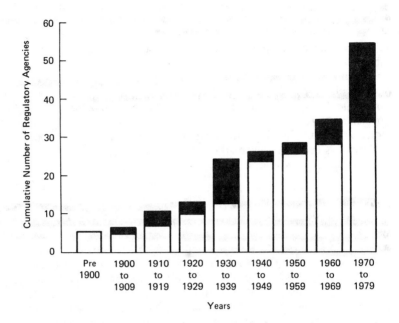

Source: Kenneth Chilton, *A Decade of Rapid Growth in Federal Regulation* (St. Louis, Mo.: Washington University Center for the Study of American Business, 1979), p. 5. Reprinted with permission.

days and hours of the Carter administration. It also ordered a halt to the issuing of any new rules for at least 60 days.

Soon thereafter, the president established a Task Force on Regulatory Relief chaired by the vice president. The major purposes of the task force were to review new proposals by regulatory agencies in the executive branch, assess regulations already in effect, and oversee the development of legislative proposals as appropriate. The task force was to be guided by the following principles: (1) federal regulations should be initiated only when there is a compelling need, (2) alternative regulatory approaches (including no regulation) should be considered and the approach selected that imposes the least possible burden on society consistent with achieving the overall statutory and policy objectives, and (3) regulatory priorities should be governed by an assessment of the benefits and costs of the proposed regulations.

A month after his inauguration, President Reagan issued an executive order that required agencies in the executive branch to prepare a "regulatory impact analysis" for each major rule being considered. This analysis involved preparing an accurate assessment of the potential benefits and costs of each major regulatory proposal. In addition, the executive order required that the agencies choose regulatory goals and set priorities to maximize the benefits to society and choose the most cost-efficient means among legally available options for securing the goals to be attained.

The president also staffed major regulatory agencies such as EPA, OSHA, FTC, and NHTSA with individuals who shared his commitment to reduce the regulatory burden on business. Budgets were cut in some of the agencies, there was a slowdown in enforcement activities, and staffing was reduced. The Reagan administration thus

TABLE 2.1 Administrative Costs of Federal Regulatory Activities in Current Dollars (Fiscal Years, Millions of Dollars)

Area of Regulation	1970	1975	1980	1981	1982	1983	1984	1985	1986	1987	1988	1989 (Estimated)	1990 (Estimated)	% Change 1970–1980	% Change 1980–1990	% Change 1989–1990
SOCIAL REGULATION																
Consumer safety and health	$710	$1,497	$2,354	$2,479	$2,461	$2480	$2,577	$2,686	$2,673	$2,850	$2,914	$3,156	$3,308	232%	41%	5%
Job Safety and other working conditions	128	364	753	807	774	807	836	860	823	884	917	959	992	488%	32%	3%
Environment and energy	278	1,114	2,201	2,173	2,276	2,260	2,671	2,976	2,793	3,615	4,094	4,428	4,618	692%	110%	4%
TOTAL Social regulation	$1,116	$2,975	$5,308	$5,459	$5,511	$5,547	$6,084	$6,522	$6,289	$7,349	$7,925	$8,543	$8,918	376%	68%	4%
ECONOMIC REGULATION																
Finance and banking	$87	$155	$362	401	$436	$415	$650	$624	$890	$774	$1,063	$1,196	$1,028	316%	184%	–14%
Industry-specific regulation	91	160	279	291	282	285	293	289	270	284	294	303	325	207%	16%	7%
General business	115	206	354	374	382	435	458	507	528	579	647	696	709	208%	100%	2%
TOTAL Economic regulation	$293	$521	$995	$1,066	$1,100	$1,135	$1,401	$1,420	$1,688	$1,637	$2,004	$2,195	$2,062	240%	107%	–6%
GRAND TOTAL	$1,409	$3,496	$6,303	$6,525	$6,611	$6,682	$7,485	$7,942	$7,977	$8,986	$9,929	$10,738	$10,980	347%	74%	2%
% Change in nominal terms		148%	80%	4%	1%	1%	12%	6%	0%	13%	10%	8%	2%			

Source: Melinda Warren and Kenneth Chilton, The Regulatory Legacy of the Reagan Revolution: An Analysis of 1990 Federal Regulatory Budgets and Staffing (St. Louis, Mo.: Washington University Center for the Study of American Business, 1989), p. 5

TABLE 2.2 Staffing for Federal Regulatory Activities (Fiscal Years, Permanent Full-Time Positions)

Area of Regulation	1970	1975	1980	1981	1982	1983	1984	1985	1986	1987	1988	1989	(Estimated) 1990	% Change 1970–1980	% Change 1980–1990	% Change 1989–1990
SOCIAL REGULATION																
Consumer safety and health	41,613	51,764	54,591	52,758	49,114	46,046	45,264	44,485	43,549	44,017	43,737	44,449	44,980	31%	−19%	1%
Job Safety and other working conditions	7,472	13,694	18,201	18,023	16,151	15,849	15,570	14,577	14,303	14,354	14,546	14,620	14,628	144%	−20%	0%
Environment and energy	4,929	15,618	19,621	18,200	16,613	16,526	16,835	18,373	19,134	20,454	20,775	21,015	21,496	298%	7%	2%
TOTAL Social regulation	54,014	81,076	92,413	88,981	81,878	78,421	77,669	77,435	76,986	78,825	79,058	80,084	81,104	71%	−13%	1%
ECONOMIC REGULATION																
Finance and banking	6,219	8,117	9,681	9,439	9,371	9,386	9,764	9,850	10,914	10,313	10,955	11,245	11,249	56%	16%	0%
Industry-specific regulation	6,072	7,221	7,365	6,946	6,403	5,921	5,715	4,969	4,792	4,792	4,806	4,952	4,942	21%	−33%	0%
General business	7,070	8,638	9,390	9,055	8,685	8,737	8,841	9,026	9,136	8,642	9,045	9,509	9,899	33%	1%	4%
TOTAL Economic regulation	19,361	23,976	26,436	25,440	24,459	24,044	24,320	23,845	24,842	23,747	24,806	25,706	26,090	37%	−3%	1%
GRAND TOTAL	73,375	105,052	118,849	114,421	106,337	102,465	101,989	101,280	101,828	102,572	103,864	105,790	107,194	62%	−11%	1%
% Change		43%	13%	−4%	−7%	−4%	0%	−1%	1%	1%	1%	1%	2%	1%		

Source: Melinda Warren and Kenneth Chilton, The Regulatory Legacy of the Reagan Revolution: An Analysis of 1990 Federal Regulatory Budgets and Staffing (St. Louis, Mo.: Washington University Center for the Study of American Business, 1989), p. 8

TABLE 2.3   Percent Changes in Real Administrative Costs of Federal Regulatory Acitivities for 5-Year Intervals 1970–1990

Area of Regulation	% Change 1970–1975	% Change 1975–1980	% Change 1980–1985	% Change 1985–1990
SOCIAL REGULATION				
Consumer safety and health	62%	11%	−12%	5%
Job safety and other working conditions	118	46	−12	−2
Environment and energy	207	39	5	32
TOTAL Social regulation	104%	26%	−5%	16%
ECONOMIC REGULATION				
Finance and banking	37%	65%	33%	40%
Industry-specific regulation	35	23	−20	−4
General business	37	21	11	19
TOTAL Economic Regulation	36%	35%	10%	24%
GRAND TOTAL	90%	27%	−3%	18%

Source: Melinda Warren and Kenneth Chilton, *The Regulatory Legacy of the Reagan Revolution: An Analysis of 1990 Federal Regulatory Budgets and Staffing* (St. Louis, Mo.: Washington University Center for the Study of American Business, 1989), p. 10.

adopted a strategy of working through the bureaucracy itself to effect change. This strategy has been called the "purse strings" approach to regulatory reform.

What has been the net effect of these measures? Tables 2.1 and 2.2 also show the trends in regulatory expenditures and staffing for the Reagan years and estimated expenditures and staffing for the first two years of the Bush administration. Spending for all regulatory activities increased 74 percent during this time period, whereas staffing decreased 11 percent. In real terms, where costs are expressed in constant 1982 dollars, spending increased only 15 percent for the decade of the 1980s. Table 2.3 shows spending in real terms for 5-year intervals, and Table 2.4 shows staffing changes for the same intervals. In both tables it is apparent that real cuts in both spending and staffing took place in the first 5 years of the Reagan administration, but in the later years of this administration and on into the Bush years, both social and economic regulation resumed a growth pattern. This pattern is shown even more dramatically in Figures 2.3 and 2.4, respectively.

The biggest cuts both in budgets and staffing during the period 1980–85 took place in the areas of social regulation, specifically in consumer safety and health regulation and job safety and other working conditions, and industry regulation because of the deregulatory trends that had been started during the Carter administration. Increased spending in environment and energy, however, is almost entirely attributable to the EPA, which experienced a 170 percent increase in spending from 1980 to 1990. Much of this increase is associated with funding of the agency's hazardous waste program.[10] Increases in both spending and staffing in the area of finance and banking are largely the result of increases in examination activities associated with bank failures and insider trading.[11]

These trends lead some to conclude that an appraisal of the purse strings approach to regulatory reform reveals more continuity than change. The rapid growth that occurred

TABLE 2.4 Percent Changes in Federal Regulatory Staffing for 5-Year Intervals 1970–1990

Area of Regulation	% Change 1970–1975	% Change 1975–1980	% Change 1980–1985	% Change 1985–1990
SOCIAL REGULATION				
Consumer safety and health	24%	5%	−19%	1%
Job safety and other working conditions	83	33	−20	0
Environment and energy	217	26	−6	17
TOTAL Social regulation	50%	14%	−16%	5%
ECONOMIC REGULATION				
Finance and banking	31%	19%	2%	14%
Industry-specific regulation	19	2	−33	−1
General business	22	9	−4	10
TOTAL Economic regulation	24%	10%	−10%	9%
GRAND TOTAL	43%	13%	−15%	6%

Source: Melinda Warren and Kenneth Chilton, *The Regulatory Legacy of the Reagan Revolution: An Analysis of 1990 Federal Regulatory Budgets and Staffing* (St. Louis, Mo.: Washington University Center for the Study of American Business, 1989), p. 10.

Figure 2.3 Trends in Regulatory Spending 1970–1990

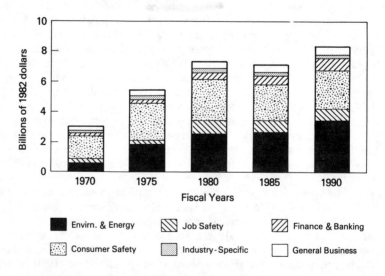

Source: Melinda Warren and Kenneth Chilton, *The Regulatory Legacy of the Reagan Revolution: An Analysis of 1990 Federal Regulatory Budgets and Staffing* (St. Louis, Mo.: Washington University Center for the Study of American Business, 1989), p. 3.

Figure 2.4 Trends in Regulatory Staffing 1970–1990

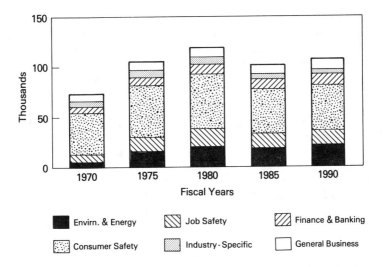

Source: Melinda Warren and Kenneth Chilton, *The Regulatory Legacy of the Reagan Revolution: An Analysis of 1990 Federal Regulatory Budgets and Staffing* (St. Louis, Mo.: Washington University Center for the Study of American Business, 1989), p. 3.

in the 1970s is no longer evident, but this is a familiar pattern for growth industries. Regulation may now have become a mature industry—one that may not be expanding rapidly, but one that is not likely to wither away either.[12] Some believe that the Reagan administration largely abandoned its attempt to bring about major changes in federal regulatory policies midway through its first term in office, when its efforts for further reductions seem to have run out of steam. Political pressures, lawsuits, and bureaucratic resistance has caught up with administrative efforts to slow down and cut back the regulatory apparatus.[13]

The presidential Task Force on Regulatory Relief was disbanded in 1983, claiming to have effected savings of more than $150 billion over the next decade through administrative and legislative changes. About $110 billion of these savings was supposed to come from modification or recision of unneccessary existing regulations and the other $40 billion (in increased income to the consumer) was supposedly to be generated by the removal of interest-rate ceilings.[14]

The task force's final report described the institutionalization of the executive oversight mechanism centered in the Office of Management and Budget (OMB) for the review and coordination of new regulations. This process, established by Executive Order 12291, ensures that all proposed federal regulations meet the requirements of benefit/cost analyses before they are published. Because of this process, the number of final regulations issued by the Reagan administration during its first 17 months was about 22 percent less than during the final years of the Carter administration—from a monthly average of 669 to 519. The number of proposed rules declined 34 percent over this same period.[15]

The number of pages in the Federal Register declined from 86,406 in 1980 to

63,554 in 1981, reflecting this same decline in rule-making. Thus the issuance of new rules was significantly slowed during the Reagan administration. With this oversight process firmly established and running smoothly, and with most of the reviews of inherited regulations completed, the task force claimed to have accomplished its basic mission.[16]

However, some were skeptical about these claims and believed that they represented savings from deregulatory actions taken by previous administrations as well as from the repeal of regulations that had been proposed but not adopted. It has also been stated that the abolishment of this task force represented the de facto abandonment of the Reagan administration's commitment to reduce government controls over corporate social conduct.[17]

Perhaps the most significant development in the regulatory area during the Reagan administration was the definite slowdown in the rate of increase in federal control over corporate social conduct. Congress went through several sessions without passing any new regulatory statutes or establishing a new regulatory agency. With just a few exceptions, the regulatory statutes enacted during the 1980s were virtually all reauthorizations of laws that had been initially approved during the previous decade. Thus the regulatory momentum was clearly slowed but not reversed.[18]

Costs of Regulation

Direct Costs.   Regulation has entailed many costs for business organizations. Most are hidden from public view, as the only visible costs of regulation are those of running the agencies themselves, those contained in the federal budget mentioned in the previous section. But the administrative costs are only the tip of the iceberg. The bulk of regulatory expense goes to compliance costs such as developing and implementing affirmative action programs, installing pollution-control equipment, and installing safety devices. Although the benefits of regulation may be shared by society at large, or at least significant segments of society, which may include business itself, the costs of regulation are largely borne by business organizations. Much regulation, especially that affecting business directly, seems to be a matter of diffused benefits to society as a whole and concentrated costs as far as business organizations are concerned.

The first study that attempted to measure these compliance costs on a comprehensive basis was completed at the Center for the Study of American Business (CSAB), a research center directed by Murray Weidenbaum.[19] The CSAB study estimated these compliance costs for 1976 by using the most reliable estimates for various areas of regulation that were available at the time. These estimates were then totaled to arrive at an overall figure believed to represent total compliance costs for the year. For example, figures from the Council on Environmental Quality (CEQ) were used for estimating compliance costs for pollution abatement. The paperwork figure came from the Commission on Federal Paperwork study. This procedure was believed to be conservative because when a range of costs was involved, the lower end was generally chosen. In some cases, no cost estimates at all were available.[20]

> The basic approach followed in the study was to cull from the available literature the more reliable estimates of the costs of specific regulatory programs, to put those estimates on a consistent and reliable basis, and to aggregate the results for 1976. Where a range of costs

was available for a given regulatory program, the lower end of the range was generally used. In many cases no cost estimates were available. Thus, the numbers in this study are low and surely underestimate the actual cost of federal regulation in the United States.[21]

Table 2.5 shows the results of this procedure. For 1976, the study showed approximately $3.2 billion in administrative costs and $62.9 billion in compliance costs.[22] This study clearly shows that the costs imposed on the private sector are much greater than the cost of running the agencies themselves. The estimated compliance costs in 1976 were 20 times the administrative costs for that year. Applying this multiple of 20 to the amounts budgeted for regulatory activities in subsequent years, approximations were generated, as shown in Table 2.6, for the total dollar impact of government regulation from 1977 to 1979.

The Business Roundtable subsequently completed a study of the compliance costs imposed on part of its membership by six regulatory agencies or programs.[23] This study, which was managed by the accounting firm of Arthur Andersen and Company, claimed to be different from other regulatory cost studies because of its specificity. It dealt only with incremental costs, defined as "the direct costs of those actions taken to comply with a regulation that would not have been taken in the absence of that regulation. These incremental costs were based upon (1) information drawn from companies' accounting, engineering, and other business records and (2) informed judgment as to which actions would have been taken in the absence of regulation."[24]

These incremental costs were classified into operating and administrative costs, research and development, product-related costs, and capital costs. Not only were the costs distributed into these classifications, they were also broken out by specific regulations. The study omitted so-called secondary costs of regulation, such as productivity losses, construction delays, inflation, and misallocation of resources.

The study, released in March 1979, covered 48 companies in more than 20 industries. All participants were considered to be large corporations. Many of them were multinational, although only their domestic operations were included. The six government agencies and programs included in the study were the Environmental Protection Agency, Equal Employment Opportunity Commission, Occupational Safety and Health Administration, Department of Energy, Employee Retirement and Income Security Act, and the Consumer Protection Bureau of the Federal Trade Commission.

TABLE 2.5   Annual Cost of Federal Regulation, by Area, 1976 (Millions of Dollars)

	Administrative Cost	Compliance Cost	Total
Consumer safety and health	$1,516	$ 5,094	$ 6,610
Job safety and working conditions	483	4,015	4,498
Energy and the environment	612	7,760	8,372
Financial regulation	104	1,118	1,222
Industry specific	484	19,919	20,403
Paperwork	—	25,000	25,000
Total	$3,199	$62,906	$66,105

TABLE 2.6 Estimated Cost of Federal Regulation of Business, Fiscal 1977–1979 (Billions of Dollars)

	1977	1978	1979
Administrative costs	$ 3.7	$ 4.5	$ 4.8
Compliance costs	75.4	92.2	97.9
Total	$79.1	$96.7	$102.7

The incremental cost for the 48 companies to comply with regulations from the six agencies and programs for 1977 was $2.6 billion. Figure 2.5 shows the breakdown of this cost by the four classifications mentioned previously. Operating and administrative costs compose the bulk (42 percent) of the total. The costs by agency (Figure 2.6) show that fully 77 percent of the total incremental costs is attributable to the Environmental Protection Agency alone.

The impact of regulation varied widely among industries. For example, the incremental cost of OSHA rules averaged $6 per year per worker in the banking industry,

Figure 2.5 Incremental Costs Summarized in Four Classifications

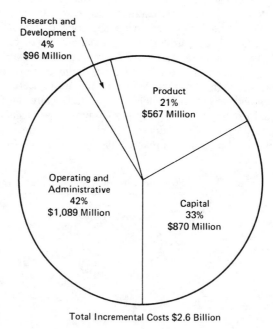

Total Incremental Costs $2.6 Billion

Figure 2.6 Incremental Costs for Each Agency

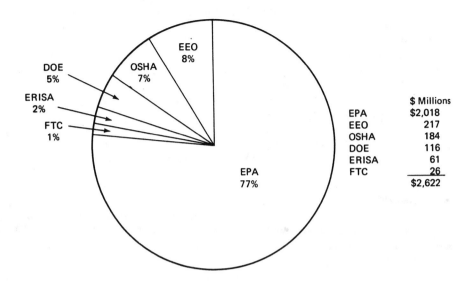

	$ Millions
EPA	$2,018
EEO	217
OSHA	184
DOE	116
ERISA	61
FTC	26
	$2,622

Source: Arthur Andersen and Company, *Cost of Government Regulation* (New York: The Business Round-table, 1979), p. 19. Reprinted with permission.

but $220 per worker per year in the chemical industry. The study also identified attributes of regulation that had a high incremental cost. These could be useful in reform efforts to help identify regulations that were going to prove costly to implement as conceived, but perhaps could be modified in some fashion to make them less costly.

A more recent study released by the National Chamber Foundation surveyed existing academic literature on regulatory costs as well as benefits focused on specific areas of regulation. Based on this survey, the authors concluded that fuel-economy standards, for example, have resulted in small energy savings at the expense of safety. Because the standards resulted in the production of lighter cars, they will be responsible for 2,200 to 3,900 additional fatalities over the next decade. Attempts to improve product safety has actually contributed to increased accident rates, as consumers were lulled into a false sense of security about the dangers of some products and modified their behavior to defeat the intentions of regulators.[25]

Regarding regulation of the workplace, studies have shown that any improvement in injury rates has been bought at excessive costs, as OSHA regulations are believed to be very inefficient. In the area of environmental protection, huge sums of money have been spent to produce small gains in environmental quality. From this survey of existing research, the authors concluded that there is a "critical mass" of scholarly work that indicates a new regulatory reform movement ought to be mounted. This movement, the authors suggest, might be compared with the deregulatory movement mounted in the late 1970s and continued into the early 1980s with respect to industry regulation. Although there are many obstacles to such a movement, there would be many benefits to consumers, taxpayers, and business organizations.[26]

It should be noted that most of these studies were done quite some time ago. In fact, no comprehensive study has been conducted since the Roundtable study that would provide something of a reasonable estimate of the overall costs of compliance. One can only guess that the costs have gone up because of inflation and new areas of regulation, such as hazardous waste disposal and cleanup. If the direct costs of regulation are still approximately 4 percent of GNP, as they were in the Weidenbaum study, the total cost of regulation is now in the neighborhood of $180 billion.

Perhaps the lack of additional studies simply reflects an acceptance of regulation—that regulation is here to stay and there is little use in conducting more studies to convince lawmakers and the public that the direct costs of regulation are excessive. Or it could be that those opposed to regulation thought the Reagan administration would begin a significant reversal of regulatory trends, thus eliminating the need for such studies. In any event, a need exists for updated information regarding the direct costs of regulation so that policymakers and the general public have some idea of the expenses involved in complying with the regulations issued by the federal government.

Other Costs.   Besides the direct, or first-order, costs of complying with government regulations, firms also face what Murray Weidenbaum calls the indirect, or second-order, effects of regulation.[27] The most serious of these costs, according to Weidenbaum, is losses in productivity. In 1975, when the movement to reform regulation first began, Weidenbaum estimated that losses of productivity and other costs of compliance amounted to about 3.6 percent of gross national product. That figure is probably higher today, but even at that rate, the costs in 1988 would have surpassed $130 billion.[28] The Chamber Foundation study mentioned earlier concluded that 30 percent of the slowdown in productivity growth in the 1970s can be attributed to OSHA and EPA regulations that affected industry efforts to be efficient.[29]

Besides this indirect effect on productivity, regulation can also affect employment. Older, marginal facilities may have to be closed down because they cannot meet regulatory standards and remain profitable. The minimum wage law also affects employment by pricing teenagers out of the market. Other plants that were proposed have been canceled because of the difficulty of obtaining all the regulatory permits from federal, state, and local agencies.[30]

A final category of regulatory costs is the induced, or third-order, effects. These are the actions that the firm takes to respond to the direct and indirect effects of regulation. Weidenbaum believes that these "difficult to measure impacts may, in the long run, far outweigh the more measurable costs resulting from the imposition of government influence on private sector decision making.[31]

One of these third-order effects is the impact regulation has on capital formation. This situation arises from closing down plants that cannot remain economically viable and meet government standards. The other side of the coin is the difficulty in obtaining all the necessary permits and clearances necessary to construct new facilities. The effect of many of these regulations is to halt or limit new capital formation and hence economic growth.

Government regulation also has an effect on innovation in some industries. In the drug industry, for example, the volume of new drug products and new chemical entities has declined since the 1962 amendments to the Pure Food and Drug Act. These amendments required extensive premarket testing of new drugs. This drop in innovation has been accompanied by increases in the cost, duration, and risk of new product development. The results have been a sharp reduction in the rate of return on research and development investment in the drug industry and an erosion of American technological leadership in new drug development.[32]

Finally, regulation diverts management attention from its basic function of running the enterprise. Management sometimes has to devote a significant portion of its time to dealing with the impacts of regulation on the economy. The net result of these third-order effects, Weidenbaum says, "can be seen in the factories that do not get built, the jobs that do not get created, the goods and services that do not get produced, and the incomes that are not generated."[33]

Information about regulation cost is important in order for people to understand that public policy in the form of government regulation is not free. Business organizations have to internalize the costs of public policy objectives related to a safe workplace, equal opportunity, product safety, clean air and water, and other public goods. These costs are reflected in the cost of products, in the wages and salaries paid to employees, and in dividends paid to shareholders. Business organizations cannot simply absorb these costs; they must pass them on to the rest of society. Thus while the costs of public policy at first glance appear to be concentrated on business organizations, they are in reality diffused throughout society. Every citizen pays for regulation in one way or another.

Deregulation

The most obvious type of reform regarding industry regulation is simply to deregulate the industry and allow it to function on a more competitive basis. Deregulation has forced industries that were protected from competition to begin to compete in the marketplace. Deregulation has taken place in the transportation industry (trucking, inner-city bus service, railroads, and airlines), the financial services industry, and the telecommunications industry. It is intended to bring about increased competition and thus provide the consumer with improved goods and services at lower prices.

The first steps toward deregulation were taken in 1968 when the Federal Communications Commission (FCC) handed down a ruling in the Carterfone case that permitted non–AT&T equipment to be connected to the AT&T system.[34] Since then, there have been a number of major decisions to bring about deregulation of the regulated sector of the economy. Freeing of interest rates on large deposits by the Federal Reserve System and the order of the Securities and Exchange Commission that barred brokers from fixing commissions on stock sales are examples of deregulation in the financial sector. Then in 1978 under pressure from the Carter administration, Congress deregulated the airlines. Deregulation of trucking and railroads came in 1980, and inner-city bus transportation in 1982. There has been an encouraging growth in innovation, productivity, and reduction of consumer prices as deregulation takes hold. By 1983, deregulation had affected a major portion of the American economy that produced a quarter trillion dollars per year.

Airlines. In 1978 Congress passed a deregulation bill (Airline Deregulation Act) aimed at air passenger service. This Act facilitated the offering of new services by the airline companies and granted them a measure of flexibility in raising and lowering their fares. The bill contained an automatic route-entry program, which granted unused route authority to air carriers willing to serve those routes. The bill was not passed without opposition, however, even from the airlines themselves. Many in the industry feared that deregulation would lead to predatory competitive practices, driving the smaller airlines out of existence or bringing about increased concentration through mergers. Small communities feared they would lose service as airlines concentrated on the more lucrative major markets.

The immediate benefits to consumers were substantial. A study published by The Brookings Institution concluded that airline deregulation saved Americans $6 billion a year because of better service and lower fares. The study also found that airlines improved their annual earnings by $2.5 billion.[35] Long-distance airfares, adjusted for inflation, fell almost 50 percent from 1976 to 1983. Fourteen new airlines have been launched since 1978, offering lower fares and/or better service. All the major carriers developed hub and spoke systems, which produce more efficient service because they provide connections between a greater number of cities. Productivity rose at the major carriers. The entire industry provided 19 percent more output with fewer than 1 percent more employees. Changes in work rules accelerated by the growth of low-cost, nonunion operators, promised even greater increases in productivity.[36]

But deregulation also contributed to the bankruptcy of one major airline, Braniff, and was a factor in the decision of Continental Airlines to operate under Chapter 11 of the Bankruptcy Code. Continental Airlines reorganized under Chapter 11 as a nonunion airline and cut the wages of its pilots, mechanics, and flight attendants almost in half, with one-third of its 12,000 employees working twice the hours they had previously. The reason given for this action was to meet the competition from low-fare nonunion airlines that had been brought about by deregulation.[37]

Many other airlines struggled. Eastern Airlines and Republic reported decreased earnings due to increased competition from nonunion carriers that have entered the market with lower cost factors, such as the wages of pilots and mechanics. Both airlines eventually agreed to merge with other carriers—Eastern with Texas Air, making it the largest airline in the country, and Republic with Northwest Airlines. People's Express, which started the competition for low fares, also fell on hard times and became part of the Texas Air empire.

Thus there is a great deal of turmoil in the industry as new forms of competition emerge and the industry is being restructured. The five largest carriers—American, Delta, Northwest, United, and Continental—controlled more of the market in 1988—70 percent—than they had when airline deregulation began. The kind of cutthroat competition that produced lower fares for several years after deregulation took place disappeared as the industry became more and more concentrated. Some carriers virtually monopolized business in their hub airports. Northwest, for example, controlled 78 percent of the boardings at its home base of Minneapolis.[38]

Airline traffic nearly doubled from 240 million trips in 1977 to a record 447 million trips in 1987, but during this time no new major airports were opened. Thus competition shifted from cut-rate fares to the control of airport departure gates and takeoff and landing slots. Many airlines that were not able to secure enough gates and slots simply went out of business. The industry as a whole reaped record profits in 1988 and was expected to do even better the following year. But airlines such as Eastern and PanAm struggled, and eventually declared bankruptcy.[39]

A cry to reregulate the airline industry rose in Congress during the fall of 1989, coming mainly from mainstream and conservative Republicans rather than liberal Democrats. Critics said airline competition has decreased dramatically in recent years, resulting in higher fares and reduced consumer choice. They argued that government must act to spur competition especially at hub airports that are dominated by one or two carriers. The Transportation Department also threatened to get into the act by stating that it may try to free up slots at congested airports for newer carriers.[40] The Department balked at USAir's plan to buy eight more gates from Eastern in Philadelphia, where it already controlled 15 gates. The Justice Department sided with Transportation and the deal was stalled. These regulatory efforts were seen as necessary to head off legislation that would further restrict the airlines.[41]

While airline deregulation may be undesirable for some people, Alfred Kahn, former chairman of the Civil Aeronautics Board (CAB) under the Carter administration and a prime mover behind the Airline Deregulation Act of 1978, points to the benefits: "generally lower fares, more choice of routes and fares in most markets, and more efficient use of assets by an industry that has seen the numbers of carriers jump from 36 in 1978 to more than 80 today." The critics of deregulation were accused of attempting to bring back the good old days before deregulation when companies were more secure and competition less intense.[42]

The CAB used to protect existing airlines from competition. The agency determined how many airlines could operate, what routes they would serve, and how much they could charge. The agency also had the last word on new entrants into the field and did not approve the creation of a single new trunk line between 1938 and 1978, even though 79 applications had been filed.[43] The CAB lost all its powers on January 1, 1985, when it ceased to exist. Some of its functions, related to smoking regulations, denied-boarding compensation, and baggage liability regulations lived on, however. They were transferred to the Transportation Department, Justice Department, or Federal Trade Commission. The remaining employees were also transferred to these departments.[44]

Trucking. In the trucking industry deregulation was accomplished by the Motor Carrier Act of 1980, although there was some controversy over the interpretation of the bill's provisions.[45] Prior to this legislation, truckers were required to obtain federal certificates of "public convenience and necessity" before they could offer their services to the public. They were also required to obtain specific approval for the routes they were to travel; sometimes the license even specified the particular roads to be taken. Prices, or "tariffs," had to be approved in advance by the ICC, and proposed tariffs that differed from those of the rest of the industry were rarely granted. Mergers involving trucking companies also required ICC approval.

The new legislation granted truckers a zone of rate-making freedom by allowing them to raise or lower rates by 10 percent a year without having to obtain ICC approval. The new law also directed the ICC to repeal its rules requiring truckers to take circuitous routes or to stop at designated intermediate points. The ICC was also asked to reduce restrictions on the commodities that could be carried by a trucking company and on the territory that the company could serve. Finally, the law lifted the burden of proof from the applicant for a permit—persons objecting to the permit would have to prove that the service would be inconsistent with public convenience and necessity.

By the end of 1983, however, about 90 percent of trucking rates were negotiated by individual shippers and carriers, whereas before most of them were set collectively. There was a marked increase in trucking contracts in which price and service were tailored even more to the shipper. A survey of 2,200 manufacturers found that 65 percent received lower rates from truckers, and many rates had fallen 30 percent since 1980. There were 50 percent more interstate carriers in 1983 than in 1979, most of them truckload (TL) carriers.[46] Some 10,000 small new operators entered the trucking industry. The ICC processed 28,700 applications for new or expanded operating trucking authority in the first year of the bill's existence.[47] Revenue ton miles for truckloads, an indicator of shipping rates, fell 22 percent from 1980 to 1986, and revenue per ton for less-than-truckload shipments declined 6 percent from 1983 to 1986.[48]

The costs to the workers was substantial. Many truckers have taken wage cuts, some as high as 10 to 15 percent at small trucking companies. During 1982 and 1983, bankruptcies ran at record levels. Layoffs left one-third of the Teamster's members without work. In 1982, the Teamsters signed off on a 37-month contract that raised total compensation costs only half as much as inflation.[49] Union contract wages, which had increased 20 percent in real terms in the 1970s, fell 12 percent in the 5 years after deregulation. A study published in 1987 calculated that the aggregate wage loss for truckers was between $990 million and $1.8 billion in 1986 dollars.[50]

In 1984, the administration considered a bill that would clear up the controversy and end the remaining regulations on the trucking industry by sparing truckers the paperwork burden of gaining formal approval of their rates and routes and lessening the chance of a return to regulation. Election-year politics intervened, however, as the Teamsters, who had supported the president in the 1980 elections, brought pressure on the administration to shelve the bill, which it did.[51]

Railroads. The Staggers Rail Act of 1980 gave railroads the freedom to set rates and removed other constraints. The railroads were thus enabled to compete with one another and against truck and barge lines. Many of the 8,000 contract-rate agreements negotiated from 1980 to 1983 contained price reductions. The railroads increased their share of the perishables market from 11 percent to 15 percent in just a year and expanded piggyback services, something they couldn't do when regulated.[52]

By most measures, railroad deregulation was a success. According to figures from the Association of American Railroads (AAR), industry earnings rose 50 percent in 1984 to $2.7 billion, up from $1.8 billion the previous year. Ton-miles for 1984 hit a record 922 billion, up 10 percent from 1983, pushing overall freight revenues to $28.5 billion. The rate of return on investment increased from 4.3 percent in 1983 to 5.9 percent the following year.[53] In 1988, a record was set in freight traffic, more than 1 trillion revenue ton-miles, up from 944 billion the year before.[54] According to one railroad executive:

> What the Staggers Act has done to this industry is revolutionary. Since its passage in 1980, not a single railroad has slipped into bankruptcy. Freight revenues are moving up, profits are starting to move in the right direction, and so is market share. . . . Staggers has done what it said it would to . . . lower costs to shippers and let the marketplace dictate rates.[55]

Workers in the railroad industry have been able to maintain their wage rates but have faced a considerable contraction in employment. Compensation for employees of major railroads rose 20 percent in real terms in the 1970s and continued to escalate at about the same rate for the first 5 years of the next decade. To counter this increase, the railroads cut employment by one-third from 1980 to 85, the net result being a sharp increase in labor productivity as the railroads continued to carry as much and even more freight with fewer workers.[56]

The industry received a scare in 1988, when the electric utility industry complained to Congress that the railroads were gouging them as well as coal companies for carrying coal to power plants. A lobby was created called the Consumers United for Rail Equity (CURE), which accused the railroads of making monopoly profits from captive shippers and pushed for legislation to undo some of the Staggers Act provisions. This bill was narrowly defeated in a House committee, and thus the issue has faded for the present. But the railroads are keeping one eye open for other issues of this nature.[57]

Financial Industry.   Deregulation in the financial industry took the following path: (1) the Federal Reserve Bank's removal of interest-rate ceilings on banks' large certificates of deposit in 1970, (2) the Securities & Exchange Commission's 1975 dictum to stop fixing brokerage commissions, (3) the creation of 6-month market-rate certificates of deposit for banks and thrifts in 1978, and (4) landmark legislation in both 1980 and 1982 clearing the way for interest-bearing checking accounts nationwide and the removal of the remaining interest-rate ceilings on bank accounts.[58] Such deregulatory measures have treated the public to an explosion of new products and services offered by a growing number of new institutions such as the multibillion-dollar Sears, Roebuck & Co. financial supermarket. The cost of buying stock for small investors using discount brokers is 60 percent below the commissions charged by the large brokerage houses.

These first steps in deregulating the financial industry met with limited resistance. Further steps, such as permitting banks and securities firms to get into each others' business more directly or permitting full interstate banking have met strong opposition.

In early 1989, the Federal Reserve Board opened a hole in the wall created by Congress to separate commercial banking from investment banking. For 55 years, the Glass-Steagall Act banned commercial banks from underwriting and dealing in corporate stocks and bonds. But on January 18, 1989, the board gave subsidiaries of five major banks authority to underwrite corporate bonds and promised that within a year it would review the bank's applications to underwrite stocks. The board said that banks are well able to assess the market price risk in a securities issue, and it encouraged Congress to repeal the Glass-Steagall Act limitations and allow bank-holding companies to engage in securities underwriting and dealing activities.[59]

Deregulation of the financial industry was blamed for the high rate of bank failures and for the collapse of the savings and loan industry. Bank failures rose sharply in the deregulatory era as 138 banks collapsed in 1986, a post-Depression high. One reason for these failures was the high cost of attracting deposits that forced banks to seek higher-paying and thus riskier loan ventures. Deregulation also provided opportunities for managers to engage in fraudulent practices that benefited themselves but led to the eventual collapse of the institutions they were managing. These failures have cost taxpayers billions of dollars as the government has acted to bail out many of these institutions.

Communications.   The big story in the communications industry was the breakup of AT&T into seven regional phone companies. Terms of the divestiture gave a federal court broad jurisdiction over industry developments. The full effects of that breakup and whether it will ultimately benefit or hurt consumers is still being debated. Most residential customers saw local phone rates rise substantially and service decrease. But supporters of deregulation pointed to the benefits of competition in the telephone equipment business that increased the variety of products on the market and the features they offered while bringing about cost reductions. Competition for long-distance calls dramatically reduced their prices. Even more competition seemed to be in the wings, as the seven regional companies asked for permission to offer computerized services and long-distance calling and to make telephone equipment, areas from which they were banned under terms of the 1984 breakup.

Meanwhile, the FCC was busy deregulating the broadcasting industry. The agency abolished scores of regulations, including radio program logs and the restrictions on the amount of time devoted to commercials on TV programs. The rules on ownership were changed, allowing a single company to own 12 TV stations, an increase over the previous 7. The rule was qualified with a provision that no owner could reach more than 25 percent of the U.S. TV audience. The chairperson of the FCC under President Reagan wanted to slash more regulations but ran into considerable opposition from Congress and public interest groups. These regulations include federal rules governing how television stations handle public affairs programming and their business practices. A repeal of certain parts of the fairness doctrine was eventually accomplished.[60] There was much criticism of the FCC in some circles, suggesting that by throwing broadcasting so quickly into the marketplace, the agency was abandoning its duty to promote quality programming and responsible ownership of the media.[61] Congress considered becoming more active in making telecommunications policy for the nation as a whole and taking the issue out of the courts and the agency.[62]

Thus winds of change have blown throughout the halls of the old-line agencies regulating industries (see Exhibit 2.2). These changes have caused severe dislocations in some cases and benefited consumers and business in other cases. Sometimes, however the effects remain uncertain. According to Murray Weidenbaum, the deregulation of the transportation, communications, energy, and financial markets over the past 10 years has been a triumph of ideas over entrenched political interests. Deregulation has lowered the cost of producing goods and services, offered a wider array of choices to the American consumer, and substantially bolstered the international competitiveness of our economy.[63]

Regulatory Reform

The costs of regulation and other problems associated with the implementation of regulation have stimulated many other efforts at reform. These reform measures have taken different forms, depending on the type of regulation and the objectives of reform measures and proponents. Most of these efforts have been directed at the area of social regulation where deregulation has not taken place on the scale it has in the area of industry regulation. Some of the most popular methods of reform are considered in the following paragraphs.

The Legislative Veto. While Congress is supposed to exercise oversight of regulatory agencies, particularly those independent agencies it created, there are many obstacles to the fullfillment of this oversight function. These obstacles include the overlapping jurisdiction between the many committees of Congress, leading to fragmented oversight, the difficulties these committees have in getting information from the agencies, and the disparity in size between congressional staffs and the agencies they oversee.

To remedy this situation, a legislative veto has been proposed from time to time to give Congress more direct control over agency actions. Under this device Congress drafts a broad statute but then incorporates a provision calling for congressional review of the executive branch's implementation. This provision permits one or both houses of Congress to block any executive action with which they disagree. Some versions of this idea provide that a ruling would take effect unless disapproved by Congress within a certain period of time. Other versions require Congress to take affirmative action before an agency ruling or new regulation could go into effect. In 1979, this idea was used as a means of curbing the power of the FTC, particularly in regard to its industrywide trade rule writing authority granted by Congress in 1975, which many believed had been used irresponsibly.

Advocates of the legislative veto believe it would provide Congress with a clear means of approving or disapproving a proposed regulation. Even the threat of a legisla-

EXHIBIT 2.2

Landmarks in Deregulation

1968	Supreme Court permits non–AT&T equipment to be hooked up to Bell System.
1969	MCI is allowed to connect its long-distance network to local phone system.
1970	Interest rates on deposits of $100,000 and over are deregulated.
1972	FCC sets domestic satellite open-skies policy.
1975	SEC ends fixed brokerage fees for stock market transactions.
	Rate bureaus for trucking firms and railroads are prohibited from protesting independent rate filings.
1977	Air cargo is deregulated; airlines are given more freedom in pricing and easier access to new rates.
1978	Congress partially decontrols natural gas.
	OSHA revokes 928 "nitpick" rules.
	CAB is phased out, ending its control over airline entry and prices.
	EPA begins emissions trading policy.
1980	FCC eliminates most federal regulation of cable TV and of consumer-premises equipment.
	Motor Carrier Act removes barriers for new entries and lets operators establish fares and routes with little ICC interference.
	Depository Institutions law phases out interest-rate ceilings and permits S&Ls to offer interest-bearing checking accounts.
	Staggers Rail Act enables railroads to adjust rates without government approval and to enter into contracts with shippers.
1981	President Reagan decontrols crude oil prices and petroleum allocations.
	FCC eliminates much radio regulation.
1982	New bus regulatory statute allows intercity bus companies to change routes and fares.
	Garn–St. Germain Act allows S&Ls to make more commercial and consumer loans and removes interest rate differentials between banks and S&Ls.
1984	AT&T agrees to divest local operating companies as part of antitrust settlement.
	Individual ocean shipping companies allowed to offer lower rates and better service than shipping conference.

Source: Murray Weidenbaum, *The Benefits of Deregulation* (St. Louis, Mo.: Washington University Center for the Study of American Business, 1987), p. 7.

tive veto might make the agencies more responsible to congressional sentiments. Critics point out, however, that such a mechanism would result in additional delays in the regulatory process and represent an added burden to Congress's already heavy workload.

These questions were rendered somewhat academic with a 1983 Supreme Court decision that rendered the legislative veto unconstitutional. The court considered it to be an unconstitutional usurpation of power that was actually a new piece of legislation that should be subject to the president's approval. Since 1932, 210 laws dealing with everything from arms sales to rules about morticians' sales pitches had contained such provisions. Some 110 of these laws were still on the books and would be affected by this ruling.[64] Congress can overcome the effects of this ruling by writing its statutes more narrowly, thus reclaiming some of the extensive authority it previously delegated to the executive branch, using its oversight and appropriation's process more effectively or forging a viable two-house veto that would pass constitutional muster.[65]

Sunset Legislation. Another idea that would enhance congressional oversight is a periodic review and reauthorization of federal agencies and programs. Time limits would be placed on a program's existence, and if no justification for its continuation could be found, it would be discontinued. Hence the term *sunset.* Such reauthorization is already required for the CPSC and FTC (3 years) and the SEC (2 years). Advocates argue that this process requires Congress to evaluate the need for regulation and eliminate waste and duplication. Again, the threat of termination could put pressure on the agencies to be more responsive to congressional sentiments. Critics point out, however, that an effective review of all the agencies, or even the most important ones, would not only be expensive but would severely increase individual committee workloads. Such a review would also lead to congressional bargaining for support of favored programs.

Presidential Intervention. In March 1978, President Carter issued Executive Order 12044, which established a new procedure for development of regulations by executive agencies. The order could not, of course, be extended to the independent commissions. Under the order, agencies were required to publish semiannual agendas of anticipated regulatory actions, write regulations in language as simple and clear as possible, seek approval of agency heads for all significant regulations before they are published for public comment, perform a "regulatory analysis" on each significant regulation, outlining the economic consequences of the proposal and its major alternatives, and periodically review all major existing regulations to determine whether they were achieving goals consistent with the order. In addition to the order, the president established a Regulatory Analysis Review Group to assess significant proposed rules and a Regulatory Council to prepare a calendar of new rules prepared by the agencies.

When President Reagan took office, a Task Force on Regulatory Relief, mentioned previously, was established to review major regulatory proposals by regulatory agencies in the executive branch, especially those proposals that have a major policy significance or that appear to involve overlapping jurisdiction among agencies. The task force also assessed executive branch regulations already in effect, oversaw the development of legislative proposals, and was to codify President Reagan's views on the appropriate role and objectives of regulatory agencies. These are examples of what the president can do to exercise oversight of the agencies in the executive branch.

Regulatory Budget. The regulatory budget idea would provide a ceiling on the compliance costs that could be imposed on the private sector during any fiscal period as well as limit the operating costs of the agencies themselves. Such a budget process would introduce some measure of control, say advocates, over compliance costs in particular. It would require that total regulatory costs be incorporated into the federal government's annual budgetary and program review mechanism. The regulatory budget would bring cost-effective considerations directly into the picture and would provide a more accurate picture of the federal government's total impact on the economy.

Analytical Techniques. Many advocate the use of more analytical techniques for all agencies before a new regulation is issued. Some assessment of the benefits and costs, it is argued, should be required of all new regulations to justify on a more rational basis the imposition of regulations. But the mere performance of a benefit-cost analysis is not enough. As stated by Murray Weidenbaum: "The key action needed by Congress is to pass a law limiting the regulations of all federal agencies to those instances where the total benefits to society exceed the costs. Government regulations should be carried to the point where the added costs equal the added benefits, and no further. Overregulation—which can be defined as regulation for which the costs exceed the benefits—should be avoided."[66]

On February 17, 1981, President Reagan issued an executive order to replace Executive Order 12044 that required agencies in the executive branch to prepare a regulatory impact analysis for each major rule being considered. This analysis should permit an accurate assessment of the potential benefits and costs of each major regulatory proposal. In addition, the executive order required that the agencies choose regulatory goals and set priorities to maximize the benefits to society, and choose the most cost-efficient means among legally available options for achieving the goals. The issuance of this executive order requiring benefit-cost analysis of executive branch agencies was called "the most thoroughgoing attempt thus far to bring the regulatory activities of executive branch agencies under White House control."[67]

The cabinet-level group that was the key actor in this decision-making process was called the Office of Information and Regulatory Affairs (OIRA). This group was located in the (OMB) and was granted broad powers of regulatory review. All important regulations must twice pass under its scrutiny before they can be issued. An agency must submit a draft regulatory impact analysis to OIRA 60 days before the agency publishes a notice of proposed rule making. If OIRA doesn't like the analysis, it can delay publication of the notice until the agency has satisfied OIRA's concerns. Then 30 days before the final rule is issued, should the rule get that far, a final regulatory impact analysis must be transmitted to OIRA, which can again object and delay issuance of the regulation.

As of mid-1983, the OMB reviewed 119 regulations already on the books, killing or revising 76 of them and proposing changes in 27 more. It had reviewed about 6,700 proposed new rules, revising or rejecting about 1 in 9. The OMB review process as described can take months or years, that can delay good as well as unnecessary changes.[68] In January 1986, a federal judge ruled that the OMB lacked authority to delay the EPA's issuance of regulations beyond statutory deadlines, a ruling that could put more force behind the deadlines that Congress inserts into environmental and health regulation. Other attacks on the OMB's authority over the regulatory process are being mounted.[69]

The Regulatory Reform Act passed by the Senate in 1981 would have required a benefit-cost analysis for all agencies that issue major new regulations costing $100 million or more to implement or that otherwise have a major impact. An agency would then be required to choose the least costly method of attaining its goal. The bill would also have given the president certain powers to determine the appropriate content of regulatory analyses and impose constraints on the ability of the courts to defer to agency judgments during judicial review. This bill constituted the first major overhaul of the Administrative Procedures Act, the statute that mandates specific methods for federal rule making. A similar bill was introduced in the House (H. R. 746) but was not acted upon.[70]

While most of the attention in government regarding the use of analytical techniques seems to have focused on benefit-cost analysis, Lester B. Lave of The Brookings Institution points out that benefit-cost analysis is only one of several decision-making frameworks that are useful in making regulatory decisions. Benefit-cost analysis is the most general of the frameworks eliciting the most information and requiring the most analysis.[71] Other decision frameworks include (1) market regulation that puts faith in consumer information and judgments; (2) the no-risk framework that is incorporated in the Delaney Clause of the Food, Drug, and Cosmetic Act; (3) technology-based standards as used in pollution control; (4) a risk-risk framework where the risk of not using a food additive or drug, for example, is balanced against the health risk of allowing it to be used; (5) a risk-benefit framework where the general benefits of a proposed regulation are balanced against its general risks; (6) cost-effectiveness analysis that is useful in determining where a given level of expenditure can be used most effectively; and (7) the use of the regulatory budget described earlier as a method of implementing cost-effectiveness analysis.[72]

These seven frameworks plus benefit-cost analysis range from simple solutions such as using market criteria to complicated ones where all the effects of the regulation must be valued in dollars. They may be applied to purely scientific problems such as identifying whether a nitrite is a carcinogen to value conflicts regarding laws requiring people to buckle their seat belts. Decision makers must understand the complexity of these problems before they can choose an appropriate framework. None of these frameworks, however, is sufficiently complete and sound to serve as an automatic way of making decisions, even if quantitative techniques are used.[73]

Alternatives to Regulation.   Finally, there may be areas where alternatives to regulation may work more effectively to achieve the objectives of regulation than the regulatory process itself. This area of reform is in effect a form of deregulation applied to the social regulatory area. Most social regulation presently involves a command and control system where laws and rules are used to more or less force people and business to meet certain objectives. The reinforcement mechanism is negative in that business and individuals are subject to penalties or lawsuits if they do not comply. Alternatives to this process involve the use of indirect methods of encouraging business to meet the same objectives.[74]

The use of a market approach to achieve regulatory objectives stresses incentives, not duties or rights. Changes in business and individual behavior can be accomplished by modifying the incentives that induce people to act in a certain way as dictated by their self-interest. Government can provide these incentives through its taxing power, for example; pollution control taxation may provide a more effective and less costly mechanism to achieve ecological objectives than the standards approach. Under such a plan, business would be induced to reduce the size of the tax by installing pollution control devices of its own choosing. Similarly provision of more accurate information to consumers on a wide range of potential product hazards may be more effective in providing safe products than outright bans or setting of safety standards that require expensive alterations.[75] The Panel on Government and the Regulation of Corporate and Individual Decisions, which was part of the President's Commission for a National Agenda for the Eighties, made the following statement.

> Nonetheless, in the current political climate, it is necessary for those who wish to see society achieve its regulatory goals to examine other ways of reaching them and to experiment with alternatives on a limited basis. To maintain an ideological rigidity by insisting that traditional ways are the only ones possible may result in a lowering of society's sights rather than in success in meeting present goals.[76]

Efforts to reduce the size and costs of the federal government's regulatory establishment are not a substitute for making substantive changes in the statutes that empower the agencies and define their responsibilities. Cutting an agency's budget or slowing down the rule-making process does not necessarily reduce the burdens imposed on the private sector. Some budget cuts may have the opposite effect to the extent that they increase delays in issuing permits or developing needed rules to clarify ambiguous requirements.[77]

The most fundamental shortcomings of government regulation may result more from statutory than from administrative deficiencies. Most statutes do not contain any provision for benefit-cost analysis or risk analysis, which may be useful tools for making regulatory decisions. Some are based on technologically questionable assumptions such as the "zero discharge" provision of clean water legislation. Others, such as the Delaney Clause of the Food, Drug, and Cosmetic Act are based on "zero-risk" assumptions that society is willing to set aside in certain situations.

In its first term, at least, the Reagan administration was unwilling to commit the political resources necessary to transform the basic statutory framework of the regulatory apparatus. Not one of the major pieces of social regulatory legislation enacted over the last decade had been repealed or even amended. Even if the administration, however, was inclined to make an effort to revise the statutory framework, it was by no means certain that Congress would go along. Revisions to the Clean Water Act were passed over the president's veto in his second term of office. Yet the basic issue remains "not whether we have too many or too few regulations," but that "too many regulations are not effective enough in accomplishing the purposes for which they were enacted." Business has a responsibility and an opportunity to take the initiative and "propose reforms that will enable the burdens on business to be reduced without decreasing—and perhaps even increasing—the benefits received by the public."[78]

At the beginning of 1987, it appeared that even in the Reagan administration, tougher regulatory enforcement was back in vogue. In response to the insider scandals on Wall Street, the chairman of the SEC asked for more enforcement funds in the agency's $140.5 million 1988 budget. OSHA increased pressure on companies to comply with accident-reporting requirements and levied substantial fines against several large companies. The Federal Aviation Administration (FAA) hit Eastern Air Lines with a record $9.5 million penalty for maintenance violations. And the EPA in 1986 referred a record 342 civil cases to the Justice Department for prosecution. Criminal charges were filed against 94 defendants. While no one expected a return to the activist days of the Carter administration, this increase in enforcement activities represented a break with the see-no-evil approach most regulatory agencies had taken in the Reagan administration.[79]

Under President Bush, regulation was expected to increase. Bush's clean air package carried an estimated $19 billion-a-year price tag, and business was expected to pick up most of the costs. The administration was also seeking to promote greater competition in the airline industry, restrain the freewheeling financial services industry, and clamp down on safety and health problems in the workplace.[80] Some said that the steam for regulatory reform seemed to be fully dissipated, and a reversal of course set by the Reagan administration was taking place as regulation was once again expanding.[81]

Further success in the area of regulatory reform would require that the administration (1) adopt a holistic approach to regulatory reform, (2) actively pursue policies to ease the transition to a less-regulated economy, (3) work with a bipartisan congressional coalition for regulatory reform, and (3) take effective actions to make certain that inefficient federal policies are not simply replaced by equally undesirable state regulations. All these recommendations would require that the administration adopt a coherent, broadly consistent approach to regulation.[82] Few expected the Bush administration to take this kind of approach.

Questions for Discussion

1. How does government regulation affect business? What functional areas does regulation affect? What changes has it made in the management function?

2. Distinguish between industry and social regulation. What are the objectives of each type of regulation? What reasons can you think of to explain the development of industry and social regulation?

3. Describe the difference between compliance costs and administrative costs of regulation. How can compliance costs be measured? Pick a specific agency, such as the EPA, and work out a methodology to measure the compliance costs in a specific business organization.

4. Is Murray Weidenbaum's multiplier of 20 a valid method of estimating compliance costs for future years? What assumptions are made in using this figure? What other methods could be developed to estimate future compliance costs?

5. Define the concept of incremental costs. Discuss implementation of this concept. Are the Roundtable guidelines specific enough? Is use of this concept valid in determining the true cost of regulation?

6. What is the usefulness of comprehensive cost studies such as the Roundtable's? Are they precise enough to be used by makers of public policy in making decisions? Should such studies continue to be performed regularly?

7. Distinguish between second- and third-order effects of regulation. Give examples of each type. In your opinion, is this distinction valid? If so, which are the most serious costs as far as society is concerned?

8. Do you believe the benefits of regulation can be quantified? In what terms? Think of a methodology to measure the benefits of consumer regulation. What value assumptions have to be made?

9. Has airline regulation been beneficial to the American consumer? In what ways? Have there been any negative effects of deregulation in this sector of the economy? Would you reregulate the airline industry? Why or why not?

10. Why have deregulatory efforts taken place to such an extent in the area of industry regulation? What forces were operative in the late 1970s that brought about this kind of major change? Are these forces present today? What implications does your answer have for future efforts of this nature?

11. Discuss the various reform measures mentioned in the chapter. Which hold the most promise for meaningful reform of social regulation? What would be the beneficial and detrimental effects of each measure? For business? For society?

12. Can the regulatory process as a whole be reformed? What alternatives to regulation exist? How can these be implemented? Why haven't alternatives been seriously considered in our society? Why regulation?

Case: Air Bags

Reducing automobile accidents in the United States is a major public policy problem because approximately 50,000 people die each year from such accidents and more than 5 million are injured. Despite improved highways and driver-training programs, accidents continue at a high level. The National Highway Traffic Safety Administration (NHTSA) was created in 1966 to develop and enforce safety standards for motor vehicles. One of the first acts of the new agency was to emphasize use of the air bag in automobiles to reduce the chance of serious injury in an accident. The agency published a notice in 1969 entitled "Inflatable Occupant Restraint System" that required air bags to be installed in all vehicles manufactured in the country. The automobile industry opposed this standard and raised questions about safety research, engineering design, financial burdens, and possible legal violations and was able to postpone implementation for nearly a decade.

Air bags are passive restraints that deploy automatically in an accident without any action by the occupants of the automobile. The bag inflates upon impact in a fraction of a second and acts as a cushion to prevent the occupants from striking the interior of the car or hitting the windshield and shattering the glass. Seat belts would perform much the same function, but the problem with such devices is that they require positive action from the occupants to buckle up, and research indicated that the percentage of people who used seat belts was very low. Use of an air bag does not require any such action and is thereby considered to be a superior technology.[1]

Initial research conducted for the NHTSA showed that air bags would be effective in preventing injuries and fatalities to adults in frontal crashes. Evaluations done by General Motors and Ford also showed air bags would be effective, especially when used in combination with seat belts.[2] Proponents of air bags stress the desirability of reducing fatalities by whatever means and that this is reason enough for requiring their installation. Automobile companies and their supporters argue that their are many unresolved problems that make the use of this technology questionable. Opponents of the air bag generally raise the following objections: (1) It is a complex and untested contraption, (2) it can go off when it shouldn't, causing a startled driver to lose control, (3) it works only in head-on crashes, (4) it needs to be used in conjunction with a seat belt to be effective, (5) it can injure a child standing on the seat or otherwise out of the normal passenger position, and (6) it is costly.[3]

The controversy over the installation of air bags continued when a passive restraint rule was adopted by the Carter administration in 1977 that would have required some 1982 models to be equipped with air bags or belts that automatically fold across front-seat occupants.[4] The Reagan administration first delayed the effective date a year and then rescinded the rule entirely. A federal appeals court overturned this decision in response to lawsuits filed by State Farm Mutual Automobile Insurance Co. and the National Association of Independent Insurers. The appeals judge called the decision "arbitrary and illogical" and said that the NHTSA had failed to consider any alternatives to recession of the requirement.[5]

The government estimated that air bags would boost car prices $300 to $1,100, and GM estimated that it would have to invest $285 million to comply with the passive-restraint requirement. Ford Motor Co. estimated an investment of $183 million.[6] The Center for Auto Safety, a Nader watchdog group, estimated a cost of $1 billion annually but stated that society pays $2.4 billion annually in medical, rehabilitation and loss-of-work time expenses linked to auto-related injuries.[7]

The head of the Transportation Department, Elizabeth Dole, issued a ruling in the summer of 1984 to deal with the controversy. Beginning with 1987 models, new cars would have to be built with either air bags or automatic seat belts. Automakers would have to equip 10 percent of their 1987 models with passive restraints for the driver and front-seat passengers. This percentage would rise to 25 percent in 1988, 40 percent in 1989, and include all 1990 models. Alternatively, new cars could be built with safer "friendly interiors" if such interiors would provide as much passenger protection as air bags or automatic belts. None of these measures would be required, however, if states representing two-thirds of the population were to enact laws requiring people to fasten their seat belts. States had until April of 1989 to pass such mandatory seat-belt laws.[8]

In mid-1986, 26 states and the District of Columbia, which accounted for 68 percent of the nation's population, had passed seat-belt laws. Legislation was pending in 26 other states. However, efforts to repeal the laws were underway in 10 states, including some in which the law hadn't yet taken effect. Compliance with the laws also seemed to be waning.[9] In September 1986, an appeals court in Washington said that none of the laws being enacted by the states to require motorists to buckle their seat belts appeared to meet the standards set by the agency. Thus in the court's opinion, it appeared unlikely that the passive restraint rule would be rescinded when the deadline for mandatory seat-belt laws was reached.[10]

Because the states failed to reach the required level of coverage with seat-belt laws, the phase-in procedure for passive restraints began. After September 1, 1986, an increasing number of automobiles had to be equipped with passive restraints on both the driver and passenger sides of the vehicle. These restraints could include air bags, passive seat belts, or other protective measures such as padded dashboards and shock-absorbent steering columns. In May 1988, Chrysler Corporation announced that it had started putting driver-side air bags in six of its car lines and by 1990 would meet the federal standard in all its passenger vehicles. Ford also stated that it was planning to install air bags on more than half of its cars before the 1990 deadline arrived.[11]

Case Notes

1. Judith Reppy, "The Automobile Air Bag," in Dorothy Nelkin, ed. *Controversy: Politics of Technical Decisions* (Beverly Hills, Calif.: Sage Publications, 1977), pp. 145–46.

2. Richard M. Hodgetts, "Air Bags and Auto Safety," *The Business Enterprise: Social Challenge, Social Response* (Philadelphia: W. B. Saunders, 1977), pp. 130–31.

3. Albert R. Karr, "Auto Air Bags: U.S. Resumes Debate on Use," *Wall Street Journal*, November 29, 1983, p. 31.

4. See Susan J. Tolchin, "Air Bags and Regulatory Delay," *Issues in Science and Technology*, Vol. 1, No. 1 (Fall 1984), pp. 66–83, for an excellent summary of the air bag controversy.

5. Albert R. Karr, "U.S. Move to Scrap Air Bags in New Cars is Overturned by a Federal Appeals Court," *Wall Street Journal*, June 2, 1982, p. 2.

6. "Cars Must Have Air Bags by 1984, U.S. Court Rules," *Wall Street Journal*, August 5, 1982, p. 4.

7. Stephen Wermiel, "High Court's Decision on Air Bags Makes it Tougher for Agencies to Rescind Rules," *Wall Street Journal*, June 27, 1983, p. 7.

8. Christopher Conte and Donald Woutat, "Rule on Air Bags Won't End Safety Battle as U.S. Agency Plan Allows Alternatives," *Wall Street Journal*, July 12, 1984, p. 3. In November of 1985, Ford announced that if would offer driver-side air bags in Tempo and Topaz models, the first company to offer such gear on nonluxury vehicles since the mid-1970s. Christopher Conte, "Ford Plans to Offer Airbags as Option on 2 Compact Cars, *Wall Street Journal*, November 4, 1985, p. 12.

9. Jan Wong, "Despite Recent Laws, Many Motorists Are Still Casual About Wearing Seat Belts," *Wall Street Journal*, March 7, 1986, p. 19.

10. Albert R. Karr, "Rule on Air Bags, Automatic Safety Belts Unlikely to Be Rescinded, Court Says," *Wall Street Journal*, September 19, 1986, p. 10.

11. Joseph B. White, "U.S. Auto Makers Decide Safety Sells," *Wall Street Journal*, August 24, 1988, p. 17.

Chapter Notes

1. Murray L. Weidenbaum, *Business, Government and the Public* (Englewood Cliffs, N.J.: Prentice Hall, 1977), p. 285.

2. Adolph A. Berle and Gardiner C. Means, *The Modern Corporation and Private Property* (New York: Macmillan, 1932).

3. Murray L. Weidenbaum, *The Future of Business Regulation* (New York: AMACOM, 1979), p. 34. One scholar characterizes the 1970–74 period as a regulatory revolution. The claim is made that over 70 percent of the current regulatory apparatus is, in one way or another, the product of this period. The amount of change that took place in those four years is said to be unmatched in any equal period in American political history. See John Adams Wettergreen, *The Regulatory Revolution and the New Bureaucratic State* (Washington, D.C.: The Heritage Foundation, 1988), p. 1.

4. Murray L. Weidenbaum, "Government Power and Business Performance." Reprinted from p. 200, *The United States in the 1980s,* Peter Dunignan and Alvin Robushka, eds., with permission of the publishers, Hoover Institution Press. Copyright 1980 by the Board of Trustees of the Leland Stanford Jr. University.

5. See Weidenbaum, *The Future of Business Regulation,* pp. 33–54.

6. George A. Steiner, "An Overview of the Changing Business Environment and Its Impact on Business," paper presented at the AACSB Conference on Business Environment/Public Policy, Summer 1979, pp. 7–8.

7. Nancy Lammers, ed., *Federal Regulatory Directory 1983–84* (Washington, D.C.: Congressional Quarterly, 1983), pp. 3–4.

8. Murray L. Weidenbaum, "The Changing Nature of Government Regulation of Business," paper presented at the AACSB Conferences on Business Environment/Public Policy, Summer 1979, p. 14.

9. Robert E. Healy, ed., *Federal Regulatory Directory 1979–80* (Washington D.C.: Congressional Quarterly, Inc., 1979), p. 5.

10. Kenneth W. Chilton, *The Effects of Gramm-Rudman-Hollings on Federal Regulatory Agencies* (St. Louis, Mo.: Washington University Center for the Study of American Business, 1986), p. 9.

11. Ibid., p. 10.

12. Kenneth W. Chilton and Ronald J. Penoyer, The Hazards of "Purse Strings" *Regulatory Reform: Regulatory Spending and Staffing Under the Reagan Administration, 1981–85* (St. Louis, Mo.: Washington University Center for the Study of American Business, 1984), p. 8.

13. David Vogel, "Business and the Reagan Administration," *Business in the Contemporary World,* October 1988, pp. 52–55.

14. The Vice President, Office of the Press Secretary, Statement by Vice President George Bush, Press Release, August 11, 1983, p. 2.

15. The White House, Office of the Press Secretary, *Fact Sheet: The Administration's Progress on Regulatory Relief,* August 4, 1982, p. 3.

16. See Office of the Vice President, *Highlights of Regulatory Relief Accomplishments During the Reagan Administration,* August, 1983.

17. Vogel, "Business and the Reagan Administration," p. 55.

18. William A. Niskanen, "The Weak Fourth Leg of Reaganomics," *Wall Street Journal,* June 30, 1988, p. 20.

19. Murray L. Weidenbaum and Robert De Fina, *The Rising Cost of Government Regulation* (St. Louis, Mo.: Washington University Center for the Study of American Business, 1977).

20. No cost estimates were available for the following regulatory activities; Animal and Plant Health Inspection Service, Packers and Stockyards Administration, Department of Housing and Urban Development, Antitrust Division, Drug Enforcement Administration, Federal Railroad Administration, Bureau of Alcohol, Tobacco, and Firearms, Customs Service, Consumer Product Safety Commission, National Transportation Safety Board, Mining Enforcement and Safety Administration, Department of Energy, Federal Maritime Commission, Commodity Future Trading Commission, Nuclear Regulatory Commission, Comptroller of the Currency, Federal Deposit Insurance Corporation.

21. Murray L. Weidenbaum and Robert De Fina, *The Cost of Federal Regulation of Economic Activity* (Washington, D.C.: American Enterprise Institute, 1978), p. 1.

22. This total of $66 billion is equivalent to: 4 percent of the gross national product; $307 per person living in the United States: 18 percent of the federal budget; twice the amount that the federal government spends on health; 74 percent of the amount devoted to national defense; over one-third of all private investment in new plants and equipment. Ibid., p. 3.

23. Arthur Andersen and Company, *Cost of Government Regulation Study* (New York: The Business Roundtable, 1979).

24. Ibid., p. ii.

25. Steve H. Hanke and Stephen J. K. Walters, "Social Regulation: A Report Card," Washington, D.C.: The National Chamber Foundation, 1990, p. 2.

26. Ibid., p. 3.

27. Weidenbaum, *The Future of Business Regulation,* pp. 16–23.

28. Wettergreen, "Regulatory Revolution," p. 3.

29. Hanke and Walters, "Social Regulation," pp. 20–22.

30. Dow Chemical Company canceled plans in January 1977 for building a $300 million petrochemical complex in California. After 2 years and a $4 million expenditure, Dow had obtained only 4 of the 65 permits that were needed from federal, state, local, and regional regulatory agencies in order to build the facility. Weidenbaum, *The Future of Business Regulation,* pp. 18–20.

31. Ibid., p. 23.

32. Jerome E. Schnee, "Regulation and Innovation: U.S. Pharmaceutical Industry," *California Management Review,* Vol. XXII, No. 1 (Fall 1979). pp. 23–32.

33. Weidenbaum, *The Future of Business Regulation,* p. 30.

34. *In the Matter of Use of the Carterfone Device in Message Toll Telephone Service,* 13 F.C.C. 420 (1968).

35. Robert E. Dallos and Lee May, "Debate Still Rages Over Deregulation," *Los Angeles Times,* November 2, 1986, p. I-1.

36. "A Painful Transition for the Transport Industry," *Business Week,* November 28, 1983, p. 86.

37. Continental's Fiesty Chairman Defends Deregulation—And Himself," *Business Week,* November 7, 1983, p. 111.

38. Janice Castro, "The Sky Kings Rule the Routes," *Time,* May 15, 1989, pp. 52–53.

39. Ibid., pp. 53–54.

40. Laurie McGinley, "Republicans Are Joining Chorus of Airline Critics Seeking Partial Reregulation to Spur Competition," *Wall Street Journal,* September 21, 1989, p. A-26.

41. Seth Payne, "How Sam The Hammer Could Nail The Airlines," *Business Week,* June 26, 1989, pp. 126–27.

42. "Rumblings of Reregulation," *Fortune,* January 10, 1983, p. 17.

43. Dallos and May, "Debate," p. I-8.

44. "The Contest Over Who Will Inherit the CAB's Powers," *Business Week,* February 6, 1984, p. 82.

45. See Christopher Conte, "ICC Nears Paralysis as Its Members Feud Bitterly About Deregulation," *Wall Street Journal,* July 18, 1984, p. 29.

46. "A Painful Transition for the Transport Industry," *Business Week,* November 28, 1983, p. 86.

47. "What Deregulation Has Done to the Truckers," *Business Week,* November 9, 1981, p. 70.

48. Thomas Gale Moore, "Transportation Policy," *Regulation,* No. 3, 1988, p. 59.

49. "Deregulating America: The Benefits Begin to Show—In Productivity, Innovation, and Prices," *Business Week,* November 28, 1983, pp. 81, 86.

50. Moore, "Transportation Policy," p. 60.

51. Rich Jaroslovsky and Christopher Conte, "Friendly Teamsters: Politics Puts Hold on Trucking Bill," *Wall Street Journal,* May 14, 1984, p. 50.

52. "A Painful Transition for the Transport Industry," *Business Week,* November 28, 1983, p. 86.

53. Brian S. Moskal, "Are Rails Headed for Re-Regulation?" *Industry Week,* May 13, 1985, p. 57.

54. Glenn Emery, "The Rail Surprise: Still Going Strong," *Insight,* May 1, 1989, p. 10.

55. J. F. Kenefick, Chair, Union Pacific System, remarks to the Western Railway Club in Chicago, January 28, 1985, permission from *Industry Week,* May 13, 1985, p. 57. Copyright, Penton/IPC, Cleveland, Ohio.

56. Moore, "Transportation Policy," p. 59.

57. Holman Jenkins, Jr., "Coal Shippers Set Their Sights on Reviving Rail Regulation," *Insight,* January 11, 1988, pp. 20–21.

58. "The Revolution, in Financial Services," *Business Week,* November 28, 1983, p. 89.

59. Christopher Elias, "Fed Blasts a Large Loophole in Ban on Bank Underwriting," *Insight,* February 13, 1989, pp. 44–45.

60. Jeanne Saddler, "Push to Deregulate Broadcasting Delights Industry, Angers Others," *Wall Street Journal,* April 16, 1984, p. 33. See also "Congress Slows the FCC's Rush to Deregulate," *Business Week,* August 20, 1984, pp. 33–34; Bob Davis, "Comment by Public On Fairness Policy Is Sought by FCC," *Wall Street Journal,* February 26, 1987, p. 42.

61. "Has The FCC Gone Too Far?" *Business Week,* August 5, 1985, pp. 48–54.

62. Jeff Shear, "Congress's Turn to Hold the Line," *Insight,* February 20, 1989, pp. 40–41.

63. Murray Weidenbaum, *The Benefits of Deregulation* (St. Louis, Mo.: Washington University Center for the Study of American Business, 1987), p. 1.

64. "An Epic Court Decision," *Time,* July 4, 1983, pp. 12–14.

65. Stuart M. Statler, "After the Legislative Veto," *Wall Street Journal,* April 6, 1984, p. 24.

66. Murray L. Weidenbaum, *Reducing the Hidden Cost of Big Government* (St. Louis, Mo.: Washington University Center for the Study of American Business, 1978), pp. 9–10.

67. George Eads, "Harnessing Regulation: The Evolving Role of White House Oversight," *Regulation,* May/June 1981, p. 19.

68. "Three Steps Forward, Two Back," *Time,* August 29, 1983, p. 13.

69. Robert E. Taylor, "OMB Lacks Power To Delay EPA's Rules, Judge Says," *Wall Street Journal,* January 1, 1986, p. 4.

70. Penoyer, *1982 Update,* p. 8.

71. Lester B. Lave, *The Strategy of Social Regulation* (Washington, D.C.: The Brookings Institution, 1981), p. 24.

72. Ibid., pp. 9–25.

73. Ibid., p. 27.

74. See Charles L. Schultze, *The Public Use of the Private Interest* (Washington, D.C.: The Brookings Institution, 1977).

75. Weidenbaum, Reducing the Cost of Government, pp. 11–12. See also Alfred E. Kahn, "Using the Market in Regulation, *Business Week,* December 15, 1980, p. 14.

76. Alan B. Morrison and Roger G. Noll, Government and the Regulation of Corporate and Individual Decisions in the Eighties, *Panel Report for the President's Commission for a National Agenda for the Eighties* (Englewood Cliffs, N.J.: Prentice-Hall, 1980), pp. 25–26.

77. Murray L. Weidenbaum, Regulatory Reform: A Report Card for the Reagan Administration," *California Management Review,* Vol XXVI, No. 1 (Fall 1983), p. 20. See also Murray L. Weidenbaum and Ronald J. Penoyer, *The Next Step in Regulatory Reform: Updating the Statutes* (St. Louis, Mo.: Washington University Center for the Study of American Business, 1983).

78. David Vogel, "Reagan and Regulation: Whence and Whither," *New Management,* Vol. 1 (Spring 1983), p. 41.

79. "Reagan's Regulators Are Suddenly Starting to Crack Down," *Business Week,* January 19, 1987, p. 45. See also Andy Pasztor, "Reagan's Top Antitrust Lawyer Surprises Critics By Stepping Up Criminal Enforcement Efforts," *Wall Street Journal,* August 18, 1986, p. 44, and Laurie McGinley, "Hands On: Federal Regulation Rises Anew in Matters That Worry the Public," *Wall Street Journal,* April 21, 1987, p. 1.

80. Tim Smart, "Regulation Rises Again," *Business Week,* June 26, 1989, pp. 58–59.

81. Albert R. Karr and Michael McQueen, "Adjusting Course: Unlike Reagan Aides, Many Bush Officials Expand Regulation," *Wall Street Journal,* November 27, 1989, p. A-1.

82. Roger G. Noll, "Regulation After Reagan," *Regulation,* No. 3, 1988, p. 20.

Suggested Reading

ANDERSON, JAMES E. *Economic Regulatory Policies.* Washington, D.C.: University Press of America, 1985.

BACKMAN, JULES, ed. *Regulation and Deregulation.* Indianapolis: Bobbs-Merrill, 1981.

BARAM, MICHAEL S. *Alternatives to Regulation.* Lexington, Mass.: Lexington Books, 1982.

BARDACH, EUGENE, AND ROBERT A. KAGAN, eds. *Social Regulation: Strategies for Reform.* San Francisco: Institute for Contemporary Studies, 1982.

GRAMLICH, EDWARD M. *Benefit-Cost Analysis of Government Programs.* Englewood Cliffs, N.J.: Prentice Hall, 1981.

KOHLMEIER, LOUIS M., JR. *The Regulators.* New York: Harper & Row, 1969.

LAVE, LESTER B. *The Strategy of Social Regulation.* Washington, D.C.: The Brookings Institution, 1981.

MACHAN, TIBOR R., AND BRUCE JOHNSON, eds. *Rights and Regulation: Ethical, Political, and Economic Issues.* Cambridge, Mass.: Ballinger, 1983.

MAXEY, MARGARET N., AND ROBERT L. KUHN. *Regulatory Reform: New Vision or Old Curse.* New York: Praeger, 1985.

McCRAW, THOMAS K. *Regulation in Perspective: Historical Essays.* Cambridge, Mass.: Harvard University Press, 1981.

MEINERS, ROGER E., AND BRUCE YANDLE, eds. *Regulation & the Reagan Era.* New York: Holmes and Meier, 1989.

MELNICK, SHEP R. *Regulation and the Courts: The Case of the Clean Air Act.* Washington, D.C.: The Brookings Institution, 1983.

MITNICK, BARRY M. *The Political Economy of Regulation.* New York: Columbia University Press, 1980.

NOLL, ROGER G., AND BRUCE M. OWEN. *The Political Economy of Deregulation: Interest Groups in the Regulatory Process.* Washington, D.C.: American Enterprise Institute, 1983.

SCHULTZE, CHARLES L. *The Public Use of the Private Interest.* Washington, D.C.: The Brookings Institution, 1977.

SHOGREN, JASON F., ed. *The Political Economy of Government Regulation.* Boston: Kluwer Academic, 1989.

SPULBER, DANIEL F. *Regulation & Markets.* Cambridge, Mass.: MIT Press, 1989.

STRICKLAND, ALLYN DOUGLAS. *Government Regulation and Business.* Boston: Houghton Mifflin, 1980.

THOMPSON, FRED. *Regulatory Policy and Practices: Regulating Better & Regulating Less.* New York: Praeger, 1982.

WEIDENBAUM, MURRAY L. *Business, Government and the Public,* 4th ed. Englewood Cliffs, N.J.: Prentice Hall. 1990.

——, *The Future of Business Regulation,* New York: AMACOM, 1979.

WHITE, LAWRENCE J. *Reforming Regulation: Processes and Problems.* Englewood Cliffs, N.J.: Prentice Hall, 1981.

3

Antitrust Policies

Federal antitrust policies began as a response to the large, modern business enterprises that first emerged at the close of the nineteenth century. Whatever one believes about the role of government in forming antitrust policies, it did appear in those years that a completely unregulated system was leading to excessive concentration in most major industries. Such power was unacceptable in American society, as it was believed that this power over markets would be used to ride roughshod over the public interest. Monopoly per se is bad, since a monopolist can set prices and output levels more or less at will, responding only to general economic conditions, not to the challenge of a business competitor.

Americans believe that through competition the best and most efficient companies will survive and prosper. Maximizing competition will cause resources to be allocated in the most efficient manner, thus minimizing the cost of products and benefiting the consumer. The ideal form of competition is, of course, pure competition, where the industry is not concentrated, where there are insignificant barriers to entry, and no product differentiation exists. In this kind of competition the firm has no other choice but to meet the competition, as buyers and sellers are so small as to have no influence over the market, thus ensuring that the forces of supply and demand alone determine market outcomes.

This kind of competition exists, however, only in textbooks. Most industries in today's economy are oligopolistic, containing a few large firms. These firms recognize the impact of their actions on rivals and therefore on the market as a whole. In oligopoly, firms deal with each other more or less directly and take into account the effect of their actions on each other. What they do depends very much on how their rivals are expected to react. Oligopolistic firms adjust prices in response to changing market conditions or to changes introduced by rivals in the industry.

Modern large corporations are not simply passive respondents to the impersonal forces of supply and demand over which they have no control. The large firms do possess some degree of economic power and do have some influence in the marketplace. Economic power can be defined as the ability to control markets by the reduction of competition through concentration or the adoption of anticompetitive practices. Markets may fail if the dominant firms in an industry are allowed to engage in predatory practices or if groups of firms are allowed to interfere with the price mechanism. The role of government in this area is to maintain a workable competition by enforcing policies that deal with the size of corporations and the structure of the industries in which they function as well as mergers and other forms of combination, and promoting fair competition by making certain forms of anticompetitive practice illegal.

> Antitrust legislation in the United States rests on two premises. The first is the English common law as it evolved through court decisions over a long time. In general, these decisions held that restraint on trade or commerce is not in the public interest. . . . The second premise is the belief that competition is an effective regulator of most markets and, with a few exceptions, that monopolistic practices can be stopped by competition. This premise is based on the economic theory espousing pure or perfect competition as the ideal, since according to the theory, competition forces firms to be efficient, cut costs, and receive no more than normal profits.[1]

American society has really never come to trust corporate power. Many people believe there is something inherently wrong with bigness, even though such bigness is a fact of life. The antitrust area keeps alive the American ideals of competition, in some sense, and provides a way for society to reaffirm its belief in the notion of a purely competitive economy where economic power is limited. The Sherman Act, for example, was supported by a coalition of small business and farm groups who were concerned about the economic power of the large trusts that existed at the end of the century and had come to dominate certain industries. In *Northern Pacific Ry.* v. *United States,* Justice Black called the Sherman Act:

> . . . a comprehensive charter of economic liberty aimed at preserving free and unfettered competition as the rule of trade. It rests on the premise that the unrestrained interaction of competitive forces will yield the best allocation of our economic resources, the lowest prices, the highest quality and the greatest material progress, while at the same time providing an environment conducive to the preservation of our democratic political and social institutions.[2]

Antitrust legislation sets guidelines to ensure that competition in the American economy remains intact in some fashion. However, the intentionally vague language of the antitrust laws allows each administration to interpret and enforce the laws in accordance with their economic philosophy. Federal agencies that are responsible for implementing the laws have the power to interpret and enforce the laws according to the philosophy that prevails in the administration in power. Courts have further power to interpret the meaning of antitrust legislation through ruling on cases that come before them.

Public Policy Measures

The Sherman Act of 1890. The most important sections of the Sherman Act are Sections 1 and 2 (see box). Section 1 attacks the act of combining or conspiring to restrain trade. This section seems to make illegal every formal arrangement among firms aimed at curbing independent action in the market. It places restrictions on market

SHERMAN ACT OF 1890

Section 1. Every contract, combination in the form of trust or otherwise, or conspiracy, in restraint of trade or commerce among the several States, or with foreign nations, is hereby declared to be illegal. Every person who shall make any such contract or engage in any such combination or conspiracy, shall be deemed guilty of a misdemeanor, and, on conviction thereof, shall be punished by fine not exceeding five thousand dollars, or by imprisonment not exceeding one year, or by both said punishments, in the discretion of the court.

Section 2. Every person who shall monopolize, or attempt to monopolize, or combine or conspire with any other person or persons, to monopolize any part of this trade or commerce among the several States, or with foreign nations, shall be deemed guilty of a misdemeanor, and, on conviction thereof, shall be punished by fine not exceeding five thousand dollars, or by imprisonment not exceeding one year, or by both said punishments, in the discretion of the court.

conduct, in particular those means of coordination between sellers who use formal agreements to reduce the independence of their actions.[3]

Section 2 enjoins market structures where seller concentration is so high that it could be called a monopoly. But the wording of the section speaks not of monopoly (the state of market structure) but of monopolizing (the act of creating a high level of seller concentration). Taken literally, this could mean that monopolies that existed before 1890 could not be touched, or those that somehow become monopolies in spite of Section 2 were immune from prosecution.[4]

The Clayton Act of 1914. The Clayton Act attacks a series of business policies insofar as they would substantially lessen competition or tend to create a monopoly. The language of the Sherman Act is quite broad, and there was a good deal of uncertainty as to what specific practices were in restraint of trade and thus illegal. The Clayton Act was passed to correct this deficiency by being more specific. It also contained a section that was designed to slow down the merger movement that had resulted in the emergence of many large corporations in the years immediately preceding its passage. The most important sections as far as these purposes are concerned are the following:

Section 2. This section bars price discrimination (charging one buyer more than another for the same item) when it tends to lessen competition in any line of commerce or tends to create a monopoly. The act prohibits a seller from granting lower prices to favored buyers, whether the price discrimination is instigated by the seller or forced upon the seller by the buyer. The Robinson-Patman Act of 1936 amended this section to strengthen it and plug loopholes. Price differentials are allowed if they are based on actual differences in the cost of manufacture, sale, or delivery resulting from different methods or quantities, or if a lower price was granted in good faith to meet an equally low price of a competitor.

Section 3. This section forbids sellers from requiring buyers of their line of goods to refrain from buying the goods of their rivals when such a policy tends to create a monopoly. There are two situations where this could happen: (1) a tying arrangement, where sellers give buyers access to one line of goods only if the buyers take other goods as well, and (2) an exclusive dealing arrangement, where sellers give buyers access to their line of goods only if the buyers agree to take no goods from any of the sellers' rivals.

Section 4. This section provides for treble damages in a private suit: it specifies that the successful claimant in an antitrust case shall recover "three-fold the damages by him sustained, and the cost of the suit, including a reasonable attorney's fee." This section thus encourages private parties such as corporations to pursue antitrust suits against alleged violators.

Section 7. This section forbids mergers that substantially lessen competition or tend to create a monopoly. It is concerned with structure and size alone rather than with specific anticompetitive practices. It reads as follows:

No corporation engaged in commerce shall acquire, directly or indirectly, the whole or any part of the stock or other share capital of another corporation engaged also in commerce where the effect of such acquisition may be to substantially lessen competition between the corporation whose stock is so acquired and the corporation making the acquisition or to restrain such commerce in any section or community or tend to create a monopoly of any line of commerce.[5]

While the language is somewhat fuzzy, this section clearly prevented the acquisition of the stock of one corporation by another in the same line of business when the effect was to lessen competition or tend to create a monopoly. The act did not say anything, however, about the purchase or sales of assets by one corporation of or to another, even in the same line of business. This proved to be a huge loophole in the law, which merger-minded companies exploited. The loophole was finally plugged by the 1950 Celler-Kefauver Amendments, which changed Section 7 to read "no corporation . . . shall acquire, directly or indirectly, the whole or any part of the stock or . . . any part of the assets of another corporation . . . where . . . the effect of such acquisition may be substantially to lessen competition, or tend to create a monopoly."[6]

The Federal Trade Commission Act of 1914. This act created the Federal Trade Commission and gave it rather sweeping powers to investigate business organizations and examine business conduct, practices, and the management of companies engaged in interstate commerce. Section 5 provides the language relevant to the antitrust area: "Unfair methods of competition in or affecting commerce, and unfair or deceptive acts or practices affecting commerce are hereby declared unlawful."

Thus unfair methods of competition are declared unlawful, but it was up to the commission itself to define what was unfair. The FTC was allowed to attack practices it defined as unlawful even though such practices did not violate the established antitrust laws (*FTC* v. *The Sperry and Hutchinson Company*).[7] No right of private action exists under this section (*Carlson* v. *Coca-Cola Co.*).[8] In 1938, the Wheeler-Lea Act amended this section to read "unfair or deceptive acts or practices in commerce," thus giving the FTC the authority to pursue deceptive advertising and other marketing practices.

Current Developments. Throughout most of the period since 1890 and the Sherman Act, violations of antitrust laws have been considered only misdemeanors, carrying very low penalties and jail terms (see Table 3.1) for corporations and individuals found guilty of violations. In 1955, the penalties were upgraded substantially, but the really significant development took place in 1974, when violations were declared a felony punishable by fines not exceeding $1 million for a corporation or an individual and imprisonment not exceeding three years.

TABLE 3.1   Penalties for Violations of Antitrust Laws

Period	Maximum Penalty for Corporations	Maximum Penalty for Individuals	Maximum Jail Term (Years)
1890–1955	$ 5,000	$ 5,000	1
1955–1974	50,000	50,000	1
1974–present	1,000,000	1,000,000	3

Another recent development in the antitrust area as far as public policy measures is concerned is the Hart-Scott-Rodino Antitrust Improvements Act of 1976. Title I of this act gave the Justice Department broadened authority to interview witnesses and gather other evidence in antitrust investigations. It gave broadened powers to obtain oral testimony and written interrogatories as well as documents from corporations that may be needed for an investigation. These provisions applied not only to formal cases actually filed by the Justice Department but also to investigations mounted in connection with planned mergers and joint ventures.

Title II provided for premerger notification, requiring large companies planning mergers to give federal antitrust authorities advance notice of their plans. This notice must describe the type of the transaction, the structure of the merging firms, the holdings of the acquiring party in the acquired firms, the horizontal overlaps, the vertical relationships, and any acquisitions made within the previous 10 years. Under this provision corporations cannot complete the merger for 30 days after the report is filed. This gives the agencies time to study the proposal and take action to block the merger before it is consummated. If the agencies find that the proposed merger raises anticompetitive concerns and the merging parties do not agree to a restructured merger, the government can file for injunctive relief in a federal district court.

Rules issued by the FTC specified that these reporting requirements applied to mergers of large companies and acquisitions of either 15 percent of the outstanding stock of a large concern or $15 million of the stock and assets of such a company. One of the companies involved must have asssets of at least $100 million for the law to apply. The reporting requirement also applies to joint ventures when the joint venture has assets of at least $10 million and one company involved has at least $100 million in assets or annual sales and another has at least $10 million in assets or annual sales. The requirement also applies if the joint venture has assets of at least $100 million and each of the two companies involved has assets of at least $10 million.

Title III of the act allows state attorneys general to sue antitrust violators in federal court for treble damages on behalf of overcharged consumers, on the assumption that each state may be a parent to its citizens. While consumers are often the victims of antitrust violations, the injuries to any one consumer are often so small that there is insufficient financial incentive to sue the violators. Thus the attorneys general of the states can sue on behalf of the aggrieved consumers. These suits may be initiated even though the state itself was not injured. The state can aggregate all the damages on behalf of all alleged victims without having to prove exactly how much each was overcharged. If the state should win, consumers would be able to claim a share of the money or the judge could also order the violator to cut prices for a while to benefit the injured class of consumers.

Goals and Purposes of Antitrust Policy

The maintenance of competition is a major explicit goal of antitrust policy, because in the real world a completely unregulated economy seems to tend toward concentration. Given the impossibility of developing a system of perfect competition, the phrase "workable competition" is often used to describe this goal of antitrust policy. Workable competition refers to a system where there is reasonably free entry into most markets, no more than moderate concentration, and an ample number of buyers and sellers in most markets. These objectives are more realistically attainable than a perfectly competitive system given the nature of modern technology and organizations.

The promotion of fair competition is another goal of antitrust policy. This goal refers to the exercise of market power in a way that will enhance the competitive process rather than undermine it. Competitors who have market power are thus prevented from engaging in anticompetitive practices that would destroy the competitive process. They are not allowed to take advantage of that market power in an anticompetitive manner. The notion of fair play is an important part of American idealism that relates to this goal of antitrust policy.

Antitrust policy also seeks desirable economic results from the system and attacks those practices and structures that adversely affect economic performance. These desirable economic results could include (1) efficiency in the use of resources, (2) progress or growth (3) stability in output and employment, and (4) an equitable distribution of income. It is generally believed that monopolies introduce allocative inefficiencies and hamper technological innovation. A competitive economy is a more efficient economy and thus should be promoted by antitrust policy.

The limitation of big business could be seen as another goal of antitrust policy. Concentrations of private or public power are not desired in American society; thus diffusion of power is a social goal of prime importance. The goal of antitrust policy is to change the relative positions of large and small firms in the economy. This goal is broader, however, than simply limiting the economic power of large firms, but extends to political power and general social leadership. There is a strong "bigness is bad" philosophy in American society because big organizations could come to dominate the society politically and socially as well as economically.

These goals are accomplished, or at least attempted, through a focus on conduct and structure. Antitrust policy does not operate directly on performance; rather it focuses on conduct and structure to affect performance. Anticompetitive conduct falls into two general classes: (1) collusive actions whereby competitive rivals act in a joint fashion to achieve monopolistic goals and (2) exclusionary policies adopted individually that bolster a firm's economic power in relation to potential rivals.[9]

Collusion may be implicit, where competitive rivals act uniformly through following the leadership of the dominant firm in an industry with regard to prices or through price signaling in press releases, or collusion may be explicit, where rivals enter into express agreements to fix prices or allocate sales territories. Exclusionary practices include predatory pricing to drive rivals out of business, price discrimination, tying arrangements, and exclusive dealing arrangements.[10]

Market structure refers to the "economically significant features of a market which affect the behavior of firms in the industry supplying that market."[11] These elements include (1) seller concentration, (2) product differentiation, (3) barriers to entry, (4) elasticity of demand, and (5) diversification. These elements are believed to be linked to market conduct and to the economic performance of firms in the market. If such a connection exists, then performance can be affected through changes in market structure.

Concentration refers to the number of firms in the industry or some other measure that indicates the extent to which the market is under the control of a few dominant firms in the industry. Usually the four-firm concentration ratio is used to measure the percentage of sales accounted for by the top four firms in the industry. It is generally believed that a four-firm concentration ratio of 50 signals the beginning of an oligopolistic industry where market power of the dominant firms is a factor in the conduct of the industry.

Product differentiation refers to the extent that similar products are perceived to be different because of design, advertising, or other selling methods. Products whose physical units cannot be distinguished, such as wheat, are largely undifferentiated in the marketplace. But when the product can satisfy many needs or uses, brand loyalty can be established. Thus product differentiation can be a source of market power, because it gives sellers power over the price of their products and reduces competition.

Barriers to entry can be natural, such as those created by technology and the capital costs of reaching an efficient level of production, or artificial though heavy expenditures on advertising or brand proliferation. Barriers to entry may also be created by government through the granting of patents or the regulation of an industry such as trucking or the airlines. These barriers tend to reduce competition because they affect the ease with which new firms can enter an industry.

The price elasticity of market demand refers to the extent to which price changes cause quantity changes, or the responsiveness of sales quantity to changes in price. Elasticity of demand is an element of market structure because it can be important in determining the incentive to collude in an industry. Where demand is highly elastic, any increase in price will bring losses in sales for the whole industry. Thus collusion may not be attractive. But if demand is inelastic, cooperative action by sellers with regard to price can add to their profits.

Diversification refers to corporations that are in many product lines and thus span several markets. Firms may become vertically integrated diversifying backward or forward into different stages of the production process, become conglomerates by diversifying into completely different markets, or spread their operations internationally to become multinationals. Diversification is an element of structure because it boosts the firm's absolute size and thus contributes to aggregate concentration, which is the total economic activity accounted for by the leading firms in the economy.[12]

Thus antitrust policy deals with conduct and structure in influencing the performance of firms in the economy. The linkage between these elements will be discussed later. This dual focus can be seen in the Sherman Act, which dealt with conduct in Section 1 and structure in Section 2. The Clayton Act deals with structure in Section 7 and conduct in the other sections. The Federal Trade Commission Act deals with both conduct and structure.

Antitrust Enforcement

Enforcement of antitrust legislation at the federal level is shared by the Antitrust Division of the Department of Justice and the Bureau of Competition within the Federal Trade Commission. There is substantial overlap between these two agencies. The main area of overlap is with regard to the Clayton Act and its amendments, where the Antitrust Division and the FTC have concurrent jurisdiction. Technically speaking, the Sherman Act is the sole province of the Antitrust Division and the FTC has sole responsibility for enforcing the Federal Trade Commission Act. But overlap occurs here also, as the FTC can reach violations of the Sherman Act under the broad mandate to deal with "unfair methods of competition." Because of these overlapping areas, the FTC and the Antitrust Division exchange notifications and clearances to assure they do not duplicate efforts and specific cases and to coordinate their efforts where necessary.[13]

The history of antitrust enforcement shows changes in notions of competition and fears about the power of big business. Enforcement efforts reflect the tensions of maintaining allegiance to the ideals of competitive markets while allowing the society to reap the benefits of large-scale production, distribution, and organization. The realities of economies of scale, technology, and modern business enterprises make a straightforward application of abstract notions about competitive markets extremely difficult if not impossible.[14] A brief look at the way antitrust laws have been enforced and interpreted will show this clearly.

EARLY YEARS: THE RULE OF REASON

The Sherman Act was first applied to unions, and it was not until 1911 that cases were decided on the Standard Oil Company and the American Tobacco Company, two giant trusts of the time. Both firms were found guilty of violating Sections 1 and 2 of the Sherman Act and ordered dissolved into several separate firms. But in doing so, the court invoked the so-called rule of reason—these firms were found guilty because they had restrained trade unreasonably, not just because they had restrained trade. This decision emphasized the vicious practices these companies had used against their competitors.

Thus Section 1 of the Sherman Act was interpreted by the courts to prohibit only "unreasonable" restraints of trade. Under this "rule of reason" test, courts would review all relevant facts and circumstances, including economic evidence, to determine whether a contract, combination, or conspiracy unduly restricts and hampers competition. A frequently cited statement of this rule of reason appears in *Chicago Board of Trade* v. *United States,* in which Justice Brandeis described the "true test of legality" to be whether the restraint merely regulates and perhaps promotes competition or whether it suppresses and even destroys competition.[15] Relevant facts identified by the court to be used in applying the rule of reason test included (1) facts peculiar to the business, (2) the condition of the business before and after the restraint, (3) the nature of the restraint and its effects, (4) the history of the restraint, and (5) the reason and purpose for adopting the restraint.

Subsequent cases against Eastman Kodak Company, United Shoe Machinery, International Harvester Company, and U.S. Steel were found in favor of the firms because they had not visibly coerced or attacked rivals; in other words, they had not restrained trade "unreasonably." Such actions as price-fixing were even allowed (*Appalachian Coals Inc.* v. *United States*) if this was done so as to promote a "fair market" and end injurious competition.[16] Under the rule of reason test, then, antitrust litigation relies upon extensive economic analysis and evidence to support pro and con positions as to whether the business practice in question is actually anticompetitive.

MARKET CONDUCT: THE PER SE APPROACH

Eventually, however, the courts came to adopt a more or less consistent per se approach to violations of Section 1 of the Sherman Act: that certain kinds of conduct are so unreasonable that they cannot be excused by evidence that they do not adversely affect competition. In the Trenton Potteries case (*United States* v. *Trenton Potteries Co.*), the court held that price-fixing per se was illegal, whether reasonable or unreasonable. "The power to fix prices," the Court said, "whether reasonably exercised or not, involves power to control the market and to fix arbitrary and unreasonable prices. The reasonable price fixed today may through economic and business changes become the unreasonable price of tomorrow."[17]

Other practices besides price-fixing were eventually treated in the same manner more or less consistently. The practices that are thus generally considered to be per se violations of Section 1 of the Sherman Act include (1) price-fixing, (2) restriction of output, (3) division of markets, (4) group boycotts, (5) tying arrangements, and (6) resale price maintenance schemes. With respect to these practices, proof can be limited to the fact and amount of damage. The establishment of a per se approach to these practices relieves the parties to the suit and the court from inquiring into the factors relevant to a rule of reason analysis. Under the per se approach, it is irrelevant to inquire into the reasonableness of the restraint or attempt to provide an economic justification for an illegal practice.

STRUCTURE: IS BIGNESS BAD?

With respect to Section 2, an attempt to monopolize can be defined as the employment of method, means, or practices that would, if successful, accomplish monopolization, or something so close as to create a dangerous probability of monopolization. To be guilty of actual monopolization, one must possess (1) monopoly power in the relevant market and (2) the intent and purpose to exercise that power. Monopoly power is the power to control prices or unreasonably restrict competition. Thus almost any combination or conspiracy to monopolize would also violate Section 1 of the Sherman Act, but unlike Section 1, which requires two separate entities for a "conspiracy," a violation of Section 2 can be based on the conduct of a single actor.

When the rule of reason doctrine was in effect, it was clear that the law did not make mere size or the existence of unexerted power an offense. Size could be an offense only if accompanied by certain predatory types of market conduct. This changed with the Alcoa case of 1945 (*United States* v. *Aluminum Co. of America*), where it was held that a high level of seller concentration in and of itself could constitute a violation. While there was no precise definition as to what share of the market constituted a monopoly, the court in this case remarked that 90 percent of the market, which apparently was Alcoa's market share at the time, "is enough to constitute a monopoly, it is doubtful whether sixty-four percent would be enough: and certainly thirty-three percent is not."[18]

The court could find no predatory conduct on the part of Alcoa; its 90 percent market share was obtained by an honest industrial effort. But Alcoa's monopoly was not thrust upon it, the court said, and by a series of normal and prudent business practices the firm had succeeded in discouraging or forestalling all would-be competitors. The Sherman Act forbade all such monopolies no matter how acquired. Furthermore, the court said, the existence of power to fix prices inherent in a monopoly position could not be distinguished from the exercise of such power. Such a distinction was purely formal, and when monopoly entered the market, "the power and its exercise must needs coalesce."[19]

Thus a standard centered on market structure replaced one that had previously depended essentially on market conduct. This decision comes close to making size in the sense of market share a per se violation of the Sherman Act, but the precedent established in this case, which was a departure from previous interpretations, was not applied consistently in later years. The question of whether mere size in itself constitutes a violation of the antitrust laws is unanswered, and the "bigness is bad" debate continues (see the subsequent discussions). This question is enormously complex, and is one of the reasons some cases drag on so long.

ANTITRUST ACTIVISM: CONGLOMERATES AND OLIGOPOLIES

In the 1960s, a new type of merger appeared on the scene, the so-called conglomerate merger. These mergers are combinations of companies in completely different lines of activity; therefore, it is argued, these mergers have no anticompetitive effects and are not subject to antitrust litigation. Since the only case filed by the government against a conglomerate (ITT) was settled out of court, no precedent has been established on interpretation of antitrust laws, and their application to these combinations. Some legislators, however, attempted to answer this question with new legislation aimed specifically at mergers between firms in different industries. For example, the Kennedy bill entitled the Small and Independent Business Protection Act of 1979 (S.600) would have amended Section 7 of the Clayton Act to (1) prohibit mergers between firms with $2 billion in sales or assets, (2) restrict mergers between firms of $350 million, and (3) restrict the right of still smaller firms to sell out to companies of $350 million in sales or assets. The proposed law assumed that big companies, regardless of their makeup, have unfair advantages, since no showing of anticompetitive dangers would have been required to bar these mergers.[20]

Finally, efforts by the FTC and Justice Department in the 1970s attempted to extend the reach of antitrust laws to oligopoly itself. This structure was referred to as a "shared monopoly," in the sense that the largest companies in some industries achieve consensus decisions on output and pricing that resemble those of a more traditional single-company monopoly. This consensus is reached through open communication, such as published price lists or news releases, that constitutes price signaling to other companies. The Justice Department proposed filing a suit on this basis to test the thinking of the courts regarding this issue.[21]

The FTC also filed suit in 1972 against the four largest U.S. manufacturers of ready-to-eat breakfast cereal, charging violations of Section 5 of the Federal Trade Commission Act (*FTC* v. *Kellogg et al.*). The four were Kellogg, General Mills, General Foods, and Quaker Oats (Quaker Oats was subsequently dropped from the case because its market share was significantly smaller than the other three companies). The case was based on economic theories of localized competition first developed in 1929 by Harold Hotelling. This theory holds that in areas where products are clearly differentiated, products compete with one or two others that share similar characteristics rather than with every other product on the marketplace.[22]

Thus companies in the cereal industry compete by introducing more and more brands. The result is brand proliferation, which gives little hope that new companies will get much of a foothold because they have to compete for ever smaller slices of the market. This was held to be an unfair method of competition because it raises high barriers to entry for new companies and is, in a sense, a shared monopoly. The FTC sought to break up these companies into smaller firms and to institute a system of trademark licensing that would have enabled new companies to imitate existing brands.

BIGNESS IS GOOD

The end of the activist era and the beginning of a more positive view of corporate bigness began in the waning months of the Carter administration. In October 1980, the FTC issued a ruling that signaled a departure from its attack on bigness. The agency dismissed charges against Du Pont Company for dominating the titanium dioxide market and defended this ruling by stating that actions that could create a monopoly are not illegal if they resulted from aggressive competition based on technological advantage. The competitive process would not be served, the FTC argued, if antitrust were used to block aggressive competition that is solidly based on efficiency and growth opportunities.[23]

Economists began to attack antitrust laws blaming the decline of U.S. competitiveness at home and abroad at least partly on outdated antitrust enforcement practices. They argued that it is wrong to look at the structure of an industry and conclude that a small number of companies automatically means less competition and higher prices. Economies of scale exist in concentrated industries that mean unit production costs and therefore prices are often lower than if the industry were more competitive. These economists called for major policy revisions in the antitrust area to give business a freer hand to compete. Even liberal economists, such as Lester Thurow of the Massachusetts Institute of Technology, urged that the government abandon almost its entire system of antitrust laws and enforcement mechanisms.[24]

These trends were accelerated with the election of the Reagan administration in 1980 that adopted a much more pro-business attitude than the previous administration. "Bigness doesn't necessarily mean badness," declared the new Attorney General William French Smith, attacking past enforcement of antitrust laws as "misguided and mistaken. Efficient firms shouldn't be hobbled under the guise of antitrust enforcement," he stated. Reflecting this philosophy, the new head of the Antitrust Division, William Baxter, stated that big businesses are "very valuable things" because they tend to be the most efficient. Antitrust enforcement should strive toward only one goal, he believed, efficiency—maximum production at the lowest price. Mr. Baxter indicated that he would rewrite the department's guidelines to allow mergers between companies that aren't competitors. Such mergers would be considered a violation only if they lessened competition by allowing entry into a concentrated market for which the merged partners could independently develop their own brand. This decision could only be made by detailed economic analysis instead of simply by the level of concentration.[25]

> Although they sometimes harm competition, mergers generally play an important role in a free enterprise economy. They can penalize ineffective management and facilitate the efficient flow of investment capital and the redeployment of existing productive assets. While challenging competitively harmful mergers, the Department seeks to avoid unnecessary interference with that larger universe of mergers that are either competitively beneficial or neutral.[26]

These words were backed up by deeds when the Justice Department settled the AT&T case and dropped charges against IBM on the same day, thus following through on its promises to relax federal antitrust actions against big business. These were two of the costliest and complex legal actions ever brought by the U.S. government against private business. The case against IBM had dragged on for 13 years and cost over $1 billion. Over this period of time, the computer industry became more competitive, making the government's case more difficult to prove. These changes led Mr. Baxter to state that "The case is without merit and should be dismissed."[27]

The case against AT&T was settled out of court. Under the agreement, AT&T would divest itself of two-thirds of its total assets by spinning off 22 local operating companies. It would retain its long-distance service, its equipment manufacturing arm, Western Electric, and The Bell Research Labs. In addition, the company would be able to enter the new fields of data processing and telecommunications. The case was based on a concern that AT&T used its local telephone monopoly to subsidize its other businesses and harm competitors. Cutting free the local monopoly, in Mr. Baxter's view, thus solved the problem.

The FTC subsequently dropped its 10-year-old case against the three largest cereal makers. Over the years, the case grew increasingly soggy. Despite spending $6 million and compiling 40,000 pages of testimony with 2,900 supporting documents, the government could never prove that the cereal makers had reaped monopoly profits.[28] An FTC hearing officer had previously stated that FTC lawyers had not proved that the cereal companies tacitly coordinated their activities when it came to pricing and the introduction of new products. Brand proliferation in response to consumer tastes, Mr. Berman ruled, is "a legitimate means of competition," inferring that it was preposterous to prosecute a company for offering consumers too much variety.[29] The full commission decided to let this judgment stand in dismissing the case, thus dealing a blow to the theory of a shared monopoly.

Further indications that the activist era had ended were provided when the FTC closed its investigation of the automobile industry in 1981, a probe that had been going on for 5 years. When the investigation began, four U.S. auto makers had dominated the domestic market for cars, and the FTC wanted to know if this domination was the result of illegal, anticompetitive practices. Since that time, foreign competition had changed the nature of the industry.[30] Later that same year, the FTC dropped a longstanding case against the nation's eight largest oil companies. The charges had been filed in 1973 and included allegations of monopolistic practices and possible price conspiracy.[31]

Merger guidelines were further loosened in 1984, when the Justice Department announced that it would give greater consideration to efficiency claims, imports limited by quotas, and other factors in considering mergers even between competitors. The guidelines were issued to correct the impression that market concentration calculations alone are used to decide whether a merger is acceptable. The new guidelines stated that even if the initial numbers made a merger appear to be unlawful, it would still be approved under either of two conditions: (1) the merger would eliminate duplication or allow the combined entity to reach economies of scale, or (2) at least one of the merger partners is so weak that its market share is likely to shrink over time if it does not team up with a stronger company. The department also indicated that it would include the current level of imports in figuring the distribution of market share among sellers both before and after the proposed merger. Thus the Justice Department was suggesting that it would be more receptive to mergers in industries facing foreign competition, in declining industries, and in situations where the merging companies could improve their efficiency.[32]

The Justice Department also encouraged joint ventures by indicating that the agency would be receptive to arguments that joint ventures can be justified, even if they involve competitors in highly concentrated markets, by expected gains in efficiency. The only conditions in which a joint venture might risk a federal suit is when the deal includes so much of an industry that there are too few companies left to compete or when the rules of the venture limit company actions. The steel industry was urged to consider joint ventures as a means to compete more effectively with foreign competition rather than resorting to mergers in an already concentrated industry.[33]

In early 1986, the administration proposed to Congress even more sweeping revisions to existing antitrust legislation that would mark the most significant changes to the Clayton Act in its 72-year history. The proposed changes, which were endorsed by President Reagan, contained the following provisions: (1) granting a 5-year exemption from the antitrust laws for mergers and acquisitions in industries that the International Trade Commission finds have been seriously injured by imports; (2) relaxing the anti-merger laws by requiring greater proof of potential harm to competition, a proposal that would codify the permissive merger guidelines that had already been put into effect by the Justice Department; (3) discouraging private antitrust suits by limiting triple damage awards to cases of price-fixing or bid rigging; (4) amending the Clayton Act's prohibition against interlocking directorates by applying it only to companies worth at least $10 million rather than the current $1 million threshold; and (5) restricting the ability of U.S. companies to file antitrust suits against foreign competitors unless damage to American consumers can be proved.[34] Many business groups believed these proposals were too ambitious to be passed by Congress and, instead, sought a more narrow objective to limit civil penalties for companies by linking them to market share in contrast to current law which says each company has "joint and several" liability for triple the total damages claimed by all victims.[35]

These words and deeds from the Reagan administration immediately touched off a boom in corporate mergers. According to W. T. Grimm and Co., acquisition specialists, during the first 6 months of 1981 there were 1,184 mergers worth $37.5 billion, compared to only 856 during the same period in 1980.[36] The merger boom kept rolling, as 2,543 deals were struck in 1984 for a total of $122 billion. The following year saw mergers between Philip Morris and General Foods and RCA and General Electric, as mergers continued at a torrid pace with companies agreeing to more than 30 deals worth at least $1 billion. In 1986, the number of mergers increased again, to 4,022, worth $190 billion, a 31.7 percent increase in dollar terms over the year before. In the fourth quarter alone, nearly 1,500 deals worth $71.6 billion were completed as companies scrambled to wrap up deals before the new tax laws took effect.[37]

Corporate takeovers, both hostile and friendly, continued to make the headlines, even after the new tax laws became effective and the stock market crashed. While merger activity fell 38 percent in 1987, it picked up again in 1988 as more mergers were announced in the first half of that year than in all of 1985, with a value greater than for all the mergers accomplished in 1984. In 1989, 3,400 deals worth almost $230 billion were completed, led by Kohlberg Kravis Roberts' acquisition of RJR-Nabisco in a leveraged buyout worth $24.7 billion, the largest-ever such acquisition.[38] Such continued activity sparked a vigorous debate about the benefits versus the evils of large-scale mergers, but there seemed to be no doubt that a bigness-is-good philosophy took hold in the Reagan administration, if not in the society as a whole, resulting in a significant restructuring of the American economy (Exhibit 3.1).

Besides relaxing enforcement of structural provisions, the Reagan administration sought to relax its enforcement of provisions related to anticompetitive conduct as well. The Justice Department argued that the legality of resale price maintenance, for example, should be judged on whether it would unreasonably restrict competition. Minimum retail prices benefit consumers, Mr. Baxter stated, because manufacturers of technologically complex products can use them to guarantee that all sellers provide such things as instruction or repair services. In the absence of such restrictions, discounters get a free ride without providing such services, endangering their continuation.[39] Subsequently,

EXHIBIT 3.1

Fifteen Largest Corporate Mergers
1981–89

Buyer	Company Bought	Value (in billions)	Date
KKR	RJR-Nabisco	$24.7	1989
Socal	Gulf	13.4	1984
Philip Morris	Kraft	12.6	1988
Bristol-Meyers	Squibb	12.5	1989
Texaco	Getty	10.1	1984
British Petroleum	Sohio	7.6	1987
Du Pont	Conoco	7.4	1981
U.S. Steel	Marathon Oil	6.5	1981
Campeau	Federated Stores	6.5	1988
General Electric	RCA	6.4	1986
BCI Holdings	Beatrice Cos.	6.2	1986
Mobil	Superior	5.7	1984
Royal Dutch Shell	Shell Oil	5.7	1985
Philip Morris	General Foods	5.6	1985
Santa Fe	Southern Pacific	5.2	1983

Data: Wall Street Journal, March 7, 1984, p. 24; *Fortune,* January 21, 1985, p. 129; January 20, 1986, p. 27; February 2, 1987, p. 69; *Business Week,* January 15, 1990, pp. 52–53.

some manufacturers began cutting off supplies to discounters and clamping down on transshipping in which discounters buy from authorized dealers with overstock instead of from manufacturers.[40] These actions were supported by a 1988 Supreme Court ruling that a manufacturer's decision to cut off a retailer who is discounting prices is not illegal per se unless it involves an explicit effort to fix retail prices. This ruling was expected to give manufacturers more freedom to persuade retailers to follow suggested retail prices.[41]

In summary, the Reagan era represented something of a revolution in antitrust enforcement. During this period, the government largely backed away from scrutinizing exclusionary or abusive conduct by dominant firms in an industry. From 1981 to 88, only three cases were initiated enforcing the Sherman Act's ban on monopolization and attempted monopolization, the lowest 8-year level of activity in this area since 1900. Rules that limited a manufacturer's choice of distribution methods were also not enforced as the Reagan administration filed no vertical restraint cases. The administration also declined to challenge mergers that increased market concentration beyond thresholds established in their own guidelines. Finally, the focus of enforcement activity seemed to shift from large firms to smaller companies, particularly in regard to horizontal price-fixing, bid-rigging, and market-allocation schemes.[42]

Economic Concentration

The question of size and structure is a crucial one as far as the antitrust area is concerned. Does the size of some corporations and the concentration of production of certain goods in the hands of a few companies make competition ineffective as a regulator of business behavior? Should the government then regulate business further by the use of public commissions and act to curb corporate growth by law to protect the public interest in good products at reasonably low prices? If, however, competition can be effective in protecting the public interest, what should be done to enhance its vigor? Should the government fragment giant enterprises to introduce more competition in industries dominated by these giants?

The answers to these questions depend in part of the degree of economic concentration that exists in our economy. Is monopoly rising, declining, or staying about the same? Conversely, what about competition: Is it increasing, decreasing, or remaining stable? How much economic power do corporations actually have in our society? Is oligopoly increasing or decreasing? And is such a structure anticompetitive in nature? It is useful to look at some studies of economic concentration that might give at least tentative answers to these questions.

Aggregate Concentration.   One way to study the structure of the economy is to deal with it in the aggregate by measuring overall concentration in the economy. This is done by taking the top 100, 200, or 500 corporations in the country and determining whether their share of total corporate assets, sales, income, or value added has increased or decreased over some period of time. If the top corporations have increased their share of total corporate assets, sales, income, or value added, it can be concluded that aggregate economic concentration is increasing. If their share is decreasing with respect to the total, aggregate concentration is declining.

One study of this type was completed in 1932 by Adolph A. Berle and Gardiner C. Means.[43] This study dealt with the 200 largest nonbanking corporations as of January 1, 1930, with size being determined by taking gross assets less depreciation as reported in Moody's *Railroad, Public Utility,* and *Industrial* manuals. They found that in 1929, the top 200 corporations controlled 49.2 percent of all nonbanking corporate wealth and received 43.2 percent of the income of all nonbanking corporations.

For the period 1909–28, the annual rate of growth of these 200 corporations had been 5.4 percent, for all corporations the growth rate was 3.6 percent per year, and for corporations other than the top 200 the growth rate was only 2.0 percent per year. Thus the 200 largest corporations were increasing in wealth 50 percent faster than were all corporations and over two and a half times as fast as smaller corporations. At these rates, they concluded, it would take only 40 years for all corporate activity and practically all industrial activity to be absorbed by the top 200 companies. The fact that this did not happen means that either there were deficiencies in their original trend data or that the trend toward increasing aggregate concentration abated.

Another study of this kind, completed in 1963 by a Senate Subcommittee on Antitrust and Monopoly, found that in 1958, the 50 largest manufacturing companies accounted for 23 percent of all the value added by manufacturing. The 200 largest companies accounted for 38 percent of value added. By 1963, these percentages had become 25 percent and 41 percent, respectively. Also in 1958, the 100 largest firms in mining, manufacturing, and distribution owned almost 30 percent of all the assets in these industries.[44]

A Conference Board study completed in 1973 looked at the growth of the largest manufacturing firms by comparing the 1947–58 and 1958–67 periods. The study concluded that the share of U.S. manufacturing attributable to the top 50, 100, and 200 largest manufacturing firms in terms of total assets, sales, and value added had grown during both periods, but the rate of growth in each case was lower in the later period than in the earlier. Thus the largest corporations were not following a trajectory that would in the foreseeable future lead to the concentration of all manufacturing activity in a few hands, an opposite conclusion from the earlier Berle-Means study.[45]

Finally, Philip Blumberg reported sales, assets, employees, and net income for the largest 500 industrial corporations for 1955, 1960, 1965, 1970, and 1973. The percentages he reported show the proportion held by the top 500 companies with respect to total industrial sales, assets, employees, and net income. These figures show a consistent increase in all respects over this time period except for 2 years with regard to net income. The largest increases in concentration took place with respect to assets and employees.[46]

These are by no means all the significant studies that have been completed on aggregate concentration, but only a representative sample. It is difficult to draw any generalizations from these studies, since they were done at different times and used different sources of information. However, many scholars in this area seem to conclude that aggregate economic concentration has increased over the years, particularly with respect to assets; that is, the share of assets owned by the top corporations in the country has increased with respect to the assets of all corporations (Figure 3.1).

Market Concentration. Some scholars argue that studies of aggregate concentration tell nothing about competition and monopoly or about corporate economic power.[47] All that these data show is that some corporations are large with respect to the total economy when aggregated across certain aspects, such as sales or assets. But the large size of these companies in the aggregate says nothing about the rivalry they face individually, the kind of market in which they function, or their price-output patterns. Therefore, a different kind of approach is recommended, one that deals with market concentration rather than aggregate concentration.

Market concentration can be defined as the percentage of total industry sales that are contributed by the largest few firms in an industry, ranked in order of market shares. The most common measure is the four-firm sales concentration ratio—the percentage of industry sales made by the leading four firms in the industry (See Table 3.2 on page 70). A concentration ratio of 75 percent indicated a highly concentrated market that was subject to a more stringent standard of review by the antitrust authorities. In a more highly concentrated market, mergers between companies with relatively small shares of the market might be challenged.

A somewhat more sophisticated method of measuring market concentration was adopted in 1982 by the Reagan administration. The Herfindahl-Hirschman Index (HHI), as this method was called, is calculated by squaring the market share of all the firms in the market and summing the squares (See box on page 71). The premerger HHI number is then compared with the increase in the HHI that will be caused by a proposed merger. If the postmerger HHI is below 1,000, the merger is unlikely to be challenged, if the postmerger index is between 1,000 and 1,800, the merger is likely to be challenged only if the increase is more than 100 points, and if the postmerger HHI is above 1,800 the merger is likely to be challenged if the increase is more than 50 points.[48]

One study focusing on market concentration was presented by Dr. Betty Bock of the Conference Board in May 1977 to the Subcommittee on Antitrust and Monopoly of the Senate Judiciary Committee chaired by Senator Edward Kennedy of Massachusetts.[49] The study showed a remarkable stability throughout the 1947–72 period, indicating that market concentration was not a rising tide that threatens to engulf the American economy. A cutoff point of 50 percent was taken to be indicative of an oligopolistic industry, one

Figure 3.1 The Long-Term Trend of Aggregate Concentration, Eight Individual Series, 1900–1980

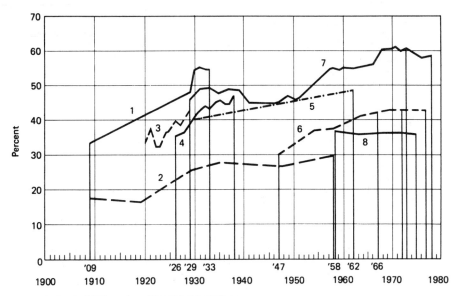

1 Assets, 200 largest nonfinancial corporations
2 Assets, 100 largest manufacturing, mining, and distribution corporations
3 Net income, 200 largest nonfinancial corporations
4 Net working capital, 316 large manufacturing corporations
5 Assets, 100 largest manufacturing corporations
6 Value added by manufacturer, 200 largest manufacturing companies
7 Assets, 200 largest manufacturing corporations
8 Assets, 150 largest nonfinancial corporations

Source: John M. Blair, *Economic Concentration,* copyright © 1972 by Harcourt Brace Jovanovich, Inc. Reprinted by permission of the publisher.
    Reprinted by permission of the publisher from *Mergers and Acquisitions: Current Problems in Perspective,* edited by Michael Keenan and Lawrence J. White (Lexington, Mass.: Lexington Books, D.C. Heath and Co. Copyright 1982, D.C. Heath and Co).

where the top four firms control 50 percent or more of the market. This 50 percent and over category remained stable at around 30 percent of all industries.

One problem, however, is that while a study such as this may show more about competition in given industries, it assumes that all industries are equal in terms of their impact on the total economy. This is undoubtedly not the case; the industries that have concentration ratios of 50 percent or more may also account for a large percentage of all manufacturing assets, sales, income, or value added. If that were true, these findings would have to be seen in a quite different perspective.

Market concentration studies thus show nothing about aggregate concentration. There is, therefore, no easy answer to questions about the degree of monopoly and competition in the American economy. One needs to ask questions and conduct research at both the aggregate and market levels to arrive at even tentative conclusions about the

TABLE 3.2 Percentages of Industry Output Produced by the Four Largest Firms in Selected High Concentration Industries

Industry	Percent of Industry Output	H-H Index[1] For 50 Largest
Hard-surface floor coverings	99%	N/A
Chewing gum	95	N/A
Household refrigerators and freezers	94	2,745
Motor vehicles and car bodies	92	N/A
Household laundry equipment	91	N/A
Electric lamps	91	N/A
Primary batteries	89	N/A
Chewing and smoking tobacco	87	2,564
Small arms ammunition	87	2,305
Flat glass	85	2,032
Tire cord and fabric	81	2,584
Household vacuum cleaners	80	1,951

[1]The Hertindahl-Hirschman Index; see text.

N/A—Not available.

Source: U.S. Bureau of the Census, *1982 Census of Manufactures, Concentration Ratios in Manfacturing* (Washington, DC: U.S. Government Printing Office, 1986), pp. 6–51.

structure of the American economy. The implications that these conclusions may have for public policy need to be carefully considered in view of the uncertainty involved.

Structure, Conduct, and Performance

The interest in these studies of economic concentration stems, of course, from a concern about size and its relationship to economic power. Such concerns give rise to the structural theory of industrial organization. This theory holds that the structure of the economy or an industry predetermines the behavior and thus the performance of firms in the economy and in particular industries. (See Figure 3.2 on page 72.) The more concentrated are all corporate assets in the largest companies, and the more concentrated are the sales of an industry in the largest few firms of that industry, the more economic power exists in society. Such concentration is bad for society because this economic power can and will be used to control markets by fixing prices in some fashion, determining which products are put on the market, restricting volume, and maintaining high or excessive profits. There are a number of basic propositions in this structural theory, including the following:

1. If an industry is not atomistic with many small competitors, there is likely to be administrative discretion over prices.
2. Concentration results in recognized interdependence among companies, with no price competition in concentrated industries.

HOW THE HHI WORKS

The HHI is calculated by summing the squares of the individual market shares of all the firms included in the market. For example, a market consisting of six firms may have this allocation of market shares:

Firm A-30%	Firm D-12%
Firm B-25%	Firm E- 9%
Firm C-20%	Firm F- 4%

The HHI for the market is 2,166, or

$$2,166 = 30^2 + 25^2 + 20^2 + 12^2 + 9^2 + 4^2$$

The increase in the HHI resulting from a merger is calculated by doubling the product of the market shares of the merging firms. Thus, if Firm E and Firm F were merged, the HHI would increase by 72, or,

$$72 = 2 \times 9 \times 4$$

The new HHI is 2,238, or,

$$2,238 = 30^2 + 25^2 + 20^2 + 12^2 + 13^2$$

The HHI ranges from 10,000 (in the case of a pure monopoly) to a number approaching zero (in the case of an atomistic market).

Source: Donlad I. Baker and William Blumenthal, ''Demystifying the Herfindahl-Hirschman Index,'' *Mergers & Acquisitions* (Summer 1984), p. 44.

3. Concentration is not natural and is due mostly to mergers, for the most efficient scale of operation is no more than 3 to 5 percent of the industry. A high degree of concentration is unnecessary.
4. There is a positive correlation between concentration and profitability that gives evidence of monopoly power in concentrated industries—the ability to elevate prices and the persistence of high profits. Entry does not take place to eliminate excessive profits.
5. Concentration is aggravated by product differentiation and advertising. Advertising is correlated with higher profits.
6. There is oligopolistic coordination by signaling through press releases or other means.[50]

The opposite point of view is the performance argument, which holds that concentration of economic power in large companies is due to underlying economic, sociological, and technological forces in society and is not based on a desire of corporate managers to monopolize an industry. Massive and complex business organizations are the tangible manifestation of the advanced technology they employ.[51] In certain industries, large companies and concentration are essential because of the heavy capital investment needed

Figure 3.2 Structural Theory of Industrial Organization

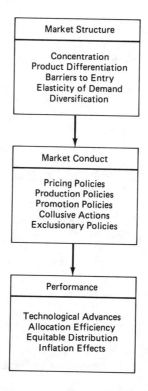

to do business and produce products. The nature of the technological processes involved provides advantages for an integrated large-scale enterprise which can coordinate all the stages of production to increase output.[52] Thus the large size of modern corporations is a function of technology more than of conscious attempts to monopolize an industry.

From a sociological point of view, Peter Drucker argues, American society has become a society of large, highly organized and professionally managed institutions. The United States has become a society of large pluralistic institutions, including business, hospitals, educational institutions, and others. Bigness is here to stay, says Drucker, and an atomistic market structure would be quite out of step with the demands of modern society. People are in no mood to do without the fruits of modern, large-scale organizations. The essence of a modern, large organization is that within it, people of very diverse skills and knowledge can work together for a common purpose. The tasks that need to be accomplished in modern society require large-scale organizations. Thus the job of society is not to abolish them but to make them perform better for individuals, for communities, and for the society as a whole.[53]

Finally, it is argued that there are sound economic reasons behind the growth of large organizations, such as (1) economies of large-scale production, (2) advantages of integrated and long-range planning, (3) advantages of large-scale purchasing and distribution economies, (4) ability to afford heavy research and development expenditures necessary for innovation, and (5) more effective competition in foreign markets. Thus there are advantages to having large organizations and society benefits through greater efficiencies and more effective use of resources.

Bigness is not necessarily bad, according to this view, but must be judged on its merits or performance. The performance of large firms must be examined independently and not inferred from the structure of the economy or the industry in which they function. Measures of performance could include product and process innovations, reductions in costs that have been passed on to consumers, whether profits are excessive or are more or less in line with other industries or whether these large firms are operating efficiently with above-average productivity gains.

Structuralists want to prevent or break up large concentrations of economic power and promote competition, and only then, they argue, will society get economically desirable performance. The performance view holds that structure is by and large irrelevant to the performance of corporations and that society should concern itself more directly with performance rather than with the structure of the economy or of particular industries. Large organizations and concentrated industries can perform as well as and perhaps better than industries that are highly competitive in the traditional sense.

Policy Implications

There are no easy answers to questions about the relationship of structure and performance. There seem to be no definitive studies at the present time that would conclusively answer some of these questions and thus have relatively clear policy implications. Many studies deal with various aspects of this question, and one can find studies of varying degrees of quality to support either the structuralist or performance position.[54] It might be not wholly inaccurate to say that the view one adopts and the policies supported depend on value preferences relative to a competitive structure versus a more concentrated one and value preferences for large enterprises versus smaller enterprises.

Thus antitrust policy represents something of a compromise between preferences for a competitive economy with small firms and preferences for large-scale diversified enterprises that may result in concentrated industries. Antitrust laws give expression to a competitive ideology where there is vigorous competition among many firms in an industry. Their application, however, is flexible to allow for large firms and concentrated industries when it is believed these will be beneficial to society.

Many feel, however, that the antitrust area needs reform. Questions exist, as stated earlier, about the way current antitrust laws apply to conglomerates and the notion of a shared monopoly. Cases could be brought before the court on these issues, forcing the court to decide them, but many believe that legislative action should be taken to modernize the antitrust area and make the laws themselves more appropriate to a market system that has grown increasingly large, complex, and multinational in scope. There is a concern that the antitrust laws may place U.S. companies at a competitive disadvantage with respect to foreign competition.[55]

One such reform measure is simply to abolish the laws altogether, either in whole or in part. Some economists, such as Yale Brozen of the University of Chicago, argue that antitrust laws are largely unnecessary, that both conduct and structure should be left up to market forces. Repeal of the antitrust laws would allow firms to engage in numerous practices now forbidden or discouraged, such as horizontal price-fixing. Critics of antitrust law generally lodge two kinds of objections: (1) economic objections to the neoclassical economic theory typically employed to justify antitrust legislation, and (2) philosophical objections to the operation of the law in the real world.[56]

Few businesspeople agree, however, that the antitrust laws should be abolished completely.[57] There is some support for limiting the antitrust area to business practices or conduct and abolishing the concern about size and structure stated in Section 2 of the Sherman Act and continued in later public policy measures. The laws could specify the rules of the game as far as fair and honest methods of competition are concerned and continue to rule out such practices as price-fixing, division of markets, price discrimination, exclusive dealing arrangements, predatory pricing, and other types of anticompetitive conduct. Certain kinds of conduct would be illegal, but the size of corporations and the structure of the economy as well as the concentration of individual industries would be left up to market forces. As long as competition is honest and fair, so the argument goes, the emergence of large companies and concentrated industries should reflect genuine economic advantages related to efficiency and productivity increases.

Another reform measure would clarify more precisely in the legislation itself exactly what business practices are unlawful. Some people complain that the vagueness of the antitrust laws causes a great deal of uncertainty about how the laws will subsequently be interpreted. Specifying more precisely what practices are unfair methods of competition would help business to know exactly where it stands. The difficulty of doing this, however, stems from the task of identifying and foreseeing all such practices when business conditions and the economy are constantly changing. It would seem to be impossible to develop an all inclusive list of anticompetitive conduct at any point in time. And even if certain practices, such as price-fixing, were specified in the law, there would still be a debate over what practices constituted price-fixing. There is uncertainty in any legislation, which is the reason legislation needs constant interpretation by the courts as conditions and society change.[58]

Replacing the antitrust laws with direct regulation is favored by some economists, including John Kenneth Galbraith, who believes that a competitive economy cannot be produced because of the technological imperatives behind the growth of large corporations. Others, such as George Stigler, point out that antitrust has not been able to bring about a more competitive economy, since the evidence shows there has been no long-term decline in concentration. Thus if bigness and concentration are inevitable, so the argument goes, regulation of the ICC type to reduce the effects of these "natural" or "shared" monopolies would seem a reasonable approach.[59]

Robert Bork in a 1978 book entitled *The Antitrust Paradox* believes that most of the problems with antitrust enforcement could be resolved by directing the courts to focus on the welfare of consumers. Thus improved productive or distributive efficiency would then be viewed as enhancing consumer welfare rather than constituting pernicious competitive advantage. Bork identifies three categories of behavior with which antitrust enforcement should be concerned:

1. Agreements by direct competitors or potential rivals to fix prices or divide markets in those cases where the agreements are not necessary for the integration of legitimate economic activity.
2. Horizontal mergers leaving fewer than three significant rivals in any market.
3. Deliberate predation, that is, charging prices below the variable cost of production with the specific intent of eliminating competitors and achieving monopoly power.[60]

Finally, there is an approach that would make size alone an offense by adopting a per se approach to the size of corporations, as has been taken in many instances toward certain forms of corporate conduct. One such bill, introduced into Congress in 1972 by Senator Phillip Hart of Michigan, called for the establishment of a federal commission with the power to break up large firms if any one of the following three conditions were present in an industry.

- An average rate of return on net worth after taxes in excess of 15 percent over a period of 5 consecutive years in the most recent 7 years preceding the filing of the complaint.
- No substantial price competition among two or more corporations in 3 consecutive years out of the most recent 5 years preceding the filing of the complaint.
- If any four or fewer corporations account for 50 percent or more of sales in any 1 year out of the most recent 3 years preceding the filing of the complaint.[61]

There have been other bills of this type, including the Kennedy bill mentioned earlier that is directed specifically at conglomerates. This approach would specify in some quantitative fashion what size was illegal and would thus make it unnecessary for government to prove the existence of monopoly power or that there was an intent to attain and maintain this power. In addition to the limitations such a structuralist approach would place on corporate growth, such a policy might deprive the society of substantial economies. It has not yet been conclusively proven that society would be better off with smaller companies.

The Future of Antitrust

In addition to all this federal activity, the states also at times become active in antitrust litigation, particularly when the federal government relaxes its enforcement of antitrust legislation. In the early 1980s, state prosecutors began going after national advertising campaigns they believed were misleading consumers. They began to share investigative resources and create models for cooperative efforts that cross state-federal boundaries. As a result of these efforts, states pressed airline advertisers to be more specific about fare discounts and frequent-flier programs, sued major insurance companies for alleged collusion to restrict certain policies, won a $16-million settlement from Chrysler Corporation for odometer fraud, won a settlement of up to $4 million from Minolta Corporation for manipulating retail camera prices, and challenged large corporate mergers ignored by federal prosecutors.[62] In early 1990, California filed a suit that in effect asked the Supreme Court to rule that states as well as the federal government had authority to break up mergers.[63] Most experts seemed to agree that this state activity was not going to fade away even if a more activist administration should be elected.

The Bush administration was not expected to pursue a much more vigorous policy toward antitrust enforcement. The changes that might come about would tend to be changes more of style than substance.[64] Early in 1990, for example, the Bush administration supported legislation that would ease antitrust restriction on joint production efforts by U.S. companies. This legislation would enable joint ventures to escape the threat of treble damages in antitrust lawsuits.[65] This action was seen to be consistent with a trend towards cooperation among manufacturers because of (1) the increasing cost, complexity, and risk of developing new technologies, (2) the globalization of markets, leading companies to seek partners to help them break into foreign markets, and (3) the emergence of powerful foreign competitors.[66]

Meanwhile, analysts and policymakers began to discuss issues related to the long-run effects of all the merger activity during the Reagan Administration.[67] Takeovers and buyouts left many companies saddled with huge debt loads from which they never recovered.[68] Concentration in many industries did increase and the final impact of this development isn't easy to forecast. Such concentration makes the economy more vulnerable to bad decisions by a few top executives, as bigger companies can make bigger and more costly mistakes. On the other hand, many companies were forced to restructure and in the process did become more efficient. Takeovers and buyouts did seem to abate as the country entered the 1990s, as the value of announced deals plunged 38 percent in the first quarter and the number of deals was off 13 percent. This slowdown was largely because of problems in the junk bond market.[69] But states also began passing tough antitakeover laws that discouraged merger activity.[70]

Questions for Discussion

1. What are the origins of antitrust as an area of public policy? What were the problems that the antitrust laws were originally designed to address? Are those problems still present in the American economy today?

2. What are the goals of antitrust policy? Have these goals been attained? What data are relevant to answering this question?

3. What is economic power? Is the existence of such power bad or good for society? How does antitrust policy attempt to place limitations on this power?

4. What is the difference between the two sections of the Sherman Act? Which section, in your opinion, is more important? Which section could have the greatest impact on business? Why?

5. What is the purpose of the premerger notification provisions of the Hart-Scott-Rodino Antitrust Improvements Act of 1976? Are you in favor of this provision? What is a good merger? What is a bad merger? What ciriteria are relevant to answering this question?

6. What is the "rule of reason" as applied to the antitrust laws? How is this different from a per se approach? Is there such a thing as a "reasonable restraint of trade?"

7. Is the size of a corporation in and of itself a public policy problem? Why or why not? What did the Alcoa decision say about this problem? Should the government pursue cases related to structure?

8. Describe a shared monopoly. Was the government justified in pursuing this concept? What was the issue in the government's case against the cereal companies? Do you approve of the outcome of the case?

9. Why was there such a merger boom in the 1980s? What factors precipitated such an unprecedented number of takeovers and leveraged buyouts that changed the landscape of corporate America?

10. What are the likely results of the restructuring of the American economy that took place in the last decade? Are all the mergers that took place going to make the United States more competitive in years to come? Or have corporations been saddled with debt that is going to make them less innovative and flexible in the future?

11. What is the difference between aggregate and market concentration? Which area is more relevant to the questions raised by antitrust policy? How are these two types of concentration related?

12. Distinguish between structure and performance as approaches to economic concentration.

What are the key assumptions behind both approaches? Where do values enter into these arguments?

13. Discuss the different dimensions to the structure versus performance argument. Are there any definitive answers to these questions? Why or why not?

14. Which of the reform measures mentioned in the text do you like best? Which would be best from a business standpoint? Which would be best for society?

15. Is it possible for antitrust laws to be more precise? Would this reform help business to relate better to public policy in the antitrust area?

16. Examine the advice to managers on antitrust policy of a typical corporation. Can you understand these guidelines? Do you believe they are relevant to the job you are considering in business? In what ways?

Case: General Sherman Goes After Higher Education

Twelve of the Northeast's most prestigious colleges and universities received civil investigative demands (CIDs) from the Antitrust Division of the Justice Department in late summer of 1989. These CIDs are rather like a subpoena from a grand jury to recipients as they are written requests intended to gather information. Receiving a CID can be a frightening experience, as it was for these colleges and universities. The CIDs focused on price-fixing that is prohibited by Section 1 of the Sherman Antitrust Act, legislation that in the past had nearly always been applied to for-profit businesses.[1]

The Justice Department's purpose in sending out the CIDs was to gather budgeting and other financial information related to a practice of two dozen or more schools that had been going on for decades. Officers from these schools met each year to agree on the amounts of financial aid they would offer top-notch students. At this meeting, the schools arrange for their aid packages to be nearly identical. In 1989, some 10,000 students were said to have been affected by this practice. Many of the schools freely admitted that they got together to fix aid awards to avoid bidding wars and defended the practice by suggesting that the conferences were held for the good of education, since the agreements helped the schools to keep their costs down.[2]

Defenders of the inquiry argued that fixing aid was an anticompetitive practice, that in a competitive environment student aid would vary, thus making the amount a student ends up paying vary proportionately. Students receiving aid would pay less if the schools were to compete on granting aid packages. The schools are no different from other institutions if they conspire to agree on what they are going to charge. Critics contended that the inquiry is novel and not an appropriate area for the antitrust law to be applied. They pointed out that the money was not going to line the college president's pocket. What the schools were talking about was a subsidy rather than a price, and thus they questioned whether antitrust should cover how much money to give away.[3]

There are three possible outcomes to the inquiry: (1) Since only one out of every five investigations ever goes anywhere after inquiries are completed, the government could simply walk away and do nothing, (2) the schools would be required to abide by some sort of injunction, and (3) the government would accept the promises of the schools to forgo price-fixing. The schools could also possibly be hit by a series of class-action suits by former students who could claim they had been hurt by the financial aid agreements and deserve damages.[4]

Such a suit was, in fact, filed by a Wesleyan University student against his school and the 11 other private colleges seeking damages on behalf of thousands of other students. The defendants were said to have "engaged in a conspiracy to fix or artificially inflate the price of tuition and financial aid." The suit sought treble damages on behalf of a class of all students who were allegedly harmed by the scheme. The Justice Department, meanwhile, widened its investigation to about 20 schools and was seeking information about not only financial aid, but the way in which the schools set tuition and salaries as well.[5]

Case Notes

1. Christopher Elias, "Northeastern Fix on Financial Aid," *Insight,* September 18, 1989, p. 48.
2. Ibid., pp. 48–49.
3. Ibid., p. 48.
4. Ibid., p. 49.
5. Gary Putka, "Twelve Colleges Named in Lawsuit On Price-Fixing," *Wall Street Journal,* September 18, 1989, p. C-17.

Chapter Notes

1. Martin C. Schnitzer, *Contemporary Government and Business Relations,* 4th ed. (Boston: Houghton Mifflin, 1990), p. 140.
2. *Northern Pacific Ry.* v. *United States,* 356 U.S. 1, 4(1958).
3. Richard Caves, *American Industry: Structure, Conduct, Performance* (Englewood Cliffs, N.J.: Prentice Hall, 1972), p. 57.
4. Ibid.
5. George A. Steiner, *Business and Society,* 2d ed. (New York: Random House, 1975), p. 420.
6. Ibid., p. 423.
7. *FTC* v. *The Sperry and Hutchinson Company,* 405 U.S. 233 (1972).
8. *Carlson* v. *Coca-Cola Co.,* 483 F. 2d 279 (9th Cir. 1973).
9. Douglas F. Greer, *Business, Government, and Society* (New York: Macmillan, 1983), p. 97–98.
10. Ibid., pp. 98–100.
11. Caves, *American Industry,* p. 17.
12. Greer, *Business, Government, and Society,* p. 97.
13. Ibid., pp. 108–109.
14. John D. Aram, *Managing Business and Public Policy: Concepts, Issues and Cases* (Boston: Pitman, 1983), p. 492.
15. *Chicago Board of Trade* v. *United States,* 246 U.S. 231 (1918).
16. *Appalachian Coals Inc.* v. *United States,* 288 U.S. 344 (1933). In this case 137 companies producing a tenth of the bituminous coal mined east of the Mississippi River and about two-thirds of that mined in the Appalachian territory had set up a joint agency to handle all their sales. The court recognized that this arrangement established common prices for the firms involved, but it went on to find that the industry was seriously depressed, that competition in the sale of coal had been subject to various abuses, and that the selling agency did not control enough of the supply to enable it to fix the market price. On this basis, the arrangement was allowed to stand. William G. Shepherd and Clair Wilcox, *Public Policies toward Business,* 6th ed. (Homewood, Ill.: Richard D. Irwin, 1979), p. 202. Copyright © 1979 by Richard D. Irwin, Inc. All rights reserved.
17. *United States* v. *Trenton Potteries Co.* 273 U.S. 392 (1927).
18. *United States* v. *Aluminum Co. of America.* 148 F. 2d 416 (1945).
19. Ibid.

20. See A. F. Ehrbar, "Bigness Becomes the Target of the Trustbusters," *Fortune,* March 26, 1979, pp. 34–40.

21. "Taking Aim at Shared Monopolies," *Wall Street Journal,* August 22, 1978, p. 18.

22. "Too Many Cereals for the FTC," *Business Week,* March 20, 1978, pp. 166–67. See also Walter Kiechell III, "The Soggy Case Against the Cereal Industry," *Fortune,* April 10, 1978, pp. 49–51; and Richard Schamalensee, "Entry Deterrence in the Ready-To-Eat Breakfast Cereal Industry," *Bell Journal of Economics,* Vol. 9, No. 2 (Autumn 1978), pp. 305–327.

23. Burt Schorr, "FTC Dismisses Charges Against DuPont in Major Statement of its Antitrust Policy," *Wall Street Journal,* October 28, 1980, p. 5.

24. "Antitrust Grows Unpopular," *Business Week,* January, 12, 1981, pp. 90–92.

25. Robert E. Taylor and Stan Crock, "Reagan Team Believes Antitrust Legislation Hurts Big Business," *Wall Street Journal,* July 8, 1981, p. 1.

26. U.S. Dept. of Justice, *Merger Guidelines—1982,* par. 4501, pp. 6881–87.

27. "Windup for Two Supersuits," *Time,* January 18, 1982, p. 38–40.

28. "Snap, Crackle, Flop!" *Time,* January 25, 1982, p. 58.

29. Margaret Garrard Warner, "FTC Case Hurt by Aide's Ruling on Cereal Firms," *Wall Street Journal,* September 11, 1981, p. 8.

30. "FTC Officially Ends its Antitrust Probe of Auto Industry," *Wall Street Journal,* May 14, 1981, p. 3.

31. Stan Crock, "FTC Ends Oil Trust Case Against 8 Firms in Another Move Away From Activist Era," *Wall Street Journal,* September 17, 1981, p. 2.

32. "Now the Antitrust Guidelines are Clearer—and Looser," *Business Week,* June 25, 1984, p. 38; Robert E. Taylor, "U.S. Revises Merger Rules to Add Weight To Efficiency Claims and Other Factors," *Wall Street Journal,* June 15, 1984, p. 4.

33. "Joint Ventures: Justice Becomes a Cheerleader," *Business Week,* November 19, 1984, p. 48; Robert E. Taylor, "Joint Ventures Likely to Be Encouraged By Friendlier Attitude of U.S. Officials," *Wall Street Journal,* November 5, 1984, p. 12. See also Stanford M. Litvak, "The Urge to Rewrite the Antitrust Laws," *Across The Board,* January 1984, pp. 13–17.

34. Andy Pasztor, "Reagan to Submit Proposals to Congress For Rewriting Much of Antitrust Law," *Wall Street Journal,* January 16, 1986, p. 52; "Closing the Antitrust Century," *Wall Street Journal,* January 21, 1986, p. 28.

35. Andy Pasztor, "Business Baffled by Reagan's Coolness To Proposed Antitrust-Law Revision," *Wall Street Journal,* November 13, 1985, p. 54; Andy Pasztor, "Cabinet Maps Easing of Antitrust Law; Business Groups Think Plan Is Too Bold," *Wall Street Journal,* December 6, 1985, p. 7.

36. Ralph Frammilino, "Justice actions follow through on Reagan policy," *Dallas Times Herald,* January 9, 1982, p. 20-A.

37. "Let's Make a Deal," *Time,* December 23, 1985, pp. 42–47.

38. "Merger Activity Fell 38% in 1987, W.T. Grimm Says," *Wall Street Journal,* February 9, 1988, p. 20; Bryan Burrough, "Takeover Boom Is Expected to Continue Through 1988 After a Strong First Half," *Wall Street Journal,* July 5, 1988, p. 3; Judith Dobrzynski, "The Top Two Hundred Deals," *Business Week,* April 13, 1990, p. 34.

39. "Antitrust Chief Suggests Price-Fixing Law Won't Be Enforced in Some Circumstances," *Wall Street Journal,* September 10, 1982, p. 4.

40. Claudia Ricci, "Discounters Alleging Price-Fixing, Are Fighting Cuts in Their Supplies," *Wall Street Journal,* June 21, 1983, p. 37.

41. Stephen Wermiel and Barbara Rosewicz, "Justice's Ruling to Help Firms Crack Down on Retailers That Discount, " *Wall Street Journal,* May 3, 1988, p. 4.

42. William E. Kovacic, "Steady Reliever at Antitrust," *Wall Street Journal,* October 10, 1989, p. A-14. See also Paula Dwyer, "The Reagan Revolution in Antitrust Won't Fade Away," *Business Week,* April 18, 1988, p. 29.

43. Adolf A. Berle and Gardiner C. Means, *The Modern Corporation and Private Property* (New York: Macmillan, 1932).

44. U.S. Congress, Senate, Committee on the Judiciary, Subcommittee on Antitrust and Monopoly, *Concentration Ratios in Manufacturing Industry,* 1963 S. Rept. 89th Cong., 2d sess., 1966, p. 2.

45. Betty Bock and Jack Farkas, *Relative Growth of the Largest Manufacturing Corporations, 1947–1971* (New York: The Conference Board, 1973).

46. Philip I. Blumberg, *The Megacorporation in American Society* (Englewood Cliffs, N.J.: Prentice Hall, 1975), p. 25.

47. See M. A. Adelman, "The Two Faces of Economic Concentration," *Public Interest*, No. 21 (Fall 1970), pp. 117–126.

48. E. Thomas Sullivan, *The Antitrust Division as a Market Regulator* (St. Louis, Mo.: Washington University Center for the Study of American Business, 1986), pp. 28–29.

49. U.S. Congress, Senate, Committee on the Judiciary, Oversight of Antitrust Enforcement, *Hearings before the Subcommittee on Antitrust and Monopoly,* 95th Cong., 1st sess., 1977, pp. 160–80.

50. J. Fred Weston, "Big Corporations: The Arguments for and against Breaking Them Up," Business and Its Changing Environment, proceedings of a conference held by the Graduate School of Management at UCLA, July 24–August 3, 1977, pp. 232–33.

51. See John Kenneth Galbraith, *The New Industrial State* (Boston: Houghton Mifflin, 1967).

52. See Alfred Chandler, *The Visible Hand: The Managerial Revolution in American Business* (Cambridge, Mass.: Belknap Press, 1977).

53. Peter F. Drucker, "The Concept of the Corporation," *Business and Society Review,* No. 3 (Autumn 1972), pp. 12–17.

54. See Arthur A. Thompson, "Corporate Bigness—For Better or for Worse," *Sloan Management Review,* Vol. 17, No. 1 (Fall 1975), pp. 37–61; Harold Demsetz, *The Market Concentration Doctrine* (Washington, D.C.: American Enterprise Institute, 1973), pp. 22, 25–26; William F. Chappell and Rex L. Cottle, "Sources of Concentration-Related Profits," *Southern Economic Journal,* Vol. 51 (April 1985), pp. 1031–1037; J. Jewkes, R. Sawers, and R. Sullerman, *The Sources of Innovation* (New York: St. Martin's Press, 1968); and Weston, "Big Corporations."

55. "Is John Sherman's Antitrust Obsolete?" *Business Week,* March 23, 1974, pp. 47–56. See also Michel McQueen, "Quayle Seeks Review of U.S. Merger Laws," *Wall Street Journal,* June 21, 1989, p. A-20.

56. Michael E. DeBow, "What's Wrong With Price Fixing," *Regulation,* No. 2, 1988, p. 45.

57. "Sherman's Antitrust," *Business Week,* March 23, 1974, p. 49.

58. Ibid.

59. Ibid., pp. 49–50.

60. Catherine England, "Bringing Antitrust Laws into the Twentieth Century," *The Heritage Foundation Backgrounder,* April 18, 1984, pp. 8–9.

61. U.S. Congress, Senate, *Industrial Reorganization Act,* 93rd Cong., 1st sess., 1973, S. 1167, pp. 2–3.

62. Paul M. Barrett, "Attorneys General Flex Their Muscles," *Wall Street Journal,* July 13, 1988, p. 13.

63. Tim Smart, "Pumping Up A State's Power to Bust Trusts," *Business Week,* January 15, 1990. Later in the year, the Supreme Court upheld the State of California in its suit by ruling that state governments have the same power as the federal government to bust up mergers that reduce competition. The merger in question involved American Stores Co. and Lucky Stores Inc., a merger that had received approval of the FTC before it was challanged by the Attorney General of the State of California. See Dean Foust and Tim Smart, "The Merger Parade Runs Into A Brick Wall," *Business Week,* May 14, 1990, p. 38.

64. Paul M. Barrett, "Bush's Apparent Pick for Antitrust Chief Is Likely to Change Style, Not Substance," *Wall Street Journal,* May 1, 1989, p. B-6.

65. Alan Murray and Paul M. Barrett, "Bush Aides Urge Antitrust Restrictions Be Eased for U.S. Firms' Joint Ventures," *Wall Street Journal,* January 22, 1990, p. A-4.

66. Christopher J. Chippello, "More Competitors Turn to Cooperation," *Wall Street Journal,* June 23, 1989, p. B-1.

67. Christopher Farrell, "The Best And Worst Deals of the '80s: What We Learned From All Those Mergers, Acquisitions, and Takeovers," *Business Week,* January 15, 1990, pp. 52–62.

68. Christopher Farrell, "The Bills Are Coming Due," *Business Week,* September 11, 1989, pp. 84–92.

69. "Leveraged Buyouts Fall to Earth," *Business Week,* February 12, 1990, pp. 62–65; Randall Smith, "Takeover Explosion of the Mid-1980s Is Being Overtaken by Junk-Bond Woes," *Wall Street Journal,* November 1, 1989, p. A-2.

70. Foust and Smart, "The Merger Parade," p. 38.

Suggested Reading

ARMENTANO, DOMINICK T. *Antitrust and Monopoly: Anatomy of a Policy Failure.* New York: John Wiley, 1982.

ARMSTRONG, DONALD. *Competition Versus Monopoly.* Vancouver, Canada: The Fraser Institute, 1982.

AUERBACH, PAUL. Competition: *The Economics of Industrial Change.* New York: Basil Blackwell, 1988.

BAIN, J. S. *Barriers to New Competition.* Cambridge, Mass.: Harvard University Press, 1956.

———. *Industrial Organization,* 2d ed. New York: John Wiley, 1968.

BLAIR, J. M. *Economic Concentration: Structure, Behavior and Public Policy.* New York: Harcourt Brace Jovanovich, 1972.

BLUMBERG, PHILIP I. *The Megacorporation in American Society.* Englewood Cliffs, N.J.: Prentice Hall, 1975.

BOCK, BETTY, AND JACK FARKAS. *Relative Growth of the Largest Manufacturing Corporations, 1947–1971.* New York: The Conference Board, 1973.

———, ET AL. *Is Antitrust Dead?* New York: The Conference Board, 1989.

BREIT, WILLIAM. *The Antitrust Casebook.* New York: Dryden Press, 1988.

BRUNNER, THOMAS W. *Mergers in the New Antitrust Era.* Washington, D.C.: BNA, 1985.

CAVES, RICHARD. *American Industry: Structure, Conduct, Performance.* Englewood Cliffs, N.J.: Prentice Hall, 1972.

CLARKSON, KENNETH W. AND ROGER LEROY MILLER. *Industrial Organization: Theory, Evidence, and Public Policy.* New York: McGraw-Hill, 1982.

DEMSETZ, HAROLD. *The Market Concentration Doctrine.* Washington, D.C.: American Enterprise Institute for Public Policy Research, 1973.

———. *The Organization of Economic Activity: Efficiency, Competition & Policy.* New York: Basil Blackwell, 1989.

GRIESON, RONALD E. *Antitrust & Regulation.* New York: Lexington, 1985.

HAYNES, WILLIAM J., JR. *State Antitrust Laws.* Washington, D.C.: BNA, 1988.

HOVENCAMP, HERBERT. *Antitrust.* St. Paul, Minn.: West, 1986.

KAYSEN, CARL, AND DONALD F. TURNER. *Antitrust Policy.* Cambridge, Mass.: Harvard University Press, 1959.

SCHERER, F. M. *Industrial Market Structure and Economic Performance.* Chicago: Rand McNally, 1970.

SCHMALENSEE, R. *The Economics of Advertising.* Amsterdam: North-Holland Publishing Company, 1972.

SHEPHERD, WILLIAM, C., ed. *Public Policies Toward Business: Readings and Cases,* rev. ed. Homewood, Ill.: Richard D. Irwin, 1979.

SHERMAN, ROGER. *Antitrust Policies and Issues.* Reading, Mass.: Addison-Wesley, 1978.

WESTON, FRED J., ed. *Large Corporations in a Changing Society.* New York: New York University Press, 1974.

CHAPTER 4

Corporate Governance

The issues that are raised in the general area referred to as corporate governance make the corporate form of organization a public policy problem in and of itself. Many critics of business question the legitimacy of the governance process as presently structured and thus strike at the heart of the corporation itself, that is, the system of internal control that has evolved over the years in which the corporate form of organization has been used by private business enterprises. These critics have advocated various reform measures, some of which would radically change the way corporations are governed.

The term corporate governance is concerned with the structure, participants, and the processes by which corporations are managed. When companies were small, the process of governing was simple and the participants were few because of the absence of other parties involved in ownership of the company. Owners of these small companies managed their businesses themselves and acted in concert with their own personal interests. But as companies grew in size and number, and went public and issued stock (incorporated), the governance process became more complex and divorced from ownership.

Why has there been a concern about corporate governance for the past several years? This concern undoubtedly stems in part from abuses of power on the part of those who manage the modern corporation—illegal campaign contributions in the United States, the maintenance of secret slush funds for payments to foreign officials or governments, the seeming unconcern of the management of some corporations for the safety of their products or the health of their employees, the unwillingness of some corporations to invest in new plant and equipment to be more competitive on world markets. But there is good reason to believe that even if such abuses had not occurred, the issue of corporate governance would still have emerged.

Corporate governance has been a latent issue in the United States since the advent of the large industrial corporation with power over vast resources. These large corporations are not run democratically even in theory, as the one-person, one-vote principle does not apply to corporate governance as it does to a democratic form of government. Instead, voting rights are based on share ownership. Most employees who have a major stake in the corporation have no influence over the decisions that are made by or on behalf of the corporation. The public at large, many of whom may be directly or indirectly affected by corporate decisions, are even further removed from having any influence over corporate behavior.

Thus for some time a fundamental value conflict has existed between the way in which economic organizations are governed and the principles upon which a democratic government is based. It seems inevitable that this conflict should have surfaced at some time, and the fact that corporate governance is a current issue at this particular time in our history may be due more to value changes with regard to participation and an emphasis on rights in recent years than to any specific abuses of power on the part of corporate managers. The concern about corporate governance may stem from more deep-rooted changes in American society relative to the uses of corporate resources for the improvement of human welfare.

Models of Corporate Governance

Traditional Model.   The traditional model of corporate governance that is dominant in the United States is based upon property rights. According to this traditional model, shareholders control the corporation and are the major factor in the governance process. They supply the capital the corporation needs and thus own the property of the corporation and have certain legal rights to see that this property is used to further their interests. The ownership of property legitimizes the shareholder's theoretical control over the use of corporate resources.

Figure 4.1 shows how this process works. The shareholders meet once a year to listen to an annual performance report from management, elect a board of directors, and dispose of other business on the agenda that may need stockholder approval. The board acts as an intermediary between the shareholders and the management of the company. The board of directors elects the management and officers of the company to run the company on a day-to-day basis and meets periodically with management to exercise an overseer function to protect the interests of the shareholders. Management, in turn, exercises a derived authority over the rest of the employees in the company to direct their activities to accomplish corporate objectives.

The legitimacy of this system of control rests on the notion that the property rights of the owners are supreme. Property rights are an important, if not the most important,

Figure 4.1   The Traditional Model

right in a free enterprise system. Stockholders have legal rights to exercise their control over the corporation through the voting mechanism described earlier, and if necessary, by challenging actions of corporate management in the courts when circumstances leave them no other feasible alternative. The final right of shareholders, of course, is to dispose of the property they own by selling their ownership certificate.

Co-Determination Model. An alternative model is found in many European countries where a form of industrial democracy has been instituted. Because of ideological differences, there has been pressure in these countries for employees to be placed on boards of directors of major corporations and play a much larger role in the corporate governance process than they do in this country. Many European countries have thus established legislation providing for worker participation in the governance process. Through the use of co-determination schemes, meaning labor and capital are both represented in the governance process, those countries have been actively promoting a form of industrial democracy.

The idea of combining labor and capital in the governance process stems from the concept of participatory decision making or participatory management. These concepts deal with the right of groups who have a major stake in an institution to have some degree of influence over what the institution does. Employees are connected with the lot of the corporation in a special way and their risk, although of a different nature than that of stockholders, is in general, larger. Investors are able to minimize their risk by diversifying their portfolio of investments across several companies. But employees cannot do this. For the most part, they are employed by only one corporation at a time, and it is not practically possible for them to work for several companies to diversify their risk.

European countries were pressured by unions and workers to recognize this special relationship and include workers in the corporate decision-making process vis-à-vis representation along with shareholders on corporate boards of directors. Co-determination thus refers to a situation where employee representatives are admitted as full members to corporate boards together with representatives of the owners. Employee representatives are those members of the work force who are directly or indirectly elected or appointed by their colleagues, with or without direct recommendation of the trade unions who may represent them.

The co-determination model in West Germany is a good example of how co-determination works in general (Figure 4.2). West German corporations have a two-tier board structure including a supervisory board and a management board. The supervisory board is much like a board of directors in this country having a broad overseer function, while the management board deals with more day-to-day operation of the company. The supervisory board can appoint and dismiss members of the management board; thus it has ultimate authority. From one-third to one-half of the seats on the supervisory board, depending on the size of the company and the industry in which it is located, must by law consist of employee representatives. The legitimacy of this system stems from the property rights of shareholders and the special relationship the employees have with the corporation.

Stakeholder Model. The stakeholder model of corporate governance is based on the notion that there are other groups in society besides owners and employees to whom the corporation is responsible and that the firm's objectives should be achieved by balancing the often conflicting interests of these different constituencies. Thus these various constit-

Figure 4.2 Co-Determination Model

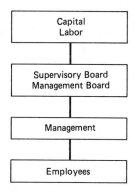

Capital Labor

| Supervisory Board
Management Board |

| Management |

| Employees |

uencies, that is, those who have a stake in the performance of the corporation (as distinguished from stock), deserve to be represented in the corporate governance process.

The stakeholder concept has been defined by Freeman as "any group or individual who can affect, or is affected by, the achievement of a corporation's purpose. Stakeholders include employees, customers, suppliers, stockholders, banks, environmentalists, government and other groups who can help or hurt the corporation."[1] The participation of these various stakeholder groups in the governance process (Figure 4.3) will assure that a wide range of interests are taken into account in corporate decision making. This complicates the governance process, but advocates also point out that corporations are more likely to respond to the interests of society as a whole when a wide range of constitutent groups have a role in the decision-making process. The legitimacy of this model stems from the interests the various stakeholders have in corporate activities and decisions.

These models thus range from a narrow conception of corporate governance based on property rights, to a conception where the interests of both labor and capital are

Figure 4.3 Stakeholder Model

Social, Political, and Economic Interests

| Stakeholder Participation
on Board of Directors |

| Management |

| Employees |

represented, to a broad model allowing for a wide range of participation representing various affected groups and interests. Many of the reform measures that have been proposed are based on one of these models. Before we discuss reform measures dealing with corporate governance, however, it will be useful to take a closer look at who actually does control the modern corporation. How does the traditional model work out in practice? What people or groups make most of the major decisions in the corporation? What evidence and theories exist that help in answering these questions?

Control of the Modern Corporation

Stockholders.   That the traditional model does not work out in practice as spelled out by theory should come as no surprise to anyone acquainted with the modern corporation. Share ownership of most major corporations is widely dispersed throughout society so that no one person owns a large enough block of stock to make a difference in the voting outcome at an annual meeting. This dispersion, with many people holding a small number of shares, means that they do not think of themselves as owners of the corporation but as investors who hope to make an adequate return on their investment. If they feel this return is not adequate, they do not go to the management of the company or the board of directors and demand better performance. They go to their stockbroker and sell the stock and invest in something else that seems to hold more promise. As far as voting rights are concerned, investors simply send their signed proxy statements back to the company, perhaps without even reading them.

Because of this dispersion of stock ownership, there has been a change in the way stockholders perceive themselves and, consequently, a change in corporate governance. This change has been described in the well-known thesis of Berle and Means regarding the separation of ownership and control in the modern corporation.[2] The owners of the large corporations do not have control over corporate resources. Individually, they have little or no power to affect change. Because of the change in stockholders' perceptions of themselves, it is difficult to organize them in significant numbers even to attend an annual meeting and exercise the collective power they have in theory.

These facts about the modern corporation were documented by Berle and Means in their 1932 classic (see Exhibit 4.1). Using data about share ownership obtained from various sources and establishing certain categories of control, the crucial one being the 5 percent cutoff point, they determined that 44 percent by number and 58 percent by wealth (assets) of the largest 200 nonfinancial corporations at that time were under control of the management. No dominant stock interest owned even so much as 5 percent of the stock in these corporations, which Berle and Means concluded was the minimum needed to exercise some influence.

This kind of study was updated in 1971 by Robert Larner, who at that time had access to different sources of stock ownership information (Exhibit 4.2). Larner also changed the critical cutoff point from 5 percent to 10 percent, concluding that it took at least a 10 percent interest by an individual or compact group that would vote as a unit to exercise any influence. Under these assumptions, Larner found that as of 1963, 85 percent of the top 200 corporations were controlled by management. Such evidence supports the idea that stock ownership is widely dispersed in many corporations, providing an empirical foundation for the theory about the separation of ownership and control.

EXHIBIT 4.1
Berle-Means Study

I. Sample

The 200 largest nonfinancial corporations ranked according to assets as of around January 1930. Used estimated asset figures. Data collection period: 1928–29, 1930–31.

II. Sources

Standard & Poor's corporation records (1929–31)
Moody's manuals (1930)
The New York Times (1928–30)
The Wall Street Journal (1928–30)

III. Classifications

Private: ownership of 80% or more of the stock by a compact group of individuals.
Majority: ownership of 50–80% of the stock.
Minority: ownership of 20–50% of the stock.
Legal Device: pyramiding arrangement which led to a considerable separation of ownership and control.
Management: dominant stock interest of less than 5%. From 5–20% classed as joint minority-management control.

IV. Findings

	Number	*Wealth*
Private ownership	6%	4%
Majority ownership	5	2
Minority ownership	23	14
Legal device	21	22
Management control	44	58

Source: Adapted from Adolf A. Berle and Gardiner C. Means, *The Modern Corporation and Private Property* (New York: Macmillan, 1932). Used with permission. Renewed © 1960 by Berle and Means.

Management. If one accepts this evidence and buys the theory of the separation of ownership and control, management not only runs the company on a day-to-day basis but also exercises ultimate control over corporate resources. Critics of the corporation are quick to point out that management controls the proxy machinery; it selects the proxies that appear on the ballots sent to shareholders and naturally will select proxies that will elect directors who will in turn reappoint the existing management. Thus management becomes self-perpetuating by controlling this process.

Furthermore, it is alleged that the board of directors is ineffectual in protecting stockholder rights. Many companies have boards composed of a majority of inside directors (officers of the company). Those outside directors who are on the board are "friends" of management—officers of other corporations, investment bankers, and the like—who share the same values as management and are not likely to raise any serious opposition to management's policies. Boards rarely question the recommendations of top management and leave the chief executive officer free to run the company as he or she chooses, as long as there is average or acceptable performance.

A study conducted by Heidrick and Struggles in 1972 showed that 49.8 percent of

EXHIBIT 4.2 ——————————————————————————————
Robert Larner Study

I. Sample

The 200 largest nonfinancial concerns ranked by assets as of 1963.

II. Sources

Corporate proxy statements stock ownership information submitted annually to the SEC on the 10K Form
Reports filed with FPC and ICC

III. Classification

Control defined as the holding of 10% or more of the voting stock. Otherwise the same as the Berle-Means study.

IV. Findings

	Number	Wealth
Private ownership	0%	0%
Majority ownership	2.5	1
Minority ownership	9	11
Legal devices	4	3
Management control	84.5	85
Nonmanagerial Interests		
Manufacturing and mining		27% of top 290
Merchandising concerns		39% of top 33
Transportation companies		13% of top 45
Public utilities		2% of top 120

Source: Adapted from Robert J. Larner, *Management Control and the Large Corporation* (New York: Dunellen, 1971). Used with permission.

the companies who responded to the survey had 50 percent or more of the board composed of inside members.[3] A study by Smith in 1970 found that 20 to 25 percent of the outside directors in large American corporations were lawyers or investment bankers, the majority of whom had business dealings with the corporations on whose boards they served.[4] They were thus unlikely to oppose the chief executive who usually controls such business dealings. A Conference Board report of 1975 stated that many of the remaining outside members of the board are either friends or colleagues of the chief executive officers.[5]

Since the chief executive officer of the company is in many cases also chairman of the board, he or she sets the agenda for board meetings and controls information going to the board members. There were instances, such as in Lockheed Corporation, Penn Central, Texas Gulf Sulphur, Bar Chis, and Anaconda, where the board members were supposedly unaware of the financial plight of the company and were as surprised as anyone when the real condition of the company became public knowledge. The Heidrick and Struggles study showed that only 17.2 percent of industrial corporations sent directors manufacturing data before board meetings, and only 21.3 percent sent marketing information. The same study found that only 6 percent sent an agenda and 11 percent sent no information at all to directors.[6] In addition to this problem, boards have no staff of their own to analyze the information they do receive or find on their own and are again dependent on management for analysis and evaluation.

These allegations project the image of a small group of unknown managers controlling the resources of the large corporations in our society, thus exercising vast powers over almost every facet of American life. They have stepped into the vacuum created by the separation of ownership and control. These managers, so the image goes, are beholden to no one but themselves, going through the ritual of directors meetings and annual meetings that have no real purpose other than to perpetuate a myth of stockholder control. Whether this image is true or not is unimportant; the crucial point is that many people believe it is true, and out of this rather marked contrast with a democratic system of control come pressures for reform of corporate governance.

The premise of management control over the large corporation has been termed "managerialism," a phrase that was popularized in a book entitled *The Managerial Revolution* by James Burnham. Published in 1941, Burham argued that capitalism was disappearing and socialism remained an abstract Marxian ideal in the Soviet Union. What was emerging in industrial countries all over the world was a managerial society, where managers of large organizations would achieve social dominance and become the ruling class in society. By managers, Burnham meant those who actually manage, on the technical side, the processes of production. The functions of management in a technological society were becoming more distinctive, complex, and specialized, and more crucial to the whole process of production. The function and legitimacy of this managerial class, Burnham argued, was not dependent on the maintenance of capitalist property and economic relations, but upon the technical nature of the processes of modern production.[7]

Family Control.   Challenging the notion of a widespread diffusion of stock ownership is the rather common knowledge that in some corporations, at least, a large block of stock is held by a prominent wealthy family, such as the Mellon family. Presumably, these families can control a corporation in which they have substantial holdings because they can be expected to vote their stock more or less uniformly and take an active interest in the running of the company because they have such a large stake in its performance. Thus they would seem to have the power to influence management policies and even replace management, if necessary, with people more to their liking.

This phenomenon was studied by Robert Sheehan in a 1967 *Fortune* article. The sources of his information were not disclosed in the article, which raises a question of validity, but in any event he determined that 17 percent of the top 200 corporations in the country were controlled by wealthy families who owned a substantial block of stock (Exhibit 4.3). In addition, he identified some of the corporations that were controlled by families.

The most complex of any of these studies that deal with stock ownership was done by Philip Burch in a 1972 book entitled *The Managerial Revolution Reassessed.* Using a variety of information sources, employing a cutoff point of 4 to 5 percent (the same as Berle-Means), and looking at representation on the board of directors in addition to stock ownership, Burch concluded that 39.5 percent of the top 200 industrial corporations in 1965 were probably under family control, and another 17.5 percent were in the possible family control category (Exhibit 4.4). That left 43 percent ostensibly under management control, with no significant stock ownership or board representation to

EXHIBIT 4.3 ───

Robert Sheehan Study

I. Sources

Not identified.

II. Classification

Corporations ranked according to volume of sales as of 1966. Control defined as holding of 10% or more of voting stock.

III. Findings

Family Control
11% of top 100
17% of top 200
24% of top 300

Ford family holds 11% of Class B shares (3.492 votes per share), which in terms of votes means 39% of the company.

Du Pont family owns 30% of Christiana Securities, which in turn owns 29% of E. I. du Pont de Nemours.

The four Firestone brothers own 15% of Firestone Tire and Rubber.

The Danforth family controls 22% of Ralston Purina.

The Pitcairn family holds 26% of Pittsburgh Plate Glass.

The Pews and their family trusts maintain 44% of Sun Oil Company.

Source: Adapted from Robert Sheehan. "Proprietors in the World of Big Business: *Fortune*, June 15, 1967, pp. 178–183. Copyright © 1967 Time, Inc. All rights reserved.

indicate family control. Burch also examined ownership for the top 50 banks, transportation companies, and merchandising establishments.

Thus there is some evidence to indicate that families do exercise control by owning large blocks of stock in some companies or being represented on the board of directors. But Table 4.1 on page 92 shows that family ownership in 43 major corporations declined over the 1929–76 period. Family holdings fell by 75 percent or more in over half the cases, and the decline was 50 percent or more in more than four-fifths of the cases. Control passed out of the hands of families during this period in 26 of the 43 companies studied, and in several other instances weakened markedly. These declines were not offset by any comparable replacements, leading some scholars to conclude that family control in general has been on the decline for several years.[8]

Even where families do still own large blocks of stock, this potential for control may not be exercised. Perhaps the members of the family have no particular interest in overseeing the running of a business but are more interested in enjoying their wealth. Unless there is someone in the family with a good business sense and an active interest in business, the potential for control may never be exercised. And even if one desires to do so, it is not always easy to exercise influence over an entrenched management. Family ownership, even in those companies where it represents a substantial percentage

Exhibit 4.4 ————————————————————————————

Philip Burch Study

I. Sample

Used *Fortune's* 1965 list of the top 500 industrial corporations, concentrating on the first 300. Also appraised the top 50 merchandising firms, top 50 transportation companies, and the top 50 commercial banks.

II. Sources

Standard & Poor's corporation records
Fortune (1950–71)
Time (1955–71)
Business Week (1955–71)
Forbes (1955–71)
The New York Times (1960–71)
Moody's manuals
1963 House Select Committee on Small Business Report

III. Classification

Probably Family Control: (1) 4–5% of stock held by family, group of individuals, or an individual; (2) inside or outside representation on the board of directors.
Possibly Family Control: definite signs of family influence but insufficient data to make a reliable assessment.
Probably Management Control: no significant stock ownership or representation on board to indicate family control.

IV. Findings

	Probably Management	*Possibly Family*	*Probably Family*
Top 50 industrials	58%	22%	20%
Top 100 industrials	44	20	36
Top 200 industrials	43	17.5	39.5
Top 300 industrials	41.3	16	42.7
Top 50 merchandising	28	14	58
Top 50 transportation	46	18	36
Top 50 banks	48	22	30

Source: Reprinted by permission of the publisher, from *The Managerial Revolution Reassessed,* by Philip H. Burch, Jr. (Lexington, Mass.: Lexington Books, D. C. Heath, 1972. Copyright D. C. Heath and Company.

of the stock, does not necessarily translate into direct control over the corporations in which they own stock.

Takeover Artists. In the 1980s, a new aspect of corporate governance appeared on the scene with the increase in the number of mergers between large companies, many of which were of the hostile variety. The availability of huge amounts of money through

TABLE 4.1 Percentage Declines in Ownership by Family Groups in 43 Large
Corporations from Peak Holding to Trough, 1929–1976

Percentage Decline	No. of Companies	Percentage
75% or more	25%	58.1%
50–74	12	27.9
25–49	3	7.0
Under 25	3	7.0
Total	43%	100.0%

Source: Edward S. Herman, *Corporate Control, Corporate Power* (Cambridge University Press, 1981), p. 78. A Twentieth Century Fund Study. Copyright © 1981, The Twentieth Century Fund, New York.

junk bond financing and bank credits allowed outsiders called raiders to capture huge companies. For all practical purposes, no company was safe from takeover attempts of this nature. These outside raiders were able to threaten and in some cases actually take over many large companies. Even where they weren't successful, they often pressured the management of target companies to restructure their organizations to ward off the takeover bid or to seek a friendlier merger partner.

Raiders such as Carl Icahn who took over TWA and T. Boone Pickens who forced Gulf Oil to merge with Standard Oil of California justified their actions by claiming to represent a grass-roots movement of shareholders who were out to shake up an entrenched management and restructure corporations to be more productive and produce greater returns to the shareholders. Stocks were undervalued because the company assets were not being used in their most productive manner. They claimed that a strongly knit corporate aristocracy existed in America that has produced a corporate welfare state consisting of an army of nonproductive workers. Thus the raiders were considered to be a kind of folk hero who were taking on corporcracy itself and forcing managers to take shareholder interests into account by being more accountable in the use of corporate assets.[9] Many companies were restructured because of these pressures by stripping away tangential operations and returning to core business operations.

Another factor in this deal making is the investment banking houses on Wall Street who put together many of these deals and managed the exchange of equity for debt that enables takeovers to proceed. From 1980 to 1985, the capital of these banks more than tripled to $22 billion, and their assets, which consisted mostly of trading inventories of stocks and bonds, increased fourfold to nearly $400 billion.[10] Investment banks such as Drexel Burnham Lambert founded the junk bond market that enabled raiders to attain huge amounts of unsecured loans and thus mount their takeover attempts on huge companies. Drexel alone raised billions in junk bond financing to support unfriendly takeover bids against Gulf Oil, Walt Disney, Union Carbide, and several other large corporations. Eventually, these investment banks began to suggest deals at their own initiative instead of just responding to the needs of an outside raider and take equity positions in companies for which they arranged leveraged buyouts and other financing. Some became outright owners of major companies by pooling their own money with pension funds and other institutions with deep pockets.[11]

From the standpoint of corporate governance, these takeover attempts forced management to adopt strategies to resist being taken over by outsiders. In some cases, they arranged deals of their own to buy the company they managed through leveraged buyout arrangements. They learned how to play the game as well as outside raiders and thus protect their position in the company. The largest buyout in history was proposed in the fall of 1988 when the CEO of RJR-Nabisco, F. Ross Johnson, and seven other managers made a $75-a-share proposal to take the company private in a leveraged buyout. The directors of the company were in a state of shock that turned to outrage when they learned about the kind of money that Johnson and the other executives would make for themselves. Some accused Johnson of raiding the company from the inside.[12]

The directors then proceeded to retaliate by taking control of the buyout process and opening the bidding for RJR-Nabisco to all comers. They believed they could get a better deal for the shareholders by putting the company up for auction rather than approving the buyout proposed by Johnson and the other managers. By taking matters into their own hands, the directors set a precedent on how boards should respond to such bids and think about the long-term interests of shareholders and other stakeholders such as employees and communities.[13] After several bids were received, the board eventually awarded the company to Kohlberg Kravis Roberts, the leveraged buyout specialists, for about $25 billion in cash and securities, or about $109 a share. This bid was even less that the $112 a share proposed by Johnson and the management group as their last offer.[14]

Some commentators saw a positive development in the trend toward leveraged buyouts. When managers become a significant equity holder, they run the company better than when they are merely agents of shareholders. They become owner-managers and run the company more efficiently because they have their own interests more directly at stake. The public corporation is fundamentally flawed, it is argued, because it separated ownership from control. The leveraged buyout recreates the close ties between commerce and finance that held sway in earlier periods of corporate history and resolves the conflict between owners and managers over the control and use of corporate resources.[15]

If management didn't proposed a leveraged buyout, it had to adopt other strategies to ward off takeovers. In some cases, it sold off lackluster divisions and laid off employees to boost cash flow and increase stock prices to make the company less attractive to takeover attempts. Once the company's stock had been put into play in the takeover game, managers had to sacrifice long-term plans and narrow their focus to immediately increase stock performance.[16] Thus managers of even the largest corporate organizations were subject to new kinds of external pressures to use corporate resources in new ways and for more short-run objectives. As a result, power has shifted somewhat from professional managers to the corporate raiders and the investment banks who manage takeover deals.

Another way for managers to protect their positions and ward off takeover attempts is through legislation. Unable to get federal antitakeover legislation, managers took their case to the states and, in many cases, received a sympathetic hearing. After the Supreme Court upheld Indiana's antitakeover law in April 1987, more than 30 other states adopted statutes designed to repel raiders. One common provision in these laws is a control-share rule, which forces raiders who accumulate a specified percentage of stock to seek approval from the remaining shareholders before these shares can be voted. Another provision imposed a lengthy moratorium on selling acquired assets to help finance the takeover.[17]

A Wisconsin law required a bidder who acquired at least 10 percent of a target company either to have approval of the company's directors or wait 3 years to complete the merger. The Supreme Court refused to hear a constitutional challenge to this law, giving a signal that states have substantial authority to regulate takeovers.[18] Even Delaware, where about 56 percent of the *Fortune* 500 companies are incorporated, adopted a law which barred hostile acquirers from merging with target companies for three years except under certain conditions.[19] Finally, the state of Pennsylvania passed the nation's toughest antitakeover law in April 1990. It forced raiders to surrender short-term profits from takeover attempts and restricted raider voting rights.[20] These laws, coupled with the collapse of the junk bond market, began to slow the takeover boom as the nation entered a new decade. Perhaps the bankruptcy of Drexel Burnham Lambert signaled the end of an era.[21]

Institutional Share Ownership. Anyone acquainted with the stock market knows that financial and other kinds of institutions own substantial blocks of stock in many corporations. One of the first people to point out this phenomenon argued that even in 1970, financial institutions, not individual investors, were the dominant influence in the stock market. Thus the market had entered the era of the institutional investor where the institutions held an ever-growing share of corporate stock. This development has implications for corporate governance.[22]

As of 1970, Barber noted, mutual funds, pension funds, and insurance companies, all with varying degrees of bank involvement, owned more than a third of all stocks listed on the New York Stock Exchange. At that time, some 10 million people were purchasing $5 billion worth of shares a year of over 200 mutual funds. In 1967, these funds reported assets of over $50 billion, which was 50 times their 1948 holdings. In 1940, only 4 million jobholders were covered by pensions, and the reserves for these pensions totaled less than $2.5 billion. But in 1970, more than 28 million people were covered by pensions, and the assets had swollen to $80 billion, half of which was invested in common stock.

Couple the holdings of these financial institutions with the holdings of universities, churches, and foundations, and institutions indeed have the potential to exercise control over many corporations. But until a few years ago, this potential was apparently not exercised, as the institutions themselves acted much like individual investors. Their major concern was financial return, and if they did not like one stock, they shifted out of it into another. They rarely opposed management on any issue and apparently routinely sent in their proxies, as did individual investors. Most institutional investors held that their fiduciary duties precluded real activism.[23]

This passive role began to change as takeovers and leveraged buyouts grew in importance. Managers of pension funds, in particular, believed they had a fiduciary duty to earn their beneficiaries the best return possible, and in many takeover situations, they earned terrific returns by tendering their shares to outsiders hostile to management. This chance for a large payoff put institutional managers at odds with company management that wanted to erect takeover defenses to protect their positions. Thus institutional-fund managers began to oppose poison pills and other such takeover defenses.[24] In 1987, 60 shareholder resolutions were filed asking companies either to rescind their poison pills or at least to put them to a vote of the shareholders.[25]

As takeovers and buyouts began to wane in the early 1990s, raiders turned to old-fashioned proxy battles to gain control of a company. Instead of trying to buy up a majority of the company's stock, raiders sought to engineer a coup of sorts by enlisting the support of other stockholders in a proxy fight. The goal of such a fight is to urge the stockholders to throw management out altogether by casting their votes for the dissident raider and his or her roster of director nominees, who promised to do a better job of running the company than the incumbents. Institutional shareholders were a major factor in this process because they owned a major portion of the stock in some companies.[26]

Pension-fund managers also were in the vanguard of dumping stocks in companies with ties to South Africa and mounting proxy fights to force companies to withdraw from that country. They also forced Exxon, after the Alaskan oil spill, to name an environmentalist to its board of directors. And they wanted to talk about how the company's environmental problems were affecting the value of the stock owned by the funds. Several of them also supported six resolutions that were presented at the Exxon annual meeting. Thus institutions came to concern themselves with social as well as economic issues, particularly when social issues had a bottom-line impact.[27]

Peter Drucker identified a more subtle influence that these institutional investors have had on corporate management. Stock ownership has become more concentrated, Drucker claims, than probably ever before in the country's history. Pension funds alone now own $1.5 trillion in corporate assets, and that figure will soon reach $2 trillion. Pension funds now own a third of the equity of all publicly traded companies in the country and 50 percent or more of the equity in large companies. Therefore, claims Drucker, any business that needs money will have to live up to the expectations of the pension-fund managers. And pension-fund managers focus on only the very shortest term, having to show immediate gains with performance judged in most cases quarter by quarter. Thus pressures from pension-fund managers are pushing managers of large corporations to subordinate long-run considerations to immediate earnings and current stock prices. This produces a threat to America's long-term economic future, according to Drucker, as the basic wealth-producing capacity of corporations is ignored.[28]

Employees. Employees in this country exercise control over corporate resources primarily through labor unions. Elected representatives of the employees choosing bargain with management every 3 years over wages and working conditions. There is thus far no direct representation of employees on boards of directors in this country on any significant scale, as is true of some countries in Western Europe. Unions seemed relatively unconcerned about having representation at the board level to exercise some influence over corporate policies as a whole, not just those concerned with wages and working conditions. The collective bargaining process, in those companies where unions exist, gives employees an indirect influence over the allocation of corporate resources.

Modern labor-management relations in the United States are based on the Wagner Act of 1935 and the Labor Management Relations Act of 1947. The Wagner Act made collective bargaining compulsory if a majority of employees in a bargaining unit agreed to form a union to represent them. The act also specified unfair labor practices for employers and created a National Labor Relations Board (NLRB) to administer the rules under which collective bargaining was to take place. Unions could order their workers to stop working and go out on strike, but once an agreement between labor and management was reached and accepted, all union workers were bound by it and had to return to work. The Labor Management Relations Act of 1947 specified a list of union practices that were banned; however, the collective bargaining process remained essentially unchanged.

Collective bargaining, rather than compulsory arbitration or legal enactment, has always been favored by American trade unions. Collective bargaining is an implied readiness to enter into a written collective agreement with employers governing all terms and conditions of employment. These terms and conditions include wages, hours, and other terms and conditions of employment. Other areas usually included in the agreement are vacations, severance pay, grievance procedures, arbitration, seniority, fringe benefits, union security, antidiscrimination provisions, and employee allowances.

John Kenneth Galbraith has developed an interesting theory about the modern corporate organization and its structure and the role of employees in the governance process.[29] He invented a new term *technostructure,* to describe decision making within the corporation. The technostructure refers to all persons who contribute specialized information to group decision making in the organization. This technostructure consists of management, technical specialists, scientists, and other knowledgeable people who may be involved, depending on the type of decision.

Galbraith's point is that the complexity of modern technology makes it impossible for top management to possess enough knowledge to make a decision that will work in the corporation's best interests. They have to rely more and more on specialists within the organization and include them in the decision-making process. This need for information from numerous individuals derives from the technological requirements of modern industry. Decision making and control have moved from the top of the organization down into lower levels, involving more and more employees. Power has thus shifted to some degree to those who posses knowledge rather than just status or position.

Employees are more directly involved in the governance of a corporation when they actually take it over through an Employee Stock Ownership Plan (ESOP). ESOPs are becoming more and more widespread. The National Center for Employee Ownership estimates that at the end of 1989, there were close to 12,000 ESOPs nationwide, covering 10 million workers[30] (Figure 4.4). Only a small percentage of these are full-fledged "buy outs" in which employees purchased an entire company. The rest are profit-sharing plans or retirement plans set up by companies to take advantage of tax breaks. In the mid-1980s, the number of new plans was increasing at a 10% annual rate largely because of tax incentives. At that pace, by the year 2000, 25% or more of all U.S. workers would own all or part of their companies.[31]

To set up an ESOP, employees form a stock ownership trust, which borrows money from banks or insurance companies. This money is used to buy newly issued stock of the company. The company then makes contributions to the trust that are used to repay the loan. These are, in effect, contributions to an employee benefit plan and as such are tax-deductible. If the company had borrowed the money directly, it would have been able to deduct only the interest as a business expense. When the money is paid to an ESOP, however, the company can deduct principal repayments as well, cutting borrowing costs further.[32] The shares in the ESOP are tax-exempt until distributed on retirement, and any capital gains on the shares are taxable only when the stock is sold. In a few ESOPs, the workers can also make contributions to the trust. Other incentives, added in the Deficit Reduction Act of 1984, included a provision allowing banks to exclude from taxable income 50% of interest received on loans to ESOPs, and another provision excluding dividends paid on stock held in ESOPs from corporate taxes.[33]

All these tax breaks were established by Congress based on the belief that employee ownership in corporate America is good for a free-market society. Many benefits are claimed for an ESOP arrangement and the virtues of employee ownership are widely touted. Some believe the idea will spur managers to invest the huge sums of money that will be needed over the next several decades to modernize U.S. industry. Others believe that ESOPs will increase productivity, improve labor-management relations, and promote economic justice. The original brainchild of the idea is said to be Louis O. Kelso, a San Francisco attorney, who has long championed various forms of "worker capitalism."[34]

Whether ESOPs will provide these benefits is open to question. Critics argued

Figure 4.4 Cumulative Growth of Employee Ownership Plans 1975–1989

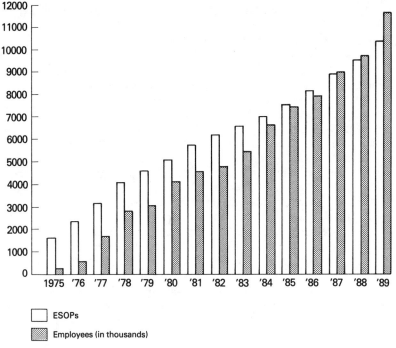

ESOPs

Employees (in thousands)

Source: National Center for Employee Ownership, Inc., Oakland, Calif.

that ESOPs seldom produce the degree of industrial democracy that advocates promise. Management in many companies refused to relinquish control either on the board of directors or on the shop floor. Thus workers in many employee-owned companies gain no voice in workplace decisions. Some studies have shown that in 85 percent of the companies with ESOPs, worker-owners do not even have voting rights.[35] The more that retirement income comes from an ESOP, the more dependent a pensioner is on the stock price of a company, making future retirees vulnerable to Wall Street as well as to management mistakes. And ESOPs cost the government money in lost tax revenues. One study by the U.S. General Accounting Office estimated that this cost for 1977 to 1983 was $12 billion.[36]

In the 1980s, ESOPs were increasingly used to help management insulate themselves against hostile takeovers through facilitating leveraged buyouts, a tax abuse whose main beneficiaries are not workers but management, investment bankers, and outside investors.[37] In 1988, for example, Polaroid set up an ESOP that initially held 14 percent of the company to ward off a takeover attempt by Shamrock Holdings, Inc. This action was upheld by a Delaware court that turned down Shamrock's challenge. Proctor & Gamble also established an ESOP that will give employees a 20 percent stake in the company. The company acknowledged that the ESOP will give the company an extra defense against a takeover.[38] In late 1989, Chevron added a new wrinkle by establishing an ESOP with only 5 percent of its stock. This 5 percent was combined with another 11 percent of its stock that had been buried in the company's employee benefit plans, giving it an effective 15 percent interest.[39]

Foreign Control.   Recently, another aspect of control over American corporations has appeared on the scene, that of foreign ownership. Foreign direct investment in the United States increased 400 percent in a decade. Foreign holdings in 1974 registered just over $25 billion. In 1983, foreign investment totaled $135.5 billion. Between 1977 and 1983, foreigners made 179 investments of at least $100 million each in the United States, and 58 of these investments exceeded $250 million. Overseas investors came to have at least a 10 percent stake in such firms as Mack Trucks, Inc., Scott Paper Co., and W. R. Grace and Company. Foreigners also held 22.2 percent of DuPont Co., 69 percent of Shell Oil Co., and 53 percent of Standard Oil of Ohio.[40]

In 1982, U.S. investment abroad exceeded foreign investment in the United States by about $137 billion. These figures began to reverse in 1985, and by 1988, foreign holdings in the United States amounted to about $1,786 trillion, whereas American investments abroad came to only $1,253 trillion. This reversal reflected America's change from a creditor to a debtor nation (Figure 4.5). Foreign direct investment, defined as ownership of at least 10 percent of a company, soared by 21 percent in 1988, as more and more foreign investors bought stock in U.S. companies.[41]

The Japanese became a major factor in foreign ownership in the late 1980s as they became buyers of U.S. government debt and began increasing their real estate holdings and stock ownership in American companies. As the dollar weakened against the yen, the stocks of American companies became a real bargain for Japanese investors. Japanese investment in the United States nearly tripled from 1980 to 1985, even though takeovers by Japanese companies in 1985 accounted for only $613.5 million of direct investment. In 1989 total direct investment by the Japanese, which included real estate acquisitions and new investment in plants and equipment as well as corporate buyouts, had increased to an estimated $26 billion. Japanese acquisitions of U.S. corporations alone climbed 8 percent in 1989 to a record $13.7 billion. If this trend continued, it was expected that

Figure 4.5   U.S. Investment Status[1]

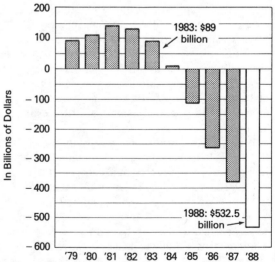

[1]Numbers reflect the difference between assets that Americans own abroad and assets that foreigners own in the U.S.

Source: "Foreign Debt Owed by U.S. Leaps 41%," *Dallas Times Herald,* June 30, 1989, p. C-1.

in 1990 the Japanese would surpass the British in U.S. takeovers for the first time in history.[42]

Japanese investment in U.S. manufacturing facilities was expected to continue growing at 14.2 percent each year until the year 2000. That would be a tenfold increase over the early 1980s and would involve the creation of 840,000 more jobs in the United States by the end of the century. Such projection raised questions as to (1) whether this investment will translate into influence over state governments and perhaps Congress, (2) whether U.S. managers working for the Japanese will find themselves cut out of decision making, and (3) what effect such control will have on union power in this country.[43]

Whether this foreign ownership will become a major factor in corporate governance remains to be seen. Nonetheless, Congress from time to time has expressed concern with rumors requiring corporations to disclose their major shareholders so any foreign influence can be seen, and putting a limit on the proportion of shares of any one U.S. corporation that can be owned by foreign sources. A task force was formed in 1981 to advise the president on foreign takeovers of U.S. companies and study the question of whether it should have the power to delay or block such sales.[44] In 1989, the Transportation Department was considering blocking foreign investments in U.S. airlines.[45] A survey conducted in 1988 showed that 78 percent of the average Americans surveyed favored a law to limit the extent of foreign investment in U.S. business and real estate, and 89 percent supported a requirement that would have foreign investors register with the government. Another 40 percent in this same survey wanted the government to ban further foreign investment in the country altogether.[46]

Reform of Corporate Governance

From this examination of the groups that have the potential to play a role in corporate governance, it seems that management is the dominant participant in the corporate governance process. Managers play the most significant role in running the modern large corporation and thus have the most influence in the decision-making process. While they may be subject to outside pressures from corporate raiders and institutional investors, they are still the dominant factor in running corporations and in making the critical decisions. The average stockholder sits on the sidelines and watches the action much like a spectator at a football game.

> Big corporations are seen as rogue elephants loose in the land, elephants which pay no attention to where they put their feet. Corporate directors are seen not as people who provide necessary windows to the outside world, but as window dressing. The election of directors and the appointment of top executives are seen as charades, simple exercises in self-perpetuation. The outside forces supposedly keeping business in check (regulation, antitrust law, market competition, collective bargaining, state chartering laws, and other agencies of constraint) are regarded as singly and severally inadequate.[47]

Corporate critics allege that the present system of corporate governance has failed to hold company managements sufficiently accountable for the use of corporate resources and have directed public attention to the internal governance system as the basic cause and cure of corporate malpractices. They view the corporation as a quasi-public institution, despite its private ownership, and believe that corporate management should be more broadly accountable to all the constituents and interests they affect, not just shareholders and the competitive marketplace. In general, there are four categories of alleged deficiencies and proposed reforms with regard to the present structure and process of corporate governance.

1. *Shareholder rights:* Management is not accountable to shareholders because management has preempted control; therefore, shareholders must have increased rights to participate in important management decisions.

2. *Boards of directors:* Management is not accountable to the board of directors because board members are too subservient to management and the chief executive officer; therefore, the board must be restructured.

3. *Employee participation:* Management is not accountable to the employees and cognizant of employee needs because employees have no voice in management; therefore, employees must be represented at some level in corporate governance.

4. *Corporate chartering:* Management is not accountable to state government because state charters are overly permissive; therefore, the large corporation must be chartered by the federal government.

Thus the present structure of corporate governance and the opportunities provided for input from various segments of society is apparently not sufficiently democratic for many critics of corporations. One of the basic questions asked by reformers is whether decisions made in large corporations are sufficiently representative of society as a whole so that not only are the private interests of the corporation a factor but that the broader public interest is also taken into account. From these concerns comes a good deal of activity to reform the internal structure of corporations and open up the process of decision making to a wider set of influences.

INCREASED DISCLOSURE

The purpose behind increased disclosure is to make the corporation more responsible to stockholders' interests and perhaps secondarily to society as a whole. Reforms in this area, in fact, could be seen as attempts to make the present system work better by providing shareholders with more information on which to base their investment decisions. Former chairman of the Securities and Exchange Commission (SEC) Harold Williams warned business that it must tell its shareholders more to make the corporate accountability process work in its present form, or the pressures may become irresistible for the more radical reform measures related to federal chartering, federal standards, or some other kind of federal governance of the American corporation.[48]

The primary force behind disclosure over the years has been the SEC, but the establishment of the Financial Accounting Standards Board (FASB) in 1972 continues the effort at self-regulation in establishing uniform standards of disclosure. The seven full-time members of the FASB are appointed by the Financial Accounting Foundation, an independent organization that oversees the operations of the Board. The purpose of the FASB is to develop standards for financial measurement and reporting. As a quasi-legal body, the board must obtain the cooperation of industry, accountants, government agencies, statement users, and the general public to set standards that will be accepted and followed. The FASB and SEC staffs are in constant communication, and over the last several years, there has been more of an "integrated disclosure" between public and SEC reporting requirements.[49]

In September 1979, the FASB issued Statement No. 33, "Financial Reporting and Changing Prices," to deal with inflation accounting. Because of the controversial nature of the subject, the standard was issued as a 5-year experiment. In 1984, the FASB issued an invitation to comment on the subject and suggest midcourse corrections in the original statement. Something had to be done during periods of increasing inflation, because the accounting system, which explicitly assumes constant prices, was increasingly being viewed as inadequate.[50] The FASB statement replaced the SEC replacement cost requirement for annual 10K forms issued in 1976, which ordered the nation's top corporations to restate their assets on a replacement cost basis and refigure the additional depreciation expense.[51] The FASB approved continuation of the experiment in July 1984 and indicated that it would put together recommendations about whether the inflation adjustments should be made permanent or continued on an experimental basis for another 3 to 5 years.[52]

Another disclosure requirement to help shareholders evaluate corporate performance is line of business reporting, a requirement imposed by the SEC after an unsuccessful effort by business in the courts to prevent such reporting. This type of disclosure requires business to report sales and earnings for each component of a company with more than 10 percent of total sales and earnings. Supposedly, this information will help investors determine which lines of business are most profitable and be a factor in their investment decisions.

Other areas of disclosure include a 1974 SEC ruling requiring companies to disclose a 5-year history of financial statistics, a 1978 SEC requirement that all proxy statements disclose the economic and personal relationship of members of boards of directors, the requirement of the Foreign Corrupt Practices Act of 1977 for disclosure of foreign payments, and SEC rulings in 1977 pertaining to disclosure of executive compensation to include not only salaries and bonuses but also deferred compensation, fringe benefits, and nonsalary compensation. The latter are commonly referred to as "perks" and are usually buried in the footnotes of annual reports. In September 1983, however, the SEC ruled that companies would not have to disclose as many details about executive stock options, incentive-pay packages, perquisites, and other forms of remuneration, watering down its previous requirements.[53]

In the midst of all the merger activity in the 1980s, another disclosure issue was put on the agenda. Shareholders filed against a company for making misleading statements in denying that there were merger talks going on with another company. The shareholders claimed that they sold their shares at an artifically low price before the takeover. The Supreme Court ruled that early merger negotiations may sometimes be "material" and thus must be disclosed to investors under certain circumstances.[54] This decision was confusing, however, and some lawyers said it confirmed the old rule of keeping quiet about merger negotiations until an agreement in principle was reached on price and structure.[55]

Regarding disclosure of social information, in 1975 the SEC conducted public hearings on the possibility of requiring the disclosure of more extensive "social" information either in statements submitted to the SEC and/or the annual report.[56] That the SEC would express such an interest in social information can be viewed as significant because of the oversight function that the SEC has assumed over corporate reporting. While corporate social reporting is not yet required in the United States, it has been required in some Western European countries for several years.[57]

ACTIVIST SHAREHOLDERS

The activist shareholder movement began in the 1960s, as small shareholders interested particularly in pursuing social goals found a way to make their voices heard at annual meetings. The SEC amended the proxy rules to allow small shareholders to place resolutions concerning social responsibility issues on corporate proxy statements. Thus the door was opened for public interest groups and others to buy a few shares of stock in a company and introduce resolutions dealing with social issues. These resolutions became quite numerous in the late 1970s and on into the 1980s, confronting management with questions of social responsibility and corporate governance.

There were 109 such resolutions voted on in 1982, and the degree of support for these resolutions increased, as a record 74.5 percent of them received the support of at least 3 percent of the shares voted. More than half received enough votes to qualify for resubmission the following year.[58] There was a big increase in 1983 to 215 resolutions, but then a sharp drop in 1984 to only 93 resolutions, and another drop to only 83 in 1985, the lowest number in a decade.[59] The reason for the drop was because so many resolutions failed to qualify for resubmission under the new SEC regulations. In 1986, there was another increase as 118 such resolutions were eligible for consideration with 79 actually being voted on and 60 receiving enough support to be resubmitted the following year. Most of these resolutions had to do with South Africa, an issue that didn't lend itself to easy agreement.[60]

In 1987, shareholder proposals were split about evenly between corporate and social issues. Resolutions on South Africa continued to dominate social-issue proposals, constituting about half the social-issue initiatives. Other social-issue proposals included religious discrimination in Northern Ireland, production of nuclear weapons, lending to Chile's repressive regime, Third World debt, overseas marketing practices of infant formula and cigarette manufacturers, environmental matters, and minority employment and purchasing practices. Corporate governance issues included prohibitions against paying greenmail, opposition to antitakeover measures, limitations of executive compensation and stock options, and increasing shareholder's ability to include proposals on proxy statements and to nominate their own slate of directors.[61]

In 1989 some 170 resolutions were filed, with the largest number still pertaining to South Africa. But some new issues, such as animal rights, were also introduced.[62] In 1990, the environment came in for increasing attention, reflecting trends in the larger society. Some 50 shareholder resolutions ranging from timber clear-cutting to the use of chlorofluorocarbons were filed with various corporations. Most of these were withdrawn before the annual meeting because they were successfully negotiated or otherwise settled.[63] Six resolutions were introduced at the Exxon annual meeting, asking the company to make public an environmental audit, encouraging it to press on with its cleanup in Alaska, and suggesting it limit emissions of carbon dioxide and other greenhouse gases.[64] None of these resolutions passed, but they did gather more of the vote than expected, leading activists to claim a symbolic victory.[65]

The resolutions introduced by these activist shareholders have never received anything approaching a majority of the shareholder vote. While their impact on corporate strategy has thus been small, these activists have at least enlivened usually staid annual meetings and made managers think twice about the social consequences of business practices. The activists claim a moral victory in voicing social concerns and a tactical victory in being able to get their voices heard. The immediate goal is to establish dialogue. Reform comes later.

Occasionally, the resolutions introduced by the activist shareholders receive the support of the large institutional investors. While mainly interested in financial return, institutions do support certain social resolutions, on occasion. The chairman of the Teachers Insurance and Annuity Association, William C. Greenough, justified this action with the following statement: "In its supporting and nudging role, the institutional investor has a potent lever to move the American corporation—the voting of corporate shares. Failure to use this lever leaves a vacuum in the responsible exercise of corporate power."[66]

During the 1970s, the SEC supported this movement toward investor responsibility. In February 1978, it reversed its earlier "1 percent rule" that permitted a company to omit a resolution that was not "significantly related" to the company's business. In reversing this rule, Chairman Williams said, "There are some issues that are so important that quantitative tests are irrelevant." The commission also ruled that a company must forward to the sponsors of the resolution a copy of its statement opposing the resolution 10 days before the preliminary filing of the proxy with the SEC so that the sponsors have a chance to challenge any alleged factual misstatement in the company's response.[67]

But in 1983, the SEC tightened the rules, forcing activist holders to alter their strategies in corporate contests. One provision required that anyone advancing a proposal must own at least $1,000 of the company's stock or 1 percent of the stock outstanding, whichever is smaller. Before this rule, an individual could become a shareholder for $25 or $50 and get management to include his or her pet proposal in proxy materials. Another requirement raised the minimum requirements for resubmitting proposals to 5 percent for the first year, 8 percent the second year, and 10 percent thereafter. Previously, the limits were 3 percent, 6 percent, and 10 percent, respectively. Other changes included a provision to permit a company to exclude a proposal if it involved less than 5 percent of assets, revenues, or sales and barring a group from submitting more than one proposal to a company each year.[68]

Because of the impact of these changes on the number of proposals submitted, the activists sued in federal court to try and force the SEC to liberalize its proxy rules once again.[69] This suit was won in September 1985, and the lower percentages were reinstituted, accounting for the increase in resolutions the following year. Thus it appears that shareholder activism is not a passing fad of the 1970s but, rather, has become a permanent feature of corporate governance in the United States.[70] While their influence on corporate policy is likely to remain limited, their influence on public policy will continue to be significant. In the words of David Vogel, a business school professor with a political science background at the University of California at Berkeley,

> Clearly, what is least important about citizen pressures has been their direct, substantive effect on corporate decisions. These have been, and are likely to remain marginal. Their impact on public policy has been more substantial. They have played a relatively important role both in bringing a number of issues before the political process, and in increasing the effectiveness of government controls over business.[71]

BOARDS OF DIRECTORS

Another attempt to make the current governance process work better is the effort to reform the board of directors to make it more responsive to the interests of the owners and less subservient to management. The board has been criticized as being nothing more than a ceremonial function that "rubber stamps" the views and policies of management. Board members have been accused of being dominated by top management who set the agenda for board meetings and are the sole source of information for many board members. As a result of these criticisms, many voluntary changes have been made over the past several years.[72]

Three trends toward reform of boards began in the late 1970s. The first was a change in the composition of boards to include more outside directors. In some cases this change went so far as to change the board from a majority of inside directors to a majority of outside directors. This is accomplished by either expanding the board or simply dropping some inside members from it. The chairman of the SEC at that time, Harold Williams, once suggested that the ideal board should have just one management director and he or she should not be the chairperson.[73]

While companies are not likely to go that far, a study conducted in 1980 by Heidrick & Struggles, an executive-search consultant, concluded that by 1990, the vast majority of companies (of all sizes) would have more outside directors than insiders. The study was based on questionnaires mailed to the 1,000 largest industrial and the 300 largest nonindustrial companies in the United States. Responses were received from 487 companies. The study found that outside directors constituted a majority on the boards of 87.6 percent of the responding companies, an increase of almost 20 percent over two years previous.[74] The prediction proved true, as by 1989, the ratio of outside to inside directors was 3 to 1 or higher. Thus during the 1980s, the boards of publicly held companies did move to a preponderance of outside directors.[75]

The second trend is that for a while, at least, these new outside directors were not necessarily quasi-insiders, such as the company's legal counsel, banker, major supplier, or retired officer. Instead they often had no ties to the company itself that would make them beholden to management. They were more likely to be college professors, executives of unrelated concerns, professional directors, or representatives of civil rights and consumer groups. The representation of women and minority-group members also increased for a while, but in the 1980s companies added female directors more slowly than they had in the 1970s.

A study conducted in 1987 by Korn-Ferry International found that only 43 percent of the 532 companies responding to the survey had at least one female director, down from 45 percent the previous year. White males held 92.1 percent of the director's chairs, which was little changed from the 1982 figures.[76] However, Heidrick and Struggles found that the percentage of all-white-male boards declined from 51.3 percent in 1983 to 38.1 percent in 1988, a significant decrease. Minorities also accounted for 7.8 percent of board memberships in 1988, up 2.2 percent from 2 years previous.[77]

Thus boards are still dominated by white males (Table 4.2), and the use of independent outside directors once advocated by chairman Williams seems to be slowing. In fact, some commentators state that the dramatic restructuring that has taken place in recent years as more and more boards are dominated by outsiders is largely a change in form rather than in substance. The selection of outside directors has continued to be heavily, if not solely, influenced by the CEO of the company. And many of the new so-called independent directors view themselves as colleagues and business allies of the CEO just like the inside directors they replaced.[78]

The third trend is the development of board committees to perform various functions. Perhaps the most important committee is the audit committee, composed entirely of outside directors. The purpose of this committee is to monitor the company's accounting procedures and ensure the accuracy of information appearing in the annual report. There is some question about the usual process of formal auditing being able to provide this

TABLE 4.2   Board of Directors Representation Nationwide

	East	Midwest	South	Southwest	West	United States
Total directors	1,671	1,514	591	354	535	4,665
White males	1,544	1,429	554	346	493	4,366
White females	80	53	18	7	25	183
Black males	30	20	16	1	9	76
Black females	15	6	0	0	1	22
Hispanic males	0	3	3	0	5	11
Hispanic females	0	1	0	0	0	1
Other males	2	1	0	0	1	4
Other females	0	1	0	0	1	2
Percent white male	92.4%	94.4%	93.7%	97.7%	92.1%	93.6%
Percent minority	7.6%	5.6%	6.3%	2.3%	7.9%	6.4%

Reflects responses from 350 of 896 *Fortune* 1000 companies surveyed nationally in late 1984. Data from Heidrick and Struggles, Inc.

Source: Ray Alvareztorres, "Minority Power: Lots of Room at the Top," *Dallas Times Herald,* October 14–20, 1985, p. 15.

assurance if management has the power to hire and fire the auditors.[79] The foreign payments controversy also played a role here, as the auditing firms failed to discover these payments in the annual review. The new SEC disclosure rules require that companies disclose the existence of audit committees as well as the number of meetings held annually and the composition of the committee.

Another very important committee is the nominating committee, which takes the power of nominating new board members away from management. Thus management cannot control the composition of the board by continuing to nominate its own friends. When these nominating committees are also made up of outside directors, management has even more difficulty in controlling the new board members and limiting the role it can play in supervising management.[80] An SEC study conducted in 1980 found that 29% of the 1,200 companies surveyed had such nominating committees.[81]

Most large companies have compensation committees to evaluate the performance of top managers and determine the terms and conditions of their employment. It was hoped that these committees would link executive pay more closely to actual performance of the company and thus prevent large pay increases from being granted to top management when the company hadn't done well and other stakeholders did not get a fair return. There is some evidence to indicate, however, that these committees have not been able to curb the continuing rise in the salaries of top management and are not as independent from top management as was hoped.[82]

Another trend that appeared in the 1980s concerned holding the board more responsible for their actions than had been true in the past, when board membership was more in the nature of a pleasant, undemanding hobby for business leaders. Shareholder suits against corporate officers and directors increased at a 10 percent annual rate in the early years of the decade, making insurance coverage for directors and officers harder to get and much more expensive (Table 4.3). In 1985, premiums for insurance coverage were 3 to 10 times higher than in the previous year, and in many cases, the higher premiums bought less coverage.[83] The mean increases for 1986 and 1987 were 506 percent and 219 percent, respectively. But in 1988, the average increase was only 87 percent, reflecting a slowing average premium increase.[84]

TABLE 4.3 Suing Directors: A Rise in Costs and Cases, 1974 and 1984

	1974	1984	Percent Change
Percentage of companies reporting one or more claims against directors and officers	7.1%	18.6%	162%
Number of claims per 100 responding companies	9.8%	35.0	257%
Percentage of claims with payment over $1 million	4.8%	8.3%	73%
Average defense cost per claim	$181,500	$ 461,000	154%
Average payment to a claimant	$385,000	$ 583,000	51%
Average total cost per claim	$566,500	$1,044,000	84%

Source: The Wyatt Company Survey data, "The Crisis in Insuring Directors," *The Corporate Board* (July–August 1986), p. 4.

Also in 1985, a landmark decision was handed down by the Delaware Supreme Court that further accelerated the trend toward accountability. The court ruled that 10 former directors of Trans Union, a railroad equipment leasing company, were financially liable for selling their company too hastily and too cheaply. The lawsuit, filed on behalf of 10,000 shareholders, claimed that the directors spent just two hours discussing a purchase offer of $55 a share, or a total of $688 million, while the company actually had been worth much more. The directors could be held responsible for the difference between what was actually paid and a "fair value" for the company. Depending on what the courts determined this value to be, each director could be liable for millions of dollars in damages.[85]

Because of this trend, many companies are finding it harder to recruit directors. A survey by Korn/Ferry International of more than 500 corporate executives in 1985 found that one company in five was turned down by a boardroom prospect. This was the highest rejection rate in recent years. Two-thirds of the executives surveyed thought that fear of public censure, excessive time demands, and potential financial loss would make the director's job still more unappealing in the future.[86] This trend continued, as about 22 percent turned down board seats in 1987, and many of them continued to mention time and legal liability as reasons for their refusal. The average director spent 114 hours a year on such things as review, preparation, and travel to attend an average of eight board meetings during a typical year.[87]

These efforts could be seen as moving in the direction of making the board a truly independent body between the shareholders and management, one that is not under the control of management, allowing the board to perform its true function of reviewing management's actions to determine if it is acting in the stockholders' best interests. Besides the RJR-Nabisco affair mentioned earlier, there were other instances where the board had acted independently of management and showed a new assertiveness.[88] Many saw this as a very healthy development in the area of corporate governance and continued to focus on reform of the board of directors as a solution to the problems of corporate governance.

A major study of corporate boards published in 1989, however, indicated that there was still a great deal of trouble in the corporate boardroom. Jay Lorsch argued that the current composition and functioning of boards constituted a major barrier to economic competitiveness. In most companies, boards were only minimal participants in corporate affairs, and their role was often restricted to ratifying the plans and preferences of top management. Three barriers, according to Lorsch, prevented boards from taking a more active role in governing the corporation.[89]

First, in many companies, the CEO also served as chairperson of the board and in this capacity determined the agenda of meetings, controlled the flow of information, and almost always possessed superior knowledge of the company. The second barrier is the composition of the boards themselves. Members, especially outside directors, typically serve on several boards, and such overcommitment leads to mediocre performance. The third barrier is what Lorsch calls the "inhibited atmosphere" of the boardroom, where board members avoid controversy and questioning of issues and policies. Many members of the board have been chosen because of their close personal ties to the CEO; others defer to the superior knowledge and experience of the CEO and the other inside directors who have knowledge of the company. The result is board meetings that are rather perfunctory in nature and do not provide a forum for real debate and discussion.[90]

FEDERAL CHARTERING

The previous reforms are actually conservative attempts to make the present system of corporate governance function more effectively–disclosure of more information to shareholders, changes in the board of directors to make it more independent of management, and activist shareholders promoting the idea of investor responsibility with regard to social issues of importance to society. Nothing in these reforms suggests radical change in the present system of corporate governance.

The proposals advocating federal chartering, however, are different. This concept means just what the term implies, that corporations would be required to obtain their charter from the federal government rather than from the states, as is the current practice. The Nader proposal, which was the most comprehensive federal chartering proposal to date, involves a law that would require all industrial, retail, and transportation corporations that sold over $250 million in goods or services or employed more than 10,000 people in the United States in any one of the previous three years to obtain their charter from the federal government. The law would bypass the 15 million smaller business associations, yet would reach some 700 industrial, retail, and transportation companies whose size clearly indicates a national impact.[91]

The arguments advanced in favor of federal chartering include the following. First, according to Nader, state incorporation makes no sense as state boundaries are not the relevant boundaries for corporate commerce. State chartering makes about as much sense, says Nader, as 50 state currencies or 50 state units of measurement.[92] Second, control of national and multinational power requires at least national authority, and federal chartering would go far toward an accessible framework for shaping and monitoring corporate power. Such an authority could remind the corporation that the charter is a compact between the government and itself to ensure business behavior in the public interest. It can also remind the corporation that it holds the charter in trust for public benefit, and if it violates that trust, it can forfeit the charter and the right to do business.

The third argument advanced by Nader is that state incorporation laws are a major impediment to proper ground rules and the functioning of corporations as public citizens. Powerful corporations can threaten to run away to a different state if such items as incorporation fees, regulatory laws, and charter provisions are not to their liking. Federal chartering could equalize the varying burden and benefits corporations obtain due to the vagueness of different state authorities.

The competition between states for chartering of corporations began with the General Revision Act of 1896 in New Jersey. This act permitted unlimited corporate size and concentration (thus corporations chartered in New Jersey could merge or consolidate at will) and allowed for the purchase of stock of other corporations by payment of the corporation's stock; it also permitted stockholders to be classified as preferred and common, with unequal power given to them. These were such attractive provisions that, by 1900, 95 percent of the major corporations were incorporated in New Jersey. The state raised so much money from incorporation fees that in 1902 it abolished property taxes and paid off the entire state debt; by 1905 had a $2,940,918 surplus in the treasury.[93]

It did not take other states long to see the benefits involved in this arrangement and some began to pass similar incorporation provisions. New Jersey, in fact, was the only state to ever reform its incorporation laws. Under Woodrow Wilson in 1913, the state passed provisions to outlaw the trust and the holding company. These provisions were later repealed, but big business would never trust New Jersey again.

Delaware took over the lead. Its self-determination provision allowed the corporation to be a lawmaker unto itself. The certificate of incorporation could contain any provision the incorporators chose to insert for the management of the business and the conduct of the affairs of the corporation and any provision creating, defining, limiting, and regulating the powers of the corporation, the directors, and the stockholders, provided such provisions were not contrary to the laws of the state. Previous to this, the corporation could only exercise powers explicitly provided or necessarily implied in the charter. Further liberal provisions were created in the 1967 revisions.

By 1971, franchise taxes and related corporate income comprised 23 percent of the state revenues. Between 1967 and 1974, 134 of the 1,000 largest companies reincorporated or incorporated in Delaware, and by 1974, Delaware was home for 448 of the largest 1,000, 251 of the largest 500, and 52 of the largest 100 corporations. About half the *Fortune* 500 companies and 40 percent of those listed on the New York Stock Exchange are still incorporated in the state.[94] Franchise taxes still provide 15 to 20 percent of the state's annual budget. Thus competition for the chartering business has rendered state incorporation ineffectual as a regulator of corporate behavior.

The federal chartering concept would provide such control because corporations who wanted to headquarter in this country would have nowhere else to go to incorporate. The federal government could insist on certain provisions regarding the corporation's structure and behavior. As an example of the form federal chartering could take, the provisions in the Nader proposal deal with internal governance of the corporation, corporate dealings with the public, company relations with employees, and industrial structure.[95]

Another proposal by Donald E. Schwartz is aimed at giant corporations and would include at least all the companies on the *Fortune* 100 list. His proposal for federal chartering would control those corporations that have a significant impact beyond their immediate vicinity. It has four major sections including corporate records and reports, directors and management, shareholders, and more fundamental changes.[96]

The concept of federal chartering is radical because it raises some fundamental questions about the proper relationship between the state and a private corporation. What gives a corporation a right to exist? If that right derives from the marketplace, that is, that a corporation gets the right to exist by serving the needs of consumers, chartering takes on a different character. Chartering, as suggested by Robert A. Hessen, research fellow at the Hoover Institution, then "merely records the existence of corporations and [is] not at all essential to their creation, any more than the registrar of births is essential to the conception of a child."[97] The federal chartering process implies that corporations get their right to exist from the state and that the state has the right to control private corporations in the "public interest."

Overview of Corporate Governance

These reform measures are summarized in Figure 4.6, which shows the major issues they are designed to address. The major area of emphasis at present is some kind of restructuring at the board level to make the governance process more responsive to shareholder interests and reduce the power that management had obtained over the past several years. These reforms are still based on the traditional model with property rights as the basis for legitimacy of the process. These reforms amount to no kind of radical change and have as their objective the goal of making the existing system work better.

At the present time, more radical measures such as federal chartering, do not seem a realistic possibility. While federal chartering is talked about occasionally, as it was during the oil embargo of the early 1970s, there have been no serious efforts to implement this concept for the past several years. Nor is there likely to be any legislation instituting some kind of co-determination scheme in this country. While there are some instances of worker participation at the board level, it is doubtful that this represents the beginning of a significant trend in the United States.

But perhaps all these changes taken together do show gradual movement toward the stakeholder model. The governance process has been opened up to more stockholder participation, even of the activist variety; the board has been changed to allow for more meaningful outsider participation; and there are some isolated instances of worker participation in the corporate governance process. Thus it would seem that more stake-

Figure 4.6 Corporate Governance Issues and Reform Measures

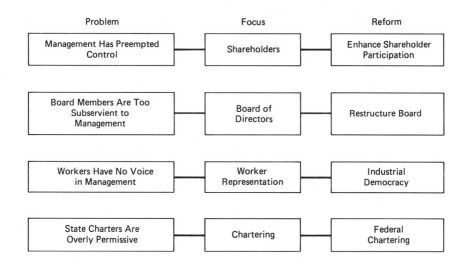

holders are presently participating in corporate decision making and that management's control has been diffused to some extent. Management is being held more accountable for its actions and has had to share power with other groups in some instances.[98]

The stakeholder approach, despite its drawbacks, has been advocated as a viable model for corporate governance to make the corporation more compatible with democratic values and more responsive to the concerns of society. Management, it is argued, is too myopic and is not in tune with the changing expectations of society. Thus a gap exists between corporate performance and public expectations that has been filled largely by government regulation. Perhaps the need for government regulation could be diminished if a wider range of interests and values were represented in the governance process of major corporations, to make the institution respond to a wider range of needs and interests in society.

The stakeholder concept, if widely implemented, would then mean that external controls could be replaced by internal controls to make the corporation respond to public issues that might otherwise find their way into the public policy process. Decision making would be shared with groups who have economic and social stakes in corporate activities. Advocates argue that stakeholder participation will assure that the interests of these groups are taken into account by corporate management and ultimately, the interests of society as a whole.

Questions for Discussion

1. Do you agree with the proposition that questions about corporate governance arise more from fundamental conflicts with democratic values than specific abuses of power? What specific conflicts exist between the way in which a corporation is run and the principles of a democratic society?

2. What has happened to the role of shareholders in the modern corporation? What legal rights do they have in relation to the corporation? What is the ultimate basis of these rights?

3. How does management control the corporation? Do you think management control is as widespread as some studies indicate? What percentage of stock ownership does it take to have influence over corporate policies?

4. Identify some important families in the nation or in your region who own a large number of shares in some corporations. Find some evidence that indicates they have actually used the power that such share ownership would imply. How have they influenced corporate policies?

5. Do you think employee representation on the board of directors will catch hold in this country to any significant degree? What ideological and cultural differences exist between the United States and Western Europe? Are you in favor of employee representation at the board level? Why or why not?

6. What new roles have institutional shareholders recently played in the corporate governance process? Why do you think their role has changed to a more activist position? Is this trend good for the corporation and the economy in the long run?

7. Do you believe that ownership of American corporations by foreign sources will increase? Should this be a cause of concern to Congress and the American public? What can be done about it? What implications does such ownership have for corporate governance?

8. What kinds of disclosure do you believe are most beneficial to shareholders? Why? Will increased disclosure satisfy critics of the corporate governance process to any significant degree?

9. Are activist shareholders a major force for reform of corporate governance? What role do

they play in the governance process? Is this role a significant one from the standpoint of shaping the agenda of public policy issues to be considered?

10. What, in your opinion, is a truly "outside" director? Should corporate boards be composed of a majority of these outside directors? Are they better able to look out after shareholders' interests? Why or why not?

11. Why is federal chartering a radical proposal as far as corporate governance is concerned? What is the purpose of the chartering process? Do you believe federal chartering of corporations would enhance corporate responsibility? In what ways?

12. What other reforms, besides those mentioned, can you think of that relate to the governance of corporations? Which reforms do you believe are most likely to take place? What impacts will these have on the management task in future years?

Case: Campaign GM

General Motors is representative of the largest of the large companies. In 1980 it was the largest corporation in the world, with 746,000 employees, 1,191,000 stockholders, assets of $34,581 million, and sales of $57,728.5 million. As such, much of the pressure aimed at large corporations to change their behavior was aimed at GM itself as representative of large corporations in general. GM was a highly visible company and subject to criticism for many of its actions and practices.

In 1965, Ralph Nader wrote *Unsafe at any Speed,* which condemned the Corvair automobile produced by General Motors. General Motors paid some private investigators to check on Nader and some of his associates. As a result, Ralph Nader filed suit for invasion of privacy; the suit was settled out of court for $425,000. With $275,000 from this settlement, Ralph Nader funded The Center for the Study of Responsive Law. This center then organized Campaign GM in 1970 to attack what it referred to as the "fiction of shareholder democracy."

Campaign GM presented three major resolutions at the 1972 GM annual meeting: "first, to establish a special shareholders' committee chosen by management, the UAW union, and the Campaign to do a year's study of GM's social impact and decision-making process; second, to expand the company's twenty-five man board to include three new members representing the public interest; and third, to amend the corporate charter to include specific prohibition of any act detrimental to public health, safety, and welfare, or of any violation of federal or state law."[1]

Other resolutions by the center called for action in the area of auto safety, new-car warranties, antipollution research, support for mass transit, and more new-car dealerships for African Americans. Thus a number of issues were raised by Campaign GM having to do with the company's response to the social environment. It was believed that GM's response to social issues was inadequate and needed to be changed in order to meet the changing expectations of the public.

The central issue, of course, was one of corporate governance. Campaign GM was asking for a change in GM's organization and its response to the social environment. Nader's group was trying to make itself a part of the governance process. Partly in response to Nader's demands, GM established a nominating committee to choose its members of the board of directors. This committee recommended candidates that were selected by the full board of directors. It was the responsibility of this committee to conduct continuing studies of the size and composition of the board, make recommendations for the enlargement or reduction of the board, to specify the procedures by which the committee recommends nominees to fill vacancies on the board, and to constitute the slate of nominees for election at the annual stockholders' meeting.

The nominating committee also reviewed and made recommendations concerning the composition and membership of each standing committee of the board, paid for board and committee members' service on other companies' boards by management personnel, and solicited proxy comments from stockholders relating to the composition of the board. The committee was also responsible for keeping abreast of current literature on the role of boards of directors affecting corporate governance.

According to GM policy, board members should have: broad experience in business, finance, or administration, familiarity with national and international business matters, and an appreciation of the relationship that a large industrial corporation must maintain with the changing needs of society. The 23-member board of directors included six management directors, an African American minister, the former U.S. Ambassador to Great Britain, a Nobel Laureate of physics, a former chairman of GM, and others with backgrounds in banking, utilities, and manufacturing.

General Motors' appointment of Rev. Leon Sullivan to the GM board of directors and GM's more recent appointments of outside members to the board of directors indicates that GM has taken steps toward the solution of governance issues. This internal movement and the accompanying impact of shareholder activism evident in programs such as Project GM has had an impact not only on GM, but on other large companies as well. The January 1971 appointment of Rev. Sullivan to GM's board of directors prompted then-President Lyndon Johnson to state that "now what's good for General Motors really is good for America."[2] Rev. Sullivan did not seek to be a token on a corporate board but vowed to resign if African Americans did not make large and measurable gains in working for and dealing with GM. He has not resigned, and by all manner of statistics African Americans have recorded those large and measurable gains at GM.

Minority members and women members on corporate boards of directors have gained much public attention, but unless these members can offer something positive to the corporation they will not continue to sit on these boards in any fashion other than ornamental. Unless these minority and women members as well as other board members solve some of the complaints about corporate governance, activists will renew their push for a legal solution to the change in corporate governance.

Case Notes

1. Ralph Nader, ed., *The Consumer and Corporate Accountability* (New York: Harcourt Brace Jovanovich, Inc., 1973), p. 327–28.
2. "Directors: The Black on GM's Board," *Time,* September 6, 1976, p. 54.

Chapter Notes

1. R. Edward Freeman, *Strategic Management: A Stakeholder Approach* (Marshfield, Mass.: Pitman, 1984), p. vi.
2. Adolf A. Berle and Gardiner C. Means, *The Modern Corporation and Private Property* (New York: Macmillan, 1932.).

3. Heidrick and Struggles, *The Changing Board—1980 Update,* p. 4. Published by Heidrick & Struggles, Inc., 225 Peachtree St., NE, Atlanta, Ga. 30303.

4. Ephraim P. Smith, "Interlocking Directorates Among the Fortune 500," *Antitrust Law and Economics Review,* Summer 1970, pp. 48–49.

5. Jeremy Bacon and James K. Brown, *Corporate Directorship Practices: Role, Selection and Legal Status of the Board* (New York: The Conference Board, 1975), pp. 28–35.

6. Heidrick and Struggles, *The Changing Board,* p. 6.

7. James Burnham, *The Managerial Revolution* (New York: John Day Co. Inc., 1941).

8. Edward S. Herman, *Corporate Control, Corporate Power* (Cambridge: Cambridge University Press, 1981), pp 78–79.

9. See George Melloan, "New Debate Over Corporate Governance," *Wall Street Journal,* November 11, 1986, p. 36, and Carl Icahn, "What Ails Corporate America—And What Should Be Done," *Business Week,* October 27, 1986, p. 101.

10. "American Business Has A New Kingpin: The Investment Banker," *Business Week,* November 24, 1986, p. 80.

11. Sarah Bartlett, "Power Investors," *Business Week,* June 20, 1988, p. 116–23.

12. Frederick Ungeheuer, "Will His Deal Go Up in Smoke?" *Time,* November 28, 1988, p. 76.

13. John Helyar and Bryan Burrough, "Nobody's Tool: RJR Nabisco Board Asserts Independence In Buy-Out Decisions," *Wall Street Journal,* November 9, 1988, p. A-1. See also Laurie P. Cohen, "Directors' Decision on RJR Offers Deemed Likely to Survive in Court," *Wall Street Journal,* December 2, 1988, p. A-4.

14. John Greenwald, "$25,000,000,000," *Time,* December 12, 1988, pp. 56–57.

15. Christopher Farrell, "The LBO Isn't A Superior New Species," *Business Week,* October 23, 1989, p. 126.

16. "More Than Ever, It's Management for the Short Term," *Business Week,* November 24, 1986, pp. 92–93.

17. Tim Smart, "More States Are Telling Raiders: Not Here, You Don't," *Business Week,* February 13, 1989, p. 28.

18. Stephen Wermiel, "Supreme Court Declines to Review Law In Wisconsin Curbing Hostile Takeovers," *Wall Street Journal,* November 7, 1989, p. 8-9.

19. Charlotte Low, "Corporate Haven Hostile to Raiders," *Insight,* May 2, 1988, p. 56.

20. Vindu P. Goel, "Pennsylvania's New Anti-Takeover Law Fuels Controversy, Faces Fight in Court," *Wall Street Journal,* April 30, 1990, p. B-1.

21. John Greenwald, "Predator's Fall," *Time,* February 26, 1990, pp. 46–52; Judith H. Dobrzynski, "After Drexel," *Business Week,* February 26, 1990, pp. 37–40.

22. Richard J. Barber, *The American Corporation* (New York: Dutton, 1970).

23. Several mutual funds have been established for customers who want to put money into stocks of companies that meet stringent standards for their response to social issues such as cleaning up the environment and doing business in or with South Africa. Assets of the six largest of these social-investment funds grew from $102 million in 1982 to $450 million in 1986, while the number of investors grew from 22,000 to 66,000 over the same period. "Moral Money: Investments for Social Activists," *Time,* October 27, 1986, p. 74. See also Paul M. Barrett, "Doing Good and Doing All Right: Investors Applying Ethical Values," *Wall Street Journal,* August 5, 1986, p. 29.

24. Christopher Power, "Shareholders Aren't Just Rolling Over Anymore," *Business Week,* April 27, 1987, pp. 32–33; Judith H. Dobrzynski, "Whose Company Is It, Anyway?" *Business Week,* April 25, 1988, pp. 60–61.

25. Edward V. Regan, "Pension Funds: New Power, New Responsibility," *Wall Street Journal,* November 2, 1987, p. 26.

26. Christine Gorman, "The Proxy Punch-Out," *Time,* April 16, 1990, pp. 40–41. See also Dean Foust, "Who's In Charge Here?" *Business Week,* March 19, 1990, pp. 38–39.

27. Larry Light, "The Power of The Pension Funds," *Business Week,* November 6, 1989, pp. 154–58.

28. Peter Drucker, "A Crisis of Capitalism," *Wall Street Journal,* September 30, 1986, p. 34.

29. John Kenneth Galbraith, *The New Industrial State* (Boston: Houghton Mifflin, 1967).

30. Christopher Farrell, "Suddenly, Blue Chips Are Red-Hot For ESOPs," *Business Week,* March 20, 1989, p. 144.

31. "ESOPs: Revolution or Ripoff?" *Business Week,* April 15, 1985, p. 94.

32. "More Worker Owners", *Time,* October 4, 1976, p. 80.

33. "ESOPs," *Business Week,* April 15, 1985, p. 102.

34. Jonathan B. Levine, "Louis Kelso's Baby Is Making Daddy Proud," *Business Week.* May 8, 1989, p. 130.

35. "ESOPs," *Business Week,* April 15, 1985, p. 95.

36. Gary S. Becker, "ESOPs Aren't The Magic Key To Anything," *Business Week,* October 23, 1989, p. 20.

37. "It's Time to Restrain ESOPs," *Business Week,* April 15, 1985, p. 174.

38. Keith H. Hammonds, "A New Way To Keep Raiders At Bay," *Business Week,* January 23, 1989, p. 39.

39. Aaron Bernstein, "How To Keep Raiders At Bay—On The Cheap," *Business Week,* January 29, 1990, p. 59.

40. John S. McClenahen, "Who Owns U.S. Industry?" *Industry Week,* January 7, 1985, p. 30.

41. "Foreign Debt Owed by U.S. Leaps 41%," *Dallas Times Herald,* June 30, 1989, p. C-1.

42. Michael R. Sesit, "Japanese Acquirers in U.S. Look Poised To Pass British, if 1989 Is Indication," *Wall Street Journal,* January 17, 1990, p. A-2.

43. "Japan, U.S.A.," *Business Week,* July 14, 1986, p. 46.

44. "Advisory Panel Studies Its Need for Power To Block Foreign Takeovers of U.S. Firms," *Wall Street Journal,* December 10, 1981, p. 10.

45. Judith Valente, "Transportation Agency May Rein In Airline Buy-Outs, Foreign Investments," *Wall Street Journal,* August 31, 1989, p. A-3.

46. Walter S. Mossberg, "Most Americans Favor Laws to Limit Foreign Investment in U.S., Poll Finds," *Wall Street Journal,* March 8, 1988, p. 48.

47. Irving A. Shapiro, *America's Third Revolution: Public Interest and the Private Role* (New York: Harper Collins. © by Irving A. Shapiro 1984), p. 234.

48. "Business Must Tell Holders More or Face Tougher U.S. Controls, SEC Chief Warns," *Wall Street Journal,* September 30, 1977, p. 10.

49. J. W. Giese and Thomas P. Klammer, *Intermediate Accounting: A Flow Approach* (Englewood Cliffs, N.J.: Prentice Hall, 1984), pp. 6–8.

50. Edward P. Swanson, "Accounting for Changing Prices: Some Midcourse Corrections," *Journal of Accountancy,* April 1984, p. 78.

51. "More Fine Tuning for Inflation Accounting," *Business Week,* June 11, 1979, pp. 93–94.

52. Lee Berton, "Big Companies' Inflation-Adjusted Data Must Still Be Reported, FASB Decides," *Wall Street Journal,* July 19, 1984, p. 8.

53. Richard L. Hudson, "Public Companies May Curb Disclosures To Holders on Executives' Pay, SEC Rules," *Wall Street Journal,* September 23, 1983, p. 4.

54. Stephen Wermiel and Thomas E. Ricks, "Supreme Court Decision Eases Filing Of Suits Over False Merger-Talks Data," *Wall Street Journal,* March 8, 1988, p. 3.

55. Wayne E. Green, "Confusion Over Merger-Disclosure Law," *Wall Street Journal,* June 24, 1988, p. 15.

56. See SEC Releases 5368, April 1973, 5627, October 15, 1975, and 5704, May 6, 1976.

57. See Report of the Task Force on Corporate Social Performance, U.S. Department of Commerce, *Corporate Social Reporting in the United States and Western Europe* (Washington D.C.: U.S. Government Printing Office, 1979).

58. David Vogel, "Trends in Shareholder Activism: 1970–1982," *California Management Review,* Vol. XXV, No. 3 (Spring 1983), p. 84.

59. Bruce Ingersoll, "Annual Meetings Are Much Calmer Affairs Under Changed SEC Shareholder Rules," *Wall Street Journal,* April 24, 1985, p. 35.

60. Investor Responsibility Research Center, *News for Investors,* Vol XIII, No. 6 (June 1986), p. 101.

61. Stanford L. Jacobs, "Corporate Issues Head Proposals By Shareholders," *Wall Street Journal,* March 16, 1988, p. 29.

62. "Shareholder Resolutions Address a Variety of New Issues," *Wall Street Journal,* April 13, 1989, p. A-1.

63. "Shareholder Groups Fire the Opening Salvo on Environmental Issues," *Wall Street Journal,* March 29, 1990, p. A-1.

64. Allanna Sullivan, "Exxon Holder's Environment Proposals Are Cleared for Proxy Statement by SEC," *Wall Street Journal,* March 8, 1990, p. A-3.

65. Allanna Sullivan and Caleb Solomon, "Environmentalists Claim Gains at Exxon Meeting," *Wall Street Journal*, April 26, 1990, p. B-1.

66. "Institutions and Antisocial Management," *Business Week*, January 19, 1974, pp. 66–67.

67. Theodore V. Purcell, "Management and the Ethical Investors," *Harvard Business Review*, Vol. 57, No. 5 (September–October 1979), p. 44.

68. Richard L Hudson, "SEC Tightens Annual Meeting Proposal Rules," *Wall Street Journal*, August 17, 1983, p. 4.

69. "Dissident Shareholders Start Shouting at the SEC," *Business Week*, December 10, 1984, p. 20.

70. Vogel, "Trends in Shareholder Activism," p. 70.

71. David Vogel, *Lobbying the Corporation: Citizen Challenges to Business Authority* (New York: Basic Books, 1978), p. 226.

72. See Murray L. Weidenbaum, *Strengthening the Corporate Board: A Constructive Response to Hostile Takeovers* (St. Louis Mo.: Washington University Center for the Study of American Business, 1985.

73. "Management Should Fill Only One Seat on a Firm's Board, SEC Chairman Urges," *Wall Street Journal*, January 19, 1978, p. 3.

74. Lawrence Ingrassia, "Outsider-Dominated Boards Grow, Spurred by Calls for Independence," *Wall Street Journal*, November 3, 1980, p. 29.

75. Tom Neff, "Let Directors Be Directors," *Wall Street Journal*, December 11, 1989, p. A-14.

76. Amanda Bennett, "Losing Ground? Surveyed Firms Report Fewer Women Directors," *Wall Street Journal*, July 17, 1987, p. 19.

77. Heidrick and Struggles, *The Changing Board—1989 Update*, p. 1. Published by Heidrick & Struggles, Inc., 225 Peachtree St., NE, Atlanta, Ga. 30303.

78. Neff, "Let Directors Be Directors," p. A-14.

79. See George Russell, "All Eyes on Accountants," *Time*, April 21, 1986, p. 61.

80. "Independent Panels of Corporate Boards to Tap New Directors Are Proliferating," *Wall Street Journal*, February 15, 1979, p. 14. See also "Survey Finds Board Nominating Panels Help Determine Management Succession," *Wall Street Journal*, January 28, 1980, p. 10.

81. "Corporate Governance Faulted in Study by SEC Staff," *Wall Street Journal*, September 5, 1980, p. 4.

82. Monci Jo Williams, "Why Executives' Pay Keeps Rising," *Fortune*, April 1, 1985, pp. 66–73. See also "Executives Face Change in Awarding of Pay, Stock Options," *Wall Street Journal*, February 28, 1986, p. 27. See also Amanda Bennett, "Top Dollar: Corporate Chief's Pay Far Outpaces Inflation And the Gains of Staff," *Wall Street Journal*, March 28, 1988, p. 1; and John A. Byrne, "Who Made The Most—And Why," *Business Week*, May 2, 1988, pp. 50–56.

83. David B. Hilder, "Risky Business: Liability Insurance is Difficult to Find Now For Directors, Officers," *Wall Street Journal*, July 10, 1985, p. 1.

84. Heidrick and Struggles, *The Changing Board—1989 Update*, p. 11.

85. "A Landmark Ruling That Puts Board Members in Peril," *Business Week*, March 18, 1985, pp. 56–57. See also Michele Galen, "A Seat On The Board Is Getting Hotter," *Business Week*, July 3, 1989, pp. 72–73.

86. Amanda Bennett, "Hot Seats: Board Members Draw Fire, and Some Think Twice About Serving," *Wall Street Journal*, February 5, 1986, p. 1.

87. Bennett, "Losing Ground?" p. 19.

88. Judith Dobrzynski, "Taking Charge," *Business Week*, July 3, 1989, pp. 66–71.

89. Philip Gold, "Trouble in the Boardroom Exposed," *Insight*, January 22, 1990, pp. 40–41.

90. Ibid.

91. Ralph Nader, Mark Green, and Joel Seligman, *Taming the Giant Corporation* (New York: W.W. Norton & Co., 1976), pp. 240–41.

92. Ralph Nader, "The Case for Federal Chartering," *Corporate Power in America*, Ralph Nader and Mark J. Green, eds. (New York: Grossman Publishers, 1973), p. 79.

93. Nader, *Taming the Giant Corporation*, pp. 44–57.

94. In the summer of 1986, the state of Delaware passed a law to help companies attract and retain qualified outside directors by allowing companies incorporated in the state to seek shareholder approval to limit the personal liability of directors or to exempt them altogether from personal liability under certain circumstances. See Francine Schwadel, "Delaware Law Might Let Firms Avoid Liability Insurance Woes for Directors," *Wall Street Journal*, June 19, 1986, p. 12.

95. "A Step Toward the Federal Corporate Charter," *Business Week*, June 21, 1976, pp. 80, 82.

96. Donald E. Schwartz, "The Case for Federal Chartering of Corporations," Robert L. Heilbroner and Paul London, eds., *Corporate Social Policy: Selections from Business and Society Review* (Reading, Mass.: Addison-Wesley, 1975), pp. 325–31.

97. "New Fire in the Drive to Reform Corporation Law," *Business Week,* November 21, 1977, p. 100.

98. See "The Battle for Corporate Control," *Business Week,* May 18, 1987, pp. 102–109; and "Shareholders Aren't Just Rolling Over Anymore," *Business Week,* April 27, 1987, pp. 32–33.

Suggested Reading

ALKHAFAJI, ABBASS F. *A Stakeholder Approach to Corporate Governance: Managing In A Dynamic Environment.* Westport, Conn.: Quorum Books, 1989.

BACON, JEREMY, AND JAMES K. BROWN. *Corporate Directorship Practices: Role, Selection and Legal Status of the Board.* New York: The Conference Board, 1975.

BARBER, RICHARD J. *The American Corporation.* New York: Dutton, 1970.

BERLE, ADOLF, AND GARDINER C. MEANS, *The Modern Corporation and Private Property.* New York: Macmillan, 1932.

BLUMBERG, PHILIP I. *The Megacorporation in American Society.* Englewood Cliffs, N.J.: Prentice Hall, 1975.

BROWN, COURTNEY C. *Putting the Corporate Board to Work.* New York: Macmillan, 1976.

BURCH, PHILLIP C. *The Managerial Revolution Reassessed.* New York: Lexington Books, 1972.

BURNHAM, JAMES. *The Managerial Revolution.* Bloomington: Indiana University Press, 1941.

The Business Roundtable. *The Role and Composition of the Board of Directors of the Large Publicly Owned Corporation.* New York: The Business Roundtable, 1978.

EISENBERG M. *The Structure of the Corporation.* Boston: Little, Brown, 1976.

GALBRAITH, JOHN KENNETH. *The New Industrial State.* Boston: Houghton Mifflin, 1967.

HERMAN, EDWARD S. *Corporate Control, Corporate Power.* Cambridge: Cambridge University Press, 1981.

KUHNE, ROBERT J. *Co-Determination in Business: Workers' Representatives in the Boardroom.* New York: Praeger, 1980.

LARNER, ROBERT J. *Management Control and the Large Corporation.* New York: Dunellen, 1971.

LORSCH, JAY W. *Pawns or Potentates: The Reality of America's Corporate Boards.* Cambridge, Mass.: Harvard Business School Press, 1990.

LOUDEN, J. KEITH. *The Effective Director in Action.* New York: AMACOM, 1975.

MACE, MYLES L. *Directors: Myth and Reality* (Boston: Harvard University, 1971).

MANNE, HENRY G., ed. *Corporate Governance: Past and Future.* New York: K.C.G. Productions, Inc., 1982.

MINK, PHILLIP D., ESQ., ed. *The American Law Institute and Corporate Governance: An Analysis and Critique.* Washington, D.C.: National Legal Center for the Public Interest, 1987.

NADER, RALPH, AND MARK J. GREEN, eds. *Corporate Power in America.* New York: Grossman Publishers, 1973.

NADER, RALPH, AND JOEL SELIGMAN. *Taming the Giant Corporation.* New York: W.W. Norton & Co., 1976.

STECKMEST, FRANCIS W. *Corporate Performance: The Key to Public Trust.* New York: McGraw-Hill, 1982.

STONE, CHRISTOPHER D. *Where the Law Ends: The Social Control of Corporate Behavior.* New York: Harper & Row, 1975.

VOGEL, DAVID. *Lobbying the Corporation: Citizen Challenges to Business Authority.* New York: Basic Books, 1978.

WEIDENBAUM, MURRAY L. *Strengthening the Corporate Board: A Constructive Response to Hostile Takeovers.* St. Louis, Mo.: Washington University Center for the Study of American Business, 1985.

CHAPTER 5

Wealth and Poverty

The market system offers large rewards, in some cases, to winners of the competitive race, but it can also impose severe penalties on some of the losers. Those losers often fall so far behind that they end up in a seriously deprived condition. They have so few and such low-quality resources at their disposal that the market places a very low value on what they do have to offer. The market system often promotes wide disparities in income and wealth, allowing the "haves" to amass increasing wealth and the "have nots" to fall further into relative poverty.

Often, people end up in this condition through no fault of their own, as poverty is most likely a function of slack labor markets and general economic and social conditions. During the depression, for example, there were simply not enough jobs to go around, even for skilled workers who were willing and able to provide for themselves. Even in prosperous times, there are sometimes not enough jobs for young people and others who have not had a chance to develop skills and gain experience useful to employers. Discrimination plays a role in poverty by preventing some people from getting jobs commensurate with the skills and ability they do have. There are never enough good-paying jobs for people with severe physical and emotional handicaps who could still be productive. The downsizing and restructuring of American industry throws many people out of jobs and necessitates training for new opportunities.

An unregulated market system can produce inhumane results, locking some people into a vicious cycle of poverty and preventing them from ever really entering into the race for the rewards society has to offer. As Arthur Okun states: "Vast disparities in results—living standards, income, wealth—inevitably spawn serious inequalities in opportunity that represent arbitrary handicaps and head starts . . . The children of the poor are handicapped in many ways—their nutrition, their education, their ability to get funds to start businesses and buy homes, and their treatment on many of the hiring lines for both private and public jobs."[1]

Poverty can become a vicious cycle that is perpetuated from one generation to the next. Children born into conditions of poverty have a high probabilty of remaining in poverty because of a lack of good education, poor health, psychological depression, and more, all of which places them at a severe disadvantage to people born into better conditions. Such disadvantaged people do not have much to offer employers and thus the market places a low value on their services.

A commitment to equality of opportunity requires, says Okun, some correction of the inequality of results that an unregulated market system produces. Severe poverty cannot be accepted in a democratic society. Even if the race is fair, condemnation to a life of deprivation is not necessarily a fair penalty for the losers. Such a result is not consistent with the goals and values of a democratic society.[2]

> . . . Poverty cannot be ignored by a society that proclaims democratic values, insisting upon the worth of all its citizens and the equality of their political and social rights. Our commitment to freedom of speech, equality of suffrage, and equality before the law rests on a broader commitment to human values that is violated by the persistence of economic misery in an affluent society. I cannot imagine how a sane society could decide deliberately to guarantee every citizen a fair trial before a judge and jury and at the same time permit some citizens to be condemned to death by the marketplace.[3]

Almost all modern industrial societies have some kind of welfare system designed to alter unequal market outcomes through public policy measures.[4] Such outcomes are unacceptable and are changed by a system of transfer payments that takes money from some groups in society through taxation and gives it to other groups in the form of benefits. Modern industrial societies also have programs designed to help disadvantaged people gain education and training so they can have something valuable to offer employers or can start their own businesses to compete in the marketplace.

The welfare system in the United States took shape in the New Deal era, when the goals of humanitarian aid to people in need and the goals of economic management were highly compatible. The eventual acceptance of Keynesian economic theories dispelled the sense of impotence and resignation that had accompanied economic downturns in the past, and destroyed the underlying fatalism that business cycles must run their course no matter what their toll in human suffering. These theories legitimized federal efforts to improve the functioning of a market system during a recession or depression and helped extend the notion of government responsibility to those who found themselves in desperate economic conditions. Public recognition and support of a federal role in assisting the least fortunate members of society has remained relatively strong since that time even when the economy is growing and most people are prospering.[5]

The New Deal saw the beginning of income transfer programs and collective bargaining on a large scale, which helped to check the tendency of free markets to promote wide disparities in income and wealth. Transfer programs provided cash assistance and in-kind programs for those who were in need, and collective bargaining enabled workers to obtain higher incomes, better working conditions, and greater job security. These interventions in free market outcomes constituted an explicit recognition that an unregulated system did not result in a morally acceptable distribution of income and wealth nor did it provide meaningful opportunities to those at the bottom of the income ladder.[6]

The Nature of Poverty

Poverty can mean many different things depending on who is doing the defining and what policies are being considered. Poverty can mean a shortage of money to buy the essentials that people or families need to support themselves. The official poverty level established by the U.S. government is based on an estimation of the level of income that it would take for various categories of people, such as a family of four, to provide themselves with a minimum level of food, clothing, shelter, and other essentials. These estimates are made for single people as well as for other size families, but the family of four is the most widely cited figure.

Others argue that to view poverty as merely a lack of income is much too unrealistic and simplistic. George L. Wilber, for example, views poverty as a system that has multiple properties capable of measurement. He defines this system as the relative lack of resources and/or the inability to utilize resources.[7] The word "relative" is important, as Wilber also points out that poverty can be defined in either relative or absolute terms. When people's basic needs for food, clothing, shelter, and medical care are not met, these people are in need in an absolute sense. But whether or not these basic needs are taken care of, people may or may not feel "relatively deprived," as this feeling depends on one's position with respect to the relevant reference group in society at any particular time and place.[8]

Defining poverty solely in terms of income or subsistence levels does not seem to capture the entire meaning of the concept. Martin Rein, of the Bryn Mawr College School of Social Work, argues that even "subsistence measures of poverty cannot claim to rest solely on a technical or scientific definition of nutritional adequacy. Values, preferences, and political realities influence the definition of subsistence."[9] What is adequate for one person may not be adequate for another. Thus no absolute measurement of poverty in subsistence terms is possible either.

Others make a distinction between economic poverty, which is based on the income level of the poor, and material poverty, which tells us about their health and welfare. Economic measures commonly used to depict the degree of poverty in the United States provide little insight into the physical and material well-being of poor people. Traditional indicators of deprivation, such as health and nutrition, might give us a less ambiguous and more consistent idea of how the poor are doing. Information about life expectancy, infant mortality, suicides, birth weights, undernutrition, and diet may tell us more about the material condition of those in poverty than conventional statistics about income.[10]

Some scholars have developed the idea that there is something called a culture of poverty, which can help in understanding the dynamics of poverty and also has policy implications. The culture of poverty, as described by Oscar Lewis, for example, "is both an adaption and a reaction of the poor to their marginal position in a class-stratified, highly individuated, capitalistic society. It represents an effort to cope with feelings of hopelessness and despair that develop from the realization of the improbability of achieving sucesss in terms of the values and goals of the larger society.[11]

> People with a culture of poverty produce very little wealth and receive very little in return. They have a low level of literacy and education, do not belong to labor unions, are not members of political parties, generally do not participate in the national welfare agencies, and make very little use of banks, hospitals, department stores, museums, or art galleries. They have a critical attitude toward some of the basic institutions of the dominant classes, hatred of the police, mistrust of government and those in high position, and a cynicism that extends even to the church. These factors give the culture of poverty a high potential for protest and for being used in political movements aimed against the existing social order.[12]

This culture of poverty is thus an adaption to a set of economic and social conditions and tends to perpetuate itself from generation to generation. Children born into the culture of poverty absorb the basic values and attitudes of this subculture and are not psychologically equipped even to take advantage of more favorable conditions or better opportunities that may occur in their lifetime. They tend to remain in the culture of poverty because it has become a way of life for them and not just a condition to be overcome. This concept has important implications for public policy measures designed to eliminate poverty.

Another way to look at poverty is to consider it as a cyclical phenomenon, rather than as a cultural condition. The poor get sick more than other people, live in unhealthy conditions, have inadequate diets, cannot get decent medical care or a good education. Thus they cannot get and hold good-paying jobs to earn a decent income, which means they cannot afford good housing, medical care, and a decent education. Poverty becomes a vicious cycle that tends to perpetuate itself, but the cycle can be broken into somewhere. If poor people could be given a good job, for example, and receive the extra training and attention necessary to keep it, they might be able to climb out of poverty, breaking out of the cycle. This view of poverty has other policy implications.

> The argument between those who think that poverty can best be eliminated by providing jobs and other resources and those who feel that cultural obstacles and psychological deficiencies must be overcome as well is ultimately an argument about social change, about the psychological readiness of people to respond to change, and about the role of culture in change. The advocates of resources are not concerned explicitly with culture, but they do make a cultural assumption: Whatever the culture of the poor, it will not interfere in people's ability to take advantage of better opportunities for obtaining economic resources. They take a situational view of social change and of personality: that people respond to the situations—and opportunities—available to them and change their behavior accordingly. Those who call attention to cultural (and psychological) obstacles, however, are taking a cultural view of social change, which suggests that people react to change in terms of prior values and behavior patterns and adopt only those changes that are congruent with their culture.[13]

If poverty has aspects of a culture, dealing with it and helping people to climb out of poverty is a much more serious problem than if it is only a cyclical phenomenon. Attempting to change people's values and ingrained habits and behavior patterns is a much more difficult than is simply developing programs to improve health, education, or job opportunities. And yet such programs are likely to fail if they are implemented in a cultural situation where the value assumptions on which they are based do not hold true. If people in poverty do not share the same values regarding work and wealth as people in the larger society, then programs designed to help them climb into the mainstream of society may be counterproductive.

The Extent of Poverty

The official figures with regard to poverty in the United States over the past several years are rather depressing. The figures for 1982 showed 34.4 million or 15 percent of the population below the government's official poverty line, the highest poverty rate since 1965, and the fourth consecutive annual increase. The 1982 figures reflected the impact of the recession and cutbacks in entitlement programs made by the Reagan administration.[14] The Census Bureau's figures for 1983 showed that poverty had again increased to 15.2 percent from 15 percent the year before, the highest level since the 17.3 percent recorded in 1965. The number of poor people increased by 900,000 to 35.3

million. While the bureau didn't consider this increase statistically significant, it was attributed to the increase in the number of people living alone and the lingering effects of the deep and lengthy 1981–82 recession.[15]

However, in 1984, the poverty rate actually dropped, according to the official figures, to 14.4 percent, a decline of 1.8 million people to a total of 33.7 million. This was the first statistically significant decline since 1976; it was attributed by the administration to the president's economic policies. Median family income rose to an inflation-adjusted $26,430, a jump of 3.3 percent from the year before. This was the fastest rate of gain since 1972 and was the second consecutive increase. Poverty among the elderly fell to its lowest level since the Census Bureau began tracking this indicator. The improvement was broad-based, with even the African American poor showing significant gains.[16]

Further gains were made in 1985 as the poverty rate declined to 14 percent. In 1985, 33.1 million Americans lived below the poverty threshold, but this decrease of 600,000 from the year before was statistically insignificant. Median family income rose only 1.3 percent to $27,735 and was the smallest gain in 3 consecutive years of increases.[17] In 1986, the poverty rate declined further to 13.6 percent, the third year in a row the rate had declined, and median family income increased significantly faster than inflation.[18] The poverty rate continued to decline, reaching 13.4 percent in 1987 and 13.1 percent in 1988, but the Census Bureau said the 1988 drop was not statistically significant (Figure 5.1). The poverty threshold for 1988 was $12,092 for a family of four people.[19]

As a result of the decline in poverty, the number of people living below the poverty line declined by about 500,000 for the year. Per capita income hit a record in 1988, rising 1.7 percent after adjustment for inflation. But the median income of American families fell 0.2 percent, the first time it failed to rise in 6 years. Experts said the divergence in the two measures reflected changes in family size and structure, including the rising number of female-headed families and a sharp increase in income reported by Americans who were not living in families. Income levels rose sharply in the Northeast and Midwest and fell slightly in the South and parts of the West.[20]

The poverty rate for children under 18 years old dropped to 19.7 percent in 1988 from 20.5 percent the year before but remained far higher than it was a decade earlier. These figures reflected a continuing problem with child poverty that boded ill for the future of American society. The increases of poverty in this category were said to be the result of a drop in the real earnings of many working Americans over the past several years, the rise in the incidence of out-of-wedlock births and of female-headed households, and cutbacks in the major welfare programs aimed at the young.[21] An index of the social health of children and youth, which included infant mortality, child abuse, children living in poverty, teenage suicide, teenage drug abuse, and high school dropouts, showed a decline to 37 in 1987 from a high of 72 in 1973, providing further evidence of a problem with children's health in this country.[22]

The problem of families headed by females and the child poverty that results is a social welfare challenge likely to plague society for many years to come. This so-called feminization of poverty is a deep, long-term poverty problem. Mothers without husbands and the children of these women are the only poverty category whose total number is currently higher than when poverty first began to be officially measured in 1959.[23] Teenage pregnancies are one of the reasons for this increase in child poverty, as many of these children are raised in fatherless homes with little economic opportunity. In 1987, the United States had the highest rate of teenage pregnancy in the developed world. One out of six newborn children was the child of a teenager, and fewer than half of these teenage mothers had graduated from high school.[24]

Figure 5.1 Poverty Rate, 1968–1988

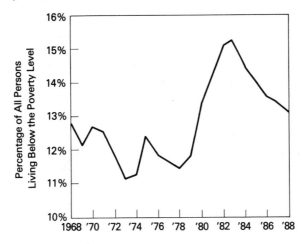

Source: U.S. Department of Commerce, *Statistical Abstract of the United States, 1989,* 109th ed. (Washington, D.C.: U.S. Government Printing Office, 1988), p. 452.

This problem is especially prevalent in the African American community. As of 1987, some 60 percent of African American children were born out of wedlock, and African American families were three and one-half times as likely as white families to be headed by a female. More than three-fourths of poor African American families were headed by women. This disparity explains much of their lag in economic and social status, as female-headed African American families suffer from crime and drug abuse to a larger extent than other groups. Most single mothers with children under age six do r●t work, and given the high costs of day care for very young children, relatively few could ever work effectively. Thus they have no choice but to turn to welfare for support.[25]

This increase in child poverty has resulted in a disparity between children and elderly people, who were previously a major poverty problem. As child poverty has increased, poverty among the elderly has fallen sharply, since the elderly were able to get the attention of lawmakers and win out over children and their advocates in the battle for society's resources. Because of cost-of-living increases, the buying power of the average Social Security check has jumped about 25% since 1970, while during the same period, the buying power of Aid to Families with Dependent Children (AFDC) checks has dropped by a third. The poverty rate for the elderly is lower than for the rest of the nation as a whole and much lower if in-kind benefits such as food stamps and medical care are considered.[26]

The Urban League in its 1990 report on the "State of Black America" report stated that in a few respects the state of African Americans is improving, but that in most areas the gains are only marginal. For the most part the "state of black America remains critical.[27] The Census Bureau figures for 1988 showed that 31.6 percent of African Americans lived in poverty compared with 10.1 percent for whites and 26.8 percent for Hispanics. In constant dollars, the median income for African American married families was $27,722 in 1978 and fell to $27,182 in 1987, whereas parallel figures for white married families showed a slight increase. In 1978, 8.4 percent of African American families had incomes under $5,000 per year, but by 1987, that figure had grown to 13.5 percent. The average income of the poorest fifth of African American families plunged 23.6 percent during this same time period.[28] In 1989, the average African American-family income was only 57 percent that of whites, and the African American unemployment rate was stuck at about double that of whites. Median African American household wealth was one-eleventh that of whites.[29]

A Census Bureau study released in 1986 found that the typical white American household in 1984 had a net worth of almost $40,000, about 12 times greater than the figure for the typical African American household. Almost one-third of all African American families reported they owned no assets at all or had a negative net worth; more than half (54 percent) had assets of less than $5,000. In comparison, 11 percent of white families had no assets or a negative net worth, and only 26 percent owned less than $5,000 in assets. This disparity was due partly to the large number of African American households headed by women and partly to low African American income over generations, which has retarded the accumulation of wealth.[30]

These economic conditions contribute to instability among African American families and mean that African American children are more likely than whites to have no father at home, to be born out of wedlock, to drop out of school, and to be victimized by the divorce of their parents. One out of 12 African American children lives with neither parent. The crumbling African American family is seen as a severe problem that may produce a lost generation of African American youths unequipped to enter the labor force or to form their own families. Thousands of African American youths may be drifting into a netherworld of unemployment, welfare, and crime from which they will not escape. African American leaders have declared this instability a major concern that threatens the survival of African American culture.[31]

More and more evidence indicated that this African American underclass was growing and represented a serious problem not only for African Americans, but for the entire society. These people were isolated from the nation's economic and social mainstream, and constituted a culture of poverty that was difficult to fathom. The underclass was composed of unemployed males and welfare mothers concentrated in crime-ridden, desperately poor, inner-city neighborhoods and was estimated to be at least 1.5 million and growing. This problem may have been exacerbated by the civil rights legislation of the 1960s, as middle-class African Americans who could take advantage of new job and housing opportunities fled the ghettos, leaving behind the truly disadvantaged, who no longer had role models to tell them about work opportunities.[32]

In the mid-1980s, a new aspect of poverty appeared in the plight of the homeless, those in our society with no fixed address who wandered the streets and found shelter in bus stations, cardboard boxes, or whatever else was available. The immediate cause of the problem was a shortage of affordable housing. But diverse circumstances helped to cause the problem. Some of the homeless were mentally ill, others were poor families who had no money to pay rent, and still others were single men without work or family. Estimates of the homeless population ranged from 250,000 to more than 3 million. Any estimate was suspect as homelessness may be temporary, episodic, or long-term.[33]

Federal support for housing was slashed 77 percent, from $32.2 billion in 1981 to $7.5 billion in 1988. The Department of Housing and Urban Development authorized the construction of only 88,136 subsidized dwellings in 1987, compared with more than 224,000 in 1981. Some 2.5 million units of low-income housing disappeared between 1980 and 1988 through a combination of market forces and government indifference. Tenements that provided housing for the disadvantaged were torn down or renovated to make way for high-priced apartments or high-rise office buildings. During the past decade, half of the single-room occupancy hotels in the nation were lost. These often provided the housing of last resort for the poor. An additional 200,000 units of low-income housing are expected to disappear over the next 5 years as loans expire from the tax-break programs of the 1970s and 1980s. The result could be hundreds of thousands more people in shelters.[34] Clearly this is an aspect of poverty that will continue to be a serious national problem.

Other Aspects of Poverty

The Census Bureau figures are often criticized as being inaccurate in measuring the real extent of poverty in the United States. The official poverty statistics, it is said, overstate the problem because of the way poverty is defined and measured. The official definition of poverty begins with the concept of a nutritionally adequate diet as estimated by the Department of Agriculture. This concept is then extended by a food-total-expenditure multiplier to cover a minimum adequate amount of other necessities. Families with money income that is insufficient to purchase this minimum amount of food and other necessities are officially considered low-income families and are included as such in the *Current Population Surveys* (CPS) published by the Bureau of the Census.

The problem is that the measuring rod used in the *Current Population Survey* is only money income—no attempt is made to measure the impact of such in-kind programs as food stamps and Medicaid, which were among the fastest-growing part of transfer payments during the 1970s and now constitute about 60 percent of the transfer-payment budget. When these in-kind programs were small, this omission was of minor consequence. But in recent years, their exclusion results in a gross distortion of the poverty problem that has not been corrected despite many attempts to raise the issue and draw attention to the problem.[35]

One of the first studies that attempted to deal with this distortion was conducted by Morton S. Paglin, who computed these in-kind transfers at market value for three program areas: housing, food and nutrition, and medical services. When these estimates are factored into the final estimates of overall poverty, some dramatic differences show up when compared with the official poverty statistics. Figure 5.2 shows that when in-kind transfers are taken into account, poverty continued to decline throughout the entire 1959–75 period instead of leveling off from 1968 to 1975 as the official CPS figures suggest. The 1968–75 period was one in which the market value of in-kind transfers in the housing, food and nutrition, and medical areas went from $3.5 billion to $14.1 billion, making quite a difference in the final outcome. As shown in Figure 5.2, the census and final revised figures were much closer together in 1959 than in 1975, again reflecting the impact of in-kind programs. The census cash-income measure of poverty, Paglin concludes, has departed further and further from reality.[36]

If in-kind subsidies are included, a *Fortune* article stated that U.S. poverty drops to about half the official level. This estimate is based on valuing the subsidies conservatively at their calculated worth to recipients. If these subsidies are valued at their full cost to the government, the article states that it is possible to argue that poverty virtually disappeared in the United States. Based on this procedure, G. William Hoagland, a congressional budget analyst, concluded that poverty fell to only 4.1 percent of the population in 1980. These kind of estimates led some to conclude that the war on poverty had been won.[37]

Another report released by the Census Bureau itself in 1986 concluded that the

Figure 5.2 Persons in Poverty, 1959–1975

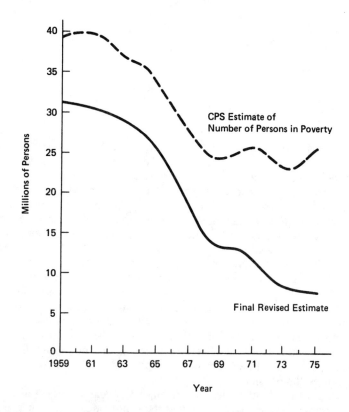

(Official and final revised estimates after all in-kind transfers have been taken into account.)

Source: Morton Paglin, "Poverty in the United States: A Reevaluation," *Policy Review,* No. 8 (Spring 1979), p. 23. Reprinted with permission.

number of Americans living in poverty may be as much as 11.5 million lower than previous official figures indicated. Computing the value of noncash federal assistance nine different ways, the bureau estimated that between 21.5 million and 30.4 million Americans were poor in 1985, reflecting a poverty rate of between 9.1 and 12.8 percent of the population. These noncash benefits were valued at $56.2 billion for 1985 compared with $30.2 billion for cash assistance. Fifteen years ago, these two types of benefits were nearly equal. Inclusion of this noncash assistance produced a lower count of people in poverty than the official figures for every year since 1979, reflecting the importance of this component.[38]

In 1984, a study was released by the Survey Research Center of the University of Michigan that introduced yet another dimension into the debate about the extent of poverty in the United States. Studies of poverty do not say anything about income dynamics and assume that the poor are a group of people who are always at the bottom of the income ladder and are incapable of changing their relative status in society. The evidence contradicts this assumption, however, and shows that the society is characterized by a great deal of income mobility. Income dynamics refers to the processes by which individuals and families change their economic fortunes and may tell us something quite different from what their economic fortunes are at any one point in time.[39]

By looking into the dynamics of poverty, the persistently poor represent a much smaller population than had previously been believed. More than half the people in poverty in any one year remain in this status for only one or two years. While one in every four Americans experienced poverty in the 1969–78 decade, most did not remain in this status very long. The persistently poor who are locked into their status make up no more than 1–3 percent of the total population of the nation (Figure 5.3). These are most likely to be the elderly, African American, rural, and southern, and come from families headed by women.

Thus more than half the poor in any given year represent a "turnover population" of the temporarily poor. Welfare programs have not created a poverty caste but provide short-term help to those who face temporary misfortune and serve as a safety net to those few who are burdened with severe economic handicaps. Furthermore, there is evidence that income mobility is intergenerational in the United States, as less than half of young adults with parents in the lowest income group remained there themselves. These findings offer a real challenge to social scientists and policymakers alike in understanding the nature of poverty and in developing policies to deal with the problem.

Workfare: Providing Economic Opportunities

One approach to the problem of poverty is to try to increase the range of economic opportunities available to poor people so they can help themselves out of poverty and work their way into the mainstream of society. Such programs are based on the assumption that poverty is a condition to be overcome and not a cultural phenomenon, and that

Figure 5.3 Incidence of Short- and Long-Run Poverty, Using Official Census Bureau Definition of Poverty, 1969–1978

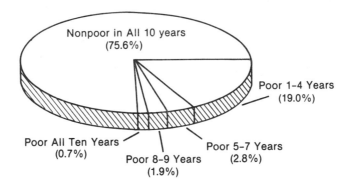

Source: S. Anna Kondratas, "Poverty and Equity: Problems of Definition," *The Journal/The Institute for Socioeconomic Studies,* Vol. 9, No. 4 (Winter 1985), p. 44. Adapted from Greg J. Duncan et al., *Years of Poverty, Years of Plenty* (Ann Arbor: Institute for Social Research, University of Michigan, 1984), pp. 41–42. Reprinted with permission.

poor people need assistance to break out of the cycle. This assistance can take the form of helping disadvantaged people to become more employable in the marketplace, providing help for starting small businesses by providing economic opportunities (particularly to minority entrepreneurs), and building plants in disadvantaged areas to provide income and jobs for the community.

The immediate cause of poverty for many families is that the adult members of the family do not have full-time work. According to statistics from the Census Bureau, only 17 percent of the heads of poor families worked full time in 1984, and 51 percent did not work at all, even though only 10 percent of them were elderly. Work effort among the poor has fallen since 1959, when 32 percent of poor family heads worked full time and only 31 percent did not work at all, even though 22 percent were elderly. Thus the connection between poverty and nonwork seems to be strong, as nonwork promotes poverty by sharply reducing income.[40]

EMPLOYMENT OF THE DISADVANTAGED

Disadvantaged people are shut out of many employment opportunities. Public policy measures aimed at eliminating discrimination in employment are not necessarily going to help them. Many disadvantaged people are white, so that racial discrimination is not necessarily a factor. They simply do not have much to offer employers by way of skills or experience and thus find it difficult to obtain decent employment to provide for themselves or their families. This lack of skills and experience for some may indeed be due to past discrimination, but the reason they cannot get jobs is because the market places a very low value on what they have to offer, not because they are necessarily discriminated against in the selection process.

People with these characteristics were once referred to as *hard-core unemployed,* a term with rather negative connotations. This term has subsequently been changed simply to disadvantaged. Disadvantaged people are those who, perhaps through no fault of their own, have never learned any skills that are marketable, may have poor health, undoubtedly have a poor education, or may never have learned appropriate work habits. Thus they simply are not qualified for most employment opportunities.

As the workplace continues to change, this problem will become more severe. Jobs are expected to continue to decline in manufacturing, mining, and other industries where unskilled men traditionally found entry-level employment as laborers. Most of the job growth in the future will be in fields like information processing and services and will require not only the ability to read and write but considerably more skills and training. According to a Hudson Institute study, by the year 2000 people with less than a high school education will be able to fill only 14 percent of all jobs, compared to 18 percent currently.[41] In an economy that will require an increasingly sophisticated work force, the productive role of the unskilled and illiterate may become nearly irrelevant.

What is needed to bring the disadvantaged into the marketplace is some effort to help them obtain the skills and experience necessary to get and hold employment. The emphasis of public policy must be placed on programs to equip them with the skills, abilities, and habits that are fundamentally necessary to compete for a job in the marketplace. As the nature of jobs changes, these programs must also change to provide skills and training that are relevant for the new kinds of work that are developing. There are both public and private sector programs directed toward this purpose.

Public Sector Programs. There are different kinds of public sector programs designed to increase the productivity of people, including training programs that attempt to equip people with skills so they can enter the market with something to offer employers and public works programs that provide people with actual work experience and enable them to earn an income. An example of a public policy program that was both a training and a public works program is the Comprehensive Employment and Training Act (CETA). This act became law in 1973, replacing the federally controlled Manpower Development Training Act with a program that allowed distribution of federal funds by local officials. This shift of control to prime sponsors at the county and municipal levels was based on the theory that local officials knew more about local conditions than federal bureaucrats.

CETA was originally passed to provide new skills for the nation's disadvantaged people. This population was referred to as the ''structurally'' unemployed—those people who are left out of the competitive labor market for reasons of race, poor education, lack of opportunity, or other social and economic reasons. But in the late 1970s an increasing share went to hire the unemployed in public service jobs. These jobs were only temporary. Their purpose was to tide some people over rough spots in the economy, while people without skills were able to get some experience that would help them to get permanent jobs after their CETA stint. The public service employment part of CETA grew from $440 million in 1974 to about $6 billion in 1979, leaving approximately $4 billion for various job-training programs.[42]

The CETA program, however, had serious problems. The program made no noticeable dent in the number of disadvantaged people unemployed, and billions of dollars were wasted on ill-defined and hastily executed relief programs. In addition, the slackness of its management was an invitation to widespread abuse and fraud. Thus CETA's image was one of an abuse-ridden, make-work employment agency rather than a training agency to equip people for meaningful jobs. Many members of Congress and the Reagan administration came to believe it was time to scrap the program entirely.

In 1981, the federal jobs portion of CETA was dismantled and about 306,000 public service jobs subsidized through CETA vanished. Former CETA participants and cities that used them had to adjust to a world without the jobs program. The federal government tried to find other jobs for former CETA workers without much success. Most of the 38 percent who did find other work stayed on public payrolls, only to be faced with layoffs when states and cities had to eliminate jobs during the recession.[43]

The Reagan administration tried to return CETA to its original role of improving the employability of the structurally unemployed. The successor to CETA was a $1.8 billion job training program called the Job Training Partnership Act (JTPA). Under this program, private industry councils were to be created in cities of 200,000 or more and in communities designated by the government. These councils would be similar to CETA sponsors, but most of the membership and its chairman would have to be business leaders. The council, along with local governments, decides what kind of jobs were locally available and then creates a training program to match the available jobs. The JPTA was designed to ensure that public funds would be spent effectively. Seventy percent of all funds must be used for training programs that lead to private sector employment.[44]

The goal of the program is to prepare groups of adults and youth for employment through training or placement. Preparation for a job is undertaken by local government officials working with the private sector. Four categories of the unemployed are targeted by the program. These include disadvantaged adults, disadvantaged youth in search of summer jobs, dislocated workers, and a miscellaneous category consisting of Native Americans, migrant and seasonal farm workers, and veterans.[45]

Federal funding of the JPTA is about $3.5 billion annually, with most of the money distributed to more than 600 local programs or service delivery areas around the country. These programs include a training program for the poor, a summer jobs-for-youth program, and a special program for workers who have lost their jobs because an industry is depressed or in decline. Officials say that about 800,000 people a year received training under this program, and about 60 percent of them get placed. This placement rate is much higher than CETA achieved.[46]

But critics say that the program emphasizes low-cost, short-term results at the expense of long-term solutions. Only about one in every 20 workers who qualify for the program can be helped. Thus the program is said to focus on those who could probably find jobs on their own and turns its back on those who need help the most.[47] Others say that the program is a boondoggle for the private sector, with the money spent on questionable activities. At least the program is not as bad as CETA, they say, because it wastes less money.[48]

Private Sector Programs. The National Alliance of Business (NAB) was founded in 1968 in response to President Johnson's labor message to Congress. In this message he announced a joint business-government effort to expand employment and training of what were then called the hard-core unemployed. The NAB, under the initial leadership of Henry Ford II, formed the Job Opportunities in the Business Sector (JOBS) program to carry out this objective. The rationale for the program was to bring the disadvantaged into the mainstream of the economy. There was a claim that the program also had a payoff for the free enterprise system by proving that business and private citizens could help solve an urgent social problem that had not been able to be solved by government alone.

In 1977, the White House and Labor Department held discussions with leaders of NAB and other business organizations. There was a concern that the primary thrust of government employment programs at that time involved fully subsidized public jobs with a very small fraction of government money supporting job training and hiring in the private sector. The decision was made to try and bring the government's work force employment apparatus into closer collaboration with the private sector, including the universe of small businesses that were largely overlooked by past programs.[49]

Thus was born Title VII, an amendment to the 1973 Comprehensive Employment and Training Act. Enacted in October 1978, Title VII authorized $400 million for what was called a Private Sector Initiative Program (PSIP). This program called for the establishment of business-led organizational units called Private Industry Councils that would share with CETA prime sponsors—the local government units that operate CETA programs—the responsibility and authority for administering Title VII funds.

The NAB was given leadership responsibility for organizing the private sector response and began developing the professional staff expertise to fulfill this new assignment. It began working with the local prime sponsors to assist in the organization of the Private Industry Councils (PICs), 300 of which were expected to have been organized by October 1979. Late in 1978, the NAB negotiated a $13 million contract with the Labor Department, $2.9 million of which was earmarked for PISP. These funds were to make it possible for the NAB to provide leadership for the program, technical assistance to business and prime sponsors, and serve as an information clearinghouse for processing, analyzing, and disseminating information on the results of local programs.

These PICs became the focal point of the government's alternative to CETA in 1982, and billions of dollars from programs funded under CETA were diverted to about

460 PICs to see if business input into training programs would improve the ability of disadvantaged workers to find jobs of a permanent nature.[50] With the passage of the Job Training Partnership Act, the NAB channeled its resources to supporting and strengthening the PIC network, and to developing mechanisms for expanding corporate involvement in this new form of public/private partnership. The NAB offers expertise, services, and products to businesses, private industry councils, and state and local governments to help them resolve local employment problems.[51]

In addition to these efforts to hire and train the disadvantaged, the NAB since its inception has also developed programs for unemployed youth. The youth programs seek to provide students with the motivation, guidance, and on-the-job work experience that will enable them to pursue productive careers. The Alliance aids in the development of partnerships among business, education, job training, and community-based organizations to create "compacts" to reduce dropout rates among youth, improve educational achievement among high school graduates, and boost youth employment. These compacts attempt to link educational improvement with increased job opportunities for youth who attain certain educational goals.[52]

Besides this kind of a comprehensive program supported by the private sector, many business organizations themselves are instituting training programs for the disadvantaged. The labor market is changing as the baby-boom generation passes into middle age, and by the year 2000, 20-year-old entrants to the work force will fall by a total of 2 million, or 8 percent, from 1985. About 80 percent of these entrants will be women, minorities, or immigrants, groups that in general are the least educated. Literacy is a particular problem, as many 21- to 25-year-olds cannot locate specific information in a news article or decipher a bus schedule. Thus business organizations are developing training programs to equip these people with basic skills that they will need to be successful in the workplace.[53]

MINORITY BUSINESS ENTERPRISE

Another approach to creating equality of economic opportunity is through the development of minority businesses. This approach involves giving minorities in this country special assistance in establishing businesses, obtaining capital, finding markets for their products, and building a managerial class. From this effort, the minority community should obtain a substantial measure of social and economic benefit. The goal of this approach is not to eliminate discrimination from the employment opportunities in the institutions of society run by the white majority but to promote the development of more economic institutions owned and operated by minorities themselves. Disadvantaged areas of cities are much like developing nations and need similar assistance to begin the process of social and economic development. If this effort could be successful and minority businesses established on a wide enough scale throughout minority communities, equality of opportunity might become more a reality and the effects of past discrimination overcome through the economic and social growth they would generate.

The need for this approach was recognized in the late 1960s, when statistics showed that there were few minority manufacturing firms in the country. The major reasons for this lack were the substantial amounts of capital needed to start such businesses and the lack of markets where the products produced by minority firms could be sold. In 1969, for example, minorities accounted for 17 percent of the total U.S. population, but they owned only 4.3 percent of the businesses, and these firms accounted for only 0.1 percent of business receipts. Well over 80 percent of these minority firms were in the services or retailing industries and thus were very small in comparison with most companies. Discrimination was, of course, a factor in these dismal figures. Minorities found it difficult to obtain financing from banks and other institutions, people were reluctant to buy products from minority firms because of concerns about quality and service, and aspiring minority businesspeople often found it difficult to get an education that would prepare them for an entrepreneurial position.

A new business needs capital, a market for its products, and managerial talent. The government became a supplier of capital for this effort at promoting minority business enterprises. Executive Order 11625, issued in October 1971, formed the Office of Minority Business Enterprise (OMBE), whose purpose was to initiate programs in both the public and private sectors geared toward increasing minority-owned and -financed businesses. In the 1970s OMBE spent $318 million funding over 200 "business assistance organizations" to counsel minority businesspeople, help them obtain financial assistance, and provide them with a variety of technical services.[54]

The Small Business Administration (SBA) also began a program called MESBIC (Minority Enterprise Small Business Investment Corporation), which provided direct and guaranteed loans to minority entrepreneurs. The MESBIC program was an attempt to apply the Small Business Investment Corporation concept to minority-owned businesses. The program invites private investors to establish a corporation that offers equity financing to entrepreneurs. These private investments are then matched by federal funds, but the programs are administered locally. In 1986, MESBICs invested in 1,658 companies, a dramatic increase over the 431 at the beginning of the decade.[55]

In 1969, the Minority Business Development Agency (MBDA) was established as a bureau in the U.S. Department of Commerce. The agency awards grants and establishes cooperative agreements with state and local government agencies, profit and nonprofit development organizations, and trade associations to offer management, marketing, financial, and technical assistance to minority enterprises. MBDA programs assist minority-owned businesses with acquisitions, mergers, capital development, technical commercialization, management development, and international trade.[56]

The larger business community itself has been active in providing a market for minority businesses. Many corporations voluntarily have instituted what is called a minority purchasing program to increase their purchases from minority enterprises. An organization originally called the National Minority Purchasing Council (NMPC) was formed by business to coordinate and promote these efforts throughout the business community. About half of the *Fortune* 500 companies established minority purchasing programs to contribute to this effort.[57]

The government has also provided markets for minority businesses. Winners of federal contracts of more than $500,000 have been required to do their best to find minority subcontractors. Efforts to locate them had to be recorded on forms filed with the federal government. Changes in this procedure (Public Law 95-507) now require contractors to work out a plan for subcontracting to minority businesses before the contract is awarded rather than simply show they did their best to find them. These new regulations require contractors to spell out goals for the amount of business they expect to place with minority-owned small businesses. This procedure is very similar to the affirmative action requirement for federal contractors with respect to equal employment opportunities.[58]

Under the SBA's 8(a) set-aside program, government agencies such as the Department of Defense or Transportation can pluck contracts from their competitive procurement channels and allocate them to the SBA, which then becomes the prime contractor and gives the work to minority firms on its roster. In fiscal 1978, 3,406 contracts were awarded under this program, totaling $767 million. This was an increase from eight contracts totaling $10.5 million awarded in 1968.[59] However, in the early 1980s, the Reagan administration told African-American businesses to shoulder more responsibility for their own future and tightened controls on the procurement program. Consequently, the percentage of federal contracts awarded to minority firms began to drop substantially.[60] But in 1986, the value of federal contracts awarded to minority-owned firms rose to $8.65 billion, which was a significant increase over the 1980 figure of $3.1 billion.[61]

Critics of the set-aside program argued that set-asides added to federal procurement costs through reduced competition and rewarded firms that have not necessarily suffered from discrimination. Furthermore, they encouraged the creation of dummy companies that are owned by minorities and women in name only. Thus the set-aside programs were said to be ineffective and rife with corruption, as the case at the end of the chapter illustrates. They also noted that minority firms have difficulty weaning themselves from the set-aside programs and competing for government contracts in the traditional manner. A study conducted by the Senate Committee on Small Business found that nearly 30 percent of minority firms had gone out of business when they were taken off the program, and another 22 percent said they were facing financial troubles. These figures suggested that fewer than half the firms weathered the transition to a competitive environment. Despite these criticisms, however, there seems to be little political pressure to kill the program and little heart to examine its operation too closely.[62]

Efforts were made to deal with some of these problems when a new law was passed in 1988 that tightened several provisions of the program. The law required companies in the program to compete among themselves for federal contracts in manufacturing worth at least $5 million and nonmanufacturing contracts worth at least $3 million. The SBA could also decide to open other contracts to competition. In addition, firms who have been in the program for 5 years will have to get 25 percent of their revenues from nonprogram sources. This share will rise to 75 percent by the ninth year. Another aspect of the law stated that each government agency must aim to spend 5 percent of its contracting dollars with disadvantaged companies. This provision extended a program adopted by the Pentagon in 1987 to award 5 percent of all contracts worth as much as $7 billion a year to minority-owned small businesses.[63]

Another form of set-asides appeared when Congress set a precedent in 1977 by writing into a $4 billion Commerce Department public works appropriation bill a clause that 10 percent of this total be reserved for minority contractors and subcontractors. This action did not make the construction industry very happy, and 27 suits were filed charging that this 10 percent set-aside was unconstitutional. The issue was one of reverse discrimination, that such a quota for minority business constitutes discrimination against nonminority enterprise. The Supreme Court agreed to hear one of these cases and thus deal with this aspect of preferential treatment. In its decision, the court said that Congress, under the Constitution, had special power to make up for the effects of past discrimination and can legitimately require innocent whites to "share the burden" as long as that burden is not unreasonable. This decision, however, did not address the rights of local governments.

In the wake of this decision, cities and counties began to set aside construction contracts for African American-owned businesses. Dade County in Florida, for example, established a program after the Liberty City race riots in 1980 that awarded a portion of county projects to African American-owned businesses until they reached a level comparable to the African American portion of the local population. Similar programs were set up in New York City, Hartford, Connecticut, and Richmond, California. In

1984, however, the Justice Department attacked the Dade County program, claiming that local governments lack the authority to reserve contracts for any racial group as that action would put other groups at a disadvantage. Only the federal government may do this, the department stated, when duly authorized by Congress and when that power is used only to benefit the actual victims of discrimination. Preferential treatment by local governments can be constitutional if limited to granting enough contracts to proven victims of discrimination to provide them with what they would have attained in the absence of discrimination.[64]

The Supreme Court dealt this form of set-aside a severe blow in early 1989, when it ruled in a case involving the city of Richmond, Virginia, which had awarded a substantial percentage of its contracts to minority-owned businesses. The decision sharply limited the ways state and local governments can favor minority companies by requiring local officials to document instances of past discrimination and determine whether some more neutral program not based on sex or race would be more effective in remedying the problem of bias. This ruling affected about 236 state and local jurisdictions, some of whom halted all or part of their set-aside programs, while others had suits pending against such programs.[65]

In 1988, the top 100 African American-owned businesses had gross revenues of $6.75 billion, which was an increase of 10.2 percent from the previous year. While traditional African American enterprises—for example, construction and food and beverage retailing companies—dominated the top 100 firms, there was some indication that more minority entrepreneurs are moving into fields such as electronics, health care, advertising, real-estate development, insurance, and computer software. Stronger educational credentials, greater access to financing, government assistance, and a growing support network among minority-owned businesses have helped to bring about this change.[66]

But the effort to promote economic opportunity in this manner is difficult. Exhibit 5.1 shows that even the top ten African American-owned firms are small in comparison to other corporations in the United States. Large pools of equity funds must be made available under realistic conditions, but many banks are reluctant to loan money to African Americans because they do not have a track record of success. There are not enough minority clients to make some minority businesses profitable, and white people are reluctant to patronize minority businesses. Large numbers of white-run organizations will have to do business with minority companies if those companies are ever to develop a market for their products. The business and technical skills of minorities must be developed if they are to compete successfully in the marketplace and move out from under the shelter of government and business.

BUILDING PLANTS IN DISADVANTAGED AREAS

Another strategy to promote equality of economic opportunity is for corporations to build plants in economically depressed inner-city areas. The idea behind these plants is the same as the idea behind minority business enterprises, that they will provide an impetus for economic development of the immediate community. Priority for employment should be given to community residents so that jobs will be available to them. The plants should also provide a mixture of job levels to create opportunities for advancement, even into management levels. The availability of entry-level positions and training

EXHIBIT 5.1

The Top 10 African American Industrial/Service Companies

Rank	Company	Location	Chief Executive	Year Started	Staff	Type of Business	1987 Sales*
1	TLC Beatrice International Holdings, Inc.†	New York, New York	Reginald F. Lewis	1983	20,365	Processing & distribution of food products	1,800.000
2	Johnson Publishing Company, Inc.	Chicago, Illinois	John H. Johnson	1942	1,903	Publishing, broadcasting, cosmetics & hair-care products	201.563
3	Philadelphia Coca-Cola Bottling Co., Inc.	Philadelphia, Pennsylvania	J. Bruce Llewellyn	1985	875	Soft-drink bottling	166.000
4	H.J. Russell & Company	Atlanta, Georgia	Herman J. Russell	1958	610	Construction & communications	141.902
5	Motown Industries	Los Angeles, California	Berry Gordy	1958	257	Entertainment	100.000
6	Soft Sheen Products, Inc.	Chicago, Illinois	Edward G. Gardner	1964	756	Hair-care products manufacturer	81.260
7	Trans Jones, Inc./ Jones Transfer Company	Monroe, Michigan	Gary L. White	1986	1,200	Transportation services	79.300
8	Systems Management American Corp.	Norfolk, Virginia	Herman E. Valentine	1970	635	Computer systems integration	62.675
9	The Maxima Corporation	Rockville, Maryland	Joshua I. Smith	1978	1,300	Systems engineering & Integration	56.086
10	M&M Products Company, Inc.	Atlanta, Georgia	Cornell McBride	1973	165	Hair-care products manufacturer & distributor	47.250

* In millions of dollars, to nearest thousand.

† Formerly TLC Group, Inc.

Source: "The Top 100 Industrial/Service Companies," *Black Enterprise*, June 1988, p. 121. © June 1988 by The Earl G. Graves Publishing Co., Inc., 130 Fifth Ave., New York, NY 10011. All rights reserved.

programs is an important ingredient for the success of these efforts. These facilities are built to provide jobs for inexperienced people and give them the opportunity to begin careers in the mainstream of industry.[67]

Control Data Corporation adopted this strategy and built at least four such inner-city plants (see box) while it was still headed by William Norris, who advocated this kind of social responsibility. In 1978 Control Data helped form City Venture Corporation, a Minneapolis-based consortium company committed to the revitalization of economically distressed inner cities through business development and job creation. Control Data was to manage the concern initially as its major shareholder, but other major corporations, such as Dayton-Hudson Corporation and Northwest Bancorporation, also bought equity positions. The company eventually had 14 stockholders, including 10 companies, two church groups, and two community organizations. Initially capitalized at $3 million, the

INNER-CITY OPERATIONS NORTHSIDE PLANT

Northside was Control Data's first inner-city plant. It was opened in January, 1968, in leased space on the near north side of Minneapolis. In February 1969, the operations were moved into a new 90,000 square foot plant at 277 Twelfth Avenue North.

Northside is Control Data's sole manufacturing source for CY 18/255X computers. Employees at the plant also perform subassembly tasks and operate an extensive sheet metal fabrication shop.

The Northside plant employs 260 full-time workers, with an annual payroll of $6 million. Sixty percent of the employees represent minority races, compared with the 30% minority make-up of the Northside community.

Jobs range from entry-level to management, including electrical/mechanical assembly, electrical technical, sheet metal working, administrative, line supervision and management. The wage and salary rates paid at Northside are identical to those paid to all other Twin Cities Control Data employees in similar job classifications.

Northside's efficiency and productivity are comparable to those of other Control Data plants engaged in similar production.

Northside is the first Control Data manufacturing plant to go more than three years and 1.5 million hours without a lost-time accident. The Northside employees received the President's Safety Award in 1983 and 1984 for this achievement.

Source: Control Data Corporation, *Fact Sheet*, May 1984.

corporation's major effort was to bring jobs to the inner city by constructing and operating plants in poverty areas as well as other programs designed to stimulate business development. The ultimate goal of all City Venture programs is community economic self-sufficiency.

The Reagan administration proposed to extend this concept by creating "enterprise zones" in economically troubled areas of the country. The basic idea of this plan is to offer a series of open-ended tax breaks for employers who decided to locate plants in these enterprise zones. Such breaks could include special investment tax credits on top of the investment tax credit already available, tax credits for hiring disadvantaged workers, tax credits of 10 percent for employers and 5 percent for employees on wages earned in a zone, and elimination of capital gains taxes on the sale of qualified property. The administration hoped these incentives would lead to the creation of many more new jobs for these zones.[68] The Reagan administration had hoped that as many as 25 of these zones could be approved each year over a 3-year period, but the plan became bogged down in Congress mainly over a debate as to how much these zones were going to cost the government.[69]

While the national bill was blocked, states began creating similar zones of their own. Studies showed that as of 1987, close to 1,500 enterprise zones were operating in 37 states. These zones were said to have created $10 billion in new investment and generated or saved 200,000 jobs.[70] The state of Louisiana alone planned to create 411 zones, in which one-eighth of its people lived. The state contacted nearly 1,000 localities with high unemployment, enlisting those that were willing to cooperate in the program by giving up some local taxes. Florida picked 26 cities and 4 counties in which to establish zones. Connecticut's program focused on Hartford, New Haven, and four other cities with severely depressed neighborhoods.[71]

After several years' experience, however, it appears that the building of inner-city plants is not the answer to poverty in the disadvantaged areas of cities and states. Out of 15 inner-city factories built by major corporations in the mid-1960s, 9 have been either sold or closed. Enterprise zones appear to be an ineffective lure, and tax breaks do not necessarily make a company interested in moving into a depressed area of a city or state. Government must get involved in training disadvantaged workers for the kinds of skills needed by private industry and must ask employers to reserve some of these jobs for minorities. Based upon these recommendations, the Secretary of Labor proposed a 20 percent increase in the department's job training budget for fiscal 1988, predicting that labor shortages would start to occur in the 1990s and that one largely untapped pool of workers will be inner-city minorities who need job training.[72]

Welfare: Providing Income, Goods, and Services

What started out as an effort to relieve the distresses of the depression era grew into a full-fledged welfare system designed to relieve the deprivation of those who, for one reason or another, have not been able to provide for their own needs in a market economy. All modern industrial societies have some kind of a welfare system designed to provide income support and/or actual economic goods and services to those in need. These programs are costly, but are believed to be a necessary overhead expense to deal with the harsh outcomes of a market economy where some fall farther and farther behind in the race for the rewards of society and simply are not able to provide for themselves.

PUBLIC POLICY BENEFITS

The types of benefits provided differ widely, but they can be categorized as in Exhibit 5.2 according to the type of benefits provided. There are social insurance programs where beneficiaries have actually contributed something to the program throughout their lifetimes. There are also programs that are designed to provide people with cash income assistance. Finally, other programs provide actual goods and services to people that are usually referred to as in-kind assistance.

The Social Security program was established in 1935 as a national insurance scheme to supplement the retirement funds citizens had available. Since this program was set up on a pay-as-you-go basis, it is a simple transfer of money, year by year, from the working to the retired population. Thus it is not an actuarially sound insurance program, despite the fact that the program was conceived as social insurance rather than a government giveaway program. Defining it as a social insurance program helped to legitimize the program and assure its passage. The program provides at least half the household income for 62 percent of its beneficiaries. It accounts for more than 25 percent of all federal tax revenues and expenditures and provides benefits for one out of every seven Americans.[73]

Social Security also provides benefits for the survivors of workers who die before retirement and offer disability protection. Medicare covers many of the medical needs

EXHIBIT 5.2 ————————————————————————————

Income/Support Programs

I. Social insurance programs

  A. Social Security, Old Age, and Survivors Insurance

  B. Public employee and railroad retirement

  C. Unemployment insurance

  D. Medicare

II. Cash income assistance

  A. Public assistance to the aged, blind, and disabled

  B. Veterans' compensation and pensions

  C. Aid to Families with Dependent Children

III. In-kind assistance

  A. Medicaid

  B. Food stamp program

  C. Student aid

  D. Housing subsidies and public housing

  E. Nutritional programs for children

of the aged and disabled who receive Social Security and is linked with Social Security for financing purposes. Thus it is usually classified as a social insurance program even though it provides in-kind benefits. Unemployment compensation is designed to tide people over while they are between jobs when the termination of their previous employment was involuntary. Unemployment compensation is managed by the states with a federal subsidy.

With regard to cash income assistance programs, there are programs that provide public assistance to aged, blind, and disabled people; the AFDC, which provides broad-scale public assistance; and veterans' compensation and pensions. The various benefit areas that provide in-kind assistance include Medicaid, which provides medical benefits to the poor who are aged, permanently disabled, or are in single-parent families. The food stamp program started out small in 1962 but escalated in the mid-1970s to become the second largest in-kind transfer program. It provides benefits in the form of food vouchers to all poor persons on a scale that varies by income. Also included in this category are various kinds of student aid programs to provide scholarships for higher education, housing subsidies or low-rent public housing, and free school lunches for elementary and secondary school children.

GROWTH OF BENEFITS

The growth of these benefits can be looked at in two ways: (1) the growth of specific programs and (2) the growth of transfer payments overall. Table 5.1 shows the growth of social welfare expenditures by the federal government from 1960 to 1986 by program areas. The graph in Figure 5.4 on page 140 shows the growth in selected programs for the years 1970 and 1980. The big gainer was the food stamp program, increasing by 490 percent in a 10-year period. Most of the other programs also had a substantial

TABLE 5.1 Social Welfare Expenditures by the Federal Government: 1960–1986

| Year | Social Welfare Outlays | | Social insurance | Public aid | Health and medical programs[1] | Veterans programs | Education | Housing | Other social welfare | All health and medical care[2] |
	Total	Annual percent change								
1960	24,957	[3]11.3	14,307	2,117	1,737	5,367	868	144	417	2,918
1970	77,337	12.0	45,246	9,649	4,775	8,952	5,876	582	2,259	16,600
1975	167,426	16.7	99,715	27,186	8,521	16,570	8,629	2,541	4,264	34,100
1980	302,631	12.6	191,162	48,666	12,703	21,254	13,452	6,608	8,786	68,801
1981	344,120	13.7	224,574	55,946	13,650	23,229	13,372	6,045	7,304	80,560
1982	367,620	6.8	250,551	52,485	14,528	24,463	11,917	7,176	6,500	90,706
1983	401,413	9.2	274,315	56,709	15,440	25,561	12,399	9,961	7,028	95,719
1984	420,399	4.7	288,743	58,480	16,622	25,970	13,010	10,226	7,349	103,927
1985	452,860	7.7	313,108	61,985	18,630	26,704	13,796	11,088	7,548	118,955
1986	472,364	4.3	326,588	65,615	19,926	27,072	15,022	10,164	7,977	125,730

[1]Excludes program parts of social insurance, public aid, veterans, and other social welfare.

[2]Combines "Health and medical programs" with medical services included in social insurance, public aid, veterans, vocational rehabilitation, and antipoverty programs.

[3]Change from 1955.

Source: U.S. Department of Commerce, *Statistical Abstract of the United States 1989*, 109th ed. (Washington, D.C.: U.S. Government Printing Office, 1989), p. 346.

increase, showing that welfare programs in general experienced a good deal of growth during this decade.

As far as the overall growth of transfer payments is concerned, Table 5.2 on page 141 shows social welfare expenditures as a percentage of GNP and total government outlays from 1960 to 1986. According to Michael E. Levy of the Conference Board, fiscal year 1965 marks a clear dividing line between the moderate growth of these transfers during the first half of the decade and the much higher growth rates that began with fiscal 1966 and finally slowed in fiscal 1978 to a lower level. Payments to individuals grew at an average annual rate of 15.3 percent during fiscal years 1966 to 1979, compared with 6.6 percent during fiscal years 1961 to 1965. Fiscal 1965 saw the beginning of a new "social activism" period, when many new welfare programs were enacted (See Figure 5.5 on page 142). Those programs included the Economic Opportunity Act, the Permanent Food Stamp Act, and the Social Security Amendment of 1965, which created Medicare and Medicaid.[74]

New Directions

The Reagan administration, which took office in January 1981, saw its election as a mandate to reverse this trend by enacting deep budget cuts in some of the entitlement programs. These budget cuts coupled with a 10 percent tax cut over each year of a 3-year period, were supposed to bring government spending under control, bring inflation down, stimulate increased saving and investment, and promote economic growth. These

Figure 5.4 A Decade of Growth in Entitlement Programs

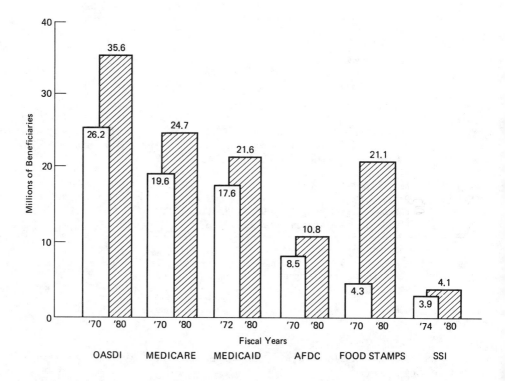

Source: L. Douglas Lee, "The Deficit Dilemma—and Its Solution," *The Journal/The Institute for Socioeconomic Studies,* Vol. VIII, No. 1 (Spring 1983), p. 16. Data from *Social Security Bulletin, Annual Statistical Supplement,* U.S. Department of Health and Human Services.

changes, formalized in the Economic Recovery Tax Act of 1981, altered the nature of the trade-offs as the cut in entitlement programs disproportionately affected the lower-income groups because they received most of the benefits from these programs, and the tax cuts disproportionately benefited the upper- and middle-income groups because they received the most income.

Regarding budget cuts in entitlement programs, food stamp funding was trimmed by 2 percent to $11.1 billion a year and the program was restricted to the "truly needy," defined as those whose incomes fell below 130 percent of the poverty level. Under this rule, a family of four must earn less than $13,260 to qualify for food stamps.[75] The AFDC program was cut 2 percent to $7 billion, which along with new eligibility rules, was expected to reduce or eliminate benefits for 670,000 of 4 million AFDC recipients.[76] Unemployed adults who received AFDC support would be required to work about 20 hours each week performing community service work. Certain exemptions from this rule were allowed.[77] By reducing the number of students eligible for free and reduced price lunches, Congress carved about $1.5 billion from the school lunch programs $4.7 billion budget. Funding for the Legal Services Corporation established to provide legal assistance to low-income people was cut 25 percent in 1982 to $241 million from $321 million the previous year.[78]

As a result of these budget cuts and changes in eligibility rules, a Congressional

TABLE 5.2 Social Welfare Expenditures Under Public Programs as Percent of GNP and Total Government Outlays: 1960–1986

	Total Expenditures				Federal				State and Local Government			
		Percent of—				Percent of—				Percent of—		
Year	Total (bil. dol.)	Annual percent change[1]	Total GNP[2]	Total govt. outlays	Total (bil. dol.)	Annual percent change[1]	Total GNP[2]	Total Federal outlays	Total (bil. dol.)	Annual percent change[1]	Total GNP[2]	Total State and local outlays
1960......	52.3	9.9	10.3	38.4	25.0	11.3	4.9	28.1	27.3	8.7	5.4	60.1
1970......	145.9	10.8	14.7	48.2	77.3	12.0	7.8	40.1	68.5	9.6	6.9	64.0
1975......	290.1	14.7	19.0	57.3	167.4	16.7	11.0	52.0	122.7	12.4	8.0	65.3
1980......	492.5	11.2	18.5	56.5	302.6	12.6	11.3	54.3	189.9	9.1	7.1	60.8
1985......	730.4	8.2	18.5	51.2	452.9	8.4	11.5	47.8	277.5	7.9	7.0	59.0
1986......	770.5	5.5	18.4	47.9	472.4	4.3	11.3	47.6	298.2	7.4	7.1	58.2

[1]Change from prior year shown; for 1960, change from 1955.
[2]Gross national product.

Source: U.S. Department of Commerce, *Statistical Abstract of the United States 1989*, 109th ed. (Washington, D.C.: U.S. Government Printing Office, 1989), p. 348.

Budget Office study said that 325,000 families lost eligibility for Aid to Families with Dependent Children and an additional 325,000 to 350,000 had their benefits reduced. About 1 million people lost eligibility for food stamps, and the number of pupils fed in the federally subsidized school lunch program dropped by about 3 million.[79]

The stated intent of these changes was not to cut aid to the truly needy but to force people off the welfare roles who were able to work for a living and reduce the level of government spending for entitlement programs. The administration maintained that it was not actually cutting entitlement programs in most instances, but only slowing their growth. They argued that the so-called safety net remained for those who are truly needy in our society and in need of government assistance. The Reagan administration was concerned to provide at least a subsistence income for the deserving poor, those who are clearly incapable of self-support.

But beyond this support for the truly needy, it became clear that the administration was attempting to redefine poverty as largely a moral rather than a social problem. Many of the poor were seen as morally deficient who lacked the discipline and incentive to support themselves. Poverty was not the result of unemployment in a changing economy or other barriers to work and self-sufficiency, but was rather the result of individual behavior and the lack of personal responsibility. Many of the poor had thus become dependent on the welfare system that had become too large and penalized the productive members of society while rewarding the unmotivated and making them welfare dependent. Thus they needed to be taken off the welfare roles and, when faced with deprivation, would find jobs or some other means of support. Welfare and not poverty was thus the problem, as the current welfare system caused poverty or at least provided disincentives for people to climb out of poverty.

Conservatives argue that government interventions are harmful by definition in that they weaken links between individual behavior and income among groups already plagued by

Figure 5.5 Payments for Individuals, Fiscal 1961–1979

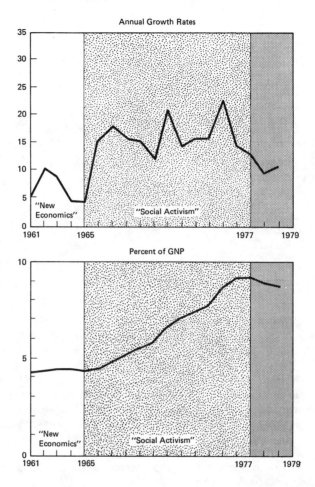

Note: Includes all direct and indirect transfer payments except unemployment compensation, which was excluded here as the major cyclical component.

Source: Michael E. Levy, "Federal Budget Policies of the 1970s: Some Lessons for the 1980s," *Stabilization Policies* (St. Louis, MO: Washington University Center for the Study of American Business, 1980), p. 166. Reprinted with permission.

an inadequate sense of personal responsibility. . . . Public assistance presumably destroys families and communities, inhibits individual advancement, hinders broader economic growth, and weakens the capacity of state, local, and private agencies to provide for the truly needy. Through such assults on federal intervention welfare programs were considered to be a threat to the nation's moral fiber and a disruption of the propitious functioning of private markets and local governance.[80]

Critics, particularly the Democrats who opposed this philosophy and the actions taken to cut welfare programs, argued that the Reagan administration was dismantling social programs that had been built up over the past 50 years to help people in distress. The Reagan philosophy was said to be one of "every person for himself or herself and the devil take the hindmost." Cuts in welfare programs were hurting those who were truly needy and meant that they were not getting adequate food and shelter or medical care. Some commentators referred to the decade of the 1980s as the mean decade, where the poor were blamed for their condition and were hit hardest by changes in social and tax policies.[81]

The final returns in regard to the change in direction represented by the cutbacks in entitlement programs are not yet in, but some figures show trends that have developed over the past decade. Inequality continued to increase throughout most of the decade, as the top fifth of all families received 44 percent of the income in 1988—an increase from 41.5 percent a decade earlier. Meanwhile, the bottom fifth of all families received 4.6 percent of the income, a decrease from 5.2 percent a decade earlier. Some 17.2 percent of all money income received by families in 1988 went to the wealthiest 5 percent of all families, which was the greatest share for these families since 1950, although changing definitions over the years distort the comparison to some extent.[82]

Statistics released by the House Ways and Means Committee showed that the income of the poorest fifth of income earners fell 8.8 percent between 1979 and 1987, while their income after taxes and transfers fell 9.1 percent. In comparison, the income of the richest 20 percent of the population increased 19.9 percent, while their income after taxes and transfers increased an even larger 18.7 percent. The people in the top 5 percent of the income distribution received a 48 percent increase in income over the same time period and were rewarded with a 12.5 percent drop in their tax rates. Effective tax rates (the ratio of taxes to family income) rose for the 10 percent of families at the bottom income levels and fell for the 10 percent of families at the highest levels. It thus appeared that the rich were getting richer and the tax structure was doing less to reduce inequality than in previous years because of increases in payroll taxes such as social security and the shrinkage of corporate income taxes.[83]

In 1987, a consensus seemed to be emerging regarding reform of the welfare system. Any reform should discourage long-term dependency, promote family stability, and provide work incentives. Furthermore, states should be given more administrative discretion and more latitude to experiment with new approaches to welfare. This new consensus included both liberals and conservatives, who began to develop new strategies that might help make welfare less a government dole and more a way to salvage human lives. These new strategies were based on two major changes to welfare, (1) tying welfare payments to jobs or job training and (2) giving the states primary responsibility for finding ways to move people from welfare dependency to productive employment. Useful work began to be seen as critical to developing self-esteem and a sense of personal responsibility. And it was felt the federal government should give states and localities financial incentives to move people off welfare roles into becoming productive members of society.[84]

This emphasis tried to tie welfare more directly to workfare and link income maintenance to employment preparation. This philosophy changes the nature of the welfare bargain. The receipt of welfare is conditioned on participation in a detailed, supervised program of preparation for self-support. Willingness to participate in such efforts becomes a test of need for public assistance.[85] Based on this philosophy, Congress passed the Family Support Act in 1988 emphasizing work programs to help welfare parents become self-supportive. Welfare parents with children over the age of three are required to enroll in state basic-education, job-training, work-experience, and job-search programs.[86]

Questions for Discussion

1. Describe the nature of poverty. What are the different factors that contribute to a poverty condition? Which of these factors, in your opinion, are most significant? What are the effects of poverty?

2. Is there any discernable trend with respect to the level of poverty in the United States in the past several years? What factors seem to be most closely related to the level of poverty in the country? What are the policy implications of your answer?

3. How has the nature of poverty changed in the United States as far as the groups affected are concerned? Why have these changes occurred? Are there any new changes that may come about in the next few years that you can foresee? What should the nation do to deal with these problems?

4. Examine closely the studies that take in-kind transfers into account. Do you agree with the methodology used to cash out these transfers? Are the conclusions valid? Is there less poverty than the official figures would lead us to believe? If in-kind transfers have such an impact, then why haven't policymakers taken these into account? What would you recommend be done to make the figures more realistic?

5. Describe a disadvantaged person. What handicaps do disadvantaged people take with them into the marketplace? What can public policy do in general to help overcome these handicaps?

6. What is a minority business enterprise? How would the development of more of these enterprises promote equality of economic opportunity? What ingredients are necessary for their success?

7. Should the government help provide markets for these minority enterprises? Is this fair to the white businessperson? Is there an element of reverse discrimination in allocating a certain percentage of public works money to minority enterprises? How would you rule on this issue if you were a federal judge?

8. Describe the origins of the welfare system. Does the market system, indeed, condemn some people to death? Are the rewards and penalties that the market allocates fundamentally arbitrary?

9. Does a democratic government owe its citizens some form of aid if they have not been able to provide for themselves through the market system? Are transfer payments a legitimate area of public policy?

10. Distinguish between cash-income assistance and in-kind assistance. If you were a recipient of assistance, which form would you rather have? Is there any basic difference in these forms of assistance from society's point of view?

11. Study the Social Security system in more detail. What was the rationale for making it a mandatory system for most people in the country? Why was it designed as a pay-as-you-go-system? Should the benefits be indexed to keep up with inflation? How will or do you feel about supporting the aged—seeing some of your paycheck directly transferred to the Social Security system for the benefit of other people?

12. Think of some alternative methods to provide for the needs of the aged in this country. Which are most feasible? Should the mandatory retirement age be removed entirely? How would this affect your job or prospects of finding work?

13. Explain the growth of transfer payments throughout the late 1960s and early 1970s. Does this growth represent a fundamental shift in the thinking and values of the American people? What implications do your answers have for the free-enterprise system?

14. Is there a trade-off between equality and efficiency? What measures are relevant in trying to determine the nature of this trade-off? What guidelines could you suggest for policymakers who are concerned about taking this trade-off into account in their decision making?

15. Do you agree that welfare reform is likely to be only incremental at best? Why? What are the political realities? What are current trends regarding welfare at present and what does

the future hold with respect to the growth of social expenditures on the part of the federal government?

16. Why are the results of all these efforts to promote equality of economic opportunity rather dismal? Is there no good solution to this problem, either through the market or public policy? What are the implications of your answer for the future of the welfare system in this country?

Case: Wedtech Corporation

In 1965, John Mariotta, a high school dropout, invested $3,000 to start a small manufacturing company in a desolate area of the South Bronx. The company struggled along for 5 years, when Mariotta entered into a partnership with Fred Neuberger, a mechanical engineer. The firm, named Welbilt Electronics, was eligible for loans directed to minority contractors from the Small Business Administration. The SBA had a set-aside program that allowed minority firms to obtain federal contracts without competitive bidding. By the early 1980s, Welbilt began winning million-dollar contracts for navy pontoon bridges and army smoke-grenade launchers. Eventually, about 95 percent of its business came from these set-aside contracts.[1]

The company changed its name to Wedtech in 1983 and moved to new facilities in the shadow of Yankee Stadium. The company hired more than 1,000 African American and Hispanic workers from the local neighborhood, an area that had lost 40 percent of its manufacturing base during the decade previous. The company's profits increased from $8 million in 1981 to more than $72 million by 1984 and went public with a $30 million stock offering that made millionaires of Mariotta, Neuberger, and other executives. The company became a symbol of minority achievement, as President Reagan lauded the company's success and called John Mariotta a hero for the 1980s. The company was hailed as a success story and an example of what minorities could achieve.[2]

But then federal and local prosecutors entered the picture, and a different story began to unfold. The prosecutors alleged that Wedtech prospered as a result of promiscuous bribery of city, state, and federal officials and engaged in a conspiracy to win government contracts by fraudulently depicting itself as a minority-owned business. The company was depicted as a racketeering enterprise dependent on bribes to public officials to win minority contracts. Payoffs were so routine, the prosecutors alleged, that the company maintained a secret bank account for depositing kickbacks from contractors and greasing public officials.[3]

When Wedtech wanted a multimillion-dollar contract for engines, for example, it hired Attorney E. Robert Wallach as a consultant; he was allegedly given some $500,000 worth of the company's stock over several years in addition to a retainer for his services. Wallach was an old friend and lawyer of then–Presidential counselor Edwin Meese, who was kept informed of Wedtech's efforts to win the engine contract. Meese later became Attorney General for the Reagan administration. The company also retained Lyn Nofziger, who had formerly worked for the White House and left to set up his own consulting firm. Nofziger had written a letter on behalf of the company to Meese's chief deputy, who then set up a White House briefing on Wedtech that was attended by top officials and representatives of the army and the SBA. Soon after this meeting, Wedtech was awarded the first of its many military contracts.[4]

When the stock sale took place, Mariotta was no longer the majority shareholder, which meant Wedtech no longer qualified as a minority-owned company. The local SBA office thus began proceedings to remove the company from the set-aside program. The company then quickly transferred 1.8 million shares of company stock to Mariotta's nominal control and retained the law firm of Richard Biaggi, the son and former partner of South Bronx Congressman Mario Biaggi. The law firm received more than $1 million in fees and stock for representing the company. Soon after these actions, the SBA approved Wedtech's stock transfer and allowed it to remain eligible for minority set-asides.[5] Eventually, Mario Biaggi and his son, along with five others, were indicted by a federal grand jury on charges of extortion, racketeering, and conspiracy. Prosecutors claimed that Biaggi received $3.6 million in Wedtech stock after he threatened to undermine SBA support for the company. A former SBA regional administrator was also indicted.[6]

Soon thereafter, Mariotta was replaced as Wedtech's chairman by Neuberger after they disagreed about management policies. The stock that Mariotta controlled was then returned to the company and it lost its status as a minority contractor. By October 1986, the stock had dropped from $11.44 a share in March to $6.50 a share. By the end of the year, the company had laid off 1,000 people and filed for bankruptcy. Debts were listed at $212 million. Four former executives, including Neuberger, pleaded guilty to a range of charges that included bribery and mail fraud. Mariotta himself was not indicted.[7]

The company tried to recover. New management took over and obtained a $500,000 loan from Chemical Bank and $38 million in government contracts that were not under investigation. However, the Cadillacs and limousines used by Wedtech's former officers were gone and a $305,000 condominium purchased in 1985 for entertainment purposes was put on the market. The scandal was a blot on the minority set-aside program and stimulated several proposals for reform. The incident also cast aspersions on the minority work force that some considered undeserved. In any event, the unfolding story was another example of how difficult it is to implement programs to aid disadvantaged people and avoid corruption and favoritism.[8]

Case Notes

1. Bruce van Voorst, "A Tale of Urban Greed," *Time*, April 20, 1987, p. 30.
2. Ibid.
3. Ibid.
4. Ibid.
5. Ibid., pp. 30, 32.
6. Walter Shapiro, "$4 Billion Worth of Temptation," *Time*, June 15, 1987, p. 20.
7. van Voorst, "A Tale of Urban Greed," pp. 30, 32.
8. Ibid., p. 32. Also see Paula Dwyer, "Wedtech: Where Fingers Are Pointing Now," *Business Week*, October 5, 1987, pp. 34–35.

Chapter Notes

1. Arthur M. Okun, "Our Blend of Democracy and Capitalism: It Works But Is In Danger," (Washington, D.C.: The Brookings Institution, Reprint #351, 1979), p. 73.
2. Ibid.
3. Ibid.

4. Sar A. Levitan and Clifford M. Johnson, *Beyond the Safety Net: Reviving the Promise of Opportunity in America* (Cambridge, Mass. Ballinger, 1984), pp. 3–7.

5. Ibid., pp. 4–5.

6. Ibid., pp. 5–6.

7. George L. Wilber, ed., *Poverty: A New Perspective* (Lexington: University of Kentucky Press, 1975), pp. 3–4.

8. Ibid., p. 37.

9. Martin Rein, "Problems in the Definition and Measurement of Poverty," *Poverty in America,* Louis A. Ferman, Joyce L. Kornbluh, Alan Haber, eds. (Ann Arbor: University of Michigan Press, 1968), p. 130.

10. Nick Eberstadt, "Economic and Material Poverty in the U.S.," *The Public Interest,* No. 90, Winter 1988, pp. 51–52.

11. Oscar Lewis, "The Culture of Poverty," *On Understanding Poverty,* Daniel Moynihan, ed. (New York: Basic Books, 1968), p. 188.

12. Ibid., p. 190.

13. Herbert J. Gans, "Culture and Class in the Study of Poverty: An Approach to Anti-Poverty Research," *Understanding Poverty,* Daniel Moynihan, ed. Copyright © 1968, 1969 by the American Academy of Arts and Sciences, Basic Books, Inc., New York, pp. 205–206.

14. "15% of Population Below Poverty Line," *Dallas Times Herald,* August 3, 1983, p. A-1.

15. Joann S. Lubin, "U.S. Poverty Rate Increases to 15.2%, Highest Since 1965," *Wall Street Journal,* August 3, 1984, p. 20.

16. Joann S. Lubin, "Poverty Rate Fell in 1984; White House Hails the Decline, but Critics Dismiss It," *Wall Street Journal,* August 28, 1985, p. 40. See also Leslie Lenkowsky, "Long and Short of Poverty Trends," *Wall Street Journal,* August 30, 1985, p. 10.

17. Joann S. Lubin, "U.S. Poverty Rate Slipped to 14% in '85, But Number of Poor Still Relatively High," *Wall Street Journal,* August 27, 1986, p. 5.

18. Michel McQueen, "Poverty Rate Falls To 13.6%; Decline Is Third Straight," *Wall Street Journal,* July 31, 1987, p. 34.

19. David Wessel, "Poverty Rate Eased to 13.1% in 1988, But Income Disparities Widened Again," *Wall Street Journal,* October 19, 1989, p. A-2.

20. Ibid.

21. " . . . But U.S. Children Are Slipping Past The Safety Net," *Business Week,* October 12, 1987, p. 26.

22. "U.S. Children's Health Plummeting," *Times-Picayune,* October 19, 1989, p. A-6.

23. "Children Having Children: Teen Pregnancies are Corroding America's Social Fabric," *Time,* December 9, 1985, pp. 79–90.

24. Alan S. Binder, "Improving The Chances of Our Weakest Underdogs—Poor Children," *Business Week,* December 14, 1987, p. 20.

25. Karl Zinsmeister, "Illegitimacy in Black and White," *Wall Street Journal,* November 16, 1987, p. 24.

26. Karl Zinsmeister, "The Poverty Problem of the Eighties," *Public Opinion,* Vol. 8, No. 3 (June–July 1985), pp. 8–12; Joe Davidson, "Differing Social Programs for Young, Old Result in Contrasting Poverty Levels for Two Groups," *Wall Street Journal,* June 27, 1985, p. 58. See also Thomas E. Ricks, People's Perception of the Elderly As Being Poor Is Starting to Fade," *Wall Street Journal,* December 19, 1985, p. 23.

27. James J. Kilpatrick, "Plight of American Blacks: What Has Gone Wrong?" *Times-Picayune,* February 6, 1990, p. B-7.

28. Roger Wilkins, "The Last Word: The Limits of Tolerance," *Mother Jones,* January, 1989, p. 60.

29. James E. Ellis, "What Black Families Need To Make The Dream Come True," *Business Week,* January 22, 1990, p. 29.

30. "Race, Net Worth Linked in Study: Whites Far Outpace Minorities," *Dallas Times Herald,* July 19, 1986, p. A-1.

31. "A Threat to the Future," *Time,* May 14, 1984, p. 20. See also "Teenage Orphans of the Job Boom, *Time,* May 13, 1985, pp. 46–47, and "Today's Native Sons: Inner-city Black Males are America's Newest Lost Generation," *Time,* December 1, 1986, pp. 26–29. See also Charles Murray, "Here's the Bad News on the Underclass," *Wall Street Journal,* March 8, 1990, p. A-14.

32. Susan B. Garland, "Why The Underclass Can't Get Out From Under," *Business Week*, September 19, 1988, pp. 122–23.

33. Elizabeth Ehrlich, "Homelessness: The Policy Failure Haunting America," *Business Week*, April 25, 1988, pp. 132–38.

34. Jacob V. Lamar, "The Homeless: Brick by Brick," *Time*, October 24, 1988, pp. 34, 38.

35. Morton Paglin, "Poverty in the United States: A Reevaluation," *Policy Review*, No. 8 (Spring 1979), pp. 8–9.

36. Ibid., p. 22.

37. Gurney Breckenfeld, "Has Reagan Hurt the Poor?" *Fortune*, January 24, 1983, p. 80.

38. Joann S. Lubin, "Number of U.S. Poor May Be Much Lower Than Reported Earlier, Census Data Say," *Wall Street Journal*, October 3, 1986, p. 50.

39. Mark Lilla, "Why the Income Distribution is So Misleading," *The Public Interest*, No. 77 (Fall 1984), pp. 62–76.

40. Lawrence M. Mead, "The Hidden Jobs Debate," *The Public Interest*, No. 91, Spring 1988, pp. 40–58.

41. Alan L. Otten, "Poor Will Find Many Jobs Will Be Out of Reach As Labor Market Shrinks, Demand for Skills Rise," *Wall Street Journal*, May 27, 1987, p. 54.

42. "Why CETA is in Trouble," *Business Week*, October 2, 1978, p. 124.

43. Joann S. Lubin, "Demise of CETA Jobs Affects Urban Services—And Changes Lives," *Wall Street Journal*, May 12, 1982, p. 1.

44. Pete Earley, "CETA Program Reborn," *Dallas Times Herald*, December 15, 1982, p. F-3. See also William H. Kolberg, "Employment Policy 2000," *The Corporate Board*, March–April 1987, pp. 6–7.

45. Karen Diegmueller, "Quayle's Job Act a Costly Dud?" *Insight*, September 26, 1988, pp. 20–21.

46. Karen Blumenthal, "Off Target: Job-Training Effort, Critics Say, Fails Many Who Need Help Most," *Wall Street Journal*, February 9, 1987, p. 1.

47. Ibid.

48. Diegmueller, "Quayle's Job Act," pp. 20–21.

49. National Alliance of Business, *1978 Annual Report* (Washington D.C.: NAB, 1978), p. 8.

50. "Business Tackles Hard-Core Unemployment," *Business Week*, September 20, 1982, p. 86.

51. National Alliance of Business, *Let's Work Together . . . to Get All of America Working*, Washington, D.C., undated.

52. National Alliance of Business, *1986 Annual Report*, p. 13.

53. Carolyn Lockhead, "Even the Most Basic Jobs Now Require Basic Skills," *Insight*, May 23, 1988, pp. 38–40.

54. Irwin Ross, "The Puny Payoff from Affirmative Action in Small Business," *Fortune*, September 10, 1979, pp. 100–101.

55. Linda M. Watkins, "Minority Entrepreneurs Venturing Into Broader Range of Businesses," *Wall Street Journal*, March 25, 1987, p. 29.

56. U.S. Department of Commerce, *A Minority Owned Business: Growing for America* (Washington, D.C.: U.S. Government Printing Office, undated).

57. Donald E. Gumpert, "Seeking Minority Owned Business as Suppliers," *Harvard Business Review*, Vol. 57, No. 1 (January–February, 1979), p. 111.

58. See "Minority Contracting Gets a Federal Overhaul," *Business Week*, February 5, 1979, p. 32.

59. Ross, "Puny Payoff," p. 103.

60. Cathy Trost, "Minority Firms Get Smaller Share of U.S. Contracts Under Reagan," *Wall Street Journal*, April 10, 1984, p. 31.

61. Watkins, "Minority Entrepreneurs," p. 29.

62. Shapiro, "$4 Billion Worth of Temptation," p. 20.

63. Jeanne Saddler, "SBA Program's Toughened Rules Upset Minority Firms," *Wall Street Journal*, January 5, 1989, p. B-2.

64. Robert E. Taylor, "U.S. Joins Group in Challenging the Right Of County to Set Aside Jobs for Black Firms," *Wall Street Journal*, March 6, 1984, p. 56.

65. Jeanne Saddler, "Set-Aside Jobs for Minorities, Women Are Evaporating," *Wall Street Journal*, December 21, 1989, p. B-2.

66. Watkins, "Minority Entrepreneurs," p. 29; Jube Shiver, Jr., "State's Black Firms Crowd List," *Los Angeles Times*, May 10, 1989, p. IV-1. Sales of the top 100 black-owned industrial and service companies

fell 3.8 percent in 1989 because of a sluggish economy. Some companies were hurt by the slowdown in defense spending and cutbacks in government set-aside programs. See Leon E. Wynter, "Top 100 Concerns Owned by Blacks Had '89 Sales Fall," *Wall Street Journal,* May 9, 1990, p. C-15.

67. *Social Responsibility Report 1978* (Minneapolis: Control Data Corporation, 1978), p. 5.

68. Timothy D. Schellhardt, "Reagan's Plan to Revitalize Inner Cities To Include Creation of 'Enterprise Zones,' " *Wall Street Journal,* January 20, 1982, p. 6.

69. "The Hidden Costs of Enterprise Zones," *Business Week,* May 10, 1982, p. 175.

70. Ron Stodghill II, "Enterprise Zones—Or Twilight Zones?" *Business Week,* February 27, 1989, p. 113.

71. "States Prove More 'Enterprising,' " *Business Week,* November 29, 1982, p. 63.

72. Ibid.

73. Nathan Keyfitz, "Why Social Security Is In Trouble," *The Public Interest,* No. 58 (Winter 1980), pp. 102–19.

74. Michael E. Levy, "Federal Budget Policies of the 1970s: Some Lessons for the 1980s," *Stabilization Policies* (St. Louis, Mo.: Washington University Center for the Study of American Business, 1980), pp. 169–70.

75. Janey Guyon, "Doleful Problem: Food-Stamp Red Tape Raises Tension Levels in Understaffed Offices," *Wall Street Journal,* June 27, 1984, p. 1.

76. "Why Welfare Rolls May Grow," *Business Week,* March 29, 1982, pp. 165–66.

77. "Putting the Poor to Work," *Time,* March 23, 1981, p. 10.

78. Scot J. Paltrow, "Cutbacks Force Legal Aid to Reject Cases, After Leaving Poor Helpless," *Wall Street Journal,* January 28, 1982, p. 23.

79. Jane Mayer, "What's Behind Divorce, Teen-Age Pregnancies? Head of White House Policy Team Blames Welfare," *Wall Street Journal,* June 13, 1986, p. 36.

80. Levitan and Johnson, *Beyond the Safety Net,* p. 56.

81. Jim Henderson, "The Mean Decade," *Dallas Times Herald,* December 24, 1989, p. A-1.

82. Wessel, "Poverty Rate Eased to 13.1% in 1988," p. A-2.

83. Henry Aaron, "If U.S. Is Unequal, Don't Blame the Payroll Tax," *Wall Street Journal,* February 14, 1990, p. A-18.

84. "Fixing Welfare: A Consensus is Emerging on the Need for Radical Reform," *Time,* February 16, 1987, pp. 18–21. See also Joe Davidson, "Welfare Policy Requiring Recipients To Work Is Approved By Governors," *Wall Street Journal,* February 25, 1987, p. 52; and "What to Do About Welfare," *Wall Street Journal,* December 2, 1986, p. 36.

85. Michael Wiseman, "How Workfare Really Works," *The Public Interest,* No. 89, Fall 1987, pp. 36–47.

86. "House Passes Bill Revamping Welfare System," *Dallas Times Herald,* October 1, 1988, p. A-1.

Suggested Reading

ATKINSON, A. B. *Social Justice and Public Policy.* Cambridge, Mass.: MIT Press, 1982.

AULETTA, KEN. *The Underclass.* New York: Random House, 1983.

CARENS, JOSEPH H. *Moral Incentives and the Market.* Chicago: University of Chicago Press, 1981.

CROMARTIE, MICHAEL, ed. *Gaining Ground: New Approaches to Poverty and Dependency.* Washington, D.C.: Ethics and Public Policy Center, 1985.

DALPHIN, JOHN R. *The Presistence of Social Inequality in America.* New York: Schenkman, 1982.

GANS, HERBERT J. *More Equality.* New York: Vintage Books, 1974.

GILBERT, NEIL. *Capitalism and the Welfare State:* Dilemmas of Social Benevolence. New Haven, Conn.: Yale University Press, 1983.

GREEN, PHILIP. *The Pursuit of Inequality.* New York: Pantheon, 1981.

HOWIE, JOHN, ed. *Ethical Principles for Social Policy.* Carbondale, Ill.: Southern Illinois University Press, 1982.

JORDAN, BILL. *Rethinking Welfare.* New York: Basil Blackwell, 1987.

KLEIN, RUDOLF, AND MICHAEL O'HIGGINS, eds. *The Future of Welfare.* New York: Basil Blackwell, 1985.

LEE, PHIL, AND COLIN RABAN. *Welfare Theory and Social Policy: Reform or Revolution?* New York: Sage Publications, 1988.

LEVITAN, SAR A. AND CLIFFORD M. JOHNSON. *Beyond the Safety Net: Reviving the Promise of Opportunity in America.* New York: Ballinger, 1984.

LEVY, FRANK. *The Logic of Welfare Reform.* Washington, D.C.: Urban Institute, 1980.

LEWIS, MICHAEL. *The Culture of Inequality.* Boston: University of Massachusetts Press, 1978.

MEENAGHAN, THOMAS M., AND ROBERT O. WASHINGTON. *Social Policy and Social Welfare: Structure and Applications.* New York: Free Press, 1980.

MURRAY, CHARLES. *Losing Ground: American Social Policy 1950–1980.* New York: Basic Books, 1984.

OKUN, ARTHUR M. *Equality and Efficiency, The Big Tradeoff.* Washington, D.C.: The Brookings Institution, 1975.

RAWLS, JOHN A. *A Theory of Justice.* Cambridge, Mass.: Harvard University Press, 1971.

SNIDERMAN, PAUL M., AND MICHAEL G. HAGAN. *Race and Inequality: A Study in American Values.* New York: Chatham House Publications, 1984.

SOMMERS, PAUL M. *Welfare Reform in America.* The Netherlands: Kluwer Academic, 1982.

STASZ, CLARICE. *The American Nightmare: Why Inequality Persists.* New York: Schocken, 1983.

TAWNEY, RICHARD H. *Equality.* London: Unwin Books, 1964.

TULLOCK, GORDON. *Wealth, Poverty and Politics.* New York: Basil Blackwell, 1988.

WILENSKY, HAROLD L. *The Welfare State and Equality: Structural and Ideological Roots of Public Expenditures.* Berkeley: University of California Press, 1975.

ZASTROW, CHARLES. *Introduction to Social Welfare, Social Problems, Services, and Current Issues,* 4th ed. Belmont, Calif.: Wadsworth, 1989.

CHAPTER **6**

Equal Employment Opportunity

The concept of equal opportunity is consistent with free-enterprise philosophy, because the most efficient combination of resources should result if those with the best abilities and talents get the best economic opportunities—the best jobs, the best chances to start a new business, the best investment opportunities. Society is better off because people will end up in positions where their abilities can best be utilized, and those who are unfit for their positions will have to find jobs elsewhere. The principle of equal opportunity helps to ensure that the best performers in society, no matter where they were born, what they believe, or what race or sex they are, have a chance to rise to the top based on their proven ability to use society's resources efficiently and wisely, or, in other words, to do something society wants done and is willing to reward commensurately.

This concept of equal opportunity never held that people would be of equal ability or that such free and open competition for existing opportunities would bring about equal results in terms of economic condition. Nor does equal opportunity raise questions about the results of the competitive process, since it assumes that unequal results are morally right and just. People with superior ability will obviously get ahead and are morally justified in receiving a greater share of the rewards society has to offer if they use their abilities to the fullest and contribute to society's well-being. The important thing about equal opportunity is that people should be free to compete equally on the basis of merit for the rewards society offers and be free to go as far as their abilities, interests, ambition, and performance will take them.

Merit is at the heart of this concept of equal opportunity. Merit dictates that opportunity should go to those who deserve it because they have the ability to take advantage of the opportunity to its fullest. Equality of opportunity means that everyone in our society should be able to compete fairly and honestly for the rewards society has to offer on the basis of merit, where merit refers to the ability of an individual to perform in some capacity. Irrelevant considerations such as race, sex, religion, creed, or national origin are not supposed to be a factor in the distributive outcomes of our society. The rewards are supposed to go to those who perform the best and thus are able to compete most effectively.

For much of our history, equal opportunity along with equality before the law has been an important ideal and a part of free-enterprise ideology and folklore. In the 1960s, however, many recognized that equal opportunity never existed in this country for some groups, since they recognized what the institution of slavery had done to opportunities for African Americans, understood the effects of poverty on the opportunities a person had to develop native abilities, and may even have recognized the phenomenon of role stereotyping in regard to women. Such beliefs became rather widespread and it was recognized that because of prejudice and stereotyping, something called systemic discrimination was built into our major institutions, preventing members of some groups, most notably minorities and women, from being free to compete on an equal basis with white males for available opportunities and to utilize or develop their abilities to go as far as they might. Built into the employment practices of businesses and other institutions were barriers to starting a new business, and barriers to an equal education that prevented members of these groups from gaining experience and training to become qualified and thus having a true equal opportunity to compete with the predominant white male culture.

Thus it came to be recognized that the market was not by itself effectively implementing the concept of equal opportunity and making it a reality for all members of society. The people making the key decisions about who got what opportunities (employment decisions, loan decisions, purchasing decisions) were by and large white males, and not surprisingly, most of these decisions were made in favor of other white males who were in advantageous positions. Women and minorities were simply not "qualified" for better positions in society.

The implementation of equal opportunity, then, which is much more difficult and complicated than its definition, became a matter of public policy. Many public policy measures were adopted in the 1960s and 1970s that were directed at rooting out systemic discrimination and overcoming the disadvantages of race and sex to give members of disadvantaged groups a fair and equal chance at the opportunities and rewards society has to offer. Fair and equal in this context means that they should be able to compete on the basis of merit, and irrelevant factors such as race, sex, religion, national origin, and creed should not hamper their ability to compete.

This approach to equal opportunity focuses on the workplace and is aimed at rooting out the kind of discrimination that prevents members of certain groups, most notably minorities and women, from having an equal chance at the job opportunities that are available. The basic issue here is not necessarily one of poverty or disadvantages that make it difficult to compete in the marketplace because of the lack of fundamental skills or work habits. It is one of prejudice and discrimination that prevent certain groups from utilizing to the fullest the skills and abilities they already possess, or from gaining the experience and training that is necessary to become qualified for the better opportunities society has to offer.

To discriminate in employment is to make an adverse decision (or set of decisions) against employees (or prospective employees) based on their membership in a certain class. Discrimination of this sort involves three basic elements: (1) it is a decision against one or more employees based solely on the fact that they are members of a certain group and not on their ability to perform a given job, (2) the decision is based on the assumption that the group is inferior to other groups and therefore less worthy of equal treatment, and (3) the decision has a harmful or negative effect on the interests of the employees, perhaps costing them jobs, higher positions, or better pay.[1]

Public Policy Measures

One of the first efforts to promote equal employment opportunity as a matter of public policy was Executive Order 8802, issued in 1941 by President Franklin D. Roosevelt. This order prohibited racial discrimination by companies under federal contract and established the first Fair Employment Practices Committee. The effect of this order was significant, as most companies had some kind of a federal contract because of the war effort. This order in combination with the severe work force shortage provided many job opportunities for African Americans and women that would otherwise not have been available. After the war ended, however, many African Americans were fired because they were no longer needed, and many women left the work force to return to their traditional role as homemaker.

Then, in 1961, President John F. Kennedy issued Executive Order 10925, establishing a President's Commission on Equal Employment Opportunity with the power to investigate complaints by employees and enforce a ban on discrimination by federal contractors. The Commission had the power to terminate contracts if necessary or prevent companies from obtaining new contracts from the government. The order also required government contractors to take affirmative action to make certain that minority group members were treated equally in terms of job opportunities and informed of job openings. This was the first time the word "affirmative action" was used in a public policy measure.

States also passed what are called fair employment practice (FEP) acts to prohibit discrimination in employment. Most of these acts are aimed at employers, unions, and employment agencies, forbidding them to discriminate in any term or condition of employment. The first such act was passed by New York in 1945, and since that time most other states have adopted such measures. These statutes generally take one of three forms: (1) statutes that provide for an administrative hearing and judicial enforcement of orders of an administrative agency or official, (2) statutes that do not provide for any type of administrative agency or enforcement of orders but do make employment discrimination a misdemeanor, and (3) statutes that call for voluntary compliance only and have no enforcement provisions.

Thus there was some action on the equal employment opportunity front prior to the 1960s, but it was during the 1960s that major public policy measures were passed in response to the civil rights movement and the feminist movement. These measures dealt primarily with discrimination against minorities and women, although other groups, such as the handicapped and aged, are also victims of discrimination. Efforts to promote equal treatment of these groups are mentioned as far as public policy measures are concerned, but are not discussed in detail because of space limitations.

The Civil Rights Act of 1964. The cornerstone of public policy regarding equal employment opportunity is Title VII of the Civil Rights Act of 1964, which forbade discrimination in employment by an employer, employment agency, or labor union on the basis of race, color, sex, religion, or national origin, in any term, condition, or privilege of employment. The law forbids discrimination in hiring and firing practices, wages, fringe benefits, classifying, referring, assigning, or promoting employees, extending or assigning facilities, training, retraining, apprenticeships, and other employment practices.

The ban on employment discrimination based on sex was inserted as an amendment during the debate about the bill on the floor of the House. Presumably this was done in an effort to defeat the bill. Thus there is little legislative history to clarify congressional intent with respect to sex discrimination, and as a result the Equal Employment Opportunity Commission and the courts have had difficulty in applying the sex provision.[2] This may be part of the reason that many women deemed the Equal Rights Amendment to be so important.

The Civil Rights Act established the Equal Employment Opportunity Commission (EEOC) as the administrative agency to implement the act, but it gave the Commission no enforcement powers. Prior to 1972, the EEOC only had authority to investigate complaints filed by individuals and to attempt to settle them by conciliation. For an employer to be taken to court, the EEOC had to convince the Justice Department that the case was worth considering. Consequently, not many cases were pursued through litigation.

An important provision of the act, called the "quota" provision, expressly forbade preferential treatment of groups discriminated against, emphasizing that the intent of the act was to promote equal opportunity for individuals. Section 703(j) of Title VII stated that

> nothing in the title should be interpreted to require an employer, an employment agency, a union or a hiring hall, to grant preferential treatment to any individual or to any group because of the race, color, religion, sex, or national origin of such individual or group on account of an imbalance which may exist in such employment as compared with the total or percentage of such persons in any community, state, section, or other area, or in the available work force in any community, state, section, or other area.[3]

Equal Employment Opportunity Act of 1972. This act was an amendment to Title VII, broadening its coverage and giving the EEOC power to bring enforcement action in the courts. This amendment also provided that discrimination charges may be filed by organizations on behalf of aggrieved individuals as well as by employees and job applicants themselves. As amended, Title VII now covers the following main categories of employers:

- All private employers of 15 or more persons. Bona fide, tax-exempt private clubs, however, are excluded from this definition.
- All educational institutions, public and private. Title VI of the Civil Rights Act also applies to educational institutions.
- Public and private employment agencies, defined as any person regularly undertaking with or without compensation to procure employees for an employer or to procure for employees opportunities to work for an employer.
- Labor unions with 15 or more members, including not only local unions, but national and international unions and collateral bodies.
- Joint labor-management committees that control apprenticeship or other training and retraining programs. There is an exception when religion, sex, or national origin is a bona fide occupational qualification for employment. This exception does not apply to race or color.

Pregnancy Discrimination Act of 1978. Title VII was further amended in 1978 when Congress passed the Pregnancy Discrimination Act. This amendment prohibits disparate treatment of pregnant women for all employment-related purposes. Specifically the act (1) prohibits termination or refusal to hire or promote a woman solely because she is pregnant; (2) bars mandatory leaves for pregnant women arbitrarily set at a certain time in their pregnancy and not based on their individual inability to work; (3) protects reinstatement rights of women on leave for pregnancy-related reasons, including rights in regard to credit for previous service, accrued retirement benefits, and accumulated seniority; and (4) requires employers to treat pregnancy and childbirth the same way they treat other causes of disability under fringe benefit plans.[4] Regarding the last provision, a court of appeals ruled that the 1978 amendments required employers to pay maternity benefits not only to female workers but also to wives of male workers whenever the workers were covered by the employer for other disabilities.[5]

The Equal Pay Act of 1963.   This act prohibits discrimination because of sex in the payment of wages, including overtime, for equal work on jobs that require equal skill, effort, and responsibility, and that are performed under similar working conditions. This law was aimed at the long-established practice of paying women lower wages than men for essentially the same work, including differential rates of pay set by union contracts. The law specifically prohibits employers from reducing the wage rates of any employee to equalize pay between the sexes. The act originally covered employees subject to the minimum wage requirements of the Fair Labor Standards Act, but in 1972 coverage was extended to include executive, administrative, and professional employees and outside salespeople.

The Age Discrimination in Employment Act.   As originally passed, the act prohibited employers, employment agencies, and labor unions from discriminating on the basis of age, against people between the ages of 40 and 65 in hiring, firing, and promotion, or other aspects of employment. The law applies to employers of 20 or more employees, labor unions of more than 25 members, and public employees. In 1978, this act was amended to raise the top age to 70 effective April 6, 1978 for employees then under 65 and effective January 1, 1979 for employees then between the ages of 65 and 69, subject to an exemption for employees covered by collective bargaining contracts.

Executive Orders.   Executive Order 11246 (as amended by E.O. 11375), issued by President Lyndon B. Johnson in 1965, forbade employment discrimination based on race, color, religion, sex, or national origin by prime contractors and subcontractors who had government contracts in excess of $10,000, and called for them to develop affirmative action plans in ''good faith'' for the hiring and training of minorities. Originally, no administrative machinery was set up to define what ''affirmative action'' meant or ensure its implementation. Eventually, it became apparent that rules and regulations were needed to guide contractors as well as compliance officers to fulfill the spirit of the order.

Thus Revised Order No. 4 was issued by the Office of Federal Contract Compliance in 1970, requiring employers with contracts of over $50,000 and 50 or more employees to develop written affirmative action programs identifying areas of minority and female underutilization and establishing goals and timetables to correct existing deficiences in the employment of minorities and women. Specifically, a contractor covered by Executive Order 11246 must do the following:

- Refrain from discriminating against any employee or job applicant because of race, color, religion, sex, or national origin.
- Take affirmative action to ensure that applicants are employed and employees are treated without regard to race, color, religion, sex, or national origin. (The obligation extends to working conditions and facilities, such as restrooms, as well as to hiring, firing, layoff and recall, promotions, and compensation.)
- State in all advertisements or help solicitations that all qualified applicants will receive consideration without regard to race, color, religion, sex, or national origin.
- Advise each labor union with which the contractor deals of its commitments under the order.

- Include the obligation under the order in every subcontract or purchase order unless specifically exempted.
- Comply with all provisions of the order and the rules and regulations, furnish all information and reports required, and permit access to books, records, and accounts for the purpose of investigation to ascertain compliance.
- File regular compliance reports describing hiring and employment practices.[6]

Underutilization was defined as having fewer minorities or women in a particular job classification than would reasonably be expected by their availability. The goal of this order was to increase the utilization of minorities and women at all levels and in all segments of the work force where such deficiencies existed. Failure to meet these provisions satisfactorily could lead to cancellation of a contract and being barred from issuance of future government contracts. This order is an example of the government using its power as a buyer to promote social goals and values.

The Vocational Rehabilitation Act of 1973. This act again applies only to federal contractors and requires them to take affirmative action to employ and promote qualified handicapped persons. The act applies to employers with federal contracts over $2,500 and requires an employer to make reasonable accommodations in hiring physically and mentally handicapped persons. Employers who have contracts worth $50,000 or more and employ 50 or more people must also prepare a written affirmative action program and make it available to all employees. The act defines a handicapped person as one "who has a physical or mental impairment which substantially limits one or more of such person's major life activities."[7] Failure to comply with these regulations can again result in contract termination, debarment from future contracts, or withholding of contract payments as necessary to correct any violations.

The Vietnam Era Veterans Readjustment Assistance Act. Applying to employers with government contracts of $10,000 or more, this act requires these contractors to take affirmative action to employ and advance disabled veterans and qualified veterans of the Vietnam era. In addition to this affirmative action requirement, the act also imposes an obligation on all covered employers to list all suitable job openings with an appropriate public or private local employment service. Priority for referral will then be given to Vietnam era veterans. Enforcement of the act is by complaint to the Veteran's Employment Service of the Department of Labor.

Equal Rights Amendment. While not a public policy measure, the Equal Rights Amendment was approved by Congress in 1972 and submitted to the states for ratification. If ratified by three-fourths (38) of the states, this amendment would have become the 27th amendment to the constitution 2 years after the final date of ratification. The states originally had 7 years to complete the approval process. Time was subsequently extended for two more years after approval was not granted by enough states during the original ratification period. In July 1982, 10 years after being passed by Congress, time ran out and the ERA was finally defeated. The amendment had been approved by 35 states, 3 short of ratification, but no state had voted for the amendment since Indiana in 1977, despite repeated efforts by its supporters. They then moved to reintroduce the measure in Congress thus starting a new ratification drive. A Lou Harris poll conducted in 1983 showed that 63 percent of the sample believed that the amendment would become part of the Constitution sooner or later.[8] The amendment itself consists of the following three sections:

> *Section 1.* Equality of rights under the law shall not be denied or abridged by the United States or by any state on account of sex.
>
> *Section 2.* The Congress shall have the power to enforce, by appropriate legislation, the provisions of this article.
>
> *Section 3.* This amendment shall take effect two years after the date of ratification.

The effects of the ERA are subject to a number of misconceptions. The possibility of women being drafted into the armed forces and serving in combat is a subject of concern when there is talk about reviving the draft system. The U.S. Code of Federal Regulations might have to be rewritten, as the U.S. Civil Rights Commission identified more than 800 sections as sex biased. Other effects of a national ERA would probably be similar to what has happened in states that have written equal rights for women into their own constitutions. Sixteen states have such laws binding their governments to observe sexual equality, but not since 1977 have any states added such an amendment to their constitution. The effects of such laws include abolishing the assumption that all household goods belong to the husband and allowing wives to share control of family assets, providing women prisoners with rehabilitation programs previously available only to men, extension of rape laws to protect both men and women against sexual assault, and equal application of antiprostitution laws, which has resulted in the arrest of male patrons in some states.[9] While state ERAs get mixed reviews, women believe that a national ERA would have importance in establishing sex equality as a clear national policy.[10]

Administrative Structure

The Equal Employment Opportunity Commission. Established by the Civil Rights Act of 1964, the EEOC is a five-member commission (including the chairperson) appointed by the president with the advice and consent of the Senate. The responsibilities of the EEOC include (1) issuing guidelines on employment discrimination, (2) investigating charges of discrimination, and (3) settling cases where discrimination exists through conciliation or, if necessary, litigation (see Exhibit 6.1). Prior to the 1972 amendments to the Civil Rights Act, the EEOC could pursue cases where it found evidence of discrimination only through conciliation aimed at reaching an agreement between the parties concerned to eliminate aspects of discrimination revealed by the investigation. The 1972 amendments gave the EEOC power to take a case to court itself if conciliation fails. Since that time, the number of cases taken to court has substantially increased and the EEOC has established litigation centers around the country with a substantial legal staff to provide rapid and effective court action.

In July 1979, a reorganization plan submitted by the president and approved by Congress transferred administration and enforcement of the Equal Pay Act and the Age Discrimination in Employment Act to the EEOC. These had formerly been the responsibility of the Wage-Hour Division of the Labor Department. The EEOC also has authority to require covered employers, employment agencies, and labor unions to keep and preserve records and to file numerous reports with the agency.

EXHIBIT 6.1 ——

Equal Employment Opportunity Commission
2401 E. Street NW, Washington, D.C. 20506

Purpose: To enforce antidiscrimination provisions of the 1964 Civil Rights Act (Title VII) as regards discrimination based on race, sex, color, religion, or national origin in hiring, promotion, firing, wages, testing, training, apprenticeship, and all other conditions of employment.

Regulatory Activity: The EEOC (1) issues guidelines on employment discrimination, (2) investigates charges of discrimination and makes public its decisions, and (3) litigates noncompliance cases. (The U.S. Attorney General in the Department of Justice brings suit when a state government, governmental agency, or political subdivision is involved in a charge of employment discrimination.) Under Reorganization Plan No. 1 of 1978, EEOC is also responsible for all compliance and enforcement activities relating to equal employment opportunity among federal employees, including handicap discrimination.*

Established: 1964

Operational: July 2, 1965

Legislative Authority:
    Enabling Legislation: Title VII of the Civil Rights Act of 1964 (78 Stat. 241), as amended by the Equal Employment Opportunity Act of 1972 (86 Stat. 103: P.L. 92-261) and by the Pregnancy Discrimination Act of 1978 (P.L. 95-555)
    The EEOC is also responsible for the administration of:
        Equal Pay Act of 1963 (77 Stat. 56), as amended
        Age Discrimination in Employment Act of 1967 (81 Stat. 602), as amended
        Rehabilitation Act of 1973 (87 Stat. 355)
        Executive Orders relating to equal employment opportunity
        Reorganization Plan No. 1 of 1978

Organization: This independent agency is headed by five commissioners who are appointed by the President with the advice and consent of the Senate.

*These EEO activities were transferred from the Civil Service Commission and the Department of Labor.

Budgets and Staffing, Fiscal 1970–90

	1970	1975	1980	1985	1986	1987	1988	(Estimated) 1989	1990
Budget ($ millions)	13	55	124	163	158	170	180	181	189
Staffing	780	2,384	3,558	3,107	3,125	3,052	3,062	2,948	2,948

Source: From Ronald J. Penoyer, *Directory of Federal Regulatory Agencies*, 2d ed. (St. Louis, Mo.: Washington University Center for the Study of American Business, 1980), p. 28. Reprinted with permission.

During the Reagan administration, Clarence Thomas, a black lawyer, was approved to head the commission. He promised to reorganize the commission to give himself and the four other commissioners more direct control over the 3,200 lawyers and bureaucrats in the agency, play down pattern and practice cases in favor of individual complaints, and use goals and timetables to measure progress by employers in countering bias less rigidly than in the past.[11]

Under Thomas's leadership, the EEOC began to change its direction and emphasis. Three themes seemed to emerge that indicated the new directions in which the EEOC was moving. These themes included (1) a suspicion of discrimination charges based on statistics rather than on evidence of bias against identified workers, (2) a belief that remedies for past bias should be more narrowly focused to aid the particular persons actually injured by bias, and (3) definitions of affirmative action that place emphasis on recruiting techniques and training programs geared to minority workers rather than specific minority hiring goals and objectives. Critics of these themes argued that by adopting a narrow focus and rejecting broad class-action suits where discrimination may pervade an entire company, backlogs would again increase, resulting in piecemeal, rather than sweeping, improvements in hiring and promotion policies.[12]

The Office of Federal Contract Compliance Programs. The OFCCP (formerly OFCC), which is located in the Labor Department, is responsible for administration of Executive Orders 11246 and 11375, the Rehabilitation Act of 1973, and the Vietnam Veterans Readjustment Assistance Act of 1974, all programs requiring equal employment opportunity and affirmative action by federal contractors and subcontractors. This compliance authority was consolidated in the OFCCP in 1978; previously, the Labor Department had shared this authority with 11 other governmental departments and agencies. The reason for this consolidation was to establish accountability and to promote consistent standards, procedures, and reporting requirements.

The basic enforcement tool of the OFCCP is a comprehensive review process encompassing all aspects of a contractor's hiring and promotion policies for handicapped workers, veterans, minorities, and women. During 1980, the OFCCP was expected to carry out 7,000 such compliance actions. Some of these could result in the termination of government contracts. Only 27 companies have been declared ineligible for government contracts since the program became effective in 1967, but 13 of these were ordered cut off during the Carter administration.[13]

This effort to implement equal opportunity was also embroiled in controversy during the Reagan administration. Early in the administration's tenure, the Labor Department announced plans to ease the job bias rules that had been established for federal contractors. For example, the department wanted to narrow the number of companies required to submit written affirmative action plans by raising the limits to 250 employees and $1 million worth of contracts. This provision would have exempted about 75 percent of the 200,000 companies with federal contracts, but who employ only about 25 percent of the 30 million workers on federal projects. Thus most of the workers would still be covered even under the new provisions.[14] The department also sought to limit backpay awards and encourage contractors to reduce their affirmative action efforts. Most of these proposals were finally dropped as they pleased neither business organizations who viewed them as inadequate tinkering and civil rights groups who feared the steps would gut the program entirely.

In 1985, the administration drafted another revision of the executive order that would have eliminated rules which force companies to increase their employment of minorities and women through the use of goals and timetables and also questioned the legality of corporations' voluntary use of goals and timetables to correct discrimination. If this version had prevailed, it would have opened companies up to reverse-discrimination litigation as the result of affirmative action programs instituted to eliminate manifest racial imbalances in the work force. Under a compromise reached late in the year, businesses with federal contracts would still be required to increase their employment of women and minority group members through a less rigid set of goals and timetables.[15]

Implementation of Equal Employment Opportunity

The implementation of these public policy measures has been very difficult, given the nature of prejudice and the complexities involved in attempting to interpret the meaning of key concepts in the legislation and determining the intent of Congress in writing and passing legislation related to equal opportunity. There are questions about affirmative action, reverse discrimination, preferential treatment, retroactive seniority, the meaning of equal pay for equal work, and sexual harassment. These issues will be treated in this section.

AFFIRMATIVE ACTION

The Civil Rights Act of 1964, taken literally, ruled out any form of preferential treatment, thus forbidding such devices as quotas, and seemed to treat discrimination as an intentional, deliberate act of exclusion. It ignored both the moral question of whether groups that had been discriminated against in the past were owed something more than simply an equal chance to compete with those who had benefited from past discrimination, and the more practical question of how discriminated groups were supposed to get the education and experience necessary to qualify themselves for jobs—particularly those professional and managerial jobs that commanded the most money and status—without some kind of preferential treatment that would make up for deficiencies in education and experience that were the result of discrimination.

It was recognized early in the federal contracting procedure that a passive approach to implementing the concept of equal opportunity would not work. What was needed was some kind of an "affirmative action" program where positive steps would be taken to hire more minorities and women and promote them into better paying positions. Federal contractors were required to analyze their work force to determine where deficiencies existed and then file an affirmative action plan with goals and timetables to show how these deficiencies were going to be corrected. These written affirmative action plans were to contain the following information.

- An analysis of all major job classifications, with an explanation of any "underutilization" of minorities in any of the job classes.
- Goals and targets and affirmative action commitments designed to relieve any deficiencies. (But the order specifies that a contractor's compliance will not be judged solely by whether it reaches its goals and meets its timetables. Instead, a contractor's compliance will be judged by reviewing the contents of the program, the extent of the contractor's adherence to it, and the contractor's good faith efforts to make its program work toward realization of the goals within timetables set for completion.)

The guidelines under Order No. 4 also outline suggested procedures for use in establishing, implementing, and judging an acceptable affirmative action program. The contractor must consider such factors as the following in developing an acceptable affirmative action program that would meet with approval.

TYPES OF AFFIRMATIVE ACTION PROGRAMS

1. **Passive nondiscrimination.** This involves a willingness, in all decisions about hiring, promotion, and pay, to treat the races and sexes alike. However, this posture may involve a failure to recognize that past discrimination leaves many prospective employees unaware of present opportunities.

2. **Pure affirmative action.** A concerted effort is made to expand the pool of applicants so that no one is excluded because of past or present discrimination. At the point of decision, however, the company hires (or promotes) whoever seems most qualified, without regard to race or sex.

3. **Affirmative action with preferential hiring.** In this posture, the company not only ensures that it has a larger labor pool to draw from but systematically favors women and minority groups in the actual decisions about hiring. This might be thought of as a "soft" quota system, i.e., instead of establishing targets that absolutely must be met, the top officers of the company beef up employment of women and minority-group members to some unspecified extent by indicating that they want those groups given a break.

4. **Hard quotas.** No two ways about it—specific numbers or proportions of minority-group members must be hired.

Source: Daniel Seligman, "How Equal Opportunity Turned Into Employment Quotas," *Fortune,* March 1973, p. 162. Copyright © 1973 Time, Inc. All rights reserved.

- Minority population of the labor area surrounding the facility and the size of the minority unemployment force.
- General availability of promotable minority employees within the contractor's organization.
- Availability of promotable minority employees within the contractor's organization.
- Anticipated expansion, contraction, and turnover in the labor force.
- Existence of institutions capable of training minorities in the requisite skills.
- Degree of training which the contractor is reasonably able to undertake as a means of making all job classes available to minorities.
- The written programs "must relate to all major job categories at the facility with explanations if minorities or women are currently being underutilized." Where there are deficiencies, goals and timetables are required to utilize minorities and women at all levels and in all segments of the work force.[16]

There are various approaches to affirmative action (see box), but the use of quotas and goals became fairly widespread as the most useful device to ensure compliance with the executive order as applied to federal contracting. Eventually, the courts came to regard the Civil Rights Act as requiring similar procedures to implement the intent of Congress. The use of quota systems and implementation goals became a preferred means of correcting deficiencies where they were known to exist and to demonstrate to the government that a company was making a "good faith" effort to comply with equal opportunity legislation.

The difficulty of proving intent to discriminate is obvious. One would have to find some internal memoranda that clearly indicated race or sex was a factor in the employment decision or find someone who was in on the decision who would testify in court to that effect. It is much easier to infer that discrimination exists from the composition of the work force, by comparing the percentage of minorities and women employed overall with some relevant population parameter such as the percentage of minorities or women in the labor force from which the company could be expected to draw its employees and by comparing the percentage of minorities and women in various occupational categories within the company itself. Where there was an obvious lack of women or minorities in the total work force, or where they were obviously concentrated in lower-paying occupations, discrimination was inferred to exist. The best way to correct these deficiencies was through the use of quotas and goals, which in effect gave preferential treatment to women and minorities to bring them up to some kind of statistical parity. The assumption behind this approach, of course, is that skills and abilities are randomly distributed throughout the population.

Thus the concepts of equal opportunity and affirmative action are not the same. Equal employment opportunity means that everyone gets an equal chance at a job or promotion. Affirmative action implies a set of specific result-oriented procedures designed to achieve equal employment opportunity at a pace beyond that which would occur normally. The objective of an affirmative action program is to achieve within a reasonable period of time an employee work force that in all major occupational categories reflect the makeup of the relevant external labor market. Affirmative action programs establish specific goals (quotas) and timetables designed to accomplish this objective.

REVERSE DISCRIMINATION

The widespread use of goals or quotas to implement affirmative action meant that inevitably reverse discrimination would be a factor. This phenomenon occurs when a minority or a woman is equally qualified when compared with a white male and is given preference over the latter for a job or promotion, or where quotas resulted in hiring minorities or women who are actually less qualified than white male applicants for the same position. While the phenomenon was tolerated for a while, cases of reverse discrimination began to receive attention, and eventually the courts began to rule that civil rights laws applied to whites as well as African Americans and preferential treatment was a violation of these laws. The EEOC itself was found guilty of discrimination against white male professionals in its hiring and promotion practices.[17]

One of the first cases of this kind was brought by two white employees of the Santa Fe Trail Transportation Co. who were accused of misappropriating a shipment of antifreeze and subsequently fired. An African American worker, who was also accused of being involved in the misappropriation, was retained. The Supreme Court ruled against this procedure, stating that the 1964 Civil Rights Act banned employment discrimination against whites as well as African Americans.[18]

Then a lower court ordered AT&T to pay damages to a male employee who was passed over for promotion in favor of a less experienced woman with lower seniority. This promotion had apparently been made to fulfill the terms of a 1973 federal consent decree in which AT&T agreed to hire and promote thousands of women and minorities into jobs previously held mostly by white males. The male employee bringing the suit alleged that he had suffered sex discrimination when he was denied a promotion. Federal Judge Gerhard A. Gesell agreed and awarded damages to the employee. He stated that AT&T "relied upon and properly applied the consent decree" in promoting the woman but that Mr. McAleer, the male employee who was passed over, was "an innocent employee who had earned promotion.'' The judge felt that the courts should attempt to protect innocent employees by placing this burden on the wrongdoing employer wherever possible. Thus, he concluded, ''AT&T should bear the principal burden of rectifying its previous discriminatory conduct. An affirmative award of some damages on a rough justice basis is therefore required and will constitute an added cost which the stockholders of AT&T must bear.'' Rather than appeal this decision, AT&T settled out of court to prevent this ruling from becoming a legal precedent that could be used by other passed-over employees.[19]

Next, the California Supreme Court, in a 6-to-1 ruling, banned minority quotas in the graduate schools of California's state university system.[20] The case was brought by Allan Bakke, who contended that he was denied admission to the medical school at the University of California's Davis campus in 1973 and 1974 because of reverse discrimination. Of the 100 openings for entering classes in those 2 years, 84 places went to those selected by normal admissions standards, which emphasized college grades and entrance examination scores. The other 16 openings were filled under an admissions program giving preference to nonwhite applicants.

The university acknowledged that it admitted minority applicants it rated substantially below Bakke. The court said the medical school's reserved places for minority students who did not necessarily score as high as white students violated the Constitution's Fourteenth Amendment guarantees of equal protection to all persons regardless of race. Universities could consider factors other than grades and test scores in admitting students—such as the needs of society—but without regard to race. The University of California appealed this ruling to the U.S. Supreme Court, which agreed to hear the case. Many people thought the country would finally have a definitive ruling on preferential treatment and reverse discrimination.

Such a definitive ruling, however, was not the result. The court split 5-to-4 on the decision, which essentially had two parts.[21] On the one hand, the court affirmed by a 5-to-4 margin the lower court order admitting Bakke to medical school at the University of California at Davis, because its special admissions program for minorities did violate Title VI of the Civil Rights Act of 1964, which forbade racial discrimination in any program or activity receiving federal financial assistance. Quotas based entirely on race where no previous discrimination had been found were held to be illegal. This provision left open the use of quotas to correct deficiencies as part of a settlement where previous discrimination had been found.

On the other hand, a majority of the court, again by a 5-to-4 margin, with Justice Lewis Powell being the swing vote in both cases, ruled that a university could continue to take race into consideration in admissions. Exactly how this was to be done was unstated, but Justice Powell referred to the admissions policies at Harvard as a possible model. Race is a factor that is considered at Harvard along with geographical location or athletic or artistic ability. Other factors Justice Powell mentioned that could be considered along with race included unique work or service experience, leadership potential, maturity, demonstrated compassion, or a history of overcoming disadvantage.[22]

The justices of the Supreme Court wrote six different opinions, reflecting their own diversity as well as that of the nation as a whole (see box). This case attracted more briefs than any other case that had ever been considered by the court. Yet the decision was hardly the landmark decision many had hoped for—the court ruled narrowly and delicately, trying to find a middle ground. The decision was not definitive and left room for further development, which on the whole may have been a positive approach to such a complex situation.

Another case that dealt with this issue that had more relevance to business organiza-

Preferential programs may only reinforce common stereotypes holding that certain groups are unable to achieve success without special protection. . . . There is (also) a measure of inequity in forcing innocent persons in (Bakke's) position to bear the burdens of redressing grievances not of their making (Supreme Court Justice Lewis Powell writing for the majority in the Bakke decision). I suspect that it would be impossible to arrange an affirmative action program in a racially neutral way and have it successful. To ask that this be so is to demand the impossible. In order to get beyond racism, we must first take account of race. There is no other way. And in order to treat some persons equally, we must treat them differently (Supreme Court Justice Harry Blackmun in a dissenting opinion on the Bakke decision).

Source: Regents of the University of California v. Bakke, 98 S.Ct. 2752, 2807 (1978).

tions was the so-called Weber case, in which an employee of Kaiser Aluminum and Chemical Corporation sued his employer and the Steelworkers Union, claiming that he had been illegally excluded from a training program for higher-paying skilled jobs in which half the places had been reserved for minorities. The Fifth Circuit Court of Appeals agreed with Weber, observing that the quota system used by the company improperly favored African Americans who had not been the subject of prior unlawful discrimination.[23] The Supreme Court disagreed, however, and by a 5-to-2 vote ruled that employers can give African Americans special preference for jobs that had traditionally been all white.[24] Whether or not it has had discriminatory job practices in the past, the court said, a company can use affirmative action programs of this type to remedy "manifest racial imbalance" without fear of being challenged in these efforts by the courts. The court emphasized the temporary nature of the program and the fact that it was not intended to maintain racial balance, but simply to eliminate a manifest racial imbalance. The program would end when the percentage of African American skilled craft workers in the plant approximated the percentage of African Americans in the local labor force. Thus the Supreme Court backed job preference programs for minorities that had been voluntarily established to eliminate conspicuous racial imbalance in traditionally segregated job categories.[25] This ruling was consistent with EEOC guidelines issued in 1978 dealing with affirmative action programs.

The key elements in this decision were that the program was designed to correct a manifest racial imbalance, that it was voluntary in nature, and that it was only temporary until such time as the manifest imbalance was corrected. These principles seemed to be upheld in further decisions by the high court. In the summer of 1986, the Supreme Court upheld a court-approved settlement between the city of Cleveland and minority firefighters that called for the promotion of one minority for every white, and another federal court order that established a 29 percent minority hiring goal for a sheet metal workers union in the New York area that was found to have excluded nonwhite applicants. This goal was based on the percentage of nonwhites in the local labor pool. The justices indicated that affirmative action plans were acceptable if they were based on sound legal principles, were of limited duration, did not unnecessarily trammel the rights of white workers, and were carefully tailored to remedy the precise discrimination that was in question.[26]

More support for affirmative action came from decisions made in 1987, where the Supreme Court first upheld affirmative action plans directed to promotion as well as hiring activities. In a case involving the Alabama police, the court upheld a lower court–ordered plan to promote one African American trooper for every white promoted to higher ranks, if there were qualified African Americans available, until they constituted 25 percent of that rank. The court said that in this case the discrimination against African Americans was "pervasive, systematic, and obstinate" and that this pattern had created a firm justification for race-conscious relief.[27]

An even more significant decision was handed down later in the year, when the court upheld an affirmative action plan voluntarily adopted in 1987 by the Santa Clara County, California, transportation agency. The primary goal of the plan was to correct a conspicuous imbalance of women in skilled and managerial positions. Among skilled craft workers, none of the 238 jobs had ever been held by a woman. It was a temporary plan designed to fill 36 percent of skilled jobs with women to mirror the percentage of women in the area labor market. Thus when the job of road dispatcher opened up in 1979, the agency interviewed nine people and found seven qualified. Among those qualified, was Diane Joyce, a road maintenance worker, who was eventually given the promotion even though she had an interview score that was two points lower than a white male who wanted the same job and eventually sued the county.[28]

The court argued that the Santa Clara plan merely set up flexible goals that didn't put male workers at a disadvantage. The plan established realistic guidance for employment decisions which visited minimal intrusion on the legitimate expectations of other employees. This decision was said to provide the clearest declaration yet on the role of affirmative action as a remedy for inequality in the workplace and give employers greater freedom to engage in broad affirmative programs without having to prove or admit prior discrimination against individuals. All that is necessary to support an affirmative action program is evidence of a manifest imbalance in the number of women or minorities holding the positions in question. The case also established the rights of women as well as African Americans and other minorities to receive preferential treatment in certain situations.[29]

PREFERENTIAL TREATMENT

The key issue in affirmative action programs and reverse discrimination is, of course, whether African Americans and women deserve some kind of preferential treatment to compensate them for past wrongs or to promote certain social goals such as reducing social injustice. Regarding the issue of compensation, supporters of preferential treatment argue that since we think veterans are owed preferential treatment because of their service and sacrifice to the country, we may similarly think African Americans and women are owed preferential treatment because of their economic sacrifices, systematic incapacitation, and consequent personal and group losses. Under preferential treatment, no one is asked to give up a job that is already his, as the job for which the white male competes belongs to the community. Thus the community takes the job away from him so that it may make amends. White males as a whole have profited from the wrongs of the community, and many have been direct beneficiaries of policies that excluded or downgraded African Americans and women.[30]

Opponents argue that preferential treatment violates the requirements of compensatory justice by requiring that compensation should come from all the members of a group that contain some wrongdoers and requiring that compensation should go to all the members of a group that contain some injured parties. Only the specific individuals who discriminated against minorities and women in the past should be forced to make reparation of some sort, and they should make reparation only to those specific individuals against whom they discriminated. Affirmative action programs are unfair because the beneficiaries are not the same individuals who were injured by past discrimination and the people who must pay for their injuries are usually not the ones who inflicted these injuries.[31]

Preferential treatment has also been justified as necessary to attain equal justice and strive for a society with greater equality of opportunity. Preferential treatment neutralizes the competitive disadvantage with which women and minorities are currently burdened and helps bring them up to the same starting point. The goal of such programs is the reduction of a great social injustice, not proportional representation of the races in all institutions or professions.[32] Equality for all can only be achieved through temporary preferences given to groups that have historically suffered discrimination. It is perverse to use civil rights law to block the very goals these laws were intended to further.

Opponents argue that affirmative action programs discriminate against white males and thus violate the principle of equality itself by allowing a nonrelevant characteristic to determine employment decisions. They harm women and minorities because such programs imply that women and minorities are so inferior to white males that they need special help to compete. Thus programs based on preferential treatment to attain social justice create social injustices of their own.[33]

Civil rights legislation has been in effect for more than 20 years and affirmative action programs have been in place for more than a decade. While affirmative action may only have been intended as a temporary measure, should corporations now assume that they will be required to indefinitely maintain affirmative action plans based on goals and timetables monitored by the federal government? Or will we look back on affirmative action as a program that peaked in the 1970s and then was phased out as burdensome and associated with reverse discrimination?[34] When will the debt owed to minorities and women because of past discrimination be paid and the books balanced.

> The broad public policy problem is how to recognize and pay the general debt in ways that do not damage investment incentives and that impose no unfair penalties on anyone. A heavy handed approach by government, unions, or corporations risks inflicting a new injustice. Affirmative action is not a punitive concept. It is intended to help produce a fairer distribution of income and opportunity, such as the distribution that presumably would exist today had there been an open and fairly competitive society all along.[35]

The Reagan administration took a stand against preferential treatment when in 1983 the Justice Department asked a federal appeals court to strike down a consent decree in which the New Orleans Police Department agreed to promote one African American for every white officer promoted until half the supervisory jobs were held by African Americans.[36] The Justice Department argued that the court-approved decree violates constitutional protection against discrimination by giving preference to African American workers. Such preferences, the department added, can be given only to compensate individuals rather than classes, who are proven victims of discrimination.[37] "Any promotion quota or other class-based racial preference included in a court-ordered consent decree is unconstitutional," the department argued, "because it would create or establish a racial classification among police officers for which there is no compelling government interest."[38]

These instances were part of a sweeping effort on the part of the administration to reassess and redirect the federal government's civil rights program. The attack on affirmative action policies could eventually affect every employer, public and private, and millions of workers. The administration maintained that it wasn't against affirmative action in principle, but was against the use of quotas and numerical goals to attain civil rights objectives. The administration charged that policies utilizing these techniques, which had been encouraged by the federal government over the past 20 years, were excessive. Quotas and goals don't help African Americans in low-salary jobs, they cause unnecessary paperwork burdens on federal contractors, and give African Americans and women preferential treatment. Affirmative action should be limited to recruitment programs.[39]

This effort to eliminate preferential treatment picked up steam with the appointment in 1985 of Edwin Meese to the office of attorney general. Meese stated that preferential treatment in the form of quotas, goals, and set-asides made no sense either in principle or practice and was nothing short of a moral, legal, and constitutional tragedy.[40] Meese attacked the executive order requiring affirmative action on the part of government contractors, supported the changes already in effect at the EEOC to eliminate the use of statistics to assess complaints of discrimination, and threatened to take action against the policy of giving minority-owned business the right to fixed percentages of federal contracts.[41]

The Bush administration backed off from some of these attacks. It indicated that the foundations of affirmative action would not be attacked. The president would not attempt to rescind the executive order that required federal contractors to adopt preferential hiring and promotion plans. Nor did the administration have any intention of challenging existing consent decrees. However, the Supreme Court began to take the lead in changing the interpretation of affirmative action by a series of 5-to-4 decisions, reflecting the new conservative majority that was put in place during the Reagan administration.[42]

In *Wards Cove* v. *Atonio,* the court ruled that those bringing race bias charges must prove that an employer has no business reason for imposing the job requirement they are contesting. This ruling reversed a 1971 precedent established in *Griggs* v. *Duke Power* where the court ruled that employers must show their hiring and promotion practices were related to job performance even if the practices were not intended to discriminate. The burden was placed on the company to show that a requirement of employment had a manifest relationship to the employment in question. The reversal of this practice was expected to make it more difficult for minorities and women to win cases based on statistics that show disparities in the number of jobs held by white men and those held by women and minorities.[43]

In another case involving firefighters in Birmingham, Alabama, the court allowed white firefighters to challenge an 8-year-old court-approved affirmative action plan if they could show reverse discrimination. The plan had originally been approved in 1981 with federal court approval to settle lawsuits filed by black firefighters charging the city with discrimination in its hiring and promotion practices. The white firefighters alleged in their suit that the plan denied them promotions because of their race and thus was a violation of civil rights legislation. In supporting the decision, Chief Justice Rehnquist stated that "A voluntary settlement . . . between one group of employees and their employer cannot possibly settle, voluntarily or otherwise, the conflicting claims of another group of employees who do not join in the agreement." Thus the challengers were not barred by the consent decree, to which they were not parties, from challenging the preferential promotion of allegedly less-qualified African American firefighters. The challengers had a right to their day in court.[44]

Finally, in *Patterson* v. *McLean Credit Union,* the high court ruled that an 1866 civil rights law does not apply to cases of racial harassment or other discrimination by an employer after a person is hired. This law was passed to allow newly freed slaves to negotiate and enforce contracts. The court ruled that the law prohibits discrimination in hiring but does not allow lawsuits involving harassment on the job or other conditions of employment. This ruling narrowed the application of the law, and as a result, federal judges dismissed at least 96 discrimination claims, 22 of which involved racial or ethnic harassment. The ruling was said to have caused confusion among judges and lawyers, discouraged new litigation, and hampered efforts to settle pending cases out of court.[45]

The effects of these rulings was to make it more difficult to prove discrimination and harassment and opened up more avenues for white males to pursue reverse discrimination suits. Lawyers were said to be turning away clients because many job-discrimination claims were viewed as impossible to win under the new rules and too costly to litigate. The ranks of civil rights lawyers were expected to be thinned.[46] Meanwhile, a coalition of Democrats and liberal and moderate Republicans introduced comprehensive legislation in Congress that would overturn the effects of these decisions. Among other things, this legislation would (1) specify that the 1866 civil rights law covers lawsuits alleging racial harassment on the job, (2) force employers to justify employment practices shown to have a discriminatory impact, and (3) allow workers to challenge discriminatory seniority plans when those plans affect them, rather than when they are adopted.[47] Such legislation passed both houses of Congress in late 1990, but was vetoed by the President.

LAST-IN, FIRST-OUT

Although affirmative action programs have been helpful in getting minorities and females into jobs and more recently have helped them in getting promotions, during a recession the problem becomes one of keeping them in jobs they may have only recently acquired. Because of the last-in, first-out (LIFO) principle, many of the gains that minorities and women may have made during prosperous times are wiped out by a declining economy. The issue here, of course, is one of seniority. Should retroactive seniority be granted to women or minorities or some kind of quota system be adopted for layoffs so the effects of a declining economy are spread across all groups? Or do women and African Americans without seniority or with less seniority than white males have no protection?

Section 703(h) of Title VII seems to exempt bona fide seniority systems and insulate them from discrimination charges, even though the system may be discriminatory in effect. The courts have upheld this exemption as long as the system is not a guise for unlawful discrimination. Thus employees must look to other laws to challenge seniority systems.

One of the first cases dealing with seniority involved African American truck drivers who were hired for city driving only and were kept there because of a discriminatory transfer policy that prevented them from transferring to over-the-road trucking. Finding that African Americans had been denied over-the-road jobs because of this discriminatory policy, the Supreme Court held that granting retroactive seniority back to the date of application was an appropriate remedy.[48]

In 1977, the Supreme Court added some qualifications to the doctrine. In the Teamsters case, the court ruled that even if a seniority system perpetuated preact or even postact discrimination, its bona fide status was not affected.[49] Section 703(h) immunizes all bona fide seniority systems. The key to whether or not a system is bona fide is if it was adopted without a discriminatory motive. This doctrine was upheld in another case involving an employee who was discharged and later rehired, and then sued to obtain seniority back to the date of her original employment even though the seniority system of the company was based solely on current employment. She was originally discharged because of the company's policy of not hiring married flight attendants, a policy that was later abandoned, enabling her to be rehired. The court, however, again said that the seniority system was bona fide and insulated from attack.[50] Lower courts have applied the same interpretation to the application of executive orders, which may not be interpreted as making a bona fide seniority system unlawful.

In 1982, the Supreme Court agreed to hear appeals by the Boston police and firefighters unions, which challenged a federal judge's order that layoffs forced by budget cuts in 1981 should bypass state seniority laws and preserve the level of court-ordered minority employment previously established. Both departments had been under court order since the mid-1970s to increase minority employment to almost 12 percent, but layoffs by seniority would have led to firing half of the African American and Hispanic employees in both departments.[51] The Supreme Court dismissed the case because most of the laid-off workers had been recalled by the time the case was considered and a state law protected them from any further layoffs. In a related case, a ruling by a district judge in New Jersey required that the federal government must compensate white firefighters who are laid off when affirmative action programs protect minority workers with less seniority. The ruling applied to 12 New Jersey cities that had entered into a consent decree with the federal government to admit more African Americans and Hispanics into their fire departments.[52]

But then, in 1984, the Supreme Court upheld seniority again. In a case involving the Memphis Firefighting Department, the court ruled that when seniority systems are involved, only individuals who can prove they are victims of discrimination by an employer may benefit from affirmative action. The case began in 1977, when African American firefighters charged the Memphis department with race discrimination. The city and the African American workers agreed on an affirmative action plan in 1980 that was approved by a federal judge. But in 1981, when Memphis began laying off workers, recently hired African Americans were the first to go because of lack of seniority. The judge then ordered an injunction to preserve the affirmative action percentages while laying off workers. A federal appeals court in Cincinnati upheld this order. But the Supreme Court overruled the order and said it conflicted with Title VII that protects legitimate seniority systems unless the plans are intentionally discriminatory or African American workers can show that they were individually the victims of hiring discrimination.[53]

The Reagan administration used this decision as a wedge to go after consent decrees that had been agreed to in settling previous antidiscrimination suits in cities, counties, school districts, and state agencies across the nation. These decrees involved the use of goals and timetables to assure compliance. Although the decision in the Memphis case addressed layoffs rather than hiring, the administration argued that the Supreme Court decision justified doing away with hiring preferences as well. Under resistance from the jurisdiction themselves, who wanted to avoid lengthy court battles and political problems, the administration eased off somewhat from this attack.[54]

In 1986, the Supreme Court again upheld seniority. In May of that year, the court in a close 5-to-4 vote struck down a Michigan school district plan that was developed to protect minority hiring gains by laying off white teachers ahead of African Americans with less seniority. While most of the teachers were eventually rehired, they filed suit charging that their constitutional rights were violated and sought back pay, damages, and restoration of seniority. In its majority opinion, the court said that these layoffs were too burdensome on the white teachers and that a less intrusive remedy could accomplish much the same purpose with fewer disruptive effects. The court did not, however, reject the concept of affirmative action in remedying the effects of past discrimination.[55]

Thus, the LIFO principle seems to apply in the case of layoffs, and seniority systems that may in effect discriminate are legitimate. Nothing like an affirmative action program on the layoff end of the employment cycle can be adopted. Unions, of course, are not going to give up hard-won seniority provisions to keep new employees on the payroll. But civil rights advocates claim that the Weber decision allows companies and unions to change the seniority system without fearing charges of reverse discrimination. About 80 percent of the nation's work force is not covered by union contracts, however, and companies not involved with unions are not legally bound to use seniority as a basis for layoffs.

Women and Equal Opportunity

COMPARABLE WORTH

The Equal Pay Act made it unlawful for an employer to pay wages "at a rate less than the rate at which he pays employees of the opposite sex in such establishments for equal work on jobs the performance of which requires equal skill, effort, and responsibility, and which are performed under similar working conditions."[56] Thus skill, effort, responsibility, and working conditions were tests to be applied in judging the equality of work. Equal work did not mean, however, that jobs had to be identical or performed with the same frequency. The controlling factor in applying the equal pay standard was job content—actual job requirements and performance—not job titles or classifications.

Perhaps a case will help to clarify the meaning of this standard. Several years ago, Northwest Airlines was found guilty of violating the law by a federal appeals court in Washington.[57] The airline had been paying its 137 male cabin pursers 20 to 55 percent more than its 1,746 female Stewardesses. The men also received such fringe benefits as a laundry allowance for their uniforms and better hotel rooms than the women. The court held that despite the differences in job classification, there were no essential differences in duties between the job of purser and stewardess.[58] Northwest was ordered to pay about $52.5 million in back wages, interest, and other charges to the stewardesses who were discriminated against, the largest reward for an employment discrimination case up to that time.[59] This award was increased to about $60 million by an appeals court that increased the time period used to calculate back pay.

After several years of civil rights laws, however, there is still a disparity between the median incomes of men and women, primarily because women are still channeled into lower-paying jobs, such as secretarial or clerical work. This gap has fluctuated between 57 and 65 percent over the past several years (Table 6.1). Census Bureau figures showed that over the span of their lifetimes, men will probably earn twice as much as women with comparable educational backgrounds. A woman completing high school will earn an average of $381,000 in her lifetime, compared with $861,000 for a man with comparable education. A women with 4 years of college will earn $523,000, whereas a man with a similar education will earn $1,190,000 over his lifetime. The

TABLE 6.1   Median Annual Earnings: 1955–1987

Year	Women	Men	Women's Earnings as % of Men's
1955	$ 2,719	$ 4,252	63.9%
1960	3,293	5,417	60.8
1965	3,823	6,375	60.0
1970	5,323	8,966	59.4
1973	6,335	11,186	56.6
1976	8,099	13,455	60.2
1979	10,151	17,014	59.7
1980	11,197	18,612	60.2
1981	12,001	20,260	59.2
1982	13,014	21,077	61.7
1983	13,915	21,881	63.6
1984	15,607	24,517	63.7
1985	15,926	24,644	64.6
1986	16,232	25,256	64.3
1987	17,504	26,722	65.5

Source: U.S. Department of Labor, Bureau of Labor Statistics, *Handbook of Labor Statistics* (Washington D.C.: U.S. Government Printing Office, various years); U.S. Department of Commerce, *Statistical Abstract of the United States, 1989,* 109th ed. (Washington, D.C.: U.S. Government Printing Office, 1988), p. 448.

bureau's projections assumed a zero growth rate for productivity and were based on 1981 dollars.[60]

Another Census Bureau report, entitled "American Women: Three Decades of Change," showed that from 1947 to 1980, the number of women in the labor force increased 173 percent, from 16.7 million to 45.6 million. But between 1955, when the bureau started keeping such figures, and 1981, salaries of full-time women workers had actually declined from 60.2 percent to 59.7 percent of men's earnings. The earnings disparity was even worse for female managers. Between 1960 and 1980, salaries of such women declined from 58 percent to 55 percent of male manager's earnings, even though the percentage of female managers doubled from 14.5 percent to 28.2 percent over the same period. In 1986, women from the vice-president's level on up were still earning only about half as much as their male counterparts, $124,623 for female executives compared with $213,000 for male executives.[61]

The reason for these disparities, say the feminists, is that women still tend to be concentrated in traditional "women's jobs," which are low-paying. The National Academy of Sciences released a report in 1985 stating that almost half of all employed women work in occupations that are at least 80 percent female, whereas slightly more than half of all men are in occupations at least 80 percent male. Women's average wages are about 60 percent of men's wages for full-time jobs, and as much as 40 percent of that gap, the report claimed, is caused by the segregation of women and men into different occupations.[62]

One way to correct this situation would be for women to step into higher-paying jobs, a process that is taking place, albeit very slowly. There are still strong incentives to channel women into segregated job slots including (1) the cost savings that result from paying women less than comparably qualified men, (2) the fact that women have traditionally acted in nurturing or supporting roles and these are the roles they are assigned in the workplace, and (3) the tendency to treat women as part of a class that is more likely to be absent and temporary without regard to individual characteristics. Thus women are typically channeled into the secondary labor market of dead-end, low-paying jobs.[63]

A faster way of reducing this wage and salary gap would be to stretch the meaning of the equal pay standard to mean equal pay for work of comparable worth. Women's groups argue that job evaluation systems themselves are discriminatory, that jobs held primarily by women, such as secretarial and electronics assembly positions, are just as important to a company as are jobs held primarily by men, such as supervision, engineering, sales, and the like. Thus these traditional women's jobs should receive equal pay because they are of equal worth. Rather than let the market determine pay scales, jobs ought to be evaluated according to their intrinsic worth, a concept with social as well as economic meaning. Such a concept, if implemented, would have a major impact on the way jobs are evaluated and pay scales developed. Content would be rejected as the basis for pay differentials, and worth would be substituted.

The EEOC commissioned the National Academy of Sciences to study whether it is feasible and desirable to develop job evaluation systems that are "fair, objective, comprehensive, and bias-free."[64] The study noted that for "full-time year-round workers, the difference in earnings between men and women is greater than between minorities and non-minorities, and the difference between men and women has not declined while the difference in earnings between minorities and non-minorities has declined."[65] The study concluded that the major reason for this differential was due to persistent discrimination in the labor market, rather than worker characteristics or some other variables. Concerns seeking to eliminate such discrimination by revising job evaluation systems should consider the comparable worth concept, the study stated, because women are often paid less than men because they hold women's jobs that are valued less than men's jobs by employers. However, the study also stated that the value of jobs cannot be determined by scientific methods because hierarchies of job worth are always, at least in part, a reflection of values. Thus the study failed to recommend any specific remedies for the problem.

There are a variety of types of job evaluation systems, but a typical system is based on points assigned to factors that are deemed important in evaluating the worth of a job to the employer. Typical factors of this kind include skill and knowledge requirements, working conditions, physical and mental effort required, amount of responsibility for people and materials, complexity, and consequences of decisions and actions. These points for all the factors are then totaled and these totals for the different jobs are used to determine pay scales.[66]

Critics argue that these job evaluations upon which implementation of the comparable worth concept is based vary considerably according to who is doing the evaluating. Such evaluations are frequently made by an agency's personnel staff, management and employee committees, unions, and consulting firms. All these groups have their own subjective preferences, and all use different evaluation methods. Thus, there is disagreement among such experts as to the true comparability of any set of jobs, and the results of job evaluations are likely to be subjective and reflect the opinions of the evaluator. Studies have been done that show the variability of job evaluation systems in those states that have adopted some form of comparable worth.[67] Such studies raise serious questions about the ability of comparable worth to deliver on its promise of a scientific, objective determination of a job's worth.

The Supreme Court at least opened the door to comparable worth by ruling in favor of women in a case involving prison matrons who were paid only 70 percent as much as prison guards in Washington County, Oregon.[68] The court stated that it did not intend to endorse the principle of comparable worth, but it did rule that Title VII's prohibition of discriminatory employment practices was meant to be broadly inclusive, and thus women were not limited to the instances of unequal pay for equal work when it came to discrimination suits over wages or salaries.[69]

Then in 1983, a federal district judge ruled that the state of Washington was guilty of wage discrimination in paying women employees less than men performing similar kinds of work and must start paying back wages and pay increases to women workers that would cost the state $800 million to $1 billion.[70] The judge said that a special master would work out pay formulas that would raise by about 32 percent the pay of women workers. The thrust of the decision went further than job discrimination within a job category and extended to sex discrimination between and among job categories, thus supporting the comparable worth concept. A study conducted by the state itself showed that employees in job classifications dominated by women were paid an average of 20 percent less than those in male-dominated classifications for work with comparable requirements.

The suit was brought under Title VII of the Civil Rights Act and was the first action to implement the 1981 ruling mentioned earlier. Some believe that this suit would be the "crack in the dam of sex discrimination that has held back women's wages for so long," because it would lend support for dozens of pending suits in other cities, counties, and states.[71] However, an appeals court ruling in 1985 overturned this decision. The appeals court questioned whether comparable worth is a feasible approach to employee compensation and stated that neither law nor logic deems the free market a suspect enterprise. This decision was opposed by the supporters of comparable worth who intended to challenge the ruling. And the governor of the state of Washington stated that despite the decision, the state had every intention of implementing a program aimed at pay equity as directed by the state legislature.[72] Such a program, costing $482 million, was eventually agreed to by state and union negotiators and approved by a federal judge.[73]

In 1985, Los Angeles became the largest city in the nation to adopt the system by adjusting pay scales for men and women so they would be comparable in value based on such factors as education, responsibility, and work conditions. Pay-equity raises will cost the city an estimated $12 million.[74] By 1986, 13 states had laws requiring both public and private employers to pay equally for work that was comparable. Some 30 other states had comparable-worth bills pending or formed commissions to study the issue further. The House of Representatives had passed a bill that requires a comparable-worth study of federal workers. Then in 1987, Ontario, Canada, passed a law that required public sector organizations and private companies with 10 or more employees to restructure pay rates so that women and men would be compensated equally for work that is comparable.[75] In the United States, several companies actually began to implement comparable-worth concepts into their job evaluation systems.[76]

There is some evidence that further progress in closing the wage gap is unlikely. The recent narrowing of the gap is said to have occurred partly because wages for males were hit harder than those for females in the 1981–82 recession, when many layoffs took place in manufacturing, where male workers predominate. Female workers employed in services got off more lightly. But government projections indicate that for the next dozen years or so, the economy will generate fewer of the higher-paid professional jobs in which women have made recent inroads. Of the 21 million new jobs expected to be created from 1986 to 2000, only 17 percent are projected to be in professional fields. Most of the new jobs will be in the clerical and service sectors, which pay below-average wages and are dominated by women. Women have made little progress breaking into the traditional male blue- and white-collar occupations.[77]

SEXUAL HARASSMENT

The issue of sexual harassment received increased attention during the later 1970s and on into the 1980s. When the federal government and the courts began to insist that sexual harassment constituted illegal discrimination in employment, it was no longer a laughing matter. After some major employers lost lawsuits charging them with failure to act against harassment, hundreds of corporations, colleges, hospitals, and other institutions took steps to deal with the problem and protect themselves against lawsuits. Many issued formal policies and some attempted to make employees more sensitive to the problem through training and strengthening internal grievance procedures. The continuing surge of women into the work force, many of them single parents who are particularly vulnerable because of their financial situations, increases the potential for sexual harassment.

The number of sexual harassment lawsuits increased in the early 1980s and were as likely to be filed against a small company as a large corporation. Harassment was charged in 6,342 job-discrimination cases filed in 1984, an increase from the 5,110 claims filed the previous year. In 1985, the number of complaints rose again to 7,273 cases. During the previous 6 years, federal courts had heard about 300 sexual harassment cases.[78] These lawsuits can be divided between so-called quid pro quo cases, where an employee has been promised promotion for sexual favors or has not been advanced because of refusing such sexual advances, and work-environment cases, where sexual harassment creates an environment that is abusive, hostile toward women, and intimidating.

Defining sexual harassment is difficult, let alone proving that it has taken place. In November of 1980, the EEOC issued guidelines to deal with sexual harassment. The EEOC defined sexual harassment as sexual advances of a verbal or physical nature that are unwelcome. To constitute sexual harassment, these types of behavior must meet the following conditions: (1) Submission to such conduct is made explicitly or implicitly a term or condition of employment, (2) submission to or rejection of such conduct is used as a basis for employment decisions affecting the individual, or (3) such conduct has the purpose or effect of unreasonably interfering with an individual's work performance or creating an intimidating, hostile, or offensive working environment.[79]

The employer has strict liability for sexual harassment perpetuated by its agents and supervisors. When the employer knows or should have known of sexual harassment in the workplace and does not take immediate and appropriate action, it will also be held responsible for the actions of nonsupervisory employees and nonemployees. The guidelines also state sex discrimination will be charged against an employer if an employee can prove he or she was qualified but was refused advancement, while a person who submitted to a request for sexual favors received preferential treatment. This provision was upheld by a 1984 decision concerning the first case to be brought under this section of the guidelines. Employers were urged to crack down on such affairs between supervisors and subordinates.[80]

A series of court decisions since 1977 have generally upheld the EEOC's guidelines. Courts have ruled that sexual harassment encompasses not only requested sexual favors but also off-color jokes, sexual leers, pats on the bottom, and requirements for sexually revealing uniforms. In 1986, the Supreme Court ruled that workers may sue their employers for sex discrimination on the grounds that sexual harassment by supervisors created a hostile job environment even if loss of a job or promotion wasn't involved.[81] After this decision, more cases were filed in which the whole environment was alleged to be a source of sexual harassment, rather than the actions of a single individual. In such an environment women are viewed as men's sexual playthings rather than as their equal coworkers.[82]

In order to deal with this problem of sexual harassment, it has been suggested that companies develop formal sexual harassment policies that clearly specify the types of behaviors perceived as sexual harassment. These policies should be communicated, along with the potential penalties for engaging in sexual harassment. In addition, companies should also establish in-house grievance and complaint procedures to be followed in the event of sexual harassment. Established systems of this nature should allow for the resolution of sexual harassment problems before they reach the litigation stage.[83]

Other research has shown that (1) both supervisors and coworkers can sexually harass, (2) sexual harassment can occur when people have just started working together or after they have been working together a long time, (3) sexual harassment can occur in a private or a public place, (4) offensive behavior can be personal comments, asking for a date, or sexual advances, and (5) a harasser need not have harassed repeatedly nor a victim have been victimized repeatedly for a given incident between them to be a case of sexual harassment.[84] These findings have implications for a sexual harassment policy.

One point to remember is that sexual harassment guidelines cover both men and women. In 1982, a male employee of the Wisconsin Department of Health and Social Services won $196,500 in damages for sexual harassment. The plaintiff contended that his female superior demoted him from his job as a disability-insurance supervisor because he refused her sexual advances. The jury believed his contention and also held a higher-level administrator of the agency liable for not remedying the plaintiff's harassment complaints.[85]

RESULTS

By 1986, women constituted 44 percent of the labor force, compared with 12 percent in 1900 and 29 percent in 1950. They provided services that ranged from teaching, air traffic control, medicine, and legal advice to administrative and technical support. The majority of adult women in 1986 (two-thirds of those between the ages of 25 and 54) worked outside the home, and most of these women were married. The sharpest increases have been for women with very young children. About 54 percent of married women with children under the age of six participate in the labor force. The rate for married women with infants is almost 50 percent. Probably because of family responsibilities, more women than men worked part-time, although since 1970 the percent of women with the strongest time commitment to the labor force (full-time and full-year) has risen, whereas the percent with the weakest time commitment (part-time and part-year) has fallen.[86]

Over the next decade, only 15 percent of new entrants to the workforce will be native white males, compared with 47 percent in that category in the late 1980s. Non-whites, women, and immigrants together are expected to make up more than five-sixths of the net additions to the work force between 1990 and the year 2000, although they make up only about half of the work force presently. Almost two-thirds of the new entrants will be women. Some 60 percent of all women of working age are expected to have jobs by the year 2000, and about 47 percent of the work force will be women.

This increase means that demands for day care and for more time off from work for pregnancy leave and child-rearing duties will increase.[87]

During the 1970s and 1980s, women chose a greater variety of occupations. They increased their participation in highly skilled occupations that have been male-dominated. For example, in 1970, when only 38 percent of the total work force was female, women constituted a mere 3 percent of lawyers in the country. By 1988, 20 percent of lawyers were women, and women constituted 40 percent of law students.[88] The number of female doctors has increased from 15,672 in 1960 to 108,200 in 1989, and the number of engineers, from 7,404 to 174,000 over the same time period. The number of women in elected office has more than tripled since 1975 at the local level, although their presence in the U.S. Congress has barely changed.[89]

In 1988, at least 3.7 million of the more than 13 million sole proprietorships in the country were owned by women, which was nearly double the 1.9 million such enterprises they owned 10 years before. These firms generated revenues estimated to be more than $100 billion a year and paid $37 billion in federal taxes and another $13 billion in state and local taxes. The majority of these enterprises were service companies, as women owned nearly half of all retail businesses in the country. But female entrepreneurs were also making headway in manufacturing, construction, mining, and other industries. The Small Business Administration expected that one-half of all self-employed people would be women by the end of the century.[90]

Women remain underrepresented in science and engineering. Only 15 percent of undergraduate engineering students are women, and at the doctoral level, they represent only 7 percent. Just 15 percent of all high-tech professionals are women, and women account for only 4 percent of American's engineers. Part of the problem is the lack of female mentors in engineering schools. Nationwide, women make up a mere 2 percent of the engineering faculty, and they are usually clustered at the assistant-professor level. To break that pattern, The National Science Foundation spent $13 million in 1988 to provide women scientists with research funds and appointments as primary researchers at universities.[91]

Women have actually lost ground in academia. The relative pay of female professors has fallen in recent years. In 1976, women earned 90 percent of what men made, but by 1986, this ratio had fallen to 88 percent. This drop is partly explained by recent hirings of female academics, which means many women are in lower-paying positions as assistant professors. This could change over time as they advance to associate and full professorships. But women are also concentrated in the arts and humanities, in which the jobs pay less than in science, engineering, and business, where men still predominate.[92]

Women presently constitute about 37 percent of corporate managers, compared with about 24 percent a decade earlier. The economic shift from manufacturing to services gives women better opportunities at landing top managerial jobs because this sector accepted women managers earlier. And as the number of women expanded in business schools, man became accustomed to them as peers and were less threatened by women managers moving into corporate positions.[93] In spite of these gains, however, less than 2 percent of top executives of *Fortune* 500 companies are women, and the wage gap increases as women move up the corporate ladder. A report issued by the U.S. Chamber of Commerce found that corporate women at the vice-presidential level earned 42 percent less than their male counterparts.[94]

In early 1989, a firestorm was set off by a *Harvard Business Review* article written by Felice Schwartz in which she proposed formalizing a two-track system for the promotion of women into higher-management positions. The plan would relegate working mothers to a slower career path called the "mommy track," and only women who were willing to set aside family considerations would be placed on the fast track to higher executive positions. Schwartz argued that corporations must find a way to segregate "career-primary" women from "career and family" women in order to cope with high turnover rates of women who quit high-pressure jobs when they cannot reconcile the conflicting needs of work and family. Working mothers would gladly trade advancement and high pay, she argued, for the chance to spend more time with their families, and corporations would benefit from retaining them in less-demanding middle-management positions.[95]

While Schwartz seemed to think her proposal would give women the best of both worlds, many women did not agree. Critics feared that corporations might accept the notion that it was a bad investment to groom working women for higher-level positions, thus reducing the opportunities for women to move into the top ranks of management. Others argued that the idea of a mommy track harked back to the old-fashioned notion of singling out women rather than men to make all the sacrifices to raise children. If such a thing as a mommy track makes sense for companies, why not also a daddy track? Another problem is that such a system would put a woman on a slow track for her whole career, even though the years spent in raising a child constitute only one phase of a woman's life.[96]

Nonetheless, the glass ceiling that prevents many women from moving beyond middle-management still seems to exist in corporate America. Many women feel stuck on the lower rungs of the executive ladder, which is why they leave to become self-employed. These women are more vulnerable to layoffs during downturns in the economy or restructuring of companies. During the recession in the early 1980s, white-collar cutbacks fell more heavily on women than men because women lacked seniority or held managerial positions in such vulnerable support functions as personnel, marketing, finance, and public relations.[97] Many women believe that the playing field for the higher-paying positions in corporate America is anything but level.

The enrollment of women in professional education, however, shows a significant change. By 1989, women made up about 54 percent of all college undergraduates, compared with 20 percent in the 1950s. In 1985, women received 30 percent of the degrees in medicine (up from 13 percent in 1975), 21 percent in dentistry (up from 3 percent in 1975), and 38 percent in law (up from 15 percent in 1975). In the fall of 1985, only 10 percent of women beginning college intended to major in education, whereas 28 percent chose a business major, making it the most popular major for women. While women still represented only 13 percent of engineering majors, this was a significant increase from the 2 percent of a decade earlier.[98]

When these women graduate and begin to take jobs, they are certainly going to make major inroads into management and other white-collar professions. The participation rate for women is expected to average about 60.3 percent by 1995, compared with 53.7 percent in 1985, a jump of almost 7 percent. A 1-percentage-point rise in the participation rate increases the number of women in the job market by nearly 1 million. Thus no matter what wage differential now exists, the forces set in motion by the changing employment patterns of women are expected to prevail during this decade and beyond. Women's income has become essential to maintaining the income levels of most families, as only 19.6 percent of families now fit the traditional pattern of the male breadwinner and female homemaker that was dominant just a few decades ago. Thus the dynamics of the labor market and prevailing social and economic trends are geared to providing increasing opportunities for women, strengthening the pressures against sex-based wage and salary discrimination.[99]

The Experience of African Americans

Some of the figures concerning gains for African Americans in terms of economic progress are not very encouraging. According to some studies, over the past 20 years, the real income of African Americans has fallen by about a third, and their chances of getting into or staying in the middle-class ranks has been cut in half. Some research shows a widening gap between the earnings of similarly educated African Americans and whites. In the mid-1980s, the income of a 20-year-old African American man who graduated from high school was only $6,200 a year, representing a 32 percent drop in real terms from the mid-1960s. For African American men in large cities, the decline in income was 42 percent. By way of comparison, the real incomes of 20-year-old white men fell only 12 percent, no matter where they lived.[100]

African American women who graduated from high school experienced a 32 percent decline in real family income from 1980 to 1985 compared with the 1967–72 period. Comparable white women suffered a decline of only 7 percent. Only 27 percent of African American women ended up with a family income of more than $25,000, whereas 15 years earlier, 51 percent of such women had a comparable middle-class household income. These were women who graduated from high school and did not give birth out of wedlock in their teens. Comparable white women showed a drop to 58 percent in the early 1980s, compared with 66 percent in the 1967–72 period.[101]

Other studies show that in 1984 the average yearly earnings of African American male college graduates, who were most likely to benefit from affirmative action programs, were just 74 percent of their white counterparts. Between 1970 and 1986, the proportion of African American families with inflation-adjusted incomes over $35,000 only increased from 18 to 22 percent.[102] Overall median income of African American families was just 57 percent of whites in 1985, down from 60 percent 15 years earlier. African Americans were twice as likely as whites to be poor and twice as likely to be unemployed. African Americans with at least 1 year of college education have about the same unemployment rate as whites who did not even go to high school.[103] Labor-force participation rates of African American males also seemed to be declining in the late 1980s compared with white males, whereas in 1960 the rates were about equal.[104]

Regarding African American and white families, a Bureau of Labor Statistics report in 1986 indicated that African American families were not keeping up with white families in terms of income gains. From 1985 to 1986, the median weekly earnings of white families rose 5 percent, whereas for the same period the increase for African American families was only 2 percent. The median income in 1986 for white families was nearly 50 percent greater than that for African American families. Much of this disparity was because of the relatively large number of African American families headed by women. According to the study, 43 percent of the 4.7 million African American families with at least one or more wage earners were headed by women, compared with 13 percent of the 36 million white families.[105]

African American families have little accumulated wealth to fall back on in emergency situations. A Census Bureau study released in 1984 showed a median African American household net worth of only $3,397, which was one-eleventh of the median for white families. Some 30 percent of African American households had a zero or negative net worth. Even middle-class households with incomes over $4,000 a month had a median net worth 54 percent below white households with similar incomes. In 1987, African Americans owned fewer than 1 percent of all stocks and bonds held by individuals in the United States. Thus the inequality of African American income seemed to be overshadowed by the inequality of African American wealth.[106]

Although impressive strides were made in the 1970s, in the 1980s campus enrollments of African Americans began to decline. The American Association of State Colleges and Universities found that although the number of African American high school graduates grew between 1975 and 1982, the percentage enrolling in college declined from 31.5 to 28 percent during the same period. This decline was attributed to cuts in federal financial aid and cutbacks in recruitment efforts for minority-group students. Many of these schools were experiencing financial problems of their own and could not aid minority students.[107] In 1988, only 26 percent of African Americans who finished high school went on to college, reflecting further declines. As fewer African Americans finish college, graduate school enrollments decline, and so the number of emerging African American teachers, physicians, and lawyers is declining. African Americans enrollment in MBA programs stalled at 3.7 percent. Fewer African Americans seemed to be traveling the upward-mobility path to better-paying careers.[108]

The situation regarding African American managers shows room for improvement. An article in the June 1982 *Monthly Labor Review* pointed out that African Americans have actually made smaller gains in the workplace during the past 10 years than they did during the previous decade. In 1972, African American men filled only 2.6 percent of all management positions and only slightly more, 3.2 percent, in 1980. African Americans commonly filled positions such as restaurant managers or school administrators, jobs that pay poorly and provide little status. The study concluded that "Blacks were still much less likely to be employed as managers or administrators than their white counterparts during the decade."[109]

Political gains of African Americans made the headlines as the country headed into the decade of the 1990s. David N. Dinkins was sworn in on January 1, 1990, as the first African American mayor of New York City. L. Douglas Wilder became the first African American governor in history, winning his campaign in the state of Virginia. In Seattle, Norman Rice won the race for mayor. More than two decades after enactment of the Voting Rights Act, there were more than 6,500 elected African American officials in the United States, representing a 60 percent increase in a decade and a fourfold increase over the past 15 years. Yet African Americans still hold fewer than 2 percent of the nation's elective offices despite representing 12 percent of the population. There is only one African American governor, and only one state has ever elected an African American U.S. senator.[110]

Questions for Discussion

1. What is discrimination? How does it differ from the other kinds of social relationships that can exist among human groups? Where does the relationship change from friendliness to hostility? How does discrimination enter into employment decisions?

2. Describe the important provisions of the Civil Rights Act with respect to business. What was the general philosophy behind the legislation? What important provisions were added by the 1972 amendments?

3. Describe how Executive Order 11246 and Revised Order No. 4 are examples of the power government has in its role of buyer. Do you think this is a legitimate use of government power? Why or why not? As a taxpayer and as a citizen, how would you vote on this issue?

4. What are the main functions of the Equal Employment Opportunity Commission? What have been some of its major problems? What changes would you recommend to make the EEOC more effective?

5. What is the difference between equal opportunity and affirmative action? What types of affirmative action programs or approaches are there? Why did quotas come into widespread use? Is there a difference between goals and quotas? What is the objective of affirmative action programs?

6. Is preferential treatment of minorities and women morally justified? How can preferential treatment be awarded without reverse discrimination? Does reverse discrimination violate the civil rights laws?

7. Describe the difference between proving intent to discriminate and a result-oriented approach. Which approach seems to be currently favored by the courts? The administration? Why?

8. Describe the Bakke case. Was it a definitive case in its implications for business organizations? Did the Weber case provide more guidance for employers? What were the key provisions of this decision that gave employers some indication of the kind of affirmative action programs that were acceptable?

9. What implications do the cases decided in 1989 have for affirmative action programs? Do the rulings represent a significant departure from the guidelines that had been supported by the courts for many years? Will Congress take steps to change the legal status of affirmative action programs in view of these decisions?

10. What is the relationship between equal employment opportunity and seniority systems? What are the issues that the courts had to consider? Would you be in favor of retroactive seniority for women and minorities? How would this be determined?

11. What was the original meaning of equal work? What does work of comparable worth mean? Are job evaluation systems in and of themselves discriminatory? What makes one job worth more than another?

12. Define sexual harassment and think of some examples from your own experience where this definition might have applied. Do you feel sexual harassment is a serious problem in the workplace? What can be done to make it less of a factor in employee relationships?

13. Why haven't the results of the emphasis on equal opportunity been more promising? Will it take more time for the results to manifest themselves? Is the public policy approach to equal employment opportunity basically flawed? Is there a market approach?

Case: Price Waterhouse _____

Ann Hopkins was a successful manager at Price Waterhouse's Washington office. In 1982, she sought to become a partner in the firm. At that time, Price Waterhouse had 668 partners; only seven were women. Ms. Hopkins was the only woman among the 88 partnership candidates being considered for promotion that year. According to some reports, there was little doubt that Ms. Hopkins was qualified for the position, as she had won at least $34 million worth of major consulting contracts for the company, the best record of all the candidates, and had billed more hours than any of the other candidates in the fiscal year prior to the partnership nominations.[1]

Of the 32 partners who submitted written reviews, 8 abstained from making a recommendation because they didn't know her well enough, 13 wanted her made a partner, 8 did not want to make her a partner, and 3 wanted her candidacy held over for the next go-around. After a lengthy evaluation process, the firm put her candidacy on hold for at least another year and then later decided not to propose her for partnership again. The firm deemed her unsuitable for promotion because she was an overbearing, arrogant, and abrasive manager. In their reviews, some of the partners wrote that Ms. Hopkins had "an abrasive personality and poor interpersonal skills." They noted her "impatience, insensitivity, and use of profanity in dealing with the staff."[2] Others described her as being too "macho" and in need of a "charm school."[3]

After being denied partnership, although 47 of the male candidates were selected, she met with the chief partner in the Washington office, who was one of her big supporters. He offered her a few tips to enhance her chances in the future. In court testimony, Ms. Hopkins said that the chief partner suggested that she "walk more femininely, talk more femininely, dress more femininely," and that she wear makeup, have her hair styled, and wear jewelry. Disgusted by this advice, Hopkins resigned and filed a lawsuit under Title VII of the Civil Rights Act, which says that an employer may not discriminate against an employee because of race, color, religion, sex, or national origin. She claimed that her stridency and occasional cursing would have been overlooked had she been a man because of her exceptional record.[4]

The district judge in the court where she filed ruled in her favor, a decision that was upheld by an appeals court. The district court found that Price Waterhouse had discriminated against Ms. Hopkins by "filtering her partnership candidacy through a system that gave great weight to negative comments and recommendations, despite evidence that those comments reflected unconscious sexual stereotyping by male evaluators based on outmoded attitudes toward women." The court stated that an inability to get along with staff and peers was a legitimate reason to deny partnership, but the "evident sexism" in the firm's evaluation system raised concerns that stereotyping had caused the denial. While Ms. Hopkins had not proved discrimination to be the direct cause of the denial, the firm's decision was tainted because it had failed to root out such evident sexism from its evaluation system.[5]

In upholding the decision, the appeals court was convinced that Price Waterhouse had discriminated against Ms. Hopkins in "subtle and insidious" ways and that it "took no steps to discourage sexism, to heighten the sensitivity of partners to sexist attitudes or to investigate negative comments to ascertain whether they were the product of such attitudes." The appeals court also ruled that it was up to the firm to prove that sex discrimination was not a decisive factor in the decision, and it would have to do this by presenting "clear and convincing" evidence rather than by the less rigorous requirement of a "preponderance" of evidence.[6]

The case was appealed to the Supreme Court, which in a 6-to-3 ruling upheld the decisions of the lower courts. Justice William Brennan, who wrote the lead opinion, stated: "An employer who objects to aggressiveness in women but whose positions require this trait places women in an intolerable and impermissible Catch-22: out of a job if they behave aggressively and out of a job if they don't." The burden of proof was shifted to Price Waterhouse in that it would have to establish that it would have considered Hopkin's partnership application based on purely nondiscriminatory factors. However, the firm would not have to present "clear and convincing" evidence to establish its position but only meet the less-rigorous standard of a "preponderance" of evidence. The firm had been held to too high a standard in earlier rulings, and thus when the case was reheard in a lower federal court, its task would be less onerous.[7]

Women hailed this decision as a victory, believing that this decision would put pressure on firms to root out bias from their evaluation systems. Personnel making promotion decisions would have to be properly trained to ensure that race and sex were not part of the decision. Hopkins, who had become a senior budget officer at the World Bank, declared herself delighted by the decision. The prolonged litigation was an embarrassment for the firm, but even after the litigation was ended, only 28 of the firm's 900 partners were women.[8]

Case Notes

1. Michael J. McCarthy, "Supreme Court to Rule on Sex-Bias Case," *Wall Street Journal*, June 14, 1988, p. 33.
2. Ibid.
3. Andrew Sachs, "A Slap at Sex Stereotypes," *Time*, May 15, 1989, p. 66.
4. McCarthy, "Supreme Court," p. 33.
5. Ibid.
6. Ibid.
7. Sachs, "Sex Stereotypes," p. 66.
8. Ibid.

Chapter Notes

1. Manuel G. Velasquez, *Business Ethics: Concepts and Cases* (Englewood Cliffs, N.J.: Prentice Hall, 1982), p. 266.
2. Howard J. Anderson, *Primer of Equal Employment Opportunity* (Washington, D.C.: The Bureau of National Affairs, Inc., 1978), p. 25.
3. Ibid., p. 35.
4. Reprinted by permission from Michael D. Levin-Epstein, *Primer of Equal Employment Opportunity,* 3d ed. (Washington D.C.: The Bureau of National Affairs, Inc., 1984), pp. 24–25. Copyright © by The Bureau of National Affairs, Inc., Washington, D.C.
5. *Newport News Shipbuilding and Dry Dock Co.* v. *EEOC,* 667 F2d 448 (1982).
6. Levin-Epstein, *Primer,* 1984, p. 58. Copyright © 1984 by The Bureau of National Affairs, Inc., Washington, D.C. Reprinted by permission.
7. Anderson, *Primer,* 1978, p. 60.
8. "For Most Americans, Passage of the ERA is Just a Matter of Time," *Business Week,* August 1, 1983, pp. 92–93. See also "Five Years Later, ERA is Back," *Dallas Times Herald,* January 12, 1987, p. A-4.
9. "Evolution, not Revolution," *Time,* March 26, 1979, p. 25. See also Jane Mayer, "Women's Movement Seeks to Turn Tide for ERA But Faces Barrage by Conservatives in Vermont," *Wall Street Journal,* July 17, 1986, p. 48.
10. Victoria Irwin, "Assessing the Impact of State ERAs," *Christian Science Monitor,* September 29, 1981, p. 18.
11. "The Conservative at the EEOC," *Business Week,* August 9, 1982, p. 54.
12. "A New Drive to 'Reaganize' Equal Opportunity," *Business Week,* March 11, 1985, p. 42.
13. "The New Bias on Hiring Rules," *Business Week,* May 25, 1981, pp. 123–27.
14. "Every Man for Himself," *Time,* September 7, 1981, pp. 8–9.
15. Joann S. Lubin and Andy Pasztor, "White House Softens Its Draft Proposal to Lift Job-Bias Rules for Contractors," *Wall Street Journal,* September 12, 1985, p. 8. See also Joann S. Lubin, "Tentative Affirmative-Action Accord Is Reached by Top Reagan Officials," *Wall Street Journal,* December 11, 1985, p. 5.
16. Levin-Epstein, *Primer,* 1984, pp. 130–31. Copyright © 1984 by The Bureau of National Affairs, Inc., Washington, D.C. Reprinted by permission.
17. "When Antibias Efforts Seem to Discriminate," *Business Week,* October 11, 1982, p. 40.
18. *McDonald* v. *Santa Fe Transportation Co.,* 427 U.S. 273 (1976).
19. *Daniel McAleer and Local #2350, Communications Workers of America* v. *American Telephone and Telegraph Co.* 416 F.Supp. 435 (1976).
20. *Allan Bakke* v. *the Regents of the University of California,* 553 P.2d 1152 (1976).
21. *Regents of the University of California* v. *Bakke,* 98 S.Ct. 2733 (1978).
22. "Bakke Wins, Quotas Lose," *Time,* July 10, 1978, p. 11.
23. *Weber* v. *Kaiser Aluminum Corp.,* 563 F.2d 216 (5th Cir. 1977).
24. *United Steelworkers of America* v. *Weber,* 99 S.Ct. 2721 (1979).

25. "What the Weber Ruling Does," *Time,* July 9, 1979, p. 48.

26. "Court Backs Affirmative Action Plans," *Dallas Times Herald,* July 3, 1986, p. A-1; "A Solid Yes to Affirmative Action," *Time,* July 14, 1986, pp. 22–23.

27. Stephen Wermiel, "High Court Upholds Affirmative Action In Alabama Plan on Police Promotions," *Wall Street Journal,* February 26, 1987, p. 5; "Replying in the Affirmative: For the First Time, The Court Approves Promotion Quotas," *Time,* March 9, 1987, p. 66.

28. Stephen Wermiel, "Supreme Court, in 6–3 Vote, Backs Hiring Goals to Correct Sex Bias," *Wall Street Journal,* March 26, 1987, p. 3.

29. "Balancing Act: In a Sweeping Decision, The High Court Expands Affirmative Action," *Time,* April 6, 1987, pp. 18–20.

30. Judith Jarvis Thomson, "Preferential Hiring," Tom L. Beauchamp and Norman E. Bowie, eds., *Ethical Theory and Business,* 2d ed. (Englewood Cliffs, N.J.: Prentice Hall, 1983), pp. 487–92.

31. Velasquez, *Business Ethics,* pp. 281–82.

32. Thomas Nagel, "A Defense of Affirmative Action," Tom L. Beauchamp and Norman E. Bowie, eds., *Ethical Theory and Business,* 2d ed. (Englewood Cliffs, N.J.: Prentice Hall, 1983), pp. 483–87.

33. See Sonia L. Nazario, "Policy Predicament: Many Minorities Feel Torn by Experience Of Affirmative Action," *Wall Street Journal,* June 27, 1989, p. A-1.

34. Daniel Seligman, "Affirmative Action is Here to Stay," *Fortune,* April 19, 1982, p. 144.

35. Richard F. America, "Affirmative Action and Redistributive Ethics," *Journal of Business Ethics,* Vol. 5, No. 1 (February 1986), p. 77.

36. Robert E. Taylor, "New Attack on Affirmative Action Quotas Begun by U.S. in New Orleans Police Case," *Wall Street Journal,* January 10, 1983, p. 5.

37. "EEOC Reverses Stand on New Orleans Suit Due to Pressure From Justice Department," *Wall Street Journal,* April 7, 1983, p. 17.

38. John H. Bunzel, "Hiring and Firing by Quotas," *Wall Street Journal,* January 21, 1983, p. 14.

39. Joe Davidson and Linda M. Watkins, "Jobs Debate: Quotas in Hiring are Anathema to President Despite Minority Gains," *Wall Street Journal,* October 24, 1985, p. 1.

40. Ibid. See also William B. Allen, Drew S. Days III, Benjamin L. Hooks, and William Bradford Reynolds, "Is Affirmative Action Constitutional?" *Regulation,* Vol. 9, No. 4 (July–August 1985), pp. 12–45.

41. Stephen H. Wildstrom, "Ed Meese is Taking a Jackhammer to Affirmative Action," *Business Week,* September 2, 1985, p. 41.

42. Paula Dwyer, "The Blow To Affirmative Action May Not Hurt That Much," *Business Week,* July 3, 1989, pp. 61–62.

43. Stephen Wermiel, "Standards for Proving Bias Charges Are Toughened in High Court Ruling," *Wall Street Journal,* June 6, 1989, p. A-28.

44. Stephen Wermiel, "Workers Hurt By Affirmative Action May Sue," *Wall Street Journal,* June 13, 1989, p. A-3.

45. "Report: Civil Rights Set Back By Ruling," *Times-Picayune,* November 20, 1989, p. A-4.

46. Arthur S. Hayes, "Job-Bias Litigations Wilts Under High Court Rulings," *Wall Street Journal,* August 22, 1989, p. B-1.

47. John E. Yang, "Job-Bias Bill Is Introduced By Coalition," *Wall Street Journal,* February 8, 1990, p. A-3. See also John E. Yang, "Job-Bias Measure Aimed at Overturning High Court Decisions Clears Senate Unit," *Wall Street Journal,* April 5, 1990, p. A-22.

48. *Harold Franks* v. *Bowman Transportation Co.,* 419 U.S. 1050 (1976).

49. *Teamsters* v. *U.S. (T.I.M.E.-D.C., Inc.)* 14 FEP Cases 1514 (1977).

50. *United Airlines* v. *Evans,* 14 FEP Cases 1510 (1973).

51. Stephen Wermiel, "Justices to Hear Case Involving Seniority Layoffs," *Wall Street Journal,* November 2, 1982, p. 3.

52. "U.S. Must Pay Affirmative Action Victims, Judge Says," *Dallas Times Herald,* May 4, 1984, p. A-5.

53. Stephen Wermiel, "Justices Limit Affirmative Action Plans When Seniority of Other Workers Affected," *Wall Street Journal,* June 13, 1984, p. 2.

54. Andy Pasztor, "Opposition Is Growing to U.S. Attempt to End Hiring Quotas of Municipalities," *Wall Street Journal,* May 24, 1985, p. 8; Andy Pasztor, "Justice Agency Eases Its Effort to Stop Racial Quotas in Hiring by Localities," *Wall Street Journal,* June 5, 1985, p. 10. In the summer of 1986, the Justice appeared to finally end these efforts. Andy Pasztor, "Justice Department Ends Bid to Overturn Affirmative Action Plan in Indianapolis," *Wall Street Journal,* August 5, 1986, p. 4.

55. "Court Rejects Minority Job Protection," *Dallas Times Herald,* May 20, 1986, p. A-5.

56. Anderson, *Primer,* 1978, p. 65.

57. *Laffey* v. *Northwest Airlines,* 13 FEP Cases 1068 (1970).

58. Lee Smith, "The EEOC's Bold Foray into Job Evaluation," *Fortune,* September 11, 1978, p. 59.

59. "Northwest Air Ordered to Pay $52.5 Million in a Sex-Bias Case," *Wall Street Journal,* December 1, 1982, p. 24.

60. "Battle of the Sexes Isn't Much of a Fight in the Salary Arena," *Wall Street Journal,* March 14, 1983, p. 5.

61. Timothy D. Schellhardt, "Despite Surge in Women Workers' Ranks, Pay Slid to 59.7% of Men's, Agency Finds," *Wall Street Journal,* October 11, 1983, p. 41; Michael J. McCarthy, "Women's Salaries Reflect Disparities in Executive Suites," *Wall Street Journal,* December 1, 1986, p. 29.

62. Cathy Trost, "Restrictions Keep Women in Low-Pay Jobs, Study Says," *Wall Street Journal,* December 12, 1985, p. 15.

63. Frances C. Hunter, *Equal Pay For Comparable Worth: The Working Woman's Issue of the Eighties* (New York: Praeger, 1986), p. 10.

64. Ibid., p. 60.

65. Donald J. Treiman and Heidi I. Hartman, eds., *Women, Work, and Wages: Equal Pay for Jobs of Equal Value* (Washington, D.C.: National Academy Press, 1981), p. 16.

66. Hunter, *Equal Pay For Comparable Worth,* p. 16.

67. See Richard E. Burr, *Are Comparable Worth Systems Truly Comparable* (St. Louis, Mo.: Washington University Center for the Study of American Business, 1986).

68. *County of Washington et al.* v. *Alberta Gunther et al.,* 452 U.S. 161 (1981).

69. "Breakthrough in the Wage War," *Time,* June 22, 1981, p. 70.

70. *American Federation of State, County, and Municipal Employees, et al.* v. *State of Washington, et al.,* 578 F. Supp 846 (1983).

71. "Group Predicts Sex-Bias Suits Against Employers to Increase," *Dallas Times Herald,* December 21, 1983, p. D-7.

72. Carrie Dolan and Leonard M. Apcar, "Washington State Union to Fight Ruling That Hurts Equal Pay-Equal Jobs Drive," *Wall Street Journal,* September 6, 1985, p. 6.

73. "Comparable Worth Pay Plan Approved," *Dallas Times Herald,* April 12, 1986, p. A-7.

74. "Typist-Driver: Los Angeles Adjusts its Salaries," *Time.* May 20, 1985, p. 23.

75. Jolie Solomon, "Pay Equity Gets a Tryout in Canada—And U.S. Firms Are Watching Closely," *Wall Street Journal,* November 28, 1988, p. B-1. See also Lynne Kilpatrick, "In Ontario, Equal Pay for Equal Work Becomes a Reality, but Not Very Easily," *Wall Street Journal,* March 9, 1990, p. B-1.

76. Comparable Worth: It's Already Happening, *Business Week,* April 28, 1986, pp. 52, 56.

77. Aaron Bernstein, "So You Think You've Come A Long Way, Baby?" *Business Week,* February 29, 1988, pp. 48–52.

78. Sexual Harassment: Companies Could Be Liable," *Business Week,* March 31, 1986, p. 35.

79. 29 CFR, Sec. 1604.11.

80. "An Office Romance Unfairly Discriminated Against a Worker, a Court Says," *Wall Street Journal,* March 20, 1984, p. 1.

81. Stephen Wermiel and Cathy Trost, "Justices Say Hostile Job Environment Due to Sex Harassment Violates Rights," *Wall Street Journal,* June 20, 1986, p. 2.

82. Joseph Pereira, "Women Allege Sexist Atmosphere In Offices Constitutes Harassment," *Wall Street Journal,* February 10, 1988, p. 19.

83. David E. Terpstra and Douglas D. Baker, "Outcomes of Sexual Harassment Charges, *Academy of Management Journal,* Vol. 31, No. 1 (1988), p. 193.

84. Kenneth M. York, "Defining Sexual Harassment In Workplaces: A Policy-Capturing Approach," *Academy of Management Journal,* Vol. 32, No. 4 (1989), p. 847.

85. "Role Reversal: Man Wins Office Sex Suit," *Business Week,* August 2, 1982, p. 19.

86. *Economic Report of the President* (Washington, D.C.: U.S. Government Printing Office, 1987), pp. 209–212.

87. Task Force on Economic Growth, Louisiana Department of Labor, *Louisiana 2000,* December 1988, pp. 10–11.

88. Anastasia Toufexis, "Now for a Woman's Point of View," *Time,* April 17, 1989, pp. 51–52.

89. Claudia Sallis, "Onward, Women!" *Time,* December 4, 1989, p. 82.

90. Janice Castro, "She Calls All the Shots," *Time*, July 4, 1988, pp. 54–57.

91. Naomi Freundlich, "Making Science More Seductive To Women On Campus," *Business Week*, August 28, 1989, p. 89.

92. Bernstein, "So You Think You've Come A Long Way," p. 52.

93. Laurie Baum, "Corporate Women: They're About To Break Through To The Top," *Business Week*, June 22, 1987, pp. 72–78.

94. Sallis, "Onward, Women!" p. 85.

95. Janice Castro, "Rolling Along the Mommy Track," *Time*, March 27, 1989, p. 72.

96. Ibid. See also Elizabeth Ehrlich, "The Mommy Track," *Business Week*, March 20, 1989, pp. 126–34; Robert J. Samuelson, "The Daddy Track," *Newsweek*, April 3, 1989, p. 47.

97. Joann S. Lubin, "White-Collar Cutbacks are Falling More Heavily on Women Than Men," *Wall Street Journal*, November 9, 1982, p. 29. See also Carol Hymowitz, "Layoffs Force Blue-Collar Women Back Into Low-Paying Job Ghetto, *Wall Street Journal*, March 6, 1985, p. 33.

98. *Economic Report of the President*, pp. 216–17.

99. "The Lasting Changes Brought by Women Workers," *Business Week*, March 15, 1982, p. 64. See also Peter Dubno, "Attitudes Toward Women Executives: A Longitudinal Approach, *Academy of Management Journal*, Vol. 28, No. 1 (March 1985), pp. 235–239.

100. "Blacks Play by the Rules and Still Lose, Study Says," *Times-Picayune*, November 5, 1989, p. A-16.

101. Ibid.

102. Dick Thompson, "Unfinished Business," *Time*, August 7, 1989, pp. 12–15.

103. Michel McQueen, "Dream Deferred: Despite Their Wider Influence, Black Leaders Find Goals for Black Poor Elusive," *Wall Street Journal*, July 30, 1987, p. 46.

104. James J. Heckman, "Murky Numbers on Black Economic Progress," *Wall Street Journal*, August 22, 1989, p. A-14.

105. "Incomes of Whites Soar Over Blacks," *Dallas Times Herald*, April 22, 1986, p. A-2. See also Mark August, "For U.S. Blacks, Parity is Still a Dream," *Dallas Times Herald*, January 1, 1987, p. K-1.

106. James E. Ellis, "The Black Middle Class," *Business Week*, March 14, 1988, pp. 62–70.

107. Linda M. Watkins, "Losing Ground: Minorities' Enrollment In College Retreats After Its Surge in '70s," *Wall Street Journal*, May 29, 1985, p. 1. See also "Dramatic Drops for Minorities," *Time*, November 11, 1985, p. 84.

108. Ellis, "The Black Middle Class," pp. 62–70.

109. "The Myth of the Black Executive," *Time*, December 6, 1982. See also Larry Reibstein, "Many Hurdles, Old and New, Keep Black Managers Out of Top Jobs," *Wall Street Journal*, July 10, 1986, p. 25.

110. McQueen, "Dream Deferred," p. 46.

Suggested Reading

AARON, HENRY, AND CAMERAN LOUGY. *The Comparable Worth Controversy*. Washington, D.C.: Brookings, 1986.

ALLPORT, GORDON. *The Nature of Prejudice*, Cambridge, Mass.: Addison-Wesley, 1954.

ANDERSON, HOWARD J. *Primer of Equal Employment Opportunity*, Washington, D.C.: The Bureau of National Affairs, Inc., 1978.

BOLES, JANET K. *The Politics of the Equal Rights Amendment: Conflict and the Decision Process*. New York: Longman, 1979.

BOWIE, NORMAN E., ed. *Equal Opportunity*. New York: Westview, 1988.

BROWNLEE, W. ELLIOT, AND BROWNLEE, MARY M. *Women in the American Economy: A Documentary History, 1675 to 1929*. New Haven, Conn.: Yale University Press, 1976.

COYLE, ANGELA, AND JANE SKINNER, eds. *Women and Work*. New York: NYU Press, 1988.

FULLINWIDER, ROBERT K. *The Reverse Discrimination Controversy: A Moral and Legal Analysis*. Totowa, N.J.: Rowman and Littlefield, 1980.

GLAZER, NATHAN. *Affirmative Discrimination: Ethnic Inequality and Public Policy.* New York: Basic Books, 1975.

GOLDMAN, ALAN H. *Justice and Reverse Discrimination,* Princeton, N.J.: Princeton University Press, 1979.

GORDON, FRANCINE E., AND STROBER, MYRA H., eds. *Bringing Women into Management.* New York: McGraw-Hill, 1975.

GUTEK, BARBARA A. *Sex and the Workplace.* San Francisco: Jossey-Bass, 1985.

HUNTER, FRANCES C. *Equal Pay for Comparable Worth: The Working Woman's Issue of the Eighties.* New York: Praeger, 1986.

JENKINS, RICHARD, AND JOHN SOLOMOS, eds. *Racism and Equal Opportunity: Policies in the 1980s.* Cambridge: Cambridge University Press, 1987.

KELLOUGH, J. EDWARD. *Federal Equal Employment Opportunity Policy and Numerical Goals and Timetables: An Impact Assessment.* New York: Praeger, 1989.

LEVIN-EPSTEIN, MICHAEL D. *Primer of Equal Employment Opportunity,* 4th ed. Washington D.C.: Bureau of National Affairs, 1987.

MASON, PHILIP, *Race Relations.* London: Oxford University Press, 1970.

PINKNEY, ALPHONSO. *The Myth of Black Progress.* New York: Cambridge University Press, 1984.

PLAYER, MACK A. *Employment Discrimination Law: Cases and Materials,* 2d ed. St. Paul: West, 1984.

RAPOPORT, JOHN D., AND BRIAN L. ZEVNIK. *The Employee Strikes Back.* New York: Macmillan, 1989.

REICH, MICHAEL. *Racial Inequality: A Political-Economic Analysis.* Princeton, N.J.: Princeton University Press, 1981.

REID, PETER C. *The Employer's Guide to Avoiding Job-Bias Litigation.* New York: McGraw-Hill, 1986.

REMIK, HELEN, ed. *Comparable Worth and Wage Discrimination: Technical Possibilities and Political Realities.* Philadelphia: Temple University Press, 1985.

TORRINGTON, DEREK, AND TREVOR HITNER. *Management and the Multi-Racial Work Force.* New York: Gower, 1982.

TREIMAN, DONALD J., AND HEIDI I. HARTMANN, eds. *Women, Work, and Wages: Equal Pay for Jobs of Equal Value.* Washington, D.C.: National Academy Press, 1981.

7

Occupational Safety and Health

The safety problem in workplaces relates to injuries that result from hazardous conditions that go uncorrected. Occupational injuries are generally noninfectious and nonchronic and are usually traumatic events that happen to workers. The causes of injuries are not difficult to recognize and define as being work related. There is usually some hazardous condition such as an unguarded machine or unsafe ladder that is directly related to the injury. Thus a program aimed at reducing injuries in the workplace must reduce these hazardous conditions in the workplace.

Illnesses, on the other hand, are more often than not difficult to define operationally, and it is not always clear that an illness can be attributed to a specific workplace hazard. Illnesses such as cancer have long latency periods and multiple causes, and employees with varying levels of susceptibility are exposed to many substances both on and off the job that may or may not act in a synergistic fashion to cause the illness. Thus the health problem in workplaces is much more complex than is the safety problem, and a program directed at dealing with illnesses in the workplace must deal with reducing exposure to hazardous substances in the work environment.[1]

The Bureau of Labor Statistics (BLS) in 1984 estimated the number of work-related deaths and disabling injuries at 5.75 million workers.[2] This estimate was based on industries that employ 11 or more workers. The National Institute for Occupational Safety and Health (NIOSH) estimated the total number of workers injured each year to be 10 million, a number that represents about 7 percent of the total labor force in the United States. The Division of Safety Research (DSR) in NIOSH estimated that during an 8-hour day, a worker is injured every 1.5 seconds. Another worker experiences a fatal injury about every 12 minutes.[3] The BLS survey also showed that about 98 percent of lost workdays are due to injuries; in comparison only 2 percent are due to illnesses. These data suggest that the occupational safety and health problem is largely a safety problem related to injuries in the workplace.[4]

Safety and health problems in the workplace are nothing new, even though it sometimes seems as if they did not exist until relatively recently. This is obviously not the case, since accidents have always occurred in the workplace. Even before the use of power machinery was widespread, people still suffered injuries from falls, dropped equipment or materials, and horse bites. Some of these injuries were all the more serious then because inadequate medical attention often turned a minor injury into a serious one or in some cases even a permanent physical impairment.[5]

The coming of industrialization and the increased use of power machinery ushered in a new era of occupational hazard and danger. ''The introduction of machinery with its moving gears, cutting blades, and power operation that continued until shut off, regardless of fingers or hands that might be caught, brought a new type of hazard and a tremendous number of work injuries.''[6] Industrialization brought a rapid expansion of facilities and jobs where new hazards (power machinery, chemicals, heat, electricity) were combined with large numbers of workers (without much training or experience) working long hours. The results in terms of an increased number of accidents were predictable.

While the possibility of accidents was most prevalent during the early years of industrialization, problems of occupational health were not entirely unknown. Such problems as "brass chills," "painter's colic" (from lead poisoning), and "grinder's consumption" (from inhaling dust) were known to exist. Other problems, such as those exhibited by hat makers who used mercury in curing beaver furs, were also fairly common.

Society, however, gave little or no thought to the notion of occupational safety and health. The dramatic oversupply of labor in the late 1800s and early 1900s made workers so cheap that labor was thought of as a commodity to be secured at the lowest possible price rather than a human resource to be carefully husbanded for humanitarian or economic reasons. Because much of the work done was of an unskilled nature, investment in training and experience was low, making replacement of injured workers much cheaper than efforts to protect them from hazards in the workplace.

Safety efforts were seen as directly conflicting with the maximization of profits, and many owners and managers tended to take an extremely cavalier attitude toward them. Statements such as "I don't have money for frills like safety," "we're not in business for safety," or "some people are just accident prone and no matter what you do, they'll hurt themselves in some way" were representative of employers' feelings on the subject.[7]

Interestingly enough, employees' attitudes were often similar. Accidents were accepted as simply part of working for a living and it was believed they could not be eliminated. This attitude may have been fostered by the protestant ethic, which contained a certain sense of fatalism and created the expectation of a life full of adversity. Workers did not expect safety to receive much attention from employers and learned to accept the unsafe conditions that existed in many of the nation's workplaces.

The attitude of the courts and common law doctrine toward workplace injuries reflected this social climate. These legal defenses were available to employers that in effect barred employees from recovering damages. These defenses were "assumption of risk," "contributory negligence," and the "fellow servant" doctrine. The courts generally held that employees accepted all the customary risks associated with an occupation when they took a job and that if injured they could sue and collect damages from an employer only if (1) they could prove the employer was negligently at fault, (2) they could prove that they had not contributed to the accident through their own negligence, and (3) none of their fellow employees contributed to the accident through their negligence.[8]

Given the difficulty of making these proofs, suits against employers were uncommon and awards to employees rare. Employees were understandably reluctant to risk their jobs to sue an employer, and fellow employees were similarly reluctant to risk their jobs to testify on the injured party's behalf. Even if an injured employee should be brave enough to sue and fortunate enough to win, legal fees usually ate up a good portion of any award. Thus the liability law of these early years failed to protect employees, proved wasteful of time and money (for legal action), and failed to stimulate any action toward accident prevention.

The first substantial effort to promote safety and health in the workplace came from the states in the form of worker's compensation laws. These laws required the employer to either carry insurance to cover damages or to pay out of pocket damages to employees injured on the job regardless of who was at fault. There was at first some question about the constitutionality of such laws since they did in effect seize property without any determination of guilt or fault, but it was held that in view of the public interest involved, it should be a matter of public policy that the employer be liable for injuries occurring to employees on the job. Medical care or compensation for workers should be one of the costs of doing business.

These laws left business free to deal with the safety problem as it saw fit. If business could reduce accidents and lower its insurance premiums (usually based on a 3-year moving accident average) and operating costs and thus save money overall, it was free to take this course of action. If, on the other hand, measures to reduce accidents would be prohibitively costly, business was not forced to undertake them with subsequent loss to itself and society through higher costs, lower production, and economic inefficiency. Business, however, would be required to pay the costs of doing business associated with injuries in the workplace.

Worker's compensation laws brought insurance companies into the accident-prevention field. They were able to interest business in substantial accident-prevention programs because lower accident frequency and severity rates meant lower insurance premiums. Many firms thus discovered that safety is good business—an effective safety program so increased efficiency and decreased accident costs that cost savings outweighed the program's expenditures. For example, A. H. Yound, when vice president of U.S. Steel, estimated that his company saved $117 million in a 30-year period as a result of a safety program costing only $25 million. There were also examples where safety modifications of existing systems more than tripled output while eliminating safety hazards, or where safety redesign turned a wood-working department's operations around from a loss to a profit.[9]

Such examples, however, were not widespread enough to make a significant impact on the safety and health problem as a whole. The system of worker's compensation laws was criticized by a temporary National Commission on State Worker's Compensation Laws. In 1972, the Commission noted that only 22 of the 50 states met even half of the criteria suggested by the Labor Department for state systems. Its recommendations included the extension of coverage to all workers, increased benefit levels, removal of dollar and time limits on compensation, and fuller coverage of occupational diseases.[10]

State regulation was also attempted, but state laws varied widely in their stringency and coverage, and many were enforced only weakly. The weight of testimony at the congressional hearings on the subject of occupational safety and health established the bankruptcy of the state system of regulation. Among the numerous complaints were the failure of state laws to provide authority for entry into plants, grossly inadequate funding and staffing, advance notification to employers of an inspection, obsolete standards with little or no provision for updating them, and failure to furnish reports of inspections to employees affected.[11]

Then a coal-mine explosion in Farmington, West Virginia, in 1968 killed 78 miners. This event, coupled with revelations of the extent of black-lung disease, promoted a national compaign for federal legislation, which eventually resulted in the Federal Coal Mine Health and Safety Act of 1969. This experience of the coal miners was not lost on organized labor in other industries as they increasingly became aware of the hazardous conditions under which they were working.

Pressures mounted for a federal system of regulation covering all industries. The final impetus came from studies such as one by the National Safety Council in 1970, which estimated that more than 14,000 workers died on the job and another 2.2 million suffered disabling injuries each year as a result of accidents at work. Other studies estimated that there might be at least 100,000 deaths and 390,000 new cases of disabling diseases each year caused by exposure to such substances as asbestos, lead, silica, carbon monoxide, and cotton dust.[12] Supporters of federal regulation also cited what the House Committee on Education and Labor called the "on-the-job health and safety crisis." Injury rates had reversed their long-term downward trend and had been rising since the mid-1950s, so the report claimed. From 1960 to 1970, for example, the rate of accidents in manufacturing rose 26.7 percent, an increase explained only in part by cyclical economic factors and the changing composition of the labor force. [13]

Provisions of the Occupational Safety and Health Act

Thus the federal government finally came to the workplace to deal with the safety and health problem in the form of the Occupational Safety and Health Act of 1970 (Williams-Steiger Act). The act was passed by a bipartisan Congress "to assure so far as possible every working man and woman in the Nation safe and healthful working conditions and to preserve our human resources."[14] Under the act, the Occupational Safety and Health Administration (OSHA), which has legislative and executive functions with respect to safety and health programs, was created. Congress outlined several specific means for OSHA to implement this mandate by giving it responsibility to

- Encourage employers and employees to reduce workplace hazards and to implement new or improved existing safety and health programs.
- Provide for research in occupational safety and health and develop innovative ways of dealing with occupational safety and health problems.
- Establish "separate but dependent responsibilities and rights" for employers and employees for the achievement of better safety and health conditions.
- Maintain a reporting and record-keeping system to monitor job-related injuries and illnesses.
- Establish training programs to increase the number and competence of occupational safety and health personnel.
- Develop mandatory job safety and health standards and enforce them effectively.
- Provide for the development, analysis, evaluation and approval of state occupational safety and health programs.[15]

At the time of its passage, OSHA covered every employer in a business affecting commerce that had one or more employees. The act did not affect workplaces covered under other federal laws such as the Coal Mine Health and Safety Act and the Federal Metal and Nonmetallic Safety Act. It also did not cover self-employed persons and farms on which only immediate members of the family were employed. Federal, state, and local government employees were covered under separate provisions in the act for public employment.

EXHIBIT 7.1

Department of Labor
Occupational Safety and Health Administration
200 Constitution Avenue NW, Washington, D.C. 20210

Purpose: To develop and enforce worker safety and health regulations.

Regulatory Activity: This agency (1) sets standards to protect workers against safety and health hazards: (2) conducts workplace inspections to enforce these regulations and may issue citations and propose financial penalties for alleged violations: (3) approves, provides, and monitors half the funding for state-administered occupational safety and health programs: (4) requires employers to report workplace accidents that result in fatalities or the hospitalization of five or more workers; and (5) requires employers with 10 or more employees to keep and post in the workplace records of job injuries and illnesses.

Established: December 29, 1970

Legislative Authority:
  Enabling Legislation: Occupational Safety and Health Act of 1970 (84 Stat. 1590; P.L. 91-596)
  OSHA develops standards that supersede those issued under the following acts:
    Longshoremen's and Harbor Workers' Compensation Act of 1927 (44 Stat. 1444)
    Walsh-Healey Act of 1936 (49 Stat. 2036)
    Service Contract Act of 1965 (79 Stat. 1034: P.L. 89-286)
    Construction Safety Act of 1969 (83 Stat 96: P.L. 91-54)

Organization: OSHA, an agency with the Department of Labor, is headed by an assistant secretary.

Note: OSHA regulations do not cover self-employed persons or any family-owned and operated farms and workplaces already regulated by other federal agencies. Federal agencies are not covered by OSHA workplace standards but must submit annual reports to OSHA on the status of their job safety and health programs.

Budgets and Staffing, Fiscal 1975–90

	1975	1980	1985	1986	1987	1988	(Estimated) 1989	1990
Budget ($ millions)	97	191	220	209	228	234	245	253
Staffing	2,435	3,015	2,176	2,092	2,141	2,352	2,415	2,403

Source: Adapted from Ronald J. Penoyer, *Director of Federal Regulatory Agencies,* 2d ed. (St. Louis, Mo.: Washington University Center for the Study of American Business, 1980), p. 68. Reprinted with permission.

ADMINISTRATIVE STRUCTURE

Occupational Safety and Health Administration. Located in the Department of Labor, this agency has legislative and executive functions with respect to the federal safety and health program (see Exhibit 7.1). The major responsibilities of OSHA are to set and enforce standards related to safety and health in the workplace, work with the states in developing their own safety and health programs, and establish record-keeping requirements that employers are required to follow.

EXHIBIT 7.2

Occupational Safety and Health Review Commission
1825 K Street NW, Washington, D.C. 20006

Purpose: To rule on contests initiated by employers or employees subsequent to a workplace inspection by the Occupational Safety and Health Administration (OSHA).

Regulatory Activity: The Commission acts as a court to rule on alleged job safety and health violations cited by OSHA that are contested by employers or employees after a workplace inspection.

Established: April 28, 1971

Legislative Authority:
  Enabling Legislation: Occupational Safety and Health Act of 1970 (84 Stat. 1590)

Organization: This is an independent agency consisting of three commissioners appointed by the president with the advice and consent of the Senate, and 45 Administrative Law Judges in nine regional offices.

			Budgets and Staffing, Fiscal 1975–90				*(Estimated)*	
	1975	*1980*	*1985*	*1986*	*1987*	*1988*	*1989*	*1990*
Budget ($ millions)	5	7	6	5	5	5	6	6
Staffing	172	165	94	90	90	90	90	88

Source: From Ronald J. Penoyer, *Directory of Federal Regulatory Agencies,* 2d ed. (St. Louis, Mo.: Washington University Center for the Study of American Business, 1980), p. 44. Reprinted with permission.

National Institute for Occupational Safety and Health. This agency is located in the Department of Health and Human Services and is the research arm of the program. NIOSH conducts research into safety and health-related problems and recommends criteria to OSHA for consideration in setting of standards. It also undertakes education and training programs and performs work in the area of safety engineering.

When conducting research, NIOSH can make workplace inspections and gather testimony from employers and employees about workplace hazards. NIOSH can require that employers measure and report employee exposure to potentially hazardous materials and provide medical examinations and tests to determine the incidence of occupational illness among employees.

Occupational Safety and Health Review Commission. This commission is the judicial arm of the safety and health program (see Exhibit 7.2). It handles the appeals of employers on violations and penalties because of OSHA inspections. Because of its need to be objective, it was established as an independent agency. The commission has three members who are appointed by the president for staggered 6-year terms. When an appeal is filed with OSHRC, an administrative law judge normally hears the case and makes a decision. This decision can be appealed to the full commission which may review the judge's decision. The final judgment of OSHRC can be appealed to a U.S. Court of Appeals and possibly reach the U.S. Supreme Court if certiorari is granted.

STANDARD SETTING

A safety or health standard has been defined as "a legally enforceable regulation governing conditions, practices, or operations to assure safe and healthful workplaces."[16] There are two types of standards on safety: (1) horizontal regulations that apply to all industries and relate to such items as fire extinguishers, electrical groundings, railings, machine guards, and the like and (2) vertical provisions that apply to particular industry groups, such as the maritime industry and construction. OSHA safety standards fall into four major categories: general industry, maritime, construction, and agriculture.

Health standards relate to particular substances such as benzene, lead, or cotton dust that workers may come into contact with in one way or another. These standards are published in the *Federal Register* along with all amendments, corrections, insertions, or deletions involving standards. The standard-setting process can begin at the initiative of OSHA or on petitions from other parties such as the secretary of Health and Human Services (HHS), NIOSH, state and local governments, employer or labor representatives, any nationally recognized standards producing organization, or any other interested person. Once it is determined that a specific standard is needed, any one of several advisory committees may be called on to develop specific recommendations. There are two standard committees of this kind (see box), and ad hoc committees may be appointed to examine special areas of concern.

OSHA must follow standard procedures for adopting a standard such as publishing its intentions in the *Federal Register* as a "Notice of Proposed Rulemaking," providing time for comments or public hearings, and publishing the full and final text of the standard and the date it becomes effective. Since OSHA is located in the executive branch, it is also subject to the provisions of executive order requiring a benefit-cost analysis. Once a final standard is issued, persons adversely affected can apply for a judicial review of the standard. Employers can also ask for variances to be granted if they cannot fully comply by the effective date or can prove their facilities already provide protection at least as effective as required by the standard. These variances can be temporary, permanent, or experimental. The latter has to be approved by the secretary of either HHS or Labor.

Under certain limited conditions, OSHA is authorized to set emergency temporary standards that take immediate effect and remain in force until replaced by a permanent standard. To issue an emergency standard, OSHA must determine that workers are in grave danger due to exposure to toxic substances or agents determined to be toxic or physically harmful or due to new hazards that provide a serious safety problem. The validity of an emergency temporary standard can be challenged in an appropriate court.

- National Advisory Committee on Occupational Safety and Health (NACOSH), which advises, consults with, and makes recommendations to the Secretary of HHS, and to the Secretary of Labor on matters regarding administration of the Act.
- Advisory Committee on Construction Safety and Health, which advises the Secretary of Labor on formulation of construction safety and health standards and other regulations.

Source: All About OSHA, U.S. Department of Labor, OSHA 2056, 1982 (rev.), p. 7.

ENFORCEMENT

The enforcement mechanism consists of inspections by OSHA safety and health officers. These inspectors visit business facilities to check compliance with the national safety and health standards that have been established. The inspector is concerned with what standards apply in a given facility and whether the employer and employees are in compliance with these standards.

Obviously, not all the 5 million workplaces covered by the act can be inspected. OSHA simply does not have that much staff. Therefore, it has established a system of inspection priorities to give the worst situations attention before those where the safety and health conditions are likely to be better. These priorities include (1) investigating imminent danger situations, (2) investigating companies that have had catastrophes and fatal accidents, (3) responding to valid employee complaints, (4) developing programs of inspection aimed at specific high-hazard industries, occupations, or health substances, and (5) reinspecting establishments cited for alleged serious violations.[17]

The original act prohibited advance notice of inspections. This has since been changed by a court ruling (see next section) requiring search warrants. Once admitted, the compliance officer conducts a walkaround of the facility with a representative of both the employer and employees. The inspector takes notes and photographs of particular situations that may violate standards. The employer's records of deaths, injuries, and illnesses are also checked for compliance. During the walkaround, employees may bring any conditions they believe to be a violation of standards to the attention of the compliance officer. Trade secrets observed by the compliance officer must and will be kept confidential. An inspector who releases confidential information without authorization is subject to a $1,000 fine and/or one year in jail. The employer may require that the employee representative have confidential clearance for any area in question.

After the walkaround is finished, the compliance officer discusses with the employer what he or she has seen and reviews probable violations. The officer then returns to his or her office and writes a report. The area director of OSHA or his or her superiors determine what citations will be issued and what penalties, if any, will be proposed. These are eventually mailed to the employer. These citations must (1) include a detailed description of the violation, (2) state which standard has been violated, and (3) provide a reasonable time period for abatement of the violation. In some cases, the compliance officer may issue citations at the worksite following the closing conference. But if all the citations resulting from the inspection cannot be issued at the worksite, none will be issued.

VIOLATIONS

The workplace may, of course, be found in compliance with OSHA standards, in which case no citations will be issued or penalties imposed. If violations are found, citations may be issued and civil penalties proposed. In order of significance, these violations are placed in one of the following categories.

> *Other than serious violation:* A violation that has a direct relationship to job safety and health but probably would not cause death or serious physical harm. A proposed penalty of up to $1,000 for each violation is discretionary. A penalty for anything other than a serious violation may be adjusted downward by as much as 80 percent, depending on the employer's

good faith (demonstrated efforts to comply with the act), history of previous violations, and size of the business. When the adjusted penalty amounts to less than $60, no penalty is proposed.

Serious violation: A violation where there is substantial probability that death or serious physical harm could result and when the employer knew, or should have known, of the hazard. A mandatory penalty of up to $1,000 for each violation is proposed. A penalty for a serious violation may be adjusted downward, based on the employer's good faith, history of previous violations, the gravity of the alleged violation, and size of the business.

Willful violation: A violation that the employer intentionally and knowingly commits. The employer either knows that what he or she is doing constitutes a violation or is aware that a hazardous condition existed and made no reasonable effort to eliminate it. Penalties of up to $10,000 may be proposed for each willful violation. A proposed penalty for a willful violation may be adjusted downward, depending on the size of the business and its history of previous violations. Usually, no credit is given for good faith. If an employer is convicted of a willful violation of a standard that has resulted in the death of an employee, the offense is punishable by a court-imposed fine of not more than $10,000 or by imprisonment for up to 6 months, or both. A second conviction doubles these maximum penalties.

Repeated Violation: A violation of any standard, regulation, rule or order where, upon reinspection, a substantially similar violation is found. Repeated violations can bring a fine of up to $10,000 for each such violation. To be the basis of a repeat citation the original citation must be final; a citation under contest may not serve as the basis for a subsequent repeat citation.

Failure to correct prior violation: Failure to correct a prior violation may bring a civil penalty of up to $1,000 for each day the violation continues beyond the prescribed abatement date.

Additional violations for which citations and proposed penalties may be issued include the following: (1) falsifying records, reports, or applications can bring a fine of $10,000 or up to 6 months in jail, or both; (2) violations of posting requirements can bring a civil penalty of up to $1,000; and (3) assaulting a compliance officer, or otherwise resisting, opposing, intimidating or interfering with a compliance officer in the performance of his or her duties is a criminal offense and is subject to a fine of not more than $5,000 and imprisonment for not more than 3 years.[18]

Upon receipt of the citations and proposed penalties, the employer has 15 working days in which to notify the area director, in writing (Notice of Contest), that he or she intends to contest the citation, penalty, or the time set for abatement. The area director then sends the case to the Occupational Safety and Health Review Commission. The Commission assigns the case to an administrative law judge, who eventually hears the case and issues a decision. The judge's decision may be reviewed by any member of the Commission, or by the Commission itself, but such a review is not required. The final decision of the Commission may be further appealed to the U.S. Circuit Court of Appeals for the circuit in which the case arose. If the employer does not contest within the 15-day period, the OSHA action becomes a final order of the Review Commission and it is not subject to further appeal or review.

RECORD KEEPING

The OSHA Act of 1970 requires employers to prepare and maintain records of occupational injuries and illnesses. These records assist compliance officers in making inspections and investigations. They also provide the basis for a statistical program that

What is considered to be an occupational injury or illness? An occupational injury is any injury such as a cut, fracture, sprain or amputation which results from a work-related accident or from exposure involving a single incident in the work environment. An occupational illness is any abnormal condition or disorder, other than one resulting from an occupational injury, caused by exposure to environmental factors associated with employment. Included are acute and chronic illnesses which may be caused by inhalation, absorption, ingestion or direct contact with toxic substances or harmful agents.

Source: All About OSHA, U.S. Department of Labor, OSHA 2056, 1985 (rev.), p. 13.

produces reliable injury and illness incidence rates and other measures. This information is also believed to be helpful to employers in identifying many of the factors which cause injuries and illnesses in the workplace. Before the act became effective, no centralized and systematic method existed for collecting data on occupational safety and health problems. With OSHA's record keeping requirements came the first consistent and nationwide procedures for collecting statistics.

While the original legislation called for the maintenance of three forms, this has subsequently been changed to only two types of records.[19] The Log and Summary (OSHA No. 200) is provided to classify injury and illness cases (see box) and note their extent and outcome. All occupational illnesses must be recorded if they result in (1) death, (2) one or more lost workdays, (3) restriction of work or motion, (4) loss of consciousness, (5) transfer to another job, or (6) medical treatment other than first aid.[20]

The Supplementary Record (OSHA No. 101) is used for recording additional information about every recordable injury or illness. These records do not have to be sent to OSHA, but they must be maintained on the premises of the facility for 5 years after the year to which they relate. These records can be inspected or copied at any reasonable time by authorized federal or state government representatives. From time to time, employers may be selected to participate in an annual statistical survey of occupational injuries and illnesses. If selected, they will be sent OSHA No. 200s for this purpose, which must be filled out and returned to the Bureau of Labor Statistics.

EMPLOYER RESPONSIBILITIES AND RIGHTS

Employers have certain responsibilities and rights under OSHA. Some of the more important responsibilities include (1) providing a workplace free from recognized hazards that are causing or are likely to cause death or serious physical harm to employees, (2) becoming familiar with mandatory OSHA standards and making copies available to employees for review upon request, (3) informing all employees about OSHA, (4) examining workplace conditions to make sure they conform to applicable standards, (5) making sure employees have and use safe tools and equipment is properly maintained, (6) establishing or updating operating procedures and communicating them so that employees follow safety and health requirements, (7) providing medical examinations when required by OSHA standards, (8) abating cited violations within the prescribed period, (9) keeping OSHA-required records of work-related injuries and illnesses, (10) informing employees of their rights and responsibilities, (11) providing employees, former employees, and their representatives access to the Log and Summary of Occupational Injuries and Illnesses at a reasonable time and in a reasonable manner, and (12) not discriminating against employees who properly exercise their rights under the act.[21]

The most important rights of employers include (1) seeking advice and off-site consultation as needed by writing, calling, or visiting the nearest OSHA office; (2) requesting and receiving proper identification of the OSHA compliance officer prior to inspection; (3) being advised by the compliance officer of the reason for an inspection; (4) having an opening and closing conference with the compliance officer; (5) filing a notice of contest with the OSHA director within 15 working days of receipt of a notice of citation and proposed penalty; (6) applying for temporary or premanent variances from standards for justifiable reasons; (7) taking an active role in developing safety and health standards; (8) being assured of the confidentiality of any trade secrets observed by an OSHA compliance officer during an inspection; and (9) submitting a written request to NIOSH for information on whether any substance in the workplace has potential toxic effects in the concentrations being used.[22]

EMPLOYEE RESPONSIBILITIES AND RIGHTS

OSHA does not cite employees for violations of their responsibilities, but each employee is expected to comply with all occupational safety and health standards and all rules, regulations, and orders issued under the act that apply to his or her own actions and conduct on the job. Some of these responsibilities include (1) complying with all applicable OSHA standards, (2) following all employer safety and health rules and regulations, (3) reporting hazardous conditions to the supervisor, (4) reporting any job-related injuries or illnesses to the employer and seeking treatment promptly, (5) cooperating with the OSHA compliance officer conducting an inspection, and (6) exercising employee rights under the act in a responsible manner.[23]

Some employee rights include (1) requesting information from the employer on safety and health hazards in the workplace and on procedures to be followed if an employee is involved in an accident or is exposed to toxic substances, (2) requesting the OSHA area director to conduct an inspection if hazardous conditions or violations of standards are believed to exist in the workplace, (3) having one's name withheld from the employer if a complaint is written and signed, (4) having an authorized employee representative accompany the OSHA compliance officer during an inspection, (5) reviewing the Log and Summary of Occupational Injuries at a reasonable time and in a reasonable manner, (6) requesting a closing discussion with the compliance officer following an inspection, (7) submitting a written request to NIOSH for information on whether any substance in the workplace has potential toxic effects in the concentrations being used, (8) objecting to the statement period set in the citation issued to the employer, (9) being notified by the employer if he or she applies for a variance from an OSHA standard and to testify at a variance hearing, and (10) submitting information or comment to OSHA on the issuance, modification, or revocation of OSHA standards.[24]

CONSULTATION SERVICE

In the early 1980s, OSHA began to provide a free on-site consultation service that helps employers to identify hazardous conditions and determine corrective measures to be taken. The consultative visit consists of an opening conference, a walkthrough of a company's facility, a closing conference, and a written summary of findings. During the walkthrough, the employer is told which OSHA standards apply to the facility and where violations exist, and where possible, is given suggestions on how to reduce or eliminate the hazards that violate OSHA standards.

There is a clear separation between the consultative and enforcement staffs, with the former coming from state governments or private contractors rather than from OSHA itself. No citations are issued and no penalties are proposed during a consultative visit, and the consultant's files cannot be used to trigger an OSHA inspection. However, an employer must agree to eliminate hazardous conditions where death or serious harm could result. If a condition presents an "imminent danger" of death or serious physical harm, the hazard must be removed immediately. When appropriate action is not taken within a reasonable period of time, the consultant is required to notify OSHA, which may then itself investigate the condition and begin enforcement action if necessary.

STATE PROGRAMS

The OSHA Act encourages states to develop and operate their own job safety and health programs. State programs are required to provide standards and enforcement procedures that are at least as effective as the federal program. Such a provision prevents the states from watering down any part of federal requirements. Once a state plan is approved, OSHA funds up to half of the program's operating costs, thus providing an incentive for states to develop their own programs. At the present time, about half the states have their own approved programs and are not operating directly under the federal program.

A state must be certified by OSHA that it has the legal, administrative, and enforcement means necessary to operate a safety and health program effectively. If after a period of at least 1 year after initial certification, it is determined that a state is effectively providing safety and health protection, final approval is granted and federal authority ceases in those areas over which the state has jurisdiction. However, OSHA continues to monitor and evaluate the state program to assure the level of effectiveness is maintained. If this level should decline, OSHA can begin proceedings to withdraw approval of the state program and reinstitute federal enforcement authority. Anyone who finds problems in the state program may file a complaint with the appropriate regional administrator of OSHA and ask that his or her name be kept confidential.

Experience with the Federal Program

Soon after its creation, OSHA became the most hated federal agency of any that had been created since the turn of the century. Mention the word OSHA, and employers would become flush with anger over what they perceived as nitpicking standards, incompetent enforcement officers, and needless and even unconstitutional intrusion into the rights of private citizens. OSHA was criticized for issuing standards that were design-oriented, thus giving employers no discretion in fashioning their own methods of reaching safety and health objectives, for not paying more attention to the costs of implementing a standard, for focusing its enforcement efforts on technical compliance with every aspect of a standard no matter how minor an impact it had on safety and health, and for being unclear under what circumstances OSHA would cite employers for violations within the various categories that had been established. How did OSHA get this kind of reputation? Was it deserved? And what has subsequently been done to improve the program and make it more acceptable and effective?

COVERAGE

As originally passed, the act extended to all employers and employees in the 50 states, the District of Columbia, Puerto Rico, and all other territories under federal government jurisdiction. An employer was defined as ''a person engaged in a business affecting commerce who has employees, but does not include the United States or any state or political subdivision of a state.''[25] Federal agencies were covered under separate provisions of the act and were required to establish and maintain an effective and comprehensive job safety and health program that was consistent with standards for private employers.[26]

There have been several attempts to limit the coverage of OSHA throughout the years of its existence. Many of these attempts focused on exemptions for small business, because many people believed that the inspection procedures and record-keeping requirements were particularly burdensome for these businesses. Finally, in late 1979, OSHA itself, under pressure from Congress, agreed to exempt businesses with 10 or fewer employees in industries with good safety records from safety inspections. Forty-nine industries that had fewer than seven injuries or illnesses per 100 workers annually qualified for the exemption. This exemption would include, OSHA said, about 1.5 million establishments employing 5 million workers. The agency would still conduct safety inspections in response to employee complaints.[27]

The paperwork requirements for small business were also reduced by an OSHA ruling. Most employers with 10 or fewer workers—3.4 million of the 5 million companies covered by job safety laws—were spared from keeping the employee accident and illness records originally required. They have to complete government forms only if a worker is killed or two or more are hospitalized.[28]

OSHA adopted a new policy as far as coverage is concerned in 1982 that was predicted to exempt about 75 percent of U.S. manufacturers from regularly scheduled inspections. With only 1,200 inspectors to cover 3 million workplaces, OSHA argued it needed to concentrate its limited resources on the most hazardous workplaces. Thus firms with below-average safety records and with 10 or more employees would be the only ones to be subject to regularly scheduled inspections. Companies with good safety records and fewer than 10 employees would be exempted from inspections.[29]

OSHA also changed its policy regarding response to employee complaints, responding only to those complaints that established grounds to believe a violation threatened physical harm or an imminent danger and limiting the inspection, when conducted, to only the complaint area rather than the entire facility for those companies that had good safety records.[30] Employers generally praised these changes, saying they would save them both time and money, but labor viewed the changes as stripping some 13 million workers of OSHA protection and interfering with the rights of workers to file complaints.[31]

This policy was changed again in 1986 in response to an increase in the rates of injuries and illnesses in workplaces in 1984 as reported by the Labor Department. The agency said it would continue to focus its targeted inspection efforts on high-hazard manufacturing companies, but it would also expand inspections to include spot checks at manufacturing concerns in industries with injury rates below the national average and nonmanufacturing companies in statistically less-hazardous industries such as retail sales, services, and transportation. These inspections would total about 10 percent of OSHA's safety inspections in the 1986 fiscal year.[32] In 1988, this policy was slightly altered when inspectors were given authorization to do a walkthrough inspection after studying factory records for those companies whose records show a low rate of injuries or illnesses.[33]

The agency also encouraged the development of voluntary inspection programs by exempting companies from routine and complaint inspections for at least 3 years if the company had a good health and safety record and a labor-management safety committee. The latter would take over monitoring of the workplace from OSHA inspectors. This enthusiasm for self-inspection grew out of the so-called Bechtel plan, where a labor-management safety committee at a Bechtel Group, Inc., nuclear power plant project conducted safety and health inspections once a month.[34]

STANDARD SETTING

Much of the hostility to OSHA that is behind the efforts to curb its power stems from the standard-setting process. Nichols and Zeckhauser criticize the way OSHA was structured on three grounds: (1) No attempt was made to analyze the problem of occupational safety and health in terms of likely causes and cures, (2) economic costs, which are a major consequence of any regulatory effort, were systematically excluded from being considered, and (3) serious thought was not given to any approach other than direct regulation. These fundamental questions were ignored, they state, in the haste to set up a federal program to respond to what was perceived as a crisis situation. Given the way the program was set up, Nichols and Zeckhauser believe that most of OSHA's failings were predictable.[35]

With regard to the first point, some critics believe that the worker's own behavior, not the work environment, is the major cause of accidents. Thus the effort to set standards related to the work environment is misguided. If there is any truth to this view, efforts to improve supervision and training should be more effective in reducing accidents than capital equipment regulations. Most accidents are probably a combination of worker behavior and the environment (lack of guards, etc.), but more research must be done to establish the true causes of most accidents, which would then provide a basis for developing an effective program to reduce them.[36]

The area of economic costs, the second point made by Nichols and Zeckhauser, is an important area that was overlooked in the legislation establishing the federal program. No economic impact statement or benefit-cost analysis was required in the process of issuing regulations. This problem was further exacerbated by court rulings that held that standards must be technologically and economically feasible, but interpreted these provisions rather broadly. For example, a standard could be technologically feasible even if it required employers to develop novel technologies existing at the outer edges of scientific development. And economically feasible came to mean that the costs of implementing the standard should not bankrupt the entire industry covered by the standard. The fact that one enterprise might be put out of business because of compliance costs would not render a standard economically infeasible.

Finally, other approaches to the safety and health problem were not considered, such as the use of incentives to encourage employers to improve their safety and health records. The basic business of OSHA is setting and enforcing standards, many of them specifying in great detail the physical conditions of various aspects of the workplace. This form of intervention was adopted without looking at other methods that might be

A means of egress is a continuous and unobstructed way of exit travel from any point in a building or structure to a public way and consists of three separate and distinct parts: the way of exit access, the exit, and the way of exit discharge. A means of egress comprises the vertical and horizontal ways of travel and shall include intervening room spaces, doorways, hallways, corridors, passageways, balconies, ramps, stairs, enclosures, lobbies, escalators, horizontal exits, courts and yards.

Exit access is that portion of a means of egress which leads to an entrance to an exit.

Exit is that portion of a means of egress which is separated from all other spaces of the building or structure by construction or equipment as required in this subpart to provide a protected way of travel to the exit discharge.

Exit discharge is that portion of a means of egress between the termination of an exit and a public way.

(*Federal Register,* Vol. 37, No. 202 (October 18, 1972), p. 22130.

more effective. The command and control system that was adopted could be expected to provoke resistance, as it only further contributes to the adversarial relationship between business and government.

The history of OSHA with regard to standard setting shows the difficulty of implementing regulatory legislation. Within one month of its creation, OSHA adopted, in wholesale fashion, about 4,400 consensus standards from previous federal regulations that were already in existence and from voluntary codes written by such organizations as the American National Standards Institute (ANSI). They had been written by safety experts and originally intended as no more than voluntary industry guidelines. Since many of these experts had little or no knowledge about production or costs, industry regarded many of the standards as unreasonable and ignored them. When OSHA made them legally binding, however, and backed them up with inspections and fines, many problems resulted.[37]

Some of these standards were trivial and unrelated to safety and health, such as the requirement that toilet seats be split and not round. Others were obsolete, such as the prohibition against ice in drinking water, which dated from the time ice was cut from polluted lakes. Still other standards were unnecessarily complex and difficult to understand (see box), such as the 140 standards covering wooden ladders and the six pages devoted to fire protection equipment.[38]

These nitpicking regulations came in for severe criticism, and finally, in 1978, OSHA revoked 928 that were of little value in protecting safety and health. Included were standards requiring split-seat toilets, prescribing the type of wood to be used in portable ladders, and specifying the number of inches from the floor that portable fire extinguishers had to be mounted. The total number of regulations relating to ladders was reduced from 10 pages to 2. This process of revocation, however, took months of consultations, publications, and hearings, demonstrating that it is sometimes easier to establish regulations than it is to get them off the books.[39]

Many of these consensus standards were adopted under pressure to do something quickly, and thus their relevance to safety and health was not reviewed. Some years later, however, they still constitute the majority of OSHA's standards. The process of establishing new standards is complex and lengthy. Most standards begin with a recommendation from NIOSH, which is then reviewed by an OSHA advisory committee. When proposed standards are finally issued in the *Federal Register,* many delays are caused by public hearings and court challenges by affected industries before a final standard can be issued and enforced.

The complexity of this process is well illustrated by OSHA's attempt to focus more of its attention on the health aspects of the workplace and issue more health standards. Between 1970 and 1977, NIOSH identified some 25,000 toxic substances used in American Industry and made recommendations to OSHA for approximately 80 of them. But by the end of 1978, OSHA had issued standards for fewer than 25 of these substances. For some 400 other substances, it adopted legal standards referred to as threshold limit values (TLV) that specified the maximum allowable concentrations of specific hazardous materials permitted in the workplace.[40]

OSHA must proceed on a substance-by-substance basis in regard to health standards. This process is subject to many delays and frustrations. There are many unresolved issues in the standard-setting process with regard to health that make it tremendously complex and lengthy. Many of these issues may have to be decided by the Supreme Court as it agrees to hear cases dealing with health standards. There seems to be no conclusive scientific evidence to resolve some of these issues, given the current state of knowledge and medical technology. Thus these standards are subject to political pressures from interested parties with ideological biases.

The process of setting safety and health standards is filled with controversy. The use of consensus standards on such a broad scale without adequate screening or careful consideration was, in retrospect, a big mistake. But regarding health standards, by 1985 OSHA had issued only 12 new or revised health standards that survived legal challenges plus 3 broad rules covering workplace labeling, employee access to records, and its policy toward substances that cause cancer. Of the 12 health standards, only 2 were issued by the Reagan administration, and 1 of these was later overturned in court. The director of OSHA in early 1985, who later resigned, attributed the slow pace of regulation to the lengthy rule-making process and to the effort devoted to designing standards that are both cost-efficient and capable of withstanding legal challenges.[41]

In early 1989, the agency adopted a proposal to establish broad workplace health standards instead of proceeding on a substance-by-substance basis. In its 17-year history, OSHA had issued individual standards for only 24 specific substances. The agency set tighter exposure ceilings for 212 chemicals and first limits for another 164, which it claimed would significantly reduce the risk or potential risk of illness caused by chemical exposure for more than 21 million workers. These new limits should save nearly 700 lives per year and were expected to cost industry $788 million annually. Employers had until September 1, 1989, to comply with the new limits by using any combination of engineering controls, new work practices, or protective equipment.[42]

ENFORCEMENT

OSHA got off to a flying start in its enforcement program. In its first fiscal year, the agency made 32,700 inspections, issued 23,230 citations charging 102,860 violations, and proposed $2,300,000 in penalties .[43] While these figures sound impressive, the inspections represented only a small fraction of the total number of workplaces covered by the program. OSHA simply did not have enough inspectors to cover more workplaces. It became apparent that some kind of a priority system was needed to focus on the industries or companies where the more serious problems existed. There was universal agreement that steps should be taken to put OSHA's compliance officers in the right place at the right time. In fiscal 1979, for example, OSHA issued no serious citations in 71 percent of the 58,000 inspections it conducted and found no rule violations in 46 of these cases. According to a study by the General Accounting Office (GAO) fewer than 5 percent of inspections that are the result of worker complaints uncover serious violations.[44]

In addition to not covering enough workplaces, or at least the most hazardous ones, the inspection system was also criticized because of the lack of trained enforcement personnel and because, in its early years, inspectors were trained to look for safety violations rather than health hazards. Very few industrial hygienists were employed by OSHA in its early years. Since that time, the quality of workplace safety and health inspections has been substantially improved through better use of the enforcement staff, 33 percent more training of OSHA compliance officers, and "crossover training" so that safety inspectors can also recognize health hazards.[45]

Finally, the inevitable constitutional challenge to the inspector's right to have unannounced access to private property came along. When an OSHA inspector tried to walk unannounced into Ferrol G. Barlow's shop in Pocatello, Idaho, the proprietor refused him entry. Barlow claimed that the inspector needed a search warrant, that the Fourth Amendment to the constitution prohibited unreasonable searches of private property. The Supreme Court eventually ruled that Barlow was legally correct, that employers can bar OSHA inspectors who do not have search warrants.[46]

This was not an undiluted victory for business, however, as the court released OSHA from having to show probable cause, as in criminal searches, to get the warrant. Also, the warrant need be obtained only if the employer refuses access to an inspector. The immediate effect of the ruling was not significant, as most businesses did not demand warrants because they believed OSHA would have no difficulty obtaining them. To obtain a warrant, OSHA only has to demonstrate a reasonable basis for selecting a workplace for inspection. This reasonable basis could be established by employee complaints, high accident rates, a history of employer noncompliance, or the passage of a long interval since the last inspection.[47]

The agency continues to experience a serious problem with its enforcement efforts. In 1988, OSHA had only 1,125 inspectors, enough to inspect only about 2 percent of the nation's 3.4 million workplaces covered by the federal law. The agency does about 70,000 inspections annually. To inspect every workplace would require about 125,000 inspectors at a cost of about $13.8 billion. Under the Bush administration, OSHA was seeking funds from Congress for another 179 inspectors, which would be the first increase in inspectors in a decade. Under the Reagan administration, the inspection force was cut 25 percent.[48]

VIOLATIONS

As might be expected, the caseload of the Occupational Safety and Health Review Commission increased over the first years of OSHA as more and more employers appealed the citations and penalties they were issued. This has, of course, necessitated the hiring of additional personnel, as these cases can be quite complex and lengthy. Beginning in 1982, however, a declining trend in the caseload appeared. The caseload was off about 48 percent, as employers contested only 6 percent of OSHA's citations, down from 22 percent 2 years earlier. About 15 of its 40 law judges were laid off. Union officials stated this trend reflected OSHA's reduced fervor to issue citations for serious violations. By 1985, the average proposed penalty for serious health and safety violations had dropped to less than $200, hardly a strong incentive to reduce hazards in the workplace. However, OSHA explained these declines by stating that its inspectors were now looking at health and safety instead of crime and punishment, which actually resulted in more rapid abatement of hazards.[49]

The right of OSHA to assess penalties administratively and commit the fact finding to an administrative law court without trial by jury was challenged on the basis of the Seventh Amendment to the constitution. This amendment says that "in suits of common law" where the controversy involves more than $20, "the right of trial by jury shall be preserved." The Supreme Court did not uphold this challenge, claiming that the amendment was "never intended to establish the jury as the exclusive mechanism for fact finding in civil cases." Thus Congress was not prevented from committing new types of litigation to administrative agencies with special competence in the relevant field. In a footnote, the court also barred any challenge to OSHA's constitutionality through the Sixth Amendment, which grants the right to a jury trial in criminal proceedings.[50]

Another area that drew criticism was OSHA's penalty structure. In 1978, an Interagency Task Force reported that the average fine for a serious violation was only $800.[51] A previous study showed that between 1971 and 1976, 8,000 citations were issued, with the average fine being only $33.[52] Thus the penalty structure was attacked as not being effective in altering business behavior in protecting workers, and suggestions were made to increase the fines for serious violations to match the compliance costs, which would neutralize the economic reasons for delayed abatement. However, if a firm is cited and fined a substantial amount for a violation that would be costly to abate, it would appeal the citation. The review process could take as long as 3 years, during which time the penalized firm would not have to correct the violation unless it posed an imminent danger. From a worker's perspective, this delay means exposure to a safety or health hazard for 3 more years, unless a serious accident or fatality occurred. Nolan Hancock, OSHA's legislative director, summarized the situation by saying, "most fines are pocket change for employers." It is far cheaper to kill a worker than it is to spend the money to prevent his or her death.[53]

In 1986, the use of cover-up tactics was said to be on the rise, as violations of federal record-keeping rules were said to have increased 71 percent in a 6-year period. These violations were probably a response to the policy of basing inspections on employer's records and inspecting those facilities with injury and illness rates above the national average. In November of 1986, OSHA fined Chrysler $911,000 for failing to report 182 job-related injuries in one of its assembly plants.[54] The final settlement was for $285,000, the largest safety fine ever paid by a company. Under terms of the settlement, Chrysler did not admit having committed any violations but agreed to make sure its record-keeping procedures complied with OSHA regulations. In 1986, OSHA proposed a $1.4 million fine against Union Carbide for alleged health and safety violations in its Institute, West Virginia plant.[55] That fine was eventually reduced to $409,000 in a negotiating process. Other fines of this magnitude followed (Table 7.1).

OSHA was criticized for picking out a few highly visible companies upon which to propose headline-making fines and then allowing these fines to be reduced an average of 67.5 percent through a bargaining process. Instead of penalizing violators, it was said that OSHA allowed employers to negotiate and finance their safety compliance through penalty reductions. OSHA defended the practice by saying that the agency settles with offenders in order to get the company to make immediate safety improvements and avoid lengthy court battles over the citations.[56] It was also alleged that since the agency is unable to conduct a high number of time-consuming plant-floor inspections, it usually looks only at record books in most of the facilities it inspects annually.[57]

TABLE 7.1   The Largest Penalties in OSHA's History

Initially proposed penalties and settlements as of March 1, 1988

Date	Company	Reason for Penalty	Penalty/Settlement (In thousands of dollars)
2/11/88	Doe Run[1]	Safety/health violation	$2,780/not settled
1/14/88	Kohler	Record keeping	$1,398/not settled
11/4/87	Bath Iron Works	Safety/health violation	$4,200/not settled
10/22/87	TPMI/Macomber[2,3]	Building collapse	$2,475/not settled
	Texstar Construction[3]		$2,524/not settled
9/25/87	Scott Paper	Record keeping	$813/$475
7/21/87	IBP[4]	Record keeping	$2,598/not settled
7/6/87	Chrysler		
	(Newark, Delaware)	Safety/health violation	$1,576/not settled
11/5/86	Chrysler		
	(Belvidere, Illinois)	Record keeping	$911/$285
4/1/86	Union Carbide	Record keeping	$1,378/$409
2/27/80	Newport News		
	Shipbuilding	Safety/health violation	$804/$121

[1]A joint venture of St. Joe Minerals and Homestake Mining

[2]A joint venture of TPM International and George B.H. Macomber

[3]Joint contractors involved in a building collapse

[4]A unit of Occidental Petroleum

Source: Cathy Trost, ''Occupational Hazard,'' *Wall Street Journal,* April 22, 1988, p. 25R. Reprinted by permission, © 1988 Dow Jones & Company, Inc. All Rights Reserved Worldwide.

Continuing Problems

One important issue for business is whether executives can be prosecuted for criminal charges by state and local officials. The Justice Department has prosecuted only 4 of the 30 cases referred to it for criminal investigation since 1980 by OSHA because prosecutors complain that penalties are so weak that the Justice Department is reluctant to go to court. Criminal negligence is also difficult to prove under the 1970 Act because prosecutors must prove that employers intentionally disregarded safety regulations, not just that they were negligent.[58] State and local prosecutors have tried to fill this void by bringing criminal charges against business, but business argues that it is unfair for companies that comply with OSHA regulations to be prosecuted for criminal conduct. Nonetheless, some states have opened the door by ruling that OSHA does not bar states from prosecuting corporate officials for work-related injuries and deaths.[59]

One such case involved Film Recovery Systems, a small company outside Chicago that specialized in recovering silver from used film by mixing it with sodium cyanide and water in large vats that were open to the surrounding atmosphere. These open vats released hydrogen cyanide gas directly into the air, where it was inhaled by workers. In 1983, a 61-year-old worker died of cyanide poisoning. The State of Illinois filed suit against the company charging that company officials were fully aware of the life-threatening dangers posed by the operation but had failed to train or equip the workers to ensure their protection. The corporation was charged with manslaughter and the company officers with murder.[60]

In June 1985, a Cook County judge found three corporate officials of the company, including the president, plant manager, and the plant supervisor, guilty of murder. The convictions carried a minimum sentence of 20 years. Film Recovery and Metallic Marketing Systems, Inc., which owned half the stock of Film Recovery, was convicted of involuntary manslaughter and 14 counts of reckless conduct. The judge, who heard the case without a jury, said the evidence clearly showed the worker had died from inhaling cyanide under "totally unsafe" workplace conditions. This was the first time that corporate officers were convicted of murder for management actions and inactions that contributed to a worker's death. The verdict sent a signal to management that employers who knowingly expose workers to dangerous conditions leading to injury or death can be held criminally responsible for the results of their actions.[61]

Another case in Texas resulted in the sentencing of Joseph Tantillo, the president of Sabine Consolidated, Inc., a construction company, to 6 months in prison because of negligence. Two workers had been killed when the walls of a 27-foot trench in which they were working collapsed and buried them beneath tons of earth. Both men were smothered. The president was not believed to have intentionally killed the men, but showed a disregard for basic safety measures in the light of obvious risks to employees. The state alleged that the trench should have been adequately shored up or the walls sloped less sharply to prevent buckling. Tantillo's clean record earned him probation and no jail time, but this was said to be the first time an executive had been sentenced to a jail term because of negligence.[62]

Another issue of interest to business concerns what might be called "inferred rights," rights that may be implied under a broad mandate to guarantee workers "hazard-free" workplaces. One such right recently debated concerned the right of employees to refuse to work in protest of allegedly hazardous working conditions. A case involving workers at Whirlpool Corporation went to the Supreme Court. Two maintenance men employed by this company refused to walk out on a wire-mesh screen suspended high above the factory floor when ordered to do so by their superior. The company suspended them for 6 hours, docked their pay, and issued written reprimands.[63]

In the OSHA Act, Congress passed certain employee rights and provided that a worker could not be discharged or discriminated against for exercising them. The question is whether the right to refuse highly dangerous work was one of them. OSHA said that in addition to rights specifically enumerated, certain other rights exist by necessary implication. The company argued that if Congress had wanted to create such a right, it would have done so, and to give workers the right to decide for themselves what is unsafe and reject assignments accordingly would open the door to mischief and abuse.

The Supreme Court unanimously upheld the right of workers to refuse, free from employer retaliation, to perform jobs they consider too dangerous. The regulation supporting this right "clearly conforms to the fundamental objective of the [OSHA] Act—to prevent occupational deaths and serious injuries," the Court said. Employees are legally protected when they refuse work of such a nature that a reasonable person under the circumstances then confronting the employee would conclude that there is a real danger of death or serious injury and there is insufficient time to eliminate the danger through resort to the regular enforcement channels. The court made clear, however, that employers are under no legal obligation to pay workers who refuse to perform assigned tasks.[64]

Another employee right that has been the subject of debate concerns employee access to health and safety records of employers. The access rule was first issued in 1980 and gave the right to employees or their representatives to inspect records kept by companies on worker exposure to dangerous substances and on job-related medical examinations, complaints, and treatment. In the spring and summer of 1982, the Labor

Department announced plans to narrow the scope of that rule by limiting the number of workers covered by the rule, reducing the number of hazardous substances for which companies must maintain records and reduce the limit on how long those records must be retained. It was estimated that the proposals would reduce the number of workers covered by the rule from 28 million to 17 million and the number of substances covered to 3,500 from 39,000 substances covered by the 1980 rule.[65] In a related development, a federal district court upheld the 1980 rule rejecting a challenge brought by the Louisiana Chemical Association, which claimed that OSHA didn't have the legal authority to issue such general rules. The court held that a rule that establishes a data base for medical research, as does the record access rule, falls within the authority of the job safety agency. This ruling was expected to make it more difficult for OSHA to justify narrowing the scope of the rule.[66]

A related issue concerns the so-called right-to-know laws regarding toxic or hazardous substances used by workers. These laws require businesses to disclose to their employees and the public the names and potential health hazards of any toxic substances workers are exposed to in the workplace. Proponents of these laws argue that if the right to know in the workplace is to be adequately protected, there must be an affirmative duty to disclose information about health hazards to workers in addition to a duty to honor worker-initiated requests for access to records. Employees should be aware of hazards that they may encounter so that they can make an informed decision as to whether they wish to work in that environment and know the precautions which they should take to avoid or minimize the possibility of suffering any adverse effects from the hazards.

Several states and local communities passed such right-to-know laws, that took effect within their jurisdiction. Pressure built for a federal preemptive law in this area because of the proliferation of state and local legislation. Finally, on November 25, 1983, OSHA issued a Hazard Communication Standard that was believed to be one of the costliest rules in its history. The initial toll for industry was estimated to be about $600 million, but by and large industry supported federal action to make compliance easier. The standard covers an estimated 75,000 chemicals and affects about 14 million employees.

In the standard, OSHA cited several reasons for the regulations. According to the National Occupational Hazards Survey conducted in 1972, 25 million Americans are potentially exposed in the workplace to one or more of nearly 8,000 hazards. Moreover, approximately 23 percent of the U.S. population may have been exposed at some time to one or more of the hazardous chemicals regulated by OSHA. The Bureau of Labor Statistics has compiled figures indicating that a total of more than 174,000 occupational illnesses in 1977 and 1978 were linked to chemical exposures.[67]

The Hazard Communication Standard has a threefold purpose: (1) to establish uniform requirements to ensure that all chemicals produced, imported, or used within the United States' manufacturing sector are evaluated to determine physical and health hazards, (2) to ensure that all employers and employees in the manufacturing sector are made aware of these hazards and that hazard-communication programs are instituted for affected employees, and (3) to preempt inconsistent state and local laws, reduce the burden on interstate commerce, and ensure that all employees in the manufacturing sector receive equal protection.[68]

The OSHA rules require manufacturers and importers of chemicals to alert workers to the harmful effects of hazardous chemicals through labeling and training. They have to provide workers and customers with detailed data sheets and warning labels that identify the chemicals and describe the health and safety standards. By May 1986, they

Figure 7.1 Label for Chemical Product

BERYLLIUM POWDER PRODUCT

DANGER — INHALATION OF DUST OR FUMES MAY CAUSE SERIOUS CHRONIC LUNG DISEASE

POTENTIAL CANCER HAZARD BASED PRINCIPALLY ON ANIMAL TESTS

This product contains beryllium. Overexposure to beryllium by inhalation may cause berylliosis, a serious chronic lung disease. Hazard Communication Regulations of the Occupational Safety & Health Administration require that caution labels for materials listed as potential carcinogens in either the International Agency for Cancer Research Monograph Series or the National Toxicology Program Annual Report on Carcinogens must contain a cancer warning. Beryllium has been so listed.

- Use only with exhaust ventilation or other controls designed to meet OSHA standards.
- Avoid contact with clothing.
- Keep stored container tightly closed. Flush container clean before discarding.
- Avoid spillage.
- Not to be taken internally.
- Sold for manufacturing purposes only.

See Material Safety Data Sheets on file with your employer for further details concerning OSHA standards, precautionary measures and special procedures in case of spillage.

Assistance in establishing safe procedures may be obtained by contacting Brush Wellman Inc., South River Road, Elmore, Ohio 43416, telephone: 419-862-2745.

Source: Beryllium Powder Product Label, Brush Wellman, Inc., Cleveland, Ohio.

were to have trained workers how to understand the sheets and labels and to handle the substances safely.[69] The specific provisions of the standard included the following.

- Placing labels on all containers identifying the chemical, possible hazards in its use, and the name and address of the manufacturer. (Figure 7.1).
- Developing a manual for its employees to explain the company's hazardous material program and to list the hazaradous material it uses.
- Offering training to employees about the hazards associated with these chemicals and how to work with them properly.
- Developing information flyers—called "material safety data" sheets—that explain, among other things, the known health effects, precautionary measures, and emergency and first-aid procedures related to exposure to the chemical. These sheets must be made available to employees and to purchasers of the product.[70]

Companies were concerned about disclosure of trade secrets; thus the labeling requirements had to allow for an exception where legitimate trade secrets were involved. Trade secrets are protected by giving companies the right to refuse to identify a substance if the information is a legitimate trade secret. The company may use symbols in these cases to indicate hazards rather than identify the actual chemical. Safety and health professionals from outside a company would have to justify a health need in order to force the company to identify a trade-secret substance.[71]

The standard was immediately attacked by unions and environmental groups, who campaigned successfully for state and local laws in the absence of federal standards. The federal rule is less stringent than some of those already passed by states and localities. Unions also charged that the provisions to protect trade secrets give companies an important loophole. Some called the new right-to-know standard a "right to snow rule."[72] Because of these perceived inadequacies, legislation was introduced into Congress in 1986 to establish a national program to assess occupational health risks and notify workers who are at greatest risk and direct them to medical monitoring programs.[73]

Several states and unions, along with public interest groups, took legal action against the standard. In May 1985, a federal appeals court found in their favor and rejected major parts of the standard. The court ordered the Secretary of Labor to substantially broaden and toughen the Hazard Communication Standard. The standard must be extended to cover workers in industries such as construction and services. The department must also come up with a less restrictive rule on disclosing trade secrets. The preemptive nature of the federal law, however, wasn't overturned.[74]

The standard was revised in 1987 to cover all workers exposed to hazardous substances. The new standard requires all nonmanufacturing employers with employees exposed to hazardous chemicals to initiate a written hazard communication program to inform employees of these hazards in the workplace. The expanded scope of coverage would include 18 million additional workers in more than 3.5 million workplaces. OSHA estimated that expansion of the standard would reduce the number of work-related cancer deaths by 143,000 over a 40-year period.[75] The cost of the expanded standard would be approximately $687 million for the first year of compliance, decreasing 83.5 percent over 20 years.[76]

Another area of responsibility for worker's health that grew in the 1980s was the area of emotional stress on the job. The number of stress claims had increased, expanding the liability of the worker's compensation system in many states. In 1985, all but nine states paid compensation for job-related emotional problems. Worker-compensation premiums covering this problem hit $35 billion in 1988, which was double the 1980 level. Many of these states had no legislation limiting the nature of these claims, creating an open-ended possibility for filing claims. The National Institute of Occupational Safety and Health also put psychological disorders on its list of leading work-related illnesses and cited reducing stress in high-tech offices as a primary objective.[77]

In the late 1980s, more attention began to be paid to hazards in the workplace that may affect workers' ability to reproduce. Some evidence suggested that a variety of chemicals and even video-display terminals may pose such health risks. In late 1989, IBM announced plans to reduce radiation in video-display terminals built by the company.[78] But at present there is little consensus on what action to take, and only 15 of the 500 largest U.S. companies in 1987 had comprehensive policies covering reproductive hazards. This issue has been called one of today's most sensitive workplace hazards because attempts to deal with the problem, usually by banning pregnant or fertile women from certain types of work, have often caused controversy and even lawsuits alleging discrimination.[79]

Repetitive-motion injuries also received increasing attention in the late 1980s. It was estimated that more than 5 million people, or about 4 percent of the work force in the U.S., suffered from motion injuries in 1986, and the cost to employers through lost earnings and expenses for medical costs and treatment amounted to more than $27 billion annually. These injuries stem from thousands of repetitive movements in jobs such as typing and meat cutting; they result in painful nerve conditions, such as carpal tunnel syndrome, that debilitate the hands and arms. The number of reported cases almost doubled in 1987, making repetitive-motion injuries the fastest-growing occupational injury in the 1980s.[80] In 1988, 115,400 cases were reported, representing 48 percent of workplace injuries.[81]

Finally, something called the "sick building syndrome" began to emerge as a health hazard. Complaints about headache, nausea, sore throat, or fatigue, commonplace among workers at the office, usually cleared up after they left the building. Many buildings were found to have inadequate ventilation, which allowed indoor contaminants from smoking and vapors from photocopying machines, cleaning liquids, and solvents to accumulate. The Environmental Protection Agency estimated that the economic cost of indoor air pollution totaled tens of billions of dollars annually in lost productivity, direct medical care, lost earnings, and employee sick days.[82]

Benefits and Costs

The economic costs of workplace injuries alone is staggering. The National Safety Council in 1984 estimated the cost of work injuries to be $33 billion dollars. Each person in the work force must produce $320 worth of goods and services each year to offset some of the costs of these injuries.[83] In 1978, the average cost of a lost-work-day injury to an employer was estimated at $14,000.[84] OSHA itself estimated that the value of each fatality avoided through the existence of a safety standard to be $3.5 million.[85] These costs, of course, must be compared with the costs of running the federal program and related to the effectiveness of the program.

There have been numerous attempts to estimate the costs of the government's safety and health program. For example, a study completed by *Dun's Review* estimated that compliance with OSHA standards would raise costs in many industries by 5 to 10 percent. The study also cited estimates that OSHA compliance would cost the metal-stamping industry $6 million over a 5-year period and would add $2,000 to $3,000 to the cost of an average new home.[86] McGraw-Hill's annual survey of business capital investments showed that between 1970 and 1981, business spent almost $43 billion for employee safety and health.[87] Another study found that the impact of OSHA regulation on productivity was greater than that of the Environmental Protection Agency, even though the EPA has a much larger budget and staff. During the period studied, OSHA regulations slowed productivity growth by 0.27 percentage points.[88]

Thus OSHA imposes substantial costs on business that vary a good deal by type of industry. The key question is, of course, whether the benefits being provided to workers and society exceed these costs, making the federal effort to regulate safety and health a worthwhile program. Without getting into the valuation of human life, the benefits that legitimately could be expected from the program include the following:

> Greater productivity of those who would have sustained a job-related injury or illness in the absence of government regulation.
>
> Greater enjoyment of life by those who thus avoided work-related disabilities.
>
> Resources that would have had to be used in the treatment and rehabilitation of victims of work-related injuries or illnesses that were avoided.
>
> Resources that would have had to be used to administer worker's compensation and insurance and to train those who would have been needed to replace the sick or disabled.

Reduction in the private efforts to increase occupational safety and health, which are replaced or reduced by the government's efforts.

Consequent decrease in damage to plant and equipment.

Savings that result from less disruption of work routines caused by accidents plus potential improvements in the morale and productivity of the work force.[89]

For the first few years, no good data were available to show what impact the program was having. Since OSHA also made a change in the methods by which injury-rate data were collected, it was impossible to make pre- and post-OSHA comparisons. By 1975, however, enough data had been collected to begin developing a record during the years OSHA had been in existence. The date for that year (1975) showed a drop in job-related deaths, injuries, and illnesses. While some argued that this drop reflected the high unemployment rates of 1975, which reduced the number of people working and hours worked, the Labor Department claimed that these figures were a positive indication of the success of national efforts to reduce such tragedies.[90]

Further declines appeared in 1976, but in 1977, the number of on-the-job fatalities among employers with 11 or more workers showed a sharp increase, 20 percent higher than the previous year. This kind of fluctuation raised some fundamental questions about the OSHA program and the meaning of the statistics. Did they actually reflect the efforts of government to reduce accidents and thus elucidate the failure of the regulatory effort? Or did they, as some argued, reflect such demographic factors as a young, inexperienced work force more than the results of a regulatory program? The answers to these questions are complex and cast doubts on the ability to attribute changes in accident statistics to specific causes or programs.[91]

Then in 1982, the number of workplace injuries and illnesses dropped to a 10-year low. The Bureau of Labor Statistics reported that injuries had declined from 5,278,400 in 1981 to 4,751,000 in 1982, a drop of about 10 percent, and occupational illnesses had gone from 126,100 to 105,600 cases over the same time period, a decline of about 16 percent and the lowest on record. Thorne Auchter, who headed OSHA at the time, claimed that the drop represented an endorsement of the administration's nonadversarial, cooperative approach to job safety and health. Others attributed the drop to a decline in hours worked in high-risk industries such as manufacturing and mining because of the recession.[92]

Figures released by the Labor Department in 1985 indicated there were 5.4 million cases of occupational deaths, injuries, and illnesses in 1984, an increase of almost 12 percent from the 4.9 million cases recorded for the previous year. The rate of injuries and illnesses for every 100 workers had increased from 7.6 per 100 to 8 per 100 over the same time period. This increase was reported to be the largest year-to-year jump in the rate since 1972, when OSHA first authorized a survey of injuries and illnesses in the workplace.[93] Further increases were experienced in 1987 and 1988, as the injury and illness rate rose to 8.6 for each 100 full-time workers.[94]

The difficulties that OSHA has experienced to date raise some fundamental questions about the whole program. As Nichols and Zeckhauser state, "An important question is whether the agency's failures have resulted simply from faulty execution (including the overly hasty adoption of thousands of consensus standards, excessive emphasis on safety relative to health, the inevitable start-up problems of any new agency, and, more controversially, the exclusion of economic considerations in all but extreme cases) or whether they were inherent in the basic approach taken: direct regulation through standards and inspections."[95] In any event, reducing injuries and illnesses in the workplace can result in a gain for everyone provided it is done effectively.

OSHA provides a lesson in how not to start regulatory program. As stated by Nochols and Zeckhauser, "The chain of causality in the creation of OSHA ran from perceived crisis, through political pressure, to regulatory response. At no juncture did basic conceptual questions relating to market performance or failure, and the appropriate role for government to assume in response, play an important role in the debate. The lesson, a painful one for economists, is that however relevant or powerful economic concepts may be, they are likely to be ignored when political passions are strong."[96]

Questions for Discussion

1. What were the prevailing attitudes toward safety and health in the workplace during the early years of this century? What was the basis of these attitudes? How have these attitudes changed?

2. What are the worker's compensation laws? What advantages did they have over the present system? Why didn't they work adequately in dealing with safety and health?

3. Identify the various factors behind the establishment of a federal safety and health program. Which, in your opinion, were most important? Was it inevitable that the federal government eventually intervene to regulate safety and health in the workplace?

4. Describe how the goals of the Occupational Safety and Health Act are to be accomplished. What are the functions of each piece of OSHA's administrative structure? Describe the inspection system. What problems exist with this kind of system?

5. Comment on employer and employee responsibilities and rights. Where does most of the burden fall? What are the most important rights employers have? What are the most important responsibilities of employees?

6. Should employers with good safety records be exempt from OSHA inspections? Would such a procedure increase the effectiveness of OSHA? In what ways?

7. What are the major problems with safety standards? What was the process by which OSHA adopted safety standards? What are the problems involved in setting health standards? Would some kind of a classification system work better?

8. Should benefit-cost analysis be used to set standards? Why or why not? Does the law require OSHA to do such analysis? How would you rule on this question?

9. Should OSHA be required to get search warrants? Did the court ruling requiring search warrants gut the enforcement program? Is the element of surprise important to effective enforcement?

10. What are "inferred rights" for employees? Has the Supreme Court opened up a Pandora's box with its recent ruling supporting a worker's right to refuse dangerous work free from employer retaliation?

11. Do the data on death, injuries, and illnesses actually reflect the effectiveness or ineffectiveness of the federal programs? If not, how would you measure the programs' effectiveness?

12. What new issues are appearing in the safety and health area? Are these important enough to warrant the attention of safety and health officials? What new regulations, if any, are likely to be the result? What can business organizations do to deal with these issues?

Case: Manville Corporation

On August 26, 1982, Denver-based Manville Corporation, a diversified manufacturing, mining, and forest-products company, filed for bankruptcy under Chapter 11 of the Federal Bankruptcy Act to protect itself from the overwhelming number of product-liability lawsuits relating to the manufacture and use of asbestos. The company decided to seek protection after a study showed that Manville faced a potential total of 52,000 lawsuits at a projected cost of around $2 billion, which was nearly twice the company's net worth.[1] The president of the company, John A. McKinney, said that the its businesses were in good shape but that Manville was completely overwhelmed by the cost of the asbestos lawsuits filed against the company.[2]

Manville's unprecedented bankruptcy case stunned the financial community, outraged those who had filed asbestos suits against it, put stockholders in a panic, and raised a complex tangle of issues that had far-reaching implications for toxic tort litigation. By filing for bankruptcy, Manville won at least a temporary reprieve, since all future claims were suspended. These future claimants then had to look to the bankruptcy court for relief, taking their place in line behind secured creditors. The bankruptcy court had the power to discharge or cancel any debts or potential claims against the company.

Manville was given many extensions to work out the differences with its creditors and litigants over its proposed reorganization plan. After several attempts, a plan began to take shape that eventually became the basis for a settlement. In the summer of 1985, Manville agreed to a flexible scheme to fund the claims against the company that would use some cash left over after normal operations but that could also take as much as 80 percent of the company stock. Under the plan, Manville agreed to a trust fund to deal with asbestos-disease claims. The trust would not be part of the company but would be funded by it with a $1.65 billion bond to be paid in annual installments of $75 million over 22 years, $646 million in insurance, and 50 to 80 percent of the company's common stock, depending on the size of the claims that had been filed. Voting rights on the stock would be restricted for four years after Manville emerged from bankruptcy, but after that time the trust could use its stock to essentially take over the company. The trust would be controlled by five people appointed by the bankruptcy court. The company would also pay the trust $200 million in cash and allocate 20 percent of its annual profit indefinitely if the funds were needed. Overall, the company would contribute $2.5 to $3 billion, depending on the value of the stock and future earnings.[3]

The company initially balked at giving up control when the board said it had to have the final say in who would run the company after it emerged from bankruptcy. Representatives of current and future health claimants insisted that any director be acceptable to all the creditor groups, and the company finally agreed to let creditors have the final say in board appointments, thereby removing the last major obstacle to gaining approval of the plan.[4] The board also agreed to look for an outsider to run the company after the present chief executive officer (CEO) and chair, John A. McKinney, retired in September 1986. At this news the president of the company, J.T. Hulce, who had been the heir-apparent, resigned.[5] The board then named George C. Dillon, an outside director, as chair and W. Thomas Stephens, the chief financial officer of the company, the chief executive officer.[6] The company then paid McKinney and Hulce more than $1.8 million in a severance agreement.[7]

During the time this reorganization plan was being debated, an estimated 2,000 of the 16,500 personal-injury plaintiffs died. These victims had not received a penny for their claims because the bankruptcy filing froze the litigation. The money their relatives will eventually receive is little consolation. The company itself, after a 4-year reorganization effort, is subject to be taken over by the trust, who could liquidate the company if the money isn't enough to pay claims. The only winners are the lawyers, who will make about $1 billion in fees from settlements paid by the trust.[8]

Manville thought that bankruptcy would be a quick fix to the endless stream of lawsuits it was facing and that it could emerge from Chapter 11 in a relatively short period of time, after having set aside enough money to cover these claims. It now seems that the company drastically underestimated the complexity of using the bankruptcy code to deal with toxic tort litigation. The company had to deal not only with commercial creditors and shareholders but also with about 20 representatives for the plaintiffs, another dozen or so lawyers representing co-defendants, and one representative for future claimants. Given this kind of a political context, Manville simply lost control of the situation and lost the store in the process.[9]

Case Notes

1. "Company Besieged by Claims, Files Bankruptcy," *Monthly Labor Review,* November, 1982, p. 48.

2. William Marbach, et al., "An Asbestos Bankruptcy," *Newsweek,* September 6, 1982, p. 54.

3. Jonathan Dahl, "Manville Offers $2.5 Billion Plan To Settle Claims," *Wall Street Journal,* August 5, 1985, p. 3.

4. Cynthia F. Mitchell, "Manville Is Said to Have Agreed to Let Creditors Decide Board Appointments," *Wall Street Journal,* April 30, 1986, p. 7.

5. Cynthia F. Mitchell, "Manville President Quits After Dispute with Asbestos Plaintiffs over Top Posts," *Wall Street Journal,* April 30, 1986, p. 34.

6. "Now Comes the Hard Part for Manville," *Business Week,* July 7, 1986, p. 76.

7. Cynthia F. Mitchell, "Manville to Pay Large Severance to 2 Executives," *Wall Street Journal,* June 24, 1986, p. 10.

8. Cynthia F. Mitchell, "Negative Verdict: Manville's Bid to Evade Avalanche of Lawsuits Proves Disappointing," *Wall Street Journal,* July 15, 1986, p. 1.

9. Ibid.

Chapter Notes

1. See *General Industry Digest,* U.S. Department of Labor, OSHA 2201, 1988 (rev.), pp. 1–4.

2. Bureau of Labor Statistics, *Occupational Injuries and Illnesses in the U.S. by Industry* (Washington, D.C.: Department of Labor, 1984), p. 1.

3. Division of Safety Research, National Institute of Occupational Safety and Health, unpublished, 1986, p. 1.

4. Bureau of Labor Statistics, *Occupational Injuries and Illnesses,* p. 1.

5. See Rollin H. Simonds and John V. Grimaldi, *Safety Management* (Homewood, Ill.: Richard D. Irwin, 1963), pp. 17–24; and Frank E. Bird, *Management Guide to Loss Control* (Atlanta, Ga.: Institute Press, 1974), pp. 1–14.

6. Simonds and Grimaldi, *Safety Management,* p. 17.

7. Bird, *Management Guide,* pp. 2–3.

8. John D. Blackburn, Elliott I. Klayman, and Martin H. Malin, *The Legal Environment of Business: Public Law and Regulation* (Homewood, Ill.: Richard D. Irwin, 1982), pp. 476–77.

9. J. V. Grimaldi, "Reducing Costs Through Accident Prevention Engineering," *Mechanical Engineering,* June 1951, pp. 492–93.

10. Albert L. Nichols and Richard Zeckhauser, "Government Comes to the Workplace: An Assessment of OSHA," *The Public Interest,* No. 49 (Fall 1977), pp. 40–41.

11. George Perkel, "A Labor View of the Occupational Safety and Health Act," unpublished paper presented at Industrial Relations Research Association, Spring Meeting, 1972, p. 2.

12. Fred K. Foulkes, "Learning to Live with OSHA," *Harvard Business Review,* Vol. 51, No. 6 (November–December 1973), p. 58.

13. Nichols and Zeckhauser, "Government Comes to the Workplace," p. 40.

14. Occupational Safety and Health Act, Public Law 91-596.

15. *All About OSHA,* U.S. Department of Labor, OSHA 2056, 1985 (rev.), p. 2.

16. *All About OSHA,* U.S. Department of Labor, OSHA 2056, 1982 (rev.), p. 8.

17. *OSHA Inspections,* U.S. Department of Labor, OSHA 2098, 1986, pp. 2–4.

18. Ibid., pp. 10–11.

19. See *A Brief Guide to Recordkeeping Requirements for Occupational Injuries and Illnesses,* U.S. Department of Labor, Bureau of Labor Statistics, OMB No. 1220–0029, 1986.

20. OSHA 2056, 1985 (rev.), pp. 13–14.

21. Ibid., pp. 40–41.

22. Ibid., pp. 41–42.

23. Ibid., p. 43.

24. Ibid., pp. 43–46.

25. Public Law 91-596, p. 2.

26. OSHA 2056, 1985 (rev.), p. 4.

27. "Some Small Companies Receive Exemptions on OSHA Inspections," *Wall Street Journal,* December 26, 1979, p. 8.

28. "U.S. Agency Ends Job-Safety Paper Work of Small Firms," *Wall Street Journal,* July 20, 1977, p. 7.

29. "Business Gets a Safety Break from OSHA, *U.S. News & World Report,* October 5, 1981, p. 87.

30. "OSHA Is Reducing Inspections Based On Complaints," *Wall Street Journal,* February 27, 1982, p. 16.

31. "Business Gets a Break," *U.S. News & World Report,* October 5, 1981, p. 87.

32. Cathy Trost, "OSHA to Check Safety at More Firms In an Expansion of Inspection Policy," *Wall Street Journal,* January 8, 1986, p. 48.

33. Albert R. Karr, "Agency Expands Safety Inspections Of Workplaces," March 23, 1988, p. 4.

34. "Joann S. Lubin, "OSHA Weighs Allowing Some Concerns To Take Over Routine Safety Inspections," *Wall Street Journal,* January 18, 1982, p. 3.

35. Nichols and Zeckhauser, "Government Comes to the Workplace," p. 42.

36. See Joseph Barry Mason, "OSHA: Problems and Prospects," *California Management Review,* Vol. XIX, No. 1 (Fall 1976), pp. 21–28.

37. Foulkes, "OSHA," p. 60.

38. Nichols and Zeckhauser, "Government Comes to the Workplace," p. 48.

39. "Labor Department Revokes 928 Rules Covering Job Safety," *Wall Street Journal,* October 25, 1978, p. 20.

40. The Insurance Company of North America, *Insurance Decisions: The Impact of Health Hazards at Work,* Philadelphia, undated, pp. 9–10.

41. Cathy Trost, "Health, Safety Enforcement at Work Has Eased Under Reagan, Report Says," *Wall Street Journal,* April 18, 1985, p. 62.

42. Albert R. Karr, "OSHA Sets or Toughens Exposure Limits On 376 Toxic Chemicals in Workplace," *Wall Street Journal,* January 16, 1989, p. C-5.

43. Dan Cordtz, "Safety on the Job Becomes a Major Job for Management," *Fortune,* November 1972, p. 166.

44. Vicky Cahan, "The Overhaul that Could Give OSHA Life Under Reagan," *Business Week,* January 19, 1981, pp. 88–89.

45. *The Budget for Fiscal Year 1981,* (Washington, D.C.: U.S. Government Printing Office, 1980), p. 428.

46. *Marshall v. Barlow's Inc.,* 46 L.W. 4483 (1978).

47. "Job Safety Inspectors Seldom Required to Get Warrants Despite Justices' Ruling," *Wall Street Journal,* July 17, 1978, p. 13.

48. Cathy Trost, "Occupational Hazard," *Wall Street Journal,* April 22, 1988, pp. 25–26R.

49. "Friendlier Adversaries? Companies Appeal Fewer OSHA Citations," *Wall Street Journal,* July 6, 1982, p. 1.

50. "Justices Uphold Right of Job Safety Unit to Set Penalties Without Going to Court," *Wall Street Journal,* March 24, 1977, p. 6. See also Michael A. Verespej," OSHA's Power Reaffirmed," *Industry Week,* April 25, 1977, p. 54.

51. Cahan, "Overhaul that Could Give OSHA Life," pp. 88–89.

52. Joseph W. Fallamn, Jr., *The Economics of Health,* American Medical Association, Chicago, Ill., 1978, p. 219.

53. Michael A. Verespej, "Has OSHA Improved?," *Industry Week,* August 4, 1980, p. 48.

54. Bryan Burrough and Seth H. Lubove, "Credibility Gap: Some Concerns Fudge Their Safety Records To Cut Insurance Costs," *Wall Street Journal,* December 2, 1986, p. 1.

55. "Chrysler to Pay Record Penalty In OSHA Case," *Wall Street Journal,* February 2, 1987, p. 19.

56. Clare Ansberry, "OSHA Is Criticized By a Safety Institute Over Megafine Policy," *Wall Street Journal,* June 26, 1989, p. A-3.

57. Robb Deigh, "As OSHA Flexes Its Muscle, Critics Doubt Power of Punch," *Insight,* October 5, 1987, pp. 42–43. See also Gordon Bock, "Blood, Sweat and Fears," *Time,* September 28, 1987, pp. 50–51; and Hazel Bradford, "OSHA Awakens From Its Six-Year Slumber," *Business Week,* August 10, 1987, p. 27.

58. Milo Geyelin, "Study Faults Federal Effort To Enforce Worker Safety," *Wall Street Journal,* April 28, 1989, p. B-1.

59. Susan B. Garland, "This Safety Ruling Could Be Hazardous to Employers' Health," *Business Week,* February 20, 1989, p. 34.

60. "Job Safety Becomes A Murder Issue," *Business Week,* August 6, 1984, p. 23.

61. Bill Richards and Alex Kotlowitz, "Judge Finds 3 Corporate Officials Guilty Of Murder in Cyanide Death of Worker," *Wall Street Journal,* June 17, 1985, p. 2.

62. "A Death At Work Can Put The Boss In Jail," *Business Week,* March 2, 1987, pp. 37–38.

63. Urban C. Lehner, "High Court Considers Workers' Right to Refuse Duties They See as Unsafe," *Wall Street Journal,* January 10, 1980, p. 12.

64. *Whirlpool* v. *Marshall,* 100 S. Ct. 883 (1980).

65. "OSHA Plans to Limit Rule on Employees' Access to Records," *Wall Street Journal,* July 13, 1982, p. 3.

66. "OSHA Wins Ruling on Letting Workers See Health Records," *Wall Street Journal,* November 15, 1982, p. 9.

67. American Legislative Exchange Council, *The State Factor,* Vol 10, No. 1, undated, p. 1.

68. *Federal Register,* Vol. 48, No. 228, p. 53334.

69. Joann S. Lubin, "U.S. Orders Labeling of Toxic Substances for Workplaces; Trade Secrets Protected," *Wall Street Journal,* November 23, 1983, p. 6. See also Laurie Hays, "New Rules on Workplace Hazards Prompt Intensified On-the-Job Training Programs," *Wall Street Journal,* July 8, 1986, p. 33.

70. "Labeling Rule Kicks In," *NFIB Mandate,* December 1985, p.8. See also *Hazard Communication Guidelines for Compliance,* U.S. Department of Labor, OSHA 3111, 1988.

71. "An OSHA Rule Industry Wants Despite the Cost," *Business Week,* November 7, 1983, p. 47.

72. Ibid.

73. Cathy Trost, "Plans to Alert Workers to Health Risks Stir Fears of Lawsuits and High Costs," *Wall Street Journal,* March 28, 1986, p. 11.

74. Leonard M. Apcar, "U.S. Standard for Labeling Hazards Denied," *Wall Street Journal,* May 29, 1985, p. 8.

75. *OSHA Fact Sheet,* U.S. Department of Labor, OSHA 87-25, 1987, p. 1.

76. *Occupational Safety and Health Reporter,* Vol. 17, No. 13, p. 539.

77. "Stress Claims Are Making Business Jumpy," *Business Week,* October 14, 1985, p. 152. See also Joann S. Lubin, "On-the-Job Stress Leads Many Workers To File—and Win—Compensation Awards," *Wall Street Journal,* September 17, 1986, p. 31; Sana Siwolop, "Stress: The Test Americans Are Failing," *Business Week,* April 18, 1988, pp. 74–78.

78. Bill Paul, "IBM Takes Steps to Reduce Radiation in Future VDTs," *Wall Street Journal,* November 22, 1989, p. B-1.

79. Barry Meier, "Companies Wrestle With Threats To Workers' Reproductive Health," *Wall Street Journal,* February 5, 1987, p. 21. See also "Bias or Safety?" *Time,* October 16, 1989, p. 61.

80. Maria Mallory, "An Invisible Workplace Hazard Gets Harder To Ignore," *Business Week,* January 30, 1989, pp. 92–93.

81. "Repetitive Strain Causing Job Pain, Safety Study Says," *Times-Picayune,* January 28, 1990, p. A-7.

82. Amy Docker Marcus, "In Some Workplaces, Ill Winds Blow," *Wall Street Journal,* October 9, 1989, p. B-1. See also David Holzman, "Elusive Culprits in Workplace Ills," *Insight,* June 26, 1989, pp. 44–45.

83. National Safety Council, "Accident Facts," 1985, p. 2.

84. P. J Sheridan, "What are Accidents Really Costing You?," *Occupational Hazards,* March 1979, pp. 41–43.

85. Bureau of National Affairs, Inc., *Occupational Safety and Health Reporter,* Vol. 15, No. 16 (September 19, 1985), p. 3.

86. Nichols and Zeckhauser, "Government Comes to the Workplace," p. 56.

87. National Association of Manufacturers, *Analysis and Background Report,* "Reform of Occupational Safety and Health Act of 1970," September 11, 1985, p. 5.

88. Wayne B. Gray, "The Cost of Regulation: OSHA, EPA and the Productivity Slowdown," *The American Economic Review,* Vol 77, No. 5 (December 1987), pp. 998–1006.

89. Murray L. Weidenbaum, *Business, Government, and the Public,* 4th ed., (Englewood Cliffs, N.J.:Prentice-Hall, 1990), p. 145–46.

90. "Decline in Job Injuries Seen Linked to OSHA Effort," *Job Safety and Health,* January 1977, p. 5.

91. "Accident Statistics that Jolted OSHA," *Business Week,* December 11, 1978, p. 62. See also John Mendeloff, "The Hazards of Rating Workplace Safety," *Wall Street Journal,* February 11, 1988, p. 24.

92. "U.S. Work Injuries, Illnesses Fell in 1982 to a 10-Year Low," *Wall Street Journal,* November 7, 1983, p. 45.

93. "Illness, Injury Rate In Workplace Rose In '84, Study Finds," *Wall Street Journal,* November 14, 1985, p. 10. See also Robert L. Simison, "Safety Last: Job Deaths and Injuries Seem to Be Increasing After Several Years of Decline," *Wall Street Journal,* March 18, 1986, p. 1.

94. "Job-Related Injuries, Illnesses Rose in '88 In the Private Sector," *Wall Street Journal,* November 17, 1989, p. C-10.

95. Nichols and Zeckhauser, "Government Comes to the Workplace," pp. 62–63.

96. Ibid., pp. 67–68.

Suggested Reading

BIRD, FRANK E. *Management Guide to Loss Control.* Atlanta: Institute Press, 1974.

BOLEY, JACK W. *A Guide to Effective Industrial Safety.* Houston: Gulf Publishing Co., 1977.

BUSINESS ROUNDTABLE. *Improving Construction Safety Performance.* New York: The Business Roundtable, 1982.

CHISSICK, S. S., AND R. DERRICOTT. *Occupational Health and Safety Management.* New York: John Wiley, 1981.

CULBERTSON, CHARLES V. *Managing Your Safety Manager.* New York: Risk Insurance Management Society, 1981.

DENTON, D. KEITH. *Safety Management: Improving Performance.* New York, John Wiley, 1982.

DEREAMER, RUSSELL. *Modern Safety and Health Technology.* New York: John Wiley, 1981.

GRIMALDI, JOHN V., AND ROLLIN H. SIMONDS. *Safety Management,* 4th ed. Homewood, Ill.: Irwin, 1984.

HAMMER, WILLIE. *Occupational Safety Management and Engineering,* 2d ed. Englewood Cliffs, N.J.: Prentice Hall, 1981.

MALASKY, S. W. *System Safety: Technology and Application.* New York: Garland, 1982.

MENDELOFF, JOHN. *Regulating Safety: An Economic and Political Analysis of Occupational Safety and Health Policy.* Cambridge, Mass.: MIT Press, 1979.

MILLER, JAMES C., AND BRUCE YANDLE. *Benefit-Cost Analysis of Social Regulation.* Washington, D.C.: American Enterprise Institute, 1979.

NATIONAL SAFETY COUNCIL. *Protecting Workers' Lives: A Safety and Health Guide for Unions.* Chicago: National Safety Council, 1983.

PAGE, JOSEPH A. *Bitter Wages.* New York: Grossman Publishers, 1973.

PETERS, G. A., ed. *Safety Law.* Park Ridge, Ill.: American Society of Safety Engineers, 1983.

POOLE ROBERT W., JR. *Instead of Regulation: Alternatives to Federal Regulatory Agencies.* Lexington, Mass.: Lexington Books, 1982.

POULTON, E. *The Environment at Work.* Springfield, Ill.: Charles C. Thomas, 1979.

ROTHSTEIN MARK A. *Occupational Safety and Health Law.* St. Paul, Minn.: West, 1978.

SASSONE, PETER G., AND WILLIAM A. SCHAFFER. *Cost-Benefit Analysis: A Handbook.* Orlando, Fla.: Academic Press, 1978.

SCOTT, RACHEL. *Muscle and Blood.* New York: Dutton, 1974.

SIMONDS, ROLLIN H., AND JOHN V. GRIMALDI. *Safety Management.* Homewood, Ill.: Richard D. Irwin, 1963.

STELLMAN, JEANNE M., AND SUSAN M. DAUM. *Work Is Dangerous to Your Health.* New York: Pantheon Books, 1973.

UNGER, S. H. *Controlling Technology: Ethics and the Responsible Engineer.* New York: Holt, Rinehart and Winston, 1982.

WALLICK, FRANKLIN. *The American Worker: An Endangered Species.* New York: Ballantine Books, 1972.

CHAPTER 8

Consumer Protection

Consumer protection refers to a number of activities that are designed to protect consumers from a wide range of practices that can infringe on the rights consumers are believed to possess in the marketplace. These activities stem from a broad and aggressive movement, usually called consumerism, that is supported by consumers themselves (particularly consumer advocates), by many business organizations, and by the government to see that these rights of consumers are respected.

> Consumerism is a movement designed to improve the rights and powers of consumers in relation to the sellers of products and services. It is a protest movement of consumers against what they or their advocates see as unfair, discriminatory, and arbitrary treatment. Consumerism is as old as business but has taken on new dimensions and thrusts in recent years. . . . Consumerism does not mean that caveat emptor—let the buyer beware—is replaced by caveat venditor—let the seller beware. It does mean, however, that protecting the consumer is politically acceptable and that the government will survey consumer demands for better treatment and respond to them with new guidelines for and regulations over business.[1]

This chapter focuses on the rights of the consumer that need to be protected and examines the various activities of the government, consumer advocates, and business organizations that protect these rights. Consumer protection is first looked at from an historical and institutional perspective. Current concerns that consumers have in the marketplace and public policies formulated to deal with these concerns are then examined.

History of Consumer Protection

Consumer protection is not just a current phenomenon, as some people might suspect. Consumers obviously have been concerned about various aspects of the products they buy ever since the marketplace has existed. But in terms of the development of consumer protection in this country, there are three distinct periods when something called a consumer movement can be identified. The concerns of the movements in each of these periods were different.[2]

MUCKRAKING ERA

Between 1879 and 1905, a number of bills were introduced into Congress to regulate the sale of food and drugs and protect consumers from the growing power of large business enterprises. However, these bills were apparently the work of a small group of consumer advocates because both Congress and the public at large were rather apathetic about any public policy measures directed to protect consumers. This apathy, coupled with strong business opposition to the bills, meant that no action was taken on the consumer front during these years.

Then, in 1905, a book was published that changed the public's attitude dramatically. That book was Upton Sinclair's *The Jungle,* a sordid tale of conditions in the Chicago meatpacking industry. The original intent of the book may have been to focus on working conditions, since it told the story of an immigrant who came to this country to make his fortune, only to end up on the ''scrap heap'' with his health broken and no money in his pocket after some years of working long hours in unsafe and unhealthy conditions. Thus ended the American dream.

What the public seized upon, however, were the conditions under which the food they were buying was produced and packaged. The book gave gruesome examples of the way meat was processed (see box), portraying meatpacking plants where rats and parts of the human body were often processed along with sausage meat. This book, more than any other single event, jolted the public out of its apathy and made the need for consumer protection apparent to many people. Congress responded by passing the following public policy measures.

- Pure Food and Drug Act (1906). Outlawed adulteration and misbranding of food and drugs sold in interstate commerce. This basic act has been amended many times since.
- Federal Meat Inspection Act (1907). Provided for federal inspection of meat sold in interstate commerce. Gave the Department of Agriculture power to inspect slaughtering, packing, and canning plants.
- Federal Trade Commission Act (1914). Designed to protect consumers from unfair methods of competition. Created the Federal Trade Commission to administer the act.
- Water Power Act (1920). Established the Federal Power Commission to protect consumers from public utility monopolies, making these monopolies subject to government regulation.

The focus of these efforts was to protect consumers from unsavory and unfair trade practices that were unknown to many people. The term *muckraking* is appropriate, since this movement was designed to expose unsavory and unfair practices of business and build public support for public policy measures. This movement ended, for all practical purposes, before the depression, since prosperity for all became the order of the day; but the depression finally ended concerns of this kind entirely because much of the public came to have other worries.

THE INFORMATION ERA

This era, too, was sparked by a book. Called *Your Money's Worth* and written by Stuart Chase and F. J. Schlink, this book pictured the consumer as an ''Alice'' in a ''Wonderland'' of conflicting product claims and bright promises. It focused on advertising and packaging that inundated the consumer with information designed to sell a

THE JUNGLE

All of these were sinister incidents; but they were trifles compared to what Jurgis saw with his own eyes before long. One curious thing he had noticed, the very first day, in his profession of shoveler of guts; which was the sharp trick of the floor bosses whenever there chanced to come a "slunk" calf. Any man who knows anything about butchering knows that the flesh of a cow that is about to calve, or has just calved, is not fit for food. A good many of these came every day to the packing houses—and, of course, if they had chosen, it would have been an easy matter for the packers to keep them till they were fit for food. But for the saving of time and fodder, it was the law that cows of that sort came along with the others, and whoever noticed it would tell the boss, and the boss would start up a conversation with the government inspector, and the two would stroll away. So in a trice the carcass of the cow would be cleaned out, and the entrails would have vanished; it was Jurgis's task to slide them into the trap, calves and all, and on the floor they took out these "slunk" calves, and butchered them for meat, and used even the skins of them.

One day a man slipped and hurt his leg; and that afternoon, when the last of the cattle had been disposed of, and the men were leaving, Jurgis was ordered to remain and do some special work which this injured man had usually done. It was late, almost dark, and the government inspectors had all gone, and there were only a dozen or two of men on the floor. That day they had killed about four thousand cattle, and these cattle had come in freight trains from far states, and some of them had got hurt. There were some with broken legs, and some with gored sides; there were some that had died, from what cause no one could say; and they were all to be disposed of, here in darkness and silence. "Downers," the men called them; and the packing house had a special elevator upon which they were raised to the killing beds, where the gang proceeded to handle them, with an air of businesslike nonchalance which said plainer than any words that it was a matter of everyday routine. It took a couple of hours to get them out of the way, and in the end Jurgis saw them go into the chilling rooms with the rest of the meat, being carefully scattered here and there so that they could not be identified. When he came home that night he was in a very somber mood, having begun to see at last how those might be right who had laughed at him for his faith in America.

From Upton Sinclair, *The Jungle* (New York: New American Library, 1960), pp. 66–67. Reprinted with permission.

product rather than help the consumer make an intelligent decision. The consumer had no way to sort through all these conflicting claims and rosy promises to decide which could be believed and which were pure exaggeration.

The book made a plea for impartial product testing agencies that had no vested interest in the product and thus could supply the consumer with objective and trustworthy information about the performance of the product. The 1930s, then, saw the development of independent product testing agencies, such as Consumers Union, that would test products and publish the results. In addition, the following important public policy measures were also passed in the 1930s:

- *Food, Drug, and Cosmetics Act* (1938): Amended the earlier law by strengthening the definitions of adulteration and misbranding, and extended the scope of the law to cover cosmetics and therapeutic devices. Also established the Food and Drug Administration, with authority to seize products found unfit for consumption and to prosecute persons or firms found in violation.
- *Wheeler-Lea Act* (1938): Amended the Federal Trade Commission Act of 1914 to give the FTC regulatory power over the advertising of food, drugs, cosmetics, and therapeutic devices.
- *Wool Products Labeling Act* (1939): Required labels on woolen goods to tell consumers the percentages of wool, reprocessed wool, and reused wool in the product.

The concern in this period was mainly with the provision to consumers of accurate, relevant information that could aid them in making intelligent and informed purchase decisions. The earlier concern about the quality of products continued, of course, but the major focus was on advertising and labeling of products. The Second World War marked the end of this particular consumer movement.

CONTINUING CONSUMER CONCERN

From the end of World War II until about 1965, there wasn't anything that could be clearly identified as a consumer movement. It was a period of widespread prosperity; consumers were being "blessed to death" with a proliferation of new products and apparently were generally satisfied with the treatment they were getting. Nevertheless, there was a continuing concern about product quality and provision of information, are exemplified in the following public policy measures.

- *Fur Products Labeling Act* (1951): Stated mandatory specifications for the labeling, invoicing, and advertising of fur products.
- *Flammable Fabrics Act* (1953): Prohibited making clothing from highly flammable materials.
- *Poultry Products Inspection Act* (1957): Provided for government inspection of poultry products in interstate commerce.
- *Textile Fiber Products Identification Act* (1958): Required labels on clothing to show the percentage of textile fiber content and regulated the use of names for synthetic fibers. Also required identification of the producer or distributor and country of origin.
- *Food, Drug, and Cosmetics Act Amendments* (1958): Further extended the Food and Drug Act to provide for regulation of food additives.
- *Hazardous Substances Labeling Act* (1960): Required warning labels on products used in households that were toxic, corrosive, irritating, or flammable.
- *Food, Drug, and Cosmetic Act Amendments* (1962): Known as the Kefauver-Harris Drug Amendments, these amendments required pretesting of drugs for effectiveness as well as safety and prescribed that drugs be labeled by the generic name.

MODERN CONSUMER MOVEMENT

The modern consumer movement began in 1965 with the publication of another book, Ralph Nader's *Unsafe at any Speed,* which eventually became a well-known book, if not a best-seller. The book was critical about the safety of the Corvair automobile and indicted its producer, General Motors, for a lack of concern about automobile safety. The issue received national attention when it became public knowledge that General Motors had hired private investigators to follow Nader and investigate him while he was a witness for a Senate subcommittee. The president of General Motors, James Roche, apologized to Nader for these actions at a public hearing of the subcommittee. This apology, of course, received national television coverage and was very embarassing to the company.

Not only did Nader receive instant publicity and notoriety because of this event, he also filed suit against General Motors and eventually settled out of court for $425,000, most of which was used to start his organization. Thus General Motors ironically helped Nader rise out of obscurity and financed his start in the public interest arena. This is not to suggest that without the General Motors incident a new consumer movement would never have begun. If it had not been Nader and automobile safety, it probably would have been someone else on some other issue.

The time was ripe for a new consumer movement to be concerned with a range of issues that grew out of a highly affluent population, a technologically sophisticated marketplace, and a society that in general had high expectations and aspirations for the fulfillment of higher needs. The complexity of many modern products made it difficult for the average consumer to make a rational choice among products and impossible to repair them when broken. This modern consumer movement lacked the particular focus of previous movements but was concerned about a variety of issues related to the marketplace, including product safety, quality of products, reliability and product obsolescence, truth in advertising and packaging, uses of credit, completeness of information, product warranties, product liability, and other issues. This range of issues is exemplified in the consumer legislation that came pouring out of Congress during the latter half of the 1960s and the early 1970s, most of which is listed here.

Cigarette Labeling and Advertising Act (1966): Required labels on cigarette packages warning consumers about the dangers of smoking.

Fair Packaging and Labeling Act (1966): Also known as the Truth-in-Packaging Act, this measure specified mandatory labeling requirements regarding identity and quantity of many household products.

Child Protection Act (1966): Banned the sale of hazardous toys and articles intended for children.

National Traffic and Motor Vehicle Safety Act (1966): Provided for a national safety program and establishment of safety standards for motor vehicles.

Wholesome Meat Act (1967): Required states to meet federal meat inspection standards and raised quality standards for imported meat.

Flammable Fabrics Act Amendments (1967): Broadened the authority of the federal government to set safety standards for flammable products including household products, fabrics, and materials.

Consumer Credit Protection Act (1968): Also known as the Truth-in-Lending Act, this measure required full disclosure of the terms and conditions of finance charges for consumer loans and installment purchases.

Wholesome Poultry Products Act (1968): Provided federal support for improving state-level poultry regulation.

Radiation Control for Health and Safety Act (1968): Provided for mandatory control standards and recall of faulty electronic products.

Child Protection and Toy Safety Act (1969): Broadened coverage of the Child Protection Act to include electrical, mechanical, and thermal hazards.

Public Health Smoking Act (1970): Prohibited cigarette advertising on television and radio and required a revision of the warning label on cigarette packages.

Amendments to the Federal Deposit Insurance Act (1970): Prohibited issuance of unsolicited credit cards, limited a cutsomer's liability in case of loss or theft, regulated credit bureaus, and provided consumers with access to their credit files.

Poison Prevention Packaging Act (1970): Authorized standards for child-resistant packaging of hazardous substances, such as drugs and medicine.

Lead-Based Paint Elimination Act (1971): Provided assistance in developing and administering programs to eliminate lead-based paints.

Consumer Product Safety Act (1972): Established a Federal Consumer Product Safety Commission with the authority to create safety standards for consumer products and ban those products presenting an undue risk of injury to consumers.

Not only was Congress active in responding to consumer issues, the executive branch was active as well. President Kennedy delivered a special message to Congress calling for a broad range of legislative and administrative action to assist consumers. Kennedy directed that the Council of Economic Advisers create a Consumer's Advisory Council and that heads of federal agencies concerned with consumer welfare appoint special assistants to advise them on consumer issues. In addition, Kennedy enunciated what has since come to be called the consumer bill of rights (see box).

President Johnson built consumer representation more directly into the executive branch by appointing a special assistant for consumer affairs. President Nixon extended this concept by asking Congress in another special message to create a new Office of Consumer Affairs in the Executive Office of the President with a larger budget and greater responsibilities. Legislation was introduced in the 91st Congress to establish a new Department of Consumer Affairs, headed by a secretary with full cabinet rank. Although this legislation failed to pass, President Ford built consumer representation in every cabinet department as an alternative to the Consumer Protection Agency. Finally, President Carter issued Executive Order 12160 ordering all federal agencies to review their procedures to see that consumer interests are adequately addressed. The order called for each agency to have a consumer staff, meaningful participation by consumers, informational materials for the public, adequate public access and complaint handling, and technical assistance to consumer organizations.

Government Agencies

Various agencies in the government have, of course, been a most active part of the consumer movement. Some new agencies were created during the modern consumer movement and additional responsibilities were given to some of the existing agencies. These agencies will be described in some detail because of the impact they have on businesses producing consumer products.

Federal Trade Commission. Established in 1914, the Federal Trade Commission (FTC) was a product of Woodrow Wilson's philosophy toward consumers, which advocated policies of freeing them from monopolies and restoring competition.[3] Under Section 5 of the Federal Trade Commission Act, the agency was empowered to protect consumers against all "unfair methods of competition." With this mandate, the agency

THE CONSUMER BILL OF RIGHTS

President Kennedy first listed four rights of consumers that he believed needed protection: the right to safety, the right to a choice, the right to know, and the right to be heard. These rights were later supported by presidents Johnson and Nixon. To these might be added several others of later vintage. Thus a complete consumer bill of rights contains the following:

1. *The right to safety:* The consumer has a right to be protected from dangerous products that might cause injury or illness and from the thoughtless actions of other consumers.

2. *The right to a choice:* The consumer has the right to be able to select products from a range of alternatives offered by competing firms.

3. *The right to know:* The consumer must have access to readily available, relevant, and accurate information to use in making purchase decisions.

4. *The right to be heard:* The consumer must be able to find someone who will respond to legitimate complaints about abuses taking place in the market and products that do not meet expectations.

5. *The right to recourse and redress:* The consumer has a right to expect full compensation for injuries or damages suffered as a result of unsafe products or abuses in the marketplace.

6. *The right to full value:* The consumer has a right to expect a product to perform as advertised and to meet expectations that were created so that full value is received for the money spent.

7. *The right to education:* Consumers must have access to educational programs that help them understand and use the information available in the marketplace to make rational purchase decisions.

8. *The right to representation and participation:* Consumer interests must be represented on policymaking bodies that deal with issues related to the marketplace.

became involved in consumer protection litigation as well as antitrust activities. The agency's consumer protection authority, however, was restricted in 1931 by a Supreme Court decision that held that Section 5 did not reach trade practices, no matter how injurious to consumers, that did not injure competitors or the competitive process. Seven years later Congress corrected this deficiency by amending Section 5 to give the agency a mandate to pursue "unfair or deceptive acts or practices in commerce."

Thus empowered, the FTC has broader authority to regulate business than almost any other agency. (See Exhibit 8.1.) To protect the public against all "unfair methods of competition" and all "unfair or deceptive acts or practices in commerce" is a very broad mandate. To carry out its mandate, the FTC uses a variety of enforcement techniques to bring accused violators of laws under its jurisdiction into compliance. For example, the FTC can issue "cease and desist" orders for violations of the FTC act to stop a business from continuing the proscribed conduct. Over the last few years, Congress has also given the FTC responsibility for the enforcement of a number of specialized consumer protection statutes, including the Truth in Lending Act, the Truth in Packaging Act, and the Fair Credit Reporting Act. In addition, the agency can promulgate trade regulation rules that affect entire industries. An example of such a rule is the

EXHIBIT 8.1

Federal Trade Commission
Pennsylvania Avenue at Sixth St. NW, Washington, DC 20580

Purpose: To ensure "vigorous, free and fair competition in the market place."

Regulatory Activity: The Commission has authority to act against and prevent: (1) general restraint of trade in interstate commerce; (2) false or deceptive advertising of consumer goods and other unfair or deceptive practices; (3) activities that tend to lessen competition or create a monopoly, such as price discrimination and certain mergers and acquisitions. The FTC also formulates its own "trade regulation rules," which have the force of law. When statutes are violated, it can issue a cease-and-desist order, conduct formal litigation, or seek civil penalties.

Established: 1914

Legislative Authority:
  Enabling Legislation: Federal Trade Commission Act of 1914 (38 Stat. 717), as amended (52 Stat. 111)
  The FTC also has responsibility for enforcement of the following acts:
    Clayton Act of 1914 (38 Stat. 730)
    Export Trade Act of 1918 (40 Stat. 516)
    Robinson-Patman Act of 1936 (49 Stat. 1526)
    Wool Products Labeling Act of 1940 (54 Stat. 1128)
    Lanham Trademark Act of 1946 (60 Stat. 427)
    Fur Products Labeling Act of 1951 (65 Stat. 175)
    Textile Fiber Products Identification Act of 1958 (72 Stat. 1717)
    Fair Packaging and Labeling Act of 1966 (80 Stat. 1269)
    Truth-in-Lending Act of 1969 (82 Stat. 146)
    Fair Credit Reporting Act of 1970 (84 Stat. 1521)
    Fair Credit Billing Act of 1974 (88 Stat. 1511)
    Magnuson-Moss Warranty-Federal Trade Commission Improvement Act of 1975 (88 Stat. 2123)
    Hart-Scott-Rodino Antitrust Improvement Act of 1976 (90 Stat. 1383)
    Debt Collection Act of 1977 (91 Stat. 874)

Organization: The Commission became an independent administrative agency in 1951. It is headed by a five-member commission appointed to 7-year terms by the President with the advice and consent of the Senate.

Additional Responsibilities: The Commission also regulates various aspects of the consumer credit industry, including issuance of loans and credit cards and activities of credit reporting agencies and debt collection agencies; packaging and labeling of certain consumer commodities; and certain aspects of the fur and textile industries.

Budgets and Staffing, Fiscal 1970–90

	1970	1975	1980	1985	1986	1987	1988	(Estimated) 1989	1990
Budget ($ millions)	21	39	66	66	67	66	67	67	70
Staffing	1,391	1,569	1,665	1,075	1,033	918	922	872	872

Source: Ronald J. Penoyer, *Directory of Federal Regulatory Agencies*, 2d ed. (St. Louis, Mo.: Washington University Center for the Study of American Business, 1980), p. 37. Reprinted with permission.

RULES FOR FUNERAL PROVIDERS

1. If a consumer phones a funeral provider, the provider must inform the consumer that price information is available over the phone and must reasonably answer any questions including those relating to the price of goods and services offered.

2. The various components of a funeral must be priced and offered on an itemized basis. The funeral provider must give all customers a list containing this itemized price information. The funeral provider may, however, continue to offer and sell package funerals so long as the itemization requirement is also met.

3. Funeral providers are prohibited from making misrepresentations about funeral requirements and state and local laws. Customers must be given several short written factual disclosures on funeral requirements and local laws.

4. The funeral provider must obtain permission of the family before embalming the remains of the deceased and may not suggest that embalming is required by law when that is not the case.

5. The funeral provider may not require that an elaborate casket be purchased if a direct cremation is being arranged. Funeral providers who offer to arrange direct cremations must make available a plain wooden box for use in such arrangements.

Source: "Funeral Rule, Upheld by Court, is Now in Effect for Providers," *AARP News Bulletin,* Vol. XXV, no. 5 (May 1984), p. 13.

funeral industry trade rules issued in 1984 (see box). These rules were put into effect after an 11-year fight with the funeral industry.[4]

The agency is governed by a chair and four other commissioners, all of whom are appointed by the president with the advice and consent of the Senate. The agency is organized into three major bureaus. The Bureau of Competition investigates and prosecutes antitrust cases. The Bureau of Consumer Protection is concerned with such consumer protection activities as advertising practices, marketing abuse, credit practices, energy and product information, and product liability. The Bureau of Economics provides statistical information and economic analysis to other bureaus. In addition, the agency has several regional offices engaged primarily in consumer protection matters and coordinated by the Washington headquarters.

For much of its history, the FTC was not particularly active and did not present the threat to business that it has in recent years. It responded to many individual complaints but did not take much broader corrective action against the offending parties to change industry practice. The years from 1914 to 1969 have been characterized as years of neglect as far as consumer interests were concerned. During that time, the FTC, more often than not, found itself promoting business interests. The commission became much more active on behalf of consumers in the 1970s because of the appointment of a more active chair and an exposé written by the Nader organization. This exposé constituted a blanket indictment of just about everything in and about the commission: its personnel, politics, and purpose. This report was a major disruption in the FTC's life and resulted in several reforms that made the FTC a thorn in the side of business.

In the late 1970s, there was concern that the FTC was getting too active, and Congress took steps to block some of its trade regulations pertaining to advertising on children's television programs. Talk about a legislative veto over all trade rules became widespread and was actually implemented when Congress reauthorized the agency in 1980. The first use of this veto power took place in 1982 when Congress overruled an

FTC rule requiring used car dealers to tell customers about any defects they knew about in the cars they were selling.[5] The regulation would have required dealers to attach a sticker to the window of each vehicle for sale, stating whether any warranty was being offered and disclosing any major mechanical defects of which the dealer was aware. Use of the legislative veto was curtailed when the Supreme Court found it unconstitutional.

The actions along with the election of a more conservative and pro-business administration in 1980 signaled the end of the activist era at the FTC, at least for the time being. The FTC head appointed by Reagan shared his philosophy of less government intervention and proposed major cutbacks in agency authority.[6] The FTC began to move its emphasis toward individual consumer protection cases and away from its broad rule-making authority. Instead of regulating entire industries, the agency began to emphasize the pursuit of individual violations. The agency closed some of its regional offices and reduced its antitrust and consumer protection work forces. In 1983, a congressional staff report criticized the agency for reducing its enforcement of antitrust and consumer protection laws, claiming that antitrust enforcement actions had dropped from 40 in fiscal 1981 to 19 in fiscal 1982 and that consumer protection actions had declined by 48 percent over the same period.[7] The new head, appointed in 1986, continued these trends by suggesting less stringent enforcement of deceptive advertising laws and advocating approval of mergers among major soft drink makers and other companies that were opposed by a majority of the other commissioners.[8]

Consumer Product Safety Commission. The CPSC was created by the Consumer Product Safety Act of 1972 to protect the public against unreasonable risks of injury associated with a wide range of consumer products. The background of this act was a national commission study on product safety, which found that 20 million Americans were injured severely enough each year because of product-related accidents to require medical treatment. Some 110,000 of these people were permanently disabled and 30,000 were killed, at a cost to the economy of more than $5.5 billion annually.[9] As with the background of OSHA, a crisis situation was believed to exist that demanded government attention. The solution to the crisis was again, as with OSHA, direct regulation.

The CPSC is another five-member commission headquartered in Washington, DC, with 14 field offices and testing laboratories around the country. The jurisdiction of the commission covers a broad range of consumer products, including ladders, swings, blenders, televisions, stoves, as well as stairs, ramps, windowsills, doors, and electrical wiring. The only consumer products not covered by the act are foods, drugs, cosmetics, automobiles, firearms, tobacco, boats, pesticides, and aircraft, all of which are regulated by other agencies. The agency was also given responsibility, like the FTC, for enforcing specific consumer legislation, including the Flammable Fabrics Act, the Refrigerator Safety Act, the Hazardous Substances Act, and the Poison Prevention Packaging Act. (See Exhibit 8.2.)

The CPSC has the authority and responsibility to (1) develop and enforce uniform safety standards governing the design, construction, contents, performance, and labeling of all the consumer products under its jurisdiction; (2) ban consumer products deemed to be hazardous; (3) initiate and monitor recall of hazardous products; (4) help industry develop voluntary safety standards; (5) help consumers evaluate the comparative safety of products; (6) conduct applied research and develop test methods for unsafe products; (7) collect, analyze, and publish injury and hazard data; and (8) help to harmonize federal, state, and local product safety laws and enforcement.

Regarding its enforcement powers, the commission can order a manufacturer,

Exhibit 8.2

Consumer Product Safety Commission
111 Eighteenth Street NW, Washington, DC 20207

Purpose: To protect the public against unreasonable risks of injury associated with consumer products.

Regulatory activity: The Commission has authority: (1) to issue and enforce safety standards governing the design, construction, contents, performance, and labeling of more than 10,000 consumer products; and (2) to ban hazardous consumer products.

Established: October 27, 1972

Legislative Authority:
  Enabling Legislation: Consumer Product Safety Act of 1972 (86 Stat. 1207; P.L. 92-573)

  The Commission is responsible for the administration of four acts, which were under the jurisdiction of different agencies until 1972:
    Flammable Fabrics Act of 1954 (67 Stat. 111; P.L. 83-88), as amended
    Refrigerator Safety Act of 1956 (70 Stat. 953; P.L. 84-930)
    Hazardous Substances Act of 1960 (74 Stat. 372; P.L. 86-613), as amended
    Poison Prevention Packaging Act of 1970 (84 Stat. 1670; P.L. 91-601)

Organization: This independent agency is governed by a five-member commission, appointed for seven-year terms by the President, with the advice and consent of the Senate.

Products Regulated: "Any article or component part produced or distributed (i) for sale to a consumer . . . or (ii) for the personal use, consumption or enjoyment of a consumer."

Products Exempted: Tobacco and tobacco products; motor vehicles and motor vehicle equipment; drugs; food; aircraft and aircraft components; certain boats; and certain other items.

Budgets and Staffing, Fiscal 1975–90

	1975	1980	1981	1982	1983	1984	1985	1986	1987	1988	(Estimated) 1989	1990
Budget ($ millions)	34	43	42	32	34	35	36	35	35	32	35	34
Staffing	884	871	812	631	577	558	502	476	456	459	498	498

Source: Ronald J. Penoyer, *Directory of Federal Regulatory Agencies,* 2d ed. (St. Louis, Mo.: Washington University Center for the Study of American Business, 1980), p. 23. Reprinted with permission.

wholesaler, distributor, or retailer to recall, repair, or replace any product that it determines in the course of its research to be unreasonably risky. Where the action is deemed to be justified because of the hazard involved, the commission can simply ban the product from being sold on the market. The fines involved range from $50,000 to $500,000, with a possible jail term of up to 1 year for violations. In addition, the act also requires manufacturers, wholesalers, distributors, or retailers to report within 24 hours the existence of any substantial product hazard that is known. The agency can then demand corrective action, including refunds, recalls, dissemination of public earnings, and reimbursement of buyers for expenses they incur in the process. In 1984, the Toy Safety Act was passed, which gave the Commission the power to recall dangerous toys from the marketplace much more quickly than before. Previous to this act the CPSC had to order recalls of children's products under the Federal Hazardous Substances Act, which required a lengthy banning process.

Over the course of its existence, the CPSC has adopted only six mandatory standards for products ranging from swimming pool slides to lawn mowers and has forced business to adopt several voluntary standards. It has also imposed two labeling requirements and six product bans under the Product Safety Act and forced recalls of many others. Since 1973, the Commission has initiated more than 1,300 recalls or other corrective actions that invovled over 200 million products. The agency has also issued five rules under the Federal Hazardous Substances Act and requirements for child-resistant caps for numerous products under the Poison Prevention Packaging Act.[10]

The Consumer Product Safety Amendments of 1981 changed the rule-making procedure of the Commission by placing more emphasis on voluntary standards. An advance notice of proposed rule-making has to invite the development of a voluntary standard. The Commission must then assist industry in developing a voluntary standard, and if it appears likely that this standard will eliminate or adequately reduce the risk of injury, and it is likely that there will be substantial compliance with the standard, the CPSC must terminate its mandatory rule-making effort and defer to the voluntary standard. This provision along with other provisions in the amendments, severely restricted the agency's rule-making authority.[11]

The Food and Drug Administration. The Food and Drug Administration (FDA), located in the Department of Health and Human Services, has been given the mandate to protect the public against impure and unsafe foods, drugs, and cosmetics and to regulate hazards involved with medical devices and radiation. In addition to the basic Food and Drug Act of 1906, which has been amended many times since, the FDA has also been given responsibility for specific consumer legislation such as the Fair Packaging and Labeling Act of 1966. (See Exhibit 8.3)

The FDA's responsibility for drug regulation is carried out by the Bureau of Drugs, which administers rigid premarket testing procedures. No new drug in the country can be marketed until teams of physicians, pharmacists, chemists, and statisticians from the Bureau of Drugs have completed a thorough assessment. Firms wanting to place a new drug on the market must develop data to show that it is safe and effective and must also prove to the Bureau's satisfaction that adequate controls are provided to ensure proper identification, quality, purity, and strength of the new drug. The FDA now also requires pharmaceutical companies to monitor usage and side effects of drugs after they have been placed on the market. This procedure will strengthen the FDA's "postmarketing surveillance" system to discover defective products and have them removed from commercial channels and detect previously unsuspected adverse side effects of drugs.[12]

The FDA's responsibility for medical devices was given it by 1976 amendments to the Food and Drug Act. These amendments empower the FDA to remove ineffective or unsafe medical devices from the market and require extensive testing of new devices before they are approved for sale on the market. The amendments also require companies to report significant defects they discover, to inform physicians and patients of these problems, and to repair or replace, or refund money on, such defective products. The background to this extension of authority was many reports of faulty cardiac pacemakers, unsafe X-ray machines, inaccurate thermometers, and similar problems.

The responsibility of the FDA for food safety stems from amendments to the Food, Drug, and Cosmetic Act passed in 1958, which contain the famous Delaney Clause on food additives. These amendments gave the FDA authority to develop regulations for

EXHIBIT 8.3

Department of Health and Human Services
Food and Drug Administration
5600 Fishers Lane, Rockville, Md 20857

Purpose: To protect the public against impure and unsafe foods, drugs, and cosmetics, and to regulate hazards involved with medical devices and radiation.

Regulatory Activity: The FDA (1) regulates, inspects, tests, sets standards for, and licenses the manufacture of biological products shipped in interstate or foreign commerce; (2) sets standards for, monitors the quality of, and regulates labeling of all drugs for human use; (3) develops regulation for the composition, quality, nutrition, and safety of foods, food additives, colors, and cosmetics, and inspects processing plants and marketing establishments; (4) sets standards for safe limits of radiation exposure; (5) evaluates the safety of veterinary preparations and devices; and (6) develops policy for and evaluates the safety, efficacy, and labeling of medical devices.

Established: 1931

Legislative Authority:
  Enabling Legislation: Agriculture Appropriation Act of 1931 (46 Stat. 392)
    Food and Drug Act of 1906 (34 Stat. 768)
    Food, Drug, and Cosmetic Act of 1938 (52 Stat. 1040) and the following amendments to it:
      Food Additives Amendment of 1958 (72 Stat. 1788) Delaney Amendment)
      Color Additive Amendments of 1960 (74 Stat. 403)
      Drug Admendments of 1962 (76 Stat. 704)
      Medical Devices Amendments of 1976 (90 Stat. 539)
    Fair Packaging and Labeling Act of 1966 (80 Stat. 1296)
    Radiation Control for Health and Safety Act of 1968 (82 Stat. 1173)
  FDA is also responsible for portions of:
    Tea Importation Act of 1897
    Filled Milk Act of 1923 (42 Stat. 1486)
    Public Health Services Act of 1944 (58 Stat.) 697
    Federal Hazardous Substances Act of 1966 (80 Stat. 1303)

Organization: This agency, located within the Department of Health and Human Services, is headed by a commissioner.

Budgets and Staffing, Fiscal 1975-90

	1970	1975	1980	1985	1986	1987	1988	1989 (Estimated)	1990 (Estimated)
Budget ($ millions)	80	207	334	437	415	457	487	559	523
Staffing	4,414	6,441	7,419	7,104	6,806	6,834	7,094	7,226	7,363

Source: Ronald J. Penoyer, Directory of Federal Regulatory Agencies, 2d ed. (St. Louis, Mo.: Washington University Center for the Study of American Business, 1980), p. 59. Reprinted with permission.

the composition, quality, nutrition, and safety of foods and food additives. Much of the current controversy about food safety centers on this Delaney Clause, which rigidly requires the FDA to prohibit the use of any food additive that is found to cause cancer in humans or animals (see the next section). The FDA is also involved in developing rules on food labeling specifying ingredient and nutritional information to be provided for consumers.

The FDA also has responsibility for a food inspection system to inspect processing plants and marketing establishments. The agency has about 1,000 inspectors who work in cooperation with state inspectors. They look for good management practices (GMP), which mainly involve sanitation. Where unsanitary conditions exist that need attention, the FDA must turn the case over to a federal attorney for prosecution. The agency lacks the power to prosecute directly which is held by some other regulatory commissions.

As of 1989, the FDA was responsible for monitoring 63,000 food companies, 14,000 drug companies, 13,000 medical-device manufacturers, and 1,700 cosmetic makers. During the Reagan administration, the budget and staff of the FDA were cut as part of a deregulatory effort. Congress, however, passed 23 public health bills during this period, many of which were meant to shore up the power of the agency in reaction to the regulatory cutbacks. While this action increased the FDA's workload, Congress did not restore any of the lost staff positions or add employees to meet the additional responsibilities. Consequently, the agency reached the point of bureaucratic burnout that even had business concerned.[13]

The National Highway Traffic Safety Administration.   NHTSA was created by the National Highway Traffic and Motor Vehicle Safety Act of 1966 to set safety standards for motor vehicles and motor vehicle equipment. The purpose of the commission is to protect the public from unreasonable risk of injury resulting from the usage of motor vehicles. The Energy Policy and Conservation Act and Clean Air Amendments of 1970 also gave it authority to set standards for fuel economy and emissions. The responsibilities of the agency include setting and enforcing mandatory average fuel economy standards for new motor vehicles, regulating the safety performance of new and used motor vehicles and their equipment, such as tires, and investigating auto safety defects and requiring manufacturers to remedy them. (See Exhibit 8.4)

Regarding safety standards, the agency has focused on problems that statistics show pose the greatest hazards to motorists and pedestrians. In proposing a standard, NHTSA must take into account the number of accidents and injuries that the standard will, it is hoped, reduce and the practicality and reasonableness of applying the standard under normal conditions. The determination of reasonableness must include consideration of the cost of compliance with the standard. The standard must also either reduce the likelihood of accidents or reduce injuries or death from accidents that do occur.[14]

Manufacturers are required to report defects connected with motor vehicle safety and noncompliance with standards to NHTSA within 5 days after their discovery. The agency can also conduct independent investigations to discover safety defects and noncompliance with safety standards. If the situation is serious enough, NHTSA can order the manufacturer to engage in a notification and remedy campaign, commonly known as a recall, even for defects not covered by standards. Such recalls have become rather commonplace in the automobile industry. These recalls cover a variety of defects from engine mounts, gas tanks, seat backs, faulty carburetors, transmissions, brakes, and similar problems.

EXHIBIT 8.4

Department of Transportation
National Highway Traffic Safety Administration
400 Seventh Street SW, Washington, DC 20590

Purpose: To set standards for motor vehicle safety and for motor vehicle fuel economy, and to set federal standards for various state highway safety programs.

Regulatory Activity: This agency (1) sets and enforces mandatory average fuel economy standards for new motor vehicles; (2) regulates safety performance for new and used vehicles and their equipment, including tires; (3) investigates auto safety defects not covered by standards, and can require manufacturers to remedy such defects; (4) sets standards for auto bumpers, auto ratings (e.g., for crashes), and diagnostic auto inspections; (5) enforces the uniform national maximum speed limit; and (6) administers the federal odometer law.

Established: 1970

Legislative Authority
  Enabling Legislation: National Traffic and Motor Vehicle Safety Act of 1966 (80 Stat. 718), as amended Highway Safety Act of 1966 (80 Stat. 731), as amended

NHTSA also carries out programs under the following acts:
  Clean Air Amendments of 1970 (84 Stat. 1700)
  Highway Safety Act of 1970 (84 Stat. 1793)
  Motor Vehicle Information and Cost Saving Act of 1972 (86 Stat. 947), as amended
  Energy Policy and Conservation Act of 1975 (89 Stat. 871)

Organization: This agency, within the Department of Transportation, is headed by an administrator.

Budgets and Staffing, Fiscal 1970–90

	1970	1975	1980	1985	1986	1987	1988	(Estimated) 1989	1990
Budget ($ millions)	32	104	136	114	121	136	128	139	145
Staffing	518	881	874	640	640	640	648	652	656

Source: Ronald J. Penoyer, *Directory of Federal Regulatory Agencies,* 2d ed. (St. Louis, Mo.: Washington University Center for the Study of American Business, 1980), p. 74. Reprinted with permission.

Consumer Advocates

Another factor in consumerism is the independent groups and organizations that are active in raising consumer issues and supporting consumer causes. These groups are generally referred to as consumer advocates. Although individual consumers can pursue their rights in a variety of ways, consumer groups have been formed over the years to pursue consumer concerns in a more organized fashion. Some of the more important groups of this type are the following.[15]

> *Consumer Federation of America* (CFA): Chartered in 1967, the CFA brings together about 230 affiliated organizations (mostly state and local consumer groups, labor unions, and rural electric cooperatives) with consumer interests. Its representatives lobby, testify at

congressional hearings, and submit the federation's views on consumer topics to federal agencies. Since 1971, the CFA has also compiled an annual Congressional voting record showing how each member of the House and Senate voted on key consumer legislation.

National Consumer League (NCL): Originally concerned with labor issues, the league now deals with consumer issues as well by monitoring the actions of Congress and agencies of the federal government. NCL is the oldest consumer-oriented organization in the country and currently has an individual membership of about 3,000 in addition to that of affiliates.

Consumers Union (CU): Founded in 1936, CU is primarily a consumer information organization. It runs a large product-testing operation and publishes the results in *Consumer Reports* magazine. During the early 1970s, Consumers Union also became active in public interest litigation and consumer advocacy in government, an activity it has backed away from in order to focus on product testing. The organization believes its primary mission is to test products the way people use them at home, not the way quality control personnel rate them in factories.[16] It spends only about $15,000 a year on lobbying, with most of this effort devoted to legislative activities and hearings. In 1987, the organization began to include articles on social issues in its magazine by running a series on the working poor.[17]

Center for Science in the Public Interest (CSPI): Founded in 1971, this nutritional advocacy group was formed by scientists who believed that consumers needed knowledgeable experts representing their interests before the government to counter the testimony of industry scientists. Thus the CSPI has been responsible for forcing the FDA to advise pregnant women to avoid caffeine and has worked to have the FDA urge manufacturers to label and reduce sodium levels in processed foods.

Center for Auto Safety (CAS): Originally a Nader organization, the center pressures the automobile companies to make sure auto safety standards are followed. It also works with the industry and government in the development of new standards.

The Nader Network: Includes many specialized organizations, such as the Center for the Study of Responsive Law, Congress Watch, Corporate Accountability Research Group, Public Interest Research Groups, and others.[18] The Public Interest Research Groups (PIRGs), for example, originally started out as campus organizations that were funded by students. Today they have as many nonstudent as student members and focus on environmental as well as consumer issues.

These groups were to influence public policies dealing with consumer issues in the 1960s and 1970s to a much greater extent than their numbers might suggest. With the election of a conservative administration in 1980, however, their influence waned, and these groups adopted defensive strategies to hold on to the gains made in these earlier years. In some ways, they were victims of their own success, as they had won so many battles that they had trouble finding new issues that would mobilize voters. The groups themselves became more professional and knowledgeable about public policy and thus learned to work more effectively behind the scenes. Many groups began to see more opportunities at the grass-roots level, as issues of interest to consumers were more local and regional than national.[19]

Business Reaction

The original response of business to the current consumer movement was largely negative. Business by and large opposed every piece of consumer legislation and feared that the costs of voluntary consumer programs would more than offset their public relations and marketing value. Much of this opposition was undoubtedly based on the different philosophies held by business, consumer advocates, and government about consumers and consumer behavior.

After losing so many battles in Congress, however, business gradually began to embrace the consumer movement and respond to it in a more constructive fashion. Some companies have at least adopted a posture of reasonable accommodation; others began to see a positive side of consumerism. Some of these accommodating actions included the following:

Consumer Research Institute: Founded by the Grocery Manufacturers Association, this organization studies consumer complaints and informs grocery manufacturers about those it decides are valid and widespread.

Cool-Line Service: Pioneered by Whirlpool Corporation, this program offers customers a 24-hour, toll-free telephone service to call from anywhere in the country to ask about service or lodge a complaint. It highlighted the need for companies to develop a formal system to handle customer complaints and inquiries. Since these initial efforts, many more have established toll-free 800 phone lines for customer inquiries or complaints. In addition to helping keep buyers loyal by resolving complaints quickly, toll-free lines also help producers stay closer to consumers.[20]

Better Business Bureau: This independent organization supported by business was revitalized in many respects, particularly in its ability to handle consumer complaints. Many BBBs offer a free arbitration service to settle small claims against business. In 1983, the BBB agreed to administer a nationwide arbitration program established by General Motors to settle government charges that millions of GM's late-model cars have defective transmissions, cam shafts and fuel pumps.[21] The consent agreement required GM to send notification letters to thousands of car owners who filed complaints against the company, advertise the program, and provide a toll-free number for information. Upon receiving a complaint, BBB will contact GM about the matter so that the company may offer to settle the problem. If no offer is made or if the offer is not satisfactory to the owner, an arbitration hearing can be held before the BBB, with the decision binding on General Motors.[22]

Consumer Appeals Board: First set up by Ford Motor Company, this panel was designed to hear the problems of Ford owners who, after exhausting all the usual complaint channels, still believed they had not been treated fairly. The boards are composed of two dealers and three consumer representatives. The boards will hear any complaint regardless of the car's age, mileage, or warranty terms. The "final" decision of the panel is binding only on the company and dealer. The consumer retains the right to take the issue to a regular court.[23] Similar arbitration programs were set up by other auto makers. Many of these programs were criticized at being unfair to the consumer with arbitrators who were unaware of state laws or who didn't apply state guidelines. As a result, many states took steps to strengthen their laws and make arbitration a stronger alternative.[24]

Consumer Affairs Office: Many companies have created consumer affairs offices with varying responsibilities for the quality of products and consumers' satisfaction. These responsibilities may include handling consumer complaints and inquiries, dissemination of consumer information, monitoring company advertisements, providing input for product design, researching consumer satisfaction, developing warranties and guarantees, increasing product safety, overseeing product packaging and labeling, selecting suppliers, and improving quality control.[25] A professional organization called the Society of Consumer Affairs Professionals in Business (SOCAP) has been organized to promote professionalism among the executives who head these consumer affairs offices.

Important Consumer Issues

Many issues in the consumer area deserve attention, but they all cannot be covered in one chapter. What can be done is to highlight a few of the issues that are of current concern and describe them in some detail. The following issues seem to be in the news a good deal and thus make good candidates for further discussion. These issues are analyzed in terms of their impact on consumers and business, and current policies are examined as far as effectiveness is concerned.

FOOD SAFETY

In 1906, the first federal food-safety law was enacted by Congress. Prior to this time, food manufacturers were permitted to sell adulterated and mislabeled food to consumers. The law was passed because some food packers were putting foreign substances into food in order to make it last longer or increase its bulk so it weighed more. Scandals regarding contaminated and spoiled food contributed to the public outcry which led to the first food safety law being passed.[26] The Pure Food and Drug Act was passed on June 30, 1906, by the 59th Congress. Its purpose was "to prevent the manufacture, sale, or transport of adulterated, misbranded, poisonous, or deleterious foods, drugs, medicines, and liquors.[27]

The law was renamed the Federal Food, Drug, and Cosmetic Act in the 1938 amendments. This amended law was designed to prohibit in interstate commerce the sale of adulterated and mislabeled food, drugs, and cosmetics. Food was considered to be adulterated if it contained ingredients that made it harmful to the consumer's health, or if a vital ingredient has been left out, or some other ingredient had been substituted.[28] The penalties for violating the law are a fine and imprisonment, and the contaminated articles are liable to be seized. The crime of adulterating food is considered to be a misdemeanor.

In 1958, the act was amended again to deal with food additives, which were being increasingly used in the marketplace. Food additives are defined by the FDA as "any substance the intended use of which results or may reasonably be expected to result, directly or indirectly, in its becoming a component or otherwise affecting the characteristics of any food including any substance intended for use in producing, manufacturing, packing, processing, preparing, treating, packaging, transporting or holding food, and including any source of radiation intended for any such use, if such substance is not generally recognized, among experts qualified by scientific training and experience to evaluate its safety, as having been adequately shown through scientific procedures to be safe under the condition of its intended use.[29]

Food additives can further be classified into functional groups, including both intentional and incidental food additives. Intentional, or direct, additives are purposely added to food for a specific function; they include stabilizers, colors, antioxidants, flavoring compounds, and special sweeteners. Unintentional additives have no purposeful function in food and include those materials added during production, processing, or storage of food, materials from nature, materials in water used for preparing food, and residues of both plant and animal origin.[30]

Prior to the 1958 amendments, producers could sell food that was potentially harmful to consumers until FDA scientists could prove that substances in the food were injurious to public health. To provide stronger protection for consumers, the 1958 food additives amendment contains the Delaney Clause (named after Congressman James Delaney of New York), which specifies that "no additive shall be deemed to be safe if it is found to induce cancer when ingested by man or animals, or if it is found, after tests which are appropriate for the evaluation of the safety of food additives to induce cancer in man or animals. . . ."[31] It should be noted that the clause does not apply to carcinogens that occur naturally in foods, only to food additives. Food additives also can include packaging materials that can get into the food.

The toxicology testing requirements for demonstrating the safety of food additives have evolved over the past several years as knowledge in the field of toxicology has expanded. Generally, comprehensive, long-term animal studies are required to demonstrate the safety of a food additive. Although testing in humans is not a requirement for the approval of a food additive, such testing is encouraged whenever possible and when considered appropriate in view of ethical considerations. Human data often come from industrial exposure, accidental poisonings, epidemiological studies, and controlled experiments, including metabolism studies. Availability of human data or experience based on common use in food may reduce the amount of animal safety data required, or it may influence the safety factor applied in making the ultimate safety evaluation.[32]

Aside from the problem of the massive test doses used in animal testing, the Delaney Clause is always interpreted as meaning "zero tolerance" for additives that are discovered to induce cancer in humans or animals; that is, there is no threshold level below which carcinogens are safe. Theoretically, even one molecule could be hazardous. Given that laboratory techniques can now detect the presence of food additives in proportions as tiny as one part per billion, some people believe that almost everything one eats can be shown to contain a confirmed or suspected carcinogen. The Delaney Clause is thus believed to be unnecessarily restrictive because it does not allow for controlled use of a substance or a gradual phasing out of its use, which many believe would be a better way to deal with weak carcinogens.

> Unlike most other regulatory actions, actions initiated by implementation of the Delaney Clause allow for almost no discretion by the FDA. Instead, once a test has shown that an additive causes cancer in any animal (or if a cancer test is simply judged "appropriate"), the FDA must ban the substance. The FDA has no power to determine how great the risk of cancer is, or to compare it to benefits that would be lost if the substance were banned. The ability of the FDA to measure risk is the central issue in the controversy surrounding the Delaney Clause.[33]

Amendments have been proposed to the Delaney Clause that introduce concepts of "significant risk" into the decision-making process. The Hatch-Wampler bill, for example, suggests that suspected carcinogens be assessed for risk to see if they are significant hazards and that safety decisions be based on such assessment of risks to humans when they use the additive under normal conditions.[34] The bill proposes the use of an independent group of scientists to help with these decisions. Others point out that the Delaney Clause alone is not the problem, and that the FDA is legally empowered by the "general safety" clause of the Food, Drug, and Cosmetic Act to take any action sanctioned by the Delaney Clause. The cyclamate decision, for example, was based on this "general safety" clause, not the Delaney Clause. Thus the entire law needs revision, not just one clause.[35]

The controversy over food safety continues. The animal-testing debate is not settled.[36] Whether a safe threshold level exists has not been proven one way or the other.[37] But scientists will continue to raise hard questions about both old and new additives that will have to be answered through public policy. Decisions must be made about where to draw the line between the desire of individuals for free choice and the collective need for protection when the choices are complex. What standards of safety should apply and what risk levels should be accepted? These questions continue to be asked as the public shows a continued concern over the safety of the food they consume.

Concerns erupted in the spring of 1989 when the Natural Resources Defense Council released a report stating that apples treated with the pesticide Alar were exposing children to dangerously high levels of daminiozide, a possible carcinogen. The NRDC claimed that daminiozide use may cause one case of cancer for every 4,200 preschoolers, 240 times the acceptable standard.[38] The story was shown on "60 Minutes" and Meryl Streep made several appearances on talk shows and Capitol Hill attacking pesticides. Soon after these incidents, apples were ordered removed from school cafeterias in New York City, Los Angeles, and Chicago. Other school systems followed suit, and signs were posted above produce bins all over the country advertising Alar-free apples. The state of Washington, where 50 percent of the nation's apples are grown, faced huge economic losses.[39]

While this panic was at its peak, the FDA discovered two cyanide-laced grapes out of hundreds of thousands of crates of Chilean fruit on a ship docked in Philadelphia. It was assumed that the fruit had been contaminated in Chile, since the search was conducted because of terrorist threats phoned in to the U.S. embassy in Santiago. Rather than issue a warning to examine fruit carefully before eating, the FDA impounded 2 million crates of Chilean fruit, worth $20 million, at airports and docks around the country. They also warned consumers not to eat any Chilean fruit, which included most of the peaches, blueberries, blackberries, melons, green apples, pears, and plums that were on the market at that time of year. Japan and Canada held up an additional $4 million worth of fruit en route from Chile. Another $15 million worth of fruit remained in Chile awaiting clearance for shipment. In all, some 20,000 Chilean food workers were fired and 200,000 more jobs were put in jeopardy.[40] There was a good deal of controversy over the FDA action as well as about how the grapes had actually become contaminated.[41]

Later in the year, President Bush unveiled plans to better protect consumers from dangerous pesticides, plans that would accelerate the process for removing unsafe pesticides from the market and toughen penalties for misusing pesticides.[42] The National Academy of Science also issued a report recommending that a "negligible risk" standard be adopted. This report challenged the zero-risk standard of the Delaney Clause and would replace it with a standard that allowed approval of pesticides in cases where they would produce tumors in less than one out of every million people exposed. The panel that produced the report stated that the new standard would eliminate 98 percent of the cancer risk from 28 pesticides that the EPA has linked to cancer. Current standards were said to eliminate only about half the estimated cancer risk from these compounds.[43]

DRUG REGULATION

The effects of drug regulation on the pharmaceutical industry are fairly well known, since regulation of drugs has been in existence for some time. Research has shown, for example, that the average time required for clinical study and agency approval increased from 2.7 years in 1966 to 6.6 years in 1973. The number of applications for clinical study fell to 41 in 1973, which was less than half the 85 that had been filed a decade earlier. The number of new drugs approved averaged 17 per year in the postregulation period, compared with more than three times that amount in the 5 years before the Harris-Kefauver amendments were passed.[44]

The rate of return and expenditures on research and development in the drug industry plummeted to about one-third the 1960 level. Drug companies have cut back on basic research—the discovery of new and better drugs—and have put more money into product development. During the 10-year period from 1970 to 1980, domestic research and development expenditures grew at an annual rate of only 0.3 percent, adjusted for inflation, while expenditures by United States companies abroad rose from 7.5 percent of total research and development expenditures in 1965 to 19 percent in 1980.[45]

Finally, since 1960, the cost of discovering and developing a new drug rose 18-fold, half of which has been attributed to FDA regulation. These costs have forced many smaller companies out of the market. Between 1957 and 1961, the four largest drug companies' share of innovational output amounted to 24 percent of the total industry's output. Between 1967 and 1971, the share of the four largest companies increased to 48.7 percent.[46] The number of independent firms introducing new chemical entities declined from 51 in the 1954–58 period to 41 in the 1963–67 period and to 36 in the 1976–1980 period.[47]

> There thus has been a decline in annual new drug introductions accompanied by strong upward trends in the costs, times, and risks associated with discovering and developing new drugs. In economists' terminology, there has been a shift in the "production function" for new drug innovation in the direction of lower R and D productivity—that is to say, fewer drug introductions are emanating from larger resource commitments by the industry.[48]

The drug-approval process proceeds in three phases. In Phase I, tests of a new drug are designed to assess toxicity and to determine how a drug is metabolized in the human body. These studies typically involve 10 to 50 healthy subjects and are generally completed in a few months. In Phase II, a drug is administered for the first time to patients with the condition it is intended to treat. These studies are most often randomized, controlled trials involving 50 to 200 subjects and take from several months to 2 years to complete. In Phase III, studies typically involve 200 to 1,000 patients, although some studies can require as many as several thousand people. Many of the Phase III studies stretch out over 3 or 4 years.[49]

Critics of drug regulation argue that this process denies Americans the benefit of new drugs that are available in foreign countries with a shorter approval process. Thus the health of American people is being adversely affected rather than enhanced. The FDA is held to a "substantial evidence" standard in demonstrating that a drug will work before it is allowed on the market. The law defines substantial evidence as "adequate and well-controlled investigations, including clinical investigations, by experts . . . on the basis of which it could fairly and responsibly be concluded by such experts that the drug will have the effect" it claims. This definition leaves the FDA little room to approve drugs that are probably effective and does not allow them to consider the needs of patients who have no adequate alternative drugs available.[50]

Statistics show that more than 90 percent of all decisions to abandon drug development are made before the end of Phase II, suggesting that Phase III could be considerably shortened or perhaps even eliminated under certain circumstances. This phase is apparently the least productive of all the testing phases, and yet it can be longer than any other phases under most conditions (Figure 8.1). In cases where Phase III has been waived, however, Phase II studies have been improved and consequently lengthened, and in some cases Phase IV studies have been added to study a drug after it has been marketed.[51]

Figure 8.1 Eye of the Needle

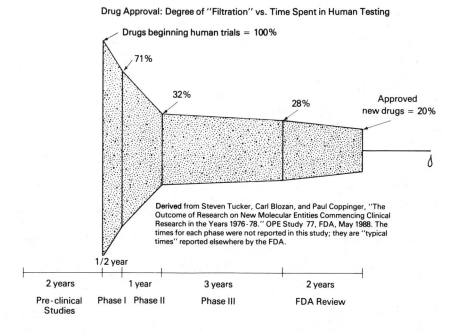

Drug Approval: Degree of "Filtration" vs. Time Spent in Human Testing

Drugs beginning human trials = 100%

71%

32%

28%

Approved
new drugs = 20%

Derived from Steven Tucker, Carl Blozan, and Paul Coppinger, "The
Outcome of Research on New Molecular Entities Commencing Clinical
Research in the Years 1976-78." OPE Study 77, FDA, May 1988. The
times for each phase were not reported in this study; they are "typical
times" reported elsewhere by the FDA.

1/2 year

| 2 years | 1 year | 3 years | 2 years |
| Pre-clinical Studies | Phase I Phase II | Phase III | FDA Review |

Source: "Dying for Drugs," *Regulation*, No. 3, 1988, p. 11. Reprinted by permission of the American Enterprise Institute for Public Policy Research, Washington, D.C.

Supporters of the FDA argue that approval delays actually protect Americans against possible hazardous drugs until the FDA is satisfied they are safe. The FDA claims that the decline in drug innovation has been largely confined to marginal drugs and is due more to depletion of research opportunities than regulation.[52] The drug regulatory apparatus in this country was developed as a response to the Thalidomide tragedy in Europe, which caused a rash of birth defects. Although the drug had not been approved in the United States, the scandal provided the political impetus for the 1962 amendments that established the current process for drug approval.

Proposals have been made to speed up the process. Some proposals would give the government power to approve breakthrough drugs before testing on them was completed. This approval could be granted in cases where lack of the drug could result in severe, life-threatening illness. Another proposal would allow approval of certain drugs for limited distribution, say only from a hospital or from people with special training and experience. Such limits could be used on a drug that otherwise would have been denied approval. Other proposals would permit approval of new drugs based solely on foreign data, if the tests are well-conducted and done by recognized researchers.

In late 1988, the FDA announced a major revision of the rules for approving drugs developed to treat diseases that are life-threatening or severely debilitating. Drugs intended for these diseases would not have to pass through Phase III testing if they show real benefit after Phase II testing. The early release of experimental drugs to patients in life-threatening situations was also speeded up by the policy change. Approval of the drug AZT used in treating AIDS was completed much faster than normal because the agency worked with company researchers on the project and released it for use before

Figure 8.2   FDA Decision Making on New Drug Applications

State of the World

		New Drug Is Safe and Effective	New Drug Is Not Safe and Effective
FDA Decision	Accept	Correct Decision	Type 2 Error
	Reject	Type 1 Error	Correct Decision

Source: Henry G. Grabowski and John M. Vernon, *The Regulation of Pharmaceuticals: Balancing the Benefits and Risks* (Washington, D.C.: American Enterprise Institute, 1983), p. 10.

it was officially approved for marketing.[53] Other beneficiaries of the policy change— victims of cancer, stroke, heart attacks, Alzheimer's disease, Parkinson's disease, blindness, osteoporosis, and rheumatoid arthritis—will also be able to obtain new drugs faster than before.[54]

Although important regulatory changes can be accomplished through administrative rule-making, this approach has its limitations as a long-run response to the incentive problems inherent in the present system of drug regulation. Grabowski and Vernon state that the legislative mandate and regulatory procedures of the FDA evolved as a response to the perceived problems of unsafe or ineffective drugs. Although an ideal system of government regulation would give comparable weight to the costs and benefits of regulatory decisions, neither Congress nor the regulators gave much initial attention to the potential adverse effects of increased regulation on drug innovation.[55] They analyze the decision problem faced by the FDA by using a standard statistical decision-making framework (Figure 8.2).

> In this decision-making situation there are two correct types of decisions and two types of errors. The correct decisions are FDA acceptance of drugs that are safe and effective and rejection of those that are not. Type 1 error is FDA rejection of a "good" drug or one whose benefits would exceed risks in clinical practice. Type 2 error is acceptance of a drug when the reverse is true. Both types of error influence patients' health and well-being since consuming a "bad" drug or not having access to a "good" drug can have deleterious effects on health.[56]

The authors go on to say that our present regulatory system does not treat type 1 and type 2 errors equally because the FDA's mandate is to protect consumers against unsafe and ineffective drugs (type 2 errors). There is no corresponding mandate to avoid type 1 errors, in fact, institutional incentives reinforce the tendency to avoid type 2 errors at the expense of type 1 errors. An FDA official who appraises a drug that is subsequently shown to be unsafe or ineffective is held politically accountable and stands to bear heavy personal cost. Such an outcome is highly visible, whereas the costs of rejecting a good drug are borne largely by outside parties such as drug manufacturers or sick patients, who are much less visible. Thus risk avoidance is emphasized at the FDA because the incentives reinforce a conservative approach to drug approval.[57]

In 1983 and 1984, the FDA came under severe criticism for its laxity in postapproval monitoring for adverse drug reactions. Doctors and hospitals are expected to voluntarily report adverse drug reactions both to the FDA and the manufacturer, and manufacturers must report data they collect on serious adverse reactions within 15 working days of discovery. The problem is that although reported adverse drug reactions increased dramatically in the early 1980s, the number of safety officers and inspectors declined because of budget cuts. In 1980, the FDA received 10,358 reports of adverse reactions, but by 1982 the number had increased more than two and one-half times.[58] In 1986, the FDA broadened its requirements that drug makers and marketers report serious ill effects from prescription drugs by adding more drugs to the list the rule covers.[59]

The General Accounting Office reported that in the case of Zomax, a popular pain reliever produced by Johnson & Johnson, many of the reports submitted by manufacturers had been misplaced, and those that hadn't took 5 months to be entered into the FDA's drug-tracking computer.[60] The company finally stopped marketing Zomax after the drug was linked to serious allergic reactions, five of them lethal. Similar surveillance problems appeared with Oraflex, an arthritis remedy manufactured by Eli Lilly & Company, which eventually pleaded guilty to 25 criminal counts for failing to inform federal authorities of four deaths and six illnesses that occurred after patients took the drug once marketed by the company.[61] These problems had their effect on the approval process, resulting in a return to a more conservative and risk-averse approach and making a change in the incentive structure more difficult than ever to attain.[62] Because of these problems, the FDA was politically embarrassed and was forced to back off from proposed reforms to deregulate the process further, until the AIDS crisis pressured the FDA to make the policy changes mentioned previously.

In 1989, the FDA was hit by a scandal involving generic drugs. Generics are designed to work as effectively as their brand-name counterparts and cost much less; thus in 1985 Congress made generics more readily available by speeding up the approval process. After the patent on a brand-name product has expired, usually after a 17-year period, a pharmaceutical company can replicate the original drug's components, making a generic much less expensive to develop. In order to speed up the approval process, companies need show the FDA only that their generic product is "bioequivalent" to its brand-name counterpart. The FDA is also allowed to rely on the manufacturer's in-house lab tests to establish a product's effectiveness. The temptation to cut corners is strong, since the first companies to gain approval of a new generic drug are likely to capture the largest market share.[63]

After a year-long investigation by the Justice Department and the FDA itself, evidence was uncovered showing that some makers of generic drugs had falsified laboratory test results and then paid off FDA chemists to gain faster approval for their products. The scandal began to unravel after Mylan Laboratories began to suspect the FDA of favoritism. The company hired its own detectives to spy on the agency, and they uncovered enough evidence to justify an investigation by federal officials.[64] In response to the scandal, the FDA investigated the nation's 12 leading generic companies (later expanded to 20 companies) for manufacturing and record-keeping irregularities and tested the potency and stability of the 30 top-selling generic products on the market.[65]

Problems were found at 10 of the 12 firms initially investigated, which raised additional questions about whether the industry can be trusted to supply accurate information to the agency. There were some proposals to drop the provision allowing the FDA to accept test results from the companies on good faith.[66] However, tests related to the drugs themselves found only 1.1 percent of the 2,000 tested generic drug samples to be deficient in meeting quality and safety standards, a rate that was comparable to regular inspections. Although 5 generic companies were accused of submitting false data or substituting brand-name drugs in premarket testing, the investigation turned up no evidence that the drugs were not safe to use as directed.[67] In response to the scandal, the FDA's generic testing division was reorganized and changes were being considered to the approval process that would undoubtedly raise the cost of generic drugs and lengthen the approval process.[68]

PRODUCT LIABILITY

In 1985, insurance costs more than doubled for 40 percent of U.S. Chamber of Commerce members. About a fourth of these companies experienced price hikes of more than 500 percent. Nearly 3 companies in 20 could not get any coverage at all, and 7 in 20 were considering going without coverage. Only the most bare-bones coverage was available for catastrophic losses such as might occur from a disaster at a chemical plant.[69] Although insurance costs have recently stabilized, they have done so at a very high level, and many risks are now excluded from coverage. In addition to high insurance premiums, manufacturers and their customers face billions of dollars in additional costs from attorney's fees, nuisance suits, and unwanted damage awards. Some estimates put the ultimate costs of product liability suits concerning asbestos alone at a potential of $40 billion.[70]

From 1974 to 1984, the number of product liability suits in federal courts grew at the astounding rate of 680 percent. Although the first million-dollar verdict did not occur until 1962, there were 401 such awards in 1984 alone. In fact, the average verdict in product-liability cases now tops $1 million. These giant awards provide a target for plaintiffs and their attorneys to try to attain and motivate defendants to make high offers to settle out of court rather than take a chance on what a jury might do with the case. Juries are prone to award compensation for nonquantifiable things such as pain and suffering, which can amount to a good deal of money, and hand out punitive damage awards that can go far beyond the actual damages incurred.[71]

These developments gave rise to a liability crisis in the United States, a crisis that sparked a national campaign against huge damage awards, which was led by insurers, doctors, defense lawyers, and part of the business community. Juries, however, did not seem to be affected by these efforts. In 1989, 10 juries handed out awards ranging from $25 million to $76 million and totaling $475 million. The largest jury award—$76 million—went to two workers who had become ill from exposure to asbestos. There were 474 awards of more than $1 million in 1988, an increase from 398 the previous year. Many of these awards are reduced by an appeals court, as studies show that 40 percent of awards of $1 million or more are reduced on appeal. Nonetheless, these awards still give evidence that the liability crisis has not abated.[72]

The liability crisis has hit some industries particularly hard. In 1979, the aviation industry produced more than 17,000 aircraft; in 1987 the industry shipped only 1,085, a decrease of more than 90 percent. Product liability is the largest single cost element in light aircraft. In 1985, the average cost of product liability coverage for each airplane delivered reached about $70,000, compared with costs of $2,111 per airplane in 1972 and only $51 in 1962. Industry-paid claims rose from $24 million in 1977 to $209 million in 1985, despite an improving safety record. Small-aircraft companies such as Beech and Cessna discovered that new-model planes, carrying a 50 percent surcharge for liability insurance, could no longer compete with used planes already on the market.[73]

These changes have caused manufacturers to abandon products and markets they have spent years in developing, have increased prices because of higher insurance costs, and have hindered product innovation.[74] The liability crisis started with a change in legal thinking regarding product liability. This change can be described as a shift from the old rule that manufacturers or sellers are liable for damages only when they have been negligent or unreasonably careless in relation to products or breached an express or implied warranty to a theory of strict liability, which holds a manufacturer or seller responsible for damages if a consumer is injured as a result of a product defect regardless of the degree of care exercised.

Strict liability thinking emerged in the 1963 case of *Greenman* v. *Yuba Power Products, Inc.*, where the Supreme Court of California ruled that "a manufacturer is strictly liable in tort when an article he places on the market, knowing that it is to be used without inspection for defects, proves to have a defect that causes injury to a human being." The court also stated that "the purpose of such liability is to insure that the costs of injuries resulting from defective products are borne by the manufacturers that put such products on the market rather than by the injured persons who are powerless to protect themselves."[75] Following this decision, state courts developed product liability law by applying the strict liability standard in their jurisdictions.

Under product liability theory based on negligence, manufacturers would be held liable only if they failed to take reasonable steps to make the product safe for consumers who are likely to use the product. Manufacturers who failed to conform to this reasonable-person standard risked liability to plaintiffs who were injured. Under warranty laws, manufacturers were liable for breach of contract. Products were expected to live up to express representations and to an implied warranty that the goods were fit for the ordinary purposes for which such goods are used.

Under a theory of strict liability, manufacturers can take every precaution in producing and distributing the product, but if it proves defective and injures consumers, they are strictly liable for damages. Thus the plaintiff's burden in proving a case has been considerably eased, and more suits are being filed. Consumers seeking damages need not prove that the manufacturer was negligent or violated an express or implied warranty. All they need prove is that the product caused the injury and that a defect in design or production made the product unreasonably dangerous. Even negligent use of the product by consumers is not always an effective defense for the manufacturer. Consumers who have improperly used products have nevertheless received sizable awards. The new climate has cost some manufacturers millions of dollars.

Thus the courts have expanded liability for insurers by reinterpreting and redefining policy language in insurance contracts, forcing them to cover risks they never intended to cover and for which they never collected premiums. Once-solid legal principles such as fault, causation, negligence, assumption of risk, and others have been undermined by judges and juries expanding liability for manufacturers. Insurance and manufacturing companies were considered to have "deep pockets"; they were expected to be able to share a greater part of the risk in using products than consumers, who are often unable to assess accurately the risk they are taking. The concept of strict liability shifts the cost burden of defective products to manufacturers, who are able to recoup losses in the form of higher prices.

Because of the increasing problem posed by substances such as asbestos, state courts began to move toward an ever-inclusive notion of the circumstances under which a company is liable for the harm its products may do to people. The idea of absolute liability began to take hold. With absolute liability there is almost no mitigating circumstance a manufacturer can cite to establish his or her innocence. A New Jersey Supreme Court, for example, held that a state-of-the-art defense may not be enough to protect manufacturers if a product later proves to be hazardous. In *Beshada* v. *Johns Manville*

Corp., a manufacturer was held liable for a hazard that could not possibly have been anticipated when the product was first introduced into the stream of commerce. The manufacturer had the responsibility of warning about dangers that were not only undiscovered but scientifically undiscoverable at the time products were first introduced.[76]

Punitive damages have received increasing attention in recent years as they have steadily grown in size and frequency along with the litigation explosion. Punitive damages are awarded in civil cases as punishment in the hopes they will deter misconduct. Such damages are awarded in addition to compensatory awards to plaintiffs for loss or injury, and they may be awarded in a variety of cases. Over the past several years, many states have set monetary caps on such damages or toughened evidentiary standards for their award. One state even abolished them entirely.[77] The Supreme Court was expected to rule on the constitutionality of such awards, but in early 1990, a state judge ruled that a company sued in a product liability case cannot use its insurance to pay for punitive damages. This ruling was seen as a setback in the effort to curb punitive damages.[78]

Because of these developments in product liability, many companies have been unable to afford product liability insurance and face risk of bankruptcy should they be hit with a product liability lawsuit. Reforms have been proposed to put some limits on the doctrine of strict liability and develop a uniform product liability law that would replace the patchwork system that currently exists. Under a bill introduced by Senator Robert Kasten (R. Wis.), a product would be held to be unreasonably dangerous if "the manufacturer knew, or, through the exercise of reasonable prudence, should have known about the danger which allegedly caused the claimant's harm, and if a reasonably prudent person in the same or similar circumstances would not have manufactured the product or used the design or formulation that the manufacturer used." Punitive damages could be awarded only to the first plaintiff and should be limited to the amount of the compensatory award. The proposal would also impose a uniform statute of limitations and allow manufacturers to defend themselves against lawsuits where products were approved by a federal regulatory agency.[79]

The Bush administration supported the Kasten bill but also proposed provisions that went beyond those endorsed by the bill's bipartisan group of sponsors. The administration proposed even stricter limits on jury awards and a cap on punitive damages. The administration also proposed limits on a legal rule that makes any defendant potentially liable for all damages to an injury victim, whether the defendant is responsible for all the harm, and suggested a state-of-the-art defense, where manufacturers would be able to defend themselves against lawsuits by proving that a product was as safe and reliable as it was possible to make it at the time of manufacture.[80]

Almost all the nation's business organizations, the insurance industry, the medical profession, and assorted groups of educators and public officials favor some kind of limitations on damage awards in personal-injury suits. On the other side, backing the consumer's right to sue, is an alliance of personal-injury lawyers, labor unions, and consumer and environmental groups.[81] Because of the difficulty of getting a product liability bill through Congress, the administration began to turn its attention to the states and concluded that the changes it seeks will more likely take shape in state legislation. In 1986, more than 30 states adopted laws that in some way limited liability claims, with many of the laws modifying the way liability is apportioned among several defendants.[82]

Product liability poses a major management problem that must be given greater consideration. Managers must give increasing attention to adequate warnings about potential dangers in using products, quality control systems to eliminate defective products, and product design to eliminate hazards by utilizing design-safety concepts. Many businesses adopted self-insurance plans, and some estimates indicated that by 1989, at least one-third, and perhaps even as much as one-half, of the commercial insurance market could be covered by self-insurance and captives. Such an increase could leave traditional insurers with the less-profitable roles of handling paperwork and selling only a last-resort layer of insurance coverage.[83]

The changes in thinking about product liability reflect the continuing increase in the safety and health consciousness of the American public and changing notions about compensatory justice. Corporations are being forced to bear more of the costs associated with unsafe and defective products because it is believed they can take greater steps to promote safety in the products they sell on the marketplace. One commentator argues that the current crisis in tort liability is really the third wave of the politics of redistribution. In the 1960s, resources were reallocated through a vast expansion of the welfare system. In the 1970s, attention shifted to regulatory agencies such as the EPA and OSHA, which imposed significant costs on the regulated parties. In the 1980s tort law became the principal means for reallocating resources away from active economic producers to passive "victims" of the economic system.[84]

In any event, modern product liability thinking seems to have made the system into some kind of insurance scheme and has spread the risks associated with products across the entire society. Insurance costs for any injury involving a product are built into its price, and consumers have to buy the insurance without having any choice in the matter. The insurance is said to be very inefficient, however, and comes with high litigation costs. And as some economists point out, the system is very regressive. Everyone pays the same premium in a sense, making higher prices more onerous for low-income consumers; high-income consumers collect more from jury awards because compensation awards are calculated according to the plaintiff's income.[85]

There are other consumer issues as well. Health claims in advertising to appeal to the health-conscious consumer received attention in the last few years because of the hype about oat bran and other ingredients that were heavily advertised as promoting the health of users. Questions were raised about the validity of these claims and how consumers could sort out fact from fiction. Other issues had to do with auto safety in terms of standards for crashes and the installation of air bags to protect occupants in the event of a crash. Another issue was the rising cost of automobile insurance and the steps some states, such as California, took to force insurance companies to roll back rates to save consumers money.

While the consumer movement is not the same as it was in the 1960s when Ralph Nader's book *Unsafe at any Speed* began a new consumer movement, there are still many issues concerning consumers that find their way onto the public policy agenda. Stephen Brobeck, executive director of the Consumer Federation of America, believes that the future of the consumer movement depends largely on the ability of the movement to retain and expand public support. Without such support, the movement's major sources of influence—active members, funding, access to the press, and influence with government officials—will diminish. The support of the public can be sustained if (1) the public continues to recognize that their interests as consumers are at risk and (2) they remain convinced that consumer advocates effectively defend and promote these interests.[86]

The primary source of frustration for many advocates is that there are so many problems they are not able to give them the attention they deserve.[87] As the service economy continues to expand, new problems will appear with respect to the quality of services consumers are receiving and the prices they are paying for these services.[88] And as the environment gets more attention, there will undoubtedly be more efforts such as those of Wall-Mart to emphasize the sale of ecologically sound products, and consumers will have to sort out legitimate claims from those that are unsound and make unsupported ecological claims.[89] There will thus be a continual need for government, consumer advocates, and business to be concerned about protecting consumer rights and responding to the changing needs of consumers in an ever-changing marketplace.

Questions for Discussion

1. Discuss the consumer bill of rights. How does the marketplace protect these rights? Why is there a need for government involvement? What can business do to better protect these rights?

2. Describe the powers of the various government agencies involved in protecting consumer rights. How do their functions differ? What rights do they protect? Why did this approach to consumer protection evolve?

3. Are you in favor of further government regulation to protect consumer's rights? Why or why not? How would you improve the present regulatory process? Can regulation be avoided by adopting other approaches with respect to consumer protection?

4. What are consumer advocates? What functions do they perform? Whose rights are they protecting? Should they be limited to specific kinds of activities? What strategies do they pursue in order to promot their interests?

5. Why was business so negative toward consumerism in its early years? Are there lessons to be learned here regarding business response to future social movements? What has business done in response to consumerism more recently?

6. Describe the food-safety controversy. What is the Delaney Clause? Should it be amended? If so, how? What are the basic issues with respect to food safety that are unresolved?

7. What have been the effects of drug regulation? Is some kind of regulation necessary? Why or why not? What reforms would you suggest? Has drug regulation on the whole been a benefit or a liability to society?

8. Describe the changes in product liability. What impacts have these changes had on business? What are the reasons for this change in thinking? What responses can management make that are likely to be effective?

9. What product liability reforms would you advocate? What would be the impact of these reforms on business and on consumers? Are they likely to be passed anytime soon? What can business do to hasten their adoption?

10. What is the future of consumerism? What new issues are likely to reach the public policy agenda that should be of concern to business? Are we seeing the end of the current consumer movement?

Case: The Rely Tampon

Procter & Gamble began developing a tampon in 1974 that they called the Rely tampon. This tampon contained new superabsorbent fibers that were supposedly able to absorb 17 times their own weight in fluid.[1] After being test-marketed, Rely was introduced nationally in 1979. In less than 6 months, it had captured an astonishing 20% share of the market.[2]

By 1980, Rely had taken over a substantial chunk of its two major competitors' market shares. Tampax, the industry leader, went from 52 to 38 percent of the market; and Playtex, owned by Esmark, went from 28 to 24 percent.[3] Industry analysts believed that Rely had the momentum to overtake Tampax. Procter & Gamble was also planning to put the product into foreign distribution.[4]

The $700-million-per-year tampon industry came under attack, however, when the Center for Disease Control (CDC) in Atlanta reported in the early spring of 1980 that the use of tampons increases the risk of developing a rare disease called toxic shock syndrome (TSS). The term was introduced in 1978 to describe an acute illness whose signs and symptoms include fever, rash, hypertension, involvement of various organ systems, and subsequent peeling of skin, especially on the palms and soles. A strong association had been shown between the occurrence of TSS and the presence of staphylococcus aureus, a bacterial species known to cause various human illnesses.[5] The CDC contended that tampons may act as a breeding ground or as a carrier of bacteria into the vagina. The bacteria causes high fever, vomiting, diarrhea, and skin disorders followed by shock.

Before 1977, all tampon products were made of cotton, rayon, or a blend of the two, according to manufacturers. Beginning in about 1977, tampon manufacturers began to make more absorbent products and to vary the composition of tampons. These new products garnered a substantial share of the market. The finding of an increased association between more-absorbent tampons and TSS in one study focused interest on the chemical composition of tampons, but the data relating composition to TSS were preliminary.[6]

Procter & Gamble first became aware of TSS in May 1980, when the CDC in Atlanta published its first indication that many new cases of TSS affecting menstruating women were being reported. On June 13, CDC contacted Procter & Gamble and other major tampon manufacturers requesting data concerning tampon usage. At this time there was no specific information linking TSS to tampon use. Then on June 19, the CDC invited tampon manufacturers to a June 25–26 meeting and asked them to provide market information for further study. After analysis, CDC confirmed that there was a statistical correlation between TSS and tampon use, but the incidence was too low to warn women to stop using tampons. CDC also found no significant link between TSS and any specific brand of tampon.

At this point, Procter & Gamble started their own study on TSS. Because they were prevented by the Federal Privacy Act from getting the names of the women whose cases had been analyzed by the CDC or their doctors, they had to find their own doctors and case histories and obtain piecemeal information and statistics from state boards of health. Procter & Gamble's study confirmed what the CDC had reported in June. There was no significant link between TSS and any particular brand of tampon, although studies released in June by the State Health Departments of Wisconsin and Minnesota had shown a statistical link to the Rely tampon.[7]

Meanwhile, the CDC continued studying TSS and found that cases reported in July and August did link the Rely tampon to TSS. The findings were announced September 15, 1980. In a sample of 42 women with TSS, 71 percent had used the Rely tampon.[8] A few days later, the Utah Health Department released findings that supported the CDC, and the Rely tampon was in trouble.[9]

The September 15 announcement by the CDC brought about a meeting between Procter & Gamble, the Food and Drug Administration (FDA), and CDC officials. When the meetings first started between Procter & Gamble and the FDA on September 18, P&G had worked up a warning statement that they were willing to put on the Rely package. After the first meeting, however, P&G realized that the FDA wanted much more; it wanted complete withdrawal of the product.

On Sunday, September 21, the Scientific Advisory Group at Procter & Gamble met to review all the available data. The group could not determine that the P&G product, Rely, was more associated with TSS than any other brand, but at the same time, there was not enough evidence for the group to say that the statistical information provided by the government could safely be ignored. Thus the company decided to pull the product off the shelves.

September 22, 1980, Procter & Gamble announced to the public that it was withdrawing Rely from the market. The next day, the FDA and P&G drafted a consent agreement under a previously unused provision of the 1976 Medical-Devices Amendment to the Food, Drug, and Cosmetics Act. In it P&G denied that Rely was defective or that the company violated any federal laws. In return, the FDA got P&G to undertake a big advertising campaign warning women not to use Rely and educating people about TSS. The agreement also required P&G to buy back any Rely tampons that consumers still had, including those received as free samples in P&G's $10 million introductory promotion. By September 26, the consent agreement was finalized, and P&G began pulling Rely out of stores.[10]

Procter & Gamble's decision to withdraw Rely was certainly both painful and expensive. The 1982 Annual Report states that a reserve of $75 million after taxes, or $0.91 per share, was established to cover the one-time loss. The company believed this reserve will cover all costs that may arise from the controversy.[11]

As of March 1982, more than 400 lawsuits had been filed against P&G.[12] It may take years before all of these cases come to trial, and it was impossible to predict whether Procter & Gamble will be held liable for damages in any of these cases. However, the company thought it likely that its product liability coverage and its $75 million reserve would prevent any seriously adverse effects on the company's operations or on its financial condition.[13]

Edward Harness, P&G's chairman and chief executive at the time, has said, "We did the right thing in suspending the brand. I don't think we could have moved any sooner than we did because we couldn't get any data. And we couldn't have moved any slower or else we would have gotten into a blood bath of wholly negative publicity." Owen Butler, P&G's vice chairman, has added, "I think we did what we could with the information we had at the time."[14]

Case Notes

1. N. Friedman, "A Major Report on Tampon Safety," *Working Woman*, January, 1981, p. 58.
2. "Rely Tampons Recalled By Maker: Linked to Toxic Shock Syndrome," *New York Times*, September 23, 1980, p. 1.
3. "Not Relied On," *The Economist*, September 27, 1980, p. 100.
4. Dean Rotbart and John A. Prestbo, "Killing a Product: Taking Rely Off Market Cost Procter and Gamble a Week of Agonizing," *Wall Street Journal*, November 3, 1980, p. 1. Copyright © Dow Jones & Company, Inc., 1980. All rights reserved.
5. Procter & Gamble Company, *1982 Annual Report*, p. 4.
6. Dean Rotbart and John A. Prestbo, "Procter and Gamble Isn't Ready To Give Up On Tampon Market Despite Rely's Recall," *Wall Street Journal*, November 5, 1980, p. 4.
7. Institute of Medicine, *Toxic Shock Syndrome: Assessment of Current Information and Future Research Needs* (Washington, D.C.: National Academy Press, 1982), p. 51.
8. Richard Severo, "Rely Tampon Recalled by Maker: Linked to Toxic Shock Syndrome," *New York Times*, September 23, 1980, p. 1.

9. "Rely Tampon Could Cost P&G Over $75 Million," *Chemical Week,* October 1, 1980, p. 22.

10. Rotbart and Prestbo, "Killing a Product," p. 1.

11. P&G, *1982 Annual Report,* p. 31.

12. "A Verdict on Tampons," *Time,* March 29, 1982, p. 73.

13. P&G, *Annual 10K Report,* p. 6.

14. Rotbart and Prestbo, "Killing a Product," p. 1.

Chapter Notes

1. George A. Steiner and John F. Steiner, *Business, Government, and Society: A Managerial Perspective* (New York: Random House, 1980), pp. 273–274. Copyright © 1980 Random House, Inc. Reprinted with permission.

2. See Ralph M. Gaedeke, "The Movement for Consumer Protection: A Century of Mixed Accomplishments," *University of Washington Business Review* (Spring 1970), pp. 31–40.

3. Thomas G. Krattenmaker, "The Federal Trade Commission and Consumer Protection," *California Management Review,* Vol. XVIII, No. 4 (Summer 1976), p. 92.

4. In 1988, the Federal Trade Commission began a review of the funeral rule to see if it should be repealed or amended in some fashion. See Horace B. Deets, "Executive Director's Report," *AARP News Bulletin,* Vol. 29, No. 9 (October 1988), p. 3.

5. Margaret Garrard Warner, "Used-Car Rule of FTC Stopped in House, 286–133," *Wall Street Journal,* May 27, 1982, p. 11. The FTC finally issued a rule that took effect on May 9, 1985, that required used car dealers to place a window sticker, called a buyer's guide, on each used car offered for sale. The guide explicitly tells the consumer whether the car has a warranty, what systems are covered by it, and the extent and duration of the warranty. The reverse side of the form lists major automotive components and possible defects that may occur in used vehicles. See Alfred King, "FTC Rule on Used Cars to Take Effect," *Dallas Times Herald,* April 10, 1985, p. B-5.

6. "A Widening Attack on the FTC," *Business Week,* April 5, 1982, p. 119.

7. Jeanne Saddler, "Antitrust, Consumer-Law Enforcement by FTC Has Been Reduced, Report Says," *Wall Street Journal,* November 10, 1983, p. 7. See also Jeanne Saddler, "FTC's New Case-by-Case Policy Irks Those Favoring Broader Tack," *Wall Street Journal,* July 3, 1985, p. 15.

8. Andy Pasztor and Jeanne Saddler, "FTC Chairman's Hands-Off View of Marketplace Prompts Scrutiny of Agency by Critics on the Hill," *Wall Street Journal,* February 4, 1987, p. 46.

9. R. David Pittle, "The Consumer Product Safety Commission," *California Management Review,* Vol. XVIII, No. 4 (Summer 1976), p. 105.

10. See Carolyn Lochhead, "A Risky Walk on the Safe Side," *Insight,* December 18, 1989, pp. 8–17.

11. Consumer Product Safety Commission, *1982 Annual Report* (Washington, D.C.: U.S. Government Printing Office, 1982), p. 4.

12. "FDA Is Requiring Pharmaceutical Firms to Conduct Postmarketing Drug Survey," *Wall Street Journal,* January 23, 1980, p. 12.

13. Dick Thompson, "What's the Cure for Burnout?" *Time,* December 25, 1989, p. 68. See also John Carey, "Why The FDA Needs A Miracle Drug," *Business Week,* February 19, 1990, pp. 108–10.

14. John D. Blackburn, Elliot I. Kayman, and Martin H. Malin, *The Legal Environment of Business: Public Law and Regulation* (Homewood, Ill.: Richard D. Irwin, Inc., 1982), p. 293.

15. "Guide to Washington," *Consumers Digest,* March/April, 1987, pp. 27–32.

16. Mary Williams Walsh, "Consumers Union Tests Products In Ways Manufacturers Won't," *Wall Street Journal,* January 14, 1984, p. 15.

17. Jeff Bailey, "Altering the Product at Consumer Reports," *Wall Street Journal,* June 5, 1987, p. 25.

18. See Susan Gross, "The Nader Network," *Business and Society Review,* No. 13 (Spring 1975), pp. 5–15.

19. Jeanne Saddler, "Holding Action: Consumer Groups Try To Keep Earlier Gains As Their Power Wanes," *Wall Street Journal,* December 31, 1986, p. 1.

20. "More Firms Use '800' Numbers to Keep Consumers Satisfied," *Wall Street Journal,* April 7, 1983, p. 29.

21. "GM Agrees to Set Up Arbitration Program to Settle Claims on Defective Auto Parts," *Wall Street Journal,* April 27, 1983, p. 10.

22. D. W. Nauss, "Arbitration Program to Aid GM Car Owners," *Dallas Times Herald,* November 18, 1983, p. B-2; "Free Phone Numbers Available to Help in GM-Owner Disputes," *Dallas Times Herald,* October 7, 1984, p. H-3. For reactions to the program see Walt Bogdanich, "Long Delays Face GM Car Owners Seeking Money for Engine Defects," *Wall Street Journal,* July 12, 1985, p. 25; and Ruth Eyre, "BBB Arbitrates GM Disputes," *Dallas Times Herald,* December 1, 1985, p. H-1.

23. "Detroit's Tonic for Lemon Buyers," *Business Week,* April 4, 1983, p. 54.

24. Bridgett Davis, "Car Buyers Discover 'Lemon Laws' Often Fail to Prevent Court Trip," *Wall Street Journal,* October 21, 1986, p. 39.

25. Richard T. Hise, Peter L. Gillett, and J. Partick Kelly, "The Corporate Consumer Affairs Effort," *MSU Business Topics,* Vol. 26, No. 3 (Summer 1978), p. 18.

26. American Council of Science and Health, *The U.S. Safety Laws: Time for a Change?,* March 1985, p. 5.

27. U.S. Statutes at Large, 1906, 59th Congress, 34:1, p. 768.

28. U.S. Statutes at Large, 1938, 75th Congress, 52:1, p. 1046.

29. Thomas E. Furia, *Handbook of Food Additives,* The Chemical Rubber Company, 1968, p. 9.

30. Ibid.

31. Thomas H. Jukes, "Current Concepts in Nutrition," *Medical Intelligence,* Vol. 297, No. 8 (August 1977), p. 428.

32. Freddy Hamburger and Judith Marqus, *Chemical Safety Register and Compliance,* 1983, p. 25.

33. American Council on Science and Health, *The U.S. Food Safety Laws: Time for a Change?,* 1982, p. 7.

34. Ibid., p. 10.

35. William R. Havender, "The Science and Politics of Cyclamate," *The Public Interest,* No. 71 (Spring 1983), pp. 17–32.

36. A new element was introduced into the debate about animal testing when animal-protection activists began protesting companies to change their testing procedures and investigate new laboratory techniques that use fewer or no animals to test products. See Richard Koenig, "Companies Begin to Use Fewer Animals When Testing New Consumer Products," *Wall Street Journal,* May 19, 1986, p. 37; John Carey, "Will Relief for Lab Animals Spell Pain for Consumers?" *Business Week,* October 30, 1969, pp. 43–44.

37. In June 1986, the Supreme Court ruled that the FDA could use informal determinations of safe levels, called "action levels," to regulate food additives. Such levels do not involve the formal procedures that usually accompany federal rule-making. These action levels were used for more than 20 dangerous substances. See Stephen Wermiel, "FDA Needn't Set Tougher Standards For Some Food Additives, Justices Rule," *Wall Street Journal,* June 18, 1986, p. 50.

38. Anastasia Toufexis, "Watch Those Vegetables, Ma," *Time,* March 6, 1989, p. 57.

39. Gisela Bolte, Dick Thompson, and Andrea Sachs, "Do You Dare To Eat A Peach?" *Time,* March 27, 1989, pp. 24–27.

40. Ibid.

41. Bruce Ingersoll, "Cyanide Mystery: In Chilean Grape Case, New Data Raise Doubt As to What Happened," *Wall Street Journal,* November 16, 1989, p. A-1.

42. Rae Tyson, "Bush Aims To Assure 'Safest Food'," *USA Today,* October 27, 1989, p. 1-A.

43. Robert E. Taylor and Art Pine, "Science Academy Urges Major Revision In U.S. Standards on Pesticides in Food," *Wall Street Journal,* May 21, 1987, p. 28.

44. "The Hidden Cost of Drug Safety," *Business Week,* February 21, 1977, p. 80. See also Henry G. Grabowski and John M. Vernon, *The Regulation of Pharmaceuticals: Balancing the Benefits and Risks* (Washington, D.C.: American Enterprise Institute, 1983), pp. 29–48.

45. Grabowski and Vernon, *The Regulation of Pharmaceuticals,* pp. 31–32. Congress approved a bill in September of 1984 that gave longer patent protection for new brand-name drugs while speeding up the availability of cheaper generic versions of older drugs with expired patents. The bill extended patent protection for as long as 5 years to compensate for regulatory delays, a move that would increase the incentive for drug companies to increase spending for new product research. At the same time, the bill gave generic drug makers a shortcut in obtaining clearances for drugs on which patents have already expired, by relying on a brand-name drug's original tests for safety and effectiveness. See Arlen J. Large, "Drug Patent Bill Clears Congress On a Voice Vote," *Wall Street Journal,* September 13, 1984, p. 20.

46. "Hidden Cost," *Business Week,* February 21, 1977, p. 82.

47. Grabowski and Vernon, *The Regulation of Pharmaceuticals,* p. 33.

48. Ibid.

49. "Dying for Drugs," *Regulation,* No. 3, 1988, pp. 9–10.

50. Ibid., pp. 10–11.

51. Ibid., p. 10.

52. Grabowski and Vernon, *The Regulation of Pharmaceuticals,* pp. 33–36.

53. "FDA to Shorten Testing Stage For Some Drugs," *Wall Street Journal,* October 20, 1988, p. B-4.

54. "Finally, the Patients Benefit," *Wall Street Journal,* October 20, 1988, p. A-16.

55. Grabowski and Vernon, *The Regulation of Pharmaceuticals,* p. 9.

56. Ibid., p. 10.

57. Ibid., pp. 10–11.

58. Michael Millenson, "Cuts are Squeezing Life from FDA, Critics Say," *St. Louis Globe-Democrat,* October 8–9, 1983, p. 5F.

59. Joann S. Lubin, "FDA Widens Rule On Posting Effects Of Certain Drugs," *Wall Street Journal,* June 7, 1986, p. 4.

60. Burt Schorr, "FDA Tracking of Adverse Drug Reactions is Sharply Criticized in Wake of Zomax Case," *Wall Street Journal,* May 24, 1983, p. 29.

61. Joe Davidson and Carolyn Phillips, "Eli Lilly Admits It Failed to Inform U.S. of Deaths, Illnesses Tied to Oraflex Drug," *Wall Street Journal,* August 22, 1985, p. 2.

62. "Federal Clearances for New Drugs Become a Bottleneck Again," *Wall Street Journal,* March 15, 1984, p. 1.

63. Christine Gorman, "A Prescription for Scandal," *Time,* August 28, 1989, p. 56.

64. Ibid.

65. Bruce Ingersoll, "FDA Finds Problems at 10 of 12 Firms Being Probed in Generic-Drug Scandal," *Wall Street Journal,* September 12, 1989, p. A-4.

66. Ibid.

67. Bruce Ingersoll, "FDA Says Tests of Generic Drugs Find Only 1.1% Deficient in Safety, Quality," *Wall Street Journal,* November 20, 1989, p. B-4.

68. Joseph Weber, "The Price of No-Name Drugs May Soon Be Hard To Swallow," *Business Week,* October 2, 1989, p. 87.

69. "The Insurance Crisis: Now Everyone Is In A Risky Business," *Business Week,* March 10, 1986, p. 88.

70. Milton R. Copulos, "An Rx for the Product Liability Epidemic," *Backgrounder: The Heritage Foundation,* May 15, 1985, p. 1.

71. "Sorry, Your Policy Is Canceled," *Time,* March 24, 1986, p. 20.

72. Amy Docker Marcus, "Juries Rule Against 'Tort Reform' With Huge Awards," *Wall Street Journal,* February 9, 1990, p. B-1.

73. "General Aviation Aircraft Directory," *Aviation Week & Space Technology,* March 16, 1987, p. 56.

74. A survey of more than 500 chief executives conducted by the Conference Board in 1988 found that 4 out of 10 believed product liability concerns have had a "major impact" on their businesses. One-third of the firms surveyed had canceled new products because of liability worries, and more than half discontinued existing product lines. Many reported that they had to close plants and lay off workers. And more than one-fifth believed they had lost market share to foreign competition because of increased product liability expenditures. Carolyn Lochhead, "Liability's Creative Clamp Holds Firms to the Status Quo," *Insight,* August 29, 1988, p. 38.

75. *Greenman* v. *Yuba Power Products, Inc.,* 59 Cal. 2d 57, 177 P. 2d 897 (1963).

76. "Unsafe Products: The Great Debate over Blame and Punishment," *Business Week,* April 30, 1984, pp. 96–104. See also Jordan Leibman, "Liability for the Unknowable," *Business Horizons,* (July–August 1983), pp. 35–40.

77. Charlotte Low Allen, "When Awards Become Too Punitive," *Insight,* April 17, 1989, pp. 46–47.

78. Wade Lambert and Wayne E. Green, "Liability Ruling Sets Back Manufacturers," *Wall Street Journal,* March 8, 1990, p. B-8. See also Elizabeth Grillo Olson, "Punitive Damages: How Much Is Too

Much?'' *Business Week,* March 27, 1989, pp. 54–56; and Stephen Wermiel, ''Punitive Damage Cases Take Spotlight,'' *Wall Street Journal,* April 14, 1989, p. B-5B.

79. Roger LeRoy Miller, ''Drawing Limits on Liability,'' *Wall Street Journal,* April 4, 1984, p. 28.

80. Michael McQueen, ''Bush Administration Strongly Backs Overhaul of U.S. Product-Liability Laws,'' *Wall Street Journal,* December 1, 1989, p. A-6.

81. Brooks Jackson, ''Proposals to Curb Damage Awards in Lawsuits Lead to Flood of Lobbying Efforts on Both Sides,'' *Wall Street Journal,* April 9, 1986, p. 56. See also Stephen Wermiel, ''Lawyers Reject Damage Award Limits, But Urge Control on Punitive Amounts,'' *Wall Street Journal,* February 18, 1987, p. 5.

82. Andy Pasztor, ''White House Switches Focus to States In Bid for Liability-Insurance Revisions,'' *Wall Street Journal,* March 27, 1987, p. 38. See also ''What Some States Have Done to Limit Liability Claims in Their Courtrooms,'' *Wall Street Journal,* August 1, 1986, p. 10; Tim Smart, ''The Liability Battle: Business Becomes A Road Warrior,'' *Business Week,* April 9, 1990, p. 25.

83. ''Business Gets The Hang Of Do-It-Yourself Coverage,'' *Business Week,* July 21, 1986, pp. 112–113. See also Lawrence J. Tell, ''United They Stand—At The Defense Table,'' *Business Week,* May 30, 1988, pp. 102–103.

84. Michael Horowitz, ''The Politics of Tort Reform,'' *Manhattan Report: The Liability Crisis,* Vol. VI, No. 2 (1986), p. 15. Not everyone agrees that there is a liability crisis. See William B. Glaberson and Christopher Farrell, ''The Explosion In Liability Lawsuits Is Nothing But A Myth,'' *Business Week,* April 21, 1986, p. 24.

85. Carolyn Lochhead, ''All Are Liable in Product Liability,'' *Insight,* February 15, 1988, p. 47.

86. Stephen Brobeck, ''The Consumer Movement: An Assessment,'' *At Home With Consumers,* Vol. 5, No. 4 (December 1984), p. 8.

87. Ibid., pp. 8–9.

88. See ''Pul-eeze! Will Somebody Help Me?,'' *Time,* February 2, 1987. pp. 48–55. See also William E. Blundell, ''When the Patient Takes Charge: The Consumer Movement Comes to Medical Care,'' *Wall Street Journal,* April 24, 1987, p. 1-D; Joan Berger, ''In The Service Sector, Nothing Is 'Free' Anymore,'' *Business Week,* June 8, 1987, p. 144.

89. Francine Schwadel, ''Retailers Latch On to the Environment,'' *Wall Street Journal,* November 13, 1989, p. B-1.

Suggested Reading

ASCH, PETER. *Consumer Safety Regulation.* New York: Oxford, 1988.

BLOOM, PAUL N., AND RUTH B. SMITH. *The Future of Consumerism.* New York: Lexington Books, 1986.

CRANSTON, ROSS. *Consumers and the Law,* 2d ed. New York: Rothman, 1984.

EILER, ANDREW. *The Consumer Protection Manual.* New York: Facts on File, 1983.

FELDMAN, LAURENCE P. *Consumer Protection: Problems and Prospects.* St. Paul, Minn.: West, 1980.

FORNELL, CLAES. *Consumer Input for Marketing Decisions: A Study of Corporate Departments for Consumer Affairs.* New York: Praeger, 1976.

HEMPHILL, C. *Consumer Protection: A Legal Guide.* Englewood Cliffs, N.J.: Prentice Hall, 1981.

HENDERSON, JAMES A., JR., AND AARON D. TWERSKI. *Products Liability: Problems and Process.* Boston: Little, Brown, 1987.

LEMOV, MICHAEL R. *Consumer Product Safety Commission.* New York: McGraw-Hill, 1981.

MAGNUSON, WARREN G., AND JEAN CARPER. *The Dark Side of the Marketplace.* Englewood Cliffs, N.J.: Prentice Hall, 1968.

MCGUIRE, E. PATRICK. *The Impact of Product Liability.* New York: Conference Board, 1988.

MCLAUGHLIN, FRANK E., ed. *The Future of Consumerism.* College Park, Md.: Center for Business and Public Policy, 1982.

MORTON, JOHN S. *Consumer Action,* 2d ed. Boston: Houghton Mifflin, 1983.

NADEL, MARK V. *The Politics of Consumer Protection.* Indianapolis, Ind.: Bobbs-Merrill, 1971.

NADER, RALPH, ed. *The Consumer and Corporate Accountability.* San Diego, Calif.: Harcourt Brace Jovanovich, 1973.

NADER, RALPH. *Unsafe at Any Speed: The Designed-in Dangers of the American Automobile.* New York: Grossman Publishers, 1972.

PERTSCHUK, MICHAEL. *Revolt Against Regulation: The Rise and Pause of the Consumer Movement.* Berkeley, Calif.: University of California Press, 1982.

SHAPO, MARSHALL S. *Law of Products Liability.* New York: Warren Gorham & Lamont, 1987.

SILBER, NORMAN I. *Test and Protest: The Influence of Consumers Union.* New York: Holmes & Meier, 1983.

STERN, LOUIS W., AND THOMAS L. EAVALDI. *Legal Aspects of Marketing Strategy: Antitrust and Consumer Protection Issues.* Englewood Cliffs, N.J.: Prentice-Hall, 1984.

UUSITALO, LIISA. *Environmental Impact of Consumption Patterns.* New York: St. Martin, 1986.

VISCUSI, W. KIP. *Regulating Consumer Product Safety.* Washington, D.C.: American Enterprise Institute, 1984.

WEBER, NATHAN. *Product Liability: The Corporate Response.* New York: Conference Board, 1987.

WEINSTEIN, ET AL. *Products Liability and the Reasonably Safe Product.* New York: John Wiley, 1987.

WHINCUP, MICHAEL. *Product Liability Law: A Guide for Managers.* New York: Gower, 1985.

CHAPTER *9*

The Physical Environment and Pollution Control

Environmentalism has been called the issue of the 1990s, and as the decade began, environmental issues once again moved to the top of the public policy agenda. The Exxon disaster stimulated concern about the environment, particularly in the United States, but this concern had been building during the 1980s, as efforts to deal with environmental problems were curbed while problems mounted. Many scientists are now saying that if we don't come to grips with some of our more serious environmental problems in the coming decade, it may be too late to prevent massive pollution problems and serious environmental degradation that will affect the lives of millions of people.

So-called global problems, such as global warming and the depletion of the ozone layer, now threaten the entire planet and require international cooperation for their solution. These problems are discussed in the chapter on the international dimensions of public policy. But all environmental problems are in some sense global rather than just regional or local in nature. It is difficult to talk about air pollution in one country and efforts being made to reduce air pollution without talking about other country's problems. The same is true of water pollution and waste disposal problems. Although public policy measures can be implemented by individual countries to deal with these problems, such problems really do not respect the boundaries of nations or localities and are fundamentally global in nature and in many cases require global solutions.

The physical environment includes, air, water, and land, without which life as we know it would be impossible. This environment provides a number of services that human beings cannot do without. Chief among them is a habitat in which plant and animal life can survive. If this habitat is seriously degraded, plant and animal life will be adversely affected. The physical environment is also called upon to provide resources that are used in the production process, whatever form that process might take to produce goods and services for the members of society. Some of these resources are nonrenewable and are thus able to be completely exhausted after having been used for many years. Others, such as timber, are renewable, but conscious effort is generally needed to replace those renewable resources that are used. This replacement usually does not happen automatically, at least not fast enough to support a growing population. The physical environment is also used as a place to dispose of waste material that results from the production of goods and services as well as from their consumption. Problems arise when this waste material overwhelms the absorption capacity of the environment, and serious degradation is the result.

This chapter focuses on pollution of the physical environment that interferes with its ability to provide a habitat in which life can survive and flourish. The ability of the physical environment to serve as a gigantic garbage disposal depends on its dilutive capacity. Pollution occurs when the waste discharged into the environment exceeds its dilutive capacity—when air can no longer dilute the wastes dumped into it without air quality being adversely affected; water can no longer absorb the wastes dumped into it without some fundamental change taking place in the quality of the water; and land cannot absorb any more waste material without producing harmful effects that relate to land usage itself or drinking-water supplies.

The amount of damage that results to a particular medium (air, water, land) varies by the type of pollutant, the amount of pollutant disposed of, and the distance from the source of pollution. These damages, however, alter the quality of the environment and render it, to some degree, unfit to provide its normal services. Thus the air can become harmful for human beings to breathe, water unfit to drink, and land unfit to live on because of toxic wastes that begin seeping to the surface to pose a threat to human health.

As far as the market system is concerned, these damages are considered negative externalities. They arise out of the transactions between producers and consumers in an industrial society but are not normally factored into the prices of products. Before the advent of pollution control legislation, air, water, and land were treated as free goods available to anyone for dumping wastes. This caused no problem when the population was sparse, factories small, and products few in number compared with today. The environment's dilutive capacity was rarely exceeded and was perceived as infinite in its ability to absorb waste. Changes in society, however, began to cause serious pollution problems. The following factors were critical in this transformation.

Population Growth and Concentration: More people mean more manufactured goods and services to provide for their needs, which in turn means more waste material to be discharged into the environment. The concentration of people in urban areas compounds the problem. Eventually the dilutive capacity of the air, water, and land in major industrial centers becomes greatly exceeded, and a serious pollution problem results.

Rising Affluence: As real income increases, people are able to buy and consume more goods and services, throw them away more quickly to buy something better, travel more miles per year using various forms of transportation, and expand their use of energy. In the process, much more waste material is generated for the society as a whole.

Technological Change: Changes in technology have expanded the variety of products available for consumption, increased their quantity through increases in productivity, made products and packaging more complex, and raised the rate of obsolescence through rapid innovation. All this has added to the waste-disposal problem. In addition, the toxicity of many materials was initially unknown or not given much concern, with the result that procedures for the abatement of these pollution problems have lagged far behind the technology of manufacture.

Increased Expectations and Awareness: As society became more affluent, it could give attention to higher-order needs. Thus expectations for a higher quality of life have increased, and the physical environment is viewed as an important component of the overall quality of life. One cannot fully enjoy the goods and services that are available in a hostile or unsafe environment. In addition, the people's awareness of the harmful effects of pollution increased due to mounting scientific evidence, journalistic exposés, and the attention given environmental problems by the media.

These forces combined in about the mid-1960s to give birth to an environmental movement that developed very quickly. Many of the energies that had gone into the civil rights movement were channeled into the environmental movement as the former matured. The result was a major public policy effort to control pollution and correct for the deficiencies of the market system in controlling the amount and types of waste being discharged into the environment. These efforts have made a major impact on business and consumers alike and have caused attitudinal and behavioral changes throughout society.

Stages of Environmental Consciousness

Concern about the environment, however, is not necessarily a new phenomenon. In earlier years in this country, a conservation movement developed that attempted to restrain the reckless exploitation of forests and wildlife that characterized the pioneer state of social development. This movement curbed the destructive environmental impacts of individuals and corporations who exploited nature for profit without regard for the larger social good or the welfare of future generations. It emphasized that resources should be used wisely and that consideration should be given to a sustainable society. This movement began to get a glimpse of natural limits to resource exploitation that would require different norms of conduct for the society to become sustainable on a long-term basis.

The Wilderness Act of 1964 ushered in a new stage, where nature was recognized as having value in its own right independent of its potential use for human purposes. Certain areas of the country were set aside to be preserved in their natural state and closed to resource development through a permanent wilderness designation. People came to believe that land and wildlife could be conserved only by leaving them in their natural state and eliminating human presence as much as possible. The Wilderness Act recognizes a wilderness ''as an area where the earth and community of life are untrammeled by man, where man himself is a visitor who does not remain.'' The important values in this movement were ecological, which means that natural systems should be allowed to operate as free from human interference as possible.

The modern environmental movement began in the 1960s with the publication of Rachel Carson's *Silent Spring,* which focused on the problems pesticides posed for society. Concern centered on destruction of the environment within or near agricultural or industrial centers that involved serious threats to human health. The movement promoted environmental cleanup as something of a quality-of-life issue and became tagged as antigrowth and elitist in nature. Nonetheless, the movement became institutionalized, as most of the environmental concerns resulted in public policy measures related to the environment and the creation of new agencies in government to implement these measures.

New-age environmentalism, as it could be called, began in the late 1980s, when concern about the environment became a survival issue rather than a quality-of-life issue. Environmental consciousness trickled down from its core of relatively affluent and well-educated supporters because (1) the less-well-off were being visibly affected by environmental problems, far more than they were suffering from environmental protection measures, (2) environmentalists became more equity-conscious and through their adoption of the sustainable growth concept have largely cast off charges of antigrowth obstructionism, and (3) the environmental movement managed successfully to mobilize informational and political resources and avoided displacement of its goals during the Reagan years.[1]

Pollution Control Policies and Objectives

There are various types of pollution, including air, water, solid and hazardous waste, noise, and visual or aesthetic pollution. Since these types of pollution and their causes are quite different, the policies to control them are also different. These policies will be discussed in detail later in this chapter. In general, however, four major types of policies or approaches have been adopted to control pollution.

The first approach is one of requiring a comprehensive environmental evaluation of an activity before it is undertaken to ensure that all possible primary and secondary effects of the undertaking are examined and all alternatives considered before the activity is approved. An example of this approach is the environmental impact statement required of all federal agencies for projects that affect the environment. A second approach is the setting of pollution standards for specific types of pollutants. These standards set limits on the maximum allowable level of these pollutants that can be discharged. Violators who exceed these standards are fined. Air pollution is controlled in this manner. Another approach is to regulate industrial and municipal discharge activities through licensing procedures, granting these facilities permission to discharge pollutants or waste using certain broad types of technology available or by following certain procedures. Except for particularly hazardous substances, such as mercury, water pollution is controlled in this fashion. Finally, another approach examines substances before they are used to determine whether they are safe or whether they constitute such a hazard that their use needs to be limited or banned. The new toxic substances control legislation is an example of this technique.[2]

There are many objectives to pollution control. One is simply an aesthetic objective: to improve the quality of the air so visibility is improved; to prevent pollution from blackening buildings; to reduce the foul odors from streams, rivers, or lakes; to reduce the level of noise so that normal conversations can be carried on; to hide offshore oil derricks behind structures that are more aesthetically pleasing.

Closely related to this objective is one of reducing the nuisance or inconvenience that pollution causes. Polluting a river or lake may make it unfit for fishing or swimming, which could cause some people a great amount of displeasure. Pollution in the air can cause a certain amount of personal discomfort, such as eye irritation, that may not actually be a health hazard but is something people can definitely do without.

There are actual direct economic losses connected with pollution that its control can reduce. This can be something as mundane as the soiling of clothes, and in this respect a reduction of pollution can reduce cleaning and washing expenses. It is said, for example, that before the days of the renaissance in Pittsburgh, executives had to take an extra white shirt to work with them in the morning if they intended to go outside of the building for lunch. Other economic losses could result from damage to vegetation or livestock, or from deterioration of buildings, particularly in cities such as Venice where many buildings are irreplaceable works of art.

Another objective of pollution control is to reduce the safety hazard that can exist due to lack of visibility. Poor visibility caused by pollution can constitute this sort of hazard for aircraft trying to land or take off and for automobiles. Accidents on the New Jersey turnpike, for example, have been attributed to the poor visibility caused by pollution from refineries and other industrial facilities in the area.

A very important objective of pollution control is to reduce the health hazards that pollutants cause. Cancer and heart and lung diseases have become the leading causes of death in our society, and a growing body of evidence links much of the occurrence of these diseases to the nature of the environment. Heart disease rates, for example, are known to be higher in areas of high air pollution, and although a direct cause may be difficult to prove, there is increasing belief that polluted air may aggravate preexisting heart conditions. The Environmental Protection Agency states that air pollution probably causes and certainly aggravates the following:

- Disease of the respiratory (breathing) system; nose, sinuses, throat, bronchial tubes, and lungs. All these organs have direct contact with breathed-in air.
- Diseases of the heart and blood vessels. Pollutants can pass through the lung membranes into the blood.
- Cancer, especially of the lungs. Airborne cancer-causing agents can enter the body through the skin as well as the lungs and be carried by the blood to any organ.
- Skin diseases, allergies, eye irritation.[3]

Water pollution also poses hazards to human health. The possibility that asbestos fibers in the taconite tailings Reserve Mining Company was dumping into Lake Superior were a health hazard was an issue in this case, the longest of all environmental controversies. Extreme noise pollution over extended periods of time can cause loss of hearing. Hazardous waste disposal that is not properly accomplished can cause many problems if people build on old dump sites or if some of the chemicals leach into the drinking water. Finally, toxic substances pose health problems for those coming into contact with them. Some 2 million chemical compounds are known, and an estimated 25,000 new ones are developed every year. About 10,000 of these have significant commercial uses, and although most are probably safe, the toxicity of many is unknown.

Administrative Structure

Council on Environmental Quality. There are two federal agencies responsible for attaining these objectives and developing policies to preserve the physical environment. The National Environmental Policy Act created the Council on Environmental Quality (CEQ), a three-member body located in the executive office of the president (Exhibit 9.1). In general, the CEQ (1) evaluates all federal programs to see that they are consistent with the national policy on the environment, (2) advises and assists the president in environmental matters, and (3) develops national policies in the environmental area.

The CEQ is responsible for administering the environmental impact statement process through the issuance of regulations to federal agencies regarding their preparation. Beyond this, however, the CEQ has no administrative authority for pollution control. Its approach is entirely preventive in nature. Another function of the CEQ is preparation of the *Environmental Quality Report,* an annual report on the state of the

Exhibit 9.1 ──

Council on Environmental Quality
722 Jackson Place NW, Washington, D.C. 20006

Purpose: To administer the environmental impact statement process and to develop and recommend to the president policies for protecting and improving environmental quality.

Regulatory Activity: The CEQ is responsible for issuing regulations to federal agencies on the preparation of environmental impact statements required under the National Environmental Policy Act. It also (1) reviews and appraises federal programs affecting the environment; and (2) assists in coordinating national environmental programs.

Established: 1969

Legislative Authority:
  Enabling Legislation: National Environmental Policy Act of 1969 (83 Stat. 852)
                        National Environmental Improvement Act of 1970 (84 Stat. 114)
                        Water Quality Improvement Act of 1970 (84 Stat. 94)

Organization: The Council, located within the executive office of the president, consists of three members appointed by the president with the advice and consent of the Senate. The Office of Environmental Quality within the Department of Housing and Urban Development provides staff for the Council.

Budgets and Staffing, Fiscal 1975–90

							(Estimated)	
	1975	*1980*	*1985*	*1986*	*1987*	*1988*	*1989*	*1990*
Budget								
($ millions)	4	8	1	1	1	1	1	1
Staffing	50	32	11	13	13	13	13	13

Note: Budget and staffing figures include the Office of Environmental Quality.

Source: Ronald J. Penoyer, *Directory of Federal Regulatory Agencies,* 2d ed. (St. Louis, Mo.: Washington University Center for the Study of American Business, 1980), p. 25. Reprinted with permission.

───

environment. CEQ responsibility for this report is analogous to the Council of Economic Advisors and the Economic Report of the President.

Despite its lack of authority, the CEQ has symbolic importance and political value to environmental interests. The agency's presence in the president's executive structure gives it visibility and implies a high national priority to environmental problems. The opportunities it has to influence the president directly gives it a role of acting as the environmental conscience of the executive branch. However, the agency can exercise no more influence than the president cares to give it, as the president can ignore any of its recommendations.

Environmental Protection Agency. The other federal agency involved in protecting and enhancing the physical environment and one with much more sweeping authority over various aspects of pollution control is the Environmental Protection Agency (EPA). Its responsibilities involve the development and implementation of programs that range across the whole domain of environmental management (See Exhibit 9.2). The EPA

EXHIBIT 9.2

Environmental Protection Agency
401 M Street SW, Washington, DC 20460

Purpose: To protect and enhance the physical environment.

Regulatory Activity: In cooperation with state and local governments, the agency controls pollution through regulation, surveillance, and enforcement in eight areas: air, water quality, solid waste, pesticides, toxic substances, drinking water, radiation, and noise. Its activities in each area include development of (1) national programs and technical policies; (2) national emission standards and effluent guidelines; (3) rules and procedures for industry reporting, registration and certification programs; and (4) ambient air standards. EPA issues permits to industrial dischargers of pollutants and for disposal of industrial waste; sets standards which limit the amount of radioactivity in the environment; reviews proposals for new nuclear facilities; evaluates and regulates new chemicals and chemicals with new uses; and establishes and monitors tolerance levels for pesticides occurring in or on foods.

Established: 1970

Legislative Authority:
   Enabling Legislation: Reorganization Plan No. 3 of 1970, effective December 2, 1970

   The EPA is responsible for the enforcement of the following acts:
   Water Quality Improvement Act of 1970 (84 Stat. 94)
   Clean Air Act Amendments of 1970 (84 Stat. 94)
   Federal Water Pollution Control Act Amendments of 1972 (86 Stat. 819)
   Federal Insecticide, Fungicide and Rodenticide Act of 1972 (86 Stat. 975)
   Marine Protection, Research, and Sanctuaries Act of 1972 (86 Stat. 1052)
   Noise Control Act of 1972 (86 Stat. 1234)
   Provisions of the Energy Supply and Environmental Coordination Act of 1974 (88 Stat. 246)
   Safe Drinking Water Act of 1974 (88 Stat. 1661)
   Resource Conservation and Recovery Act of 1976 (90 Stat. 95)
   Toxic Substances Control Act of 1976 (90 Stat. 2005)
   Clean Air Act Amendments of 1977 (91 Stat. 685)
   Clean Water Act of 1977 (91 Stat. 1566)

Organization: This independent agency, located within the executive branch, is headed by an administrator.

Budgets and Staffing, Fiscal 1970–90

	1970	1975	1980	1985	1986	1987	1988	(Estimated) 1989	1990
Budget ($ millions)	205	794	1,360	1,928	1,860	2,642	3,109	3,384	3,664
Staffing	3,856	9,144	11,004	11,615	12,041	13,197	13,589	13,739	14,417

Source: Ronald J. Penoyer, *Directory of Federal Regulatory Agencies,* 2d ed. (St. Louis, Mo.: Washington University Center for the Study of American Business, 1980), p. 27. Reprinted with permission.

began on July 9, 1970, when President Nixon sent a reorganization plan to Congress that took the various units dealing with the environment from existing departments and agencies and relocated them in a single, new independent agency. The plan became effective on December 2, 1970, when the EPA officially opened its doors.

The EPA was formed from 15 separate components of 5 executive departments and independent agencies. Programs related to air pollution control, solid waste management, radiation, and drinking water were transferred to the EPA from the Department of Health, Education, and Welfare (now the Department of Health and Human Services). The water pollution control program was transferred from the Department of Interior and the authority to register and regulate pesticides from the Department of Agriculture. The responsibility to set tolerance levels for pesticides in food was transferred from the Food and Drug Administration, and a pesticide research program came from the Department of Interior. Finally, the responsibility for setting environmental radiation protection standards came from the old Atomic Energy Commission.[4]

The EPA now has responsibility for pollution control in seven areas of the environment: air, water, solid and hazardous waste, pesticides, toxic substances, radiation, and noise. Its general responsibilities in these areas include (1) the establishment and enforcement of standards, (2) monitoring of pollution in the environment, (3) conducting research into environmental problems and holding demonstrations when appropriate, and (4) assisting state and local governments in their efforts to control pollution. The EPA is headquartered in Washington, DC, with regional offices and laboratories located throughout the country.

The research arm of the EPA is the Office of Research and Development (ORD), which directs the EPA's research program. About 70 percent of this program is in direct support of environmental problems of concern to the agency; the other 30 percent deals with long-term problems to address future regulatory needs. The major areas of research are monitoring, development of technology, determination of ecological effects, and definition of the health effects of environmental pollutants. In addition to its own research staff, a Science Advisory Board composed of preeminent non-EPA scientists was established by Congress to advise the agency on scientific issues.

The Office of Legal and Enforcement Council acts as the EPA's law firm and is responsible for carrying out all its legal responsibilities and activities. The enforcement philosophy of the EPA is to encourage voluntary compliance by communities and private industry with environmental laws and encourage state and local governments to perform enforcement actions when needed. If these efforts fail, the EPA is authorized to enforce the law through inspection procedures with respect to all aspects of its responsibilities and criminal investigation units with regard to hazardous waste disposal.

Air Pollution

The total amount of pollution in the air over the United States at any given time adds up to hundreds of millions of tons. Table 9.1 shows the total emissions over several decades of the six most pervasive pollutants. The amount of these pollutants spewed into the air during some of these years was over 200 million metric tons (a metric ton is about 2,200 pounds), nearly a ton for every many, woman and child in the country.[5] Table 9.2 shows the source of these pollutants for 1970, 1980, and 1986, the latest year for which figures were available. A glance at this table shows clearly that certain kinds

TABLE 9.1 National Air Pollutant Emissions: 1940 to 1986

[In millions of metric tons, except lead in thousands of metric tons. Metric ton = 1.1023 short tons. PM = Particulates, SO_x = Sulfur oxides, NO_x = Nitrogen oxide, VOC = Volatile organic compound, CO = Carbon monoxide, Pb = lead]

Year	Emissions						Percent Change[1]					
	PM	SO_x	NO_x	VOC	CO	Pb	PM	SO_x	NO_x	VOC	CO	Pb
1940	23.1	17.6	6.8	18.6	81.6	(NA)	(NA)	(NA)	(NA)	(NA)	(NA)	(NA)
1950	24.9	19.8	9.3	21.0	86.3	(NA)	7.8	12.5	36.8	12.9	5.8	(NA)
1960	21.6	19.7	12.8	23.8	88.4	(NA)	−13.3	−.5	37.6	13.3	2.4	(NA)
1970	18.5	28.3	18.1	27.5	98.7	203.8	−14.4	43.7	41.4	15.5	11.7	(NA)
1975	10.6	26.0	19.1	22.8	81.0	147.0	−42.7	−8.1	5.5	−17.1	−17.9	−27.9
1980	8.5	23.9	20.3	23.0	76.1	70.6	−19.8	−8.1	6.3	.9	−6.0	−52.0
1981	8.0	23.5	20.3	21.6	73.4	55.9	−5.9	−1.7	−	−6.1	−3.5	−20.8
1982	7.1	22.0	19.5	20.1	67.4	54.4	−11.2	−6.4	−3.9	−6.9	−8.2	−2.7
1983	7.1	21.5	19.1	20.9	70.3	46.3	−	−2.3	−2.1	4.0	4.3	−14.9
1984	7.4	22.1	19.7	21.9	69.6	40.1	4.2	2.8	3.1	4.8	−1.0	−13.4
1985	7.0	21.6	19.7	20.3	64.3	21.1	−5.4	−2.3	−	−7.3	−7.6	−47.4
1986	6.8	21.2	19.3	19.5	60.9	8.6	−2.9	−1.9	−2.0	−3.9	−5.3	−59.2

− Represents zero.

NA Not available.

[1]Percent change from prior year shown.

Source: U.S. Department of Commerce, *Statistical Abstract of the United States 1989,* 109th ed. (Washington, D.C.: U.S. Government Printing Office, 1988), p. 200.

of sources predominate for different types of pollution. The internal combustion engine (autos and trucks) in 1986, for example, respectively accounted for 70 and 40 percent of carbon monoxide and lead emissions. Stationary fuel-burning (power, heating) accounted for 75 and 81 percent in 1970 and 1986, respectively, of sulfur oxide emissions.

Recent public policy measures designed to reduce air pollution date from the Air Pollution Act of 1955, which authorized the Public Health Service to undertake air pollution studies through a system of grants. This act created the first federally funded air pollution research activity. The Clean Air Act of 1963 replaced the 1955 act and was aimed at the control and prevention of air pollution. It permitted legal steps to end specific instances of air pollution and authorized grants to state and local governments to initiate control programs. The 1965 amendments to the Clean Air Act (called the National Emissions Standards Act) gave the federal government authority to curb motor vehicle emissions and set standards which were first applied to 1968 model vehicles. The Air Quality Act of 1967 required the states to establish air quality regions with standards for air pollution control and implementation plans for their accomplishment. The Clean Air Act Amendments of 1970 provided the legal basis for a new system of national air quality standards to be set by the federal government and called for a rollback of auto pollution levels. In the Clean Air Act Amendments of 1977, new deadlines were set for the attainment of air quality standards.

Thus the public policy approach to pollution control is many-faceted. The management system that has evolved over the years to control pollution and improve the quality of the air that we breath is complicated and deals with various levels of control. The Clean Air Act Amendments of 1970 and 1977 laid out the following areas, where different kinds of management methods are used to accomplish the goals of pollution-control legislation with respect to air quality:

TABLE 9.2   Air Pollutant Emissions, By Pollutant and Source: 1970 to 1986

[In millions of metric tons, except lead in thousands of metric tons. Metric ton = 1.1023 short tons]

| Year and Pollutant | Total emissions | Controllable Emissions | | | | | | Misc. un-controllable | Percent of Total | | |
| | | Transportation | | Fuel combustion[1] | | Industrial processes | Solid waste disposal | | Trans-portation | Fuel combustion[1] | Industrial |
		Total	Road vehicles	Total	Electric utilities						
1970: Carbon monoxide...	98.7	71.8	62.7	4.4	.2	9.0	6.4	7.2	72.7	4.5	9.1
Sulfur oxides..........	28.4	.6	.3	21.3	15.8	6.4	–	.1	2.1	75.0	22.5
Volatile organic compounds.........	27.5	12.4	11.1	1.1	–	8.9	1.8	3.3	45.1	4.0	32.4
Particulates	18.5	1.2	.9	4.6	2.3	10.5	1.1	1.1	6.5	24.9	56.8
Nitrogen oxides.......	18.1	7.6	6.0	9.1	4.4	.7	.4	.3	42.0	50.3	3.9
Lead................	203.8	163.6	156.0	9.6	.3	23.9	6.7	–	80.3	4.7	11.7
1980: Carbon monoxide...	76.1	52.6	45.3	7.3	.3	6.3	2.2	7.6	69.1	9.6	8.3
Sulfur oxides.........	23.9	.9	.4	19.3	16.1	3.8	–	–	3.8	80.8	15.9
Volatile organic compounds.........	23.0	8.2	6.9	2.2	–	9.2	.6	2.9	35.7	9.6	.4
Particulates	8.5	1.3	1.1	2.4	.8	3.3	.4	1.1	15.3	28.2	38.8
Nitrogen oxides.......	20.3	9.2	7.2	10.1	6.4	.7	.1	.2	45.3	49.8	3.4
Lead................	70.6	59.4	56.4	3.9	.1	3.6	3.7	–	84.1	5.5	5.1
1986: Carbon monoxide...	60.9	42.6	35.4	7.2	.3	4.5	1.7	5.0	70.0	11.8	7.4
Sulfur oxides.........	21.2	.9	.5	17.2	14.3	3.1	–	–	4.2	81.1	14.6
Volatile organic compounds.........	19.5	6.5	5.3	2.3	–	7.9	.6	2.2	33.3	11.8	40.5
Particulates	6.8	1.4	1.1	1.8	.4	2.5	.3	.8	20.6	26.5	36.8
Nitrogen oxides.......	19.3	8.5	6.6	10.0	6.6	.6	.1	.1	44.0	51.8	3.1
Lead................	8.6	3.5	3.3	.5	.1	1.9	2.7	–	40.7	5.8	22.1

– Represents zero.
[1]Stationary.

Source: U.S. Department of Commerce, Statistical Abstract of the United States 1989, 109th ed. (Washington, D.C.: U.S. Government Printing Office, 1988), p. 200.

- Air quality management (ambient air quality)
- Limits on emissions from stationary sources (factories and power plants)
- Limits on emissions from mobile sources (primarily cars and trucks)
- Restrictions on industrial growth and expansion in areas where national air quality standards have not been met (nonattainment areas).
- Limitations on industrial growth in areas where the air quality is better than the national standards, termed Prevention of Significant Deterioration (PSD).

Air Quality Management.   To control ambient air quality, which refers to the air that surrounds us, the EPA sets primary and secondary standards for the seven pollutants. Six pollutants were initially identified by the EPA in 1971 as being the most pervasive of artificial pollutants and in need of immediate reduction and control. These six are sulfur oxides, particulates, carbon monoxide, ozone, nitrogen oxides, and hydrocarbons. In 1978, lead was added to the list of harmful pollutants. The nature and health effects of these pollutants are varied (Exhibit 9.3).

The primary standards concern the minimum level of air quality that is necessary to keep people from becoming ill and are aimed at protecting human health. These primary standards are intended to provide an "adequate margin of safety," which has been defined to include a "representative sample" of so-called sensitive populations, such as the elderly and asthmatics. These standards are to be set without regard to cost or availability of control technology. The secondary standards are aimed at the promotion of public welfare and the prevention of damage to animals, plant life, and property generally. These standards are based on scientific and medical studies that have been made of the pollutant's effects. Table 9.3 on page 267 shows the current standards that are in effect. As can be seen, the primary and secondary standards for some of the seven pollutants are the same.

Because air pollution problems vary from place to place throughout the country, a regional concept was adopted for air pollution control through the establishment of 247 air quality control regions. These air quality control regions were useful units for management and control as each region had individual problems and individual characteristics of pollution control. An air quality control region is defined by the EPA "as an area with definite pollution problems, common pollution sources, and characteristic weather."[6]

The states were given responsibility for drawing up plans called state implementation plans (SIPs) to attain the standards for the air quality control regions within their boundaries. The primary standards were to be attained by mid-1975 as required by the 1970 Clean Air Act. When that deadline came, however, only 69 of the 247 air quality control regions were in compliance with all the antipollution standards then in existence. Sixty regions failed the standards for particulates, 42 for sulfur dioxide, 74 for ozone, 54 for carbon monoxide, and 13 for nitrogen dioxide. Such cities as Los Angeles, Chicago, and Philadelphia violated the standards for all pollutants. Some interesting headlines appeared in the newspapers when these goals were not attained, among them, "AIR TO BE ILLEGAL—BUT BREATHE ANYWAY."

Obviously some adjustments had to be made. These were finally worked out in the 1977 amendments. Under these amendments, the primary standards were to be attained as expeditiously as possible but not later than December 31, 1982, with extensions until 1987 for two pollutants most closely related to transportation systems (carbon monoxide and ozone) if the state required an annual automobile inspection of emission controls. Each state was also required to draw up specific plans for bringing each

EXHIBIT 9.3

Major Air Pollutants and their Health Effects

Pollutant	Major Sources	Characteristics and Effects
Carbon monoxide (CO)	Vehicle exhausts	Colorless, odorless poisonous gas. Replaces oxygen in red blood cells, causing dizziness, unconsciousness, or death.
Hydrocarbons (HC)	Incomplete combustion of gasoline; evaporation of petroleum fuels, solvents, and paints	Although some are poisonous, most are not. Reacts with NO_2 to form ozone, or smog.
Lead (Pb)	Antiknock agents in gasoline	Accumulates in the bone and soft tissues. Affects blood-forming organs, kidneys, and nervous system. Suspected of causing learning disabilities in young children.
Nitrogen dioxide (NO_2)	Industrial processes, vehicle exhausts	Causes structural and chemical changes in the lungs. Lowers resistance to respiratory infections. Reacts in sunlight with hydrocarbons to produce smog. Contributes to acid rain.
Ozone (O_3)	Formed when HC and NO_2 react	Principal constituent of smog. Irritates mucous membranes, causing coughing, choking, impaired lung function. Aggravates chronic asthma and bronchitis.
Total suspended particulates (TSP)	Industrial plants, heating boilers, auto engines, dust	Larger visible types (soot, smoke, or dust) can clog the lung sacs. Smaller invisible particles can pass into the bloodstream. Often carry carcinogens and toxic metals, impair visibility.
Sulfur dioxide (SO_2)	Burning coal and oil, industrial processes	Corrosive, poisonous gas. Associated with coughs, colds, asthma, and bronchitis. Contributes to acid rain.

Source: *Environment and Health*, 2d ed. (Washington, D.C.: Congressional Quarterly Inc., 1982), p. 21.

TABLE 9.3 National Quality Standards for Ambient Air[1]

Pollutant	Averaging Time	Primary Standards (Health)	Secondary Standards (Welfare, Materials)
Particulates	Annual	75 μg/m³	60 μg/m³
	24 hours	260 μg/m³	150 μg/m³
Sulfur dioxide	Annual	80 μg/m³ (0.03 ppm)	
	24 hours	365 μg/m³ (0.14 ppm)	
	3 hours	—	1,300 μg/m³ (0.5 ppm)
Carbon monoxide	8 hours	10 mg/m³ (9 ppm)	Same as primary
	1 hour	40 mg/m³ (35 ppm)	
Hydrocarbons (nonmethane)	3 hours (6–9 A.M.)	160 μg/m³ (0.24 ppm)	Same as primary
Nitrogen dioxide	Annual	100 μg/m³ (0.05 ppm)	Same as primary
Ozone	1 hour	240 μg/m³ (0.12 ppm)	Same as primary
Lead	3 months	1.5 μg/m³ (0.006 ppm)	

[1]In micrograms or milligrams per cubic meter—μg/m³ and mg/m³—and in parts per million—ppm.

Source: EPA, Environmental Protection Agency, *Cleaning the Air: EPA's Program for Air Pollution Control* (Washington, D.C.: June 1979), p. 10.

nonattainment region up to standard and for maintaining the purity of air in regions that already meet the standards.

In order to prevent the states from failing to meet the deadlines again, the EPA was authorized to impose sanctions on counties and cities failing to meet the standards. The law allowed the EPA to withhold millions of federal dollars for highway construction, new sewage-treatment plants, and clean-air planning grants as well as ban construction or modification of most factories, power plants, and other major sources of air pollution. As the deadline approached, some 600 counties, about one-fifth of all the nation's counties, were not in compliance with at least one of the standards and thus faced possible sanctions.

The EPA, however, stalled in issuing such sanctions, hoping that Congress would amend the Clean Air Act in 1983 to give the EPA more discretion on where and when to impose sanctions and give the states more flexibility to determine how and when to clean up dirty air without the threat of federal action. Efforts to weaken the Clean Air Act, however, become bogged down in politics, and no amendments from Congress were forthcoming. Subsequently, the EPA itself became embroiled in controversy that resulted in in a change of leadership. The new EPA adopted a conciliatory approach, giving the states more time to meet national standards as long as the EPA believed they were making a good-faith effort to comply.[7] However, the agency used the threat of sanctions to force some states and cities into compliance.[8] Thus the "action-forcing" strategy was continued.

As the 1987 deadline approached, at least 60 cities were expected to be out of compliance with the standards for carbon monoxide and ozone. About a third of these cities qualified for extensions without incurring additional sanctions, and the EPA drew up a plan for coping with the other cities that were not in compliance. These cities would be subject to a construction ban, but would get new compliance deadlines, depending on the seriousness of the problem. State and local officials were to begin reducing emissions immediately in those cities by an average of 3 percent annually. This plan gave the EPA considerable discretion in setting deadlines and instituting enforcement procedures, which, according to some environmental groups, made the necessity of passing new amendments to the Clean Air Act even greater.[9]

Ozone proved to be particularly difficult to control, in 1986, 76.4 million Americans continued to live in metropolitan areas with unhealthy levels of ozone. Studies released in 1986 suggested that ozone is harmful to human health at half the level previously thought, which would put a third of the U.S. population at risk. Recommendations were made to lower the present standard of 0.12 parts per million based on these findings.[10] Another study released in 1989 indicated that at the high levels existing in some cities, ozone could cause permanent damage, affecting lung tissue over many years leading to a precipitous and irreversible loss of breathing power. Children's lungs were found to be particularly susceptible to permanent damage at levels below the federal standard.[11]

Early in 1985, the EPA announced a decision to cut allowable lead levels in gasoline more than 90 percent by January 1, 1986, and to consider a total ban as early as 1988 in light of evidence that airborne lead poses substantial health threats. Several studies had shown a strong correlation between high lead levels in gasoline and lead levels in blood (particularly in children) that could cause brain and nerve damage, mental retardation, anemia, and kidney disorders. Despite increased costs to refiners, the EPA administrator claimed that the reduction in lead content would produce a net savings of at least $6 billion in medical and automobile maintenance costs over the next 7 years and would reduce lead usage from 33,000 to 5,500 tons a year.[12] A total ban on lead in gasoline proved to be impossible to attain, because of damage to older car engines, but due to existing efforts ambient levels of lead in the air declined by 87 percent between 1977 and 1986, and emissions decreased by 94 percent.[13]

Prevention of Significant Deterioration. The 1977 amendments strengthened efforts to maintain air quality in regions where the air is already cleaner than the standards allow. Three kinds of regions were defined. A Class I region includes all national parks and wilderness areas and may include further areas named by the states. In these regions, no additional sulfur or particulate sources are permitted. Class II areas encompass every other PSD region in the nation. In these areas, some industrial development is permitted up to a specified level. Class III areas can have about twice as much pollution from new sources, sometimes even up to the minimum federal standards. Any potential new pollution sources in these regions must obtain a permit before operating and meet a number of other conditions, such as using the best available control methods (BACT). Class III areas are created by reclassifying Class II areas. Thus far only one reclassification has taken place, in part because of the complexity of the reclassification system.

Nonattainment Areas. For nonattainment areas, the EPA has adopted an offset policy. New industrial development is permitted as long as offsetting reductions are made from existing sources for the pollutants to be emitted by the new facilities. These existing sources must reduce their emissions more than enough to compensate for new sources of pollution. An example of this policy cited by the EPA was in Oklahoma City, where several oil firms agreed to put floating tops on large storage tanks to reduce hydrocarbon emissions so General Motors could build an automobile plant there.[14] Companies building new plants or expanding existing ones are also required to meet lowest achievable emission rates (LAER). This requires companies to limit emissions to the lowest rate achieved by any similar installation or plant anywhere in the United States, regardless of cost or circumstances.

Stationary Sources. Stationary sources of air pollution, as distinguished from ambient air quality, are also controlled. Typical stationary sources are power plant and factory smokestacks, industrial vents for gases and dust, coke ovens, incinerators, burning dumps, and large furnaces. The state plans required by the 1977 amendments must inventory these sources and determine how they should be reduced to bring the regions into conformance with ambient air quality standards.

The law currently makes the EPA set emission limits for certain designated pollutants for selected categories of industrial plants and for those that are substantially modified. Control technique guidelines (CTG) focus on retrofitting technology for existing plants. In addition, the EPA sets standards for all major stationary new sources. These limits are called new source performance standards (NSPS) and are specific to each industry. These standards set the maximum amount of each kind of pollutant that can be emitted from a new plant's stacks for each unit of the plant's production. As of 1981, the agency had listed 60 categories of sources, from power plants to grain elevators, for which it expected to develop standards. Rules had been issued for 33 sources, but the EPA failed to meet the 1982 deadline for developing NSPS for all 60 categories.

Although all air pollutants are regarded as hazardous to some degree, some are considered so dangerous to human health that they are limited individually through the setting of hazardous emission standards, called National Emissions Standards for Hazardous Air Pollutants (NESHAP). Presently such limitations apply to any discharge of asbestos, beryllium, mercury, benzene, arsenic, vinyl chloride, radionuclides and coke-oven emissions. These substances have strict limits in regard to the amount that can be emitted into the atmosphere from stationary sources. Other substances are also being considered for this category of control including carbon tetrachloride, chromium, chloroform, and other suspected carcinogens.

After the Bhopal, India, incident, there was increased pressure on the EPA to regulate toxic gas emissions, particularly from large plants. After several months of discussion, the EPA announced a plan to set up a new system to notify states about specific chemicals that may present substantial risk locally but little risk nationally. Each state would be required to monitor the major sources of these chemicals and publish the results but would be free to regulate these emissions as they saw fit, meaning that regulations of a few hazardous pollutants could vary widely from state to state.[15] The first report of toxic emissions was released in 1989 and showed that emissions in eight states exceeded 100 million pounds (Table 9.4). The total included 235 million pounds of carcinogens such as benzene and formaldehyde and 527 million pounds of such neurotoxins as toluene and trichlorethylene. The EPA estimated that such air toxics cause more than 2,000 cases of cancer annually.[16]

In 1982, the EPA adopted a new policy toward stationary sources of pollution called the bubble concept. This policy gives business more flexibility in meeting EPA standards. Under this policy, the agency assumes that an area that might include several

TABLE 9.4   Toxic Emissions

Of 2.4 billion pounds of toxics emitted in 1987, more than half came from 10 states.

States	Millions of pounds of toxic pollutants released into the air
Texas	229.9
Louisiana	134.5
Tennessee	132.5
Virginia	131.4
Ohio	122.5
Michigan	106.2
Indiana	103.5
Illinois	103.1
Georgia	94.3
North Carolina	92.3

Source: EPA from, "Is Breathing Hazardous to your Health?" *Newsweek,* April 3, 1989, p. 25.

plants is covered by an imaginary bubble. Companies within the bubble are allowed to expand their industrial operations so long as total emissions within the bubble don't increase. This approach gives plant engineers an incentive to find or develop the most inexpensive methods of limiting plantwide emissions of a particular pollutant to a level required in their permit to operate. Companies that reduce or limit their pollution will be allowed to sell or trade credits to other companies that are already violating clean air standards and yet want to expand operations.[17]

As of December 31, 1983, the EPA had approved nine generic bubble rules allowing eight states to approve large classes of bubbles without prior EPA approval. Another generic bubble rule had been proposed for approval and 17 more were under development. As of the same date, 35 plant-specific bubbles had been approved by the EPA, and 8 had been proposed. The total savings resulting from bubbles proposed and approved were estimated at over $200 million. The total savings resulting from all bubbles approved, proposed, or under development were estimated to be over $700 million.[18] Table 9.5 shows several representative bubbles and the cost savings that will result from them.

In 1986, the EPA expanded its bubble policy by announcing that it would approve bubbles in areas that had not met federal air pollution standards. Permission would be granted if pollution sources cut their emissions more than 20 percent below the allowable pollution level. Such bubbles must also be consistent with state air quality goals. Approval for new bubbles had ground to a halt over the previous 18 months as the EPA was in the process of revising the policy. When the policy was announced, about 125 bubble applications were pending in 29 states.[19]

Mobile Sources.   For mobile sources of air pollution, the EPA sets standards for automobile, truck, and aircraft emissions. The motor vehicle emission standards in the Clean Air Act are directed at controlling nitrogen oxides, carbon monoxide, particulate matter, hydrocarbons, and lead. This policy is based on the belief that control of these

TABLE 9.5 Representative Control Cost Savings from Approved Bubble Transactions

Firm	Industrial Category	Type of ERC[1]	Cost Savings
3M Bristol, PA	Tape and packaging	Process change VOC	$3 million capital $1.2 million annual operating costs
Kentucky Utilities Muhlenberg, KY	Electric utility	Change in control SO$_2$	$1.3 million annual operating costs
General Motors Defiance County, OH	Foundry	Change in control TSP	$12 million capital costs
National Steel Corp. Weirton, WVA	Integrated steel	Change in control TSP	$30 million capital costs
U.S. Steel Fairless Hills, PA	Integrated steel	Change in control TSP	$27 million capital costs
J. H. Thompson Kennett Square, PA	Greenhouse	Fuel switch SO$_2$	$100,000 annual operating costs
Scott Paper Co. Chester, PA	Paper mill	Fuel Switch SO$_2$	$220,000 annual operating costs

[1]Emissions reduction credit.

Source: Environmental Quality 1983: 14th Annual Report of the Council on Environmental Quality (Washington, DC: U.S. Government Printing Office, 1984), p. 191.

pollutants can best be accomplished by using control devices such as catalytic converters and electronic carburetors on autos and other vehicles. A near disaster was averted in 1977, when Detroit was producing 1978 model cars that were not in compliance with the standards for carbon monoxide and nitrogen oxides that were to go into effect that year. The auto industry claimed that the technology did not exist to meet these standards and asked for a relaxation that was finally granted, but not until a substantial number of cars had been produced for inventory.

The primary standards for carbon monoxide and hydrocarbons were set at a 90 percent reduction based on 1970 levels. Nitrogen oxide emissions were to be reduced 75 percent by 1985. The 90 percent reduction standard for hydrocarbons was achieved in 1980, and in 1981, the standards for carbon monoxide and nitrogen oxides were also achieved.[20] However, a study completed by the EPA in 1985 found that the percentage of cars meeting federal standards dropped to about 40 percent for the 1981 and 1982 model years, from about 65 percent in 1980, the year before tighter emission standards went into effect. Nevertheless, the agency didn't expect the rate of pollution-related recalls to increase, because most of the cars flunking the standards were close to compliance.[21]

The Bush administration made a proposal for improving air quality to break the impasse that had existed for several years over amending the Clean Air Act. The proposal initially called for a 50 percent reduction in acid-rain-producing sulfur dioxide emissions by the turn of the century, a 40 percent tightening of emissions standards for hydrocarbons from automobiles, a 75 percent cut in cancer-causing toxics emitted into the atmosphere over an unspecified period, and the use of alternative fuels that burn cleaner than gasoline.[22] Such fuels would be mandated in cities that have the worst smog problems. The proposal touched off a debate over the merit of the proposals, and as the bill wound its way through the House and Senate, the inevitable compromises began to be worked out that weakened some of the provisions.[23] A revised bill was finally passed in November, 1990.

Water Pollution

Controlling water pollution involves efforts in two areas of concern: (1) reducing the pollution of free-flowing surface waters and protecting their uses, and (2) maintaining the quality of drinking water. In the early 1970s, the impact of conventional pollutants on surface waters was recognized and programs were developed for their control. Later, the dangers posed by toxic pollutants on the nation's waters was recognized and steps were taken to eliminate their discharge. The need to protect drinking water became apparent in the mid-1970s as more than 50 percent of the nation's drinking water was threatened by contamination from various sources, such as underground storage tanks, fertilizers, pesticides, hazardous waste sites, and other sources.[24]

Thus a series of laws and regulations have been developed over the past several decades to protect our water resources. However, some of the laws relating to water pollution go back to the early years of the century or before. Laws to control water pollution actually began with the Rivers and Harbors Act of 1899, which prohibited discharge of pollutants or refuse into or on the banks of navigable waters without a permit. The next public policy measure on water pollution was the Oil Pollution Act of 1924, which prohibited the discharge of refuse and oil into or upon coastal or navigable waters of the United States. These laws are still enforced in situations where their application is appropriate.

Modern efforts to control water pollution began with the Water Pollution Control Act of 1948, which declared that water pollution was a local problem and required the U.S. Public Health Service to provide information to the states that would help them coordinate research activities. The Water Pollution Control Act of 1956 contained enforcement provisions by providing for a federal abatement suit at the request of a state pollution-control agency. The Water Pollution Control Act Amendments of 1961 broadened federal jurisdiction and shortened the process of enforcement by stating that where health was being endangered, the federal government did not have to receive the consent of all the states involved.

The Water Quality Act of 1965 provided for the setting of water quality standards that were state and federally enforceable. These became the basis for interstate water quality standards. This act also created the Water Pollution Control Administration within the Department of Health, Education and Welfare. The Clean Water Restoration Act of 1966 imposed a fine of $100 per day on a polluter who failed to submit a required report. Finally, the Water Quality Improvement Act of 1970 prohibited discharge of harmful quantities of oil into or upon the navigable waters of the United States or their shores. It applies to offshore and onshore facilities and vessels. The act also provided for regulation of sewage disposal from vessels.

Surface Water. Pollution of surface water occurs when the quantity of wastes entering a body of water overwhelms its capacity to assimilate the pollutants these wastes contain. Thus the natural cleansing ability of oxygen contained in the water is compromised and the water can no longer break down organic pollutants. Excessive nutrients from

EXHIBIT 9.4

Pollutants and Their Sources

	Common Pollutant Categories							
	BOD	Bacteria	Nutrients	Ammonia	Turbidity	TDS	Acids	Toxics
Point Sources								
Municipal sewage treatment plants	•	•	•	•				•
Industrial facilities	•							•
Combined sewer overflows	•	•	•	•	•	•		•
Nonpoint Sources								
Agricultural runoff	•	•	•		•	•		•
Urban runoff	•	•	•		•	•		•
Construction runoff			•		•			•
Mining runoff					•	•	•	•
Septic systems	•	•	•					•
Landfills/spills	•							•
Silviculture runoff	•		•		•			•

Abbreviations: Biological Oxygen Demand, BOD; Total Dissolved Solids, TDS.

Source: United States Environmental Protection Agency, *Environmental Progress and Challenges: EPA's Update* (Washington, D.C.: U.S. Government Printing Office, 1989), p. 70.

agricultural activities and municipal sewage also cause eutrophication, which is a state of ecological imbalance where algae growth is favored at the expense of other forms of aquatic life. Large algae formations at the surface of the water deplete available oxygen and prevent sunlight from reaching submerged vegetation. Photosynthesis is seriously hampered, reducing both support for aquatic life and the assimilative capacity of the water.

The major sources of surface water pollution are (1) organic wastes from urban sewage, farms, and industries, (2) sediments from agriculture, construction, and logging, (3) biological nutrients, such as phosphates in detergents and nitrogen in fertilizers, (4) toxic substances from industry and synthetic chemicals such as those found in pesticides, plastics, and detergents, (5) acid and mineral drainage from open-pit and deep-shaft mining, and (6) runoff containing harmful chemicals and sediment drained from streets and parking lots (Exhibit 9.4).[25]

There are both point and nonpoint sources of water pollution. Point sources are places where polluting substances enter the water from a discernible, confined, and discrete conveyance such as a sewer pipe, culvert, tunnel, or other channel or conduit. Point sources are those that come from industrial facilities and municipal sewage systems. Pollutants can also wash off, run off, or seep from broad areas of land. These are called nonpoint source pollutants because they cannot be located with much precision. Degradation of water from nonpoint sources is caused by the cumulative effect of all the pollutants that originate from large land areas within a single watershed. Common pollutants of the latter type are sediment eroded from soil exposed during construction of buildings and pesticides and fertilizers washed off cropland by rainwater.

The current system of water pollution control was established by the Federal Water Pollution Control Act Amendments of 1972, which mandated a sweeping federal-state campaign to prevent, reduce, and eliminate water pollution. This law proclaimed two general goals for the United States: (1) to achieve wherever possible by July 1, 1983, water that is clean enough for swimming and other recreational uses, and clean enough for the protection and propagation of fish, shellfish, and wildlife; and (2) by 1985, to have no discharges of pollutants into the nation's waters.[26]

The act established a national pollutant discharge elimination system (NPDES), which required permits for all point sources of pollution, providing the first major direct enforcement procedure against polluters. Under the system, it is illegal for any industry to discharge any pollutant into the nation's waters without a permit from EPA or from a state that has an EPA-approved permit program. When issued, the permit regulates what may be discharged (see box) and the amount of each identified pollutant allowed from a facility. The discharger must monitor its wastes and report on discharges and comply with all applicable national effluent limits and with state and local requirements that may be imposed. If a plant cannot comply immediately, the permit contains a compliance schedule of firm dates by which the pollutants will be reduced or eliminated.

By 1988, 39 states were issuing permits under the NPDES structure, with the EPA itself issuing permits in the remaining states and on Indian reservations. While there are currently about 48,400 industrial and 15,300 municipal facilities that have NPDES permits, the EPA estimates that about 10 percent of the major facilities are in significant noncompliance with their permit conditions. These facilities are subject to federal and state enforcement action, which can range all the way from an informal telephone call to formal judicial proceedings with possible financial penalties.[27]

This act was amended by the Clean Water Act of 1977, which made over 50 changes in the 1972 law. The most important from a business point of view was a change in the classification system of industrial pollutants and the establishment of new deadlines. This change resulted in a much greater emphasis on the control of toxic pollutants. Toxic substances such as heavy metals and synthetic chemicals have rapidly contaminated the nation's waters. One major source of these substances is industrial discharges; therefore, more attention to toxics was given in the amendments. These new categories and their deadlines as amended in 1987 are the following:

> *Conventional Pullantants:* These include BOD (biological oxygen demand), suspended solids, fecal coliforms, pH (acidity), and other pollutants so designated by the EPA. Industry is to have installed the "best conventional" technology (BCT) as expeditiously as practicable but in no case later than March 31, 1989, to control these pollutants.
>
> *Toxic Pollutants:* The 1977 amendments specify an "initial list" of toxic substances to which EPA may add or subtract. Industry is to have installed the "best available" technology (BAT) not later than 3 years after a substance is placed on the toxic pollutant list and in no case later than March 31, 1989, to control toxic substances.
>
> *Nonconventional Pollutants:* This category includes "all other" pollutants, that is, those not classified by the EPA as either conventional or toxic. The treatment required is the "best available" technology as expeditiously as possible or within 3 years of the date the

It's illegal under the 1972 Federal Water Pollution Control Act to discharge pollutants into the Nation's waters except under the NPDES permit.

Pollutants covered by this permit requirement are: Solid waste, incinerator residue, sewage, garbage, sewage sludge, munitions, chemical wastes, biological materials, radioactive materials, heat, wrecked or discarded equipment, rock, sand, cellar dirt, and industrial, municipal, and agricultural wastes discharged into water.

Excluded from the NPDES permit program are: Discharges of sewage from vessels; pollutants from vessels or other floating craft in coastal or ocean waters; discharges from properly functioning marine engines; water, gas, or other material injected into oil or gas wells, or disposed of in wells during oil or gas production, if the State determines that ground or surface water resources will not be degraded; agriculture projects; separate storm sewer discharges; and dredged or fill material.

Discharges excluded from the NPDES permit system are covered by other pollution control requirements.

Source: Environmental Protection Agency, *Toward Cleaner Water* (Washington, D.C.: EPA, 1974) p. 5.

EPA established effluent limitations, but no later than March 31, 1989. A modification of these requirements is available under certain circumstances.

Rather than regulate surface water pollution on a substance-by-substance basis, as was done in air pollution, or establishing effluent limitations for each individual industrial and municipal discharger, Congress developed technology-based standards that apply to the broad categories of pollutants as mentioned. Although there is some disagreement as to exactly what these standards mean, in general "best conventional technology" means the average level of technology that an industry has installed to control that category of pollutants, whereas "best available technology" means the most sophisticated technology that is currently available regardless of its cost and whether or not it is recognized as an industry standard.

In early 1987, Congress approved further amendments to the Clean Water Act by passing a $20 billion bill over the president's veto. The bill authorized $9.6 billion in grants and $8.4 billion in revolving construction projects for waste water treatment plants; as much as $2 billion to clean up specific lakes, rivers, and estuaries; $400 million in grants to help states plan ways to reduce the toxic runoff from farmland and city streets; and funds to eliminate "hot spots" of toxic chemicals in waterways. The bill was backed by a coalition of construction companies, municipalities, and environmentalists.[28]

Nonpoint sources of pollution are regulated under Section 208 of the Clean Water Act. These nonpoint sources of pollution are a much more difficult problem to control. They generally cannot be collected and treated in some fashion, but can only be reduced by greater care in the management of water and land resources. One reason the United States did not meet the goals of the federal Water Pollution Control Act was because a technology still does not exist to control nonpoint sources of pollution. These sources pour as much as 79 percent of all nitrates and 92 percent of all suspended solids into surface waters. Some major nonpoint sources of pollution are the following:

- Urban stormwater: water running off buildings and streets, carrying with it oil, grease, trash, salts, lead, and other pollutants.
- Agricultural runoff: rain washing fertilizers, pesticides, and topsoil into water.
- Construction runoff: earth washed into streams, rivers, and lakes from erosion.
- Acid mine drainage: water seeping through mined areas.
- Forestry runoff: water washing sediments from areas where the earth has been disturbed by logging and timber operations.[29]

Section 208 requires that states and localities establish programs to control nonpoint source pollution. In contrast to point sources of pollution where uniform national standards for controlling point source pollution have been developed, state and local governments have been assigned the major burden and responsibility for developing nonpoint source pollution controls. The reason for this approach is that soil conditions and types, climate, and topography (which are primary determinants of nonpoint source pollution) vary throughout the country. State and local authorities are required to develop a process for identifying significant nonpoint sources of pollution and to set forth control procedures, including, where appropriate, land use regulations. Best management practices (BMPs) are to be identified and implemented to reduce the amount of pollution generated by nonpoint sources to a level compatible with water quality goals.

Drinking Water. The quality of drinking water is regulated by the Safe Drinking Water Act of 1974 as amended in 1977 and 1986, which gives the EPA authority to set national standards to protect drinking water. These standards represent the Maximum Contaminant Levels (MCL) allowable and consist of numerical criteria for specified contaminants. The states bear primary responsibility for enforcing drinking-water standards assisted in part with federal funds.[30] The EPA also issues rules to protect underground sources of drinking water (aquifers) from contamination by underground injection of wastes and other materials (Figure 9.1).

The EPA took over the setting of drinking-water standards from the U.S. Public Health Service in 1975, and in a 10-year period, set limits for only 25 contaminants. Critics complained that hundreds of synthetic chemicals that were widely used were not included in drinking-water standards. In response to this criticism and growing evidence of drinking-water contamination, the EPA in late 1985 proposed standards to restrict the levels of 8 additional chemicals found in public water systems and 39 other compounds and 4 microbes found in drinking water. These standards were based on health effects of the chemicals, cost considerations, and feasibility of maintaining the limits. The EPA also proposed that water systems monitor 51 other compounds suspected of being harmful. It was estimated that about 1,300 community water systems would have to spend $280 million on treatment equipment and $21 million annually on operating expenses to meet the "maximum contaminant levels" in the proposed standards.[31]

Revisions to the Safe Drinking Water Act, passed in 1986, provided money to protect aquifers that are the sole source of drinking water for an area and authorized the EPA to review any federally funded projects that may threaten or affect their quality. The revisions also required states to develop plans to safeguard other public water supplies, and gave the EPA 5 years to set maximum levels for at least 108 of the

Figure 9.1 Sources of Groundwater Contamination

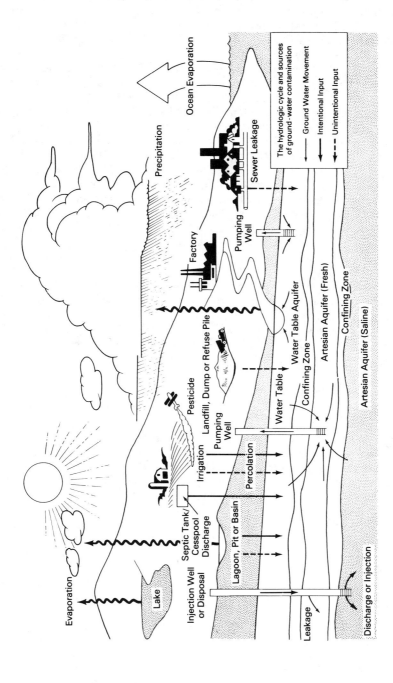

Source: United States Environmental Protection Agency, *Environmental Progress and Challenges: EPA's Update* (Washington, D.C.: U.S. Government Printing Office, 1988), p. 53.

hundreds of contaminants currently found in drinking water. Twenty-five more standards were to be issued every 3 years thereafter. The EPA was also required to issue regulations within 18 months requiring public water systems to test for contaminants not yet regulated. Public systems would have to test their water at least once every 5 years thereafter for such contaminants.[32]

In early 1990, the EPA did issue new regulations for 25 additional chemicals, which covered an additional 2.5 million metric tons of waste or wastewater generated by 17,000 businesses each year. The rules were expected to affect 13 major industries and cost them an additional $200 million to $400 million a year. The largest share of the costs would fall on petroleum refineries, pulp and paper mills, synthetic-fiber producers, wholesale petroleum marketers, and organic-chemical companies. Some 200 facilities that were disposing of industrial wastes in surface impounds that could leak contaminants into groundwater were expected to close as a result of the new regulations.[33]

In 1987, the EPA began to pay more attention to underground storage tanks that were said to be leaking motor fuels and chemical solvents into groundwater. Most of these tanks were made of bare steel without any corrision protection and were nearing the end of their useful lives. About 400,000 of these underground storage tanks were thought to be leaking. Rules were issued that required existing tanks to be monitored and repaired or replaced if leaking. Since existing tanks would also have to meet the minimum requirements for new tanks within 10 years, it was expected that most of them would have to be replaced during this time period. The rules banned installation of new bare-steel tanks that lacked corrosion protection and required double-walled tanks for hazardous chemicals. These rules were expected to cost industry about $410 million annually.[34] Changes to these regulations in 1988 required phasing in of new tanks within 5 years instead of 10, with the oldest tanks forced to comply within the first year. The new tanks were also to be installed with monitoring devices.[35]

Pesticides

Pests destroy crops worth billions of dollars each year, and with a steadily expanding population and a decrease in available land, the world must use pesticides to control these pests and maintain high crop yields. There is no other way, with existing technology, to raise crops on the scale that is required. Besides helping in the production of greater quantities of food, pesticides also help reduce loss of food in storage and control disease carriers. Each year, about 3 billion pounds of pesticides are used for these and other purposes. Agriculture accounts for 70 percent of usage; industry, forestry, and government, 23 percent; and home gardening and lawn usage, 7 percent.[36]

Yet in poisoning pests, human beings may also be poisoning themselves. Pesticides persist in the environment for long periods of time and move up through the food chain from plankton or insects to animals and humans, making dietary exposure unavoidable in many situations. They also move downward through soil to contaminate groundwater used for drinking. Through these exposures, pesticides pose a threat to human health by causing cancer or birth defects or other health and environmental problems.

One of the first people to point out these dangers was Rachel Carson. In her book *Silent Spring,* information about the dark side of pesticide use was presented to the public.[37] Before this, pesticides were by and large seen as an unqualified benefit, but after her book, fear began to spread throughout society that pesticides were unmanageable poisons. Federal pesticide regulation was toughened and enforcement responsibility transferred from the Department of Agriculture, which promoted chemical pest control, to the EPA. The use of DDT was banned in 1972, and several other pesticides such as aldrin, dieldrin, toxaphene, and ethylene dibromide have been suspended or banned since that time.[38]

Pesticides are regulated by the Federal Insecticide, Fungicide, and Rodenticide Act (FIFRA) of 1947. This act assigned the EPA responsibility for protecting human health from any commercially available product used to kill germs, insects, rodents and other animal pests, and weeds and fungi. Such products cannot be sold until they are first registered with the agency.[39] If test data show that a pesticide may be harmful to human health or the environment, the EPA can refuse to register it, restrict its use to certain applications, or require that only certified applicators apply the pesticide. Once a product is registered, manufacturers must use appropriate labels showing the approved uses of the pesticide. More than 50,000 pesticides have been registered since FIFRA was enacted.[40]

Amendments to the act in 1972 required the EPA to reregister the 35,000 pesticides previously registered and already on the market, because the long-term health and environmental effects of many of these pesticides were poorly understood. The EPA was required to do a benefit-cost analysis on these products, taking into account new information. If this analysis revealed that a particular product posed an unreasonable risk to human health or the environment when weighed against its benefits to agriculture and society, it had to be removed from the marketplace or restrictions had to be placed on its use as a pesticide.

These amendments, however, required the EPA to proceed on a product-by-product basis, even though many products have similar chemical properties. Further amendments to FIFRA in 1978 allowed the EPA to take a "generic" approach to registering pesticides. Using this approach, the agency is able to make one regulatory decision for an entire group of pesticides that have similar chemical ingredients rather than looking at them separately. It was estimated that using this method the agency would have to consider fewer than 600 active ingredients contained in the 45,000 different commercial products on the marketplace. Standards could be set for these 600 ingredients, and products would be registered according to whether they measure up to these standards.

Under the EPA's pesticide program, more than a million private users, mostly farmers, and 150,000 commercial applicators have been trained and certified in the safe use of pesticides. This program trains people in the proper use, handling, storage, and disposal of pesticides. Only such certified users are allowed to use pesticides that have a "restricted use only" classification. In late 1984, the EPA adopted a tougher policy toward pesticides thought to be hazardous, by banning or restricting the use of eight high-volume pesticides, and proposing more stringent controls on about 25 other widely used pesticides that were suspected of posing health hazards for consumers and farm workers. This action was expected to cost manufacturers millions of dollars in the next few years as they supplied the government with more extensive, up-to-date health and environmental test data on these substances.[41]

Despite these efforts, the risks to farm workers continued. It was estimated that in the course of a 30-day harvesting season, the typical farm worker might be exposed to 15 different compounds at various times, making the process of identifying which pesticide is to blame for a particular health problem impossible. Little is known about the chronic effects of many pesticides, and many of the studies that have been conducted can be faulted for one reason or another, thus making proof of a link between a specific pesticide and cancer difficult to establish. The benefit of doubt has always gone in favor of manufacturers and users of pesticides rather than the workers, and pesticides have often been assumed safe until proven otherwise. To cope with this problem, the EPA issued new regulations to protect farm workers in 1988, which some believed were still inadequate.[42]

In October of 1984, the EPA took its first step toward regulating pesticides created by gene-splicing or other methods of biotechnology. The EPA issued rules requiring all companies or individuals planning to test the effectiveness of pesticides produced by genetic manipulation to notify the agency at least 90 days before the tests are conducted. The EPA can then deny experimental permits for tests that the agency determines may pose "substantial health concerns." These rules were the first phase of a comprehensive set of proposed policies and regulations that would spell out the EPA's authority to regulate the commercial testing and use of all such pesticides in the future.[43] A framework for coordinating federal regulation of biotechnology was established in 1986 that built on existing legislation and practices but imposed additional levels of federal review for certain applications, particularly relating to new microorganisms. Further regulations were expected to be issued that would build on this policy statement.[44]

Toxic Substances

There are 7 million known chemical compounds, 60,000 of which are in substantial commercial use. Some 1,000 new chemicals are put into production—and thus into the environment—each year. Although most of these chemicals are not harmful to health or the environment, those that are must be identified, and steps must be taken to reduce the risks associated with these chemicals. Before the Toxic Substances Control Act (TSCA), previous laws that dealt with these substances authorized the government to act only after widespread exposure and possibly serious harm had already occurred. One major concept underlying TSCA is that the government has the authority to act before a substance can harm human health or the environment—the substance is, in effect, guilty until proven innocent. Under TSCA, the EPA reviews risk information on all new chemicals before they are manufactured or imported and decides whether they should be admitted, controlled, or denied access to the marketplace.

Because of TSCA, the entire chemical industry was put under comprehensive federal regulation for the first time, as the law applies to virtually every facet of the industry—product development, testing, manufacturing, distribution, use, and disposal. In addition, importers of chemical substances are treated as domestic manufacturers, thus extending EPA's control to certain aspects of the international chemical trade.[45]

The initial impact of TSCA was in the area of inventory reporting. The act required the EPA to compile and publish an inventory of chemical substances manufactured, imported, or processed in the United States for commercial purposes. The inventory was compiled from reports that manufacturers, importers, processors, or users of chemical substances were required to prepare and submit to the agency.[46] The first inventory was published in 1979 and contained information on more than 62,000 chemicals that came from manufacturers and importers and included production volume and plant location.

After publication of the initial inventory, the premanufacture provisions of TSCA went into effect. These provisions require a manufacturer who has developed a new chemical not on the inventory list to submit a notice to the EPA at least 90 days before beginning manufacture or importation of a new chemical substance for commercial purposes other than in small quantities solely for research and development. The information that has to be given to the EPA includes a description of the new chemical substance, the estimated total amount to be manufactured and processed, and similar information.[47]

In addition to this information, submitters must append any test data in their possession or control and descriptions of other data concerning the health and environmental effects of the substance. The EPA encourages, but does not require, the submitter to follow the premanufacture testing guidelines the EPA has published. In any event, all test data are to be submitted regardless of their age, quality, or results.

The administrator of the EPA has a number of options available after receipt of this information; these include extending the 90-day premanufacture review period for an additional 90 days for good cause, requiring additional testing of the substance, and initiating no action within the 90-day period because the chemical is deemed not to present a hazard to health or the environment. If a hazard is believed to exist, the administrator may issue a proposed order to take effect on the expiration of the notification period to prohibit or limit the manufacture, processing, distribution in commerce, use, or disposal of such substance or to prohibit or limit any combination of such activities.

If a total ban on the substance is not necessary, the administrator can issue further directives regarding regulation of the substance. Possibilities include setting concentration levels, limiting the use of the chemical, requiring warnings or instructions on its use, requiring public notice of risk or potential injury, and regulating methods of disposal. If the administrator has reason to believe the method of manufacture rather than the chemical itself is at fault, the manufacturer may be ordered to revise quality-control procedures to the extent necessary to remedy whatever inadequacies are believed to exist.

By the end of 1987, the EPA had screened more than 10,000 new chemicals proposed for commercial production since TSCA was enacted. The majority of these chemicals were determined to present no unreasonable risk to human health or the environment. Some 533 of these chemicals, however, required restrictions on manufacturing, and 149 of required additional health and environmental testing. After more than a decade of experience, the EPA now acts more quickly to identify potential health and environmental problems.[48]

In addition to these premanufacture notification provisions, other sections of TSCA deal with testing, evaluation, and control of existing substances. The act empowers the EPA administrator to require manufacturers or processors of potentially harmful chemicals already in use to conduct tests on these chemicals. The need for such testing must be based on the following criteria: (1) The chemical may present an unreasonable risk to health or the environment, or there may be substantial human or environmental exposure to the chemical; (2) there are insufficient data and experience for determining or predicting the health and environmental effects of the chemical; and (3) testing of the chemical is necessary to develop such data.[49]

The overall goal of the Existing Chemicals Program is to reduce unreasonable risks of injury to health or the environment from chemicals that are already in commerce. An interagency committee has been established by the act to assist the administrator in determining chemicals that should be tested, but the administrator's actions are not limited to these recommendations by the committee. This committee may designate, at any one time, up to 50 chemicals from its list of recommended substances for testing. Within 1 year, the administrator must either initiate testing requirements for these designated chemicals or publish in the Federal Register any reasons for not initiating such requirements.

By the end of 1987, the EPA had requested additional health and environmental testing by the manufacturers of 63 chemical groups for possible regulatory control. Some of the actions taken under these provisions of TSCA have shown dramatic results. Restrictions on the use and disposal of PCBs, for example, have resulted in a significant decline of these residues in the environment, food, and human tissues. The number of individuals with high PCB levels has declined from more than 8 percent to less than 1 percent of the population.[50] The EPA has also taken a number of actions to control dioxin contamination, including canceling all uses of dioxin containing pesticides. In 1987, nonessential uses of chlorofluorocarbons in aerosol sprays was banned because of concern that these chemicals caused a decrease in the ozone layer in the earth's stratosphere. And the EPA has also been working to remove or reduce the risks from the widespread use of asbestos in schools and other buildings, a program that has sparked a good deal of controversy.[51]

In 1983, a new agency was formed to study chemical dangers. This agency, called the Agency for Toxic Substances and Disease Registry, is located in the Public Health Service of the Department of Health and Human Services. It was created in response to a suit filed by the Environmental Defense Fund demanding intensive government health research into the effects of toxic chemical contamination. One purpose of the agency was to develop a list of all areas in the nation that have been closed or restricted for use because of chemical contamination and registries of people who have been exposed to toxic substances.[52]

Also in 1983, the state of New Jersey passed a worker right-to-know bill that, among other things, requires business organizations to disclose to their employees and the public the names of toxic substances used in the manufacturing process. Several states have laws mandating disclosure to employees, but this was the first law mandating disclosure to both workers and nearby communities. Under the law, companies have 18 months to label all containers used by workers that contain any of about 1,000 hazardous substances and file publicly available papers with county health departments itemizing those substances. The New Jersey Business and Industrial Association estimated that it would cost state businesses about $20 million to comply and that it would put them at a serious competitive disadvantage.[53]

After the Bhopal tragedy, community right-to-know bills were introduced into more states and both houses of Congress. Under Title III of the Superfund Amendments and Reauthorization Act (SARA) of 1986, also known as the Emergency Planning and Community Right-to-Know Act, facilities that manufacture, process, or use any of 309 designated chemicals in greater than specified amounts must report routine releases of those chemicals. The EPA is required to make information from these reports available to the public. This Toxic Releases Inventory, as it is called, is designed to assist citizen groups, local health officials, state environmental managers, and the EPA to identify and control toxic chemical problems. One of the EPA's challenges is to interpret this information to help state and local officials evaluate and manage the risks posed by substances present in their communities.[54]

In addition to reporting routine releases, the law also provides for emergency notification of chemical accidents and releases, planning for chemical emergencies, and reporting of hazardous chemical inventories. The law's purposes are to encourage and support emergency planning for responding to chemical accidents and to provide local governments and the public with information about possible chemical hazards in their communities. It requires that detailed information about the nature of hazardous substances in or near communities be made available to the public. This law is different from many other federal statutes, in that it does not preempt states or local communities from having more stringent or additional requirements. More than 30 states have such laws giving workers and citizens access to information about hazardous substances in their workplaces and communities.[55]

Waste Disposal

Solid Waste.   Almost 160 million tons of solid waste are discarded in the United States every year, or about 400,000 tons every day. This is enough waste to fill the Astrodome in Houston more than twice daily for a year and represents about a ton of waste created annually for every individual in the nation. This waste stream has increased 80 percent since 1960 and is expected to increase another 20 percent in the next 10 years. These wastes include municipal garbage and industrial refuse as well as sewage, agricultural refuse, demolition wastes, and mining residues. Each American throws out about 4 pounds of trash a day, mainly paper products and yard wastes, which make up about 59 percent of all municipal solid waste.[56]

About 80 percent of this waste material is disposed of in landfills. But many of these landfills are close to overflowing, and almost 70 percent of them are expected to reach capacity within 15 years. In more than 40 states, rising land costs, technical risks, new EPA regulations, leachate problems, increasing space scarcity, and an escalating number of NIMBY (Not in My Back Yard) movements are forcing the closing of landfills. Communities where old landfills have reached capacity are having trouble finding sites for new landfills.[57]

Many of these landfills leak pollutants that threaten groundwater supplies. To deal with this problem, the EPA proposed new regulations in 1988 that would force all municipal landfills to monitor hazardous wastes and methane gas, ban discharges of harmful wastes into underground water, and strengthen controls on rodents, insects, fire, and odor. The EPA estimates that these rules, which would take full effect in 1991, would add $800 million to $900 million a year to the nation's garbage disposal bill, now estimated at $4 to $5 billion annually. These added costs will undoubtedly force more landfills to close and prevent other ones from opening, further contributing to the problem of solid-waste disposal.[58]

An alternative disposal method is incineration, which can reduce garbage weight as much as 70 percent as well as produce heat that can be sold to generate electricity. But many of these facilities have been halted by the NIMBY movement which is concerned about the air pollution that incinerators generate. Another option, recycling, is being pursued by an increasing number of communities. At least 22 states have already passed legislation either promoting or requiring the recycling of residential garbage, and 9 states have passed mandatory deposit laws on beverage containers.[59] Other bills seek to impose bans on various solid-waste elements, implement packaging taxes or restrictions, mandate some degree of source separation and recycling, or establish state procurement guidelines for recycled products.[60]

One of the most troublesome problems is the increasing use of plastic packaging, which is difficult to burn or recycle and—because it is not biodegradable—will clog landfills for centuries. Many state and local governments have taken steps to ban or tax certain forms of plastic packaging and others are studying the problem. Bills have been introduced into Congress that would ban nondegradable beverage loops or require all plastic products that pose a threat to fish and wildlife to be degradable or recyclable. But recycling has yet to take hold because plastic cannot legally be recycled into food containers because of the possibility of contamination. And the economics of the situation does not favor other uses because consumers can buy new material for less than they would pay for recycled products.[61] There is some evidence, however, that this situation is changing as some companies are finding ways to make a profit from plastics recycling.[62]

Hazardous Wastes. Disposal of hazardous wastes is a costly and time-consuming business, requiring complex measures to control. Uncontrolled waste presents environmental and health risks that necessitates action to prevent degradation of water, soil, and air, and to protect human health. Initial concerns regarding waste disposal centered on the fire hazards that solid wastes posed. But in the latter half of the 1970s, attention focused on the problems negligent hazardous waste disposal was causing for the environment and human health because of leaching, contamination, corrosion, and poisoning of land, water, vegetation, and animals as well as human beings by deadly chemicals and heavy metals. Investigations disclosed that between 1950 and 1979, more than 1.5 trillion pounds of hazardous wastes had been dumped in about 3,300 sites around the country. Fifty-three chemical companies in 1978 alone had dumped 132 billion pounds of industrial waste.[63] Incidents such as Love Canal heightened public apprehension about the hazardous waste problem.

Hazardous wastes have been defined as wastes that (1) cause or significantly contribute to an increase in mortality or an increase in serious, irreversible or incapacitating, reversible illness, or (2) pose a substantial present or potential hazard to human health or the environment when improperly treated, stored, transported, or disposed of or otherwise managed.[64] They are wastes that cannot be managed by routine procedures because if they are improperly managed, they can cause a threat to public health and the environment. Improper disposal of hazardous wastes has also been responsible for other kinds of environmental damage—fires, explosions, pollution of surface water and air— as well as posing serious threats to human health through poisoning via the food chain or through direct contact.[65]

Hazardous wastes include wastes that pose a fire hazard (ignitable), dissolve materials or are acidic (corrosive), are explosive (reactive), or otherwise pose dangers to human health and the environment (toxic). Hundreds of potentially dangerous substances can be found in hazardous waste, but as shown in Exhibit 9.5, the most common are few in number. While there are about 14,000 regulated producers of hazardous waste, by far the majority are chemical manufacturers and allied industries. Ninety percent of the hazardous waste produced in the country comes from facilities that generate large quantities of more than 2,200 pounds per month. A much smaller amount comes from small-quantity generators that produce between 220 and 2,200 pounds per month.[66]

Responsibility for control and eradication of waste-disposal problems is lodged in the EPA's Office of Solid Waste and Emergency Response. This office implements two federal laws related to waste disposal, the Resource Conservation and Recovery Act (RCRA), which regulates current and future waste practices, and the Comprehensive Environmental Response, Compensation, and Liability Act (CERCLA), commonly called Superfund, which provides for cleaning up of old waste sites. Legislation thus focuses on preventing future contamination from improper waste disposal and the cleanup of existing waste sites where hazardous waste was disposed of improperly and poses a threat to human health and the environment.

The Resource Conservation and Recovery Act of 1976 controls the generation, transportation, storage, and disposal of wastes at existing or future waste facilities. Each year about 3,000 facilities manage 275 million metric tons of RCRA waste in the country. Specifically, the law provides for (1) federal classification of hazardous waste, (2) a "cradle-to-grave" manifest (tracking) system for waste material (See Figure 9.2 on page 286), (3) federal safeguard standards for generators and transporters, and for facilities that treat, store, or dispose of hazardous wastes, (4) enforcement of standards for facilities through a permitting system, and (5) authorization of state programs to replace federal programs.[67]

EXHIBIT 9.5

Common Hazardous Wastes

Chemical	Use	Manufacturing Hazard
C-56	Bug and insect killer	Acutely toxic, suspected carcinogen
Trichloroethylene (TCE)	Degreaser	Suspected carcinogen
Benzidene	Dye industry	Known human carcinogen
Curene 442	Plastics industry	Suspected carcinogen
Polychlorinated biphenyls (PCBs)	Insulators, paints, and electrical circuitry	Acutely toxic, suspected carcinogen
Benzene	Solvent	Suspected carcinogen
Tris	Fire retardant	Suspected carcinogen
DDT	Bug and insect killer	Acutely toxic
Vinyl chloride	Plastics industry	Known human carcinogen
Mercury	Multiple uses	Acutely toxic
Lead	Multiple uses	Acutely toxic, suspected carcinogen
Carbon tetrachloride	Solvent	Acutely toxic, suspected carcinogen
Polybrominated biphenyls (PBBs)	Fire retardant	Effects unknown

Source: Council on Environmental Quality, *Environmental Quality 1980* (Washington, D.C.: Government Printing Office, 1981), p. 217.

The basic purpose of RCRA is to protect groundwater from toxic pollution. Those who produce wastes have to obtain a permit to manage them on their own property. When shipping them to a treatment, storage, or disposal facility, they have to provide a manifest containing basic information about the waste material. All treatment, storage, and disposal operations are required to meet minimum standards to protect public health and the environment.[68]

Regulations to implement RCRA were developed in phases. The first phase included identification of solid wastes considered to be hazardous and the establishment of reporting and record keeping for the three categories of hazardous waste handlers: generators, transporters, and owners or operators of treatment, storage, and disposal (TSD) facilities (See box on page 287). In November 1980, these regulations became effective. By July 31, 1985, the EPA had identified 52,864 major generators of hazardous wastes, 12,343 transporters, and 4,961 TSD facilities.[69]

The second phase involved the development of technical standards related to the design and safe operation of the various types of treatment, storage, and disposal facilities. These standards serve as the basis for issuing permits to such facilities. Technical standards have been issued for incinerators and for new and existing land disposal facilities, along with financial responsibility and liability insurance requirements for all facilities. Landfills, for example, must now include double liners, leachate detection and collection systems, and groundwater monitoring.

Congress intended the states eventually to assume responsibility for the RCRA hazardous waste program. The EPA is authorized to approve qualified state plans for

Figure 9.2 The Hazardous Waste Manifest Trail

A one-page manifest must accompany every waste shipment. The resulting paper trail documents the waste's progress through treatment, storage and disposal. A missing form alerts the generator to investigate, which may mean calling in the state agency or EPA.

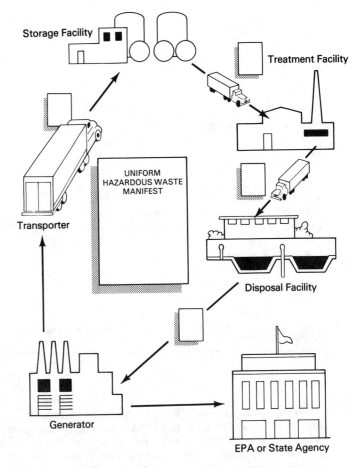

Note: A manifest is unnecessary for waste treated and disposed of at the point of generation.

Source: United States Environmental Protection Agency, *Environmental Progress and Challenges: EPA's Update* (Washington, D.C.: U.S. Government Printing Office, 1988), p. 88.

hazardous waste management. To receive final authorization to operate the entire RCRA program, states must adopt regulations fully "equivalent to" and "consistent with" federal standards. Mississippi became the first state to receive full authorization to operate its own program. States can be granted interim authorization by setting regulations that are "substantially equivalent" to EPA's regulations. All 50 states were expected to seek final authorization to manage their own hazardous waste programs.

Congress reauthorized RCRA in late 1984, imposing new and far-reaching requirements on the 175,000 enterprises that generate small amounts of waste per month (between 220 and 2,200 pounds) and those that own or operate underground storage tanks. These are called small-quantity generators (SQGs), and rules implemented in 1985 and modified in 1986 require any business producing or using hazardous materials or chemicals to register with the agency and to be able to prove that the wastes from these materials are being disposed of properly. The new RCRA also bans the land disposal of hazardous wastes unless the EPA finds they will not endanger human health and the environment.[70]

The continuing problem of dealing with waste generation is complex and expensive. The EPA itself will not estimate what portion of the estimated 264 metric tons of hazardous waste generated annually is disposed of improperly, but some estimates state that one out of every seven companies producing toxic wastes may have dumped illegally in recent years. No doubt huge quantities of such wastes go into streams, pastures, or vacant lots, where the risk of human contamination is high and the chance of detection is slim.[71] Perhaps the best solution is for manufacturers to reduce the amount of waste generated by using new materials, adopting new processes and equipment, and reusing waste material in some fashion.[72]

The Comprehensive Environmental Response, Compensation, and Liability Act (CERCLA), or Superfund, provides money to the EPA and gives it authority to direct and oversee cleanup of old and abandoned waste sites that pose a threat to public health or the environment. The law provides funding for the government to clean up inactive waste sites where responsible parties cannot be found or where those responsible are unable or unwilling to perform the cleanup, and creates liabilities for parties who were associated with waste sites, either to perform the cleanup or to reimburse the EPA for the cost of the cleanup. Superfund was first authorized in 1980 for $1.6 billion, with the total amount dependent upon the size of the National Priority List, extent of cleanup necessary, responsible party contributions, scope of the fund, and amount of money the PA could manage efficiently.

Superfund imposes liability on responsible parties for the costs of removal or remedial action, costs of response by other parties or entities, and for damage to, or destruction of, natural resources. The liability of the law is joint and several; that is, a single party may be held responsible for all cleanup costs even if other parties are involved. This might occur where other parties have disappeared or become insolvent, defunct, or bankrupt. Liability also attaches to a party without regard to fault or negligence. These costs can be high; for example, for a facility other than a vessel or vehicle, liability includes the total of all response costs plus up to $50 million for damages.[73]

The first phase of this effort was to conduct a nationwide inventory of such sites and establish priorities for cleanup. In ranking these dumpsites, the EPA takes five exposure pathways into account: (1) the population put at risk, (2) the hazard potential of substances at the sites, (3) the potential for contamination of drinking water, (4) the possibility of direct human contact, and (5) the potential for destruction of sensitive ecosystems. The EPA has broad discretion under the law in determining the appropriate remedial action to be taken in a specific instance. Once sites have been identified, the EPA can require owners of old or abandoned dumps to perform the cleanup work themselves, or, where this is not possible or where immediate action is needed, the EPA and the states can step in and do the cleanup. Proposed actions need to be cost-effective, environmentally sound remedies that are feasible and reliable from an engineering standpoint. No action can be taken in cases where attempting to clean up a dumpsite would present more danger to human health and the environment than leaving it alone.[74]

Approximately 30,000 potentially contaminated sites that may pose a threat to human health or the environment have been identified nationwide. More than 27,000 preliminary assessments have been conducted, and on the basis of these assessments, 9,000 sites have been determined to require no further action. As of 1988, 1,177 sites have been listed or proposed for listing on the national priorities list (NPL), which is a prerequisite for cleanup activities that would use federal superfund money (Figure 9.3). For sites listed on the NPL, further studies are conducted to determine the nature and extent of contamination. Such studies have been initiated at more than half the sites currently on the NPL, and more than 140 long-term cleanups have been initiated at Superfund sites around the nation.[75]

The Office of Technology Assessment estimated that there may be at least 10,000 hazardous waste sites in the United States that pose a serious threat to public health and that should be given priority in any national cleanup. The cost could easily reach $100 billion or more than $1,000 per each household. The General Accounting Office (GAO) estimated that 378,000 waste sites may require corrective action.[76] The EPA itself estimated that cleaning up abandoned waste dumps would cost another $11.7 billion beyond that already authorized. This estimate assumed that the cost of cleaning up an individual site varied between $6 million and $12 million, that 1,500 to 2,500 sites would need cleanup, and that companies that generated the wastes would pay 40 percent to 60 percent of the costs.[77]

The original Superfund authorization ran out in October of 1985, and proposals were introduced in Congress to raise the amount of money in a reauthorization that ranged from $5.3 billion to $10 billion. The chemical industry lobbied hard to oppose any increase in the $300 million a year in special taxes that were required to contribute to Superfund, and most proposals contained provisions that would spread the cost of the cleanup of abandoned hazardous waste sites to all U.S. manufacturers instead of just oil and chemical companies. Proposals were made for a 0.08 percent value-added tax levied on the manufactured goods of companies with more than $10 million in sales with an exemption for processed foods.[78]

Because of the inability to agree on a financing plan, no new bill was passed before the old one expired; thus the administration was not able to collect any more taxes to support the cleanup effort. As the money began to run out, the EPA had to abandon

Figure 9.3 Hazardous Waste Sites—June 1988

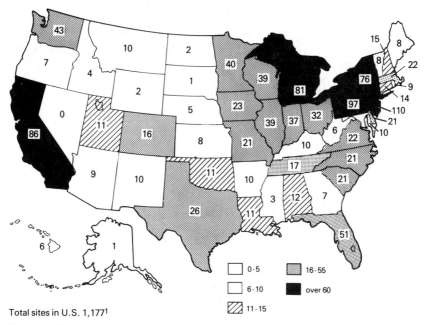

Total sites in U.S. 1,177[1]

Represents final and proposed sites on National Priority List.
[1]Includes nine in Puerto Rico; and one in Guam.

Source: U.S. Department of Commerce, *Statistical Abstract of the United States 1989,* 109th ed. (Washington, D.C.: U.S. Government Printing Office, 1988), p. 202.

new cleanup projects and put ongoing projects on hold. Without additional funds by April 1, 1986, the EPA would have been forced to terminate all cleanup contracts and start the furlough process of 1,500 Superfund personnel.[79] On April 1, 1986, the president signed a 2-month extension that provided $150 million in stopgap funding through May 31, 1986, enough to keep the program going while Congress continued to seek a compromise on a comprehensive 5-year reauthorization plan.

Finally, in October of 1986, a new $9 billion Superfund program, called the Superfund Amendments and Reauthorization Act of 1986 (SARA), was passed and signed into law by the president. The measure set more stringent toxic waste cleanup guidelines and permitted the formation of risk-retention groups to offer pollution liability coverage. It also directs communities to enhance their emergency planning efforts for chemical accidents and allows citizens to sue businesses and the EPA for violations of the measure. To fund the bill, petroleum taxes were to be increased to $2.75 billion, with a higher burden placed on imports. Another $2.5 billion was to be raised from a broad-based corporate surtax levied at a rate of 0.12 percent on corporate alternative minimum taxable income exceeding $2 million. Other sources of funding included a $1.4 billion tax on chemical feedstocks, $1.25 billion from general revenues, and $0.6 billion from interest and recoveries from companies responsible for toxic dumps.[80]

Progress under Superfund is slow, however, as there is little incentive in the program for companies to develop new cleanup technologies and a great deal of incentive for companies to spend millions of dollars on lawyers to put off spending hundreds of millions on actual cleanup. For example, Shell Oil along with its insurers spent $40 million in legal fees before agreeing to spend several hundred million dollars to clean up a site near Denver. Five companies spent $16 million in legal fees before coming to an agreement to clean up a site near St. Louis that cost $14 million. Companies sue each other over their share of the liability and sue their insurance companies to make them financially responsible. The EPA has even gone beyond site owners, operators, and transporters and has sued lenders in some situations. All this legal manuvering takes a considerable amount of time and money.[81]

Conclusions

The environmental problems of past decades are not necessarily the same as those that need to be dealt with in today's world, or at least the context in which these problems have to be dealt with has changed. The way we define and understand environmental problems cannot be based on old and outdated assumptions. Clarence Davies, executive vice president of the Conservation Foundation, makes the following observations regarding some of these changes: (1) There are now far more pollutants to monitor and control than were recognized in the mid-1970s, when we thought we could protect the environment if we controlled four or five air pollutants and a handful of water pollutants, (2) pollutants are more widely dispersed than we believed in past years and yet we do not have the scientific understanding or information to cope with long-range transport problems, and (3) chronic health problems may be more important than acute effects as the adverse effects of some pollutants may not be felt for decades or even centuries. Higher priority must be given to developing better testing techniques and improving our understanding of the biological factors involved in pollution-related health damage.[82]

These changes make it imperative to assign responsibility for coordinating research and obtaining ecological information to deal with environmental problems. Pollution problems can no longer be neatly compartmentalized into air, water, and land. We must have a better understanding of the interrelationships among these media, how pollutants travel from one to another, and the impact of our activities on natural systems. This calls for more and better ecological research.

New problems, such as indoor air pollution, have also appeared. The typical home harbors dozens of products that release toxic chemicals into the air, and conventional pollutants such as nitrogen dioxide come from gas stoves, water heaters, and furnaces. Some studies showed indoor levels at two to seven times higher than outdoor standards. Radon gas is also a problem in some areas of the country. Radon is a naturally occurring gas resulting from the radioactive decay of radium, which is found in many types of rocks and soils. It enters buildings through openings around pipes and cracks in foundations. When inhaled, this gas can adhere to particles and lodge deep in the lungs, increasing the risk of cancer.[83]

International trade in hazardous substances has contributed to the global proliferation of toxic chemicals at a time when the global scale of diffusion and danger associated with such substances is just beginning to be documented and cumulative risks to be more fully appreciated. Current U.S. laws allow domestic firms to ship hazardous or toxic substances to other countries even when their use has been suspended in the United States itself. For example, most domestic uses of DDT have been banned since 1972, but an estimated 40 million pounds of the pesticide are still exported annually. The export of such substances often ends with their return as residues on imported food destined for consumption in this country.[84]

These and other issues that remain to be dealt with may inflict upon succeeding generations a chemical plague of global proportions. Many of these chemicals are not biodegradable and may persist throughout the world ecosystem indefinitely and pose risks well into the future. Modern science and industry possess the capacity to alter the biochemical basis of future human life and change future ecosystems radically. Yet we continue to develop new technologies and manufacture new substances to enjoy present benefits these can bring us and hope most of the risks can be passed on to future generations. There are not enough incentives to take the long-term consequences of our action into account in developing policies and programs to cope with problems in our physical environment.[85]

Questions for Discussion

1. What service does the physical environment provide for human beings? Which of these services are most important? Where are trade-offs between the different services involved?

2. What is pollution? What factors have contributed to a pollution problem in this country? Are these factors still important today? What implications does your answer have for the environmental movement?

3. Distinguish among the different methods of pollution control. Give examples of each method. Is one method best, in your opinion, for all types of pollution or is some kind of a mix the best strategy as far as public policy is concerned?

4. What is the difference between the Council on Environmental Quality and the Environmental Protection Agency? For what purposes was each agency created? Which agency is of most concern to business? Why?

5. Describe the current system of air pollution control. What is ambient air quality? How does this differ from stationary sources of air pollution? What methods of control are used in each situation?

6. Describe the "bubble concept" that is used to control stationary sources of air pollution. Is this a more sensible policy than regulating stack by stack? Does it give business more flexibility?

7. What is the difference between point and nonpoint sources of water pollution? Which is easier to control? Why? Describe the way point sources of water pollution are currently controlled.

8. Name some nonpoint sources of pollution. Describe the system by which these sources are controlled. Is this a workable system as far as you are concerned? What are the best management practices? Where do they fit into the system?

9. What are toxic substances? How is the Toxic Substances Control Act going to control these substances? What impact is this system likely to make on business in general and the chemical industry in particular?

10. What is hazardous waste material? How are these materials going to be controlled? What is the likely impact on business organizations? What industries will be most affected?

11. How are pesticides regulated? How can society reap the benefits of pesticide control and yet guard against damage to the environment? Are any alternatives to pesticides currently available? Do these alternatives have any adverse environmental effects?

12. Comment on the public policies to control pollution described in this chapter. Are they necessary? Have they been effective? Would some of the alternatives mentioned later in the chapter be more effective?

Case: The Exxon Valdez

The Exxon supertanker *Valdez* entered the port of Valdez on March 22, 1989, riding high in the water because its huge cargo chambers were empty. Tugs guided it into the dock at Berth 5 at the Alyeska oil terminal. Alyeska was the name given to a consortium of oil companies that had been formed to operate the terminal. The tanker, only 2 years old and built in the San Diego shipyards, cost $125 million. It was one of the best-equipped vessels that hauled oil from the port of Valdez, having collision-avoidance radar, satellite navigational aids, and depth finders.[1]

The commander of the *Valdez* was Captain Joseph Hazelwood of Huntington, New York, a 20-year veteran of Exxon and commander of the supertanker for 20 months. Hazelwood was 42 years old and had one characteristic typical of many sailors, a drinking problem. In 1985, he had been convicted of drunken driving in Long Island, New York, and was again found guilty of driving while intoxicated in September 1988 in New Hampshire. In the span of 5 years, his automobile driver's license was revoked three times. He informed the company of his drinking problem in 1985, and Exxon immediately sent him to an alcohol rehabilitation program. The company claimed it was not aware that his drinking problem persisted after he left the treatment program; however, at the time of the incident, Hazelwood apparently was still not permitted to drive a car but retained his license to command a supertanker.[2]

On Thursday, March 23, the ship was eased out into the harbor by the port pilot, which is a customary practice in most shipping facilities. The pilot apparently noticed alcohol on Hazelwood's breath but noticed no impairment of the captain's judgement or faculties. Thus he turned over command of the ship to Hazelwood and descended over the side of the tanker to a waiting pilot boat. The tanker increased its speed to 12 knots and entered the more-open water of Prince William Sound. It was the 8,549th tanker to negotiate the Valdez narrows safely since the first tanker left Valdez fully loaded in August 1977. No serious accidents had happened during that time.[3]

There were icebergs, however, in the outgoing lane, and the ship radioed the Coast Guard for permission to steer a course down the empty incoming lane to avoid the icebergs. This permission was granted and the *Valdez* altered course. At some point after the pilot left the ship, Hazelwood left the command post and went below to his cabin, in violation of company policy, which requires the captain to stay in command of the ship until it is in open water. Third Officer Gregory Cousins was left in charge of the ship, even though he lacked Coast Guard certification to pilot a tanker in Alaskan coastal waters. The ship was in trouble almost immediately, as it had set out on a course that would take it due south on a potential collision course with Busby Island, 5 miles away.[4]

The Coast Guard station on Potato Point had been tracking the ship but had not noticed a potential problem, apparently because the ship disappeared from the screen for a while. Apparently the Coast Guard had replaced its radar unit 2 years earlier with a less powerful unit that was unable to maintain contact with the ship and warn it of potential danger. During this time, the ship rode over submerged rocks off Busby Island and minutes later plowed into Bligh Reef and began dumping its cargo. The reef had torn 11 holes in the ship's bottom, some as large as 6 by 20 feet. Eight cargo holds big enough to swallow 15-story buildings were ruptured. Although a command had been given to change the course of the ship to avoid disaster, it came too late to have effect. At 12 knots, it takes about half a mile for any rudder change to alter the course of a 987-foot ship substantially.[5]

The Coast Guard station in Valdez was notified of a vessel run aground about 12:28 A.M. on Friday. About 1 A.M. a Coast Guard pilot boat headed for the accident site, following a tugboat that had already been dispatched. At 3:23 A.M. they arrived on the site and saw that the ship was losing oil at a rate that was later reported to be 1.5 million gallons an hour. At 5:40 A.M. it was reported that the *Valdez* had lost 210,000 barrels of oil, or more than 8.8 million gallons. (There are 42 gallons in a barrel of oil, which is the standard industry measure.) Spotters aboard an Alyeska plane reported at 7:27 A.M. that the oil slick was 1,000 feet wide and 5 miles long and was spreading. Earlier a passing boat had reported encountering an oil slick about half a mile south of Bligh Reef. Later it was estimated that the *Valdez* had released about 240,000 barrels of oil, equivalent to 10.1 million gallons, into the sound.[6]

When Hazelwood's blood was tested, fully 9 hours after the ship ran aground, he still had a blood-alcohol level of 0.06, which is higher than the 0.04 the Coast Guard considers acceptable for captains. It was estimated that his blood-alcohol level at the time of the accident was about 0.19, assuming that he had not had anything more to drink after the accident and that his body metabolized at the normal rate. This level of 0.19 is almost double the amount at which most states consider a motorist to be legally drunk. After it learned of these test results, Exxon fired Hazelwood and the state filed criminal charges against him for operating a ship while under the influence of alcohol, reckless endangerment, and criminally negligent discharge of oil. The maximum penalty for the combined charges was 27 months in jail and a $10,000 fine. The state also issued a warrant for his arrest.[7]

After 1 day, the slick was 8 miles long and 4 miles wide and was clearly the worst spill in U.S. history. By the end of the week the slick covered almost 900 square miles to the southwest of Valdez, threatening the marine and bird life in the sound and spreading to the Chugach National Forest. On Thursday afternoon, the slick began taking its greatest toll on wildlife when oil began washing up on the beaches on Knight and Green islands. Scientists found many blackened animals huddled or dead on the beaches. Scores of cormorants and other birds were barely distinguishable from the oil-covered sand and gravel.[8]

The oil slick continued to spread, covering more than 1,000 square miles, hitting hundreds of miles of inaccessible beaches, and drifting into the Gulf of Alaska, where it threatened the port of Seward and the delicate shoreline of Kenai Fjords National Park. The area covered by the spill was said to be larger than the state of Rhode Island. Eventually the slick spread 100 miles out into the Gulf of Alaska, forcing federal officials to open a second front in their battle to contain its advancement. Scientists estimated that about half the oil lost by the *Valdez* had left Prince William Sound and had entered the gulf, creeping south at about 15 to 20 miles a day.[9]

One of the first effects of the accident was an indefinite postponement of the fishing season for shrimp and sablefish, to which the fishing community reacted bitterly. There was also some question as to whether the season for herring roe would also have to be canceled because of the spill. Herring roe, which are really eggs, are considered to be a delicacy in Japan and bring high prices; this gives the fishing community an economic boost to carry them through to the summer salmon season.[10] The herring lay their eggs on floating kelp beds that the community feared would be smothered by the oil slick. Millions of salmon fingerlings from the hatcheries were scheduled to be released into the sound's inlets to begin a 2-year migration cycle. These fingerlings feed on plankton that may be poisoned by the oil, thus beginning a contamination that would continue up the food chain. Clams and mussels were expected to survive, but hydrocarbons would probably accumulate in their body tissues, which would endanger any species that feeds on them.[11]

Before long, waterfowl by the tens of thousands would finish their northward migrations and settle in summer nesting colonies in the sound. More than 200 different species of birds were reported to be in the sound, and some 111 of them are water-related. The Copper River delta, which is at the east end of the sound, is home to an estimated 20 million migratory birds, including one-fifth of the world's trumpeter swans. It was later estimated that thousands of sea birds such as cormorants and loons died either because oil destroyed their buoyancy or because they were simply poisoned.[12]

Emergency teams that were sent out to clean up the oil found ducks coated with crude and sea lions with their flippers drenched with oil clinging to a buoy that was located near the damaged tanker. Environmentalists feared that a significant part of the sound's sea otter population of 12,000 would be totally wiped out by the spill. Sea otters die of hypothermia when their fur becomes coated with oil. They may also sink under the surface of the water and drown. Thus many different kinds of animals were threatened by the spreading oil slick.[13]

The long-term effect of the spill could be to change the balance of power between the oil industry and the environmentalists. The latter lost no time in getting their message across regarding oil and gas exploration on the North Slope. Although they were unable to prevent development of the North Slope fields, the *Valdez* disaster gave them new ammunition in the fight against opening up the Arctic National Wildlife Refuge (ANWR) that lies between Prudhoe Bay and the Canadian border. As the name implies, the area teems with wildlife of all kinds, and the environmentalists want to keep the oil industry out of this preserve.[14]

The oil industry has lost the trust of the Alaskan people, who felt betrayed by believing the claims of the oil companies that they could protect the environment. People will be less likely to believe that the oil industry can develop the Arctic in a responsible manner. State lawmakers want assurances that current operations will not further harm the environment but are less likely to trust the oil companies to do this on their own without state regulation.[15] Federal officials began talking about stricter enforcement of existing laws as well as new requirements that tankers be equipped with double hulls for added protection. Other suggestions had to do with tougher personnel rules that would ban drunken drivers from commanding tankers and proposals for updating the training standards for crews of tankers. Perhaps one of the most controversial proposals had to do with testing of employees for drug and alcohol abuse.[16]

Case Notes

1. "Disaster at Valdez: Promises Unkept," *Los Angeles Times,* April 2, 1989, p. I-20.
2. "The Big Spill," *Time,* April 10, 1989, p. 39.
3. "Disaster at Valdez," p. I-20.
4. Ibid.
5. Ibid., p. I-22.
6. Ibid., p. I-21.
7. "The Big Spill," p. 40.
8. Mark Stein, "FBI Starts Probe of Valdez Spill as Toll Mounts," *Los Angeles Times,* April 1, 1989, p. I-1.
9. Larry B. Stammer and Mark A. Stein, "New Front Opened in Oil Spill Battle," *Los Angeles Times,* April 8, 1989, p. I-23.
10. Mark A. Stein, "Arrest of Missing Tanker Captain Sought by Alaska," *Los Angeles Times,* April 2, 1989, p. I-1.
11. Ken Wells and Marilyn Chase, "Paradise Lost: Heartbreaking Scenes Of Beauty Disfigured Follow Alaska Oil Spill," *Wall Street Journal,* March 31, 1989, p. A-1.

12. Ibid.
13. "Smothering the Waters," *Newsweek,* April 10, 1989, p. 57.
14. "Tug of War Over Oil Drilling," *U.S. News & World Report,* April 10, 1989, p. 48.
15. Michael D. Lemonick, "The Two Alaskas, *Time,* April 17, 1989, p. 63.
16. Ibid., p. 66.

Chapter Notes

1. Denton E. Morrison, "How and Why Environmental Consciousness Has Trickled Down." Paper presented at a Conference on Distributional Conflicts in Environmental Resource Policy, Science Center, West Berlin, 1984.

2. Anthony D. Tarlock, "Environmental Law: What It Is, What It Should Be," *Environmental Science and Technology,* Vol. 13, No. 11 (November 1979), p. 1345.

3. Environmental Protection Agency, *Air Pollution and Your Health* (Washington, D.C.: EPA, March 1979), p. 2.

4. *Your Guide to the U.S. Environmental Protection Agency,* OPA 212 (Washington, D.C.: Environmental Protection Agency, 1982), p. 3.

5. *Cleaning the Air: EPA's Program for Air Pollution Control* (Washington, D.C.: Environmental Protection Agency, 1979), pp. 3–4.

6. Ibid., p. 9.

7. Andy Pasztor, "EPA Puts Aside Action Against States and Cities," *Wall Street Journal,* October 3, 1983, p. 4.

8. See "EPA Proposes End to Highway Funds for Chicago Area," *Wall Street Journal,* May 2, 1984, p. 6; and "Detroit Faces Cutoff of Highway Funding Over EPA Standards," *Wall Street Journal,* June 12, 1984, p. 3. See also Robert E. Taylor, "U.S. Is Likely to Impose Growth Curbs In Areas Not Meeting Ozone Standard," *Wall Street Journal,* February 20, 1987, p. 6.

9. Barbara Rosewicz, "EPA Prepares Plan for Cities On Clean Air," *Wall Street Journal,* November 12, 1987, p. 64.

10. Robert E. Taylor, "New Studies Indicate Ozone Is Harmful At Half Level Previously Thought Safe," *Wall Street Journal,* April 24, 1986, p. 4.

11. David Stipp, "Breathing Ozone at Cities' Current Levels May Injure Lungs, Research Indicates," *Wall Street Journal,* September 18, 1989, p. B-4.

12. Robert E. Taylor, "Lead Content of Gasoline Must Be Cut By 90% by 1986, EPA Ruling States," *Wall Street Journal,* March 5, 1985, p. 46.

13. Jim Brady, "Leaden Gas' Demise Fuels Controversy," *Dallas Times Herald,* April 4, 1987, p. A-1.

14. EPA, *Clearing the Air,* pp. 10–11.

15. Robert E. Taylor, "EPA Is Planning to Leave Regulation Of Most Toxic-Gas Emissions to States," *Wall Street Journal,* June 4, 1985, p. 5.

16. Sharon Begley, "Is Breathing Hazardous to Your Health?" *Newsweek,* April 3, 1989, p. 25.

17. "EPA is Set to Allow Factory Trade-Offs for Air Pollution," *Wall Street Journal,* April 2, 1982, p. 5.

18. *Environmental Quality 1983: 14th Annual Report of the Council on Environmental Quality* (Washington, D.C.: U.S. Government Printing Office, 1984), pp. 190–91.

19. Robert E. Taylor, "EPA Is Expanding Its 'Bubble' Policy For Air Pollution," *Wall Street Journal,* November 16, 1986, p. 18.

20. NAM, "Clean Air and the Quality of Life," p. 3.

21. Robert E. Taylor, "EPA Finds Fewer Cars Are Meeting Emissions Limits," *Wall Street Journal,* May 28, 1985, p. 12.

22. Michael Duffy, "Smell That Fresh Air!" *Time,* June 26, 1989, pp. 16–17.

23. Rose Gutfeld and Barbara Rosewicz, "White House and Senate Leaders Strike Clean-Air Bill Compromise," *Wall Street Journal,* March 2, 1990, p. A-3.

24. United States Environmental Protection Agency, *Environmental Progress and Challenges: EPA's Update* (Washington, D.C.: U.S. Government Printing Office, 1988), p. 45.

25. *Setting the Course: Clean Water* (Washington, D.C.: National Wildlife Federation, undated), p. 5.

26. *A Guide to the Clean Water Act Amendments* (Washington, D.C.: Environmental Protection Agency, 1978), pp. 1–2.

27. EPA, *Environmental Progress and Challenges*, p. 72.

28. Robert E. Taylor, "Senate Approves Clean Water Act, 86-14, Joining House in Overriding Reagan Veto," *Wall Street Journal,* February 5, 1987, p. 5.

29. *Clean Water and Agriculture* (Washington, D.C.: Environmental Protection Agency, 1977), pp. 2–3.

30. Andy Pasztor, "EPA Will Let States Retain Responsibility for Safety of Underground Water Supply," *Wall Street Journal,* December 30, 1983, p. 28.

31. Robert E. Taylor, "EPA's Plan to Regulate Contaminants Of Water Isn't Seen Satisfying Congress," *Wall Street Journal,* October 14, 1985, p. 5.

32. Environmental Protection Agency, *Safe Drinking Water Act: 1986 Amendments* (Washington, D.C.: U.S. Government Printing Office, 1986), pp. 1–5.

33. EPA Expands Rules In Battle to Control Water Contamination," *Wall Street Journal,* March 7, 1990, p. A-8.

34. Robert E. Taylor, "EPA Plans to Require the Replacement Of Many Storage Tanks Within 10 Years," *Wall Street Journal,* April 3, 1987, p. 4. See also "Costly Cleanups At The Gas Pump," *Business Week,* April 20, 1987, pp. 28–29.

35. Paulette Thomas, "EPA Issues Rules To Prevent Leaks In Storage Tanks," *Wall Street Journal,* September 14, 1988, p. 52.

36. *Your Guide to the EPA,* p. 9.

37. Rachel Carson, *Silent Spring* (Greenwich, Conn.: Fawcett, 1962).

38. Allen A. Boraiko, "The Pesticide Dilemma," *National Geographic,* Vol. 157, No. 2 (February 1980), p. 151. See also "Pesticides Leave Enduring Trail, Causing Disagreement," *Dallas Times Herald,* July 20, 1986, p. A-53.

39. *1978 Report: Better Health and Regulatory Reform* (Washington, D.C.: Environmental Protection Agency, 1979), p. 29.

40. EPA, *Environmental Progress and Challenges,* pp. 114–15.

41. Andy Pasztor and Barry Meier, "EPA Has Started to Crack Down on Use Of Pesticides Thought to Be Hazardous," *Wall Street Journal,* December 6, 1984, p. 7.

42. David Holzman, "Farm Workers Reap Cancer Risks," *Insight,* September 4, 1989, pp. 52–53.

43. "EPA Issues Rules on Pesticides Made by Biotechnology," *Wall Street Journal,* October 5, 1984, p. 37.

44. EPA, *Environmental Progress and Challenges,* p. 140.

45. *Better Health and Regulatory Reform,* p. 21.

46. Environmental Protection Agency, Office of Toxic Substances, *Reporting for the Chemical Substance Inventory* (Washington, D.C.: Environmental Protection Agency, 1977), p. 1.

47. Appendix I to Premanufacture Notification Draft Guideline, *The Chemical Reporter* (Washington D.C.: Bureau of National Affairs, 1978), p. 1124.

48. EPA, *Environmental Progress and Challenges,* p. 116.

49. Environmental Protection Agency, *The Toxic Substances Control Act,* 1976, p. 2.

50. EPA, *Environmental Progress and Challenges,* p. 116.

51. Ibid., p. 117. See also Michael D. Lemonick, "An Overblown Asbestos Scare?" *Time,* January 29, 1990, p. 65.

52. "New Agency to Study Chemical Dangers," *Dallas Times Herald,* May 28, 1983, p. 4-A.

53. "New Jersey Bill Signed Forcing Public Listing of Toxic Substances," *Wall Street Journal,* August 30, 1983, p. 2.

54. EPA, *Environmental Progress and Challenges,* p. 124.

55. United States Environmental Protection Agency, *Chemicals in Your Community: A Guide to the Emergency Planning and Community Right-to-Know Act* (Washington, D.C.: U.S. Government Printing Office, 1988), pp. 2–4.

56. EPA, *Environmental Progress and Challenges,* p. 87.

57. Ibid.

58. George J. Church, "Garbage, Garbage, Everywhere," *Time*, September 5, 1988, pp. 81–82.

59. Bill Eldred, "Changing Economics Revives Recycling," *American City and Country*, No. 102, 1987, pp. 57–63.

60. Paul Frumkin, "A Looming Crisis," *Restaurant Business*, No. 88, 1989, pp. 143–54.

61. Elliott D. Lee, "Opposition to Plastic Packaging Is Intensifying As the Nation's Solid-Waste Problem Grows Acute," *Wall Street Journal*, November 25, 1987, p. 38.

62. Susan Dillingham, "New Answers to a Plastic Life-style," *Insight*, January 30, 1989, p. 44.

63. Samuel Epstein et al., *Hazardous Wastes In America* (San Francisco: Sierra, 1982), p. 303.

64. Office of Research and Development, *Controlling Hazardous Waste Research Summary* (Washington, D.C.: Environmental Protection Agency, 1980), p. 4.

65. *The Resource Conservation and Recovery Act: What It Is; How It Works*, SW-967 (Washington, D.C.: Environmental Protection Agency, 1983), p. 3.

66. EPA, *Environmental Progress and Challenges*, p. 80.

67. Ronald J. Penoyer, *Reforming Regulation of Hazardous Waste* (St. Louis, Mo.: Washington University Center for the Study of American Business, 1985), p. 1.

68. *Better Health and Regulatory Reform*, p. 16.

69. *The Resource Conservation and Recovery Act*, SW-967, p. 5; *The New RCRA: A Fact Book* (Washington, D.C.: Environmental Protection Agency, 1985), p. 4.

70. *The New RCRA*, pp. 1–2.

71. Barry Meier, "Dirty Job: Against Heavy Odds, EPA Tries to Convict Polluters and Dumpers," *Wall Street Journal*, January 7, 1985, p. 1.

72. See Alix M. Freedman, "Firms Curb Hazardous Waste To Avoid Expensive Disposal," *Wall Street Journal*, May 31, 1985, p. 19.

73. Penoyer, *Reforming Regulation of Hazardous Waste*, p. 17.

74. Ibid.

75. EPA, *Environmental Progress and Challenges*, pp. 94–95.

76. "A Problem That Cannot Be Buried," *Time*, October 14, 1985, p. 76.

77. Robert E. Taylor, "EPA Says Cleanup Of Sites Will Cost $11.7 Billion More," *Wall Street Journal*, December 13, 1984, p. 38.

78. "Everybody Will Probably Pay To Clean Up Toxic Waste," *Business Week*, November 4, 1985, p. 30.

79. "Superfund Cleanup: What Price Delay?" *Business Week*, February 10, 1986, pp. 29–30.

80. Alexander & Alexander Government and Industry Affairs Office, *Washington News*, Vol. 4, No. 11 (October 31, 1986), pp. 1–2. See also Superfund Amendments of 1986, P.L. 99-499.

81. Amal Kumar Naj, "How to Clean Up Superfund's Act," *Wall Street Journal*, September 15, 1988, p. 26. See also Christopher Elias, "Waste Site Cleanup Liability May Be Hazardous to Lenders," *Insight*, November 13, 1989, pp. 42–44.

82. Clarence Davies, "It's Time for the EPA to Tackle New Problems," *Business Week*, October 24, 1983.

83. EPA, *Environmental Progress and Challenges*, p. 32.

84. Walter A. Rosenbaum, *Environmental Politics and Policy* (Washington, D.C.: Congressional Quarterly Press, 1985), pp. 308–11.

85. Ibid., pp. 100–101.

Suggested Reading

BALDWIN, JOHN H. *Environmental Planning and Management*. New York: Westview, 1985.

BANDOW, DOUG, ed. *Protecting the Environment: A Free Market Strategy*. Washington, D.C.: Heritage Foundation, 1986.

BEALE, JACK G. *The Manager and the Environment: General Theory and Practice of Environmental Management*. New York: Pergamon, 1980.

BERGER, JOHN J. *Restoring the Earth: How Americans Are Working to Restore Our Damaged Environment*. New York: Doubleday, 1987.

BROWN, MICHAEL. *Laying Waste: The Poisoning of America by Toxic Chemicals.* New York: Pantheon Books, 1980.

BURROWS, PAUL. *Economic Theory of Pollution Control.* Cambridge, Mass.: MIT Press, 1980.

CARSON, RACHEL. *Silent Spring.* (Greenwich, Conn.: Fawcett, 1962).

COMMONER, BARRY. *The Closing Circle,* New York: Knopf, 1971.

DiLORENZO, THOMAS, AND JAMES BENNETT. *The Politics of Environmentalism.* St. Louis Mo.: Washington University Center for the Study of American Business, 1986.

DIX, H. M. *Environmental Pollution: Atmosphere, Land, Water and Noise.* New York: John Wiley, 1980.

FREEDMAN, WARREN. *Federal Studies on Environmental Protection: Regulation in the Public Interest.* New York: Greenwood, 1987.

FREEMAN, A. MYRICK. *Air and Water Pollution Control: A Benefit Cost Assessment.* New York: John Wiley, 1982.

GILBREATH, KENT, ed. *Business and the Environment: Toward Common Ground.* Washington, D.C.: Conservation Foundation, 1984.

HAWKINS, KEITH. *Environment and Enforcement: Regulation and the Social Definition of Pollution.* New York: Oxford University Press, 1984.

HOLMES, RALSTON III, *Environmental Ethics: Duties To and Values in the Natural World.* Philadelphia: Temple University Press, 1987.

HUISINGH, DONALD, AND VICKI BAILEY, eds. *Making Pollution Prevention Pay: Ecology with Economy.* New York: Pergamon, 1982.

KAPP, K. WILLIAM. *The Social Costs of Private Enterprise.* New York: Schocken Books, 1971.

KIEFER, IRENE. *Poisoned Land: The Problem of Hazardous Waste.* New York: Atheneum, 1981.

KNEESE, ALLEN V. *Economics and the Environment,* New York: Penguin Books, 1977.

———, AND CHARLES L. SCHULTZ. *Pollution, Prices, and Public Policy.* Washington, D.C.: The Brookings Institution, 1975.

LAKE, LAURA M. *Environmental Regulation: The Political Effects of Implementation.* New York: Praeger, 1982.

LEVINE, ADELINE G. *Love Canal: Science, Politics, and People.* Lexington, Mass.: Lexington Books, 1982.

NASH, RODERICK. *The Rights of Nature: A History of Environmental Ethics.* Madison: University of Wisconsin Press, 1989.

NASH, RODERICK. *The American Environment: Readings in the History of Conservation.* New York: Knopf, 1987.

NICHOLSON, MAX. *The New Environmental Age.* Cambridge: Cambridge University Press, 1987.

PACHLKE, ROBERT. *Environmentalism and the Future of Progressive Politics.* New Haven: Yale University Press, 1989.

ROSENBAUM, WALTER A. *Environmental Politics and Policy.* Washington, D.C.: Congressional Quarterly, 1985.

SAGOFF, MARK. *The Economy of the Earth: Philosophy, Law and the Environment.* Cambridge: Cambridge University Press, 1988.

SANDBACH, FRANCIS. *Principles of Pollution Control.* New York: Longman, 1982.

TIETENBERG, THOMAS H. *Environmental and Natural Resource Economics,* 2d ed. New York: Scott-Foresman, 1988.

CHAPTER 10

International Dimensions of Public Policy

Previous chapters have focused on public policy and public issues in the United States, but this is by no means the only dimension to public policy about which a manager needs to know something and take into consideration. As business becomes increasingly internationalized, public policies that affect business in the international arena have also become increasingly important. The term internationalization refers to an increased foreign influence on national trends and policies.[1] When countries trade with each other and when they are open for foreign investment and technology, they are also more open to outside influences. The increased magnitude of international trade and investment that has taken place over the past several decades has led to greater independence among individual national economies as they have become internationalized.[2]

This internationalization of domestic economies around the world is most directly the result of decisions made by private firms to engage in international trade and investment. Thus some attention needs to be given to the role of the multinational corporation (MNC) in the international economy. Because of its role in promoting trade and investment between countries, the MNC has become a major force in internationalizing national economies. The MNC is the major institutional means through which international trade and investment is accomplished.

> The multinational corporation is probably the most visible vehicle for the internationalization of the world economic system. As the economies of different nations have become increasingly linked and functionally integrated, the multinational corporation seems to have been the institution most able to adapt to a transnational style of operation. Indeed, multinational corporations are a major result of and a prime stimulus for furthering the number and complexity of transnational interactions.[3]

A multinational corporation has been defined as any enterprise that undertakes foreign direct investment, owns or controls income-gathering assets in more than one country, produces goods or services outside its country of origin, or engages in international production.[4] Multinational corporations are generally headquartered in industrialized countries and pursue business activities in one or more foreign countries. They exercise influence over the various entities (branches, subsidiaries, joint ventures) in those countries. This allows them to adopt a common globally oriented corporate policy

Figure 10.1 U.S. Exports and Imports of Goods and Services In Constant (1982) Dollars, 1947–1987

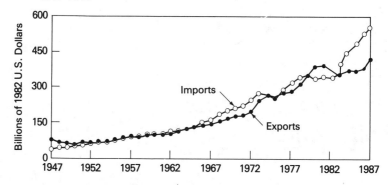

Source: Richard McKenzie, *The Global Economy and Government Power* (St. Louis Mo.: Washington University Center for the Study of American Business, 1989), p. 5.

with respect to sharing information, using resources, and dividing responsibilities. Thus the term *multinational* can refer to many different kinds of business enterprises and is not limited to a single type of business.[5]

Multinationals have gained importance over the past several years as an international economy has developed. Growth in the volume of international trade shows this internationalization quite dramatically. For the United States, growth of exports and imports since World War II has steadily increased (Figure 10.1). In 1947, exports and imports of goods and services were $82.3 million and $39.9 billion, respectively. By 1987, exports had grown to $426.8 billion, more than five times the 1947 level, whereas imports had grown more than 14 times to $560 billion, leaving a trade deficit of $135 billion. Throughout this postwar period, U.S. international trade expanded more rapidly than production for domestic markets.[6]

Internationalization of the economy is also shown by the flow of international capital. In 1960, Americans owned $434 billion in foreign assets, but by 1987, their aggregate foreign investments had nearly tripled to $1.2 trillion. Of this total, U.S. citizens held 74 percent, or $859 billion, in portfolio assets, and the remainder of $309 billion was direct foreign investment in plants, equipment, and real estate. Foreigners' total investment in the United States increased even more dramatically, rising from $280 billion in 1970 to more than $1.5 trillion in 1987, 83 percent of which was in portfolio assets and 17 percent in direct investments. Through 1984, the United States was the world's leading creditor nation, but by 1987, it had achieved the dubious distinction of being the world's leading debtor nation. In that year, total foreign investments in the United States exceeded total U.S. investments abroad by $368 billion (Figure 10.2).[7]

This kind of growth in trade between nations and international investment means that MNCs have significant economic and social impacts on national economies and political systems.[8] Their activities have become very visible, making them subject to criticism from many quarters. They have something of a love-hate relationship with many developing countries, who welcome MNCs because they have the potential to assist these countries in pursuing their own economic growth and development. Yet these same countries view MNCs as a threat to their national sovereignty and autonomy. They do not want to become economically and technologically dependent on institutions outside of their control. They often find MNCs hard to live with and yet impossible to live without.[9]

Figure 10.2 International Investment Position of the United States In Constant (1982) Dollars, 1970–1988

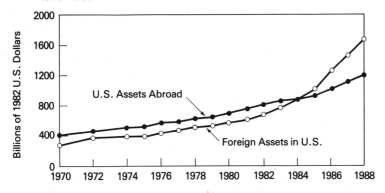

Source: Richard McKenzie, *The Global Economy and Government Power* (St. Louis Mo.: Washington University Center for the Study of American Business, 1989), p. 9; *Economic Report of the President* (Washington, D.C.: U.S. Government Printing Office, 1990), p. 409.

Generally speaking, there are at least four reasons why a business enterprise might decide to become international in scope. The first reason is to find new markets for products. These new markets may be needed to provide a sufficient demand to allow for economies of scale to be realized from large production runs. Large production runs may permit output to be produced at a level where the marginal cost of producing an extra unit is substantially less than the average cost. Thus the more goods that are produced, the lower the average cost per unit and the greater the profitability of the firm. Because of these economies, some business executives look for international markets to provide this extra demand for their products.

The second reason is the desire of business managers to find opportunities to earn greater returns on capital. These opportunities may be better in foreign countries, especially in the third world, where competition may be much less keen than it is in the United States (or other advanced industrialized countries) and where consumption is rising more rapidly. Growth of foreign consumption in the developing countries has become especially important in recent years. Firms can sometimes introduce new products overseas faster than they can in their home country, and thus start earning a return on investment sooner.

Firms may also become international in order to obtain resources that are needed for its operations. These resources may not be available in the firm's home country and thus it is necessary for the firm to go abroad and search for these resources on the best terms available. In other cases, foreign countries may have specialized skills that are significant factors in the decision to establish overseas operations. A firm that is located in an advanced industrial country where wages are relatively high may invest in developing nations in order to take advantage of low-cost labor. These lower costs may give it a competitive advantage.[10]

Finally, foreign markets are a must for corporations making products for which domestic demand has been satiated. Such corporations must either find new markets for their products or develop new lines of business. The best course of action in many of these cases is to find new markets for existing products by attempting to penetrate foreign countries. For example, infant formula companies turned to overseas markets for exactly this reason. As the baby boom generation grew up and the birthrate declined in developed countries, the developing countries offered new potential markets for such products.

TABLE 10.1   Importance of Reasons for Foreign Investment

	Mentioned by Number of Companies
1. Maintain or increase market share locally	33
2. Unable to reach market from U.S. because of tariffs, transportation costs, or nationalistic purchasing polices	25
3. To meet competition	20
4. To meet local content requirements and host government pressure	18
5. Faster sales growth than in the United States	15
6. To obtain or use local raw materials or components	13
7. Low wage costs	13
8. Greater profit prospects abroad	11
9. To follow major customers	10
10. Inducements connected with host government investment promotion programs	8

Source: U.S Department of Commerce, Domestic and International Business Administration, *The Multinational Corporation: Studies on U.S. Foreign Investment,* Vol. 2. (Washington, DC: U.S. Government Printing Office, 1973), p. 6.

The United States Department of Commerce has had a long-standing interest in the area of foreign investment of U.S. multinational corporations. Concerning the principal reasons for making investments in foreign countries, the Department conducted a series of interviews with 76 chief executives in charge of international operations, covering most U.S. manufacturing industries.[11] Table 10.1 shows the results of this survey, listing the reasons in order of importance as measured by the frequency of mention by the executives interviewed.

The growth of multinational corporations is paralleled by a growth in government regulation of economic activity, including regulation of multinational activity both within and without national borders. This growth increases the chances that the regulations of different countries will clash, with multinationals caught in the middle.[12] In effect, expansion beyond national boundaries is much more than a step across the geographical line of a country. It is also a step toward new and different social, educational, political, and economic environments. Different values and cultures mean that there are different ways of conducting business in various countries. These differences cause problems for managers of multinational corporations, as conflicts arise between MNCs and host and home countries, and find their way into public policy measures regulating the conduct of multinational enterprises. Public policies are often adopted to resolve these differences, making public policy important to companies operating in the international economy as well as in the domestic economy.

The International Regulatory Environment

Many countries find it difficult to control the activities of MNCs within their territories. The flexibility of MNCs enables them to move capital, goods, personnel, and technology across national boundaries. This flexibility enables them to play one country off against another to get the best deal for themselves. Since the activities of MNCs affect the level of social and economic development in many countries, particularly developing countries, there has been an increasing interest in developing some form of international regulation to control the activities of MNCs and give host governments some control over their activities. Third World nations in particular believe that in the absence of international regulation, MNCs would show interest only in profit maximization without any regard to the development needs of host nations.[13]

MNCs are accused of creating numerous negative externalities for host countries, including the following: (1) The benefits of foreign investments are poorly or unfairly distributed between the MNC and the host country, (2) MNCs preempt the development of an indigenous economic base by squeezing out local entrepreneurs, (3) they employ inappropriate capital-intensive technology, adding to host country unemployment, (4) MNCs worsen the distribution of income in the host country, (5) they alter consumer tastes in the host country, thus undermining the culture, and (6) foreign investors subvert host country political processes by co-opting the local elites, using their influence to keep host governments in line, and structuring the international system to respond to their needs to the detriment of host authorities.[14]

Most conflicts arise from the fact that MNCs have some degree of economic power because of the decisions they make concerning product lines, location of plants, technology employed, trade flows, and other business considerations. These decisions are made with regard to corporate objectives related to profits and market share and are not necessarily made in the interests of the host country or even the home country. MNCs do not and cannot take into account the interest of each and every country in the decisions they make because the interests of the various countries affected by these decisions very rarely coincide. MNCs must maintain that they are looking after their own interests within a worldwide strategy they have developed for themselves. Yet governments are not likely to let important decisions be made by a foreign private institution without exercising some kind of influence.[15]

Host governments influence multinationals in a variety of ways. The underlying motive is to set the rules of the game. Government regulation is theoretically nondiscriminatory, since all the parties are nominally subject to the same rules of the game. But governments in reality are political creations, often motivated by purely political considerations. Another major problem facing multinationals is that the regulatory environment varies considerably from country to country. Many regulations governing multinationals are difficult to interpret and are not consistently enforced. Moreover, in large parts of the Third World there is a distinct absence of regulations or mechanisms for enforcing those regulations that do exist. Third World countries often lack the necessary legal and administrative institutions and the technical proficiency to implement and enforce national policies.

The problems MNCs face are the result of investment decisions and operational practices that are geared to their need to survive and grow by maintaining or increasing world market shares, gaining a competitive edge over rivals, shifting operations to take advantage of access to natural resources or cheap labor markets, and other such factors where policies and strategies are developed that are global in nature, scope, and character. An international regulatory structure has developed over the years to deal with some of these problems, as it is difficult for any one country to deal with multinationals unilaterally, particularly countries in the Third World. Public policy has thus become internationalized in some sense to correspond with the internationalization of economic activity.

INTERNATIONAL LEVEL

Conceived and born amid the idealism and hopes that came with peace at the end of World War II, the United Nations is probably the best known of the international organizations. Of particular interest is the United Nations Centre on Transnational Corporations (UNCTC). It provides numerous services for member nations with respect to the operation of what it calls Transnational Corporations (TNCs) within their borders. The UNCTC has been in the process of developing an international code of conduct to regulate the activities of TNCs with regard to the internal affairs of host countries and to encourage TNCs to facilitate the achievement of the development activities of Third World countries. This code represents the first time a comprehensive international instrument is being developed for regulating a wide range of issues arising from relations between TNCs and host governments.[16]

The code is meant to provide a stable, predictable, and transparent framework that can facilitate the flow of resources across national boundaries, thereby enhancing the role of foreign investment in economic and industrial growth. The code is also meant to minimize the negative effects of TNCs by establishing the rights and responsibilities of TNCs and host governments. As a result of this twin focus, it is hoped the code will help reduce friction between TNCs and host countries and enable the flow of direct foreign investment to realize its full potential.

The first part of the code consists of a preamble and statement of objectives. The second part deals with definitions and the code's scope of application. The next portion concerns the activities of TNCs including (1) the general political implications flowing from the operations of TNCs; (2) specific economic, financial, and social issues; and (3) disclosure of information. The fourth part of the code covers the kind of treatment TNCs should expect from host governments, including issues of nationalization, compensation, and choice of jurisdiction for settlement of disputes. The fifth section deals with intergovernmental cooperation for application of the code, and the sixth and final part is concerned with development at national and international levels.[17]

The problem with all such international codes is to make them general enough to secure ratification by a number of nations with diverse interests and yet specific enough to have some real meaning in concrete situations. Another problem is implementation. Third World countries generally want such codes to be binding and are in favor of setting up some institutional machinery for enforcement purposes, whereas industrialized countries generally want such codes to be voluntary without any binding authority. This problem of international enforcement authority has undermined other efforts of this nature and is likely to produce the same result regarding the UNCTC code. Perhaps the major benefit of the code will be to provide a model for other such efforts at regulating TNCs at regional or national levels.

Some economists see this code as a dangerous activity and have attacked this attempt to regulate multinational business enterprises. Unlike domestic regulation, it has been argued, international regulation of this kind is not primarily motivated by a desire to improve business performance. This style of rule-making is said to have more political objectives in attempting to redistribute the income and wealth of member nations by stepping up regulation of private enterprise. The code in particular is seen to be the most dangerous of the proposals or actions by international agencies in connection with regulating the day-to-day operations of private companies. It is feared that the code could become the basis for treaties and other directives nations might adopt in the future.[18]

The complexity of problems on the global level, particularly with respect to international trade, has led the major trading nations to seek better solutions in the form of international trade agreements. Nations act in their own self-interest in restricting imports that may hurt domestic industries and promoting exports that will expand growth opportunities for their enterprises. The trade policies of individual nations often conflict, hampering world trade and making international cooperation desirable. Two international trade organizations that have an important impact on the international economic environment are the General Agreement on Tariffs and Trade (GATT) and the United Nations Conference on Trade and Development (UNCTAD). These organizations have been influential in dealing with the problems of international trade on a global level. A third organization, the Organization of Economic Cooperation and Development (OECD), is also discussed.

The General Agreement on Tariffs and Trade. The unhappy experience of the Great Depression led the major trading nations to seek better commercial policies after World War II. As one outcome of their efforts, the General Agreement on Tariffs and Trade was formed on October 10, 1947, as the world's trading club. Its initial membership was only 23 countries; today, GATT counts over 90 members and associates who account for well over 80 percent of total world trade. The communist countries are also represented by five members.

GATT provides a framework for multilateral trade negotiations and allows nations to work out differences in trade policies that might otherwise create a no-win situation for all the major trading nations. It was designed to provide a multilateral framework for tariff negotiations on a product-by-product basis. One of GATT's guiding principles to promote trade is that of nondiscrimination. Each contracting party must grant all others the same rate of import duties, that is, a tariff concession granted to one trading partner must be extended to all members of the organization. Another principle is the concept of consultation. When trade disagreements arise, GATT provides a forum for consultation. Disagreeing members are more likely to compromise than resort to arbitrary trade-restricting actions.

World-trade cooperation since World War II has led to a better open-door trading policy than might have been expected. GATT has been a major contributor to this policy. Since 1947, GATT has sponsored seven major tariff negotiations. As a result, the tariff rates for tens of thousands of items have been reduced, and a high proportion of the world trade has seen an easing of restrictions. The organization has undoubtedly contributed to the expansion of world trade since its inception. However, GATT has not prevented industrialized nations from adopting protectionist measures when it is in their interest to adopt such measures.

The United Nations Conference on Trade and Development. UNCTAD was formed in 1964 as a permanent organ of the United Nations General Assembly. It counts 147 member countries, which is more than the UN itself and more than any other international organization in the world. UNCTAD was established because of the dissatisfaction of less-developed countries with GATT's performance. These countries felt that the results and benefits of GATT were not equally distributed. They have been dissatisfied because their share of the world trade was declining, and because the prices of their raw material exports were not consistent with the prices of imported manufactured goods.

At least three major goals can be cited for the UNCTAD: (1) to further the development of emerging nations by trade as well as other means, (2) to improve the prices of primary goods exports through commodity agreements, and (3) to establish a tariff preference system favoring the export of manufactured goods from less developed countries.[19] However, major achievements of UNCTAD have been modest. One major achievement is organizational. A new club for world trade matters has been established with a large membership and financing from the UN budget. A second achievement is all the publicity and attention given by many countries to the trade aspects of a major world problem—the gap in economic development between the "have" and "have not" nations. UNCTAD has made few concrete achievements to date, however.[20]

The Organization of Economic Cooperation and Development.   The OECD was formed in 1960, and has since grown into an international organization uniting the views and interests of the developed market countries. One of its first efforts to regulate MNCs was in 1967 when it proposed a code for the protection of foreign private investments. In 1975, voluntary standards of conduct to be used as guidelines in regulating MNCs were proposed. These efforts were directed toward integrating the activities of MNCs into national economic and social systems. But the OECD guidelines represent an attempt by the industrialized countries to regulate MNCs to suit their objectives. Thus the organization is often in conflict with communist and developing countries regarding international economic negotiations.[21]

REGIONAL LEVEL

On the regional level, the tendency toward economic cooperation between nations of the same region to attain goals that they cannot achieve in isolation of each other has also led to the creation of a number of regional economic associations. The tendency to form regional groupings has been growing in the world economy since World War II. The expression *regional groupings* means agreements between nations in the same region to cooperate in various economic matters, even though political matters enter the picture. As described next, the European Free Trade Association (EFTA), the Latin American Free Trade Association (LAFTA), and the European Economic Community (EEC) are good examples of regional groupings. The tendency toward economic cooperation within regions is an attempt by the concerned nations to attain and achieve goals in a cooperative venture that is believed to be mutually beneficial to all the member nations.

The European Free Trade Association (EFTA) was formed in 1959 and originally included Austria, Denmark, Norway, Portugal, Sweden, Switzerland, and the United Kingdom. Finland and Iceland were added later. Tariffs between the member countries were reduced by successive cuts and in 1966 were abolished altogether. This action greatly stimulated trade between the member countries. EFTA does not maintain a common external tariff, since each member country retains its own tariff structure applicable to non-EFTA countries.

Argentina, Brazil, Chile, Colombia, Ecuador, Mexico, Paraguay, Peru, Uruguay, and Venezuela agreed to form the Latin American Free Trade Association (LAFTA) in 1961 in the Treaty of Montevideo. The treaty provided for the elimination of all customs duties, surcharges, deposits, and other obstacles to trade between the member countries by 1973. This timetable had to be set back because of difficulties between the member countries. There has not been a great number of tariff concessions granted within this regional organization; thus its success has been limited.

The European Economic Community (EEC) was established by the Treaty of Rome in 1958 and includes Germany, France, Italy, Belgium, Luxembourg, the Netherlands, the United Kingdom, Ireland, and Denmark. Greece became the tenth member in 1981, and negotiations began in 1980 regarding the membership of Spain and Portugal. A gradual reduction of internal customs duties on industrial goods resulted in their complete removal by July 1, 1968, by EEC countries. At the same time, a common external tariff applying to goods imported from other countries also was created. Since that time, a common agricultural policy has been adopted and the removal of internal agricultural duties has been completed. The EEC has also made progress in abolishing restrictions on the movement of capital between member countries, in the alignment of taxes, in developing a community policy on competition, and on restrictive practices such as price-fixing and company mergers.

In the mid-1980s, the 12 member nations of the EEC agreed to dismantle all internal barriers to trade by 1992, creating a single unified market of 320 million consumers. The member nations will transfer a good deal of power to the policy-making body of the European Community (EC) in Brussels, which will make decisions for all the member nations. The Single European Act of 1987 established majority rule in place of the unanimous vote requirement, that had previously existed in four areas: the completion of the internal market, research and technology, regional policy, and improvement of working conditions. This action will speed up the EC's decision-making process by preventing a single state from blocking decisions.[22]

If carried out this action will create one of the largest markets in the world. With the free movement of capital, goods, labor, and services across national boundaries, economies of scale could be achieved that would benefit member nations. With harmonized regulations with respect to trade, environment, and other areas, the costs of doing business in 12 separate nations, should be greatly reduced. An EC study predicted that the program could increase GNP by 5 percent, create 2 to 5 million new jobs, and lower prices by 6 percent as companies improve their efficiency with economies of scale and face fewer costly regulations.[23]

While the creation of such a market could provide opportunities for foreign investment and trade, there is also some concern that a "Fortress Europe" will be created, locking out foreign companies from meaningful participation. Barriers could arise in the areas of standards harmonization, regulations regarding local content and rules of origin, and reciprocity and government procurement. Harmonization of standards could force foreign companies that do not meet the standards to retool and lose market opportunities. Regulations regarding local content and rules of origin could force companies to buy parts in the EC or even manufacture in Europe using European suppliers to avoid tariffs and quota restrictions. And reciprocity would mean that EC trading partners might have to adopt laws identical to EC laws in order for their companies to gain access to the unified market.[24]

Most of the international trading that the communist countries do engage in comes within the framework of the Council for Mutual Economic Assistance (CMEA), the Soviet counterpart of the EEC. The CMEA includes most of the communist countries as members (U.S.S.R., Czechoslovakia, East Germany, Hungary, Poland, Romania, Cuba, and Vietnam). It has objectives similar to those of western organizations but is concerned only with the communist countries. For a time, the U.S.S.R. seemed to be directing its efforts toward turning the organization into a planning agency, with the Soviet government deciding where new factories should be built and what should be traded where.[25] The nature of this organization, however, will change drastically with the political and economic changes taking place in Eastern Europe and within the Soviet Union itself. Closer ties will undoubtedly be developed with the EC as these Eastern European countries adopt democratic forms of government and change their economies.

TABLE 10.2 Country Goals, Policies, and Policy Tools

Country Goals	Policy Areas	Policy Tools
Autarky/self-sufficiency	Price stability	Tariff controls
Economic welfare	Economic competition	Nontariff controls
Border integrity and control (national security)	Free trade	Export promotion
	Industrial and basic resource development	Import substitution
Employment stability		Foreign direct investment: disincentives/incentives
Financial performance of economy growth rates and in balance of payments	Infrastructure development	Official grants and loans
	Technology transfer	Fiscal and monetary policy
	Defense	Exchange rate adjustment or control
Economic development through technological (development)	Foreign aid	
	Ecological Balance	Design of Governmental organization
	Agriculture/food supply	
Economic/political relations	Labor/employment	Government procurement programs
External assistance	Consumer protection	
	Education/science	Cross national agreements

Source: R. Hal Mason and Robert S. Spich, *Management: An International Perspective* (Homewood, Ill.: Irwin, 1987), p. 61.

NATIONAL LEVEL

One of the major costs of joining regional groupings is having to give up some degree of sovereignty in terms of economic matters. Nations do join, however, because they expect benefits to outweigh costs. A variety of benefits are expected by economic integration, such as countervailing power, the benefits of free trade in a limited region, or economics of scale for their industries. These benefits, however, are often not enough to prevent nations from engaging in unilateral action with regard to regulations of MNCs in order to accomplish national goals and objectives.

The political and regulatory climate in which MNCs have to function flow from these goals and objectives. Governments develop policy areas that represent statements of their intentions to achieve national goals and objectives. These policy areas define national interests in terms of specific development problems that need attention. Policy tools are then available to deal with these problem areas in order to attain national goals and objectives. These tools may include monetary and fiscal policies, trade policies, policies related by technology transfer and other national policies, that directly affect a firm's operations.[26] A representative list of these goals, policy areas, and tools is shown in Table 10.2.

The United States has numerous laws and regulations that apply to the operations of MNCs, most of which deal with the operation of MNCs in foreign countries. Some of these laws relate to the competitive conduct of U.S.-based companies in their overseas operations. Others relate to technology transfer and restrict the sale of certain goods to communist countries that are believed to have implications for our national security. Other laws pertain to bribery in foreign countries and impose the standards we adhere to in this country regarding bribery on the operations of U.S. companies in overseas transactions. Still other policies deal with trade and attempts to restrict imports of foreign goods and services and promote exports of our goods and services overseas. Yet other policies deal with the imposition of economic sanctions that restrict trade to accomplish certain political objectives.

Ethics and Multinational Operations

One of the interesting problems that arises in the case of multinational operations in foreign countries is ethical in nature. Every country has its own standards with regard to the conduct of business, and these standards are often in direct conflict with the standards of acceptable conduct in the United States as expressed in custom or in formal legislation. What is a company to do when faced with this kind of conflict? To which set of standards should it adhere in the conduct of its business? These conflicts can arise in almost every area of activity, including anticompetitive conduct, marketing practices, environmental policies, and hiring practices. The multinational can be caught between different standards and expectations regarding ethical behavior.

The issue, from an ethical point of view, is one of cultural relativism. Is ethics relative to each culture such that different cultures have different standards of ethical behavior that are valid and legitimate for that culture? According to cultural relativism, moral beliefs and principles that prescribe acceptable forms of human behavior are closely connected in culture to other cultural characteristics, such as language and political institutions. Anthropological studies show that moral beliefs differ greatly from culture to culture. Thus moral standards are held to be simply a historical product sanctioned by customs that have developed over a long period of time in response to conditions under which the society functions. Moral beliefs and standards are relative to groups and individuals that make up a culture, and consequently, there are no universal norms that apply to all people and cultures.[27]

If cultural relativism is valid, then what is a multinational to do when confronted with conflicts between the host country in which it is doing business and the home country in which it is headquartered with regard to the conduct of business? Shall it adopt a "when in Rome do as the Romans do" policy and adapt its behavior to conform with the standards of each country in which it does business? Or should it adopt a uniform standard for its worldwide operations that it follows in every country with regard to, for instance, hiring practices or environmental policies? Should it attempt to do business throughout the world the way business is conducted in the United States, or should it view this approach as cultural imperialism and adopt a more relativistic approach to its conduct in foreign countries?

This dilemma is nicely illustrated by the foreign-payments controversy that erupted in the early 1970s, when it was discovered that many large corporations made contributions to political campaigns in foreign countries on a rather large scale. These payments were most often contributions to politicians for political campaigns or favors and payments made to agents of government officials to win contracts. These contributions were often referred to by the media "questionable payments" because there was some question about the ethics of them.

Revelation of the extent to which these questionable payments were made abroad to further the interests of American businesses stirred great concern among government officials and other public and private figures in the 1970s and resulted in broad condemnation of these practices. In its report on questionable foreign payments by corporations, the Ad Hoc Committee on Foreign Payments states: "No single issue of corporate behavior has engendered in recent times as much discussion in the United States—both in the private and public arenas—or as much administrative and legislative activity, as payments made abroad by corporations."[28]

The revelations rocked American corporate management, tarnished the image of American private enterprise at home and abroad, and shook foreign government officials, in Belgium, Holland, Honduras, Italy, and Japan, contributing to the decline of confidence in American business leadership. One commentator stated that ". . . the leadership of American big business has never been held in such low regard since perhaps the days of the Great Depression . . . big business is now close to the bottom rung in measures of public trust and confidence."[29]

Foreign payments were defined as "any transfer of money or anything of value made with the aim of influencing the behavior of politicians, political candidates, political parties, or government officials and employees in their legislative, administrative and judicial actions."[30] Lawful payments included contributions to political parties or candidates in countries where this behavior is not illegal as it is in the United States. Many countries allow corporations to make such contributions. Even where such payments were unlawful, it may not be appropriate to call them bribes, as they were not meant to abuse government authority. It is also true that in some cases the initiative for many payments came from foreign officials who demanded payments and may even have threatened sanctions. But in many other instances, payments were made on the initiative of American corporate officials.

Business tried to defend these practices by explaining that these payments were a necessary cost of doing business—that payments of this kind were an accepted practice in other countries. Business was transacted in many of these countries through agents who collected high fees for their services and passed some of this money on to government officials. In other cases, government officials were paid directly to award favors to companies. Customs officials were paid low salaries or wages with the expectation that their income would be supplemented by payments from foreign corporations. Thus it appeared U.S. companies should not impose their ethical standards on other countries. In addition, if companies in this country did adhere to "higher" standards, the business would simply go to a non-U.S. corporation that was not so virtuous, and the United States would be shut out of many foreign markets.

The public's concern about these payments was based, on the one hand, on the belief that such payments corrupted the free-enterprise system, under which the most efficient producers with the best products are supposed to prevail. As one treasury official explained, "When the major criterion in a buyer's choice of a product is the size of a bribe rather than its price and quality and reputation of its producers, the fundamental principles on which a market economy is based are put in jeopardy."[31] Such payments were believed to subvert the laws of supply and demand and result in free markets being replaced by contrived markets.

On the other hand, the public's concern for these payments stemmed from our beliefs about the proper relationships between the economic and political system and the behavior of public officials and private managers. The idea that official power vested by the state in government officials can be bought and sold on the marketplace is repugnant to the U.S. mind. We make a clear separation between business and government, between the commercial and the political; we draw a boundary line between marketable goods and services and nonmarketable political rights, duties, and authority.[32]

Theoretically, the best way to deal with foreign bribery would be for some international body to pass measures regulating this practice. And in fact, resolutions on foreign payments were prepared by the secretariats of both the United Nations and the Organization of American States. But these resolutions were never formulated into an international code of some kind that could be implemented in countries all over the world. Despite pressure from the United States for such a code, the issue faded away on the international level. Many countries believed their national laws were already adequate to deal with the situation. Some countries did not consider such payments to be unethical and were not motivated to eradicate them from the system. If the United States wanted to do something to stop foreign payments, at least for those corporations with U.S. headquarters, it appeared that unilateral action was the only course available.[33]

Eventually, a new public policy measure was passed by Congress and signed into law by the president. The Foreign Corrupt Practices Act (FCPA) of 1977 has been characterized as the most extensive application of federal law to corruption since the passage of the 1933 and 1934 securities acts.[34] The law contains both antibribery provisions and accounting provisions. The act makes it a criminal offense for any U.S. business enterprise—whether or not incorporated or publicly held—to pay money or give anything of value to a foreign official, foreign political party, or any candidate for a foreign political office for purposes of (1) influencing any act or decision of a foreign official, foreign political party, or party official or candidate acting in an official capacity (including a decision to fail to perform official functions); or (2) inducing a foreign official, political party, or party official or candidate to use influence with a foreign government (or instrumentality thereof) to influence any act or decision of such government or instrumentality.[35]

The law also prohibits offering money or anything of value to any person (foreign or domestic) while knowing or having reason to know that all or a portion of such money or thing of value will be used for the purposes just described. The law does not, however, cover facilitating, or "grease," payments that are intended merely to move a matter toward an eventual act or decision not involving discretionary action. (For example, payments or gifts to a customs duties officer of a foreign government to facilitate the passage of material to a facility may not be considered practices in violation of the act.)[36]

In terms of the accounting provisions, the Foreign Corrupt Practices Act consists of two basic requirements: (1) the maintenance of books, records, and accounts that accurately and fairly reflect, in reasonable detail, the transactions and dispositions of the assets (the word transactions encompasses all asset, liability, equity, income and expense accounts); and (2) the development of a system of internal accounting controls that provides reasonable assurance that transactions are executed in accordance with management's general or specific authorization, that transactions are recorded as necessary (a) to permit preparation of financial statements in conformity with generally accepted accounting principles or any other criteria applicable to such statements and (b) to maintain accountability for assets, that access to assets is permitted only in accordance with management's general or specific authorization, and that the recorded accountability for assets is compared with the existing assets at reasonable intervals and appropriate action is taken with respect to any differences.[37]

The passage of this act raises many questions related to public policy that have ethical and moral dimensions. The negative effects of bribery were generally considered to be (1) the warping of economic and social objectives in the country as a result of altered decisions, (2) the upsetting of political processes resulting in undesirable decisions, (3) a potential reduction in national security, and (4) the destabilization of international relations.[38] But who is responsible for dealing with these negative effects? In which country should ethical criteria originate to deal with this issue? And if international action proves impossible to attain, should one country act unilaterally to deal with what is an international issue? Are there universal standards with respect to this issue that should be adhered to regardless of cultural differences?

Some scholars think such universal standards do exist with respect to many business practices and that such guidelines may be found embedded in several multilateral compacts adopted by governments in recent years. Taken as a whole, these normative guidelines are believed to comprise a framework for identifying the essential moral behavior expected of multinationals, regardless of where they are conducting operations. This set of normative prescriptions embodies a moral authority that transcends national boundaries and cultural differences, thereby invoking or manifesting a universal or transcultural standard of corporate ethical behavior that should be adhered to in every country in which a multinational does business.[39]

Between 1948 and 1988, there were several international agreements, compacts, accords, and declarations that were concerned with military security, economic and social development, regulation of capital flows, slavery and genocide, political rights of women, acceptable actions by multinational enterprises, and numerous other issues. These issues reflected the kinds of problems and issues that faced governments in the latter half of the twentieth century. There are six of these compacts that provide the outlines of a transcultural corporate ethic, according to some scholars, and lay down specific guidelines for the formulation of multinational corporate policies and practices.[40] These six compacts include the following:

The United Nations Universal Declaration of Human Rights (1948)

The European Convention on Human Rights (1950)

The Helsinki Final Act (1975)

The OECD Guidelines for Multinational Enterprises (1976)

The International Labor Office Tripartite Declaration of Principles Concerning Multinational Enterprises and Social Policy (1977)

The United Nations Code of Conduct on Transnational Corporations (not yet promulgated but originating in 1972)

The first two compacts emphasize human rights and are normative in focus and intention. Although the principal emphasis of the Helsinki Act is national security, it also contains provisions dealing with human rights and environmental protection. The last three compacts are directed at the practices of multinationals and cover a wide range of issues and problems. Three of the six accords primarily involve European–North American governments, but the other three represent the views of a much wider range of governments.[41] Taken as a whole, these six compacts cover the areas of employment practices and policies, consumer protection, environmental protection, political payments and involvement, and basic human rights and fundamental freedoms. The specific guidelines that can be derived from these compacts expressed in these categories follow.

MULTINATIONAL GUIDELINES

Employment Practices and Policies

MNCs should not contravene the manpower policies of host nations.

MNCs should respect the right of employees to join trade unions and to bargain collectively.

MNCs should develop nondiscriminatory employment policies and promote equal job opportunities.

MNCs should provide equal pay for equal work.

MNCs should give advance notice of changes in operations, especially plant closings, and mitigate the adverse effects of these changes.

MNCs should provide favorable work conditions, limited working hours, holidays with pay, and protection against unemployment.

MNCs should promote job stability and job security, avoiding arbitrary dismissals and providing severance pay for those unemployed.

MNCs should respect local host-country job standards and upgrade the local labor force through training.

MNCs should adopt adequate health and safety standards for employees and grant them the right to know about job-related health hazards.

MNCs should, minimally, pay basic living wages to employees.

MNCs' operations should benefit lower-income groups in the host nations.

MNCs should balance job opportunities, work conditions, job training, and living conditions among migrant workers and host-country nationals.

Consumer Protection

MNCs should respect host-country laws and policies regarding the protection of consumers.

MNCs should safeguard the health and safety of consumers by various disclosures, safe packaging, proper labeling, and accurate advertising.

Environmental Protection

MNCs should respect host-country laws, goals, and priorities concerning protection of the environment.

MNCs should preserve ecological balance, protect the environment, adopt preventive measures to avoid environmental harm, and rehabilitate environments damaged by operations.

MNCs should disclose likely environmental harms and minimize risks of accidents that could cause environmental damage.

MNCs should promote the development of international environmental standards.

MNCs should control specific operations that contribute to pollution of air, water, and soils.

MNCs should develop and use technology that can monitor, protect, and enhance the environment.

Political Payments and Involvement

MNCs should not pay bribes or make improper payments to public officials.

MNCs should avoid improper or illegal involvement or interference in the internal politics of host countries.

MNCs should not interfere in intergovernmental relations.

Basic Human Rights and Fundamental Freedoms

MNCs should respect the rights of all persons to life, liberty, security of person, and privacy.

MNCs should respect the rights of all persons to equal protection of the law, work, choice of job, just and favorable work conditions, and protection against unemployment and discrimination.

MNCs should respect all persons' freedom of thought, conscience, religion, opinion and expression, communication, peaceful assembly and association, and movement and residence within each state.

MNCs should promote a standard of living to support the health and well-being of workers and their families.

MNCs should promote special care and assistance to motherhood and childhood.

Source: William C. Frederick, ''The Moral Authority of MNC Codes,'' Conference on Socio-Economics, Harvard Business School, March 31–April 2, 1989, pp. 6–8.

These guidelines are said to have direct implications for a wide range of specific corporate policies and practices. These include pollution-control efforts, advertising and marketing activities, childcare, minimum wages, hours of work, employee training and education, adequate housing and health care, severance pay, privacy of employees and consumers, safety and health programs, and other policies and practices. These guidelines are believed to have direct applicability to many of the central operations and policies of multinational enterprises and comprise a set of universal standards that cross national boundaries and transcend cultural differences.[42]

For both private and public policy makers, these guidelines could be taken to represent a growing consensus among the world's peoples about what is thought to be morally desirable action by both governments and private enterprises. Although these guidelines do not cover all possible issues that are of concern to people nor are they universally adhered to by all countries, they are said to represent the general outlines of a globally oriented system of normative principles governing corporate behavior.[43] Corporate leaders of multinational institutions would be well advised to take them into account when developing policies and programs for their companies and to think of them as part of the public policy environment, as the internationalization of the world proceeds and grows more complicated.

Global Environmental Problems

The environmental problems that were of concern in the 1970s were global in the sense that every industrial society had some of the same problems. Air pollution existed in every country that had factories and automobiles, and water pollution was a problem in societies that had manufacturing companies with large quantities of waste to dispose of in lakes and rivers. The disposal of solid and hazardous waste began to pose serious problems for many countries as the 1970s drew to a close. But these problems were dealt with largely on a national basis, and even sometimes on a local or regional basis. The United States, for example, passed laws and regulations related to air and water pollution that were largely implemented by states. The problem of waste disposal was also dealt with on a federal level. Every country that became concerned about these types of pollution passed some kind of laws or regulations to deal with the problem.

In the 1980s, however, problems appeared that were truly global in nature in that they affected people all over the world and required international cooperation to deal with effectively. Two problems of this nature that became of concern in the 1980s are global warming and ozone depletion. Global warming is a phenomena involving a warming of the earth's atmosphere because of the buildup of infrared absorbing trace gases such as carbon dioxide, methane, CFCs, and nitrous oxide, all of which have increased dramatically in past decades. The buildup of these gases traps heat that would normally escape into the atmosphere and leads to an increase in the temperature of the earth's atmosphere, the so-called greenhouse effect.

Scientists have documented a 25 percent increase in carbon dioxide in the past 100 years, and some scientists expect the present level to double by the year 2050. Atmospheric methane has doubled during this same time period. Regarding an increase in the temperature of the atmosphere, about half a degree of real warming has taken place with the 1980s appearing to be the warmest decade on record. Specifically, 1988, 1987, and 1981 were the warmest years, in that order. There was a rapid warming of the earth until the end of World War II, a slight cooling through the mid-1970s, and a second period of warming since then.[44] The major culprit seems to be the burning of fossil fuels, particularly coal, which releases carbon dioxide (CO_2) into the atmosphere. Deforestation also adds carbon dioxide to the atmosphere, since as trees and other vegetation absorb CO_2 as they grow and release an equal amount when they are burned or decay naturally.

A doubling of CO_2 or an equivalent increase in other trace gases would warm the earth's average surface temperature by between 3.0 and 5.5 °C, a change that would be unprecedented in human history. Such a change would mean hot, dry summers for many parts of the world and a melting of polar ice caps and glaciers that would cause sea levels to rise several feet by midcentury. Many cities near low-lying coastal areas would be flooded, and people either would have to erect sea walls or move to another location. Temperate zones would move further north, leaving areas that were primary agricultural zones, such as the midsection of the United States, useless as far as growing crops is concerned.

James Hansen, an atmospheric scientist who heads NASA's Goddard Institute, made national headlines when he testified before Congress in 1988 that the greenhouse effect had already begun and was no longer just a theory. During the first 5 months of 1988, he testified, average worldwide temperatures were the highest in all the 130 years of record-keeping. He also stated that he was 99 percent certain that the highest temperatures were not just a natural phenomenon but were the direct result of a buildup of carbon dioxide and other trace gases from manufacturing sources. His findings were based on monthly readings at 2,000 meterological stations around the world.[45]

There are few objections to the theory as a whole, and the scientific community agrees that atmospheric concentration of carbon dioxide and other trace gases is on the rise. Most believe that this increase cannot help but have some effect on the climate.[46] But whether or not the greenhouse effect is already apparent and thus needs to be dealt with now, as Hansen claimed, is a matter of some debate. Some scientists say that the the buildup of carbon dioxide and the warming of the globe is circumstantial. The warming that has been experienced could be due to natural causes and attributable to atmospheric cycles or other naturally occurring factors. The greenhouse theory has not been proven conclusively, and to take action at this time to reduce emissions of carbon dioxide or other trace gases may be spending a good deal of money unnecessarily.[47] Others question the accuracy of the models used to predict future temperature increases related to the continued buildup of carbon dioxide.[48]

To deal with this problem would require international cooperation, as one nation could not solve the problem alone. All nations of the world would have to agree to take steps to limit the release of carbon dioxide and other trace gases to have a major effect on global warming. Thus far, some countries, including the United States, have taken a wait-and-see attitude and continue to study the problem. The problem is that waiting for more direct evidence of the greenhouse effect could involve a commitment to greater climatic change than would be involved if action were taken now to slow the buildup of trace gases. In other words, waiting to solve the problem if the theory proves to be true would cost more money in the future than taking some steps now to cut back on carbon dioxide and other emissions.

Another global environmental problem that recently appeared is the depletion of the ozone layer in the stratosphere. This layer absorbs most of the ultraviolet radiation that comes from the sun, and depletion of this layer would allow higher levels of ultraviolet radiation to reach the surface of the planet. Too much ultraviolet radiation can damage plant and animal cells, cause skin cancer and eye damage to humans, and kill many smaller and more sensitive organisms. Each 1 percent drop in ozone is projected to result in 4 to 6 percent more cases of skin cancer. Increased exposure to radiation also depresses the human immune system, lowering the body's resistance to attacking organisms.[49]

The culprit was identified in 1974 by Sherwood F. Rowland of the University of California at Irvine, who theorized that chlorofluorocarbons (CFCs) eventually drifted up to the stratosphere to react chemically with ozone molecules in a destructive fashion. While many chemicals that are released into the atmoshpere decay in weeks or months, CFCs are so chemically inert that they often can stay intact for a century. This gives them ample time to rise through the atmosphere to reach higher altitudes and do their damage to the ozone layer. Because of the nature of the chemical reactions, a single molecule of chlorine can destroy thousands of ozone molecules. It was also discovered that other compounds, such as methyl chloroform and carbon tetrachloride, assist the CFCs in ozone destruction. And another family of compounds—halons, which contain bromines—were discovered to be a hundred times more efficient than the chlorine compounds at ozone destruction.[50]

When first discovered, CFCs proved to be remarkable compounds. Since they were inert, they did not react with other chemicals with which they were mixed. They were also neither toxic nor flammable at ground level. The number of CFC compounds quickly grew into the dozens; they were used as a universal coolant, refrigerating 75 percent of the food consumed in the United States, as a blowing agent in rigid insulation forms, as an aerosol propellent, as a solvent to remove glue, grease, and soldering residues from microchips and other electronic products, and as a component of foam packaging containers. Between 1958 and 1983, the average production of some forms of CFC compounds grew 13 percent a year; this growth could continue more or less indefinitely.[51]

When Roland developed his theory, the United States banned the use of CFCs as an aerosol propellant, but most of the rest of the world continued to use them for this purpose. No international action was taken until the discovery of the ozone hole over Antarctica. By the spring of 1987, the average ozone concentration over the South Pole was discovered to be down 50 percent, and in isolated spots it had actually disappeared. The report on this discovery also indicated that the ozone layer around the entire globe was eroding much faster than any model had predicted. Ozone depletion was also said to be occurring in a different pattern than had been forecast. While the role of CFCs in ozone depletion had been hotly contested after the theory was formulated in 1974, within a matter of weeks the report's conclusions were widely accepted and the need for immediate policy decisions became apparent to many of the world's leaders.[52]

On September 16, 1987, after years of debate and heated negotiation, the Montreal Protocol on Substances that Deplete the Ozone Layer was signed by 24 countries. By mid-November of 1988, that total had increased to 35 countries. The agreement includes a freeze on CFC production at 1986 levels to be reached by 1989, a 20 percent decrease in production by 1993, and another 30 percent cut by 1998. Halon production was also subject to a freeze based on 1986 levels starting in 1992. In order to obtain this many signatures, the treaty includes extended deadlines for some countries, allowances to accommodate industry restructuring, and loose definitions of products that can legitimately be traded internationally. Developing countries were given a 10-year grace period past the industrial-country deadline, during which CFC production can be increased to meet "basic domestic needs."[53]

The cumulative effect of the loopholes means that even with widespread participation, the protocol's goals of having CFC use by 1998 will not be attained. The agreement will probably only slow the acceleration of ozone depletion unless it is strengthened.[54] Because CFCs take as long as 6 to 7 years to drift up to the ozone layer, there are still many in the pipeline, so to speak, that have yet to do their damage. But this treaty was an unprecedented effort to deal with a global problem and may provide a model for agreements to deal with other global problems. And it led to the largest manufacturer of CFCs, Du Pont, to phase out the production of CFCs regulated under the protocol altogether.[55]

International Dimensions of Antitrust Problems

At first glance, one might think that antitrust problems have no international dimension and that such problems are purely domestic, since antitrust laws are largely concerned with restrictions affecting anticompetitive practices in domestic markets. But on further reflection, there is no reason to expect that antitrust problems end at the water's edge of any industrialized country. Just as corporations collude in fixing prices and allocating territories in domestic markets, it should be expected that they might engage in collusive practices to fix export prices and allocate territories in the international market.

> The antitrust aspects of multinational enterprises are part of the whole multinational picture and are bound up in the relationships of multinational enterprises to the countries in which they operate. Most countries adopt as a principle that the law of competition is of general application and make no distinction between the restrictive business practices of multinational and national enterprises. This, of course, does not mean that any present system of legislation is fully adequate to deal with all the restrictive business practices which are international in scope.[56]

In its report about the impact of multinational corporations on economic development and international relations, the United Nations Department of Economic and Social Affairs pointed out that the extraordinary growth of multinational corporations over the past 20 years and their enormous size and preponderance in key sectors of industry indicate that the multinational enterprises may be only too easily tempted to abuse their dominant position anywhere in the world.[57] The following anticompetitive effects were listed as problems caused by multinational enterprises.

1. Allocation of selling markets among subsidiaries, thus hampering the ability of some of them to export and thereby damaging the host country's foreign trade.
2. Using restrictive patent and know-how license practices to restrict exports, to prevent host country acquisition of the benefits of the technology, and to restrict sources of supply of goods needed to practice the technology licensed.
3. Using prices for the transfer of goods among the enterprise's subsidiaries that are artificial as compared with open market prices, and that may sometimes discriminate against, and sometimes for, given subsidiaries, with alleged anticompetitive consequences.
4. Making acquisitions and entering into joint ventures that may unbalance and sometimes threaten the survival of host country industries and markets.[58]

Trade restrictions imposed by multinational corporations on the international level are often referred to in the literature as international restrictive business practices or international restraints of trade. For a country to be able to control such trade restrictions in an equitable manner, it may be necessary for that country to claim, or appear to claim, what is known as "extraterritorial jurisdiction." According to Boaz Barack, "jurisdiction is a measure of the limits within which one State may prescribe and enforce rules of law without violating or infringing the sovereignty of another State."[59] The term "extraterritorial jurisdiction" implies that the antitrust rules of the country "reach out to, or bring under the purview of these rules, enterprises situated abroad and/or behavior that occurred outside the territory."[60]

Once jurisdiction has been asserted by a country, some types of legal conflicts and issues of extraterritorial enforcement are bound to arise. The most obvious types of legal conflicts are claims of jurisdiction by a country that are contested by other countries. Such conflicts result in overlapping or concurrent jurisdiction of two or more countries and may place multinational corporations in a situation of double jeopardy. In fact, the most frequent problem in international markets is the inconsistency of the antitrust laws between countries claiming jurisdiction, which raises questions of priority or paramount interest.[61] In addressing the issue of antitrust laws and divergencies in policies and interests between nations, Kingman Brewster has listed the following sources of conflict:

> first, we mention differences in legal technique . . . ; next the basic differences in national attitude and policies toward the cartel question; third, clashes of economic interest which may be fostered by antitrust enforcement; fourth, and perhaps most important, seeds of resentment against our alleged intrusion into the domestic affairs of other countries.[62]

Even when a state has jurisdiction to prescribe rules, such jurisdiction does not give it the right to engage in extraterritorial enforcement of rules in the territory of another state. Such enforcement is generally regarded, with certain exceptions in limited situations, a violation of international law unless the territorial state consents to enforcement activities. These limits apply to both the use of physical force in the territory of another state as well as the peaceful performance of acts of authority.[63]

American antitrust laws, for example, as well as the commerce clause of the U.S. Constitution, make specific reference to the trade or commerce with foreign nations as well as among the several states. Thus they may be interpreted broadly in defining the scope of "foreign commerce" as they have been in relation to the meaning of "interstate commerce." The American antitrust statutes regulating foreign commerce could in theory have an extraterritorial reach to cover the activities of American multinationals in foreign countries.

This extraterritorial scope, particularly if pushed to its outer limits, is a very controversial issue. The extraterritorial scope is most doubtful when the restraints concerned are carried out solely in foreign markets. Restraints of trade on the part of multinationals are less controversial if they are interwoven with domestic conduct. In practice, the Justice Department is generally not interested in application of American antitrust laws to activities in foreign markets, either by foreign or U.S. firms, where U.S. interests are not substantially affected. Overzealous enforcement could hurt American business abroad, and the Justice Department has declared that it does not seek to push matters to the extremes. The approach of the U.S. Antitrust Division has been formally stated as follows.

U.S. law in general, and the U.S. antitrust laws in particular, are not limited to transactions which take place within our borders. When foreign transactions have a substantial and foreseeable effect on U.S. commerce, they are subject to U.S. law regardless of where they take place . . . to use the Sherman Act to restrain or punish an overseas conspiracy whose clear purpose and effect is to restrain significant commerce in the U.S. market is both appropriate and necessary to effective U.S. enforcement.[64]

A new bill, the Foreign Trade Antitrust Improvements Act of 1986, was introduced in an attempt to clarify the applicability of U.S. antitrust laws overseas. This bill includes six factors for courts to consider in deciding whether to exercise jurisdiction over a foreign corporation. These include (1) the relative significance, to the violation alleged, of conduct within the United States as compared to conduct abroad; (2) the nationality of the parties and the principal place of business of corporations; (3) the presence or absence of a purpose to affect U.S. consumers or competitors; (4) the relative significance and foreseeability of the effects of the conduct on the United States as compared with the effects abroad; (5) the existence of reasonable expectations that would be furthered or defeated by the action; and (6) the degree of conflict with foreign law.

In addition to the legal conflicts that are likely to occur as a result of the extraterritorial application of antitrust laws, economic conflicts over economies of scale and technology transfer are also likely to occur. Such conflicts do not necessarily render domestic antitrust laws completely ineffectual in solving international disturbances caused by restrictive business practices. But they do limit the effectiveness of such laws in regulating restrictive business practices that have international ramifications and are often a cause of concern to the international community of nations.

These conflicts, and the extraordinary growth of multinational corporations, have clearly emphasized the need for some types of international cooperation on public policy matters to combat business practices that restrain trade between and among nations. Accordingly, various international organizations have considered the establishment of international mechanisms for the control of international restrictive business practices and for the avoidance and settlement of conflicts between nations when they arise. A wide range of proposals for possible remedies of international antitrust problems have been mentioned by scholars and policymakers in international committees. These include (1) harmonization of existing laws, (2) the creation of new procedures to obtain more information about multinational corporations at the national and international level, (3) the development of international consultation and conciliation and arbitration procedures, (4) the formulation of a voluntary code of good ethical conduct and standards of behavior or guidelines for enterprises and governments, and (5) the creation of a binding international antitrust law and an international agency with powers of enforcement.[65]

International Public Affairs

As foreign trade and direct foreign investment by U.S. companies in overseas countries grows, the role of international public affairs also becomes more significant. Because of the complexity of the environments faced by multinationals in overseas markets, U.S. companies need to take a long-term view of the business opportunities abroad and develop public affairs programs to influence the local, national, and regional social, political, and economic environments. Multinational companies need to cultivate markets and adjust products and services to the needs and tastes of foreign consumers and to adapt to the priorities and values of host governments. Domestic public affairs serves as a bridge between the corporation and the external environment. This is basically the same function that should be performed by international public affairs (Exhibit 10.1).

The basic components of an international public affairs program, according to one commentator, include the collection of social, political, and economic information and the analysis and forecasting of issues that are perceived to be important by a country's leadership. The forecasting task includes political and economic risk evaluation, identification of public policy issues that would be material to a company's activities in a host country, and ways in which issues are likely to affect a company's performance and operations. The assessment and management of risk in foreign environments requires skills that are often lacking in executives whose traditional business acumen was honed in the United States, and thus the public affairs function can perform a valuable service to the company by doing this assessment.[66]

Another important component of an international public affairs program is corporate strategy and policy development. This component includes benefit-cost analysis of the various policy options that are available to manage potential social, political, and economic risks, and making appropriate changes in corporate strategy as a result of this analysis. The company should also plan to reduce such risks in the future. Action programs that can be developed by the public affairs function include community action and government relations programs with participation in international, national, regional, and local organizations and programs, both public and private.[67]

The differences between domestic and international public affairs need to be addressed. The international environment is manifestly more complex and multifaceted than that of any single country, making the potential for system overload a real problem. Issues identification is more complex as MNCs face different sets of stakeholders in different countries. There are also differences with respect to corporate organizational problems. There is a tendency in many companies to leave all international responsibilities to the subsidiaries or regional offices located overseas with little or no role for public affairs. And finally, there are differences in how the international public affairs programs are focused. Each county's government is different and political power is located in different places. Thus each country needs to be analyzed independently to determine the critical junctures and influences in the development of issues and public policies that will affect the company. This complicates the process enormously.[68]

There are three different levels at which issues can arise in the international environment: (1) global issues that are often played out at the international organization

EXHIBIT 10.1

Elements of an International Public Affairs Program

Environmental assessment/issue identification and management
- Identify, track, and assess issues and trends
- Achieve systematic internal issues awareness and coordination
- Assess political, social, and cultural elements of risk in projects, products, investments, and operations
- Issue research and analysis
- Emerging issue forecasting

Government relations activities
- Washington, D.C.
- Foreign-country level
- Regional level: EEC, OECD, ASEAN, etc.
- International level: UN, ILO, WHO, WIPO, etc.

Community action/involvement
- Community outreach
- Assess company impact on communities where located
- Philanthropy
- Corporate social responsibility activities
- Development activities
- Political involvement

Corporate public affairs training and constituency development
- Public affairs staff development
- Relations with line managers and other staff groups
- Employee relations
- Shareholder relations
- Media relations
- Academic relations
- Interest group relations
- External constituency group relations, e.g., suppliers

Corporate policy and strategy development
- External factor assessment in strategy planning and management decision-making
- Effect change in corporate strategy and policy to minimize risk and/or maximize opportunity
- Cost/benefit analyses of policy options based on external factors
- Assess impact/compliance with codes of conduct and company ethical standards

Source: Douglas Bergner, "International Public Affairs: A Preliminary Report by a PAC Task Force," *Perspectives,* Public Affairs Council, Washington, D.C., April 1983, p. 3.

level, (2) regional issues that are distinct to a particular area of the world, and (3) country-specific issues. These issues will have differing impacts on the company. Some issues will involve only one division or strategic business unit; others will cut across divisions; a third type will affect the company's competitive environment and/or the entire industry; and some will relate to the company's economic environment.[69]

A survey conducted by the Public Affairs Council in 1984 of selected multinational firms with Washington offices found that 78 percent of the respondents conducted varying amounts of international public affairs from their Washington offices. More public affairs activities were being conducted by Washington-based staff and more functional responsibility for international public affairs was being located in the Washington office. Although it was still a relatively low-profile activity, there had been continued development of the Washington-based international public affairs function for 4 years. Internal functions of international public affairs included issues analysis, forecasting, planning, relations with overseas executives, political risk analysis, international philanthropy, community relations, and the development of international codes of conduct.[70]

Questions for Discussion

1. What is a multinational corporation? What role do multinationals play in the international economy? What social and political impacts do they have? What public issues arise with respect to multinational corporations?

2. What role does the United Nations play in terms of regulating multinational corporations? What advantages does it have over regional organizations? What are some of the inherent limitations that are evident in actions taken by the United Nations?

3. What are the major international trade organizations? What role do they play in resolving public policy problems? Are regional economic associations an important aspect of the international regulatory environment? In what respects?

4. What were foreign payments and for what purposes were they made? Who received these payments and how were they made? Were they really necessary to do business in foreign countries?

5. How did business attempt to defend these payments? Was this defense justified? Why didn't the public accept the "necessity" of such payments? What was basis for public concern? What was the outcome of the controversy?

6. What were the ethical issues raised by the foreign payments controversy? Did business ignore these issues? What kind of a control system could be set up to prevent such payments from being made in the future?

7. Is the Foreign Corrupt Practices Act a good law in your opinion? In what respects? Has it had an adverse impact on business? What problems exist with the law? Should it be amended? If so, what aspects of the law would change?

8. Are there universal ethical principles that apply to the conduct of business in all countries? Or do you want to develop an argument to defend cultural relativism? What do you think of the principles listed in the chapter that came from several international agreements? What would you add or delete from this list of principles?

9. What are global environmental problems and how do they differ from the more traditional environmental problems of air and water pollution? What needs to be done about them in your opinion? What does the best available evidence suggest? Are current policies adequate to protect the environment on an international scale?

10. Why did the issue of ozone depletion suddenly change from a theory that was hotly debated to essentially an accepted fact that demanded action on an international level? What was the precipitating event that caused this change? Is the same thing likely to happen with respect to global warming?

11. What antitrust problems exist on the international level? How are these problems different from domestic antitrust problems? Can these antitrust problems be resolved successfully by sovereign nations acting more or less unilaterally? Or must they be addressed by some international organization?

12. Define the concept of extraterritorial jurisdiction. What legal and political problems arise from the application of this concept? What is the position of the United States government

with regard to the application of U.S. antitrust laws to overseas activities of U.S.-based multinationals?

13. How do international public affairs differ from domestic public affairs? Is the international function more complicated? In what ways? What role will international public affairs be likely to play in the future as far as corporations are concerned?

14. What is the future going to be like for multinational corporations? Are they likely to be regulated more stringently? If so, in what respects? What effect will the changes taking place in Eastern Europe and the Soviet Union have on multinationals and international business? How can multinationals respond to these changes?

Case: Nestlé Corporation

Nestlé, a large international conglomerate, was attacked by Ralph Nader, Dr. Benjamin Spock, Cesar Chavez, Gloria Steinem, and such groups as the United Auto Workers, The National Council of Churches, the World Health Organization, the Infant Formula Action Coalition (INFACT), the Interfaith Center for Corporate Responsibility (ICCR), and a host of other church, health, and international agencies. These individuals and groups claimed that rising infant mortality rate in Third World nations was due to the aggressive sales promotions of the infant formula companies, who influenced women to switch from traditional breast-feeding methods to the more "modern" idea of bottle-feeding. Their primary target was the Nestlé Company of Switzerland, which accounted for 50 percent of Third World sales of infant formula. The decade-long debate was labeled by the press as "The Infant Formula Controversy" and "The Bottle-Baby Battle." The issues, however, were not as simple as mere "misguided propaganda" over infant formula but rather were a complex interplay of social, political, economic, and cultural factors.

Infant formula is a specially prepared food based on cow's milk and designed for infants under 6 months in age. It is scientifically formulated to approximate the most nearly perfect of foods, human breast milk.[1] A decline in breast-feeding throughout the developing world was associated with the increased availability of infant formula and modern baby bottles. The international manufacturers of infant foods and formulas mounted vigorous marketing campaigns in many of these countries, making their products available in ever-expanding areas. Because of this effort, many of them were accused of unfair marketing practices by consumer groups and health professionals.

The declining birth rate in industrialized countries, which began in the 1960s, caused all the infant-formula companies concern. The popularity of formula-feeding had greatly expanded their sales during and after World War II, but in the 1960s their sales began to diminish as the market became saturated. They viewed developing and underdeveloped countries as potential sources of new markets to restore declining sales. A large portion of the populations of many of these countries suffered from malnutrition, and this, too, encouraged the manufacturers to look to the Third World to revive sales of infant formula.

As reports began to appear indicating that women in the Third World were beginning to abandon breast-feeding, many health professionals became alarmed because of the widespread lack of basic nutritional knowledge and adequate sanitation in the Third World, two conditions that were necessary in order to use infant formula safely. It was estimated that only 29 percent of the rural areas and 72 percent of the urban areas in the Third World had potable water for mixing formula or for sanitizing feeding equipment.[2] The lack of sanitation facilities and the absence of clean water could be remedied only with further development.

The lack of education in underdeveloped countries often meant that a mother did not properly mix a formula or did not follow correct sanitary procedures. Sometimes a poor family would also stretch the formula by adding additional water. Although these practices were not the manufacturer's fault, when consumers did not have even a basic understanding of sanitation and nutrition and the company was aware of this, it would seem it should bear some responsibility to correct these conditions so its product could be used safely and would provide adequate nutrition for children.

Third World countries presented other problems for the infant formula companies, including the relatively high cost of infant formula compared to with the average earnings and the frequent lack of refrigeration. When questioned about the high cost of their product to Third World consumers, some major manufacturers argued that infant formula was a relatively free good. Although the money required to purchase equipment and formula to feed an infant for 6 months approximately equaled the per capita income of a person in one of these countries, the companies reasoned that bottle-feeding allowed the mother to work, so that the added cost was offset by additional income.[3]

Despite these problems, the infant-formula companies mounted aggressive marketing and promotional campaigns in Third World countries. These marketing and promotional practices included extensive mass-media advertising, large quantities of free promotional samples to doctors and maternity wards, gifts of equipment, trips, and conferences for medical personnel, and the use of company representatives called "milk nurses," whose jobs entailed promoting and explaining formula feeding to new mothers. Billboards and posters prominently displayed pictures of fat, rosy-cheeked babies, subtly suggesting that the healthiest babies were formula-fed.

As controversy over the marketing of infant formula in Third World countries mounted, manufacturers responded to these concerns in various ways. In 1972 Abbott Laboratories adopted a policy that limited promotion of its product to health professionals and states that where no health-care counseling is available, their product was inappropriate. Other firms suspended marketing of formula in areas where safe potable water or sanitation facilities did not exist. This policy resulted in a careful and costly segmentation of the Third World market as well as the necessity of foregoing many growth opportunities.[4]

By 1977 an organization called The Infant Formula Action Coalition (INFACT) had been formed in Minneapolis to address the problem. This organization attempted to create public awareness and economic pressure through a nationwide boycott of all Nestlé products. Nestlé was chosen because it had the largest share of the world market and also because it was based in Switzerland and could not be pressured through shareholder resolutions in the United States. The boycott, which had the support of the National Council of Churches, had little effect on Nestlé's business, but the antiformula movement did get the attention of some very powerful groups.

To combat the negative image that was developing around the world and to ascertain exactly what its responsibility was, Nestlé initiated the formation of the International Council of Infant Food Industries (ICIFI), a coalition of formula makers, to develop self-regulatory controls for the industry. Abbott Laboratories set up an office to investigate bottle-feeding practices, Borden curtailed all promotional activity of its Klim formula in Third World countries, Abbott Laboratories took its milk nurses out of white uniforms, and Bristol Meyers met with church groups to disclaim responsibility for misuse of its products and issued a report of its promotional activities.

In 1977 Nestlé also initiated a public relations campaign to describe to church and community leaders its response to the issue. They followed this with an announcement in 1978 that they had terminated their advertising and promotion practices for the sale of infant formula to the Third World. Despite Nestlé's initial reluctance to go along with an International Code of Breast-Feeding and Infant-Formula Marketing adopted by the World Health Organization in 1981, in March 1982 the company announced that it would observe the code. In a further step, Nestlé set up the Infant Formula Audit Commission, composed of doctors, scientists, and church people under the chairship of former Secretary of State, Edmund Muskie, to monitor its own conduct.

In general, the industry—through ICIFI recommendations and the World Health Organization—started to "demarket" its products. Demarketing means that efforts to sell a product are reduced or stopped completely because of risks to health or safety; it is usually initiated because of management decisions, public pressure, or government regulation. Demarketing is ordinarily carried out in declining markets or markets in which a company can no longer compete successfully, but in the developing countries, demarketing decisions were made for growing markets and in contrary to usual business practice.[5]

In January 1984, the groups that had criticized Nestlé's marketing of infant formula in Third World countries finally called off the boycott of Nestlé's products that had been instituted earlier. In negotiations with the Nestlé International Boycott Committee, the company agreed to observe the World Health Organization's marketing code for infant formula.[6] Thus ended a long and bitter controversy that involved numerous stakeholder groups and that received comprehensive coverage in the press. Perhaps Nestlé learned that public opinion and pressure is not to be ignored in setting its policies.

Case Notes

1. James E. Post and Edward Baer, "Demarketing Infant Formula Consumer Products in the Developing World," *Journal of Contemporary Business*, Vol. 7, No. 4, p. 18.

2. Ibid., p. 29.

3. Ibid., p. 19.

4. David O. Cox, "The Infant Formula Issue: A Case Study," in *Business Environment/ Public Policy: The Field and Its Future, 1981 Conference Papers*, ed. by Edwin M. Epstein and Lee E. Preston (St. Louis, Mo.: American Assembly of Collegiate Schools of Business, 1982), p. 126–31.

5. Post and Baer, "Demarketing Infant Formula," p. 23.

6. "Nestlé Alters Policy on Infant Formula: Boycott Called Off," *Dallas Times Herald*, January 26, 1984, p. A-8.

Chapter Notes

1. H. Hal Mason and Robert S. Spich, *Management: An International Perspective* (Homewood., Ill.: Irwin, 1987), p. 2.

2. Ibid., p. 9.

3. David H. Blake and Robert S. Walters, *The Politics of Global Economic Relations* (Englewood Cliffs, N.J.: Prentice-Hall, 1983), p. 83. See also William J. Holstein, "The Stateless Corporation," *Business Week*, May 14, 1990, pp. 98–105.

4. Thomas J. Biersteker, *Distortion or Development? Contending Perspectives on the Multinational Corporations* (Cambridge, Mass.: MIT Press, 1981), p. xii.

5. The term Transnational Corporation (TNC) is often used to refer to this same entity. See Kwamena

Acquaah, *International Regulation of Transnational Corporations: The New Reality* (New York: Praeger, 1986), p. 48.

6. Richard McKenzie, *The Global Economy and Government Power* (St. Louis Mo.: Washington University Center for the Study of American Business, 1989), Mo.: p. 4.

7. Ibid., p. 8.

8. See William J. Holstein, Japan's Clout in the U.S.,'' *Business Week,* July 11, 1988, pp. 64–66.

9. Acquaah, *International Regulation,* p. 44. As an indication of the power of MNCs, it is useful to note that in 1984, only 25 nations had gross national products greater than the total sales of Exxon, the world's largest MNC, and the total sales of Exxon surpassed the sum of the GNPs of 44 African countries. Ball and McCulloch, *International Business,* p. 5.

10. Mason and Spich, *Management,* p. 18.

11. U.S. Department of Commerce, Domestic and International Business Administration, *The Multinational Corporation: Studies on U.S. Foreign Investment,* Vol. 2 (Washington, D.C.: U.S. Government Printing Office, 1973), pp. 1–2.

12. Douglas E. Rosenthal and William M. Knighton, *National Laws and International Commerce: The Problem of Extraterritoriality* (Boston: Routledge & Kegan Paul Ltd., 1982), p. 1.

13. Acquaah, *International Regulation,* p. xii.

14. Jack N. Behrman, *Essays on Ethics in Business and the Professions* (Englewood Cliffs, N.J.: Prentice Hall, 1988), p. 59–60.

15. Ibid., p. 240.

16. Ibid., p. 111.

17. Ibid., p. 114.

18. Juliana Geran Pilon, ''The Centre On Transnational Corporations: How The U.N. Injures Poor Nations,'' *The Heritage Foundation Backgrounder,* No. 608, October, 1987, pp. 3, 10.

19. Vern Terpstra, *International Marketing,* 2d ed. (Hinsdale, Ill.: Dryden, 1978). p. 36.

20. Ibid., p. 37.

21. Acquaah, *International Regulation,* pp. 139–142.

22. U.S. Chamber of Commerce, ''Europe 1992,'' June 1989, p. 2.

23. Ibid., pp. 1, 4.

24. Ibid., p. 3. See also ''World Business: The Uncommon Market,'' *Wall Street Journal,* September 22, 1989, pp. R1–R9.

25. Ball and McCulloch, *International Business,* p. 511.

26. Mason and Spich, *Management,* pp. 59–60.

27. Tom L. Beauchamp, *Philosophical Ethics: An Introduction to Moral Philosophy* (New York: McGraw-Hill, 1982), pp. 34–35.

28. Ad Hoc Committee on Foreign Payments of the Association of the Bar of the City of New York, ''Report on Questionable Foreign Payments by Corporations: The Problem and Approaches to a Solution,'' March 14, 1977, p. 1.

29. Nicholas Wolfson, U.S. Senate, Committee on Banking, Housing and Urban Affairs, *Foreign Corrupt Practices and Domestic and Foreign Investment Disclosure:* Hearing on S. 305, 95th Congress, 1st Session, March 16, 1977, p. 215.

30. Neil H. Jacoby, Peter Nehemkis, and Richard Eells, *Bribery and Extortion in World Business* (New York: Macmillan, 1977), p. 86.

31. Gordon Adams and Sherri Zann Rosenthal, *The Invisible Hand: Questionable Corporate Payments Overseas* (New York: The Council on Economic Priorities, 1976), p. 3.

32. Jacoby, Nehemkis, and Eells, *Bribery and Extortion,* p. 127.

33. Berhman, *Essays on Ethics,* p. 289.

34. American Bar Association, Committee on Corporate Law and Accounting, ''A Guide to the New Section 13(b)(2) Accounting Requirements of the Securities Exchange Act of 1934 (Section 102 of the Foreign Corrupt practices Act of 1977),'' *The Business Lawyer,* Vol. 34, No. 1 (November 1978), p. 308.

35. *An Analysis of the Foreign Corrupt Practices Act of 1977* (Chicago: Arthur Andersen and Co., 1978), p. 4.

36. Ibid.

37. Ibid., pp. 8–9.

38. Berhman, *Essays on Ethics,* p. 290.

39. William C. Frederick, ''The Moral Authority of MNC Codes,'' p. 2.

40. Ibid., p. 3.

41. Ibid., p. 4.

42. Ibid., p. 8.

43. Ibid., p. 24.

44. Stephen H. Schneider, "The Changing Climate," *Scientific American,* September 1989, p. 72.

45. David Brand, "Is the Earth Warming Up?" *Time,* July 4, 1988, p. 18.

46. Bill McKibben, *The End of Nature* (New York: Random House, 1989), p. 29.

47. See Carolyn Lochhead, "The Alarming Price Tag on Greenhouse Legislation," *Insight,* April 16, 1990, pp. 10–13.

48. Carolyn Lochhead, "Global Warming Forecasts May Be Built on Hot Air," *Insight,* April 16, 1990, pp. 14–18.

49. Cynthia Pollock Shea, "Protecting the Ozone Layer," *State of the World 1989* (New York: Norton, 1989), p. 82.

50. McKibben, *The End of Nature,* pp. 39–40.

51. Ibid., p. 39.

52. Shea, "Protecting the Ozone Layer," p. 81.

53. Ibid., pp. 93–94.

54. Ibid., p. 94.

55. Laurie Hays, "Du Pont Plans to Complete Phase-Out Of Chlorofluorocarbons by Year 2000," *Wall Street Journal,* July 29, 1988, p. 16.

56. Wilbur L. Fugate, "Antitrust Jurisdiction and Foreign Sovereignty," *Virginia Law Review,* Vol. 49 (June 1963), p. 925.

57. United Nations Department of Economic and Social Affairs, *The Impact of Multinational Corporations on Development and on International Relations,* Report of Group of Eminent Persons 83-86 UN Doc. E/5500/Rev. 1 St/ESA/6 (1974).

58. Ibid., as reported in Boaz Barack, *The Application of the Competition Rules (Antitrust Law) of the European Economic Community (The Netherlands: Kluwer-Deventer, 1981), p. 418.*

59. Barack, *Application of Competition Rules,* p. 13.

60. Ibid., p. 2.

61. Ibid.

62. Kingman Brewster, *Antitrust and American Business Abroad,* 1958, p. 39., as quoted in Barack, Competition Rules, p. 3.

63. Barack, *Application of Competition Rules,* p. 219.

64. Antitrust Division, U.S. Dept. of Justice, *Antitrust Guide for International Operations* 6-7 (1977), as quoted in Barack, *Competition Rules,* p. 360.

65. See Barack, *Application of Competition Rules,* pp. 419–420.

66. Robert A. Kilmarx, "International Public Affairs," *The Public Affairs Handbook,* Joseph S. Nagelschmidt, ed. (New York: AMACOM, 1982), p. 178.

67. Ibid.

68. Douglas Bergner, "International Public Affairs: A Preliminary Report by a PAC Task Force," *Perspectives,* April, 1983, p. 2.

69. Douglas Bergner, "Managing International Issues ," *Perspectives,* July, 1982, p. 2.

70. Douglas Bergner, "Washington-Based International Public Affairs: A Growing Corporate Function," *Perspectives,* July, 1984, pp. 1–4.

Suggested Reading

ACQUAAH, KWAMENA. *International Regulation of Transnational Corporations.* New York: Praeger, 1986.

ADAMS, GORDON, AND SHERRI ZANN ROSENTHAL. *The Invisible Hand: Questionable Corporate Payments Overseas.* New York: The Council on Economic Priorities, 1976.

BALL, DONALD A., AND WENDELL H. MCGULLOCH, JR. *International Business: Introduction and Essentials,* 2d ed. Plano, Tex.: Business Publications, 1985.

BASCHE, JAMES R., JR. *Unusual Foreign Payments: A Survey of the Policies and Practices of U.S. Companies.* New York: The Conference Board, 1976.

BIERSTEKER, THOMAS J. *Distortion or Development? Contending Perspectives on the Multinational Corporations.* Cambridge, Mass.: MIT Press, 1981.

BLAKE, DAVID H., AND ROBERT S. WALTERS. *The Politics of Global Economic Relations,* 2d ed. Englewood Cliffs, N.J.: Prentice Hall, 1983.

BLANK, STEPHEN, ET AL. *Assessing the Political Environment: An Emerging Function in International Companies.* New York: The Conference Board, 1980.

BREWER, THOMAS L., ed. *Political Risks in International Business: New Directions for Research, Management, and Public Policy.* New York: Praeger, 1985.

DANIELS, JOHN D., AND LEE H. RADEBAUGH. *International Business: Environments and Operations,* 4th ed. Reading, Mass.: Addison-Wesley, 1986.

DIXON, C. J., ET AL, eds. *Multinational Corporations and the Third World.* New York: Westview, 1986.

DONALDSON, THOMAS. *The Ethics of International Business.* New York: Oxford, 1989.

DOZ, YVES L. *Multinational Strategic Management.* New York: Pergamon, 1986.

DOZ, YVES L., AND C. K. PRAHALAD. *The Multinational Mission.* New York: Free Press, 1987.

FAYERWEATHER, JOHN. *International Business Strategy and Administration,* 2d ed. Cambridge, Mass.: Ballinger, 1982.

FRANK, ISIAH. *Foreign Enterprise in Developing Countries.* Baltimore: Johns-Hopkins University Press, 1980.

GARLAND, JOHN, AND RICHARD N. FARMER. *International Dimensions of Business Policy and Strategy.* Boston: Kent, 1986.

GLADWIN, THOMAS M., AND INGO WALTER. *Multinationals Under Fire: Lessons in Management of Conflict.* New York: John Wiley, 1980.

GREANIAS, GEORGE C., AND DUANE WINDSOR. *The Foreign Corrupt Practices Act.* Lexington, Mass.: Lexington Books, 1982.

HOFFMAN, W. M., ET AL., eds. *Ethics and the Multinational Enterprise.* Washington, D.C.: University Press of America, 1985.

INTERNATIONAL LABOR OFFICE. *Multinational Enterprises and Social Policy.* Geneva: International Labor Office, 1980.

JACOBY, NEIL H., PETER NEHEMKIS, AND RICHARD EELLS. *Bribery and Extortion in World Business.* New York: Macmillan, 1977.

KENNEDY, TOM, AND CHARLES E. SIMON. *An Examination of Questionable Payments and Practices.* New York: Praeger, 1978.

KLINE, JOHN M. *International Codes and Multinational Business: Setting Guidelines for International Business Operations.* New York: Quorum, 1985.

KOBRIN, STEPHEN J. *Managing Political Risk Assessment: Strategic Response to Environmental Change.* Berkeley: University of California Press, 1982.

MASON, HAL R., AND ROBERT S. SPICH. *Management: An International Perspective.* Homewood, Ill.: Irwin, 1987.

MORAN, THEODORE H., ed. *Multinational Corporations: The Political Economy of Foreign Direct Investments.* Lexington, Mass.: D.C. Heath, 1985.

PERLMUTTER, H. V., T. SAGAFI-NEJAD, AND R. W. MOXON. *Controlling International Technology Transfer.* New York: Pergamon, 1981.

POYNTER, THOMAS A. *Multinational Enterprises and Government Intervention.* New York: St. Martin, 1985.

ROBINSON, JOHN. *Multinational Corporations and Political Control.* New York: St. Martin, 1983.

ROBINSON, RICHARD D. *Internationalization of Business: An Introduction.* Hinsdale, Ill.: Dryden, 1984.

Rosenthal, Douglas E., and William M. Knighton. *National Laws and International Commerce: The Problem of Extraterritoriality.* London: Routledge & Kegan Paul Ltd., 1982.

Rutenberg, David. *Multinational Management.* Boston: Little, Brown, 1982.

Terpstra, Vern, and Kenneth David. *The Cultural Environment of International-Business,* 2d ed. Cincinnati: South-Western, 1985.

United Nations Centre on Transnational Corporations. *Transnational Corporations in World Development: Third Survey.* New York: United Nations, 1983.

Index

E

Eastern Airlines, 36, 45
Economic concentration. *See* Concentration
Economic power, 53, 73
Economic Recovery Tax Act of 1981, 140
Economies of scale, 63, 72–73
Eli Lilly & Company, 242
Emergency Planning and Community Right-to-Know Act, 282
Emergency temporary standard, 193
Emotional stress, 209
Employees:
  and corporate governance, 95–97
  responsibilities and rights, 197
Employee Stock Ownership Plans, 96–97
Employers responsibilities and rights, 196–97
Employment, 34
Employment of the disadvantaged, 128–29
Enterprise zones, 136–37
Entitlement programs, 137–39
Environmental consciousness, 257–58
Environmental Defense Fund, 282
Environmental degradation, 255
Environmental movements, 257–58
Environmental Protection Agency, 22, 45, 210
  and air pollution, 267–71
  description, 260–62
  hazardous waste disposal, 284–90
  pesticides, 278–80
  responsibilities, 262
  toxic substances, 280–83
  and water pollution, 272–78
Environmental Quality Report, 259–60
Equal employment opportunity:
  administrative structure, 157–59
  and African Americans, 178–79
  executive orders, 155–56
  laws, 152–57
  problems, 160–70
  results, 175–79
  and women, 170–77
Equal Employment Opportunity Act, 154
Equal Employment Opportunity Commission, 153–54, 157–59, 172, 174–75
Equality before the law, 151
Equal opportunity, 151
Equal Pay Act, 155, 157, 170
Equal Rights Amendment, 153, 156–57
Ethics and Multinationals, 309–14

European Economic Community, 306–7
European Free Trade Association, 306
Exclusive dealing, 56
Executive orders, 43, 155
Existing Chemicals Program, 281
Externalities, 18, 256
Extraterritorial jurisdiction, 318–19
Exxon Valdez, 292–94

F

Fair competition, 58
Fair Employment Practice Acts, 153
Fair Employment Practice Committee, 153
Fair Labor Standards Act, 155
Fair Packaging and Labeling Act, 223
Farm workers, 279
Federal Aviation Administration, 45
Federal chartering:
  arguments for, 107
  proposals, 108
Federal Coal Mine Health and Safety Act, 189–90
Federal Communications Commission, 21, 35, 39–40
Federal Insecticide, Fungicide, and Rodenticide Act, 279
Federal Meat Inspection Act, 220
Federal Metal and Nonmetallic Safety Act, 190
Federal Paperwork Study, 30
Federal Power Commission, 21
Federal Register, 6, 29–30, 193
Federal Reserve System, 38–39
Federal Trade Commission, 21–22, 40, 59–60, 62–64, 224–28
Federal Trade Commission Act, 56, 220
Federal Water Pollution Control Act Amendments, 274
Fellow servant doctrine, 188
Film Recovery Systems, 205–6
Financial Accounting Standards Board, 100–101
Financial industry, 38–39
Food additives, 236–37
Food and Drug Administration, 230–32, 236–43, 248–49, 262
Food, Drug, and Cosmetics Act, 45, 222–30, 236–37, 249
Food inspection system, 232
Food safety, 230–32, 236–38
Food stamps, 138, 140
Ford Motor Company, 47–48, 235

Foreign Corrupt Practices Act, 311–12
Foreign ownership, 98–99
Foreign payments:
  classification, 309–10
  defense, 310–11
  definition, 310
  disclosure, 309–10
  public concern, 310
Foreign Trade Antitrust Improvements Act, 319
Freeman, R. Edward, 85
FTC v. *Kellogg et al.*, 62
FTC v. *The Sperry and Hutchinson Company*, 56
Fullilove v. *Klutznick*, 133
Funeral providers, 227

G

Galbraith, John Kenneth, 74, 96
General Accounting Office, 203, 242
General Agreement on Tariffs and Trade, 305
General Electric, 65
General Foods, 65
General Motors Corporation, 47, 111–12, 223, 235
Generic drugs, 242–43
Gesell, Gerhard A., 162–63
Glass ceiling, 177
Glass-Steagall Act, 39
Global warming, 255, 314–16
Gore, Albert Jr., 14
Grabowski, Henry G., 241–42
Greenman v. *Yuba Power Products, Inc.*, 244
Griggs v. *Duke Power Co.*, 167
Grimm, W.T. & Co., 65

H

Habitat, 255–56
Hansen, James, 315
Harold Franks v. *Bowman Transportation Co.*, 168
Harris, Lou, 156
Harris-Kefauver amendments, 238
Hart, Phillip, 75
Hart-Scott-Rodino Antitrust Improvements Act, 57
Harvard Business Review, 176–77
Hatch-Wampler bill, 237
Hazard communication standard, 207–9
Hazardous emissions, 269
Hazardous waste disposal, 284–91

National Alliance of Business, 130–31
National Center for Employee Ownership, 96–97
National Chamber Foundation, 33–34
National Commission on State Worker's Compensation Laws, 189
National Consumers League, 234
National Council on Wage and Price Stability, 19
National Emission Standards for Hazardous Air Pollutants, 269
National Environmental Policy Act, 259
National Highway Traffic Safety Administration, 46–47, 232–33
National Institute for Occupational Safety and Health, 187, 192, 202
National Labor Relations Board, 23, 95
National Minority Purchasing Council, 132
National Pollutant Discharge Elimination System, 274–75
National Priority List, 288
National Safety Council, 190, 210
Natural monopoly, 21
Natural Resources Defense Council, 238
Negligence, 244
Nestlé Corporation, 323–25
New-Age environmentalism, 257
New Deal, 119
New Source Performance Standards, 269
New York Stock Exchange, 94
Nichols and Zeckhauser, 200, 211–12
Nofziger, Lyn, 145
Nominating committee, 105, 112
Nonattainment regions, 268–69
Nonconventional pollutants, 274
Northern Pacific Ry. v. *United States,* 54
Northwest Airlines, 36, 170
Northwest Bancorporation, 135–36
Not In My Back Yard, 283

O

Occupational safety and health:
attitudes, 188
criminal charges, 205–6
hazards, 187–88
history, 187–90
illnesses, 187
injuries, 187
legal defenses, 188
Occupational Safety and Health Act:
administrative structure, 191–93
benefits, 210–11
consultation service, 197–98
continuing problems, 205–11
costs, 210–11
coverage, 199–200
employees, 197
employers, 196–97
enforcement, 194, 202–3
provisions, 190
record-keeping, 195–96, 204, 206–7
results, 211
standards, 193, 200–202
state programs, 198
violations, 194–95, 203–5
Occupational Safety and Health Administration, 22, 31–34, 45, 191–92, 228
Occupational Safety and Health Review Commission, 192, 195
Office of Consumer Affairs, 224
Office of Federal Contract Compliance Programs, 155, 159
Office of Information and Regulatory Affairs, 43
Office of Management and Budget, 29, 43
Office of Minority Business Enterprise, 132
Office of Research and Development, 262
Office of Solid Waste and Emergency Response, 284
Office of Technology Assessment, 288
Offset policy, 268–69
Okun, Arthur, 118–19
Oligopoly, 53, 62
Organization of American States, 310–11
Outside directors, 104
Ozone, 268
Ozone depletion, 255, 316–17

P

Paglin, Morton, 125–26
Passive smoking, 13
Patterson v. *McLean Credit Union,* 167–68
PCBs, 281–82
Pension funds, 94–95
Performance argument, 71–72
Perks, 101
Per se approach, 60–61
Pesticides, 238, 278–80
Philip Morris, 65
Physical environment, 255
Pickens, T. Boone, 92
Plastic packaging, 283
Pluralism, 3–4
Political Action Committees, 9
Political strategies, 8–11
Pollution:
air, 262–72
causes, 256
definition, 256
future problems, 290–91
water, 272–78
Pollution control:
objectives, 258–59
policies, 258
Population growth, 256
Post, James, 5–6
Poverty:
and African Americans, 123–24
and children, 122–23
culture of, 120–21
cycle of, 118–19, 121
definition, 119–20
dynamics of, 126–27
extent of, 121–25
feminization of, 122–23
nature of, 119–21
rate of, 121–22
Powell, Lewis, 163
Preferential treatment, 160, 165–68
Pregnancy Discrimination Act of 1978, 154–55
Prejudice, 151–52
Premerger notification, 57
Preservation, 257
Presidential intervention, 42
Presidential Task Force on Regulatory Relief, 24, 29, 42
Preston, Lee, 5–6
Prevention of Significant Deterioration, 268
Price elasticity, 59
Price Waterhouse, 180–81
Private Industry Councils, 130–31
Private Sector Initiative Program, 130
Procter & Gamble, 247–49
Product differentiation, 59
Productivity, 34
Product liability, 15, 243–47
Product safety, 228–30
Property rights, 83–84
Proxy battles, 94–95
Public affairs, 1, 320–22
Public Affairs Council, 321
Public Health Service, 276, 282
Public issues:
definition, 2

Public issues (*cont.*)
  emergence, 2
  life cycle, 6–10, 12
  nature, 2–4
  and strategic management, 10–12
Public opinion, 8–9
Public policy:
  definition, 4–5
  formulation, 9
  impacts, 1
  implementation, 9–10
Public policy agenda, 6
Public policy process, 2–3, 5–6
Public works projects, 133
Punitive damages, 245
Pure competition, 53
Pure Food and Drug Act, 220, 236

Q

Quotas, 154, 161

R

Railroads, 38
RCA Corporation, 65
Reader's Digest, 13
Reagan administration, 23–24, 34,
    42–43, 63, 66, 166–67
Recalls, 230
Recycling, 283
Reform of corporate governance,
    99–109
  activist shareholders, 102–3
  board of directors, 103–7
  disclosure, 100–101
  federal chartering, 107–9
*Regents of the University of Califor-
    nia* v. *Bakke,* 163–64
Regulation:
  administrative costs, 25, 27–28,
    31
  alternatives to, 44–45
  compliance costs, 31
  and decision-making, 43–44
  direct costs, 30–34
  and functional areas, 19–20
  growth, 23–30
  impacts, 18–19
  international, 302–9
  other costs, 34–35
  reform, 27–29, 40–45
  staffing, 26, 28–29
  types, 19–23
Regulatory Analysis Review Group,
    42
Regulatory budget, 42
Regulatory Council, 42

Regulatory Impact Analysis, 42
Regulatory reform, 40–45
Regulatory Reform Act, 43
Rely Tampon, 247–49
Repace, James L., 13
Repetitive-motion injuries, 209
Resale price maintenance, 65
Reserve Mining Company, 259
Resource Conservation and Recov-
    ery Act, 284–87
Retroactive seniority, 168–70
Reverse discrimination, 162–65
Richmond, Virginia, 134
Right-to-know laws, 207, 282
Risk assessment, 44
RJR-Nabisco, 65, 93, 106
Robinson-Patman Act, 55
Roosevelt, Franklin, 152
Rowland, Sherwood, 316
Rule of reason, 60

S

Sabine Consolidated, Inc., 206
Safe Drinking Water Act of 1974,
    276
Safety and health standards, 193
Safety standards, 201–2, 232
Santa Clara, California, 165
Schlink, F.J., 220
Schwartz, Donald E., 108
Schwartz, Felice, 176–77
Sears Roebuck & Co., 39
Securities and Exchange Commis-
    sion, 39, 45, 100–103
Senate Committee on Small Busi-
    ness, 133
Senate Subcommittee on Antitrust
    and Monopoly, 67
Seniority, 168–70
Separation of ownership and control,
    18, 86
Set-aside program, 132–33
Sexual harassment, 174–75
Shared monopoly, 62
Shareholders:
  activist, 102–3
  and corporate governance, 83–87,
    102–3
  resolutions, 102
Sheehan, Robert, 89–90
Sherman Antitrust Act, 19–20,
    59–61, 66, 77
  description, 54–55
  penalties, 56–57
Sick building syndrome, 210
Silent Spring (Carson), 278
Sinclair, Upton, 220–21
Single European Act, 307

Small and Independent Business Pro-
    tection Act, 62
Small Business Administration,
    132–33, 145–46
Small-quantity generators, 286
Smith, William French, 63
Smoking controversy, 12–15
  and advertising, 15
  and airplanes, 14
  ordinances, 14
  and public places, 13
  and the workplace, 13–14
Social changes, 1
Social information, 101
Social movements, 3–4
Social regulation, 22–23
Social Security, 137–38
Society of Consumer Affairs Profes-
    sionals, 235
Socio-political process, 3
Sole proprietorships, 176
Solid waste disposal, 283
South Africa, 5, 95, 102
Staggers Rail Act of 1980, 38
Stakeholders, 84–86, 110
Standard Oil Company, 60
State chartering, 107–8
State Implementation Plans, 265
Stationary sources, 269–70
Stereotyping, 152
Stigler, George, 74
Stockholders. *See* Shareholders
Strategic management, 10–12
Strict liability, 174, 243–46
Structure, conduct, and perfor-
    mance, 70–73
Subsistence level, 120
Sullivan, Rev. Leon, 112
Sunset legislation, 42
Superfund, 287–90
Superfund Amendments and
    Reauthorization Act, 282,
    289–90
Supreme Court, 6
Surface water, 272–74
Survey Research Center, 126
Systemic discrimination, 152

T

Teachers Insurance and Annuity As-
    sociation, 103
Teamsters v. *U.S. (T.I.M.E.-D.C.
    Inc.),* 168–69
Technology:
  and change, 256
  and corporate governance, 96
  and economic concentration,
    71–72
Technology-based standards, 275